PROPERTY LAW AND PRACTICE

PROPERTY LAW AND PRACTICE

Paul Butt LLB, Solicitor

and

Neil Duckworth BA, Solicitor

Published by

College of Law Publishing,
Braboeuf Manor, Portsmouth Road, St Catherines, Guildford GU3 1HA

© The College of Law 2008

British Library Cataloguing-in-Publication Data

A catalogue record for this book is available from the British Library.

ISBN: 978 1 905391 58 5

Typeset by Style Photosetting Ltd, Mayfield, East Sussex

Printed in Great Britain by Ashford Colour Press Ltd, Gosport, Hampshire

Preface

This book is intended as an introduction to property law and practice for those studying on the Legal Practice Course. It is hoped, however, that it will also be of use to others wanting an introduction to property practice and procedure. Its approach is essentially practical, and it does not pretend to contain a detailed analysis of the underlying law. Some background law is included, but it is assumed that readers will have the basic knowledge of land law and contract on which an understanding of property law and practice depends.

In the interests of brevity, both solicitor and client are referred to throughout the book in the male gender. Users of the book are requested to read 'he/she' every time the masculine pronoun is used, and to accept our apology for omitting specific references to both female solicitors and clients.

Although we have been responsible for the preparation of this edition, the book still owes an enormous debt to Frances Silverman who was responsible for previous editions. It has been a daunting task taking over from such a renowned conveyancer.

Thanks also to all our colleagues and students at The College of Law for their assistance, some of it unwitting.

Paul would particularly like to thank his daughters, Sarah and Siân, for putting up with a father who was always 'working on his book'.

The law is generally stated as at 1 May 2008.

Paul Butt
Chester

Neil Duckworth
Moorgate

Acknowledgements

The Standard Conditions of Sale and the Standard Commercial Property Conditions are reproduced for educational purposes only by kind permission of the Solicitors Law Stationery Society Limited and The Law Society of England and Wales.

We also acknowledge with thanks the kind permission of The Law Society to reproduce the following:

- the National Protocol for Domestic and Leasehold Property;
- the Law Society's formulae for exchanging contracts by telephone, fax or telex;
- the Law Society's code for completion by post;
- the form of undertaking to discharge building society mortgages;
- the forms of undertaking agreed with banks.

The CML Lenders' Handbook for England and Wales, Part 1, is reproduced for educational purposes only by kind permission of the Council of Mortgage Lenders. The Handbook is frequently updated and the current version can be found at http://www.cml.org.uk/handbook.

Contents

Table of Cases

Table of Statutes

Table of Statutory Instruments, Codes, Rules, Conditions and Guidance

Glossary of Terms

Absolute title	This is the best of the four classes of title that Land Registry can give to land.
Abstract of title	A summary of the title deeds and documents which prove title to unregistered land. Nowadays an epitome of title is normally used.
Acknowledgement and undertaking	A confirmation contained in a deed that the person named has the right to see a document not in his possession and a promise that the person who has possession of that document will keep it safe.
Additional rent	A sum payable under a lease (eg, service charge payments) which is to be treated as rent, giving the landlord the same remedies as if it were rent.
Adverse possession	The occupation of land without the permission of the owner. In certain circumstances after 12 years of such possession (unregistered land) or 10 years (registered land) the occupier may gain title to the land.
Adverse rights	Sometimes used to refer to the rights which someone other than the owner may have over land.
Agreement for sale	Another name for the contract setting the agreed terms of a sale.
Alienation clause	Provision in a lease which restricts the tenant's rights to assign or sub-let.
Apportionment	The process of adjusting the purchase price of land to take account of outgoings that affect it. In leasehold property, rent and service charges are normally paid in advance, so on completion of the sale the buyer will have to pay to the seller an extra sum equivalent to the payments in advance made by the seller.
Appurtenant	A right benefiting a piece of land (eg, an easement) can be said to be 'appurtenant' to that land.
Arbitration clause	A clause in an agreement (eg, a lease) requiring disputes to be referred to a third party for resolution in accordance with the Arbitration Acts.
Arm's length	A transaction between parties who are not associated in any way.
Assign	To transfer a right in property over to another. Usually used to signify the transfer of a lease.
Assignee	The person who receives the property being assigned.
Assignment	The document by which property is assigned — usually used in relation to the transfer of leases.
Assignor	The person who transfers the property.
Attestation clause	The part of a document containing the signatures of the parties.

Bailiff	An officer of the court charged with serving documents and enforcing judgments.
Banker's draft	A cheque drawn by a bank (rather than by a private individual) usually on its own head office. It is generally accepted as the equivalent of cash, although it needs to be paid in through the bank's 'clearing system' in the same way as any other cheque.
Beneficial owner	The person who is entitled to enjoy the benefit of property (as opposed to a trustee who owns land for the benefit of someone else).
Benefit (of a covenant)	The right to enforce compliance with it.
Body of deed	The operative part of a deed — as opposed to the recitals.
Boiler plate clause	Standard provision included in a legal document.
Break clause	Clause in a lease which allows one party to terminate the lease before its normal expiry date.
Bridleway	A path or road over which the public have the right to pass on foot or with horses and bicycles, but not with vehicles.
Building lease	Long lease under which the tenant is obliged to carry out some building work on the demised property.
Building regulation approval or consent	Confirmation that the plans for proposed building work show that it will comply with the Building Regulations. All building work has to comply with prescribed standards and the local authority is charged with ensuring compliance (although the NHBC will normally undertake such responsibility in relation to a new house to be covered by its structural insurance).
Burden (of a covenant)	The obligation to comply with it.
Call option	An agreement under which a party can, within a defined period, 'call' on (or compel) the other to sell his property.
Caution	Under LRA 1925 a method of protecting a third-party right in registered land. This could be entered on the register without the consent of the proprietor. Cautions can no longer be used under LRA 2002, but existing registrations remain effective.
Caveat emptor	Let the buyer beware — emphasising that it is the buyer's responsibility to discover problems with the property, not the seller's to disclose them.
Cesser	The premature ending of a right.
Charge	An interest in land securing the payment of a debt; a mortgage.
Chattels	Items of property other than land, eg, furniture. They will be excluded from the sale of land — unless there are specific provisions in the contract to the contrary.
Chief rent	Used in certain parts of the country to describe a rentcharge.
Clear lease	A lease under which the landlord is under no liability to pay for insurance and repairs, ie, the rental income is 'clear' of these obligations.

Comfort letter	A letter under which an assurance is given that the sender will behave in a particular way, eg, that the sender will provide funds for a particular purpose.
Common land	Land over which the inhabitants of a locality can exercise rights, eg, grazing.
Common parts	The parts of a development used in common by all the occupiers, eg, the hallways and stairs in a block of flats or the car park in a business park.
Concurrent lease	A lease granted to run at the same time as an existing lease. The tenant under the concurrent lease will then become the landlord of the tenant under that existing lease. Sometimes used in flat management schemes.
Conservation area	An area of special architectural or historic interest so designated by the local authority in order to preserve or enhance its character or appearance. Special planning rules will apply restricting development in the area.
Conveyance	The document used to transfer ownership to another. Usually used in unregistered land.
Corporeal hereditament	Physical property, eg, land, buildings — as opposed to incorporeal hereditaments such as easements.
Counterpart lease	A lease is normally drawn up in two identical copies: the lease signed by the landlord and the counterpart signed by the tenant. Each party then keeps the part signed by the other.
Covenant	An obligation entered into by a landowner. In certain circumstances this can be binding on subsequent owners of the land.
Covenantee	The person to whom the promise is made, ie, taking the benefit of the covenant.
Covenantor	The person making the promise, ie, bearing the burden of the covenant.
Curtilage	Old fashioned term used to refer to the land occupied along with a property, eg, the garden of a house.
Dedication	Giving rights over land for public use, eg, the dedication of land for use as a highway.
Deed	A document executed in accordance with various formal requirements. It must be signed and witnessed and then delivered.
Defective title insurance	Insurance taken out to protect a buyer and/or lender against the consequences of a specified defect in title up to the financial limit specified in the policy.
Delivery	One of the formal requirements for a deed. A deed will be delivered when the signatory intends it to be binding on him. This is usually on payment by a buyer of the purchase price.
Demise	A lease; the grant of a lease. Sometimes used to indicate the property granted by a lease.
Devise	A gift of property by a will.
Disbursements	Payments made by a solicitor on behalf of the client, eg, search fees.

Distress	Seizing possessions of a tenant to secure payment of rent.
Dominant tenement	The piece of land which benefits from an easement.
Due diligence	The proper steps to be taken by a professional in connection with a particular transaction to ensure that it is lawful.
Easement	A right over one piece of land for the benefit of another, eg, a right of way.
Enfranchisement	In leases, the process of tenants acquiring the freehold in their land.
Engrossment	The final version of a document which will be signed by the parties. Traditionally prepared on better quality paper than mere 'drafts' of the document.
Epitome of title	A chronological list of the documents which prove title to unregistered land. It will usually be accompanied by photocopies of the documents.
Escrow	A deed which has been signed but only delivered conditionally. It will not become operative until the condition (eg, the payment of money) is fulfilled.
Estate rentcharge	A rentcharge imposed on freehold land to ensure the running of the burden of postitive covenants.
Execution	Signing and delivering a deed to make it legally effective.
Fair wear and tear	Damage caused by the ordinary operation of natural causes. Sometimes in a lease a repairing obligation does not include damage caused in this way.
Fine	A non-returnable lump sum payable by a tenant to a landlord on the grant of a lease in addition to rent. A premium.
Fixtures	Items fixed to land which become part of it and will pass to a buyer on a sale unless specifically excluded by the terms of the contract.
Flying freehold	A part of a freehold property which lies over land belonging to someone else.
Forfeiture	A landlord's right to terminate a lease prematurely due to the tenant's breach of his obligations.
Good leasehold title	One of the classes of title conferred by Land Registry. It guarantees the ownership of the lease but not that the landlord had the right to grant that lease.
Ground rent	The rent payable to a landlord, particularly in relation to leasehold houses and flats where the tenant will have paid a premium on the grant of the lease to cover the cost of the house and will effectively just be renting the 'ground' on which the building stands.
Guarantee	Promise given by a guarantor
Guarantor	Person who promises to perform an obligation if there is default by the person who has taken on the obligation, eg, the tenant under a lease.
Habendum	The part of a deed which describes the property being transferred.

Head-lease	A lease granted directly by the freeholder. Used where the tenant under that lease has then granted a sub-lease of all or part of that property.
Heads of terms	The fundamental terms of an agreement which will then form the basis of the formal contract between the parties when it is drawn up by the lawyers.
Hereditament	Real property; land.
HMRC	Her Majesty's Revenue and Customs. The government department responsible for the administration and collection of taxes such as Value Added Tax and Stamp Duty Land Tax, roles formerly undertaken by the Inland Revenue and HM Customs and Excise.
Holding	The area of land demised to a tenant.
Holding over	The act of a tenant remaining in possession of the land at the end of a lease.
Improvements	Changes to property which increase its value.
Incorporeal hereditament	An intangible right over land, eg, an easement.
Incumbrance	An adverse right affecting a property, eg, a mortgage or a covenant.
Indemnity	An agreement to reimburse or compensate someone in relation to some possible future liability.
Indemnity covenant	A promise to indemnify someone against a possible future loss or expense. Often included in a transfer to protect a seller against a possible breach of obligation by the buyer for which the seller could be liable.
Indenture	A deed made between two parties. Historically, each party was given his own copy both of which had been written on. The same document was then cut into two using a wavy line.
Inhibition	Under LRA 1925 a method of protecting third-party rights over the land. Any disposition was prevented in the circumstances prescribed, eg, on bankruptcy.
Joint and several	An obligation entered into by two or more persons under which they are 'severally' or individually liable (eg, for the full amount of a debt) as well as jointly liable with the others.
Laches	Delay in enforcing a right.
Lady Day	25 March. The feast of the Annunciation of the Virgin Mary. One of the usual quarter days.
Landlord	The grantor of a lease.
Lease	Used interchangeably to mean a leasehold interest in land and also the document creating that interest.
Lessee	Tenant under a lease.
Lessor	Landlord under a lease.
Lien	The right to hold onto another's property as security for a debt.

Managing agent	Someone appointed to oversee the day-to-day maintenance of a property, eg, a block of flats or a shopping centre.
Mesne	Intermediate.
Mesne profits	Compensation due to a landowner for the unlawful occupation of his land, eg, by a tenant who holds over without the landlord's consent.
Messuage	Old fashioned term for a dwelling house.
Michaelmas	29 September. The feast of St Michael. One of the usual quarter days.
Midsummer Day	24 June. The feast of St John the Baptist. One of the usual quarter days.
Minor interest	Under LRA 1925, an interest which had to be protected by an entry on the register in order to bind a purchaser.
Office copies	The name formerly used for official copies — but still often used in practice.
Official copies	Copies of the register entries relating to a title.
Party wall (or fence)	A wall (or fence) owned jointly by adjoining landowners over which both have rights and responsibilities as to maintenance.
Peppercorn rent	A nominal rent.
Perpetuity	Forever.
Planning permission	Permission required from the local authority to develop land.
Possessory title	One of the classes of title the Land Registry may grant. Often granted when the owner claims to have lost the title deeds, or to have acquired ownership by adverse possession.
Pre-emption	A right of first refusal.
Premium	A non-returnable lump sum payable by a tenant on the grant of a lease in addition to rent.
Prescription	The acquisition of legal easements by long user — often 20 years user as of right will suffice.
Public bridleway	A path or road over which the public have the right to pass on foot or with horses and bicycles, but not with vehicles.
Public footpath	A path over which the public have rights to pass on foot only.
Public highway	A road over which the public have rights to pass on foot and with vehicles.
Put option	A contract under which a party has the right, but not the obligation, to sell his land to another.
Quarter days	25 March; 24 June; 29 September; 25 December. The days on which (traditionally) rent was payable. Still much used in commercial leases as rent payment days.
Rack rent	Open market rental.
Reddendum	The part of a lease which specifies the rent payable.

Rentcharge	A sum of money payable by the owner of freehold land.
Reversion	The interest which the lessor retains after the grant of a lease, ie, the right to repossession when the lease terminates — if the lease was granted by the owner of the freehold the grantor then has a freehold reversion.
Riparian rights	The rights of a landowner over a non-tidal river adjoining his land, eg, rights to fish.
Sale and leaseback	An arrangement in which a landowner sells the freehold and then takes back a lease of the property from the new freeholder. Often used to free up capital tied up in freehold land.
Seisin	Old-fashioned term denoting the possession of freehold land.
Service charge	Payment made by an owner of property towards the landlord's costs of the upkeep of the 'common parts', eg, the repair and maintenance of a block of flats or shopping centre.
Side letter	A letter accompanying a legal document, eg, a contract, explaining or clarifying the intentions of the parties.
Stamp Duty Land Tax	Tax payable to the Government (inter alia) on the purchase of property or the grant of a lease. Known as stamp duty until 1 December 2003.
Sub-lease	A lease granted by a person who is himself a tenant. Must be of a shorter duration than the head-lease.
Sub-lessor and sub-lessee	The parties to a sub-lease.
Surety	Person who promises to perform an obligation if there is default by the person who has taken on the obligation; a guarantor.
Surrender	The premature termination of a lease by agreement between landlord and tenant.
Telegraphic transfer/TT	Term still used to signify the transfer of money from one bank account to another, eg, from the buyer's solicitor's bank to the seller's solicitor's bank on completion. The banks's computerised system is used today, but the old term is still used. Often shortened to 'TT'.
Tenancy	Often used instead of lease for short term, eg, 10 years, 21 years or periodic tenancies.
Tenant	The person to whom a lease is granted.
Tenant's fixtures	Chattels fixed to leasehold property by a tenant which, although strictly fixtures, can be lawfully removed by the tenant.
Term	The duration of the lease.
Term of years	A leasehold interest in land (an archaic alternative to lease).
Title	The ownership of a piece of property. Often also used to signify the documents used to prove ownership.
Transfer	The document used to pass the ownership of land to another. Usually used in relation to registered land.

Travelling draft	The draft of a document that 'travels' between the parties and on which the various amendments required are made. Will nowadays often be sent electronically.
Tree preservation order	An order made by the local planning authority preventing the felling or lopping of trees without permission from the local authority.
Trigger notice	A notice required to initiate some procedure — usually used in relation to a notice required to initiate a rent review under a lease.
Turnover lease	A lease (eg, of retail premises) where the rent is fixed as a percentage of the annual turnover.
User	The use to which a property can be lawfully put.
Usual quarter days	25 March; 24 June; 29 September; 25 December. Days on which rent was traditionally payable. Still frequently used in commercial leases as rent payment days.
Vacant possession	Having no tenant or other person in occupation.
Waiver	The abandonment of a right, eg, of the right to forfeit a lease.
Warranty	A promise as to the truth of a statement.
Yield up	To give up possession at the end of a lease.

Table of Abbreviations

AGA	authorised guarantee agreement
CGT	capital gains tax
CHAPS	Clearing House Automated Payment System
CML	Council of Mortgage Lenders
CPSE	Commercial Property Standard Enquiries
DCLG	Department for Communities and Local Government
END	Electronic Notification of Discharge
EPA 1990	Environmental Protection Act 1990
FSA	Financial Services Authority
GPDO	Town and Country Planning (General Permitted Development) Order 1995
HCR	Home Condition Report
HIP	Home Information Pack
HMRC	Her Majesty's Revenue & Customs
LCR	Land Charges Registry
LPA	local planning authority
LPA 1925	Law of Property Act 1925
LRA 1925	Land Registration Act 1925
LRA 2002	Land Registration Act 2002
LRHUDA 1993	Leasehold Reform, Housing and Urban Development Act 1993
MLRO	money laundering reporting officer
NHBC	National House Building Council
NLIS	National Land Information Service
NPV	Net Present Value
nse	no subsisting entries
OMRV	open market rental valuation
PD	Particulars Delivered
PEA 1977	Protection from Eviction Act 1977
PR	Personal Representative
SC	Standard Conditions
SCPC	Standard Commercial Property Conditions
SDLT	stamp duty land tax
SEAL	Solicitors' Estate Agency Ltd
SOCA	Serious Organised Crime Agency
SRA	Solicitors Regulation Authority
SPIF	Seller's Property Information Form
TCPA 1990	Town and Country Planning Act 1990
TID	Title Information Document
TT	telegraphic transfer
VCO	Town and Country Planning (Use Classes) Order 1987
VAT	value added tax
VATA 1994	Value Added Tax Act 1994

Part I
INTRODUCTION

Chapter 1

Introduction to Property Law and Practice

1.1 What is it about?

Property Law and Practice is the law and practice involved in the transfer of ownership of land. Many – particularly the man or woman in the street – will be familiar with the older term 'conveyancing'. To the public, conveyancing inevitably means the process of buying and selling and moving home – allegedly one of the most stressful times in a person's life. It is the conveyancer – or property lawyer – who must manage this move and endeavour to make it less stressful. In 2006, Law Society research (published on The Law Society website www.lawsociety.org.uk/home.law) showed that 18% of solicitors dealt with some residential conveyancing. 'Conveyance' is the name of the deed that 'conveyed' or transferred the ownership of land from seller to buyer.

But residential conveyancing is only one aspect of the conveyancer's role. The modern property lawyer will often be much more involved in commercial transactions. These will range from the sale or purchase of a small corner shop, to the multi-million sale or purchase of a large office development or shopping centre. Property lawyers will also be involved in the sale and purchase of land that is going to be the site of some major new development – whether a housing estate, or a commercial or industrial site. But most of these major developments will not be occupied by their owners; they will be leased out to business as shops, or offices or factories. The grant and approval of commercial leases and the on-going relationships between landlord and tenant are also the field of the property lawyer.

The law and procedures involved in buying land for development are the same as those for a semi-detached house in a suburban street – or indeed those used when taking a lease of an office or a shop. This book is intended to provide an introduction to all these different aspects of Property Law and Practice.

1.2 The two systems of conveyancing

Two systems of conveyancing exist in England and Wales: the 'registered' and the 'unregistered' systems. The main difference between the two systems lies in the way in which the seller proves his ownership of the property to an intending buyer. The reason for the existence of two parallel systems of conveyancing is historical.

1.2.1 The unregistered system

Under the unregistered system, a seller proves his ownership of land (or 'title', as it is called by property lawyers) by establishing that he has been in undisturbed possession of the land for a long time. In English law, the ownership of land has for centuries been based on possession – indeed it is still possible even today, in certain circumstances, for a trespasser (or 'squatter') to acquire title to land simply by being in 'adverse' possession of it for a period in excess of 12 years.

Possession and thus ownership is proved by the seller producing the conveyances and other documents dealing with the ownership of the land for a long period of time. Collectively these are known as the 'title deeds' to the property. The seller is required to show the buyer that he can prove undisputed ownership of the land from a point in time at least 15 years before the present sale/purchase transaction down to the present day. If, for example, A owned the land in question in 1980, it would be necessary for the seller to show to his buyer documents which proved that A, the owner in 1980, had sold to B, who in turn had sold the same land to C, and so on until the land became the property of the present seller. There must be no missing links in the chain, no unexplained jumps from, say, B to E.

This method of proving ownership is logical. If the seller can prove that he has been in undisturbed possession for this length of time and has the title deeds, it is fair to assume that he is the owner. If anyone else had rights in relation to the land, the logical assumption is that they would not have let the seller remain on the land for so long without claiming possession. However, the process of producing and then checking all the documents needed to establish this chain of ownership is cumbersome, time-consuming and expensive, and must be repeated each time the land is sold. The system is also not without its flaws, since a competent forger would have little difficulty in producing an authentic and convincing set of fake documents.

1.2.2 The registered system

In order to simplify and speed up conveyancing, and to lessen the opportunities for fraud, the 'registered' system of conveyancing was introduced.

The idea of the registered system is that the Government maintains a register of title to land, land transfers take place by notifying the registry of the change of ownership, and the details recorded at the registry are amended accordingly. (This is a similar concept to the DVLA, which keeps a central record of motor vehicles and which must be notified on the change of ownership of a vehicle.)

The register for each title shows the extent of the land concerned by reference to a plan based on the Ordnance Survey map. The register sets out the benefits enjoyed by the land (eg, the benefit of a right of way over neighbouring land) and also contains details of the burdens attached to it (eg, mortgages or restrictive covenants which have to be observed by the owner).

When an intending buyer wants to check the title which he is buying, a quick search of the register at Land Registry will confirm the information which he needs.

Placing all the land in England and Wales on the register is a time-consuming process, but it will lead to the gradual elimination of the unregistered system.

1.2.3 The systems exist in parallel

The register is so much quicker, simpler and more reliable for proving ownership than checking through documents supplied by the seller that it is perhaps surprising to find that, after nearly 150 years, the registered and unregistered systems of conveyancing are still running in parallel with each other. The registered system now dominates conveyancing, but there are still large pockets of land, some in rural areas, others owned by large trusts, which continue to be unregistered.

The progress of the registered system was achieved by gradually making designated areas of the country 'compulsory' areas, so that within these areas, when land was sold, it was obligatory to register it, and, afterwards, to carry out all further dealings with the land using only the registered system. By this approach, much land was entered on the register, but it was only in 1990 that the last compulsory registration order was made, so that it became compulsory to register land on any freehold sale throughout England and Wales. It was only from 1 April 1998 that changes of ownership following death and gifts of land have become compulsorily registrable.

Although all areas of the country are now 'compulsory' as far as registration is concerned, broadly registration occurs only when land changes hands. Thus, although there will, in the future, be a steadily increasing proportion of registered land transactions, some land will be unregistered for the foreseeable future. For this reason, property lawyers need to know and to understand the mechanics of both systems. However, both the Law Commission and Land Registry think that all remaining unregistered land should be registered as quickly as possible, so that the register becomes conclusive as to the ownership of all the land in England and Wales. Land Registry is actively encouraging owners of unregistered land to register their titles voluntarily. Land Registry aims to complete the registration of all remaining unregistered titles by 2012. A brief explanation of the registered land system is set out in **Chapter 4**.

1.3   Relationship of conveyancing and land law

Conveyancing is the practical application of land law and the law of contract. It is necessary for the property lawyer to have some knowledge of these in order to understand, and so to avoid, their pitfalls. A summary of the main points of land law and the law of contract as they affect conveyancing appears in **Chapter 3**.

1.4   Approach taken by this book

This book is intended as an introductory work for those who have little or no experience of conveyancing in a practical context. It is set out in a chronological sequence, taking the reader through the steps in a simple transaction in the order in which they would occur in practice. The procedures applicable to the registered and unregistered systems of conveyancing are largely identical and are not specifically referred to except where they differ from one another.

Most land is owned freehold, and the major part of this book concentrates on the procedures relating to freehold tenure. In many cases, the procedure adopted in a leasehold transaction is identical to that used in freehold conveyancing. Where leases differ from freeholds, the differences are highlighted in **Part VII** of this book.

Similarly, the procedures used in residential and commercial conveyancing are identical to one another. Commercial transactions may involve more money than residential ones, and the large sums of money involved may increase the tension and risk for the solicitor involved, but the object of both types of transactions remains the same – the safe, speedy and efficient transfer of ownership from seller to buyer. If the solicitor does not achieve this, whether in the domestic or the commercial sphere, he will not have done his job properly and risks being sued for negligence. Where the steps to be taken differ in a commercial transaction from a residential transaction, these are indicated at the appropriate stage of the proceedings. An introduction to the drafting and approving of commercial leases and the security of tenure given to business tenants is also included in **Part VII**.

This book does not set out to be a definitive academic textbook on conveyancing. It is a beginner's guide to the law and procedures involved in the conveyancing process, and the reader is advised to use practitioner texts to supplement the information given in this book.

You will find many references in the text to the Standard Conditions of Sale used in residential transactions and this is set out in full in **Appendix 2**. References in the text to specific Conditions appear in the form SC 1.1 etc. Similarly, there are references to the Standard Commercial Property Conditions used in larger commercial transactions. This is set out in full in **Appendix 3** and references in the text to specific Conditions appear in the form SCPC 1.1 etc.

1.4.1 Practitioner textbooks

1.4.1.1 General textbooks

F Silverman, *The Law Society's Conveyancing Handbook* (14th edn, 2007). This contains The Law Society's recommended methods of practice.

1.4.1.2 Specialist works

Specialist books exist in almost every area of conveyancing from contract drafting to remedies. They are too numerous to mention in this book, but a well-stocked library should contain a selection of appropriate texts.

Of those of more general application, the loose-leaf work, *Emmet & Farrand on Title* (Sweet & Maxwell) is a recognised authority on many aspects of conveyancing law, especially those relating to legal title.

Many precedent books (which are used to trigger ideas for drafting a particular document) also exist. The well-known examples are: *The Encyclopedia of Forms and Precedents*, vols 35–38 (Butterworths), which carry a comprehensive range of model documents and clauses designed to fit most situations, and TM Aldridge, *Practical Conveyancing Precedents* (Sweet & Maxwell), which contains a selection of precedents drafted in simple, modern language.

For a fuller explanation of the land law principles on which conveyancing is based, reference should be made to a standard land law textbook such as LJ Oakley, *Megarry's Manual of the Law of Real Property* (8th edn, 2002).

1.5 E-conveyancing

At the moment, conveyancing is very much a paper-based system. Contracts for the sale of land must be in writing; a deed must be used for the actual transfer of ownership. The various searches and enquiries necessary prior to a purchase are often still made by the submission of application forms to the relevant bodies. The Government, however, is very keen that the conveyancing process should be able to be undertaken almost entirely electronically, so that the process can be speeded up. Land Registry has set up a new 'Land Registry Direct' system which allows direct access to the register via the Internet. Another part of this process involves the setting up of the National Land Information Service (NLIS) (see **18.3**) which will enable searches and enquiries to be made almost instantaneously using the Internet.

The Electronic Communications Act 2000 and the Land Registration Act 2002 (LRA 2002) together provide a framework which will ultimately allow the whole conveyancing transaction to be effected electronically. Contracts will be drafted, approved and exchanged electronically. Searches will be made, and results sent directly to your computer. Contracts and transfers will be 'signed' by a secure electronic signature. On completion, the register will be automatically changed without need for a further application. All money payments would be made electronically (and automatically) using a new Electronic Funds Transfer system.

Land Registry is introducing the new system incrementally, rather than with one big bang. In the past many large computer projects have gone spectacularly wrong and Land Registry is determined to ensure that the same does not happen with e-conveyancing. At the moment certain mortgage lenders are using a system of electronic discharge, whereby when a mortgage has been paid off the lender sends an electronic message to Land Registry and the mortgage is automatically removed from the register. It is also possible to obtain official copies of the register and make searches electronically. Certain applications to change the register, eg, to remove the name of a deceased proprietor, can also be made electronically.

One of the key parts of e-conveyancing as far as residential transactions are concerned was to be the 'chain matrix'. One of the major causes of problems in residential transactions is the 'chain'. This is the situation where buyer A is buying from B, who in turn is buying from C, who is then hoping to buy from D and so on. Every transaction is dependent on the other. If A does not buy from B, then B cannot buy from C. This means that all the transactions must proceed at the pace of the slowest, and delays and uncertainty as to what is happening where along the chain are common. To assist in solving these problems, Land Registry's e-conveyancing plans include the chain matrix. This will have to be completed by all involved in the chain and be open to be viewed by all involved. It will enable everyone to see what stage all the various links in the chain have reached and, it is hoped, by ensuring transparency, will enable any delays to be resolved speedily.

The chain matrix was piloted in Bristol, Fareham and Portsmouth in 2007, and based on this Land Registry has concluded that more work needs to be done to enable the service fully to meet the needs of professional customers and the wider home-owning public. It will thus not be proceeded with at the moment. Equally, the concept of an Electronic Funds Transfer system is also on hold for the moment, but remains part of Land Registry's 'long-term vision'. But these delays are also evidence of Land Registry's softly-softly approach to the implementation of e-conveyancing, and give assurance that when it does come, it will work.

In 2008 the focus will be on the introduction of electronic charges, electronic discharges and other types of forms commonly used by legal practitioners, paving the way for electronic transfers in 2009.

For the moment, this book must concentrate on the paper-based system currently in use, but enormous changes in conveyancing practices are inevitable.

Chapter 2

Outline of a Simple Transaction

2.1 How a conveyancing transaction works

A typical conveyancing transaction divides into three stages:

(a) the pre-contract stage;

(b) the post-contract (or pre-completion) stage; and

(c) the post-completion stage.

In terms of time, the pre-contract stage is the longest and much of the legal work involved in the transaction is done at this time. Assuming that matters proceed smoothly, the pre-contract stage of a residential transaction may take four to six weeks from the date when instructions are first received. The post-contract stage may then be much shorter, usually no longer than two weeks, and the post-completion stage represents the 'tidying up loose ends' process after the buyer has taken possession. It is unrealistic in most circumstances to expect the transaction to be accomplished in less than about eight weeks from start to finish, and sometimes, due to delays caused by parties over whom the solicitor has no control (eg, delays by a local authority in returning a search application, or delays by a lender in processing a client's mortgage application), the transaction may take much longer than either the solicitor or the client feels is reasonable. In commercial transactions, different considerations apply, and a much shorter timescale has often to be achieved in order to meet the needs of the clients. However, the procedure to be followed is basically the same.

2.1.1 Home Information Packs

2.1.1.1 Why are they needed?

There has been much criticism in recent years of the length of time taken to complete a house purchase. The delay between a prospective buyer making an informal offer for a property and the sale becoming legally binding facilitates the practices known as 'gazumping' and 'gazundering'. 'Gazumping' occurs when a buyer, having spent much time and money on surveys and legal work, is told by the seller, just before contracts are to be exchanged, that unless he is prepared to pay a higher price, the property will be sold to another buyer. 'Gazundering' occurs when the buyer, again just before exchange, informs the seller that he will proceed only if the price is reduced.

Towards the end of 1998, the Government produced a Consultation Paper proposing changes in conveyancing procedure aimed at speeding up the process and thus reducing the opportunity for these undesirable practices. The Government introduced its Homes Bill into the House of Commons on 12 December 2000 but the original Bill was lost when the May 2001 election was called.

The Housing Act 2004 received the Royal Assent in November 2004 and contains the statutory authority for the introduction of Home Information Packs (or 'HIPs' as they are sometimes called).

The Government's original plan was that before putting a house on the market, the seller should make available to prospective buyers a pack containing all the documents, information, etc that a buyer's solicitor would normally obtain during the transaction. It was also planned that the pack would contain a Home Condition Report (HCR), a form of structural survey. It was hoped that the early availability of these documents would speed up the transaction and avoid the possibility of problems being discovered at a late stage – and the delay or collapse of the sale that would then result. As will be seen (**2.1.1.2**), the result is a somewhat watered-down version of the original plan. It has to be said that the plan to introduce HIPs was not welcomed by many conveyancers and estate agents, the requirement of an HCR being particularly criticised. One factor was the cost of preparing a HIP, estimated at about £500. The current version of the HIP, without the HCR, can be obtained for about £300.

The HCR, as well as giving a report on the condition of the house was also to contain an Energy Performance Certificate (EPC; see also **2.1.1.6**). The certificate sets out the energy efficiency and environmental performance of a home. It is commissioned by the seller (or his agent) from an accredited Energy Assessor, who visits the property to collect the relevant data and creates the certificate. These data include the date, construction and location of the house, and relevant fittings (heating systems, insulation or double glazing, for example). The EPC grades the house for performance on a scale of A (most efficient) to G. This scale is similar to one that has been used for some years in relation to domestic appliances, eg washing machines, fridges, etc. The EPC states annual heating and lighting costs, assessed on a standard basis, and the amount of carbon dioxide emitted by heating and lighting the house.

The EPC also lists cost-effective measures that homeowners can take to improve the energy efficiency of the building. This can mean lower energy bills for the occupiers, and could make homes more attractive to potential purchasers. It is hoped that the EPC will influence property owners and potential purchasers to make their homes more energy efficient, and thus help to combat global warming.

By the end of 2008, all buildings in the UK that are constructed, sold or rented out will have to have an EPC. This is in compliance with the European Energy Performance of Buildings Directive (Directive 2002/91). Nearly 40% of the UK's energy consumption arises from the way in which our 25 million buildings are lit, heated and used. Even comparatively minor changes in the energy performance of each building, and the way in which we use it, would have a significant effect in reducing energy consumption and therefore carbon emissions.

In July 2006, the Government announced that the inclusion of an HCR would no longer be mandatory but would be recommended. It still remains Government policy, however, that the HCR will eventually become a mandatory part of the HIP. The requirement that an EPC should be included remains.

2.1.1.2   The contents of the Home Information Pack (HIP)

The Home Information Pack Regulations 2007 (SI 2007/992) set out the current requirements for a HIP.

The Regulations specify matters which are 'required' to be included and those which are 'authorised' to be included in a HIP. A HIP must not contain any documents which are not 'required' or 'authorised'.

Required HIP documents

The HIP must include the following:

(a)   an index;

(b)   an EPC (or a predicted energy assessment if the property is not physically complete). To emphasise its importance, the EPC must be the first document in the HIP following the index. Details of the grading of the house must also be included in the estate agent's particulars describing the house;

(c)   the sale statement setting out the basic terms of the sale;

(d)   official copies and title plan or an epitome of title;

(e)   in the case of leasehold land—

    (i)   a copy of the lease;

    (ii)   any regulations or rules made for the purposes of managing the property;

    (iii)   statements or summaries of service charges relating to the 36 months preceding the first point of marketing;

    (iv)   the most recent requests for payment with regard to services, insurance and ground rent made in respect of the property, relating to the 12 months preceding the first point of marketing;

    (v)   the names and addresses of the current or proposed landlord and managing agents;

    (vi)   any proposed amendments to the lease or regulations;

    (vii)   a summary of such works as are being undertaken or proposed, affecting the property or the building in which the property is situated;

(f)   In the case of Commonhold land, specified information and documents about the scheme (eg the Commonhold Community Statement). See **34.7** as to Commonhold;

(g)   a local search;

(h)   enquiries of the local authority; and

(i)   a drainage and water enquiries report.

Authorised HIP documents

The HIP may include any of the following:

(a)   a Home Condition Report (HCR);

(b)   an accurate translation in any language of any HIP document (under reg 8(3), HIP documents must be in English or, where the property is in Wales, English, Welsh or a combination of both);

(c)   an additional version of any HIP document in another format, such as Braille or large print;

(d)   any warranty, policy or guarantee covering defects in the design, building, or completion of the property, or its conversion for residential purposes (eg an NHBC policy – see **41.2.3**).

(e)   a summary or explanation of any HIP document;

(f)   information identifying the property including a description, photograph, map, plan or drawing of the property;

(g)   information about a HIP document or about the HIP, relating to its source or supply, or any complaints or redress procedures arising from it;

(h)   official copies of any documents referred to in the register of title;

(i)   if the property is leasehold, various other details about the leasehold arrangements which would be of interest to potential buyers of the property. These include details of any head lease or management company, details of any breaches of covenant, etc;

(j)   documentary evidence of any work carried out to the property since the date of the HCR;

(k)   any guarantees relating to work carried out to the property;

(l)   various further searches, including commons registration, environmental, chancel repairs and additional enquiries of the local authority;

(m)   any documents referred to in a search report;

(n)   further specified information which would be of interest to potential buyers of the property interest, including the property's contents, fixtures or fittings, and information about access to the property, disputes with neighbours, building works carried out on the property and the utility services connected to the property.

Time-sensitive documents contained in a HIP (eg searches and official copies) must be dated no more than three months prior to the date of first marketing. However, there is no requirement to update such documents, no matter how long the house remains on the market.

2.1.1.3   When will they be required?

The requirement to provide a HIP applies to open market sales of homes with vacant possession. It will be the responsibility of the person marketing the property to ensure that the pack is available. A HIP is required for all homes first marketed on or after 14 December 2007, the introduction having been phased in during 2007 (four-bedroom houses as from 1 August, three-bedroom houses as from 10 September). Houses that were already on the market before the appropriate date can continue to be marketed without a HIP. At the time of writing no 'drop dead' date had been fixed from when a HIP would be required for such properties.

It is not intended to catch private sales (eg, to a member of the family, a neighbour or a friend) where the property is not offered on the open market, or sales of tenanted property where the home is not offered with vacant possession.

The HIP obligation does not apply to non-residential property, mixed commercial (or industrial) and residential property, properties sold with sitting tenants and therefore unavailable for owner occupation, or portfolios of properties.

2.1.1.4   Transitional provisions

For a transitional period, a property can be marketed without a HIP, provided that a written request has been made for one to a HIP supplier. The duty to provide a HIP then runs from when the HIP is actually received. It was not clear at the time of writing when this transitional period would end.

2.1.1.5   Sanctions

The enforcement regime is to be based on civil sanctions. The regime will give local weights and measures authorities primary responsibility for enforcing the HIP obligations. Trading Standards Officers will be given discretion to determine appropriate action in each case – whether to provide information and assistance, or issue a warning or a civil fixed penalty notice. The penalty will be set at a rate determined by the Secretary of State (initially £200).

Trading Standards Officers will also be able to notify the Office of Fair Trading (OFT) of any breach by persons acting as an estate agent, which could also trigger action by the OFT under the Estate Agents Act 1979. Trading Standards Officers will have a duty to do so, where a fixed penalty notice had been issued.

In addition, a person who breached the HIP obligations will be liable to be sued by prospective buyers for recovery of the costs of obtaining documents which should have been provided in the HIP.

2.1.1.6   Energy Performance Certificates

As part of the Government's policy to reduce carbon emissions, EPCs will be a 'required' element of a HIP in relation to the sales of residential properties, but they will also eventually be required on the sale or letting of most properties. The Energy Performance of Buildings (Certificates and Inspections) (England and Wales) Regulations 2007 (SI 2007/ 991) require, where a building is to be sold or rented out, that the seller or landlord:

> . . . shall make available free of charge a valid energy performance certificate to any prospective buyer or tenant—
>
> (a)   at the earliest opportunity; and
>
> (b)   in any event before entering into a contract to sell or rent out the building or, if sooner, no later than whichever is the earlier of—
>
>> (i)   in the case of a person who requests information about the building, the time at which the relevant person first makes available any information in writing about the building to the person; or
>>
>> (ii)   in the case of a person who makes a request to view the building, the time at which the person views the building.

Certificates will be required for non-residential buildings with a total useful floor area exceeding 500 m^2 as from 6 April 2008 and for other buildings as from 1 October 2008. (There are exceptions, amongst others, for buildings about to be demolished.) The Regulations also impose obligations for air-conditioning systems exceeding stated power outputs to be subject to an energy assessment every five years.

2.1.2   Taking instructions

Whether the solicitor is acting for the seller or the buyer, the first step in the transaction is the same for both of them: instructions must be taken from the client. Those instructions should normally be confirmed to the client in writing, together with written information relating to the costs which the client will have to pay for the work to be done by his solicitor. At this stage it will also be necessary to obtain documentary proof of the client's identity – whether buyer or seller – in order to comply with anti-money laundering regulations. Following this, the seller's and buyer's solicitors must attend to different aspects of the transaction.

2.1.3   The pre-contract stage

Having taken instructions, the seller's solicitor must prepare the pre-contract package for the buyer. This comprises:

(a)   the draft contract, showing what land the seller is selling and on what terms he is prepared to sell it;

(b)   evidence of the seller's legal title to the property, to prove that he does own and is entitled to sell the land; and

(c)   sometimes, the results of pre-contract searches which the seller has made and other information about the property.

The package may also include such items as copy local authority planning permissions, which the buyer's solicitor will want to see to make sure that the property which his client is buying was permitted to be built on the site. In a residential transaction, some of the information will have been included in the HIP (see **2.1.1.2**).

When the buyer's solicitor receives the pre-contract package from the seller's solicitor, he will check all the documents supplied very carefully to ensure that the terms of the contract accord with his instructions and do not reveal any problems which might make the property an unsuitable purchase for his client. Although the seller has a limited duty to disclose defects in his legal title (but not physical defects), the *caveat emptor* principle ('let the buyer beware') applies to conveyancing, so that it is the buyer's responsibility to find out all the information which he needs to know about the property before committing himself to the purchase. Home Information Packs will, to some extent, remove the *caveat emptor* principle, but it will still be the responsibility of the buyer's solicitor to appreciate the importance and effect of the information revealed and to advise the buyer accordingly.

GENERAL FREEHOLD CONVEYANCING

OUTLINE OF A SIMPLE CONVEYANCING TRANSACTION

SELLER	BUYER
TAKE INSTRUCTIONS	TAKE INSTRUCTIONS
PREPARE PRE-CONTRACT PACKAGE	
	PRE-CONTRACT SEARCHES AND ENQUIRIES
	INVESTIGATE TITLE
	APPROVE DRAFT CONTRACT
EXCHANGE CONTRACTS	
	PREPARE PURCHASE DEED
APPROVE PURCHASE DEED	
	PRE-COMPLETION SEARCHES
PREPARE FOR COMPLETION	PREPARE FOR COMPLETION
COMPLETION	
POST-COMPLETION MATTERS	POST-COMPLETION MATTERS

The chart above shows the responsibilities of the parties' solicitors at each stage of the transaction and serves as a reminder of the various procedures which are involved and the stages in the transaction at which they take place.

2.1.3.1   Title

The pre-contract package will include documents showing proof of the seller's ownership of the land. The buyer's solicitor must check these documents carefully to ensure that the seller is entitled to sell what he is purporting to sell. Any queries arising out of the title documents are raised with the seller's solicitor by means of 'requisitions'. These are questions or 'requests' addressed to the seller, requiring him to resolve any apparent problems with the seller's ownership, or 'title' as it is usually referred to. The contract usually contains a clause excluding the buyer from questioning the seller's title once contracts for the sale and purchase have been entered into. In such a case it is essential, therefore, for any problems with title to be raised and resolved prior to a binding contract being entered into. If the buyer's solicitor discovers problems with the seller's title at this stage, the buyer can withdraw from the transaction without penalty since no formal contract yet exists between the parties.

2.1.3.2   Searches

It is the application of the caveat emptor principle which makes pre-contract searches necessary. These searches, many of them made with public bodies such as the local authority or Land Registry, will reveal a large amount of information about the property, all of which will help the buyer to make up his mind whether or not to proceed with the purchase. In some cases, the seller's solicitor will submit the search applications and pass their results to the buyer's solicitor with the pre-contract package. If this has happened, the buyer's solicitor still needs to check that the correct searches have been made and that their results are satisfactory. In most cases, the buyer's solicitor will make the search applications himself. In this situation the search applications need to be sent to the relevant authorities as soon as firm instructions to proceed have been obtained, otherwise the delay in receiving search replies may cause a delay in the transaction. The National Land Information Service (NLIS) provides an Internet-based 'one-stop shop' enabling information kept by a variety of public and other bodies to be accessed more efficiently and speedily than by requesting the information separately from each individual body. Where there is a HIP, this will include replies to various searches, but it will still be the responsibility of the buyer's solicitor to check the results and ensure that they do not cause any problems for the buyer. It will also still be necessary to check whether any further searches are required over and above those included in the Pack.

2.1.3.3   The buyer's finances

The buyer's solicitor must check that his client is able, in financial terms, to proceed with the transaction. Unless the client has sufficient available cash to purchase the property, he must have received a satisfactory offer of finance and have available sufficient money to pay the balance of the purchase price (it is unusual to obtain a mortgage for the whole of the purchase price). The client must also be able to fund the 10% deposit which traditionally is payable on entering into a contract to buy land. (Note, however, that in recent times it has become customary for the buyer to negotiate a payment of a deposit of less than 10%, and sometimes in commercial transactions, no deposit at all will be paid.)

2.1.3.4   The draft contract

When the buyer's solicitor is satisfied with his search results, with the proof of the seller's ownership (title) and with the terms of the draft contract (he may have negotiated some amendments to the contract with the seller's solicitor), he will be ready to return the draft contract to the seller's solicitor, telling him that the buyer has approved the terms and is now ready to enter the contract. The contract is then prepared for the clients' signatures. Two copies of the contract, incorporating any agreed amendments, are printed off; the seller signs one, the buyer the other. The contract comes into existence by 'exchange of contracts' (ie, the buyer receives the copy signed by the seller and the seller the copy signed by the buyer). However, prior to physical exchange, which is effected through the post, it is usual for the parties to agree over the telephone that the contract should come into existence at the moment of the telephone call. This is often referred to as 'telephonic exchange'.

2.1.4 Exchange of contracts

The exchange of contracts marks the stage in the transaction at which a binding contract comes into existence. Until exchange, no contract exists between buyer and seller, and either is free to change his mind about the transaction and withdraw from it. It is this aspect of conveyancing procedure that is most frequently criticised; remember, in a residential transaction, there could well be six weeks or more between a solicitor being instructed and contracts being exchanged, and if either party withdraws at the last minute before exchange, this can cause great inconvenience to the other party. It is with a view towards reducing this delay that the Government has introduced HIPs. Once exchange has taken place, a binding contract exists and usually neither party can withdraw without incurring liability for breach of contract. On exchange, the buyer will normally pay a deposit. This was customarily 10% of the purchase price and will be held by the seller's solicitor until completion. The money serves as a 'statement of intent' by the buyer that he is serious about the transaction and intends to fulfil his contractual obligations. If he fails to complete, the seller can usually forfeit the deposit and retain the money.

2.1.5 Post-contract stage

Since most of the important stages of the transaction have now been accomplished, the pre-completion, or post-contract, stage of the transaction should be less onerous for both sides. Although it is often necessary for the buyer to insure the property on exchange, the first step is normally for the buyer to 'raise requisitions' with the seller. Historically, the purpose of requisitions was to clarify any queries which had arisen out of the seller's proof of ownership of the property, but in modern conveyancing, where proof of title is invariably a pre-contract issue, requisitions are more likely to be directed at the resolution of procedural queries relating to the mechanics of completion itself. For example, the buyer needs to know precisely how much money is required from him to complete the transaction, where completion is to take place and who holds the keys to the property. These queries are usually raised on a standard form which is sent to the seller's solicitor for his replies.

2.1.5.1 The draft purchase deed

At the same time as sending the requisitions, the buyer's solicitor sends the draft purchase deed to the seller's solicitor, for his approval. In registered land, this will take the form of a transfer, as prescribed by the Land Registration Rules. In unregistered land, it may take the form of a traditional conveyance, although usually a modified form of Land Registry transfer is used.

Although it was the seller's solicitor's duty to prepare the contract, customarily it was the buyer's solicitor who prepared the purchase deed itself. However, it is increasingly common for the contract to provide that the seller will draft the transfer. This will then be provided to the buyer at the same time as the draft contract. This can help to prevent delays between exchange and completion. The contract states what the parties have agreed to do; the purchase deed carries it out. In other words, the purchase deed activates the terms of the contract and brings them alive; this deed must therefore be drafted to reflect the terms of the contract (no new terms can be introduced at this stage) and the seller's solicitor will check the draft deed to ensure that the buyer's solicitor has done the job properly (if the buyer's solicitor has prepared it). The seller's solicitor's approval of the draft purchase deed is normally notified to the buyer's solicitor at the stage when the seller's solicitor replies to the buyer's solicitor's requisitions. The purchase deed can then be 'engrossed', ie a copy is prepared containing any agreed amendments; this is the copy which will be signed by the parties. Only one copy of the purchase deed is prepared which is required by both parties.

The seller must always sign the purchase deed, otherwise the legal estate in the land will not pass. Usually the buyer also signs, but there are circumstances in which it is not necessary for him to do so.

2.1.5.2   The buyer's lender

At the same time as the purchase deed is being prepared, it is also necessary for some work to be done on behalf of the buyer's lender. At the time when a mortgage offer was made to the buyer, the lender would have instructed solicitors to act for him in connection with the loan. The lender needs to be certain that the property which he is accepting as security for the loan has a good title (ie, he needs to carry out the same investigations as were carried out on behalf of the buyer in this respect) and various documents need to be drawn up to put the mortgage into effect.

2.1.5.3   Acting for the buyer and the lender

Frequently, in a residential transaction, the solicitor who is acting for the buyer will also be instructed to act for the buyer's lender. Acting for more than one party in a transaction is severely restricted by Rule 3 of the Solicitors' Code of Conduct 2007, but acting for buyer and lender is usually permitted; see **Chapter 5**. The solicitor who is acting for the buyer's lender must:

(a)   draw up the mortgage deed for signature by the borrower (buyer);

(b)   certify to the lender that the legal title to the property is in order (a report on title); and

(c)   obtain a clear bankruptcy search against the borrower, since the lender will be reluctant to lend money to a person who is the subject of bankruptcy proceedings.

The buyer's solicitor must also ensure that he is put in funds to complete the transaction. The seller's solicitor will have informed him of the exact amount of money needed to complete the transaction, either in answer to the buyer's requisitions or on a separate document called a 'completion statement'. In residential transactions, the amount needed to complete is often simply the balance of the purchase price, taking into account the deposit which was paid on exchange. In other cases, other sums may be due, for example payment for stock-in-trade in the case of the purchase of a business. The buyer's solicitor will notify his client of the amount due to complete the transaction by sending him a statement of account. The client will also be sent (where appropriate) a copy of the completion statement and, in residential cases, the solicitor's bill showing the fees and disbursements payable in respect of the transaction.

Commonly in house purchases, a large part of the purchase price will be provided by way of loan from the lender and/or by the proceeds of sale of the buyer's present property. This fact will be shown on the statement of account, so that the amount which the client has to find from his own funds is comparatively small.

The money which the client has to pay the solicitor to make up the balance due on completion must be paid to the solicitor in sufficient time before completion to allow that money to be cleared (ie, the normal banking process of clearing a cheque) before the solicitor uses that money to complete the transaction. The mortgage loan from the lender must similarly be obtained, so that at the time when the money is required to be sent to the seller's solicitor, all the necessary funds are cleared and are in the buyer's solicitor's client account. Usually, however, the mortgage advance will not be paid by cheque but will be transmitted directly to the solicitor's bank account.

2.1.5.4   Preparation for completion

A few days before completion the buyer's solicitor makes his pre-completion searches to ensure that no last-minute problems have occurred with the title to the property.

At the same time as the buyer's solicitor is preparing for completion, the seller's solicitor is also taking steps to ensure that completion will proceed smoothly and without delay.

2.1.5.5   Discharge of seller's mortgage

Very often the seller will have a mortgage on the property which he has agreed with the buyer to remove on completion. The seller's solicitor must now confirm with the seller's lender the exact amount of money which is required to discharge the seller's mortgage, and generally make sure that he has in his possession all the documents required to complete the transaction. This may involve the preparation of a form of discharge of the seller's mortgage if (as is usual) the seller's solicitor is also acting for the seller's lender in connection with the discharge.

2.1.5.6   Final checks

Both parties' solicitors check through their respective files and make a 'checklist' of what is to happen at completion. This is to ensure that nothing has been overlooked: no two transactions are identical, and even the most straightforward of residential transactions can throw up unforeseen last-minute complications. An appointment can then be made for completion actually to take place.

2.1.6   Completion

Traditionally, completion took place by the buyer's solicitor attending personally at the seller's solicitor's offices to hand over the money in return for the deeds, but personal attendance at completion is an expensive and time-consuming operation, especially in the context of residential transactions. It is more common today for the parties to agree to complete 'through the post'. In effect, a postal completion means that the seller's solicitor is temporarily appointed to be the agent for the buyer's solicitor, and while acting as such must carry out all the steps which the buyer's solicitor instructs him to do (ie, all the things which the buyer's solicitor would be doing if he was physically present at completion).

The method by which completion is to be effected will have been agreed by the respective solicitors at the 'requisitions' stage of the transaction. If a postal completion is to take place, the time at which completion is due to take place will have been agreed in the course of a telephone conversation between the parties' solicitors, and the buyer's solicitor will have given the seller's solicitor precise instructions as to what is required to be done. This is in accordance with the guidelines for postal completions issued by The Law Society (the 'Code for Completion by Post') (see **Appendix 5**).

On the morning of completion day, the first priority is to transmit to the seller's solicitor the money which is required to complete the transaction. Without tangible evidence that the buyer has paid, the seller will not complete. With a postal completion, the money is usually sent to the seller's solicitor's bank account by what is still called a telegraphic transfer, but is now an electronic transmission of funds from the buyer's solicitor's bank account to the seller's solicitor's account. No physical transfer of the money takes place: the buyer's solicitor's account is debited with the requisite sum, a corresponding credit being entered in the seller's solicitor's account. Computer technology makes this possible even where the two solicitors bank at different banks in different towns.

When the seller's solicitor's bank receives the funds from the buyer's solicitor's bank, the bank should notify the seller's solicitor that the funds have arrived, so that the seller's solicitor can proceed with completion itself. In practice, this is little more than a formality. The deeds may have to be checked on behalf of the buyer's solicitor, the purchase deed dated, the estate agent informed that completion has taken place (so that he can release the keys of the property to the new owner), and the deeds themselves sent by first-class post to the buyer's solicitor. The seller's solicitor will then telephone the buyer's solicitor to inform him of the safe arrival of the money and that completion has taken place in accordance with his instructions.

The clients themselves do not attend completion but should be informed by telephone immediately after completion that it has taken place: the sellers are told that they are now in funds with the proceeds of sale; the buyers are told that they now own, and can take possession of, their new property.

2.1.7 Post-completion

2.1.7.1 The seller's solicitor

The seller's solicitor now has some loose ends to tie up. First he must send to the seller's lender the amount required to pay off the seller's mortgage, obtain a receipt for that money and send the receipt to the buyer's solicitor, who will need this receipt to prove to Land Registry that the mortgage has been discharged. He must also account to his client for the proceeds of sale and, if not already done, prepare and submit his bill of costs. The proceeds of sale should be dealt with on the day of completion, or as soon as is possible. A solicitor who delays in returning money to a client may have to pay interest on that sum to the client under the Solicitors' Accounts Rules 1998. The seller's solicitor can close his file when he has dealt with these matters.

2.1.7.2 The buyer's solicitor

The buyer's solicitor must deal with the payment of stamp duty land tax. More detail about rates of tax and the method of payment is to be found in **Chapter 31**, but where the purchase price of the property is over £125,000 (£150,000 in the case of commercial property), stamp duty land tax on the amount of the price is usually payable to Her Majesty's Revenue & Customs (HMRC) within 30 days of completion. Failure to pay or late payment attracts heavy penalties. Particulars of the transaction (ie, who has sold what to whom and at what price) must also be delivered to HMRC after completion in the form of a land transaction return. A certificate is then issued by HMRC as proof that these requirements have been complied with. Without this certificate it is not possible to register the transaction at Land Registry. Without registration the buyer will not acquire legal ownership to the property.

After these formalities have been completed, the buyer's solicitor must apply to Land Registry for his client's title to be registered. Land Registry would previously return to the buyer's solicitor a charge certificate (or land certificate if there was no mortgage over the property) containing details of the buyer's ownership of the land, the mortgages to which it is subject and particulars of any easements or covenants affecting the land. However, under the LRA 2002, land and charge certificates have been abolished as part of Land Registry's moves towards electronic conveyancing. They have been replaced by a simpler form of certificate (known as a Title Information Document, or TID) confirming the buyer's ownership of the land. When he has checked that the details contained in the TID are correct, the buyer's solicitor should forward the TID, together with any other relevant documents, to the lender or, if the property is not subject to a loan, to the buyer, for safe-keeping. However, due to increasing costs of storage, most mortgage lenders do not wish to receive any documents relating to the mortgaged property and the solicitor must either pass them to the client or store them himself. After he has received an acknowledgement from the lender or buyer and all other outstanding matters have been satisfactorily dealt with, the buyer's solicitor may send his file for storage.

2.2 Linked transactions

In many residential transactions, the client will be selling one house and buying another. His intention is to move from one to the other on the same day, using the money obtained from the sale transaction towards payment of the purchase price of the house he is buying. In such a case, the sale and purchase transactions are inextricably linked: the client cannot afford to buy his new house unless he can also sell the old one, neither does he want to sell his existing house unless he can buy a new one in which to live, since a sale without a related purchase would leave him homeless. This is often described as the 'no home/two homes' syndrome; neither situation is desirable from the client's point of view. The solicitor's objective is to ensure that at any one time the client owns only one house and that at no time is the client without a home. The sale and purchase transactions must therefore be synchronised, and failure to achieve synchronisation where the client has instructed it will prima facie be negligence on the part of the solicitor. It follows that, where the solicitor is acting in linked transactions, he will at the same time be carrying out the steps described above relating to both the seller's and the buyer's solicitor, one set of procedures being relevant to the sale transaction, the other to the simultaneous purchase.

2.3 The National Protocol

In 1990, The Law Society issued the first edition of the National Protocol for domestic conveyancing. The Protocol is known by the brand logo 'TransAction' and is intended to standardise, simplify and speed up the procedures relating to domestic conveyancing. Most firms which carry out residential conveyancing are registered with The Law Society as TransAction users.

At the beginning of a residential transaction, the solicitors acting for the parties should ascertain whether the Protocol is to be used in that transaction and, if so, whether there are intended to be any variations to the prescribed procedures. The procedures laid down by the Protocol are intended to regulate the relationship between the seller's and buyer's solicitors and do not affect dealings with third parties such as estate agents or lenders. Broadly speaking, the requirements of the Protocol reflect what is already standard practice within the profession and no special procedures are involved. However, some of the forms used in Protocol transactions are specially prescribed for use in conjunction with the Protocol and some are compulsory (eg, a particular form of contract is compulsory). In this book, reference is made to the Protocol in the context of the particular procedural steps being discussed where those procedures differ from accepted practice. If the Protocol is not mentioned specifically, this indicates that the procedure under the Protocol is identical to the procedures described for that particular stage of the transaction. The text of the Protocol is set out for reference in **Appendix 1** and provides a further useful checklist of the procedural stages in a simple transaction.

2.3.1 Disclosure of related transactions

When a solicitor is instructed to buy or sell a residential property on behalf of his client, he will explain the use of the Protocol to the client and will discuss with him the advantages and disadvantages of disclosing information to the other party about the progress of any related sale or purchase transaction. Disclosure of such information may be helpful to the other party, but might not be helpful to the solicitor's own client if, for example, the client is experiencing difficulties in selling his own property. Disclosure of information about related transactions can be made only with the client's consent, and the client's refusal to give such consent is not deemed to be a departure from the Protocol.

The Government's proposals for e-conveyancing include the appointment of a Land Registry official as 'chain manager' in relation to every use of a chain matrix (see **1.5**) and the chain of related sales and purchases. The idea is to provide openness throughout the chain of transactions so that all parties can see at which stage the various transactions are. Following a pilot in 2007, Land Registry announced that the chain matrix proposal would not be proceeded with in the short term.

2.3.2 Non-solicitors

Where it is in the interests of a client to use the Protocol, a licensed conveyancer acting for the other party should be invited to adopt it. Licensed conveyancers are regarded in the same light as solicitors, so it is possible to rely on a licensed conveyancer's agreement to use the Protocol in a transaction. Since the Protocol procedures are to an extent dependent on undertakings, it is unwise to attempt to use it in a situation where an unqualified person is purporting to represent one of the parties to the transaction, since an undertaking given by an unqualified person is not enforceable in the same way as a solicitor's or licensed conveyancer's undertaking.

Chapter 3
Essential Background Law

3.1 Introduction

Conveyancing is about the practical application of land law, and for that reason this chapter contains a brief reminder of some basic principles. It does not pretend to be a comprehensive guide to land law, for which the reader is referred to one of the standard texts on the subject.

Please re-read sections as necessary, when referring to the later chapters, to refresh your knowledge of particular land law topics as they arise. This chapter attempts to put the basic principles of land law into the context in which you will come across them in a conveyancing transaction.

3.2 Legal estates, legal interests and equitable interests

3.2.1 Legal estates

Since 1925 there can be only two legal estates:

(a) an estate in fee simple absolute in possession (the freehold estate); and

(b) a term of years absolute (the leasehold estate).

3.2.2 Legal interests

The most important legal interests which can subsist today are:

(a) an easement for an interest equivalent to a fee simple absolute in possession or term of years absolute; and

(b) a charge by way of legal mortgage.

3.2.3 Equitable interests

Virtually all other estates, interests and charges in or over land other than those mentioned above will take effect as equitable interests (LPA 1925, s 1).

3.2.4 Deeds

As a general rule, a deed is required to convey or create a legal estate or interest, but there are exceptions: certain leases for not more than three years and some assents do not need to be by deed. See **27.7** as to the formalities required for a document to become a deed.

3.3 Third-party rights

It is often necessary to determine whether or not a buyer of a legal estate in land is to buy free from or subject to a particular existing right or interest in that land belonging to someone else, ie, a third party.

For example, assume S owns land which is subject to an easement in favour of E. Will a buyer from S take free from or subject to E's easement?

The way in which third-party rights are protected depends upon whether the title to the land is registered or unregistered.

3.3.1 Unregistered land

The protection of third-party rights in land with an unregistered title largely depends on whether or not the particular right concerned is capable of registration under the Land Charges Act 1972.

3.3.1.1 Land charges

The following classes of land charge should be noted:

Class C(i)	A puisne mortgage (ie, a legal mortgage not protected by the lender's possession of the title deeds).
Class C(iv)	An estate contract (ie, a contract to create or convey a legal estate, eg a contract to sell land or grant a lease).
Class D(ii)	A restrictive covenant entered into on or after 1 January 1925.
Class F	A spouse's right of occupation of the matrimonial home under the Family Law Act 1996.

If the third party has registered his right, it will be binding on all persons (such registration being deemed to be actual notice).

If it is registrable but has not been registered then the precise effect of failure to register will depend on the nature of the right, but in broad terms failure to register will render the right void as against a buyer. The fact that the buyer may actually know of the third-party right is irrelevant.

If the right or interest is incapable of registration then whether or not it is binding on a buyer will depend on whether it is legal or equitable.

3.3.1.2 Legal interests

Legal easements and legal leases (no matter what the length) and legal mortgages protected by the lender's possession of the title deeds are binding on all persons irrespective of notice.

3.3.1.3 Equitable interests

Equitable interests (eg, an interest under a resulting trust) bind a buyer unless the buyer falls within the definition of a bona fide purchaser for value of the legal estate without notice.

Notice here includes not only actual notice (ie, within the buyer's own knowledge), but also imputed notice (ie, within the actual or constructive knowledge of his solicitor) and constructive notice (ie, of matters a person would have discovered had he made the enquiries he ought reasonably to have made). However, equitable interests arising under trusts can be overreached (ie, transferred to the purchase money) on a sale by two trustees. In such a case they will not be binding on a buyer, even if he has notice of them.

3.3.2 Registered land

How third-party rights are protected in registered land depends upon whether they are classified as:

(a)   registrable dispositions;

(b)   unregistered interests which override registered dispositions (usually referred to as 'overriding interests'); or

(c)   interests affecting a registered estate (sometimes still referred to by the LRA 1925 designation 'minor interests').

Registrable dispositions are listed in the LRA 2002, s 27. The most important of these are:

(a)   legal easements (only if expressly created by deed); and

(b)   legal charges (mortgages)

Overriding interests are defined in the LRA 2002, Sch 3. If a third-party right is classified as an overriding interest, it will not appear on the register but it will bind a buyer, irrespective of whether that buyer has notice of it (see **4.8.2**).

All other third-party rights are classified as interests affecting a registered estate and must be protected by some entry on the register if they are to bind a buyer. Failure to register (as a notice or restriction) will mean that a buyer for valuable consideration in good faith will take free from the interest.

3.4 Easements

An easement confers the right to one landowner to use the land of another in some way, or to prevent it being used in a certain way. Examples are a right of way and a right of light.

There are certain conditions which must be satisfied before an easement can exist:

(a)   there must be a dominant and a servient piece of land;

(b)   the right must accommodate (ie, benefit) the dominant land;

(c)   the dominant and servient pieces of land must not be both owned and occupied by the same person; and

(d)   the right must be capable of being granted by deed and therefore must usually be:

(i)   within the general nature of rights capable of being easements; and

(ii)   sufficiently definite.

3.4.1 Creation of easements

As with covenants, easements are frequently (though not exclusively) created on a sale of part of land.

Example

S owns West and East. He proposes to sell East to B. S may wish to retain ('reserve') for the benefit of West rights of drainage over East. (Perhaps there is a building on West with drains running through East and S wishes to continue to use those drains after the sale.)

S may have agreed to grant to B the right to use a driveway across West.

Both the above are easements. The parties will agree their terms in the contract for sale of East and they will then appear as clauses in the deed which transfers the legal estate in East to B.

S West	B East
Driveway	
Drain ◥	

3.4.1.1   Acquisition

In the above example the easements are acquired by express grant (right to use driveway) and express reservation (drainage). Since the grant and reservation are by deed the easements will be legal.

Easements may be acquired by:

(a)   statute;

(b)   express grant or reservation;

(c)   implied grant or reservation;

(d)   prescription.

Express grant or reservation

To create a *legal* easement, the grant or reservation must be by deed and the easement must be equivalent to (ie, not granted for longer or shorter than) an estate in fee simple in possession or a term of years absolute.

(a)   Where the land has an unregistered title a legal easement is automatically binding and needs no registration.

(b)   Where the land has a registered title a legal easement should be registered on the charges register of the servient tenement.

(c)   Where both the servient and dominant titles are registered (which is often the case), a legal easement (except those already in existence on 13 October 2003) should be registered against both titles.

Example

If the titles to West and East above were registered:

(i)   the right to use the driveway would be noted in the charges register of the title to West and the property register of the title to East; and

(ii)   the right of drainage would be noted in the charges register of the title to East and the property register of the title to West.

Where a deed is not used the easement will be equitable if granted in writing and for value (Law of Property (Miscellaneous Provisions) Act 1989, s 2).

Where the land has an unregistered title an equitable easement should be registered as a Class D(iii) Land Charge against the name of the servient owner.

Where the land has a registered title an equitable easement should be registered as a minor interest on the charges register of the servient tenement.

Implied grant or reservation

Implied grant

This arises where a seller disposes of part of his land, retaining part. In certain circumstances legal easements may be impliedly granted to the buyer of the part sold even though the parties have failed to provide for the express grant of an easement.

Implied grant in a conveyancing transaction

Standard conveyancing practice would be to exclude the operation of the implied grant rules on a sale by agreement between the parties. This would be on the basis that any easements required by the buyer would be expressly granted by the seller.

The right to exclude the implied grant rules must be agreed as a term in the contract of sale. The exclusion clause is then inserted in the deed transferring the legal estate to the buyer.

Implied reservation

The general rule is that if the seller wishes to reserve easements on a sale he must do so expressly by agreeing the reservation as a term of the contract of sale and then inserting it as a clause in the deed of transfer.

Prescription

A legal easement may be presumed to have been granted if the claimant can show long and continuous user as of right.

A claim may be made under common law rules but more usually it is made under the Prescription Act 1832 where the period of uninterrupted user must be at least 20 years.

3.4.2   Extinguishment of easements

Easements may be extinguished by:

(a)   Unity of ownership of the dominant and servient tenements. (If this happens the easement will not automatically revive if the tenements are subsequently split up again.)

(b)   Express release by deed by the dominant owner.

(c)   Implied release, ie, where the circumstances imply that the dominant owner has abandoned the easement, eg, non-user for more than 20 years.

3.4.3 Public rights of way

A public right of way, often encountered in conveyancing, is not an easement but a right exercisable by anyone, by virtue of the general law, to cross another's land. The surface of the land over which a public right of way exists is known as a highway.

A public right of way can be created at common law by dedication by the owner to the public either expressly or by implication, and by the public accepting that dedication as a highway. It can also be created by statute, for example, under the Highways Act 1980.

Whether or not such a highway is maintainable at the public expense is a separate matter.

3.4.4 Easements and conveyancing

Easements have a dual importance in a conveyancing transaction. First, a buyer needs to ensure that the land being purchased has the benefit of all easements over adjoining land that are necessary for the full enjoyment of the land being acquired. So, for example, if the only access to the land is over land belonging to another, a right of way over that land should be in existence. Secondly, a buyer is concerned to see what easements affect the land being bought. So, if land is being bought for development purposes, the existence of rights of way, or drainage or other easements over it could cause problems to that development, and thus need discovering at an early stage.

3.5 Covenants

3.5.1 Covenants affecting freehold land

A covenant is simply a promise made in a deed. Land may be subject to ('incumbered' by) covenants which affect its use in some way.

Such covenants are usually first imposed on a sale of part of land.

Example

S owns a large plot of land and he is selling the northern part ('North') to B. S will retain the southern plot of land ('South'). (Maybe he already has a house on it or factory or office premises.) S wants to ensure that B will not be able to use North in a way that will interfere with S's use of South or devalue it. S makes it a condition of the sale to B that B will enter into covenants over North for the benefit of South. The drafting of these covenants is first agreed in the contract for sale of North and they are then inserted as clauses in the deed that transfers the legal estate in North to B.

B   North
S   South

3.5.2 Positive and restrictive covenants

Covenants imposed on land may be positive or restrictive. Positive covenants usually involve expenditure of money or labour, restrictive covenants restrict the use of the land in some way. The test is the substance of the covenant not its wording. Thus a covenant 'to leave the land uncovered by buildings' is restrictive even though it is worded in a positive form – it means 'not to build'. Set out below are some examples of the sort of covenants you might meet in a conveyancing transaction.

3.5.2.1 Restrictive covenants

(a)   'not to build without the consent of S';

(b)   'not to build without submission of the plans for approval by S';

(c)   'to use only as residential/factory/office premises' (with commercial property the *type* of factory or office may be further specified);

(d)   'not to do anything on the property which may become a nuisance or annoyance to S'.

3.5.2.2 Positive covenants

(a)   'to fence along the boundary between the points marked "A" and "B" on the plan' (the height of the fence/materials to be used/time limit for building it, etc is then generally specified);

(b)   'to maintain the fence...';

(c)   'to pay one half of the cost of maintaining the shared driveway coloured brown on the plan attached'.

3.5.3 Enforcement of covenants by and against successors in title

In the example in **3.5.1** above, as between B and S, B will obviously be bound by the covenants since, as a matter of contract, he entered into them, but there are two further questions:

(a)   if B sells North to X, could the covenants be enforced against X? (ie, does the 'burden' run with North?)

(b)   if S sells South to A, could the covenants be enforced by A? (ie, does the 'benefit' run with South?)

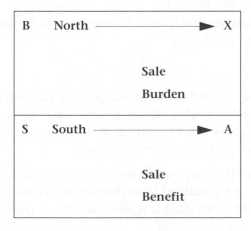

3.5.3.1 Burden

The burden of a positive covenant (eg, to fence) *cannot* run with the land. Thus it will not be directly enforceable against X.

Note: Although the burden of a positive covenant cannot run with the land there is a common law rule that a person who claims the benefit of a deed must also submit to any burdens contained in it (*Halsall v Brizell* [1957] Ch 169). In that case an easement of way over the roads on a housing estate had been granted to house owners, coupled with a positive covenant to contribute to maintenance of the road. It was held that a subsequent purchaser of one of the houses who wished to use the roads must submit to the burden of the covenant. In order for this principle to work, the burden assumed must be linked to the benefit enjoyed, eg, a payment related to services that the payer actually uses (see *Thamesmead v Allotey* [1998] 3 EGLR 97).

Under the rule in *Tulk v Moxhay* (1848) 2 Ph 774, the burden of a restrictive covenant *can* run with the land in equity if:

(a)   it touches and concerns the burdened land (North); and

(b)   it was entered into for the benefit of the retained land (South) and is capable of benefiting that land; and

(c)   the parties (S and B) intended that the covenant should run with the burdened land (North) and not be a purely personal matter between them; and

(d)   X and all successors in title to North buy with 'notice' of the covenant.

The first three requirements are normally clear from the wording of the covenant. A well-drafted covenant will always say that the burden is intended to affect the land and each and every part of it and to run with it so as to bind successors in title of B (LPA 1925, s 79 anyway implies this).

To ensure that X and all successors in title have notice of the covenant it must be registered.

(a)   If North has an unregistered title it must be registered as a D(ii) Land Charge against B's name in the Central Land Charges register. Unregistered D(ii) Land Charges are void against a purchaser of the legal estate for money or money's worth. Volunteers, such as donees or assentees will, however, be bound by them even though unregistered. (Covenants created before 1926 are not registrable as Land Charges and are subject to the old doctrine of notice – a purchaser without notice, actual or constructive, will take free. Generally purchasers will have actual notice since the covenant will be a clause in one of the title deeds.)

(b)   If North has a registered title it must be registered as a minor interest on the charges register of North's title.

3.5.3.2   Benefit

The benefit of both positive and restrictive covenants can run with the retained land (South) at common law and in equity. In practice however, since the *burden* of a positive covenant cannot run with the land, the issue of running of benefit is generally of more concern with restrictive covenants.

Well-drafted covenants will always state that the benefit of the covenant is given for each and every part of S's retained land (South) and is intended to run with it to benefit successors in title of S (that it is 'annexed' to it). (Annexation is anyway implied by LPA 1925, s 78.)

3.5.4   Covenants in the context of a conveyancing transaction

When X buys North he will want to know what, if any, incumbrances affect the land. He may want to change the current use of the land and/or build on it. He will also be concerned about being liable for any existing breaches of covenant. X's solicitor will check the title for covenants. If the land is unregistered he will search in the Central Land Charges Register. If the land is registered he will check the charges register of the official copy of the registered title.

3.5.5   Personal indemnity covenants

The original party who enters into the burden of a covenant ('the original covenantor') remains liable in contract for breach of the covenant even after he has parted with the burdened land; ie, he can be sued for a breach committed by a successor in title.

Example

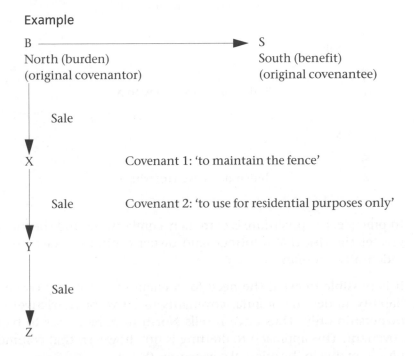

B ————————————————▶ S
North (burden)   South (benefit)
(original covenantor)   (original covenantee)

| Sale

X   Covenant 1: 'to maintain the fence'

| Sale   Covenant 2: 'to use for residential purposes only'

Y

| Sale

Z

Suppose that Z breaches covenants 1 and 2.

Covenant 1: S can only sue B (for damages). This is a positive covenant – the burden does not run directly to Z.

Covenant 2: S can sue Z **or** B as this is a restrictive covenant. (He could seek an injunction against Z or damages from B. He cannot seek damages from Z as the restrictive covenant only gives him an equitable interest and damages are a common law remedy.)

3.5.5.1   Indemnity covenants

Since B is at risk of a claim for breach of either covenant by a successor the standard conveyancing approach is as follows:

(a)   When B sells to X, he requires X to enter into a personal indemnity covenant in his (B's) favour.

(b)   X will covenant 'to observe and perform' covenants 1 and 2 and 'to indemnify B against any claim for breach by X or by his successors in title'.

(c)   X, in turn, when he sells to Y, will require Y to enter into an indemnity covenant with him (X) and Y will take one from Z. Thus a chain of indemnity covenants is created on the title with each buyer entering into the same personal promise when he buys. Note that these covenants are personal – the burden of them will not pass to a successor.

(d) If B is sued for Z's breach B will sue X for indemnity. X will sue Y for indemnity and Y will sue Z. Thus, in theory, Z is made indirectly liable for the breach he commits.

Example

B ——————————————————————▶ S
North (burden)   South (benefit)

    ⏐ Sale
    ▼
X   Indemnity covenant with B

    ⏐ Sale
    ▼
Y   Indemnity covenant with X

    ⏐ Sale
    ▼
Z   Indemnity covenant with Y

In practice, the procedure is extremely cumbersome and the longer the chain the greater the risk that a former land owner cannot be traced or did not give an indemnity covenant.

It is possible to avoid the need for a chain of indemnity covenants by limiting liability under the original covenants (positive or restrictive) to the period of ownership only. Thus once B sells North to X he ceases to be liable on either covenant. This approach to drafting is not, however, that common as it may not be acceptable to the original covenantee (S).

3.6 Settlements

A settlement consists of a disposition of property in a form which creates a succession of interests in the property. Previously they could exist either as strict settlements under the Settled Land Act 1925, or as trusts for sale under the LPA 1925.

The Trusts of Land and Appointment of Trustees Act 1996 now prohibits the creation of new strict settlements, but those which were in existence at the date when the Act came into force remain valid. All settlements created on or after 1 January 1997 will take effect as trusts of land.

3.7 Trusts of land

A trust of land is defined as 'any trust of property which consists of or includes land'. This includes express, implied, resulting and constructive trusts, trusts for sale, and bare trusts. Trusts of land are governed by the Trusts of Land and Appointment of Trustees Act 1996. Such a trust can be expressly created or will arise under statute, for example where land is held by co-owners or where land passes to personal representatives on the death of the owner.

Under a trust of land the legal estate is vested in the trustees. Trustees have all the powers of an absolute owner, but restrictions may be imposed on such powers by requiring that consent be obtained, for example from a beneficiary, before a power is exercised.

On the death of a trustee, the legal estate automatically vests in the surviving trustee(s) without the need for any document.

On a sale by trustees, a buyer is protected, and need not be concerned with the trusts affecting the proceeds of sale if he pays the purchase money to all the trustees, being at least two in number, or to a trust corporation. In such cases, the trusts which affected the property are detached from it and are overreached.

3.8 Co-ownership

Co-ownership arises whenever two or more people have simultaneous concurrent interests in land. The most common example is two people buying a house together. Whenever co-ownership occurs, the legal estate can be held only by those to whom it is conveyed as trustees of land, and trustees of land must hold as joint tenants. Thus, the right of survivorship applies to the legal estate.

So far as the beneficial interests in the property are concerned, these may be held either as joint tenants (where the right of survivorship applies) or as tenants in common (where it does not).

A conveyance to co-owners should state how the beneficial interests are to be held and this is conclusive. If it does not, they will be held as joint tenants unless either words of severance have been used (eg, 'in equal shares') or an equitable presumption of a tenancy in common arises (eg, when the purchase money is provided in unequal shares or where property is purchased by a business partnership).

3.8.1 Joint tenancy

The characteristic of a joint tenancy is the 'right of survivorship' – when a joint tenant dies their interest automatically accrues to the remaining joint tenants.

Joint tenants are all equally entitled to the whole property and do not have individual shares. If the property is sold they are entitled to share the sale proceeds equally. Thus three joint tenants would receive a third each.

The word 'jointly' will create a joint tenancy but any words creating individual shares (known as 'words of severance') will create a tenancy in common. Thus phrases such as 'in equal shares', 'equally', 'half and half' will usually create a tenancy in common.

A joint tenancy in equity is suitable where the parties wish the survivor to own the whole property.

Example

Husband and wife buy the matrimonial home together. They wish the survivor to own the whole property.

1. H and W   legal estate as joint   2.   H dies – W acquires whole legal
               tenants   estate and equitable interest by
                                                   survivorship
               on trust for

    H and W   equitable interest
               as joint tenants

3.8.2   Tenancy in common

Where the equitable interest is held as tenants in common the right of survivorship does not apply and, on the death of one of the co-owners, the equitable interest passes under the will or intestacy of the deceased co-owner. (The legal estate passes by survivorship.) Tenants in common may hold equal or unequal shares in equity.

A tenancy in common is usually created by use of the term itself, eg, 'the transferees declare they hold the property as tenants in common'. Any words of severance (see **3.8.1** above) will, however, create a tenancy in common.

A tenancy in common in equity is suitable where the co-owners wish to control the devolution of the equitable interest either in a private or in a commercial context. Private individuals may decide to hold as tenants in common but it is also particularly appropriate for partners in a business who would not normally wish their share in the partnership to accrue to their surviving partners automatically.

Example

A and B, an unmarried couple, who contributed to the purchase price of the property $\frac{1}{3}$ and $\frac{2}{3}$ respectively, wish to be free to leave their share in the jointly owned property to their respective families.

1.   A and B   legal estate as joint tenants

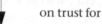
                    on trust for

       A $\frac{1}{3}$ and B $\frac{2}{3}$ – equitable interest as tenants in common

2.   A dies – result is:

       B – legal estate (by survivorship)

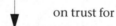
                    on trust for

       A's estate $\frac{1}{3}$ and B $\frac{2}{3}$ – equitable interest as tenants in common

In order to avoid subsequent disputes and litigation, it is essential that the shares of each tenant in common are expressly agreed and recorded in a deed of trust (or certified copy transfer) which is signed by the co-owners and kept in safe custody. This statement or declaration as to the division of the beneficial interest can be altered only by mutual consent of the parties.

3.8.3   Land Registry practice

Where the co-owners have indicated on the transfer that they will be holding the property as tenants in common, Land Registry will place the following restriction on the proprietorship register of the title:

> No disposition by a sole proprietor of the registered estate (except a trust corporation) under which capital money arises is to be registered unless authorised by an order of the court.

This serves as a warning to any third party dealing with the proprietors that a trust is in existence, and that any disposition of the legal estate must be effected by a minimum of two trustees. This restriction indicates that a tenancy in common exists, but it does not state the proportions in which the co-owners have divided the equitable interest between them. The division of the equitable interest is not a matter with which Land Registry is concerned; it is a private matter between the co-owners. No such restriction appears on the proprietorship register if the co-owners have indicated that they wish to hold the beneficial interest as joint tenants. In the absence of a restriction, a third party is entitled to assume that a joint tenancy exists, and may therefore safely deal with the survivor of the joint tenants and need not insist on dealing with two trustees.

3.8.4 Severance of a joint tenancy

It is possible to 'sever' a joint tenancy of the equitable interest (though *not* of the legal estate). Severance turns the joint tenancy into a tenancy in common in equity.

Severance may be achieved, inter alia, by written notice by one joint tenant to the other. Severance must be inter vivos, it cannot be by will. Bankruptcy of any joint tenant also automatically severs their interest.

3.8.5 Sale by a sole surviving co-owner

Where land has been owned by co-owners and all but one have died, a buyer purchasing from the survivor will be concerned to check that the survivor has power to dispose of the land alone.

The sole survivor of tenants in common does not have power to sell the land alone since the equitable interest passes by will or intestacy. After the death of one of two tenants in common therefore, the trust will still subsist. A single trustee of land cannot give a good receipt for capital money and a second trustee must be appointed to overreach the equitable interests on any sale.

The position for the buyer is as discussed below.

3.8.5.1 Sole survivor of joint tenants

If A and B own land as joint tenants in equity and A dies, the law of survivorship will result in B, the sole survivor, becoming absolutely entitled to the whole legal estate and equitable interest. B can therefore sell the property on his own as a sole beneficial owner.

The problem for the buyer is how to be sure that the equitable interest was not severed before A's death, so turning it into a tenancy in common.

The position varies depending on whether the land is registered or unregistered.

Registered land

Here the buyer is entitled to rely on the register of title. If the parties are tenants in common there should be a restriction in the proprietorship register preventing the sole survivor selling alone. If there is no restriction the buyer may assume they were joint tenants and will take a good title from the survivor.

The buyer should obtain a copy of the death certificate of the deceased joint tenant.

Unregistered land

Here the buyer is protected by the Law of Property (Joint Tenants) Act 1964. He should check:

(a)   That the conveyance, which transferred title to the joint tenants, expressly states that they are joint tenants and does not contain any words of severance. (If there is no express statement the buyer should not rely on the Act.)

(b) That there is no 'memorandum of severance' endorsed on the conveyance which originally transferred title to the joint tenants. Where a joint tenancy is severed it is standard conveyancing practice to type a note recording the date and method of severance on the back cover of the conveyance to warn all future buyers.

(c) That there are no bankruptcy registrations in the Land Charges Register against any of the joint tenants. (Bankruptcy severs a joint tenancy.)

(d) That the conveyance to the buyer by the sole surviving joint tenant states that he is solely and beneficially entitled to the land.

The buyer should obtain a copy of the death certificate of the deceased joint tenant.

If the above conditions are not satisfied the buyer cannot rely on the Act and should require the seller to appoint a second trustee to overreach the equitable interests.

Note that the Act does not apply to registered land.

3.8.6 Sale by the sole survivor of tenants in common

Since the sole survivor of tenants in common cannot sell the land alone, a second trustee must always be appointed to overreach the equitable interests under the trust.

3.8.6.1 Registered land

There will be a restriction in the proprietorship register.

3.8.6.2 Unregistered land

The conveyance which originally transferred title to the co-owners should declare how they hold the property.

The buyer should obtain a copy of the death certificate of the deceased tenant in common.

The sole survivor should appoint a second trustee by deed of appointment. The second trustee can be appointed at any time before completion of the transaction and does not have to be appointed before the contract for sale is made. If, however, he is appointed before the contract his name should appear as one of the sellers (ie, he should be a party to the contract). This is because he now holds the legal estate as trustee and must act jointly with the other trustee.

The second trustee could be any third party, eg, the seller's solicitor – it does not have to be the beneficiary who has inherited the equitable interest.

3.8.7 Implied trusts

Consider the following situation:

S owns land and is purporting to sell it to B. Only S's name appears on the documents of title but O is also living there.

B will be concerned to discover what rights, if any, O has in the property.

If O has rights and B does not ensure that he takes the land free of them, he may be involved in a dispute on completion and may not be able to obtain vacant possession.

3.8.7.1 Rights under a trust

O may have acquired rights under a constructive or resulting trust by virtue of contribution, eg, to the original purchase price or to mortgage repayments or substantial improvements to the property.

Enforcement against a purchaser

The position depends on whether the land is registered or unregistered.

Registered land

If O is in actual occupation of the property, the right (if it amounts to an interest under a trust, ie, an interest in land) may be overriding under Sch 3 to the Land Registration Act 2002. It will bind B irrespective of notice.

If O is not in actual occupation, the right must be protected by a restriction in the proprietorship register of S's title.

Unregistered land

Interests under trusts are not registrable as Land Charges. The old doctrine of notice, actual or constructive applies. If B is a bona fide purchaser of a legal estate for value without notice he will take free of O's right. However, occupation by O fixes B with constructive notice of O's rights and puts him on inquiry. In practice, it is often difficult to establish lack of notice.

Overreaching

If O has an equitable interest under a trust S must be required to appoint a second trustee, as a sole trustee cannot give a valid receipt for capital money. A conveyance by all trustees being at least two in number will overreach the equitable interests under the trust and B will take title free of them. This principle applies to registered and unregistered land.

3.8.8 'Non-owning spouses' or civil partners

Suppose that H and W, who are married, both occupy the matrimonial home but that only one of them, say H, owns the legal title. The risk is that in the event of a dispute between them H could seek to exclude W from the property relying on his sole legal ownership.

3.8.8.1 Family Law Act 1996

Where one spouse or civil partner owns the matrimonial home and the other does not, the Act gives statutory rights of occupation (called 'home rights') to the non-owning spouse or civil partner. These rights apply only to married couples or civil partners, not to cohabitees.

Home rights

The home rights are:

(a)   if the spouse or civil partner is in occupation of the matrimonial home, a right not to be excluded from it without a court order; and

(b)   if the spouse or civil partner is not in occupation, a right to enter into occupation with a court order (s 30(2)).

The home rights belonging to the owner will only bind a purchaser for value if they are registered. They can be registered at any time before the owner completes the sale of the home. They are registered as:

Registered land

A notice on the charges register of the owner's title. (Home rights cannot be overriding interests under Sch 3 to the LRA 2002.)

Unregistered land

A Class F Land Charge in the Central Land Charges Registry against the name of the owner.

Family Law Act rights cannot be overreached by appointment of a second trustee. They must be waived (or removed, if already registered) by the non-owning spouse or civil partner.

Even if such rights are not presently protected by registration, the spouse or civil partner may still effect a registration at any time until actual completion of the sale of the home. It will be a condition of the contract that any such registration is removed before completion (Family Law Act 1996, Sch 4, para 4). Negotiations must be entered into with the spouse's or civil partner's solicitors for the removal of the charge and a satisfactory solution obtained before exchange of contracts.

It is unsafe to assume that the spouse or civil partner will not exercise the right to register a charge under the Family Law Act 1996 prior to completion and instructions should be obtained directly from the spouse or civil partner (through a separate solicitor if there is any possibility of conflict of interests) to confirm his or her agreement to the proposed sale. A formal release of rights and agreement not to enforce any such rights against the seller should be prepared for signature by the non-owning spouse or civil partner before exchange.

A registration under the Family Law Act 1996 can be removed on production of one of the following:

(a) an application made by the person with the benefit of the rights;

(b) a decree absolute of dissolution of the marriage or civil partnership;

(c) a court order for removal of the charge;

(d) the death certificate of the spouse or civil partner.

Equitable interests

If it is thought that the spouse or civil partner may also be entitled to an equitable interest in the property (eg, because of financial contributions to the property), it should be assumed that the property is held by the seller on constructive trust for himself and his spouse or civil partner. Independent confirmation of agreement to the sale must be obtained (in writing) from the spouse or civil partner.

3.8.9 Sharers and cohabitees

Sharers and cohabitees may also be able to establish an equitable interest in the property through contribution to the purchase price. Investigation must be made of the exact status of each occupier. If the occupier has an equitable interest, this will be binding on a buyer of registered land as an overriding interest under Sch 3 to the LRA 2002. In unregistered land it would be binding under the doctrine of notice. The occupier should, therefore, be required to release these rights in the contract; see **19.4.3**.

3.9 Mortgages

A mortgage is a transaction where the borrower borrows money from the lender and transfers to the lender, as security for the loan, a legal or equitable interest in land.

3.9.1 Creation of legal mortgages

To be legal a mortgage must be created by deed. The position then depends on whether the mortgaged land is registered or unregistered.

3.9.1.1 Unregistered land

A first legal mortgage of a freehold or a leasehold with more than seven years to run will trigger first registration of the title to the land. The mortgage will appear as a registered charge on the charges register of the title.

Second and subsequent mortgages of *unregistered* land ('puisne' mortgages) will not trigger first registration of the title and the mortgage must be registered as a C(i) Land Charge against the name of the mortgagor (borrower) in the Central Land Charges Register.

3.9.1.2 Registered land

If the mortgaged land already has a registered title, all legal mortgages must be registered, as registered charges, in the charges register of the mortgagor's title. The mortgagee does not obtain a legal interest until this is done.

3.9.2 The power of sale

The power of sale is one of the mortgagee's most important remedies in case of default by the mortgagor on the loan.

(a) A mortgagee who has a mortgage by deed has a statutory power to sell the mortgagor's legal estate (LPA 1925, s 101).

(b) If the mortgaged land is registered, a mortgagee who has a registered charge can execute a transfer that will lead to the registration of the buyer as the new proprietor of the land (LRA 1925, s 34).

The power of sale *arises* 'when the legal date for redemption is past', ie, when the loan is repayable. Most mortgages contain a condition providing that the power of sale will arise as soon as the mortgage is created.

Under s 103 of the LPA 1925 the power of sale is not *exercisable*, ie, should not be used by the mortgagee, until:

(a) the mortgagor has defaulted in a repayment of capital for three months; or

(b) a repayment of any interest due is two months or more in arrear; or

(c) the mortgagor has broken some provision in the mortgage.

This section can be changed by agreement to the contrary and most mortgages say that the power shall be exercisable as from the creation of the mortgage.

Note that a purchaser from a mortgagee exercising a power of sale will take a good title if the power of sale has *arisen*. He does not have to check whether it has become exercisable and still takes the legal estate if in fact it has not. (The mortgagee will, however, be liable to the mortgagor for wrongful exercise of the power.)

3.9.3   Effect of a sale

Sale by a mortgagee vests the mortgagor's legal title in the buyer, subject to incumbrances prior to the mortgage but free from those subsequent to the mortgage.

> **Example**
>
> X owns a freehold factory site.
>
> The land is subject to:
>
> (a) restrictive covenants created in 1978;
>
> (b)   an easement of services for neighbouring property created in 1996;
>
> (c)   a first legal mortgage in favour of M Finance Co created in 1997;
>
> (d)   a second legal charge in favour of N Bank Plc created in 1998.
>
> X defaults on his mortgage to M Finance Co and they exercise their power of sale to B.
>
> B takes the legal estate subject to the restrictive covenants and the easement but free from the charge in favour of N Bank (and also free from the M Finance Co's charge since it will repay itself from the sale proceeds).

The mortgagee (M Finance Co) will use the purchase price to pay off the expenses of sale and its own mortgage and then hand the entire balance to the mortgagee next in priority (N Bank Plc). The mortgagor, X, will be paid any balance left after all the mortgages have been paid off. If there is not enough money to go round, any disappointed mortgagee will sue the mortgagor for debt.

The mortgagee who is selling cannot defeat a prior mortgage. However, his statutory power of sale entitles him to promise to sell free of this prior mortgage. To fulfil the promise, the selling mortgagee will have to redeem (ie, pay off) the prior mortgagee from the proceeds of sale before paying off his own mortgage, and handing on any balance.

Note: If the mortgagor is in occupation of the mortgaged property the selling mortgagee will first have to obtain a possession order from the court so that the sale can be made with vacant possession.

3.9.4   Mortgage of a dwelling house

The Administration of Justice Acts 1970 and 1973 apply where the mortgage is of a dwelling house and the mortgagee is bringing a claim for possession. If the court is satisfied that the mortgagor is likely to be able, within a reasonable period, to pay sums due under the mortgage or to put right a breach of any other obligation in the mortgage, it can adjourn the proceedings or suspend the effect of an order for possession for a period the court thinks to be reasonable.

If the mortgage is an instalment mortgage with a provision that, if any instalment is unpaid, the entire principal becomes instantly due, the mortgagor has only to satisfy the court that he can pay off the outstanding instalments within a reasonable time, not the entire capital.

3.9.5   Leases of mortgaged property

Where mortgaged property is subject to a lease and the mortgagee seeks to exercise a power of sale, the lessee will need to know whether his lease is binding on the mortgagee. If it is not, the mortgagee can sell free of it and the lessee will have to vacate the property.

3.9.5.1   Leases granted prior to the creation of the mortgage

Registered land

A mortgage of a registered title will be subject to a lease existing at the date of the mortgage if the lease is an overriding interest or was noted on the register of title at the date of the mortgage.

Unregistered land

A mortgage of an unregistered title will be subject to an existing lease if the lease was legal or, if equitable, it was registered as a C(iv) Land Charge at the date of the mortgage.

If the mortgage is subject to a lease, the mortgagee will have to sell subject to it.

3.9.5.2   Leases granted after the creation of the mortgage

Section 99 of the LPA 1925 gives a mortgagor who is in possession of the mortgaged property a power to grant leases that will bind the mortgagee, providing the leases meet certain criteria. This power is unpopular with mortgagees and can be, and invariably is, removed by a provision in the mortgage deed.

If the lease is granted without the consent of the mortgagee, the mortgagee who wishes to sell can obtain a court order for possession against the tenant. The tenant will have no security of tenure against the mortgagee and will have to leave.

3.9.6   The mortgagor's spouse/civil partner

3.9.6.1   Spouses who co-own the legal estate

If husband and wife/civil partners co-own the legal estate, both will have executed the mortgage and both are likely to be evicted if the mortgage payments are not made (subject to obtaining relief under the Administration of Justice Acts). However, either may be able to claim that he or she is not bound by the mortgage if he or she only executed the mortgage under the undue influence of the other (see **3.9.7.4** below).

3.9.7   Home rights

A spouse or civil partner who does not co-own the legal estate will have 'home rights' under the Family Law Act 1996, s 30 whether or not he or she co-owns in equity.

3.9.7.1   Co-ownership of the equitable interest

A mortgagee lending to a spouse or civil partner (H) on the security of the matrimonial home is always concerned about the possibility of being bound by an equitable interest belonging to the other spouse or civil partner (W). If the mortgagee is so bound it might mean that:

(a)   the mortgagee cannot get an order for possession against W. This is because W is a beneficiary of a trust of land and the court may not order possession if W has a right to occupy the trust land (see Trusts of Land and Appointment of Trustees Act 1996, s 12).

(b)   even if the mortgagee can get vacant possession he will have to share the proceeds of sale with W.

3.9.7.2   Where the loan is to acquire the house

Suppose that H, a spouse or civil partner, is buying a house and is going to live there with his spouse or civil partner, W. W is contributing £10,000 towards the purchase price. H is raising the balance of the purchase price by a loan from the building society. The legal estate is conveyed into the name of H alone and only H executes the mortgage deed. Later H defaults on the mortgage payments. The building society wants to sell the house with vacant possession. W claims that she owns part of the equitable interest in the house and is therefore entitled to a share in the proceeds of sale. If W's claim to co-own is correct, the building society might nevertheless be protected both by case law and from action taken by the building society's solicitor at the time of the purchase.

The case of *Abbey National Building Society v Cann* [1990] 1 All ER 1085 is authority that W's interest will be postponed to the mortgage. The reason is that the purchase and the mortgage are indivisible events. W's claim is against the house acquired by H. He acquired it subject to a mortgage so W's claim is against the mortgaged property.

What the building society's solicitor would invariably have done is to have obtained W's written consent to the postponement of her claim to that of the building society. Alternatively, the building society could have insisted that W was a party to the mortgage deed. This protection is not strictly necessary because of case law but a signed consent is obviously a clearer argument to raise against the wife than case law is.

3.9.7.3   Where the loan is secured on a house already owned by the spouse or civil partner

If the house has already been bought, and the purpose of the mortgage is to secure later borrowings by H, it is probable that any equitable interest owned by W will pre-date the mortgage. The *Cann* case will not, therefore, assist the bank. The bank needs W's agreement that her interest will be postponed to the bank's mortgage. Her signature is needed either to an agreement to that effect, or to the mortgage deed.

The bank must be very careful as to how that signature is obtained. If W has been induced to sign because of the undue influence of H, her signature will not bind her as against H. Nor will it bind her as against the bank if she can prove either:

(a)   that when he obtained the signature, H did so as agent for the bank. For this reason the bank should approach W directly. It should not hand the documents to H and ask him to procure W's signature on the bank's behalf; or

(b)   that the bank had actual or constructive notice of H's undue influence.

3.9.7.4   Undue influence

Suppose that husband and wife or civil partners live together in the family home. H wishes to raise money to meet his business debts. He intends to borrow money from the bank. The bank insists that any loan be secured by a mortgage of the house. W thinks this is imprudent and is reluctant to sign the mortgage documents. H puts pressure on W to do this and she finally agrees. They both therefore sign mortgage documents in favour of the bank. H is unable to make the mortgage repayments.

The bank could be at risk in these circumstances unless it took reasonable steps to try to ensure that W understood the nature and effect of the transaction and that her consent to it was an informed consent.

The reason for the risk is that W might be able to claim that she was unduly influenced by her husband into signing the mortgage deed. If this were so she would have the right to ask that the mortgage deed be set aside.

The leading case on this area is *Royal Bank of Scotland v Etridge (No 2)* [2001] 4 All ER 449. The procedures to be followed to avoid the risk are considered at **5.3.3**.

The principles apply 'in all cases where there is an emotional relationship between the cohabitees'. It covers all cohabitation, whether heterosexual or homosexual. It can apply to other relationships, eg, to child and parent, if the co-owner 'reposes trust and confidence' in the borrower.

The principle can apply not only where the co-owner is asked to execute the mortgage because he or she is a co-owner of the legal estate, but also where he or she is asked to execute a mortgage or to sign any form of waiver because it is thought that he or she might have an equitable interest in the property.

3.10 Leases

3.10.1 Definition of a lease

A lease is an interest in land for a fixed period of certain duration usually granted in consideration of the payment of rent. To be a lease the tenant must have been granted exclusive possession of the premises (see **3.10.6** below).

3.10.2 Types of leases

Leases may be fixed term or periodic.

3.10.2.1 Fixed-term leases

A lease may be granted for any period of certain duration, no matter how long or short, eg, one week, 99 years, 2,000 years, etc.

Fixed-term leases automatically expire at the end of the term by 'effluxion of time' – at common law there is no need to serve any notice to determine them.

3.10.2.2 Periodic tenancies

Periodic tenancies continue indefinitely, from one period to the next, until determined by the appropriate period's notice to quit (see **3.10.10.2** below).

The most common examples are yearly, quarterly, monthly and weekly.

Such tenancies may be granted expressly but they will also arise by implication of law where the tenant goes into occupation, eg, under an oral agreement and pays rent on a periodic basis. The tenant will acquire a legal periodic tenancy, the period depending on the period over which he paid his rent.

Such tenancies also arise by implication where the tenant 'holds over', ie, remains in possession, with the landlord's consent, after the expiry of a fixed-term tenancy.

Example

T had a 10-year lease under which he paid rent of £300 per quarter.

T's lease expired on 1 January 2002 but he continued to occupy the premises and to pay rent, which the landlord accepted, on a quarterly basis.

T has a legal, quarterly periodic tenancy by implication of law, on the same terms as those of his original lease to the extent they are not inconsistent with a periodic tenancy.

3.10.3 Grant and assignment of leases

3.10.3.1 Grant of a lease

The grant of a lease amounts to the creation of a new estate in land, ie, a leasehold estate. In terms of procedure, it will involve the negotiation of the terms of the lease between the lessor and lessee.

The owner of a freehold estate (L) can grant a lease of any length. He has the right to take possession of the property at the end of the lease – the freehold reversion.

The tenant of the head lease (T) may in turn grant a 'sub-lease' or 'under-lease' out of his lease. The sub-lease cannot be granted for a term longer than the unexpired residue of T's head lease. T has the right to take possession of the property at the end of the sub-lease – a leasehold reversion.

> **Example**
>
> L   landlord/lessor – owner of freehold reversion
> ↓
>   head lease, eg, for 99 years
> T   tenant/lessee – owner of lease
> ↓
>   sub-lease/under-lease, eg, for 21 years
> ST   sub-tenant/sub-lessee

In the above example the only person actually entitled to occupy the land is the sub-tenant (ST). However, three estates in the land exist concurrently, ie:

(a)   the freehold;

(b)   the head lease;

(c)   the sub-lease.

ST could himself grant a lease for no longer than the unexpired residue of his sub-lease. This would be called a sub-underlease. Further grants are in theory possible but not that common, at least in residential property.

3.10.3.2 Assignment of a lease

The owner of a lease may transfer the unexpired residue of the term of the lease to a third party unless the terms of the lease prohibit this. The transfer is called an assignment. The parties are the assignor and the assignee. Any number of assignments may take place during the term of the lease.

> **Example**
>
> L   owner of freehold

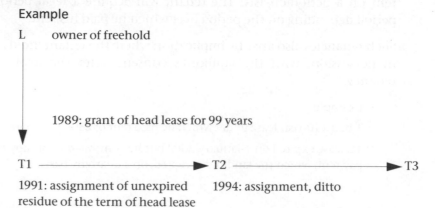

Note that, unlike the grant of a lease, the assignment of a lease merely transfers an existing estate in land, it does not create a new one. The terms of the lease cannot be varied by the assignor and assignee. The consent of the landlord is necessary for this.

The reversion on a lease, whether freehold or leasehold, may also be assigned.

In the following example the reversion on the head lease (freehold reversion) and the reversion on the sub-lease (leasehold reversion) have both been assigned. The events are numbered in order of occurrence.

Example

    (iv)   1993: assignment of freehold reversion

L1 ——————————————————▶ L2

    (i)   1989: grant of head lease for 99 years

T1 ——————————————————▶ T2 ——————————————————▶ T3

    (iii) 1991: assignment   (v) 1994: assignment
                                 of leasehold reversion

ST   (ii)   1990: grant of sub-lease for 21 years

The assignee of a reversion acquires the right to receive the rent and also the right to repossession of the property when all subsidiary leases determine.

3.10.4 Characteristics of a lease

A lease is a *contract* between lessor and lessee. The consideration is usually rent and mutual covenants and agreements, eg, to repair, insure, etc.

In addition, however, a lease creates an interest in land, which means that its terms may bind successors in title of the original parties. The privity between successors in title is known as 'privity of estate'.

3.10.5 Certainty of duration

A lease must be for a certain duration, not for an indefinite period of time.

3.10.6 Exclusive possession (lease or licence?)

To be a lease the lessee must have been given the right to exclusive possession of the premises, that is, he must have the right to exclude all others, including the landlord.

If the person to whom the 'lease' is granted does not have exclusive possession then it may be that he merely has a personal right to occupy, generally known as a licence. A licence does not create an interest in land.

Whether a lease or a licence has been created depends on the intention of the parties in so far as it can be inferred from all the circumstances. The court will look at the substance of the agreement not the form (see, eg, *Street v Mountford* [1985] 2 All ER 289, HL).

A licence may be revoked at any time or according to its terms.

3.10.7 Legal or equitable?

A lease may be legal or equitable. A legal lease must be created using the correct formalities (see below).

3.10.7.1 Legal leases

A term of years absolute

To be capable of existing as a legal estate a leasehold interest must be 'a term of years absolute' (LPA 1925, s 1(1)):

(a)   term of years, ie, a period having a fixed and certain duration, eg, 99 years. Note: a periodic tenancy *is* within this definition;

(b)   absolute, ie, not determinable on the happening of some uncertain future event.
Note: The possibility of premature determination by, eg, notice, surrender or forfeiture will not prevent the lease being 'absolute'.

Note: A lease does not have to take effect in possession. It can be granted to take effect at some future time provided it is within 21 years of its grant (LPA 1925, s 144(3)).

> **Example**
>
> | 1 January 2002 | L grants a 99-year lease of Blackacre to T |
> | 1 June 2002 | the term commences, ie, T is entitled to take possession and the 99 years begins to run |

The date when the term of the lease begins (ie, when the right to possession arises) is usually referred to as the commencement date.

The commencement date can also be backdated to a date *before* the date of grant of the lease. This is sometimes done where a landlord grants a number of leases, eg, of flats or offices, in the same building over a period of time and wishes the terms of all the leases to expire on the same day. All the commencement dates for the terms will be expressed to be the same regardless of the date of grant of the individual leases.

Formalities

A legal lease must be created by deed (LPA 1925, s 52(1) and Law of Property (Miscellaneous Provisions) Act 1989, s 1) unless it is within s 54(2) of the LPA 1925, below.

The LPA 1925, s 54(2) provides that a lease which:

(a)   takes effect in possession;

(b)   for a term of years not exceeding three years (this includes a periodic tenancy);

(c)   at the best rent reasonably obtainable without taking a fine,

may be merely in writing or even oral and will still be legal.

Note: A deed is always necessary to effect a legal assignment of a lease even if the lease itself has been created informally under s 54(2).

Enforcement

Legal leases are prima facie binding on all comers; however this position is modified by the LRA 2002 and depends on the length of the original term of the lease. Leases granted for a term of more than seven years must be registered with their own separate title number. The position then depends on whether or not the reversionary title is registered.

Leases exceeding seven years

Unregistered reversion   The grant of the lease triggers first registration of title to the lease (but does not affect the title to the reversion, which will remain unregistered).

Registered reversion   If the lease is granted out of a reversion with a registered title the grant of the lease amounts to a 'dealing' with the registered title and the lease must be registered with its own title and in addition noted on the reversionary title.

Leases for seven years or less

Unregistered reversion   The lease is automatically binding and requires no form of registration.

Registered reversion   The lease is an overriding interest under Sch 3 to the LRA 2002 whether or not the tenant is in actual occupation. No form of registration is required.

3.10.7.2   Equitable leases

A lease which has not been created by deed and is not within s 54(2) of the LPA 1925 (see above), may take effect as an equitable lease (in effect as contract to create a lease) provided that it is:

(a)   for value; and

(b)   satisfies the requirements of the Law of Property (Miscellaneous Provisions) Act 1989, s 2, ie, it is in writing, incorporating all terms expressly agreed and signed by or on behalf of each party.

Enforcement

Equitable leases usually require some form of registration to make them binding on a purchaser of the reversion.

Unregistered reversion

The lease must be registered as a C(iv) Land Charge against the name of the owner of the immediate reversion. If unregistered, it is void against a purchaser of the legal estate for money or money's worth.

Registered reversion

The lease must be registered as a minor interest on the charges register of the reversionary title. If, however, the tenant is in actual occupation the lease is an overriding interest under Sch 3 to the LRA 2002 and binding without registration.

3.10.8   Enforcement of leasehold covenants

See **34.5** below for discussion of the enforcement of leasehold covenants.

3.10.9   Options in leases

The terms of the lease may contain the grant of an option to the tenant to renew the lease for a further term or to purchase the reversion. Such options are binding between the original parties to the lease by privity of contract.

Does the benefit and burden of the option run with the lease and the reversion respectively?

3.10.9.1   Option to renew the lease

Where the lease has been assigned, an option to renew a lease has been held to be a 'touching and concerning' covenant. The benefit of the covenant will therefore pass automatically to an assignee of the lease unless the wording of the option confines the benefit to the original grantee.

Example

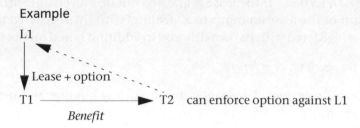

Where the reversion has been assigned the burden of an option to renew will *not* pass automatically to the assignee of the reversion. To be enforceable against the assignee the option must be registered.

Example

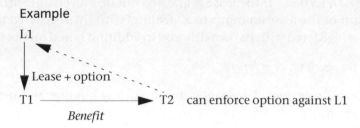

For the current lessee to enforce against L2 – the option must be registered.

If L1's title is unregistered the option should be registered as a C(iv) Land Charge against L1's name before he assigns to L2.

If L1's title is registered the option should be protected, as a minor interest, by a notice on the charges register of L1's title before he assigns to L2. If however, the tenant is in actual occupation, the option will be an overriding interest under Sch 3 to the LRA 2002.

3.10.9.2   Option to purchase the reversion

Where the lease has been assigned, an option to purchase the reversion has been held *not* to be a 'touching and concerning' covenant. Thus the benefit does not automatically pass to the assignee of the lease.

The benefit may be expressly assigned (with or without the lease). It may also be held to have been impliedly assigned, as in *Griffith v Pelton* [1958] Ch 205, where the term 'the Tenant' was defined to include the tenant's successors in title. A grant of an option to 'the Tenant' was therefore held to include assignees of the lease on any assignment.

The burden of an option to purchase the reversion will not bind an assignee of the reversion unless it registered. Registration requirements are the same as for options to renew the lease (see **3.10.8.1** above).

3.10.10   Determination of leases

3.10.10.1   Expiry by effluxion of time

This applies to fixed-term leases. No notice to determine them is necessary at common law – they automatically expire at the end of the term.

3.10.10.2   Notice to quit

Periodic tenancies are determined by the appropriate period's notice to quit. At common law the notice period does not have to exclude the day of service and the day of expiry, ie 'clear' notice is not necessary. If the terms of the tenancy do not provide, the common law implies the following length of notice:

Yearly tenancies

These are determined by at least half a year's notice expiring at the end of a completed year of the tenancy.

Either the last day of the year of the tenancy (ie, the day *before* the anniversary of the commencement of the year) or the next following day may be specified in the notice as the expiry day.

If the tenancy began on one of the usual quarter days 'half a year' means two quarters, otherwise it means 182 days, ie, the odd half day is ignored.

Example

T has a yearly tenancy. The period starts on 1 January and ends on 31 December each year.

It is 2008 and L wishes to give T notice to quit to leave at the end of that year.

The last day in 2008 when L can give notice is 3 July. The notice may be expressed to expire on 31 December 2008, ie 182 days.

If L serves notice later than 3 July he cannot obtain possession until 31 December 2009 because the notice served must be at least half a year *AND must expire at the end of a completed year of the tenancy.* In effect, L would then be forced to give more than a year's notice in order to comply with the rules.

Quarterly, monthly and weekly tenancies

These are determined by one full period's notice (ie one quarter, month, etc) expiring at the end of a completed period of the tenancy.

Example

T has a monthly tenancy – the period starts on the 1st of each month.

It is 14 August and L wants to give T notice to quit. The earliest date L can specify for expiry of the notice is 30 September, ie, the notice must be at least one month long *and must expire at the end of a completed month.*

If L had wished T to quit at the end of August he would have had to serve notice *no later than* 1 August to expire on 31 August.

Note: Any notice to quit premises occupied as a dwelling house must be given at least four weeks before it is to take effect, must be in writing and must contain certain prescribed information (Protection from Eviction Act 1977, s 5).

It will be seen, from the above examples that, in order to give the minimum period of notice required at common law, careful attention must be paid to the latest date for service. Serving too late will mean that a longer period of notice must be given to ensure that the notice expires on the correct day. The consequences are particularly severe in the context of a yearly tenancy (see above).

Notice periods are strictly enforced and the court will not grant equitable relief because of negligence or forgetfulness.

3.10.10.3 Surrender

Surrender occurs where the tenant yields up his lease to his immediate landlord who accepts the surrender. The lease is said to merge in the landlord's reversion and is extinguished. To be legal, surrender must be by deed (LPA 1925, s 52).

3.10.10.4 Merger

This occurs where the tenant acquires the immediate reversion on his lease (ie, acquires his landlord's estate in land). It can also occur where a third party acquires both the lease and the reversion. It is the converse of surrender. As with surrender, the lease automatically merges with the reversion and is extinguished unless the contrary intention appears.

3.10.10.5 Statutory protection

Note, however, that many types of leases have the benefit of statutory protections which will only allow them to be terminated in prescribed ways. Often the landlord will have to prove a 'ground', or statutory reason for wishing to obtain possession.

3.11 Landlord's remedies for breach of covenant

3.11.1 Against former tenants

Before proceeding against a former tenant or his guarantor for a 'fixed charge', the Landlord and Tenant (Covenants) Act 1995 requires the service of a 'default notice' within six months of the current tenant's default. A 'fixed charge' is rent, service charge or any other liquidated sum due under the lease.

3.11.2 For non-payment of rent

Only six years' arrears is recoverable. As well as suing for the rent, the landlord may consider the following remedies:

(a)   Forfeiture (see **3.11.5**).

(b)   Distress: this consists of entry to the demised premises and seizing chattels to the value of the debt. It is subject to very complex rules and is generally not available in the case of residential properties. Under the Tribunals, Courts and Enforcement Act 2007, distress will be replaced by a new commercial rent arrears recovery procedure. This will allow (in relation to commercial lettings only) an authorised enforcement agent to seize possession of a tenant's goods in defined circumstances.

(c)   Collecting the rent from a sub-tenant: this is possible under s 6 of the Law of Distress Amendment Act 1906, the sub-tenant being required to pay his rent direct to the head landlord. Under the Tribunals, Courts and Enforcement Act 2007, the new commercial rent arrears recovery procedure will enable recovery of rent from a sub-tenant.

(d)   Bankruptcy and winding up: if the debt exceeds £750 a statutory demand can be served with a view to commencing bankruptcy or winding-up proceedings.

3.11.3 Other covenants

(a)   forfeiture (see **3.11.5**);

(b)   injunction: this is most appropriate for breach of a negative covenant such as a user covenant, or to prevent an anticipated breach of covenant such as an assignment in breach of covenant;

(c)   damages: these are recoverable under normal contractual rules as laid down by *Hadley v Baxendale* (1854) 9 Exch 341.

3.11.4   Special rules for breaches of tenant's repairing covenant

3.11.4.1   Forfeiture

See **3.11.5**.

3.11.4.2   Damages

Under s 18 of the LTA 1927, damages recoverable are not to exceed the diminution in the value of the landlord's reversion, ie they are not necessarily based on the cost of doing the repairs. However, s 18 does not apply to a breach where a landlord has used his self-help remedy. So it is common in a lease for the landlord to be allowed to enter the premises and carry out the repairs if the tenant has failed to comply with a landlord's notice to repair. The lease clause will then provide that the tenant should pay to the landlord the landlord's costs incurred in effecting the repairs. The case of *Jervis v Harris* [1996] Ch 195 confirms that the amount thus recoverable is not limited by the s 18 rules.

There are further limitations on a landlord's claim for damages which can also be avoided by use of the self-help remedy. So if the lease was originally granted for seven years or more and has at least three years unexpired, then the provisions of the Leasehold Property (Repairs) Act 1938 apply. This Act provides that where a landlord is serving a notice under s 146 of the LPA 1925 prior to forfeiture, the notice must include a statement of the tenant's right to serve a counter-notice within 28 days. The 1938 Act also provides that before the landlord can enforce a claim for damages against a tenant under such a lease, the landlord must serve a s 146 notice on the tenant and the notice must again include a statement of the tenant's right to serve a counter-notice within 28 days. If the tenant does so, the landlord can proceed with his claim (ie, either to damages or forfeiture) only if he gets the leave of the court. Such leave will be granted only in specified circumstances, eg, that the value of the reversion has been substantially diminished.

3.11.5   Forfeiture

This is a right to retake possession of the premises and so prematurely determine the lease. The right must generally be expressly reserved by the lessor.

Note: Where premises are let as a dwelling, it is unlawful to enforce forfeiture otherwise than by court proceedings while any person is lawfully residing on any part of the premises (Protection from Eviction Act 1977, s 2).

In all other circumstances, the landlord may forfeit by *peaceful* re-entry onto the premises – ie, court proceedings are unnecessary.

3.11.5.1   Forfeiture for non-payment of rent

The tenant may be able to claim relief if he pays all arrears of rent and costs before the hearing, or if he pays them after the hearing and the court considers it just and equitable to grant relief.

3.11.5.2 Forfeiture for breach of other covenants

The landlord must first serve a notice on the tenant under s 146 of the LPA 1925, which:

(a)   specifies the breach; and

(b)   requires it to be remedied if capable of remedy; and

(c)   requires compensation if desired.

The tenant must be allowed a reasonable time within which to remedy the breach, and if he does so there can be no forfeiture and the landlord's costs are not recoverable unless the lease otherwise provides (which it generally does).

If the tenant does not remedy the breach the landlord may forfeit the lease by applying to the court for a possession order.

The tenant may apply to the court for relief against forfeiture and the court may grant such relief as it thinks fit (LPA 1925, s 146).

3.11.5.3 Additional rules for breach of a repairing covenant

If the lease was originally granted for seven years or more and has at least three years unexpired, then the provisions of the Leasehold Property (Repairs) Act 1938 apply. This provides that whether a landlord is seeking to claim damages or to forfeit for breach of a repairing covenant, he must serve a notice on the tenant under s 146 of the LPA 1925. In addition to the normal requirements of such a notice (see above) it must also include a statement of a tenant's right to serve a counter notice within 28 days. If the tenant does so, the landlord can only proceed with his claim (ie, either to damages or forfeiture) if he gets the leave of the court. Such leave will only be granted in specified circumstances, eg, that the value of the reversion has been substantially diminished.

3.12 The law of contract

A working knowledge of the basic law of contract is also essential for an understanding of the underlying framework of a conveyancing transaction.

For a legally binding contract to exist, certain essential elements are required. There must be:

(a)   an offer (as opposed to a mere invitation to treat);

(b)   unconditional acceptance of the offer;

(c)   consideration; and

(d)   an intention to create legal relations.

3.12.1 Legal formalities for a contract for the sale of land

In addition to the items in the list in **3.12** above, a contract for the sale of an interest in land must comply with the Law of Property (Miscellaneous Provisions) Act 1989, s 2. This requires all contracts for the sale or other disposition of land or an interest in land to be made in writing and signed by the parties. The writing must incorporate all the terms which have been expressly agreed by the parties and the document must then be signed by or on behalf of all the parties.

Where contracts are to be exchanged each part of the contract must contain all the agreed terms and be signed by the appropriate party; it is not necessary for both parties to sign both parts of the contract. It is possible for the signed document to refer to another document which itself contains some or all of the agreed terms. If the document does not contain all the agreed terms, an order for rectification may be sought. The requirement for a written contract does not apply to contracts:

(a)   to grant a lease for a term not exceeding three years taking effect in possession at the best rent without a fine (premium);

(b)   made at public auction;

(c)   regulated under the Financial Services and Markets Act 2000.

However, options, equitable mortgages and side letters (variations of contract) issued in connection with sale of land transactions do need to satisfy the requirements of s 2 of the 1989 Act. Failure to satisfy the requirements of s 2 results in there being no contract at all between the parties, and the court has no equitable jurisdiction to allow the enforcement of a contract which does not comply with s 2. The statutory requirements are normally satisfied by the preparation by the seller's solicitor of a formal contract which is usually prepared in two identical parts based on standard conditions of sale amended to fit the particular circumstances of the transaction.

3.12.2 Unfair contract terms

The Unfair Terms in Consumer Contracts Regulations 1999 (SI 1999/2083) require all contracts to which they apply to be drafted in plain English, and also allow a buyer to challenge any term which has not been individually negotiated between the parties on the grounds that the term is unfair. Although the Regulations do not expressly state that they apply to land contracts, it is generally accepted, in the absence of an express exclusion, that they do. The Regulations apply only where the seller is a 'supplier', ie, acting in the course of a business, and the buyer is a 'consumer', ie, a private individual. Therefore, the 'normal' residential conveyancing transaction between a private seller and a private buyer is not affected by the Regulations. Similarly, a commercial lease between a landlord who is in business and a tenant who is in business falls outside the Regulations since in this case the transaction is made between two 'suppliers' as defined in the Regulations. The principal land transactions to which Regulations apply are:

(a)   new house sales by a seller/developer (acting in the course of a business) to a private buyer;

(b)   tenancy agreements made between a landlord (in business) and a tenant (private individual);

(c)   mortgages where the lender is acting in the course of business and the borrower is a private individual;

(d)   contracts for financial services made between a broker (in business) and a private individual;

(e)   sales by a mortgagee to a private individual.

Where the Regulations do apply, the burden is on the buyer to prove unfairness. A term will be regarded as unfair if, contrary to the requirement of good faith, it causes a significant imbalance in the parties' rights and obligations arising under the contract to the detriment of the consumer. Various factors, similar to those contained in the Unfair Contract Terms Act 1977 (which does not apply to land contracts), are included in Sch 2 to the Regulations to act as guidelines as to whether 'good faith' exists, for example the strength of the bargaining position of the parties, the circumstances surrounding the contract, whether the consumer has received any special inducement, such as a discount, to agree to the term. An illustrative list of terms which may be regarded as unfair is set out in Sch 3. If a term is held to be unfair, that term is to be treated as void, but the rest of the contract remains binding on the parties, so long as it is capable of continuing without the offending term.

3.13 Further reading

C Harpum, *Megarry and Wade: Law of Real Property* (6th edn, 1999).

Chapter 4

Registered Land

4.1 Introduction

The two systems of conveyancing currently in use in England and Wales, registered and unregistered conveyancing, were introduced in **Chapter 1**. The substantive law and procedure relating to both systems is broadly similar. Where differences exist, it will normally be found that the registered system is less complex than its unregistered counterpart.

Most of the statutes relating to land transactions have equal application to both systems. In particular, the LPA 1925 applies to both. However, there are some provisions which are exclusive to registered land. The principal statute governing registered land is the LRA 2002. This came into force on 13 October 2003 and replaced the LRA 1925. This chapter sets out the general principles relating to registered land as they apply from 13 October 2003. The 'fundamental objective' of the LRA 2002 is to lay the foundations for electronic dealing with land so that the register will be a complete and accurate reflection of the state of the ownership of any given piece of land.

To administer the registration of title to land in England and Wales, a system of Land Registry Offices has been established. Each Office deals with the registration of the title to the land in the area of the country allocated to it. This is generally on a regional basis; for example, the Office in Swansea covers the whole of Wales. However, several of the London Boroughs are allocated to Offices some distance from the capital (eg, Birkenhead).

4.2 What title may be registered

The register is a register of the 'title' (or ownership) of various rights over the land. The following may be registered:

(a) the freehold (ie, the fee simple absolute in possession);

(b) a lease that has more than seven years unexpired;

(c) leases of any length where the right to possession is discontinuous (eg, a time share);

(d) leases of any length granted to take effect in possession more than three months after the date of grant;

(e)   a rentcharge that is either perpetual or for a term of which more than seven years are unexpired;

(f)   a *profit à prendre* in gross (eg, a fishing right) that is either perpetual or for a term of which more than seven years are unexpired;

(g)   a franchise (eg, a right to hold a market) that is either perpetual or for a term of which more than seven years are unexpired.

It should be noted that it is the title to each of these rights that is registrable. So, there will be a separate entry on the register for each of these rights, even though they relate to the same piece of land: there will not be one entry which deals with the ownership of all the rights affecting a given piece of land.

4.3   When title must be registered

The owners of the above rights can voluntarily apply for registration at any time, but, due to the slow take-up of voluntary registration, a system of compulsory registration was introduced many years ago. The requirement to 'convert' land from the old unregistered system to the registered system occurs when one of the following events happens in relation to unregistered land:

(a)   a transfer of the freehold, whether for valuable consideration or by way of gift (eg, an assent or inter vivos gift) or in pursuance of a court order;

(b)   a grant of a lease for more than seven years;

(c)   a grant of a lease where the right to possession is discontinuous (eg, a time share) provided that the periods of possession when added together total more than seven years;

(d)   a grant of a lease of any length granted to take effect in possession more than three months after the date of grant;

(e)   an assignment of a lease which at the time of assignment has more than seven years unexpired;

(f)   a first legal mortgage of the freehold or of a lease which at the time of the mortgage has more than seven years unexpired.

Once the title has been registered, any subsequent dispositions must themselves be registered in order to be legally effective.

4.3.1   Conveyancing implications

If the title is not registered within two months of any of the above, the disposition will become void as regards the legal estate. It is, however, possible to apply to the Registrar for an extension of this period (on payment of a fee).

Unfortunately, the requirements for compulsory registration have been brought into force at different times. So, although the requirements for compulsory registration have applied on a sale of the freehold to the whole of England and Wales since 1 December 1990, different areas of the country became subject to compulsion at different times prior to this. This is because the requirement to register was imposed gradually over a period of more than 50 years. Similarly, it is only since 1 April 1998 that registration became compulsory after a gift, the grant of a first legal mortgage or an assent, and only since 13 October 2003 that leases with more than seven years unexpired are registrable. Prior to this, only leases for more than 21 years were capable of registration.

When buying unregistered land, it is therefore always necessary to check the date when the area in which the property is situated became subject to compulsory registration. If it is discovered that the land should have been registered after some earlier disposition but has not been, the seller must be required to register the title before the transaction to the buyer proceeds. It is not satisfactory to purchase the unregistered title from the seller and then for the buyer to apply for first registration, because the buyer has no guarantee that the unregistered title being offered to him by the seller will be accepted for registration by Land Registry. The buyer's lender will also insist that the defect in the seller's title is corrected before completion of the buyer's purchase.

4.4   Land and charge certificates

Once land is registered, title to that land depends on what is entered on the register at Land Registry; thereafter the State guarantees the title. Proof of ownership no longer depends on the deeds to the land.

However, prior to 13 October 2003, a copy of the entries on the Register in the form of a land certificate was issued to the registered proprietor. If there was a mortgage over the land, a charge certificate in similar form, but having the original mortgage deed attached, was issued instead to the lender, the land certificate being retained in the Registry. Generally speaking, either the land or charge certificate had to be submitted to the Registry before any subsequent disposition could be registered. Land and charge certificates were abolished as from 13 October 2003 and existing certificates are no longer required on a subsequent registration. However, Land Registry now issues a TID to a registered proprietor which contains a copy of the entries on the register. It is not admissible as evidence of ownership, though, and does not need to be produced on a subsequent disposition of the land. It is the register itself which is the proof of ownership, and official copies (previously called 'office copies') can be obtained and these are admissible as proof of ownership.

4.5   Devolution of registered land

Once an estate in land becomes registered, all devolutions from that title must also follow the registered system. A separate title number identifies each estate in registered land, so that each separate estate in one physical parcel of land will have its own distinctive title number. If, for example, a landowner registered the freehold estate in a parcel of land, a register entry would be made, identifying the physical area of land which belonged to him. The title would also identify the estate as freehold and give him a title number by which to identify the land. If that landowner then grants a 999-year lease of the whole of the land to a tenant, the tenant under that lease has a registrable interest in the land and, on registration of the lease, a new entry would be made showing the physical extent of the land (in this example this will be identical to that shown on the freehold title), stating that the interest held is leasehold, giving brief details of the lease itself, and giving the tenant an identifying title number which is different from that used by the freehold estate.

On registration of the lease, the freehold title will be cross-referenced to show the existence of the lease. Similarly, the leasehold title will contain a reference to the freehold title. This cross-referencing system ensures that the tenant of a registered lease is able to trace his landlord should the need to do so arise, and that, because the existence of the lease is noted on the freehold title, a buyer of the freehold cannot do so in ignorance of the existence of the lease.

The 999-year lease used in the above example would probably be a building lease, and the tenant under the lease might then build a block of flats on the land and sell off each flat on a 99-year lease. Each of the tenants under the 99-year leases will also have his own title number. Each of these will show only part of the land, ie, the part which is the subject of the lease – the flat itself – and each will be cross-referenced to the superior titles. It is, therefore, possible for there to be several titles in existence at any one time, all of which relate to the same physical plot of land, but each is distinguished from the other because each relates to a separate estate in that land, and each has its own distinctive title number. The title number of an estate in registered land is its sole distinguishing feature and must be referred to in every dealing with that estate.

4.6   Classes of title

Once land is entered on the register, the State guarantees the title and compensation is payable in certain circumstances if a defect is found in a registered title. Four classes of title are available and, when an application is made for first registration, the Registrar will decide which class of title should be allocated to the interest which is being registered. The class of title which has been given to the interest is shown on the proprietorship register of the title (see **4.7**).

4.6.1   Absolute title

The vast majority of registered titles are classed as 'absolute', which in effect means the title is as near perfect as it can be (see further below). This class of title can be given to either a freehold or a leasehold interest in the land.

The proprietor of an interest which is registered with an absolute title has vested in him the legal estate, together with all appurtenant rights, and subject only to:

(a)   entries on the register;

(b)   unregistered interests within Schs 1 or 3 to the LRA 2002 (see **4.8.2**);

(c)   where the proprietor is a trustee, minor interests (third-party rights) of which he has notice, for example the interests of the beneficiaries under the trust; and

(d)   where the land is leasehold, the express and implied covenants and obligations under the lease.

On an application for first registration, the Registrar has a discretion under s 9(3) of the LRA 2002 to overlook minor defects in the title and to grant an absolute title, so curing the defect.

It must not be assumed that just because a piece of land is registered with absolute title this means that the title to the land is perfect. The State guarantee takes effect subject to entries on the register (eg covenants and easements) which might make the land totally unsuitable for a client's needs. Further, Land Registry often makes 'non-guaranteed' entries on an absolute title, ie entries that do not carry the State guarantee. So the register might state that a particular deed 'is expressed' to have some effect. This means that Land Registry does not guarantee that it does have that effect.

4.6.2   Possessory title

Registration with a possessory title has the same effect as registration with absolute title, except that the proprietor is also subject to all adverse interests existing at the date of first registration. Possessory title will be granted where the applicant is in possession of the land and, for example, he has lost his title deeds or is claiming title through adverse possession under the Limitation Act 1980.

Although initially only a possessory title will be granted in these circumstances, it may be possible to upgrade the title to absolute after a period of time. Possessory titles are encountered quite frequently in practice, although statistically they represent less than 1% of all registered titles. This class of title can be given to either a freehold or a leasehold interest in the land.

4.6.3   Qualified title

A qualified title, which in practice is very rare, is granted where the title submitted for registration shows a specific identified defect which the Registrar deems to be of such a nature that he cannot use his discretion to overlook the defect and grant an absolute title. The registration has the same effect as registration with an absolute title, except that the State's guarantee of the title does not apply to the specified defect. Such a title might be awarded where, for example, the title submitted for first registration showed that a transaction within the title had been carried out in breach of trust. In this situation, the proprietor would take his interest in the land subject to the interests (if any) of the beneficiaries under the trust. This class of title can be given either to a freehold or to a leasehold interest in the land.

4.6.4   Good leasehold title

As its name suggests, a good leasehold title applies only to leasehold estates. This class of title will be awarded where the Registrar is satisfied that the title to the leasehold interest is sound but, having no access to the title to the superior reversionary interest, he is not prepared to guarantee the lease against defects in the freehold title, or to guarantee that the freeholder had the right to grant the lease. Such a title will therefore be given only where the title to the freehold reversion is unregistered, or where the freehold is registered with less than an absolute title and where the applicant for registration of the leasehold interest does not submit evidence of title to the freehold reversion when making his application. A good leasehold title is regarded by lenders as being unsatisfactory, and for this reason is sometimes difficult to sell or mortgage.

4.6.5   Upgrading title

The Registrar may upgrade a title on his own initiative, or the proprietor may apply for upgrading.

4.6.5.1   Possessory title

A possessory title may be upgraded to an absolute title (or, in the case of leasehold land, to a good leasehold title) if either:

(a)   the Registrar is satisfied as to the title; or

(b)   the land has been registered with possessory title for at least 12 years and the Registrar is satisfied that the proprietor is in possession.

4.6.5.2   Qualified title

A qualified title may be upgraded to absolute (or, in the case of leasehold land, to a good leasehold title) if the Registrar is satisfied as to the title.

4.6.5.3   Good leasehold title

A good leasehold title may be converted to an absolute title if the Registrar is satisfied as to reversionary freehold title and any intermediate leasehold title. This could occur after the registration of the reversion or of a superior lease.

4.7 The form of the register

The register kept at Land Registry shows the true state of the title. Land Registry Offices now have computerised records and the official copy issued is a computer-generated printout of the register entries. The register is divided into three sections:

(a)   the property register;

(b)   the proprietorship register; and

(c)   the charges register.

An example showing typical register entries is shown below.

LAND REGISTRY

TITLE NUMBER: **LM 12037**

Edition date: 1 May 1985

A: Property Register

This register describes the land and estate comprised in the title.

COUNTY	DISTRICT
CORNSHIRE	MARADON

1. (19 February 1960) The freehold land shown and edged with red on the plan of the above title filed at the Registry and being 47, Queens' Road, Loamster, Maradon, Cornshire CS1 5TY

B: Proprietorship Register

This register specifies the class of title and identifies the owner. It contains any entries that affect the right of disposal.

Title Absolute

1. (1 May 1985) Proprietor (s): ROGER EVANS of 47, Queens' Road, Loamster, Maradon, Cornshire CS1 5TY

C: Charges Register

This register contains any charges and other matters that affect the land.

1. (19 February 1960) A Conveyance of the land in this title dated 9 August 1952 made between (1) Sir James Fawcett (Vendor) and (2) Harold Hawtree (Purchaser) contains the following covenants:
    "The Purchaser with the intent and so as to bind the property hereby conveyed and to benefit and protect the retained land of the Vendor lying to the south of the land hereby conveyed hereby covenants with the Vendor that he and his successors in title will at all times observe and perform the stipulations and conditions set out in the schedule hereto."
    THE SCHEDULE ABOVE REFERRED TO
    "Not to build or allow to be built on the property any building without the written consent of the Vendor or his successors in title."

2. (1 May 1985) REGISTERED CHARGE dated 19 April 1985 to secure the moneys including the further advances therein mentioned.

3. (1 May 1985) Proprietor(s): HUMBERSHIRE AND COUNTIES BANK PLC of County House, Westford, Humbershire HS11 8YU.

END OF REGISTER

Note: A date at the beginning of an entry is the date on which the entry was made in the Register.

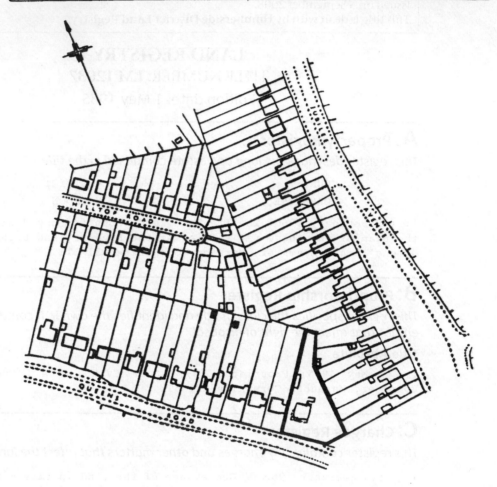

H.M. LAND REGISTRY		TITLE NUMBER	
		LM 12037	
ORDNANCE SURVEY PLAN REFERENCE	ZZ 8987	SECTION M	Scale 1/1250
COUNTY CORNSHIRE	MARADON DISTRICT	© Crown Copyright 1969	

4.7.1 The property register

The property register describes the estate in land which is registered (ie, freehold or leasehold), identifies the property by a short verbal description (eg, its postal address) and shows the physical area of the land which is the subject of the registration, usually by reference to a plan. The plan (known as 'the title plan') is based on the Index Map, which is a large-scale map, based on Ordnance Survey maps, showing the extent of the land which is registered. A copy of the plan is supplied with the official copies of the register entries. The property register will also give details of any rights which benefit the land (eg, the right to use a pathway over adjacent land). It may also contain reference to easements to which the property is subject. In appropriate cases, the register will contain cross-references to superior and inferior titles (eg, to the freehold reversion in the case of a head lease and to any sub-leases granted out of the head lease).

Although the right does exist for a land owner to have his boundaries determined by Land Registry, this right is rarely used and the boundaries shown on the plan supplied by the Registry will give only a general indication of the position of the boundaries. Extraneous evidence (eg, from pre-registration deeds) may be required to prove the exact position of boundaries.

Where the land is leasehold, brief details of the lease under which the land is held will be given on the property register.

4.7.2 The proprietorship register

The proprietorship register states the class of the title which is registered. Although the vast majority of titles are absolute, this part of the register must be checked carefully to ensure that a registration with a title other than absolute is not inadvertently overlooked. This part of the register will also give the name(s) and address(es) of the registered proprietor(s). The address entered on the register is the address which the Registrar will use if for any reason he needs to contact the land owner about the land. It is therefore important that this address is kept up-to-date, eg on a company changing its registered office. It is possible for a proprietor to have up to three addresses for service noted on the register, one of which can be an e-mail address.

If there are any restrictions on the proprietors' powers to deal with the land (eg, if they hold as trustees for another person) a note of the restriction will be entered on this part of the register. The register shows only the position of the legal estate in the land. As with unregistered land, equities are kept 'behind the curtain'. The register may, therefore, reveal the existence of a trust, but will never reveal the details of the trust, such as who the beneficiaries are or their respective interests in the trust.

If, on the transfer to the current proprietors, they entered into personal covenants, for example an indemnity covenant binding only on them and not on future proprietors of the land, this will also be noted on the proprietorship register.

In the case of proprietors registered on or after 1 April 2000, the register will also normally include details of the price paid for the property by those proprietors.

4.7.3 The charges register

The charges register contains details of charges or incumbrances which currently affect the title. Here will be found a note of the burden of easements and covenants which bind the land, often with a reference to a schedule attached to the register. The schedule will contain extracts of the documents which imposed the easements or covenants, with a verbatim copy of the wording of the incumbrance. Only covenants which endure through a change of ownership of the land are noted on the charges register. Covenants which are purely personal in nature, such as an indemnity covenant, are commonly noted on the proprietorship register.

Positive covenants (eg to repair a fence) can also sometimes be seen in the charges register, particularly if they are mixed up with negative covenants. However, the fact that a positive covenant is on the register does not make it binding; under normal land law rules, the burden of a positive covenant cannot run with the land even if it is on the register (see **3.5.3.1**).

Details of mortgages of the land are also found on the charges register. Two entries are recorded for each mortgage, the first stating the fact that the mortgage exists and the date on which it was created, the second showing the name and address of the proprietor of the charge, ie lender.

4.8 Third-party rights

Third-party rights in registered land fall into one of the following three categories:

(a)   registered charges;

(b)   unregistered interests which override the disposition;

(c)   interests which must be protected by an entry on the register.

4.8.1 Registered charges

The most usual way of protecting a mortgage of registered land is by substantive registration of the charge, which will be noted in the charges register of the mortgaged land.

The priority of mortgages in registered land is governed by the date of registration of the charges. The LRA 2002 has changed the rules with regard to the tacking of further advances, but this is beyond the scope of this book.

Other methods of creating a mortgage of registered land do exist, but they are rare in practice and beyond the scope of this book.

4.8.2 Unregistered interests which override a registered disposition

The LRA 1925 set out various rights which would be binding on the proprietor of registered land, even though they did not appear on the register and irrespective of whether he had notice of them. These were known as 'overriding interests', although the LRA 2002 no longer uses this terminology.

The LRA 2002 has introduced important changes, as the existence of overriding interests is incompatible with the objective of the LRA 2002 that the register should be a complete and accurate reflection of the state of the ownership of any given piece of land. The principle behind the Act was that interests should have overriding status only where protection against buyers was required but where it was unreasonable to expect an entry to be placed on the register.

The first change is that the LRA 2002 now makes a distinction between those unregistered interests which will override a first registration and those which will override a disposition of land already registered. This is because whether a first proprietor is bound by an interest depends upon the rules relating to the purchase of unregistered land and his first registration merely reflects that existing position.

4.8.2.1   Unregistered interests which will override a first registration

These are set out in Sch 1 to the LRA 2002. There are 15 such interests, the most common being:

(a)   leases for seven years or less;

(b)   an interest belonging to a person in actual occupation;

(c)   a legal easement or profit;

(d)   a local land charge (see **18.5**).

4.8.2.2   Unregistered interests which will override a registered disposition

These are set out in Sch 3 to the LRA 2002. There are 15 such interests, the most common being:

(a)   leases for terms for seven years or less;

(b)   an interest belonging to certain persons in actual occupation (see below);

(c)   certain legal easements and profits (see **4.8.2.5**);

(d)   local land charges;

(e)   occupiers' rights.

Occupiers' rights

It is this head that has produced the most case law under the old system laid down by the LRA 1925, and this case law will still be relevant to the provisions under the LRA 2002, despite the changes made. As from 13 October 2003, the rights of a person in actual occupation will override a disposition *except* for:

(a)   an interest under a Settled Land Act settlement;

(b)   an interest of a person of whom enquiry was made before the disposition and who failed to disclose the right when he could reasonably be expected to do so;

(c)   an interest of a person whose occupation would not have been obvious on a reasonably careful inspection of the land at the time of the disposition and of which the person to whom the disposition was made did not have actual knowledge at the time of the disposition;

(d)   a lease granted to take effect in possession more than three months after the date of the grant and which had not taken effect in possession at the time of the disposition.

An interest in the property might be claimed under this head by a spouse or civil partner who had contributed to the mortgage repayments or otherwise made contributions towards the purchase or upkeep of the property. Equally, rights might be claimed by a cohabitee of the legal owner, or by a tenant in possession of the property. Note, however, that a spouse's or civil partner's home rights under the Family Law Act 1996 are not overriding, even though the spouse or civil partner will be in occupation of the land.

To have a right binding on a buyer, the claimant must:

(a)   be in actual occupation at the date of completion of the transaction; and

(b)   have a right recognised under normal land law principles.

Note that the provisions of the LRA 1925 giving persons in receipt of rents and profits overriding interests have been discontinued by the LRA 2002.

The House of Lords decision in *Abbey National Building Society v Cann* [1990] 1 All ER 1085 emphasises the need for both occupation and a right in the land before an overriding interest can exist under this head. It also shows that a lender making an advance to finance a purchase will not be bound by any rights claimed by an occupier who has contributed to the purchase price, even though he or she might have been in occupation when the mortgage was created (see **3.9.7**).

It remains to be seen what interpretation the courts will place on the requirement under the LRA 2002 that an occupier will not have overriding rights if the occupation would not have been obvious on a reasonably careful inspection of the land at the time of the disposition. What is meant by 'obvious' and what constitutes a 'reasonably careful inspection' are new problem areas introduced by the Act in addition to the existing problem as to what amounts to occupation.

4.8.2.3   Overreaching

An overriding interest which arises under a trust of land can be overreached on a disposition by two trustees: see *City of London Building Society v Flegg* [1988] AC 54. Note that a trust of land will arise in all cases of co-ownership, and a situation where an occupier has contributed to the purchase of a property will thus give rise to a trust of land. The occupier's rights will therefore be capable of being overreached.

4.8.2.4   Spouses and non-owning occupiers

A non-owning occupier (of either sex) may be able to claim both a beneficial interest in the property through his or her contribution to it, and rights under the Family Law Act 1996 (these are a minor interest). In appropriate circumstances both possibilities must be considered and dealt with (see **3.8.8**).

4.8.2.5   Easements and profits

Under the LRA 1925, all legal easements (and some equitable easements) were capable of being overriding interests. Under the LRA 2002, an easement that is expressly granted or reserved on or after 13 October 2003 can never be overriding. Nor can equitable easements. Other legal easements and profits (ie, those created impliedly or by long user under the Prescription Act 1832) will be overriding *except* for an easement or profit which, at the time of the disposition:

(a)   was not within the actual knowledge of the person to whom the disposition was made; and

(b)   would not have been obvious on a reasonably careful inspection of the land; *unless*

(c)   it had been exercised within the 12 months ending with the day of the disposition.

However, there are again transitional provisions. Any easement or profit that was an overriding interest immediately prior to 13 October 2003 will retain that status.

4.8.2.6   Ensuring that unregistered interests are registered

Although these interests that override a first registration or a registered disposition form a major flaw in the concept that the register itself should be conclusive as to ownership, this should prove to be less so over a period of time. The Land Registration Rules 2003 (SI 2003/1417) contain provisions requiring an applicant for registration (whether on a first registration or a disposition) to provide details to the Registry of any interests that would override the disposition so that they can then be entered on the register. They will then cease to override, although they will be binding by virtue of their registration.

4.8.3   Interests which must be protected by an entry on the register

All interests affecting a registered estate except registered charges and those that override a disposition even though not registered (see **4.8.2**) have to be protected by some entry on the register in order to bind a successor. Under the LRA 1925, these were referred to as 'minor interests', but the LRA 2002 no longer uses that term. The easiest way to recognise which interests need protecting by an entry on the register is by a process of elimination. Is the interest a registered charge? If not, does it override even though unregistered? The unregistered interests which override a disposition are set out in Schs 1 and 3 to the LRA 2002. If the list of such interests is consulted and the interest in question does not appear on that list, it must be protected by an entry on the register.

4.8.4   Hybrid interests

An interest which should be protected by an entry on the register can sometimes be binding on a successor to the proprietor if it satisfies the conditions set out in Sch 3 to the LRA 2002 of an unregistered interest that will override a disposition. Thus, an option should be protected by an entry on the register. But if the person with the benefit of the option is in occupation of the land, the option may override the disposition even though unregistered. This, however, should not be relied upon, as under the LRA 2002 the occupation needs to be obvious on a reasonably careful inspection, and it may not be.

4.8.5   Notices and restrictions

The LRA 1925 set out four methods of protecting 'minor interests' by entries on the register. These were notices, cautions, restrictions and inhibitions. Under the LRA 2002, cautions and inhibitions are abolished for the future (although existing registrations will remain). Notices are now the appropriate method of protection for interests intended to be binding on future proprietors of the land. Restrictions operate to prevent a disposition being registered without conformity with the conditions laid down in the restriction.

4.8.5.1   Cautions

Under the LRA 1925, a notice could be entered only with the consent of the registered proprietor. Where the entry of a notice was not possible (eg, where the proprietor did not consent to the application – perhaps because he disputed the claim) a caution could be used. This, however, provided only temporary protection for the owner of the interest claimed. On an application to register a subsequent disposition, the claimant would be given a limited period of time to establish his rights. Also, at any time the proprietor could require the Registrar to 'warn off' the caution. The claimant would be warned that unless he could justify his claim to an interest, the caution would be removed from the register. If he could justify the claim, the interest would receive permanent protection (eg, by the entry of a notice).

Cautions appeared on the proprietorship register. Although no new cautions can be entered on or after 13 October 2003, existing ones will remain until 'warned off'.

4.8.5.2 Inhibitions

Inhibitions were used under the LRA 1925 to prevent dispositions being made in certain defined circumstances. So, an inhibition would be used when a court injunction had been obtained to freeze the disposition of land, or on the insolvency of the proprietor to prevent any disposition which might be in breach of the insolvency laws. Although no new inhibitions can be registered on and from 13 October 2003, existing registrations will remain.

4.8.5.3 Agreed notices

Notices have always been the usual method of protecting third-party rights and appear on the charges register. So, easements, restrictive covenants and estate contracts will be protected in this way. Under the LRA 1925, most interests could only be protected by notice and could be registered only with the consent of the registered proprietor, hence the need for cautions (see **4.8.5.1**). As from 13 October 2003, there are two types of notice: agreed and unilateral. Agreed notices will usually still need the consent of the registered proprietor. As before, a spouse's matrimonial home rights under the Family Law Act 1996 can still be entered as an agreed notice without the proprietor's consent.

4.8.5.4 Unilateral notices

Unilateral notices are registrable on and from 13 October 2003 and replace cautions. Unlike cautions, however, they appear in the charges register. As the name suggests, unilateral notices can be entered on the register without the consent of the proprietor. A similar system of 'warning off' applies to unilateral notices as applies to cautions.

4.8.5.5 Restriction on the proprietorship register

Where the registered proprietor's powers of disposition are restricted in some way, this will be signified by the entry of a restriction in the proprietorship register. The restriction must be complied with, otherwise any disposition will not be registered. Typically, such an entry is made where co-owners hold as beneficial tenants in common, where the land is held on trust or strict settlement, or where the proprietor is a limited company or charity which is subject to the Charities Act 1993, s 36. Where tenants in common are registered as proprietors the following restriction will be entered:

> No disposition by a sole proprietor of the registered estate (except a trust corporation) under which capital money arises is to be registered unless authorised by an order of the court.

Under the LRA 2002, restrictions will be used in circumstances where inhibitions were used under the LRA 1925 (eg, on insolvency).

4.8.5.6 Personal covenants

Positive covenants, which do not run with the land, are personal obligations which affect only the proprietor who entered into the covenants. They are commonly noted on the proprietorship register of the title, although there is no obligation on Land Registry to make reference to them on the title. Such covenants may, however, be enforceable through a chain of indemnity covenants and, in order to give a subsequent buyer of the land notice of the existence and wording of the covenants, a separate copy of the deed imposing the covenants should be kept with the title deeds.

4.9 Caution against first registration

A caution against first registration should not be confused with the caution which was used under the LRA 1925 to protect third-party rights and which has been abolished as from 13 October 2003 (see **4.8.5.1**). A caution against first registration can be lodged by a person who has an interest in land which is currently unregistered. The caution warns any person who attempts to deal with the land that another person purports to have an interest in that land. When a dealing with the affected land is lodged at Land Registry, the cautioner is 'warned off' and given a limited period of time in which to establish his rights over the land, failing which the dealing will proceed and the cautioner will lose his interest. This procedure might be used, for example, by a landowner where the precise boundaries of the land are uncertain. Registration of a caution against first registration would ensure that the landowner was notified of any purported dealing with the land and would be given an opportunity to defend his rights if a neighbour deliberately or inadvertently attempted to register the land as his own.

However, the LRA 2002 limits the use of cautions against first registration as from 13 October 2003. They cannot be used if the applicant is the owner of the freehold or a lease for more than seven years in the land over which the right is being registered. So, a caution could no longer be used in the example given above. An application for first registration should be made to resolve the problem. A caution against first registration is now used to protect someone who has the benefit of an easement or profit and wants to ensure that it will be noted against the servient land if that is registered.

4.10 Mistakes on the register

Where there is a mistake on the register, it may be possible to seek rectification of the register. Compensation (indemnity) is payable where an error in the register is not rectified, where the register is rectified but loss is still suffered, where loss is suffered as a result of rectification or for any other error in the registration system, such as an error in the result of an official search. The conditions for claiming rectification and/or indemnity are stringent and are beyond the scope of this book. Note that the LRA 2002 has changed the rules relating to both rectification and indemnity.

4.11 Adverse possession (LRA 2002, ss 96–98)

Under the LRA 1925, the rules for adverse possession were basically the same for both unregistered and registered titles, ie, that after the requisite period of adverse possession (often 12 years) a squatter was able to claim ownership to land. However, this did not fit in well with the principle that the register should set out the precise details of ownership of land. So, the register might state that X was proprietor, but if a squatter could claim adverse possession, then the squatter would be the owner. Important changes were made under the 2002 Act.

The usual 12-year limitation period has been disapplied to registered land; the law remains unchanged for unregistered land.

A squatter in adverse possession for 10 years can apply to be registered as proprietor of the land.

Notice of the application will be given to the registered proprietor and certain others (eg, the proprietor of any registered charge). Any such person so notified has the right to give notice of objection to the Registrar within the specified time limit. If such notice is given then the squatter will not be registered unless certain conditions are complied with.

One of three sets of conditions must be met. A squatter will become registered only if:

(a)   it would be unconscionable because of an equity by estoppel for the registered proprietor to dispossess the applicant and the circumstances are such that the applicant ought to be registered; or

(b)   the applicant is for some other reason entitled to be registered as proprietor; or

(c)   the land in question is adjacent to land belonging to the applicant and the exact boundary has not been determined under Land Registry rules. Also, for at least the last 10 years of the adverse possession prior to the application, the applicant (or any predecessor in title) reasonably believed that the land belonged to him and the estate in the land in question was registered more than 12 months prior to the date of the application.

Where the squatter is not entitled to be registered under these provisions, the registered proprietor then has two years to obtain possession as against the squatter. If he does not do so, and the squatter remains in possession for the further two years, the squatter can once again apply for registration as proprietor. He will then be registered as proprietor.

Note, however, that there are transitional provisions (set out in Sch 12 to the LRA 2002) which preserve the position of a squatter who had been in adverse possession for the requisite period (say 12 years) as at 13 October 2003. Such a person will still be entitled to apply to be registered under the old rules.

4.12   Further reading

RB Roper et al, *Ruoff and Roper: Registered Conveyancing* (looseleaf, 1991)

C Harpum and J Bignell, *Registered Land: Law and Practice under the Land Registration Act 2002* (2nd edn, 2004).

Chapter 5
Conduct Issues Relevant to Conveyancing

5.1 Introduction

The principles of professional conduct apply to conveyancing as they do to every other aspect of the solicitor's business.

This chapter contains a summary of the conduct issues which are likely to be encountered during the course of a conveyancing transaction. Those matters which are exclusive to conveyancing are dealt with in detail. Other more general principles are mentioned in outline only and further detail of these can be found in *Legal Foundations*.

For many years a solicitor's conduct was governed by the Solicitor's Practice Rules 1990. However, these were replaced as from 1 July 2007 by the Solicitors' Code of Conduct 2007.

5.2 Acting for more than one party

5.2.1 Conflict of interests

As a general principle of professional conduct, a solicitor or his firm should not accept instructions to act for two or more clients in the same transaction where there is a conflict or a significant risk of a conflict between the interests of those clients. Nor should a solicitor or his firm continue to act for two or more clients where a conflict of interests arises between those clients.

5.2.2 The Solicitors' Code of Conduct

Rules 3.07 to 3.21 lay down a basic rule that, subject to various exceptions (see **5.2.2.2**), a solicitor (or a firm of solicitors or associated practices) cannot act for more than one party in connection with conveyancing, property selling or mortgage-related services. The prohibition applies to the transfer of land for value at arm's length, the grant or assignment of a lease for value at arm's length and the grant of a mortgage of land. The prohibition applies to all types of conveyancing transactions, whether commercial or residential. The general rule is that separate representation is required because conveyancing is an area where the risk of a conflict arising between two parties is high and where any conflict may affect a conveyancing chain.

5.2.2.1 Transactions not at arm's length

Under r 3.08, a solicitor may act for seller and buyer if the transaction is not at arm's length, provided that there is no conflict or significant risk of conflict.

Whether a transaction is at arm's length will depend on the circumstances of the case and, in particular, the relationship between the parties. A transaction will not usually be at arm's length if the parties are:

(a) related by blood, adoption or marriage, or living together;

(b) the settlor of a trust and the trustees;

(c) the trustees of a trust and its beneficiary or the beneficiary's relative;

(d) personal representatives and a beneficiary;

(e) the trustees of separate trusts for the same family;

(f) a sole trader or partners and a limited company set up to enable the business to be incorporated;

(g) associated companies (ie, where one is a holding company and the other is its subsidiary within the meaning of the Companies Act 1985, or both are subsidiaries of the same holding company); or

(h) a local authority and a company of which the local authority is a shareholder or guarantor, or to which it has the power to appoint officers.

However, even though the rule does not apply in these situations, the general rules of conduct must still be followed. Thus, it would not be possible to act if there was a conflict of interest, or a significant risk of a conflict arising.

5.2.2.2 Exceptions

A solicitor may act for seller and buyer only in one of the following circumstances:

(a) both parties are established clients; or

(b) the consideration is £10,000 or less and the transaction is not the grant of a lease; or

(c) seller and buyer are represented by two separate offices in different localities, and:

    (i) different solicitors who normally work at each office conduct or supervise the transaction, and

    (ii) no office of the practice (or an associated practice) referred either client to the office acting for that client; or

(d) the only way in which the solicitor is acting for the buyer is in providing mortgage-related services; or

(e) the only way in which the solicitor is acting for the seller is in providing property selling services through a SEAL (see **5.2.3**).

However, even if one of the above circumstances exists, a solicitor still cannot act for buyer and seller:

(a) without the written consent of both parties; or

(b) if a conflict of interest exists or arises; or

(c) the seller is selling or leasing as a builder or developer.

Many solicitors take the view that it is always best never to act for both buyer and seller in a transaction, even where the Code allows. If acting for seller and buyer under the provisions of rr 3.07 to 3.15, a solicitor would have to stop acting for at least one of the clients if a conflict were to arise during the course of the transaction. The Solicitors' Regulation Authority recommends that clients should be made aware of the consequent disruption and additional expense involved in such circumstances, and of the advantages of separate representation, before giving their written consent.

5.2.2.3 Established clients

The test of whether a person is an 'established client' is an objective one – is it reasonable to regard the person as an established client? A seller or buyer who instructs a solicitor for the first time is not an established client. A former client is not necessarily the same as an established client. There needs to be a degree of permanence in the solicitor–client relationship as exemplified by some continuity of instruction over time and the likelihood of future instruction. An individual related by blood, adoption or marriage to an established client, or who is living with an established client, counts as an established client. A person also counts as an established client if selling or buying jointly with an established client.

5.2.3 Property selling

A solicitor is permitted to sell property on behalf of his client (see **5.10**). In such a case, special rules apply governing whether a solicitor can also act on behalf of the buyer. This property selling business might be conducted directly by the solicitor himself, or through the medium of a Solicitors' Estate Agency Ltd (a SEAL). This is a separate company owned by at least four firms of solicitors which conducts business from separate premises from those of any of the owning solicitors.

When a solicitor (including a SEAL) acts in the property selling for the seller and the same solicitor acts for the buyer, the following conditions must be complied with in addition to those set out in **5.2.2**:

(a)   different persons must conduct or supervise the work for the seller and the buyer; and

(b)   the solicitor must inform the seller in writing before accepting instructions to deal with the property selling of any services which might be offered to a buyer; and

(c)   the solicitor must explain to the buyer before the buyer gives consent to the solicitor acting for both parties:

   (i)   the implications of a conflict of interest arising, and

   (ii)   the solicitor's financial interest in the sale going through, and

   (iii) if the solicitor proposes to offer mortgage-related services to the buyer through a SEAL which is also acting for the seller, that the solicitor cannot advise as to the merits of the purchase.

5.2.4 Joint buyers

It is acceptable to act for joint buyers provided that no conflict of interest exists or is likely to arise between them (see **Chapter 9**).

5.2.5 Contract races

The same solicitor must not act for both seller and buyer, nor for more than one buyer, in a transaction where a contract race is in existence (see **5.5**).

5.3 Acting for borrower and lender

5.3.1 General principles

In residential transactions, the buyer's lender will frequently instruct the buyer's solicitor also to act for him in connection with the grant of the mortgage. The same situation commonly occurs in relation to the discharge of an existing mortgage when acting for a seller client.

As soon as the solicitor receives instructions to act for the lender, he is effectively acting for both parties in one transaction (ie, for both lender and borrower). He has two clients and owes a duty to both (see *Mortgage Express v Bowerman & Partners (A Firm)* [1996] 2 All ER 836). Acting for buyer and lender is governed by rr 3.16 to 3.22 of the Solicitors' Code of Conduct.

A solicitor can act for borrower and lender in the case of a standard mortgage provided that the following conditions are complied with:

(a)   no conflict of interest arises;

(b)   the lender's instructions to the solicitor do not extend beyond the limitations contained in rr 3.19 and 3.21;

(c)   if the property is to be used as a private residence, the certificate of title set out in r 3.20 is used.

A mortgage is a standard mortgage where:

(a)   it is provided in the normal course of the lender's activities;

(b)   a significant part of the lender's activities consists of lending; and

(c)   the mortgage is on standard terms.

Basically, standard mortgages are mortgages from lending institutions such as banks and building societies.

Rules 3.19 and 3.21 state that the lender's instructions must be limited to certain matters if the solicitor is to be able to act for both parties. These limitations are lengthy and complex. However, most mortgage lenders have adopted the Council of Mortgage Lenders' *Lenders' Handbook*. This is a standardised set of instructions, subject to variations in certain respects by individual lenders. Adoption of this by the lender guarantees compliance with the r 3.16 limitations on the content of the instructions. The current version of the *Lenders' Handbook* is set out in **Appendix 7**.

Rule 3.20 also sets out a certificate of title to be used when acting for both lender and borrower. This delineates the solicitor's responsibilities and duties towards the lender client, and must be used by the solicitor when the mortgaged property is to be used solely for residential purposes.

If the solicitor or a member of his immediate family is the borrower, the lender must first be notified in writing of the circumstances of the transaction. Many lenders will not allow the solicitor to act in such circumstances.

The solicitor may not act for seller, buyer and lender in the same transaction unless the lender has been notified of the circumstances of the transaction.

If a conflict does occur, the solicitor must decline to act for both parties unless he can, with the consent of one party, continue to act for the other.

Conflict may arise if, for example:

(a)   the terms of the mortgage offer are unfair to the borrower (eg, an extortionate rate of interest is being charged);

(b)   instructions reveal that the buyer would be in breach of one of the terms of the offer (eg, by allowing tenants into possession of the property);

(c)   the buyer or seller is unable to comply with the lender's terms (eg, to provide the balance of the purchase price from his own funds).

5.3.2   Individual mortgages

An individual mortgage is any mortgage which is not a standard mortgage. Rule 3.16 prohibits a solicitor acting for both lender and borrower unless:

(a)   the transaction is not at arm's length; and

(b)   no conflict of interest exists or arises.

5.3.3   Acting for joint borrowers – undue influence

Provided no conflict of interest exists or is likely to exist, there is no rule of law or conduct which prevents the same solicitor acting for joint borrowers. However, problems can arise in the common situation where (say) a husband needs to borrow money for the purpose of his business. The bank requires security, but the only asset is the matrimonial home and that is in joint names with the spouse.

The wife agrees to a mortgage over the house for the benefit of her husband's business, but the husband defaults. The bank seeks to enforce its security and the wife then claims that the mortgage is not valid as her signature was obtained only because of the undue influence of her husband. The same kind of problems could also arise in any situation where there is a 'special relationship' between the parties, eg co-habitees or civil partners.

The House of Lords, in the case of *Royal Bank of Scotland v Etridge (No 2) and Other Appeals; Barclays Bank plc v Coleman; Bank of Scotland v Bennett; Kenyon-Brown v Desmond Banks & Co (A Firm)* [2001] 4 All ER 449, has laid down detailed guidance for solicitors acting in such a loan situation.

The burden of proof that a landowner entered into a charge because of undue influence rests on the landowner. Where there is a special relationship (parent and child; solicitor and client; but not husband and wife), there is a rebuttable presumption that there has been undue influence. In the case of husband and wife, there is no presumption of undue influence as there are many occasions where both parties are fully aware of the nature of the transaction and clearly understand what they are doing.

However, where a wife proposes to charge the matrimonial home as a security for a bank loan to her husband, or to a company through which he operates his business, a lender is put on enquiry because, prima facie, such transaction is not to the wife's advantage. There is thus a substantial risk of undue influence, giving rise to a right on the part of the wife to have the charge set aside.

Where the lender is put on such enquiry, it need do no more than take reasonable steps to satisfy itself that the practical implications of the proposed transaction have been brought home to the wife in a 'meaningful way', so that she enters into the transaction with her eyes open so far as its basic elements are concerned. Normally, it will be reasonable for the lender to rely on confirmation from a solicitor acting for the wife, that he has advised the wife appropriately.

In ordinary cases, the deficiencies in the advice given by the solicitor are matters between the wife and her solicitor. The lender is entitled to proceed on the basis that the solicitor advising the wife has done so properly.

The solicitor should:

(a)   explain to the wife the purpose for which he (the solicitor) has become involved;

(b)   explain that, if it becomes necessary, the lender will rely on the solicitor's involvement to counter any suggestion that the wife has been unduly influenced or has not fully understood the nature of the transaction;

(c)   obtain confirmation from the wife that she wishes the solicitor to act for her in the transaction and to advise her on the legal and practical implications of the transaction.

The nature and extent of the advice given will depend on the facts of the case, but must include the following:

(a)   an explanation as to the nature of the documents and the practical consequences to the wife of her signing them;

(b)   a warning as to the seriousness of the risks involved.

It must be clearly explained to the wife that she has a choice as to whether or not to go ahead with the transaction, emphasis being placed on the fact that the choice is hers and hers alone.

The solicitor must check if the wife wishes to proceed. She should be asked whether she wants the solicitor to write to the lender confirming that matters have been explained to her.

The solicitor must not write to the lender confirming these matters unless he has express instructions from the wife to do so. The solicitor should ensure that all the relevant documents have been received from the lender and should refuse to make the confirmation to the lender until they have been received. The lender should supply the following financial information:

(a)   the purpose for which the facility is being made available;

(b)   the current amount of the husband's indebtedness;

(c)   the amount of the current overdraft facility;

(d)   the amount and terms of the new facility;

(e)   a copy of any written application made by the husband for the facility.

The lender cannot release this information without the consent of the husband, and if the consent is not forthcoming, the transaction cannot proceed.

The solicitor's discussion with the wife should take place at a face-to-face meeting in the absence of the husband and the advice should be given in non-technical language. It is not for the solicitor to veto the transaction, but if the solicitor thinks that the transaction is not in the wife's best interests, he should give reasoned advice to that effect. However, ultimately, the decision is one for the wife. If she wishes to enter into a financially unwise transaction, that is a matter for her.

However, if it is 'glaringly obvious' that the wife is being 'grievously wronged', the solicitor should decline to act.

Note that although the *Etridge* case involved husband and wife, the same principles will apply to any situation where property is being charged in return for a loan that is not being made to the property owners. So if parents mortgage property to secure a loan made to a child, or cohabitees mortgage property to secure a loan being made to finance a business operated only by one of them, the same guidelines should be followed.

5.4 Confidentiality

All information received by the solicitor from his client is confidential and remains so even after termination of the retainer. Where, for example, the solicitor is told by his client that the client intends to breach the terms of the mortgage offer by letting the premises to a tenant and will not agree to the lender being told of this, the solicitor, when informing the lender that he can no longer act for him, must tell the lender that the reason for the termination of the retainer is because a conflict of interests has arisen, but he is not at liberty to disclose the nature of the conflict without the buyer client's consent.

5.5 Contract races

5.5.1 Solicitors' Code of Conduct, r 10.06

Where a seller's solicitor is asked by his client to deal simultaneously with more than one prospective buyer, he is required to comply with r 10.06, the text of which is as follows:

> **Dealing with more than one prospective buyer in a conveyancing transaction**
>
> (1)   Each time a seller of land, other than in a sale by auction or tender, either:
>
>   (a)   instructs you to deal with more than one prospective buyer; or
>
>   (b)   to your knowledge:
>
>   (i)   deals directly with another prospective buyer (or their conveyancer); or
>
>   (ii)   instructs another conveyancer to deal with another prospective buyer;
>
>   you must, with the client's consent, immediately inform the conveyancer of each prospective buyer, or the prospective buyer if acting in person.
>
> (2)   If the seller refuses to agree to such disclosure, you must immediately stop acting in the matter.

Compliance with the rule is mandatory, and breach can lead to disciplinary action being taken against the solicitor. It is the seller's instruction to 'deal' with more than one buyer that triggers the obligation to disclose. This cannot be delayed until a contract is submitted to another purchaser. Any instruction that indicates a decision to deal with more than one party (eg, to send out official copy entries to another prospective buyer) requires the disclosure of the decision. The rule applies to freehold and leasehold transactions, and to commercial transactions as well as residential ones.

5.5.2 Withdrawal of papers

Where, having supplied a prospective buyer with a draft contract, the seller later receives a further offer for the property, which offer he would prefer to accept, the seller may withdraw his offer and the draft papers from the first prospective buyer before accepting the second prospective buyer's offer and submitting draft papers to him. In this situation, only one buyer is in possession of a draft contract at any one time, thus a contract race does not exist and the rule does not apply.

5.5.3 Solicitor acting for seller

Where a solicitor is acting for the seller, he must explain to his client that the solicitor is required to comply with r 10.06 (see **5.5.1**). If the seller refuses to allow the solicitor to notify all the prospective buyers of the contract race, the solicitor must decline to act.

Since buyers are themselves wary of entering into contract races, the seller should also be warned of the danger of losing all the prospective buyers if a race is commenced. It is normally preferable to avoid a contract race if at all possible.

5.5.4 Disclosure of race to buyers

Having obtained his client's authority, the seller's solicitor must at once disclose the seller's decision to conduct a contract race direct to the solicitor acting for each prospective buyer, or, where no solicitor is acting, to the prospective buyer(s) in person. Such disclosure must be made immediately by the 'most suitable means'. If the disclosure is made orally or on the telephone, there is no requirement that this should be confirmed in writing, but this is advisable. When the seller's solicitor informs the prospective buyers of the race, he must make clear to each of them the precise terms of the race, ie, what has to be done by a buyer in order to secure the property. Commonly, the terms of the race are that the first buyer who presents a signed contract and deposit cheque at the seller's solicitor's office will secure the property.

5.5.5 Acting for more than one party

A solicitor must not accept instructions to act for both seller and buyer, even where one of the exceptions contained in r 3.09 would otherwise apply (see **5.2.2.2**). Neither must the solicitor act for more than one prospective buyer where a contract race is involved.

5.6 Undertakings

An undertaking is any statement, made by a solicitor or his or her firm, that the solicitor or the firm will do something or cause something to be done, or refrain from doing something, given to someone who reasonably relies upon it. It can be given orally or in writing and need not include the word 'undertake'. However, it is recommended that oral undertakings be confirmed or recorded in writing for evidential purposes. Once an undertaking is given and the recipient has relied upon it, it can be withdrawn only by agreement.

There are many situations in conveyancing where a solicitor will be asked to give an undertaking on his client's behalf. For example, an undertaking may be required to enable the buyer client to obtain a bridging loan for the deposit. Similarly, an undertaking may be required from the seller's solicitor that he will discharge his client's mortgage over the property. All the general rules on undertakings apply equally in the context of conveyancing. Failure to honour an undertaking is professional misconduct. Because of the personal liability which attaches to undertakings, it is important that both the giver and recipient of the promise understand precisely what the terms of the promise are. To avoid any misunderstanding, it is recommended that undertakings are always given in writing.

5.6.1   Bridging finance for the deposit

Where bridging finance is being extended for the deposit on the client's purchase, the bank or other lender will normally require the solicitor to give an undertaking to repay the loan, usually out of the proceeds of sale of the client's existing property. Such an undertaking should be given only where:

(a)   the solicitor is sure that sufficient funds will be available on completion to repay the loan with interest;

(b)   the solicitor knows the client well enough to feel confident of making a binding commitment on that client's behalf;

(c)   the client has given his irrevocable authority for the undertaking to be given – if in doubt, obtain the authority in writing.

Until contracts have been exchanged on the client's related sale transaction, there is no guarantee that any funds will be available to repay the loan. Ideally, therefore, an undertaking should not be given until contracts have been exchanged on the sale. In practice, it may be necessary to give the undertaking shortly before exchange in order to ensure the availability of funds for a simultaneous exchange on both sale and purchase contracts.

5.6.2   Terms of an undertaking on bridging finance

The Law Society has agreed a form of wording for use by solicitors when giving undertakings to banks for bridging finance. Even where an undertaking is presented to the solicitor in the standard form or in a familiar and frequently used form of wording, the entire wording should be read carefully in the light of the particular transaction to ensure that the wording is appropriate for those circumstances. If the wording is not wholly appropriate to the circumstances in hand, the undertaking should be amended to reflect the particular requirements of the transaction. The terms of the undertaking should be restricted to repayment:

(a)   of a stated figure, plus interest on that sum if so instructed;

(b)   from a defined source (eg, the proceeds of sale of a named property);

(c)   of the net proceeds of sale, having defined what is understood by the word 'net', ie, after deduction of specified loans, estate agent's commission, solicitor's fees, disbursements on the sale and purchase, and any other known and defined liabilities which will reduce the amount available to repay the loan;

(d)   when the proceeds of sale are actually received by the solicitor, thus protecting the solicitor against having to honour the undertaking in circumstances where the sale of the property is completed but for some reason the funds are never received by him, for example, the client intercepts the money and absconds with it.

5.6.3   Change of circumstances

If, having given an undertaking, the circumstances of the client's sale and purchase transactions change – for example the price of the sale property is reduced to take account of a structural defect – the terms of the undertaking must be considered carefully to ensure that they are still capable of performance. The recipient of the undertaking must be informed of the changed circumstances, irrespective of whether they affect the obligations covered by the undertaking.

5.7   Estimate for costs

5.7.1   Duty to give estimate

Whenever possible, a solicitor should give a client an estimate of the costs of the transaction. If it is not possible to give an estimate, a general indication of the approximate costs should be given. In residential conveyancing it is normally possible to give the client an estimate of the costs. A precise estimate of costs may not be possible in commercial transactions, but the client should still be given a general forecast of likely costs and the method of calculation of those costs at the outset of the transaction, and informed if that figure is likely to vary substantially.

5.7.2   Giving an estimate

In order to avoid misunderstandings an estimate should, if possible, be given in writing. If an oral estimate is unavoidable (eg, in response to a telephone enquiry from a client), the estimate should be confirmed in writing either immediately or, at the latest, when the solicitor is instructed to act for the client. In residential conveyancing, it is frequently not possible to avoid giving an estimate over the telephone; many potential clients 'ring round' to obtain the lowest possible price. In such circumstances the prospective client should be advised that the estimate is given on the basis of information supplied by the client and may be subject to variation if unknown factors later emerge which complicate the transaction.

The estimate should be as comprehensive as possible and should be clear as to whether VAT and/or disbursements are included in the given figure. Minor expenses, such as postage and telephone, must be included in the estimate, not added as a disbursement.

5.7.3   Change in circumstances

If events occur which cause the original estimate to become inaccurate, the solicitor must immediately inform the client in writing of the change in circumstances and revise his estimate accordingly. Failure to advise the client of a change in the likely level of fees may render the solicitor liable to prosecution for giving misleading information relating to charges under the Consumer Protection Act 1987, s 20.

5.7.4   Quotations for costs

The solicitor should make it clear to the client that an estimate for costs is not a fixed price ('a quotation') for the work unless he intends to charge a fixed price which will not be altered in any circumstances. Many firms do handle residential conveyancing matters on a fixed fee basis. It is also becoming increasingly common for clients wishing to instruct in a commercial conveyancing matter to require a fixed fee quotation. In residential conveyancing, many firms will charge a separate fee for completing the stamp duty land tax return on behalf of the client (see **31.7**). It is also recommended that any fee for acting for a lender should be itemised separately.

Where a quotation is given, the solicitor is not permitted to charge the client more than the fixed fee, even if the transaction turns out to be more difficult or complex than had been anticipated. Petty expenses, such as postage and telephone, must be included in the fixed fee quoted to the client. If a fixed fee is quoted, the client should be informed of that fee in writing and told that the quotation will be valid for a stated period (eg, three months). If the solicitor has not been instructed by the client within this period, he will then be entitled to issue a revised quotation.

5.7.5 Value added tax on solicitors' charges

Where a firm is registered for VAT, it will be payable by the client on the solicitor's bill and on some of the disbursements paid by the solicitor on the client's behalf. When giving an estimate or quotation of costs to the client, the solicitor must make it clear whether or not that estimate or quotation includes VAT. If no mention of VAT is made, the client is entitled to assume that the quoted figure is VAT inclusive.

Where an individual or firm is registered for VAT, the firm's VAT registration number must appear on the bills issued by the firm or, if a separate tax invoice is issued, on the tax invoice.

5.8 Introductions and referrals

Many solicitors will have an arrangement with third parties such as estate agents and building societies for the mutual referral of clients. The building society may send the solicitor a client who needs legal advice, and the solicitor may refer to the building society a client who needs to obtain a mortgage. These arrangements must comply with r 9 of the Solicitors' Code of Conduct. This provides (inter alia) that the client must be advised, before instructions are accepted, of the amount of any referral fee payable to the introducer.

5.9 Dealing with non-solicitors

Where the other party to the transaction is not represented by a solicitor, precautions may have to be taken to ensure that the transaction proceeds smoothly and that the interests of the solicitor's client are properly protected. The Law Society has issued notes for guidance for solicitors which are summarised below.

5.9.1 Licensed conveyancers

Licensed conveyancers are bound by rules made by the Council for Licensed Conveyancers which relate to conduct, discipline, insurance and accounts. These rules are similar to those which bind solicitors. It is therefore possible to deal with a licensed conveyancer as if the conveyancer was a fellow solicitor.

5.9.2 Dealing with unqualified persons

Section 22 of the Solicitors Act 1974 makes it an offence for an unqualified person to carry out certain acts, including preparing a contract or transfer for the sale of land for gain or reward. At the commencement of a transaction which apparently involves an unqualified person, the solicitor should write to the unqualified person drawing attention to The Law Society's guidelines on this matter and asking for satisfactory evidence that no offence will be committed. The solicitor's client should also be informed of the situation.

Undertakings should not be accepted from unqualified persons because there is no method of enforcing them. Therefore, where a seller who is represented by an unqualified person has a mortgage to be discharged at completion, the buyer's solicitor must require the seller to produce a signed Form DS1 (or receipted mortgage) at completion and must not accept an undertaking for its discharge.

5.9.3 Acting for the lender

A solicitor acting for a lender where the borrower is represented by an unqualified person is under no obligation to undertake work which the buyer's solicitor would normally carry out (eg, drafting the purchase deed) and should not give the unqualified person additional assistance. However, in such a situation, the solicitor must bear in mind that the interests of his lender client in obtaining a good title to the property are paramount. The advance cheque should be drawn in favour of a solicitor, licensed conveyancer or person properly authorised to receive the money by the borrower. Similar principles apply on redemption of a mortgage.

5.9.4 The buyer is not represented at all

Where it appears that the buyer will not be represented or assisted by a solicitor or professional adviser, the seller's solicitor should not prepare a form of contract which he knows will be placed before the buyer for signature without the buyer having had an opportunity to obtain legal advice. This duty in conduct means that the seller's solicitor should advise the buyer in writing to obtain legal advice before signing the contract, but he is under no duty to explain the terms of the contract to the buyer. The solicitor is under a general duty in conduct never to act in a way which is fraudulent or deceitful, nor to act in a way which would gain an unfair advantage either for himself or his client. This provision means that the seller's solicitor must draft a contract which, although properly protecting his own client's interests, does not unfairly disadvantage the unrepresented buyer. Similar considerations apply where it is the seller who is unrepresented.

5.10 Property selling

A solicitor is permitted to sell property on behalf of his client, ie he can act as an estate agent for the purpose of selling the property. This activity may be carried out by a solicitor as part of his practice, either through the solicitor's own office or through a separate property display centre. Even when acting in his role as an estate agent, the solicitor is still considered to be a solicitor and therefore remains bound by the Solicitors' Code of Conduct, the Solicitors' Accounts Rules 1998 and all other rules, regulations and principles of conduct which affect solicitors in practice. There are special rules relating to advertising and fees which apply where the solicitor is acting as an estate agent. A solicitor can run or be a partner in an estate agency business which is separate from his practice. In this case he must comply with r 21 of the Solicitors' Code of Conduct.

5.10.1 Surveys and valuations

A solicitor is allowed to carry out a valuation of the property which he has been instructed to sell in order to advise the client on the price at which the property should be advertised for sale. He can also prepare the sale particulars, but may not describe himself as an 'estate agent' nor carry out any other types of surveys or valuations. A qualified surveyor employed by the solicitor may carry out surveys on behalf of a client or prospective client. The solicitor, as the surveyor's employer, would nevertheless remain liable for breach of duty if the surveyor carried out the survey negligently.

5.10.2 Application of the Estate Agents Act 1979 and the Property Misdescriptions Act 1991

The Estate Agents Act 1979 does not apply to solicitors who are engaged in property selling as part of the solicitor's business, but the Property Misdescriptions Act 1991 does. The 1991 Act makes it an offence for a person selling property to attach a misleading description to the property which is being sold. The liability is similar to that incurred under the Trades Descriptions Act 1968. If the solicitor provides estate agency service through a separate business, then that business will be subject to the provisions of the Estate Agents Act 1979.

5.11 Money laundering

Broadly speaking, money laundering is the conversion, concealment or disguise of the proceeds of crime, so as to make it appear that it comes from a legitimate source. Conveyancers need to be aware of the possibility of clients using their services in order to launder money. The Money Laundering Regulations 1993 (SI 1993/1933) only had a limited effect, but did require reporting of suspicions of money laundering in relation to drug trafficking and terrorism. The Money Laundering Regulations 2003 apply (inter alia) to all 'legal professionals' acting in any 'real property transaction' and extend to the proceeds of any criminal activity.

They require solicitors involved in all conveyancing transactions (whether a sale or a purchase) to:

(a)   obtain satisfactory evidence of the identity of each client;

(b)   keep copies of the evidence and details of all transactions carried out for five years; and

(c)   appoint someone in the firm as a money laundering reporting officer (MLRO), to whom members of staff can report suspicious transactions. The MLRO must consider the report and, if he considers that it does give rise to such suspicion, he must report it to the Serious Organised Crime Agency (SOCA). Within seven days, the SOCA must advise the solicitors whether they are allowed to continue with the transaction or not.

The Law Society has issued a 'Blue Card' warning of the signs to watch out for to try to spot a money laundering transaction. These include clients making payment by using large sums of cash.

There are criminal sanctions for failure to comply with these provisions.

The Law Society has published revised guidelines on preventing money laundering for solicitors acting in conveyancing transactions. These emphasise the need to 'know your client' and take a risk-based approach to the problem. This involves identifying and concentrating on higher risk transactions rather than on transactions with a lower risk. For further reading, see *Solicitors and Money Laundering* (2nd edn, 2007) (The Law Society).

Chapter 6

Capital Gains Tax and Value Added Tax

6.1 Liability to capital gains tax

A liability to capital gains tax (CGT) may arise on the disposal of an interest in land. A seller's solicitor should be aware of the possibility of potential liability and advise his client accordingly. Similarly, a buyer who is purchasing property other than for use as his principal private dwelling should be made aware of potential tax liability which may be incurred in his subsequent disposal of the property.

6.1.1 Chargeable assets

The definition of 'chargeable assets' within the Taxation of Chargeable Gains Act 1992 includes an interest in the proceeds of sale of land held by co-owners. Thus, a disposition by a beneficiary of his equitable interest in land could give rise to a charge to CGT (*Kidson v Macdonald* [1974] Ch 339). Some transactions which are incidental to the sale of land also give rise to a charge to CGT, for example, where a separate payment is made for the release or modification of an easement or covenant. Subject to certain reliefs, gifts fall within the meaning of 'disposal'.

6.2 The principal private dwelling house exemption

The disposal of an individual's principal private dwelling house (including grounds of up to 0.5 hectares) is exempt from CGT (Taxation of Chargeable Gains Act 1992, s 222).

6.2.1 Qualifications

To qualify for the exemption, the seller must have occupied the dwelling house as his only or main residence throughout his period of ownership. If an individual has more than one residence it is a question of fact which one constitutes his 'only or main' residence. However, the taxpayer can determine the question by making an election within two years of acquiring a second property, backdated for up to two years.

6.2.2 Absences

Under s 223 of the Taxation of Chargeable Gains Act 1992, certain periods of absence are disregarded when calculating the amount of relief:

(a) The last 36 months of ownership (in order to facilitate the purchase of another property).

(b) By extra-statutory concession, the first 12 months of ownership (in order to facilitate the sale of another property). If there are good reasons for the period exceeding one year, which are outside the individual's control, it will be extended up to a maximum of two years.

(c)   Any period(s) not exceeding three years in total throughout the period of ownership. Absence within this exception may be for any reason (eg, an extended holiday) and can be made up of several separate periods of absence, provided that the total under this exception does not exceed three years.

(d)   Any period(s) during which the individual was working outside the UK. This exception applies to employees only, not to self-employed persons.

(e)   Any period(s) not exceeding four years in total during which the individual was prevented from living in his dwelling house because he was employed elsewhere. This exception would apply, for example, to a school caretaker who was required to live in accommodation provided by the school, or an employee taking a job in another part of the country.

If the taxpayer is absent for longer periods, the proportion of the gain attributable to periods in excess of those mentioned in cases (c) to (e) above loses the benefit of the exemption, and so becomes chargeable.

Example

X spent four years wandering through Central Asia in the middle of his 12-year ownership of 'Home'. He makes a gain of £120,000 on its sale.

Three of the four years' absence fall within case (c): 'any reason' exemption. So the gain attributable to one year out of the 12 years' ownership will be chargeable.

$1/12 \times £120,000 = £10,000$ of the gain will be chargeable.

6.2.3   Letting the property

To the extent that the property is let during the period of ownership, it ceases to be the individual's only or main residence (unless such absence can be disregarded under 6.2.2). The proportion of the gain attributable to the period of letting will be chargeable, but only to the extent (if any) which it exceeds the lesser of £40,000 and the part of the gain which is not a chargeable gain.

Example

If X in the example in 6.2.2 above had let his house during his absence, the £10,000 gain would be exempt as it is under £40,000 (and £40,000 is less than the £110,000 gain attributable to his occupation).

On the other hand, if the gain attributable to the period of letting had been £50,000 and the non-chargeable gain still £110,000, then £10,000 (ie, the excess of £50,000 over £40,000) would be chargeable.

6.2.4   Houses with large grounds

Where a dwelling house has grounds of more than 0.5 hectares, the excess is prima facie taxable, but HM Revenue & Customs (HMRC) has a discretion to allow land in excess of 0.5 hectares to be included within the principal private dwelling house exemption if the extra land can be shown to be necessary for the reasonable enjoyment of the house.

6.2.5   Sale of land alone

The sale of land alone, where the ownership of the house is retained, may enjoy the benefit of the exemption so long as the area of the grounds does not exceed 0.5 hectares. If the house is sold and land retained, a subsequent sale of the land will usually attract CGT.

6.2.6 Duality of user

Where part of a principal private dwelling house is used exclusively for business purposes (eg, a doctor who has a consulting room in his home), a proportion of the exemption may be lost, relative to the area of the 'business premises' in relation to the total area of the dwelling house. If a 'duality of user' can be shown, the full exemption may be available. Thus, a person who works from home, but who does not have a separate room for his business from which the other members of the family are excluded, may still take full advantage of the principal private dwelling house exemption.

6.2.7 Married couples

Only one exemption is available to married couples. Where a married couple own more than one house they must choose which property is to take the benefit of the exemption. However, an election is not irrevocable and can thus be changed (eg, if one property is increasing in value more than the other).

6.2.8 Trustees

The principal private dwelling house exemption is available where the disposal is made by trustees, provided that the person in occupation of the property was a person who was entitled to be in occupation under the terms of the settlement (eg, a tenant for life) (see the Taxation of Chargeable Gains Act 1992, s 225). By virtue of s 12 of the Trusts of Land and Appointment of Trustees Act 1996, a beneficiary under a trust of land now has a statutory right to occupy the trust property.

6.2.9 Tenants in common

Tenants in common may be liable for CGT on their respective shares in the equitable interest in the property.

6.3 Chargeable gains

The gain is calculated by deducting the purchase price of the property (or its base value in 1982 if purchased earlier than this) from its current sale price. Any gain which is chargeable on the disposal is subject to indexation allowances for periods of ownership falling before 6 April 1998. For ownership from that date, the amount of the gain will be 'tapered', ie, reduced according to the number of complete years of ownership that have elapsed since 6 April 1998. The taper is greater for business assets than for non-business assets. Any gain is then subject to the individual's annual exemption at the current rate; for details of this and indexation and tapering, see *Legal Foundations*. Over and above this, the gain is chargeable at the highest rate at which the individual pays income tax. Separate taxation is applied to married couples, so each spouse has his or her own annual allowance for CGT purposes. Corporations pay CGT at the corporation tax rate applicable to them, subject to roll-over and other reliefs.

6.4 Four key questions

When taking instructions from an individual in relation to the sale of a dwelling house, the answers to the following four questions will indicate whether there is likely to be a CGT liability on the property. If the client's answers to all the questions set out below match the suggested answers, there is unlikely to be a CGT liability on the transaction. If any of the client's answers differ from those suggested, further enquiries should be raised with the client.

Question 1:   Did you move into the house immediately after you bought it?

Answer: Yes.

Question 2:   Have you lived anywhere else since moving into this house?

Answer: No.

Question 3:   Does the garden extend to more than 0.5 hectares?

Answer: No. (The answer to this question may be self-evident from the estate agent's particulars of the property.)

Question 4:   Do you (or your spouse) own another house?

Answer: No.

6.5 Value added tax

6.5.1 Introduction

A property lawyer will frequently have to consider the impact of value added tax (VAT) on the transaction. VAT is chargeable in respect of a supply of goods or services made in the course of a business. Supplies can be exempt, zero-rated or standard-rated depending upon the circumstances. Standard-rated supplies are subject to VAT at the then current standard rate (17.5%); zero-rated supplies are taxable, but, as the name suggests, are subject to VAT at a zero rate. Exempt supplies are not subject to tax. Tax paid by a business on supplies made to it ('input tax') can be recovered from HMRC, provided that it was incurred in making taxable supplies, ie, standard-rated or zero-rated, but not exempt, supplies. The tax charged by a business on supplies it makes ('output tax') has to be accounted for to HMRC. In practice, the input tax incurred in making those supplies is deducted from the output tax and only the balance is paid over to HMRC.

VAT affects property transactions as follows:

(a)   Residential properties:
    (i)   sale of a green field site: exempt, but subject to option to tax (see **6.5.2**);
    (ii)   construction and civil engineering works: zero-rated;
    (iii)   legal and other professional services: standard-rated;
    (iv)   sale or lease of a new house: zero-rated;

(b)   Commercial properties:
    (i)   sale of a green field site: exempt, but subject to option to tax (see **6.5.2**);
    (ii)   construction and civil engineering services: standard-rated;
    (iii)   legal and other professional fees: standard-rated;
    (iv)   sale of a new freehold building: standard-rated;
    (v)   sale of an old freehold building: exempt, but subject to option to tax;
    (vi)   grant or assignment of a lease; exempt, but subject to option to tax.

6.5.2 The option to tax

When an exempt supply is made, any input tax incurred is not recoverable from HMRC. The purpose of the option to tax is to enable the developer to convert an exempt supply into a taxable supply. This will then enable him to recover any input tax incurred in connection with that supply. The details of how to effect this election are outside the scope of this chapter.

6.5.3 VAT and residential property

In the case of residential property, the impact of VAT is relatively uncomplicated. The purchase of land by a developer will be an exempt supply, unless the seller has elected to charge tax. The construction work will be zero-rated and so no input tax will be incurred on this. Input tax will be paid on the professional fees, however. The sale of the houses will be zero-rated. However, this is a taxable supply, albeit at a zero rate, and so any input tax incurred (eg, the professional fees or if the seller of the site elected to tax) will be recoverable from HMRC.

6.5.4 VAT and new commercial property

The VAT implications here are much more extensive. The sale of the development land is again exempt, but subject to the option to tax. However, the construction and other works will be standard-rated. The developer will thus be incurring substantial amounts of input tax. The sale of the new building is, however, standard-rated and so the seller will be able to recover the input tax paid on the construction, etc. A 'new' building is one completed within the three years prior to the sale, and VAT must be charged on the sale.

If a lease is granted of the new building, this is an exempt supply and so no input tax is recoverable. However, it is subject to the option to tax to enable the recovery of input tax.

6.5.5 Old commercial buildings

Dispositions of commercial property more than three years old are exempt, but subject to the option to tax. The only point in electing to tax is to enable you to recover any input tax incurred; if you incurred none, you will not elect. However, VAT may have been incurred in carrying out repair and refurbishment works on the building. This cannot be recovered on making an exempt supply. Hence again, there is the option to tax, whether on a sale of the freehold or the grant of a lease, to enable the input tax to be recovered by setting it off against the output tax being charged.

6.5.6 Conveyancing points

Unfortunately, making a taxable supply or electing to tax does not necessarily mean that the buyer/tenant will have to pay VAT *in addition* to the agreed consideration. The agreed price might be deemed to be *inclusive* of VAT. The terms of the contract between the parties and the operation of s 89 of the Value Added Tax Act 1994 (VATA 1994) have to be considered.

6.5.6.1 Seller and buyer

On a sale of a new commercial building there is mandatory VAT on the purchase price. The price agreed is deemed to be inclusive of VAT, unless the contrary is agreed. Where the Standard Conditions (SC) are used, note that SC 1.4.2 states that the price is exclusive of VAT. The buyer's solicitor should point this out to the client at the earliest opportunity, as the extra amount payable (17.5%) may affect the buyer's financial arrangements.

On the sale of an old commercial building the position may depend upon when the seller makes the election to tax. If he elects before contract, the position is as above; if he elects after contract then s 89 of the VATA 1994 allows the VAT to be added to the purchase price unless the contract expressly states that the price is inclusive of VAT. If the Standard Conditions are used, the position will be the same in both cases. In any event, the buyer should be warned of the danger of the seller electing and should try to negotiate a provision in the contract that the seller will not elect before completion, or that the price is deemed to be inclusive of VAT. Otherwise, the buyer should again be advised to make his financial arrangements on the assumption that VAT will be payable in addition to the agreed price.

Where the Standard Commercial Property Conditions (SCPC) are used, SCPC 1.4 provides that the sale does not constitute a supply for VAT purposes and that the seller will not elect to charge VAT. Thus if VAT is chargeable or the seller wishes to elect to tax, the optional condition A1 in Part 2 should be expressly incorporated into the contract.

6.5.6.2 Landlord and tenant

The grant of a commercial lease, whether of a new or old building is an exempt supply, subject to the option to tax. If the election is made after the grant of the lease, s 89 of the VATA 1994 allows the rent to be increased by the amount of VAT, unless there is a clause in the lease making the rent inclusive of VAT. If an election is made before the grant of a lease, s 89 will not apply and so the landlord will be able to add VAT to the rent only if there is a provision in the lease permitting this. In every lease, therefore, there ought to be such a provision.

6.5.6.3 What if the seller/landlord cannot add on VAT?

If an election is made, or a standard-rated supply is made and the seller/landlord is unable to add VAT on to the agreed price, the seller is still liable to account for VAT to HMRC out of the agreed price. So, for example, a price of £1 million is agreed for a sale of land. If the seller can add VAT, the buyer will hand over £1,175,000, £1 million of which will be kept by the seller, the other £175,000 being handed over to HMRC. If the seller is unable to add on the VAT, the buyer need only pay £1 million on completion. Out of this the seller will have to account for £148,936 to HMRC and will thus keep only £851,064 himself.

Part I Summary – Essential Background: Outline of a Conveyancing Transaction, Underlying Law, Professional Conduct and Taxation

Sub-section heading	Summary
Outline of a conveyancing transaction – Overview	A typical conveyancing transaction divides into three distinct parts: first, the stage up to exchange of contracts; secondly, the stage from exchange through to completion; and finally, post-completion.
Up to exchange	The pre-exchange stage begins with a seller and buyer agreeing terms. At this stage, there is no legally binding contract between the parties and either is free to withdraw from the transaction.
	From the buyer's perspective, this part of the transaction is primarily concerned with ensuring he is willing and able to commit himself to buying the property. This will involve carrying out extensive investigations, including checking that title is satisfactory and carrying out a survey to check the physical state of the property. The results of this process may involve renegotiation of the original deal, such as the purchase price, should, for example, the survey reveal structural problems.
	The seller will be heavily involved in this investigation process and his solicitor will draft the contract embodying the terms of the agreement to which the parties will commit themselves.
	During this stage, the buyer will also need to ensure that he is in a financial position to buy the property, including arranging a mortgage if necessary.
	Assuming all matters are resolved satisfactorily, the parties will 'exchange contracts', legally binding each other to the transaction. At this stage, it is usual for the buyer to pay a deposit to the seller's solicitor.
From exchange to completion	Exchange of contracts does not transfer title: instead, it commits the parties to transfer the property at a date specified in the contract (called the completion date) for the price agreed between them.
	Prior to completion, the deed that will effect transfer needs to be drafted and executed by the parties. The terms of this deed will have been fixed in the contract. In addition, the buyer will need to carry out some last-minute checks on the property, and arrange for the money payable on completion to be made available. This will include the money being advanced by any mortgage lender.
	On completion, the buyer will pay over the balance of the purchase money to the seller and the property will be transferred to the buyer by the purchase deed.

Sub-section heading	Summary
Post-completion	This stage essentially involves tying up the loose ends of the transaction. The buyer will need to pay any stamp duty land tax due on the transaction and register his ownership of the property at Land Registry. As part of this latter process, the seller's solicitor will need to provide evidence to discharge any mortgage that his seller-client had over the property prior to sale. Once the buyer has been correctly registered as the new owner, the transaction reaches its end.
Underlying law – Overview	It is essential to have a firm understanding of the underlying principles concerning land law. An owner of freehold land can choose to sell that freehold or carve a lease out of it. The creation and subsequent disposal of leases is considered in Part VII of this book.
Registered land	Title to most land in England and Wales is registered. A seller will need to provide a buyer with an official copy of the title and title plan. The title will identify the owner together with details of rights and matters that benefit the property and those which burden it. Burdens revealed on the title, such as restrictive covenants, will bind a buyer, and so the buyer's solicitor will need to check these carefully to anticipate any difficulties. In addition, a buyer will be bound by any overriding interests affecting the property, even if no mention is made of them on the register. The most commonly encountered overriding interests are legal leases granted for a term of seven years or less and the rights of individuals in occupation of the property. Note that it is the right that is protected: the mere fact of occupation does not confer any benefit within itself.
Positive and restrictive covenants	The burden of restrictive covenants can run with the land burdened. In registered land, the covenant must be entered on the register in order to be binding. The burden of positive covenants cannot run with the land. This does not mean a buyer need not be concerned with them, as methods exist to make such covenants indirectly enforceable. In essence, a positive covenant is one that requires positive action in order to ensure compliance (such as an obligation to repair), whilst a restrictive covenant is one that can be complied with by inactivity (such as an obligation not to cause a nuisance).
Professional conduct – Overview	The rules governing professional conduct apply as much to conveyancing transactions as they do to any other aspect of a solicitor's practice. Particular areas of concern are as follows.
Acting for borrower and lender	It is common, especially in residential transactions, for the buyer's solicitor also to act for the buyer's lender. As such, the solicitor has two clients. This is permitted by the Solicitors' Code of Conduct in the case of a 'standard mortgage' provided that:

Sub-section heading	Summary
'Contract races'	• no conflict of interest exists; • the lender's instructions do not extend beyond the detailed limitations contained in paras 3.19 to 3.21 of the Code. In the case of a mortgage for the purchase of the buyer's home, this includes using a prescribed form of certificate of title when reporting to the lender. A 'standard mortgage' is one provided by a lender in the normal course of its activities, where lending is a significant part of those activities, and which is on standard terms. A seller may find himself dealing with more than one prospective buyer at the same time. Where this is the case, the Code imposes strict requirements on the seller's solicitor. He must, with the seller-client's consent, inform each prospective buyer. If the seller-client does not give this consent, the seller's solicitor should immediately stop acting. 'Dealing with' is widely defined and includes any communication intended to progress the transaction, such as sending out a draft contract.
Taxation – Overview	There are three major forms of taxation that need to be considered in a conveyancing transaction. These are Capital Gains Tax (CGT), Value Added Tax (VAT) and Stamp Duty Land Tax (SDLT). SDLT is considered in more detail in Part V.
CGT	CGT is payable by a seller on any gain made between the price paid to buy the property and the price for which it is sold. This sum is subject to adjustment to allow for inflation. The disposal of an individual's principal private dwelling may be exempt from CGT provided certain conditions are satisfied. If CGT is payable, the inflation-adjusted sum, after deduction of an annual exemption, is payable at the highest rate at which the individual pays income tax. In the case of companies it is payable at the applicable corporation tax rate for that company.
VAT	Payment of VAT is not generally an issue for a buyer of residential property. In the case of commercial property, the sale of freehold property completed within three years of sale is standard rated. The sale of other freehold land and the grant or assignment of a lease is exempt, subject to an option for the seller to choose to charge VAT. A purchaser of commercial property should therefore establish its VAT status. If it is understood that an election will not be made, appropriate provisions should be included in the contract to prevent the seller electing to charge VAT. In the absence of this, the seller it is otherwise able to elect at any time before completion.

Part II

THE FIRST INTERVIEW

Chapter 7

Taking Instructions

7.1 Purpose of taking instructions

The purpose of taking instructions is for the solicitor to obtain from his client sufficient information to enable him to carry out the whole of the client's transaction, not just to enable him to take the first or next step in that transaction. This does not mean that the client is contacted only once during the course of the whole conveyancing transaction; the client must be regularly informed as to the progress of the transaction. From time to time, his further instructions will be needed. However, obtaining as much information as possible in one interview at the commencement of the transaction will save time (both the client's time and that of the solicitor) and will enable the solicitor to obtain a full picture of the transaction and thus to advise the client fully and correctly about his proposals.

Unless full instructions are taken, the solicitor is in danger of overlooking matters which are relevant to the transaction but which the client had not thought to mention specifically to him (eg, a liability to pay CGT on the proceeds of sale).

7.1.1 Personal interview

Wherever possible, instructions should be taken from the client in person. The personal interview gives the client the opportunity to ask questions of the solicitor, and the solicitor the benefit of being able to explain matters to the client in an informal and friendly manner. The Law Society's Guidance on Money Laundering and on Property Fraud both advise of the need for taking special care in cases where the solicitor never meets the client.

7.1.2 Indirect instructions

Indirect instructions, for example where an estate agent sends the solicitor instructions to act on behalf of one of the estate agent's clients, must be confirmed directly with the client, preferably by personal interview, to ensure that there is no misunderstanding about the instructions and that they comply in all respects with the Solicitors' Code of Conduct. This principle applies equally to the situation where instructions are taken from one only of two or more co-sellers or co-buyers (see *Penn v Bristol and West Building Society and Others* [1995] 2 FLR 938). Direct confirmation of instructions must be obtained from all persons who are to be clients of the solicitor.

A solicitor who acts for a client without authority may be liable to anyone who suffers loss as a result of this under the principle of breach of warranty of authority. Under the law of agency, an agent (ie the solicitor) is deemed to warrant that he has the authority to act on behalf of his principal (ie the client) and is liable for any loss suffered by someone who relies on this. So, in the *Penn* case (above) a solicitor who had no instructions to act for one co-owner was liable to the buyer's lender who advanced money to fund a purchase in which that co-owner's signature on the transfer had been forged by the other co-owner. The forgery rendered the transfer (and thus the mortgage) void.

7.1.3   Preparing for the interview

The methods of preparation for the interview and interviewing techniques are dealt with in *Skills for Lawyers* and are not further discussed in this book, except for the comments which appear below which are particularly relevant to conveyancing.

Before the interview, the solicitor should find out whether the firm has acted for this client previously in property matters. If it is found that the firm acted on the client's purchase of the property which he is now proposing to sell, the old purchase file should be retrieved from storage and its contents examined before interviewing the client for the purpose of taking instructions on the sale. Much of the information required on the sale transaction may already be contained in the purchase file (eg, who owns the boundaries of the property) and it will save time at the interview if this information can be confirmed with the client (to ensure that it has not changed) rather than fresh and full instructions being taken on every point.

7.1.4   Acting for both parties

Rule 3.07 of the Solicitors' Code of Conduct prevents a solicitor from acting for both seller and buyer in the same conveyancing transaction, except in the limited circumstances covered by r 3.07 (see **Chapter 5**). Before interviewing the client, the solicitor should check that the firm has not already accepted instructions to act for the other party in the same transaction or that, if it has, acting for this client is covered by one of the exceptions to r 3.07, complies with the general principles relating to conflict of interests and does not infringe any other practice rule or principle of professional conduct.

7.1.5   Protocol cases

Under the terms of the Protocol (see **Chapter 2**), the seller's solicitor is required to obtain his client's answers to the questions contained in the SPIF (a standard form of pre-contract search, see **18.7**), to obtain from his client any relevant documents relating to such matters as guarantees, building regulation control, etc, and to ask his client to complete the Fixtures Fittings and Contents Form showing which items are to remain at the property after the sale and which are to be removed (see **Chapter 10**). He must also obtain details of all financial charges over the property (including second and subsequent mortgages), and ascertain the identity of all persons aged over 17 who are resident in the property in order to establish whether or not such persons have an interest in the property.

7.1.6   Using checklists

Although checklists cannot be expected to cover every eventuality in every transaction, they are useful in standard transactions to ensure that all necessary information is acquired during the course of the interview. Checklists focus the interviewer's mind on the relevant information, reducing preparation time and, ultimately, saving time in the interview itself, but they do need to be used sympathetically so that the client does not feel he is being processed in an impersonal way. Where checklists are used, it is helpful to have them printed on a distinct colour of paper so that they are easily located in the file, either by the solicitor himself or by another member of his staff who has to work on the file.

An example of an attendance note made using such a checklist appears at 7.6.

7.1.7 Evidence of identity

Money laundering and fraud of all types is on the increase. Since 1 March 2004 solicitors have been required to play their part in combating such criminal activity by obtaining documentary proof of the identity of clients involved in property transactions, whether as a seller or a buyer. This should be obtained as soon as possible after first contact with the client is made. See 5.11 for details of the requirements of the Money Laundering Regulations.

7.2 Matters on which instructions must be obtained

A reminder of the matters which will be discussed at a first interview with a client is set out in 7.3 and 7.4. Although much of the information needed when acting for a seller is the mirror image of, or identical to, the information needed when acting for a buyer, some issues are exclusive to each side of the transaction. For that reason, separate checklists for seller and for buyer are given.

7.3 Acting for the seller

7.3.1 Full names and addresses of seller(s) and buyer(s), and home and business telephone numbers of seller(s)

The full names and addresses (including post codes) of all parties involved in the transaction are needed because they have to be inserted in both the contract and purchase deed. 'Full names' includes all middle names (ie, names exactly as they appear on the client's birth certificate or passport). The client's home and business telephone numbers are needed in order to be able to contact him during the course of the transaction. If a limited company is involved, details of the company's registered office and its registered number should also be obtained. The company's articles should also be checked to ensure that it does have the power to buy, sell or mortgage land, as the case might be.

7.3.2 Name, address and person to contact at estate agents

Where an estate agent is involved in the sale, the name, address and telephone number of the person at the agents who is dealing with the sale is needed for contact purposes and in case any queries need to be resolved with the agents. Where an HIP has been provided, the seller's solicitor should obtain a copy of this from the estate agent and carefully check the accuracy of its contents.

7.3.3 Name and address of other party's solicitors

The name, address and telephone number of the person dealing with the matter as solicitor or representative of the other party to the transaction must be obtained for contact purposes.

7.3.4 Full address of the property to be sold

The full address (including post code) and description of the property to be sold is required for insertion in the draft contract and, later, in the purchase deed.

7.3.5 Tenure

Whether the property is freehold or leasehold will need to be stated in the contract. Where the property is held on a lease, the terms of the lease must also be set out in the contract. The client may well not know this information. In any event, it should always be checked with the title documents, when they have been obtained.

7.3.6 Price

The price at which the property is agreed to be sold must be stated in the contract and the purchase deed.

7.3.7 Has any preliminary deposit been paid?

There is no requirement for the buyer to pay any money to the seller before the contract is entered into. However, sometimes a small sum of money (a preliminary deposit) is paid by the buyer to the seller's estate agent pending negotiations for the sale. This sum should be noted on the seller's solicitor's file, with a copy of the receipt for its payment, and taken into account when calculating the deposit needed later in the transaction (see **Chapter 21**). The commonest situation in which a preliminary deposit is payable is when the seller is a builder or developer selling a new house (see **Chapter 41**).

7.3.8 Fixtures and fittings

It is essential to obtain clear instructions relating to which fixtures and fittings are to remain at the property after completion of the sale, and which are to be removed by the seller (see **Chapter 10**). Where the Protocol is being used, the client should be asked to complete the Fixtures Fittings and Contents Form. Consideration should be given to whether any fittings (eg, carpets and curtains) which are included in the sale are included in the purchase price or are to be paid for separately by the buyer. Where a Home Information Pack (HIP) has been provided, it may contain this information. If it does, the seller's solicitor will need to check that the contents do reflect the seller's current intentions.

7.3.9 Seller's Property Information Form

In cases where the Protocol is being used, the seller should be asked to complete this form. This is a standard form of enquiry dealing with matters such as boundary disputes or whether any alterations have been made to the property. It is usual for the client to be given the form to complete in his own time and then return to the solicitor as soon as possible. However, it is then necessary for the solicitor to check the seller's replies to ensure that they are accurate. Failure to do this may amount to the provision of an inadequate professional service, or even to negligence. See **18.7** for details of the form.

Where a HIP has been provided, it may contain answers to such enquiries. If it does, the seller's solicitor will need to check that the answers provided are still correct.

7.3.10 Anticipated completion date

The client should be asked when he anticipates completion taking place. A 'normal' residential transaction takes on average 8–10 weeks from start to finish, although in certain circumstances a shorter time-span can be achieved. Sometimes a longer period of time may be desired by the client owing to particular circumstances (eg, where the client finds a buyer for his property in September, but he does not want to move until his children have completed the full academic year at their school the following July).

7.3.11 The present use of the property

Information relating to the present use of the property should be checked against its authorised use for planning purposes (see **Chapter 17**) and any restrictive covenants affecting the use of the property to ensure in both cases that no breaches have been committed.

7.3.12 Does the transaction attract VAT?

Most residential property transactions are not within the scope of the charge to VAT; VAT is, however, an important consideration in a commercial sale. In the case of a 'new' commercial property it is mandatory for VAT to be charged on the sale; in the case of other commercial properties, the seller may elect to charge VAT. He will need to elect if he wishes to reclaim any input tax incurred in connection with the property. If VAT is chargeable on the sale, the seller's solicitor should ensure that the terms of the contract with the buyer enable VAT to be added on to the agreed price (see **6.5**).

7.3.13 Who is in occupation of the property?

If someone other than the seller(s) is in occupation of the property, it will be necessary to ensure that they will vacate on or before completion. Details of any tenancies to which the property is subject must also be obtained as these will have to be disclosed to the buyer.

7.3.14 Synchronisation

Whether the transaction is dependent on the purchase or sale of another property is one of the most important questions to be raised at the first interview. In residential transactions, the client will often wish to sell his existing house and to use the proceeds of sale to purchase another house in which he will then live. The purchase of the new house cannot be undertaken without the proceeds of sale of the old house. Similarly, if the old house is not sold, the client has no use for the new house – he does not want or need two houses. Where the sale and purchase transactions are interdependent, the solicitor must ensure synchronisation of the two transactions, ie no sale without purchase and vice versa. Failure to do this constitutes professional negligence.

7.3.15 Whether any terms have been agreed between the parties

It is usually a good idea to ask whether the parties have agreed any other terms between them, ie terms which have not come to light in the interview so far. These terms may have been agreed informally by conversation between the parties, or may be recorded in correspondence between them. The solicitor should be aware of all the terms which have been agreed so that they can be incorporated into the contract which is drawn up between the parties.

7.3.16 Money

The client must be advised as to the costs of the transaction and a financial calculation should be made to ensure that the sale will yield sufficient funds to carry out the client's proposals (eg, to pay off the existing mortgage and to purchase a new house).

7.3.17 Whereabouts of title deeds and documents

The seller's solicitor will need to obtain the title deeds to the property to check that the seller does own and can sell the property, and to enable the contract to be drafted. The whereabouts of the deeds should, therefore, be ascertained from the seller. Often they will be in the possession of an existing lender. Under the LRA 1925, a land certificate was issued to the registered proprietor and this was needed before any subsequent registration could be made. However, under the LRA 2002, land certificates are no longer issued and any existing certificate is no longer required on a disposition.

7.3.18 Outstanding mortgages

Where the client has an outstanding mortgage on the property, the solicitor will need to contact the lender to obtain the title deeds. The client should be asked to supply his mortgage roll number or account number so that the solicitor can obtain the information and documents which he needs from the client's lender. Under the LRA 1925, a charge certificate was issued to each mortgage lender and this was needed before any subsequent registration could be made. In recent years, mortgage lenders frequently requested the Registry to retain the certificate in the Registry and the LRA 2002 has now abolished them. Any existing certificates are no longer required on a disposition. However, the mortgage lender may have other documents in its possession (eg, planning permissions) that will be required on the sale. Increasingly, however, mortgage lenders are unwilling to store any documentation, and it may well be that the client or the client's previous solicitors will have custody of this documentation. Most clients will have a mortgage over their property, some have more than one. All outstanding mortgages will normally need to be discharged before completion of the sale, and therefore the solicitor needs to enquire of the client:

(a)   whether there are any further charges over the property;

(b)   if so, how many;

(c)   who the lender is in each case; and

(d)   in each case, how much money (approximately) is outstanding on the loan. The information yielded by this question affects the financial calculation.

7.3.19 Amount of deposit

It is customary for a deposit equivalent to 10% of the purchase price to be paid by the buyer to the seller when a contract is entered into. If it is contemplated that a lower deposit will be paid in this case, the seller should be fully advised of the consequences of this step (see **Chapter 21**).

7.3.20 Proceeds of sale

In many residential cases, the question of what is to happen to the proceeds of sale of the property will be self-evident – the proceeds are to be used towards the purchase of another property. If the answer to this question is not clear from the information already supplied by the client, the solicitor must find out what the client's wishes are. The proceeds of sale must be dealt with as quickly as possible after completion takes place, otherwise the client may be entitled to interest on his money from the solicitor. If the proceeds are to be sent to the client's bank account, the solicitor needs to know the name and address of the relevant bank and the client's account number.

7.3.21   Capital gains tax

In certain cases, the sale of the property will be a disposal for CGT purposes (see **Chapter 6**).

If CGT is payable this should be pointed out to the client at the earliest possible opportunity. The fact that tax is chargeable on the disposition may affect the financial viability of the sale and the seller's decision to sell.

7.4   Acting for the buyer

Most of the information required when acting for a buyer client is either the same as, or the mirror image of, that required when acting for the seller, with the following modifications.

7.4.1   Use of the property

In addition to knowing what the present use of the property is, the buyer's solicitor will need to know what the buyer intends to use the property for after completion. In many cases, the answer to this question will be apparent from the circumstances of the transaction (eg, the client wants to buy a house to live in it). Any change of use of the property or alteration to its physical structure may require planning permission (see **Chapter 17**). This issue must be addressed before the client is committed to buy the property.

7.4.2   Money

A financial calculation must be undertaken to ensure that the client potentially has sufficient money to purchase the property and pay the related costs of purchase including, in appropriate cases, Land Registry fees and stamp duty land tax. Land Registry fees are payable for registering the land or registering a dealing at Land Registry after completion; fees are payable on a scale published by Land Registry and the client can therefore be told the exact amount of this cost.

Stamp duty land tax is payable at the rate of 1% on the whole of the consideration paid for the property where that price exceeds £125,000 for residential properties or £150,000 for commercial properties, or residential properties in certain disadvantaged areas (see **31.7.1**), but does not exceed £250,000. Where the price exceeds £250,000, but does not exceed £500,000, tax will be payable at 3% of the price. If the price exceeds £500,000 the tax is 4% of the price. In each case, the stated rate of tax is payable on the whole of the price. Thus a purchase for exactly £125,000 will incur no tax, but a purchase for £126,000 will attract £1,260 in tax.

Tax is payable only on the consideration for the land, not on that separately attributed to chattels. In marginal cases like this, if the sale includes chattels, it is sometimes possible to reduce the liability to tax by apportioning some of the price to the chattels included in the sale, for example carpets and curtains. The amount apportioned to the chattels must, of course, be a fair reflection of their value, otherwise both solicitor and client could be liable to criminal sanctions. However, in the example given of a purchase for £126,000, if £1,000 could be specifically attributed to the purchase of the carpets etc, this would reduce the consideration for the land to £125,000 and thus no tax would be payable, a saving of £1,260 for the client. Even bigger savings can be made where the purchase price is around the £250,000 or £500,000 thresholds for the higher rates of tax. The rates of tax are changed from time to time by the Finance Act. The rates cited above are those which are current at the time of publication of this book.

As mentioned above, stamp duty land tax is not payable on purchases of residential property within specified disadvantaged areas of the country where the purchase price does not exceed £150,000. The exemption from tax is based on postcodes, and the solicitor should therefore check whether the property being purchased is within such an area. This can be checked online from HMRC's website: www.hmrc.gov.uk/so/.

The source of the funds should also be considered. Where a residential property is being purchased with the aid of a mortgage, the *Lenders' Handbook* (para 5.9) (see **Appendix 7**) requires the solicitor to ascertain the source of the remainder of the purchase price and advise the lender if it is not being provided from the buyer's own funds. Very often family members will provide part of the purchase price, and this must then be reported to the lender with the client's authority. If authority is not forthcoming then the solicitor must cease to act as a conflict will have arisen.

The Law Society Money Laundering Guidance (paras 16–21) also reminds solicitors of the need to exercise caution in this area from a money laundering point of view. If, for example, a client states that £100,000 of the purchase price is to be provided from savings, this will be a factor to take into account in deciding whether the transaction should be referred to the firm's MLRO. The key factor in money laundering issues is to 'know your client'. Is it reasonable to expect that this client has £100,000 in savings, or could the money be the proceeds of crime?

Particular care should be taken if the buyer advises that part of the purchase price has been/is to be paid directly to the seller. Again, according to the *Lenders' Handbook*, this should be reported to the lender (para 6.3), and again may give rise to money laundering issues.

7.4.3 Deposit

The buyer will usually be required to pay a deposit of 10% of the purchase price on exchange of contracts, although often the seller can be persuaded to accept a lower figure. The client may not have ready access to cash to be used for the deposit and the solicitor will have to discuss with his client how the deposit is to be funded. Often it will be possible to use the deposit paid to the client on the sale of his existing property to fund the deposit required on his purchase. Otherwise a bridging loan may be necessary (see **21.4.2**).

7.4.4 Mortgage

Most clients will require some type of mortgage funding to assist with the purchase of the property. Some clients will already have arranged finance before going to see the solicitor, residential clients may require assistance with the sources and types of finance available (see **Chapter 8**).

7.4.5 Survey

The maxim 'caveat emptor' applies (with limited exceptions) to conveyancing; it is for the buyer to make sure of his bargain. It is sensible for the buyer to commission an independent survey of the property to ensure that the property does not have more problems associated with it than the client had bargained for. The solicitor should therefore discuss with his buyer client the need for a survey in appropriate cases (see **Chapter 11**). The need for an environmental survey should also be discussed (see **17.6**). Where a HIP is in place, this may contain a Home Condition Report (HCR). This is a pro-forma report on various aspects of the structure and condition of the property. It will also contain an energy efficiency rating. It is not, however, a substitute for a full structural survey and the buyer should be advised of its limitations. Particular care should be taken where the HCR recommends further investigation into a particular problem.

7.4.6 Situation of the property

Enquiries should be made as to the situation of the property, for example, its proximity to canals, rivers, etc, which may indicate the need for special searches to be undertaken (see **Chapter 18**).

7.4.7 Insurance

The risk in the property for insurance purposes will often pass to the buyer when a contract is entered into. The client should be warned of this and that the solicitor will arrange such insurance on his behalf at his expense. Additionally, there may be a need to discuss with the client arrangements for life assurance (it may be a term of the client's mortgage offer that he takes out a life policy) and buildings contents insurance.

7.4.8 Who is buying the property?

Where the prospective buyer is married or is intending to live in the property with a cohabitee or friend, the lender who is providing the mortgage finance for the property will insist that the legal title to the property is held in joint names or that they sign a waiver of any rights they may have in favour of the lender. Where the purchase is to be in more than one person's name, the clients must be advised in relation to co-ownership (see **Chapter 9**). The problems of conflict of interests must be borne in mind when dealing with this issue.

7.4.9 Custody of deeds

Where there is to be a mortgage of the property, the client's lender would normally in the past have taken custody of the charge certificate and other documents after completion. The LRA 2002 abolished charge certificates and many mortgagees are no longer prepared to store documents because of the costs involved. In all cases, therefore, the client's instructions in relation to custody of the deeds should be obtained. The client may, for example, wish to have the deeds sent to his home, or to his bank, or for the solicitor to keep them in his own strong room.

7.4.10 The client's present property

In a residential transaction, it must be ascertained where the client is presently living, and whether it is necessary to sell the client's present house before buying the new one (see **7.3.14**). If the client is presently living in rented accommodation, he may need to be advised about giving notice to his landlord to terminate that tenancy.

7.5 Instructions in special cases

Information additional to that outlined above will be required where the transaction concerns a newly constructed property (see **Chapter 41**), a leasehold (see **Chapter 35**), or a dealing with part only of the seller's property (see **Chapter 40**).

7.6   Specimen instructions

Set out below is an example of an attendance note recording instructions from a client which would have been obtained using the sort of checklist referred to in **7.1.6**. Many firms have their own checklists and this is merely one suggested format. The client, Roger Evans, is the current owner of 47, Queens' Road, Loamster, the title to which has already been seen at **4.7**.

Bucks & Co Solicitors
Attendance Note

Client:	Roger Evans
Matter:	Sale of 47, Queens' Road, Loamster. Purchase of 10, Bladen Road, Overton.
In attendance:	A Solicitor Roger Evans
Date:	1 September 2008

Money laundering identity check

Passport seen and copy on file.[1]

Sale

Property and tenure	47, Queens' Road, Loamster, Maradon, Cornshire, CS1 5TY. Freehold
Seller:	Roger Evans (tel mob 08875 456987).
Buyer:	Catherine and Joanne Reade, 24 Leeming Road, Bridgeton, Cornshire, CS3 4DD.
Buyer's solicitors:	SLT Solicitors (contact details to be confirmed).
Estate Agents:	Mercury Estate Agents (Anne Norwood – mob 08877 324536).
Price (including fixtures and fittings)	£350,000. Various items of garden furniture and, washer drier and fridge freezer being sold for an additional £500.
Deposit:	No preliminary deposit paid. £20,000 deposit agreed.
Completion date:	As soon as possible, but ideally before the end of October as this fits in with buyer's plans.
SPIF and FFC:	Handed client SPIF and FFC and explained purpose. Client to complete and return next week.
Mortgage:	Mortgage with Humberside and Counties Bank, £50,000 outstanding. Title documents at the Loamster Branch.
Miscellaneous:	
• Current use • Any works carried out to property • Occupiers • CGT/VAT	The property is the client's home. Apart from minor decoration, the client has not carried out works to the property. There are no other occupiers.

Purchase

Property and tenure:	10, Bladen Road, Overton, Cornshire, CS1 6AU. Freehold.
Seller:	Neil Stuart. Address as above.
Seller's solicitors:	Fining and Co, Overton Office. Jayne Peters (01366 695444)
Estate Agents:	Cranswick Properties. Overton Office.
Price (including fixtures and fittings):	£252,000 including £2,000 for chattels (antique dining furniture).
Deposit:	No preliminary deposit paid. 5% deposit agreed. Explained that the deposit received on sale of 47, Queen's Road might be used to fund this.[2] Client would prefer this but has savings to fund if necessary.
Completion date:	As with sale. Seller is moving abroad but has no deadline.
Survey:	Client has already commissioned a survey.
Mortgage:	None. Purchase to be funded from equity released on sale of current property.
Miscellaneous:	Roger Evans is retiring and buying 10, Bladen Road as his retirement home. The seller, Neil Stuart, is recently widowed and is moving overseas. NS is keen to complete as soon as possible, but has no specific deadline for doing so.
	Explained to client that apportioning the £2,000 specifically to fixtures and fittings will save SDLT. Client confirmed that £2,000 represents proper market value for the items in question.
	10, Bladen Road has recently been extended (client thinks in 2002) with a conservatory to the rear overlooking the nearby river. This was one of the selling points to the client as there is also access to the river for the purposes of fishing.

Financial	Reviewed estimate of figures with client and will confirm in writing:[3]			
	Sale		**Purchase**	
	Sale price	350,000	Purchase price	250,000
			Furniture	2,000
	Less:			
	Mortgage	50,000	Plus:	
	Our fees (incl VAT)	[ ]	Our fees (incl VAT)	[ ]
	Estate agents fees (incl VAT	[ ]	Disbursements	[ ]
			Survey	[ ]
			SDLT	2,500
			Land Registry fee	220

Balance of proceeds of sale to be sent to client on completion. Recommended Private Client department for advice on financial and estate planning.

Notes

1. For more detail on this issue, see **7.1.7**.

2. For more information on funding the deposit, see **Chapter 21**.

3. This specimen attendance note identifies the major financial elements of a typical residential transaction. Clients may be unaware of some of the costs involved (particularly significant sums such as SDLT) and so must be made aware of them when taking instructions. Disbursements would include searches and enquiries, for which see **Chapter 18**. Note that potential clients will often shop round before choosing a solicitor and so care needs to be taken in explaining the basis of, level of, and reasons behind the fees charged.

Chapter 8

Finance for the Buyer

8.1 Introduction

The buyer's solicitor should check that the client has sufficient funds available to meet the cost of his purchase and related expenses. This matter should be raised with the client when taking instructions and a further check should be made just before exchange of contracts to ensure that any factors which have altered since instructions were first obtained have been taken into account in calculating the client's financial situation. The client should be advised against entering into a binding contract for purchase unless the financial arrangements are settled and adequate to meet the commitments involved.

The methods used to finance commercial purchases are outside the scope of this book and this chapter concentrates on finance for the purchase of residential property. However, whatever the type of transaction, the buyer's solicitor should always ensure that his client has sufficient funds available.

8.1.1 The client has already arranged a mortgage

Many clients will have already considered the financial implications of the transaction before instructing the solicitor to act, in which case all that the solicitor needs to do is to check through the figures with the client to ensure that all necessary items of expenditure have been taken into account. In this situation, the client is likely already to have submitted a mortgage application to a lender and will not require advice on the sources and types of finance available for the purchase of property. The solicitor should not interfere with arrangements which the client has made but, if it appears that the mortgage arrangements are patently unsatisfactory (eg, an exorbitant interest rate is to be charged on the loan), there may be a duty on the solicitor to suggest that the client reconsiders his choice of finance on the basis that more advantageous terms could be obtained from another source.

8.1.2 Financial services

When advising on finance, regard must be had to the Financial Services and Markets Act 2000. Solicitors who wish to advise on 'mainstream' investment business, eg advising on specific investments, must be authorised so to do by the Financial Services Authority (FSA). Most solicitors firms, however, are not so authorised and rely on regulation by the Solicitors Regulation Authority (SRA). The SRA is a Designated Professional Body under the 2000 Act, and as such has issued rules as to what solicitors can and cannot do. A mortgage as such is not an investment and so does not come within the scope of the 2000 Act. So a solicitor can give general advice as to what type of mortgage loan a client should obtain, or arrange a repayment mortgage for a client. However, advising on a specific investment product to support a loan, eg, an endowment policy, or a pension policy or an ISA, would amount to mainstream investment business for which authorisation from the FSA would be necessary.

8.2 Sources and types of finance

Where the client has not made any financial arrangements prior to instructing the solicitor, he may require advice on the sources of mortgage finance and types of loan available. In some cases, the client may require assistance with making his mortgage application. The solicitor may have an arrangement with a lender for the introduction of clients; such arrangement must comply with the Solicitors' Code of Conduct 2007.

8.2.1 Sources of finance

The main sources of mortgage finance available for the purchase of land in England and Wales are:

(a)   banks;

(b)   building societies;

(c)   insurance companies;

(d)   the client's employer;

(e)   a private mortgage (eg, a loan from a relative or from a trust fund); and

(f)   finance houses.

8.2.1.1 Building societies and banks

Loans from building societies and banks represent the largest slice of the mortgage market, accounting between them for approximately 85% of all residential loans. There is little to distinguish between the terms offered by these two types of institutions: both will offer long-term loans (eg, 25 years) at commercially competitive interest rates.

Banks have the reputation of being slightly more flexible in the application of their lending criteria and of being more willing to consider unusual property (eg, a derelict barn which is to be converted) and higher-value loans. Loans for commercial property and business expansion are also more likely to be funded by banks.

8.2.1.2 Insurance companies

Although loans from insurance companies for house purchase represent a small percentage of the loan market, their lending terms are broadly similar to those offered by the banks and building societies. A loan from this source would normally be supported by an endowment policy on the borrower's life. Several insurance companies have now set up their own banking subsidiaries to compete in the mortgage market.

8.2.1.3 The client's employer

Some large company employers (eg, banks) offer mortgages at concessionary rates to their employees. The terms of these loans may enable the employee to borrow a substantially higher sum at a lower rate of interest than could be obtained on the open market.

Where the rate of interest payable on such a loan is less than the commercial rate being charged by other lenders, the employee may be deemed by HMRC to be in receipt of a benefit in kind which is taxable in the hands of a higher-paid employee. Even with this tax burden, the loan from the employer still usually represents good value for money. The main drawback to such an arrangement is that the employee with this type of loan will find it more difficult to change his job, since ending his employment will result in the withdrawal of the concessionary rates and a consequent increase in mortgage repayments.

8.2.1.4 Individual mortgage

A client may sometimes be able to arrange mortgage finance through a loan from a relative or from a private trust fund. The terms of such a loan are a matter for agreement between the parties involved, who must always be separately advised. The Solicitors' Code of Conduct, r 3.16 prohibits the same solicitor from acting for both lender and borrower in this situation except where the transaction is not at 'arm's length' (see **5.2.2.1**). It is suggested that, even where the loan is not at arm's length (eg, a loan from father to son), the potential conflict of interests between lender and borrower will preclude the same solicitor from acting for both parties.

8.2.1.5 Finance houses

Mortgage funding is available from finance houses, but they are not generally considered to be a primary source of finance for a client who is seeking a loan for the purchase of property. The terms offered by a finance house may be less generous than those offered by the banks and building societies (eg, a shorter period of loan and higher rate of interest).

However, a client who already owns his house might approach a finance house for a second loan (eg, for the purchase of a new car or for improvements to the property). Second mortgages from finance houses for sums not exceeding £15,000 may be affected by the notice provisions contained in s 58 of the Consumer Credit Act 1974.

8.2.2 Amount of loan

All lenders have slightly different criteria or status qualifications for granting a loan. If the state of the mortgage market means that funds are readily available, the lender may be less stringent in the application of its criteria than at a time when funds are in short supply.

In broad terms, the maximum sum that a borrower can hope to obtain on mortgage is linked to a multiplier of his and his co-owner's salary. For example, a lender may stipulate that it is prepared to lend up to three times the main salary earner's salary plus one times the lesser earner's salary. Thus, if a client earns £40,000 per annum, and his co-owner earns £10,000 per annum, the maximum loan which the couple could apply for would be £130,000.

This overall limit is usually subject to the further qualification that the amount of the loan does not exceed a fixed percentage of the lender's valuation of the property (not the purchase price). The fixed percentage will vary depending on the lender and the type of property involved, but as a general rule it is unrealistic to expect to obtain a loan of more than 90% of the valuation (except perhaps for first-time buyers) and the percentage will decrease with the age of the property being purchased. A 90% limit may be placed on a modern property; this figure may drop to 80% or 70% with an older house. It must also be remembered that the lender's valuation of the property is frequently less than the asking price of the property. Where the lender agrees to lend a sum in excess of the normal percentage of the valuation, it may be a term of the loan that the borrower pays for a single premium insurance policy ('a guarantee policy') which is taken out by the lender. If the lender has to exercise its power of sale, it is insured against any loss it may incur due to having lent more than the normal percentage of the value.

These mortgage guarantee policies have been much criticised as, although they are paid for by the borrower, they protect only the lender. The borrower has no rights under them on a sale at a loss. Indeed, the insurer often has a right of subrogation to reclaim any loss it has had to meet from the borrower. Many lenders now no longer require such policies, or will meet the cost themselves.

8.2.3 Types of mortgage

Each lender will apply a different name to the various loan packages which it advertises. These are mainly variations of the four main types of mortgage available, which are:

(a)   a repayment mortgage;

(b)   an endowment mortgage;

(c)   a pension mortgage; and

(d)   Islamic mortgages.

8.2.3.1 Repayment mortgage

A repayment mortgage is the most straightforward type of loan available. In return for the loan, the borrower grants a mortgage of the property to the lender. Throughout the term of the loan (eg, 25 years) the borrower will make monthly repayments to the lender, part of which represents a repayment of the capital sum borrowed. The balance is interest on the loan. At the end of the mortgage term, the loan has been completely repaid and the mortgage is discharged. If the borrower wants to sell the property before the end of the mortgage term, he will pay off the mortgage out of the proceeds of sale of the property, and any sum over and above this amount will belong to him.

The main disadvantage of this type of mortgage is that if the borrower dies before the mortgage is paid off, the whole of the outstanding balance of the loan becomes immediately repayable from the deceased's estate. This can cause problems if the deceased borrower was the main salary earner for a family, leaving a non-earning spouse and children to cope with the repayment of the mortgage. This difficulty is easily surmounted by the borrower taking out a 'mortgage protection policy' to cover the amount of the loan. Such a policy will guarantee to repay the balance outstanding on the mortgage in the event of the borrower's death. Some policies will also cover permanent disability through accident or illness which prevents the borrower from earning his living. These policies are readily available, inexpensive (a small monthly premium is payable) and, in the case of co-owners, should be taken out over joint lives, so that even if one co-owner is not contributing financially to the mortgage, the repayment of the loan is guaranteed in the event of the death of either of them.

8.2.3.2 Endowment mortgage

An endowment mortgage provides additional security for the loan over the property by means of an insurance policy taken out on the borrower's life. The borrower mortgages the property to the lender and takes out a life policy in the same sum as the amount of the loan. He may also be required to mortgage or to deposit the policy with the lender for safe-keeping. During the mortgage term the borrower makes monthly repayments of interest only to the lender. No capital is repaid during the term of the mortgage. If the borrower dies during the term of the mortgage, the proceeds of the insurance policy will discharge the loan. At the end of the term, the policy 'matures' and should yield sufficient money to discharge the capital sum owing on the mortgage. Most endowment policies do not actually guarantee to repay the amount of the loan on maturity, although they do guarantee to discharge the loan on the death of the borrower. They are 'with profits' policies, which means that the policy holder shares in the profits made by the insurance company over the term of the policy. 'Bonuses', representing this share in the profits, are then added to the amount due on maturity, the expectation being that this will then be sufficient to repay the whole of the loan. Sometimes the profits will be such that there will be an excess over the amount needed to repay the loan and this will then be payable to the borrower.

In the event of the borrower wanting to sell the property before the expiry of the mortgage term, he will have to repay the whole of the mortgage debt out of the proceeds of sale of the property. The insurance policy may then be terminated or transferred as security for another loan. Not all policies can be transferred in this way. The cash value of a policy which is surrendered during the early years of the mortgage will be very small. This type of mortgage may not always therefore be suitable for a borrower who is intending to resell the property within a few years. Since the borrower has to pay monthly premiums on the life policy, in addition to his monthly payments to the lender, this type of loan may be more expensive than a repayment mortgage. This, however, will depend upon the age and state of health of the borrower. Insurance companies will apply normal actuarial principles in assessing the amount of the premium, so that a young, fit and healthy borrower will pay less than an older borrower suffering from a chronic illness.

There has been much controversy in recent years with regard to the mis-selling of endowment mortgages. The danger is that when the endowment policy matures it may not produce enough money to pay off the full amount of the loan, leaving the borrower to find the shortfall from his own funds. It now seems to be accepted that for many people an endowment mortgage is not a good investment. This has particularly proved to be the case following falls in share prices in the 1990s.

8.2.3.3 Pension mortgage

As its name suggests, a pension mortgage links a mortgage of the property which the client is buying with pension arrangements for the client's retirement. This type of mortgage is generally available only to self-employed people and is beneficial (in terms of tax relief on the pension contributions) to high earners.

8.2.3.4 Islamic mortgages

Most loans require the payment (and receipt) of interest. There are, however, various finance schemes that are Sharia compliant and avoid the payment of interest.

The Murabaha involves a bank buying the property and then reselling it to the actual buyer at a higher price. This price is then paid to the bank by instalments over a period of years.

Alternatively, the Ijara and Diminishing Musharaka schemes allow the bank to purchase the property and then lease it to the buyer in return for rent. At the end of the lease, the bank agrees to transfer the property to the buyer.

8.2.4 Lender's powers

Almost all mortgage deeds will give the lender power, expressly or impliedly, to repossess and sell the property in the event of default by the borrower. Some borrowers are unaware of this fact and the solicitor, without unnecessarily frightening the client, should point out to the client that these powers do exist and will be exercised by the lender if the need arises. It may therefore be sensible to check that the client is aware of his liability to make monthly repayments of the loan, and insurance premiums where appropriate, and that the amount of these monthly outgoings does not represent an unrealistically high proportion of the client's income. As a very rough guide, the amount of the client's net monthly mortgage repayment should not exceed about 25% of his net monthly income.

8.3 Further reading

P Camp, *Solicitors and Financial Services* (3rd edn, 2002).

Chapter 9

Advising Joint Buyers

9.1 Advising the client

Where it is apparent from instructions that the property is to be occupied and/or financed by two or more adults, the solicitor should discuss with his client(s) the advantages and disadvantages of co-ownership and the various methods by which the client's wishes can be carried out. A note of the client's instructions should be made on the file to ensure that they are implemented at the appropriate stage of the transaction (ie, in the purchase deed).

There are three possible alternatives which need to be discussed with the clients:

(a) sole ownership by one of the clients; or

(b) ownership by all as joint tenants; or

(c) ownership by all as tenants in common.

The following points should be borne in mind.

(a) Instructions should be obtained directly from all proposed co-owners. It is not sufficient to accept the word of one co-owner that his or her co-buyer agrees to the proposals.

(b) Advising more than one party in the same transaction (ie, the two or more co-buyers) may give rise to a conflict of interests between them, for example, where the beneficial interest in the property is to be held in unequal shares. The solicitor must ensure that the co-owners receive separate independent advice in any situation where a conflict arises or is likely to arise (see **Chapter 5**).

9.2 Suitability of each method

9.2.1 Sole ownership

This is generally suitable only where the other occupier is not contributing to the purchase price in any way. It will mean, however, that the non-owning occupier will legally have no say in any future disposition of the property. However, a spouse or civil partner will have rights of occupation under the Family Law Act 1996 and may prevent a sale by registering those rights.

If the occupier is making a financial contribution, it may well be preferable to consider one of the forms of co-ownership. Whatever type of co-ownership is chosen, all co-owners have to join in (and thus agree to) any disposition. However, if there is to be a mortgage on the property, all co-owners will be required to join in this and thus make themselves personally liable to repay the loan. This may well not be what the parties intend.

If an occupier making a contribution were not to become a legal co-owner, it may well still not be possible for a sale or other disposition to be made without his consent. He will have an overriding interest under Sch 3 to the LRA 2002 and, as such, will be required to release those rights on a disposition; otherwise they will be binding on a purchaser irrespective of notice. In theory, the sole owner of the legal estate can appoint another trustee and thus overreach the overriding interest of the occupier (see *City of London Building Society v Flegg* [1988] AC 54). However, in practice, if a sale is contemplated and the occupier is refusing to leave, it may well still be necessary to obtain a court order to evict the occupier and thus give a buyer vacant possession.

The possibility of a conflict of interest arising should be very carefully borne in mind in advising in this area.

9.2.2 Joint tenancy

All cases of co-ownership give rise to a trust of land (see **3.8**). The maximum number of legal owners is four. As with any form of co-ownership, all of the legal co-owners must join in any future disposition of the property. In case of a dispute, an application can be made to the court under s 14 of the Trusts of Land and Appointment of Trustees Act 1996. The court can make whatever order it thinks fit, but will particularly take into account the purpose for which the land was bought.

On the death of a joint tenant the right of survivorship will apply, and this will make a joint tenancy particularly suitable for married couples and others in a permanent relationship who want their interest in the house to go to the other party on their death. If the parties wish to be able to leave their respective shares by will, eg where they have children from a previous relationship, then a tenancy in common will be necessary.

A joint tenancy can subsequently be 'severed', ie converted into a tenancy in common. This will then destroy the right of survivorship and allow an owner's share to be left by will to whomsoever he pleases.

However, joint tenants always have equal rights in the property, irrespective of their contributions to the purchase price. Thus, if A and B buy as joint tenants, A having contributed 90% of the price and B only 10%, on a subsequent severance B will acquire a half share in the land. If the parties want recognition to be given to their respective contributions then a tenancy in common will be required from the outset.

9.2.3 Tenancy in common

This would be usual in the case of business partners and other circumstances where the parties do not wish the right of survivorship to apply, for example where the parties are not co-habiting or not in a long-term relationship, or want to be able to make provision for others out of their interest on death, or want the amount of their contribution to the purchase price to be recognised in the size of their share in the land.

It is essential in a tenancy in common for the respective shares of the co-owners to be expressly recorded. This will be included in the transfer passing the legal estate to them, but this will be retained by Land Registry for registration purposes. It is sensible, therefore, for a duplicate transfer to be drawn up and executed by the parties; this should then be kept in a safe place as evidence of the parties' rights.

As with a joint tenancy, all of the co-owners of the legal estate must join in a disposition. Disputes can again be resolved by the court under s 14 of the Trusts of Land and Appointment of Trustees Act 1996.

In the case of business partners, it is preferable for the exact shares of the partners not to be recorded in the transfer itself. This is because those shares might change due to a reorganisation of the partnership, for example on the admission of a new partner. It is preferable for the shares of the co-owners to be dealt with exclusively by the partnership agreement and for the transfer to make it clear that they hold as tenants in common in the shares as set out in the partnership agreement.

Chapter 10

Fixtures and Fittings

10.1 Fixtures

Fixtures are generally items which are attached to and form part of the land (eg, fitted wardrobes) and will therefore be included as part of the property on sale of the land unless the seller expressly reserves the right to remove them, ie, by including a contractual condition to this effect such as 'the seller reserves the right to remove the garden seat and stone ornaments from the property before completion'.

Except where the seller has reserved the right to remove specific items, the buyer can expect to take over the ownership of fixtures on completion; they are part of the property which he has purchased and their value is included in the purchase price.

10.2 Fittings

Fittings, or chattels (eg, carpets and curtains) do not form part of the land and so are not included as part of the property on sale of the land unless the seller expressly agrees to leave them behind. Any fittings which are to be included in the sale should be specifically itemised in the contract or, in residential transactions, a special condition in the contract may refer to the Fixtures Fittings and Contents Form attached to the contract (see **10.6**).

Some fittings may be included in the sale price of the property. These are normally expressly mentioned in the estate agent's particulars of sale; otherwise the seller and buyer will need to reach agreement over an additional price which the buyer is to pay for the purchase of the fittings.

10.3 Practical distinction

The legal distinction between fixtures and fittings as outlined above is quite clear, but the practical distinction between the two categories is sometimes less obvious. Moveable objects which are not attached to the land, such as carpets, curtains and free-standing furniture, clearly fall within the definition of fittings, but items which are attached to the land are not always classified as fixtures. Case law in this area is unclear and there have been reported cases where items such as greenhouses and garden ornaments have been held to be fixtures, and other cases where the same types of items have been held to be fittings (see *TSB Bank plc v Botham* (1997) 73 P & CR D1).

10.4 Need for certainty in contract

Disputes over the unexpected removal of fixtures and fittings are common, and frequently cost more to resolve than the value of the disputed items. The estate agent's particulars should be scrutinised to see which items are listed as being included or excluded from the sale, and checked with the client to ensure their accuracy. When taking instructions, it will be necessary to ascertain from the client which items are to be removed, which items he expects to remain at the property, and whether any price in addition to the price of the land is required for the fittings.

In view of the uncertainty of the status of some items in law, it is essential that in appropriate circumstances the contract expressly deals with:

(a)   fixtures which the seller intends to remove on or before completion;

(b)   fittings which are to remain at the property;

(c)   any additional price which the buyer is to pay for the fittings;

(d)   postponement of passing of title to fittings until completion; in the absence of such a condition, s 18 of the Sale of Goods Act 1979 will provide that title to the fittings passes to the buyer on exchange (this provision is contained in SC 10);

(e)   a warranty that fittings are free of incumbrances (eg, subsisting hire-purchase agreements). In the absence of an express special condition dealing with this matter, SC 10, by making the contract one for the sale of goods, implicitly imports s 12 of the Sale of Goods Act 1979 which contains such a warranty.

10.5 Apportionment of purchase price

The sale of chattels does not attract stamp duty land tax. The value of chattels which have been included in the purchase price of the land can therefore be deducted from the total purchase price, producing a reduction in the value of the land and a possible consequent reduction in the amount of tax payable by the buyer. This apportionment of the purchase price between the land and the chattels is of most value to the buyer when the value of the land and chattels together is marginally above the current stamp duty land tax threshold. Thus, assuming a residential property not in a disadvantaged area, a purchase for exactly £125,000 will pay no tax, but a purchase for £126,000 will attract £1,260 in tax. So if £1,000 can be attributed to the chattels, the purchase price of the land will be reduced to £125,000 and will be exempt from tax, a saving of £1,260 for the buyer. Similar savings can be made if the purchase price is just above the £250,000 and £500,000 thresholds for the higher rates of tax (see 7.4).

Only the true value of the chattels may be deducted from the purchase price for this purpose. Any overvaluation of the price of the chattels is a fraud on HMRC which may render both the solicitor and his client liable to criminal sanctions. Such conduct would also be conduct unbefitting a solicitor which could result in disciplinary proceedings being brought against the solicitor concerned. A further consequence of an overvaluation is that the contract for the sale of the land would be unenforceable by court action, since it could be construed by the courts as being a contract to defraud HMRC; such contracts are unenforceable on the grounds of public policy (see *Saunders v Edwards* [1987] 2 All ER 651). If necessary, the advice of a professional valuer should be obtained.

10.6 Fixtures Fittings and Contents Form

The Protocol requires the seller's solicitor to obtain information relating to fixtures and fittings from the seller, using the standard Fixtures Fittings and Contents Form. The completed form should then be sent to the buyer's solicitors with the draft contract. Special Condition 3 on the reverse of the Standard Conditions of Sale form makes reference to the Fixtures Fittings and Contents Form and, in appropriate cases, requires it to be annexed to and form part of the contract.

Where a HIP has been provided, this may contain details of the items included in the sale. This may not be in the form of a Fixtures Fittings and Contents Form as this is Law Society copyright. However, as it is 'authorised' rather than 'required' content of a HIP, it is likely that most HIPs will not contain such information. If such information is included in the HIP, the seller's solicitor must ensure that it still reflects the seller's current intentions. If it does not, the buyer should be informed immediately.

Chapter 11

Surveys

11.1 When should a survey be commissioned?

In an ideal world, the client should always have a survey carried out before exchange of contracts, but many buyers of residential property, particularly first-time buyers for whom the expense of a survey is a major consideration, do not commission an independent survey, preferring to rely instead on the valuation undertaken by their lender. Most lenders disclose their written valuation reports to their customers.

Where a HIP is in place, this may contain a Home Condition Report (HCR). This is a form of structural survey in a standard format (see **11.3.4**) and may obviate the need for the buyer to commission his own survey. However, it will not contain a valuation of the property, so mortgage lenders will still need to commission their own valuation (see **11.3.1**). In any event, as the HCR is not 'required' content of a HIP, it seems likely that most sellers will be unwilling to bear the expense of such a report, although the Government does recommend that one should be included.

11.2 Reasons for a survey

The *caveat emptor* rule places on the buyer the onus of discovering any physical faults in the property agreed to be sold. For this reason alone, a survey is always advisable in order to discover physical defects which are not readily apparent on inspection of the property by the lay client.

11.3 Types of survey

The client has four main choices open to him:

(a)   to rely on the valuation made by his lender;

(b)   to commission a 'Home Buyer's Valuation and Survey Report';

(c)   to commission a full structural survey;

(d)   to rely on the Home Condition Report.

11.3.1 Valuation

A valuation will be undertaken by the buyer's lender in order to establish whether the property being purchased will be adequate security for the amount of the loan. The buyer pays the cost of this valuation and is usually permitted to see the valuer's report, but the report will not necessarily reveal sufficient information about the state of the property to allow the buyer to make a reasoned judgement as to whether or not to proceed with his purchase. As its name suggests, it just assesses the value of the property; it will not contain a detailed commentary on the state of the structure of the property.

11.3.2 Home Buyer's Valuation and Survey Report

The Home Buyer's Valuation and Survey Report represents a compromise between the mortgage valuation and the full survey and is an attractive option for a residential client who is reluctant to commission a full survey. In many cases the buyer's lender will agree (for an additional fee) to instruct the lender's valuer to undertake the survey at the same time as the mortgage valuation is carried out, with consequent savings in time and expense for the client. Although of much more value to the client than a mere valuation, this type of survey is still relatively superficial in scope.

11.3.3 Full survey

The potential expense of a full survey deters many clients, but the client might be reminded that £500 abortive expense on a survey is preferable to discovering that many thousands of pounds need to be spent on carrying out structural repairs to the property he has just purchased without the benefit of a survey. A full structural survey will provide a detailed commentary on the condition of the structure of the building.

11.3.4 Home Condition Report (HCR)

This may be included as part of the HIP. It is an objective report about the physical condition and energy performance of the house prepared, in a standard format, by a qualified 'Home Inspector', ie, not a surveyor. It is likely to contain similar information to the Home Buyer's Valuation and Survey Report (see **11.3.2**) plus the energy efficiency report. Buyers should be advised that it is not a substitute for a full survey. See **11.4** as to the factors indicating the need for a full survey. In any event, clients should be advised to be particularly wary of HCRs prepared more than (say) two months previously as the condition of the house may have changed since the HCR was prepared.

11.4 Factors indicating desirability of a full survey

The need for a full structural survey may be indicated by the presence of one or more of the following factors:

(a)   the property is of a high value;
(b)   the amount of the buyer's intended mortgage represents a low proportion of the purchase price (eg, 70% or less);
(c)   the property is more than 100 years old;
(d)   the buyer intends to alter or extend the property after completion;
(e)   the property is not of conventional brick and mortar construction;
(f)   the proximity of the property to features which may cause subsidence or other structural problems (eg, mines, rivers, clay sub-soils);
(g)   the property is not detached.

11.5 Surveys in special cases

A surveyor, even when instructed to carry out a full structural survey, will not normally investigate drainage or electrical systems. A property which does not have the benefit of mains drainage will require a separate drainage survey from an expert in that field, since the cost of repair or replacement of a private drainage system can be prohibitive. Liability for escaping effluent can also involve civil and criminal penalties. An environmental survey may also be required – see **17.6**.

11.6 Flats and other attached properties

Where the property to be purchased is a flat or is a property which is structurally attached to neighbouring property, a full survey is desirable. The structural soundness of the property being bought is, in these circumstances, dependent on the soundness of the neighbouring property too, and the surveyor must therefore be instructed to inspect the main structure of the building and the adjoining property (if possible) as well as the property actually being purchased.

11.7 Surveyor's liability

The surveyor owes a duty of care to his client to carry out his survey with reasonable skill and care. This common law duty is reinforced by s 13 of the Supply of Goods and Services Act 1982, which implies into a contract for services a term that the work will be carried out with reasonable skill and care. Where a client suffers loss as a result of a negligent survey, a claim may lie against his surveyor, subject to the validity of any exemption clause which may have formed part of the surveyor's terms of work. The normal rules relating to remoteness of damage apply, thus the client will not sustain a successful claim unless the area of the client's complaint lies within the scope of what the surveyor was instructed to do, hence the importance of giving full and explicit instructions when the survey is commissioned.

Where the client suffers loss after having relied on a lender's valuer's report, a claim in tort may lie against the surveyor. No claim in contract can be sustained because the survey was commissioned by the lender, and so there is no contractual relationship between the buyer and the surveyor. The success of such a claim may again depend on the validity of any exclusion clause contained in the valuation. However, it was held by the House of Lords in *Smith v Eric S Bush (a Firm)* [1990] 1 AC 831 that a valuer instructed by a lender to carry out a mortgage valuation of a modest house, in the knowledge that the buyer would rely on the valuation without obtaining an independent survey, owed a duty of care to the buyer to exercise reasonable care and skill in carrying out the valuation.

Chapter 12

Action Following Instructions

12.1 After the interview: both parties

12.1.1 Attendance note

An attendance note (see **7.6**) should be made as soon as possible after the interview, recording exactly what took place at the interview, the instructions received and the advice given. The time spent in the interview should be noted on the attendance note for time-recording purposes.

It is important that a detailed written record of the interview exists on the solicitor's file. The written record provides a reminder to the solicitor of what needs to be done, and evidence of what took place between solicitor and client in case of a later dispute between them.

12.1.2 Confirming instructions to the client

In order to ensure that no misunderstanding exists between solicitor and client, instructions should always be confirmed to the client in writing as soon as possible after the interview has taken place. The letter should contain a full record of what happened at the interview, including a repetition of the instructions given by the client and the advice given by the solicitor. The letter should also deal with information as to costs, confirm any action agreed to be taken by the solicitor, and remind the client of anything which he promised to do (eg, obtain his building society account number). To comply with the Solicitors' Code of Conduct, the letter must also give details of who in the solicitor's firm is dealing with the client's matter and whom the client should contact in the event of a complaint about the solicitor's services.

12.1.3 Letters to other parties

If not already done, contact should be established with the representatives of the other parties involved in the transaction, such as the other party's solicitor, the estate agent, and the client's lender. Any such letter is likely to be merely introductory, saying that the solicitor has been instructed to act in the transaction, on what terms the client has agreed to proceed, and that the solicitor will contact the third party further in due course.

12.1.3.1 'Subject to contract'

For historical reasons, it used to be customary for all correspondence preceding the contract, including this type of introductory letter, to be headed 'Subject to contract'. The purpose of the inclusion of this phrase was to ensure that no contract was inadvertently entered into between the seller and buyer before they fully intended to do so. In view of the provisions of the Law of Property (Miscellaneous Provisions) Act 1989 (see **3.12.1**), it is extremely unlikely that a client could inadvertently form a contract by letter, so the inclusion of the 'Subject to contract' phrase is unnecessary on pre-contract correspondence, but it is still encountered in practice.

12.1.3.2   Telephone call

A telephone call to the third party (provided it is recorded by means of an attendance note on the file) would suffice in place of a letter in these circumstances. The object of the exercise is to establish contact between all the parties who are involved in the transaction, and any method of doing this quickly is therefore acceptable. Sending correspondence by fax is also routinely used to speed up transactions; more and more solicitors also use e-mail as a method of communication.

12.1.3.3   The estate agent

Apart from confirming to the estate agent that the solicitor is instructed, it is always useful to have a copy of the estate agent's particulars of sale on file. These particulars can provide useful information relating to the area in which the property is sited, which may indicate to the solicitor that particular searches and enquiries may be required. They will also contain details of the fixtures and fittings at the property, and whether or not these are to be included in the sale (see **Chapter 10**).

In residential transactions, both seller's and buyer's solicitors should ensure that they obtain a copy of the HIP relating to the property.

12.2   For the seller

12.2.1   Obtain title deeds and documents

The seller's solicitor needs to have access to the title documents in order to check that the seller owns and is entitled to sell what he has instructed the solicitor to sell, and to draft the contract of sale.

If the seller does not have a subsisting mortgage on the property, he may have the title documents himself, or they might be kept, for example, in the solicitor's strongroom or in a bank safe deposit box. The whereabouts of the documents will have been ascertained from the seller in the initial interview.

Although land and charge certificates have been abolished by the LRA 2002, they will be already in existence for all titles registered prior to 13 October 2003. Although they are not required in order for a disposition to be registered, it will still be necessary to ask the client for the title documents. There may be other documents accompanying the land or charge certificate which will be required for the sale (eg, planning consents or guarantees for any building work carried out).

Where there was a subsisting mortgage over the property, it used to be the case that the deeds (charge certificate in registered land) and other documents would be kept by the mortgage lender. However, in recent years, mortgage lenders have been concerned about the cost of storage of such documents. Increasingly, therefore, they took advantage of s 63 of the LRA 1925, under which a lender could request the Registry to retain the charge certificate in the Registry. Where this has happened, an entry to that effect will be found in the charges register. In such a case, it will still be necessary to obtain any other documents held by the lender, as explained above. However, some lenders are reluctant to retain any documents after completion of the mortgage, and in such a case it will be necessary to ascertain their whereabouts from the client.

Where the lender is holding documents, it will be reluctant to hand them over without a guarantee that the loan will be repaid. The lender will thus require an undertaking from the solicitor with regard to repayment.

When writing to the lender to ask for the title deeds, it is customary to pre-empt the lender's request about the repayment of the loan, and to include in the letter an undertaking that the solicitor will either repay the loan to the lender (thus ending the mortgage and entitling the seller to the return of his deeds) or, at the lender's request, return the deeds to the lender. This type of undertaking is normally acceptable to the lender, who will then release the deeds to the solicitor on the terms of the undertaking. The undertaking is a solicitor's undertaking, subject to the usual rules as to enforceability, and care must therefore be taken in wording it to ensure that what it promises to do is within the solicitor's control to perform (see *Legal Foundations*).

12.2.2 Amount outstanding on mortgage

When writing to the lender, it may also be prudent to ascertain the approximate amount outstanding on the seller's mortgage (a redemption figure) to ensure that there will be sufficient funds from the sale to pay off (redeem) the mortgage and the costs associated with the sale, and that the surplus (if any) is sufficient for the seller's requirements (eg, to put towards the purchase of another property). At this stage, an approximate redemption figure only need be obtained (eg, to the nearest £500); nearer completion an exact figure can be confirmed with the lender. Where the seller has several mortgages on the same property, redemption figures should be obtained from each lender.

12.2.3 Official copies of the register

When the land being sold is an interest in registered land, the seller's solicitor should make an application to the Land Registry Office for the area in which the land is situated for official copies of the register entries. This application is usually made on Form OC1 (see **Appendix 8**), which is an application for copies of the register entries and filed plan only. Where additional documents are known to be filed at Land Registry (eg, a copy of a conveyance imposing restrictive covenants), it may be necessary to apply for copies of these documents on Form OC2.

The application may be sent to the appropriate Land Registry Office by post, although Offices will accept applications by telephone and fax. An online computer service (Land Registry Direct) is frequently used, giving direct access to the register and enabling a solicitor to print off copy entries immediately. A fee is payable for obtaining official copies, but this can be paid by credit account, provided the solicitor's 'key number' (account number) is entered on the application form.

In a residential transaction the HIP will contain official copies. However, as Land Registry rules prevent a pre-completion search being made in relation to official copies dated more than 12 months ago (see **28.5.1**), it should be checked to see if more up-to-date copies are required. In any event, if the copies are more than a few months old, it may be prudent to obtain up-to-date copies to ensure that no further entries have been made which may affect the sale.

12.2.4 Investigation of title

The purposes of obtaining official copies are:

(a)   To check that the information supplied by the seller in relation to his title, and that contained in the land or charge certificate or TID, is supported by the information contained in the official copies. The official copies are an official and up-to-date copy of the actual register entries, which therefore represent the true state of the title at the date of their issue. The land or charge certificate or TID in the solicitor's possession may not have been updated by Land Registry for several years (eg, since the seller bought the land) and it is important for the seller's solicitor to know precisely what entries are now present on the register so that he can take account of these in drafting the contract of sale.

(b)   During the course of the transaction, the seller will need to prove his ownership of the property to the buyer. In registered land this is done by supplying the buyer with (inter alia) official copies of the register entries.

When the official copies are received from Land Registry, they should be examined to ensure that they do not contain anything of which the solicitor was previously unaware (if they do, instructions must be obtained immediately), and a photocopy should be taken. The seller's solicitor will need to keep a copy of the register entries in his own file to refer to during the transaction, and he must supply the buyer with the original of the official copies.

This procedure is known as 'investigating title' and has to be carried out by the seller's solicitor before the contract can be drafted. The precise procedure to be followed in investigating title to both registered and unregistered titles is set out in **Chapter 14**.

In all cases where the seller is a company, a company search should be commissioned to ascertain that the company:

(a)   exists (it could have been struck off the register for failure to file annual returns);

(b)   has powers to buy and sell land (although these are normally implied);

(c)   has no undisclosed fixed or floating charges which affect the land being sold; and

(d)   is not in administration, receivership or liquidation.

A solicitor acting for a company which has been struck off or lacks legal capacity may be personally liable to a buyer or a lender who suffers loss as a result of this under the principle of breach of warranty of authority (see **7.1.2**).

In the case of unregistered land, the deeds should be studied (see **14.4** as to the procedure to be followed) to ensure that the seller does have the power to sell the property and to ascertain what third party rights affect it. Also, the date at which the area became subject to compulsory registration should also be ascertained from Land Registry Practice Guide 51, to ensure that there have been no dealings since that date that would have induced compulsory registration. In all cases an Index Map search should also be commissioned from Land Registry using Form SIM (see **Appendix 8**) to ensure that the land has not already been registered and that no caution against first registration affects the land.

12.2.5   Home Information Pack

In residential transactions, the contents of the HIP should be studied to ensure that they do not reveal any problems (eg, entries on the local search) that might cause difficulties in the sale. Any problems, eg, missing planning consents, are best resolved as early as possible during the transaction.

The HIP will also include official copies, but as these may well be several months old, it will often be advisable to obtain up-to-date copies to ensure that there have been no further entries on the register which, when discovered by the buyer, could cause problems at a late stage of the transaction. Similarly, if the HIP contains a Property Information Form and/or a Fixtures Fittings and Contents Form (or similar information), the seller's solicitor should go through it with the client to ensure that the information contained in the form is still accurate. If not, the buyer should be advised immediately. If the title to the land is unregistered, the HIP will also contain a search of the Index Map; again this may need repeating, depending upon its age.

12.2.6   Preparation of the pre-contract package

The seller's solicitor should then start preparing the pre-contract package which will have to be sent to the buyer. This will contain, as a minimum, two copies of the draft contract (see **Chapter 15**) and details of the seller's title to the property (see **Chapter 13**), but if the Protocol is being adopted it will also need to contain the following:

(a)   the Seller's Property Information Form: this was handed to the seller for completion at the initial interview;

(b)   the Fixtures Fittings and Contents Form: this was also given to the seller for completion at the first interview;

(c)   in unregistered land, an Index Map search at Land Registry. This is to ensure that the land is indeed unregistered and that there are no interests registered at Land Registry adverse to the seller's title;

(d)   in unregistered land, a land charges search against the seller and all other previous estate owners revealed by the title deeds against whom there is not already a search with the deeds upon which it is safe to rely (see **Chapter 18**). This will reveal incumbrances affecting the property and whether any insolvency proceedings have been commenced against the seller;

(e)   copies of planning permissions relating to the property; and

(f)   copies of any other certificates, consents, etc, relating to the property (eg, a guarantee in relation to the insertion of a new damp proof course).

The object of this package is to supply the buyer with all the information he needs to make his mind up whether or not to proceed with the transaction. If the buyer is supplied with a complete package of information at the start of the transaction, it is likely to run more smoothly and speedily, as time will not be wasted in the buyer having to make repeated requests for information and documents from the seller. Although this information is required only in a Protocol transaction, similar packages are also being provided in other transactions.

12.3   For the buyer

12.3.1   Search applications

The buyer's solicitor should, as soon as is practicable, put in hand such pre-contract searches as are appropriate to the property in question (see **Chapter 18**).

12.3.2   Mortgage and survey arrangements

The buyer's solicitor should deal with his client's mortgage and survey arrangements if required to do so. In many cases, the client will already have approached a lender and submitted a mortgage application form before seeing the solicitor, and this step will therefore be unnecessary (see **Chapter 8**). Surveys are dealt with in **Chapter 11**.

12.3.3   The pre-contract package

When the pre-contract package is received from the seller's solicitor, its contents must be studied carefully to ensure that what is being offered for sale by the seller matches the instructions given by, and expectations of, the buyer (see **Chapter 19**).

12.3.4   Home Information Pack (HIP)

Where a HIP is in place, the buyer's solicitor should obtain a copy of this from the estate agent and study its contents. In particular, the searches included should be studied to ascertain what other searches will be required in relation to the property (see **Chapter 18**). The buyer's solicitor should also ensure that if the Seller's Property Information Form and/or the Fixtures Fittings and Contents Form are included in the HIP, there is nothing in the pre-contract package supplied by the seller's solicitor indicating any changes to the information contained in these forms. The buyer client should be advised of any such changes as soon as possible.

Part III

PROCEDURE LEADING TO EXCHANGE

Chapter 13

Deduction of Title

13.1 Deduction of title

'Deduction of title' is the expression used to signify the seller's obligation to prove to the buyer his ownership of the interest which he is purporting to sell. Ownership is proved to the buyer by producing documentary evidence of title. The method of doing this varies according to whether the land in question is registered or unregistered.

13.2 Time for deduction

Historically, deduction of title took place only after contracts had been exchanged, so that the buyer had to take the seller's title on trust up until that time and to rely on his right to rescind the contract if the title later turned out not to reflect what the seller had contracted to sell.

Modern practice (reflected in the Protocol) is for title to be deduced before exchange. Where a HIP is in place, the requisite title documentation will have been included in the HIP. As the buyer will therefore have entered into the contract with full knowledge of the title, his right to raise questions about the title after exchange should be limited. This is reflected in both the Standard Conditions of Sale and Standard Commercial Property Conditions (SC 4.2.1 and SCPC 6.2.1).

13.3 Seller's obligations

The seller's obligation in relation to the deduction of his title is to supply sufficient documentary evidence to the buyer to prove that he has the right to sell the land.

13.4 Method of deduction for registered land – official copies

Both the Protocol and SC 4.1.2 (SCPC 6.1.2) require the seller to supply official copies of his title to the buyer. Official copies are copies prepared directly from the register and should always be supplied since they show the up-to-date position of the register. The seller should pay for the official copies.

13.5 Method of deduction for unregistered land – epitomes and abstracts

13.5.1 Format

Title to unregistered land is proved by the title deeds which, obviously, the seller will not be prepared to release to the buyer until completion. Instead, the seller will prove his ownership of the title by supplying the buyer with an abstract or epitome of the documents comprised in it. In some cases the evidence supplied will be made up of a combination of these two styles of presentation. An example of an epitome appears in **Chapter 14**.

An abstract of title is in essence a précis of all the documents comprised in the title. Abstracts of title have largely been superseded by the practice of supplying an epitome of the title supported by photocopies of all the documents referred to.

An epitome of title is a schedule of the documents comprising the title accompanied by photocopies of the documents themselves. On the epitome, the documents should be numbered and listed in chronological order. Each document should be identified as to its date, type (eg, conveyance, assent, etc), the parties to it, whether a copy of the document is supplied with the epitome and whether the original of the document will be handed to the buyer on completion. Photocopies of the documents which accompany the epitome must be of good quality and marked to show the document's corresponding number on the list shown by the epitome. Any plans included in the documents must be coloured or marked so that they are identical to the original document from which the copy was made.

13.5.2   The root of title

Whatever format is chosen, title in unregistered land begins with what is known as the root of title. At common law the epitome must commence with a good root of title at least 15 years old (LPA 1925, s 44 as amended). A good root of title is a document which:

(a)   is at least 15 years old;

(b)   deals with or shows the ownership of the whole legal and equitable interest contracted to be sold;

(c)   contains a recognisable description of the property; and

(d)   contains nothing to cast any doubt on the title.

Both the Standard Conditions of Sale and Standard Commercial Property Conditions contain space for the seller to specify the document that is to form the root of title for that transaction (see **Chapter 15**). This document could in theory be of any age, but a buyer should not generally accept a root that does not comply with the common law position (ie, is not a 'good' root). The reason for this is explained in **13.5.2.2**.

13.5.2.1   Documents capable of being good roots of title

A conveyance on sale or legal mortgage which satisfies the above requirements is generally acknowledged to be the most acceptable root of title, because it effectively offers a double guarantee. The buyer in the present transaction will be investigating the seller's title back for a minimum period of 15 years, and the buyer under the root conveyance would similarly have investigated title over a period of at least 15 years prior to when he bought the property. Thus the present buyer is provided with the certainty of the soundness of the title over a minimum period of at least 30 years.

In the absence of both a conveyance on sale and legal mortgage, title may be commenced with either a voluntary conveyance or an assent dated after 1925. Since voluntary conveyances and assents both effect gifts of the land, no investigation of prior title may have taken place at the time when they were executed, and therefore they do not provide the double check which is given by the conveyance on sale or legal mortgage. For this reason they are less satisfactory to a buyer when offered as roots of title.

13.5.2.2 The dangers of accepting a 'short root'

A good root of title (ie, one that satisfies the buyer's statutory entitlement under s 44 of the LPA 1925) effectively acts as a longstop in the buyer's investigation of title. Under s 44, a buyer is bound by matters that would be revealed by a title that begins with a good root, but does not have notice of any additional matters that would have been revealed by a title that began with an earlier root. The danger for a buyer who accepts a title that begins with a document that does not satisfy s 44 – such as one that is less than 15 years old – is that the buyer will therefore be bound by matters that would have been revealed had the title begun with a good root, but he will be unaware of what those matters are. In addition, the title is unlikely to be registered with absolute title at Land Registry.

In fact, it is only in rare cases that the seller will be unable to provide the buyer with a good root of title. However, a buyer who is offered a short title should not accept the situation until he has received a satisfactory explanation from the seller of the reasons for the short root. It will also be necessary to get the agreement of his lender before accepting such a root of title. The possibility of obtaining defective title insurance should also be considered.

13.5.2.3 Documents and events to be included in the abstract or epitome

All documents and events affecting the ownership of the land from the root to the present day must be included. There should be an unbroken chain of ownership from the root to the present seller. This includes the following:

(a) conveyances on sale and by gift;

(b) deaths;

(c) grants of representation to deceased owners' estates;

(d) changes of name of estate owners (eg, on marriage, or by deed poll or statutory declaration);

(e) leases;

(f) mortgages;

(g) discharge of legal mortgages;

(h) documents prior to the root which contain details of restrictive covenants which affect the property;

(i) memoranda endorsed on documents of title (eg, recording a sale of part, assent to a beneficiary, or severance of a beneficial joint tenancy);

(j) powers of attorney under which a document within the title has been executed.

13.5.2.4 Documents which need not be included in the abstract or epitome

Certain documents need not be included in the abstract or epitome, although in some cases their inclusion will be helpful to the buyer. These include:

(a) documents of record (eg, death and marriage certificates) and land charges department search certificates. It is, however, good practice to include search certificates so that the buyer can see which searches have been correctly made in the past, in which case he need not repeat the search during his own investigation of the title. Documents of record should also always be abstracted so that the buyer receives a complete picture of the title;

(b)   leases which have expired by effluxion of time;

(c)   documents which pre-date the root of title, except where a document within the title refers to the earlier document (LPA 1925, s 45). Where a document within the title has been executed under a power of attorney, the power must be abstracted whatever its date.

13.5.3   Production of original documents

Standard Condition 4.1.3 (SCPC 6.1.3) requires the seller to produce to the buyer (at the seller's expense) the original of every relevant document, or an abstract, epitome or copy with an original marking by a solicitor of examination, either against the original or against an examined abstract or against an examined copy. 'Marking' is a certification by a solicitor that the copy has been examined against, and is a true copy of, the original.

13.5.4   Documents which will not be handed over on completion

The epitome must specify which documents will be handed to the buyer on completion and which will be retained by the seller. The buyer is entitled on completion to take the originals of all the documents within the title, except those which relate to an interest in the land which is retained by the seller. For example, on a sale of part, the seller will retain the title deeds in order to be able to prove his ownership of the land retained by him. Similarly, a general power of attorney will be retained by the seller, because the donee of the power needs to keep the original document in order to deal with other property owned by the donor, and personal representatives will retain their original grant in order to administer the remainder of the deceased's estate.

13.6   Leaseholds

Deduction of title to leaseholds is discussed in **Chapter 36.**

Chapter 14

Investigation of Title

14.1 Introduction

Investigation of title is one of the most important and intellectually rewarding elements of a conveyancing transaction. As such it is important to grasp the fundamental technical issues and techniques involved in carrying out this process. To achieve this, the chapter is divided into five main parts. It begins by considering the reasons why the various parties to a transaction need to carry out investigation of title in the first place. The form in which title will be deduced depends upon whether the title is registered or unregistered and so, secondly, the chapter considers how to approach investigation of title in each of these situations. Next, whether the title is registered or unregistered, there are certain situations which can throw up particular challenges to a conveyancer: what these issues are and how they can be resolved is dealt with in part three. Fourthly, issues relating to verifying title and raising queries on issues raised during the investigation of title are considered. Finally, the chapter ends with a worked example of an investigation of first a registered and then an unregistered title.

The key to successful investigation of title is the keeping of systematic and thorough notes of issues raised by that investigation and the steps taken to resolve those issues. The precise format of this may vary from individual to individual (and the worked examples at the end merely reflect one approach). The fact that the format may vary should not detract from the need to keep a thorough and systematic record.

14.2 Reasons for investigating title

14.2.1 Seller's investigation of title

There are two main purposes behind the seller's solicitor investigation of title. First, it is the seller's solicitor's responsibility to draft the contract for the sale of the property. This will contain the terms of the agreement between the parties including what it is that the seller is actually selling to the buyer: ie, the title to the property (see **Chapter 15**). The seller's solicitor will therefore need to carry out a thorough investigation of title in order to be able to embody the detail of this accurately in the contract. Secondly, investigation of title will enable the seller's solicitor, at an early stage, to anticipate and if possible deal with any likely problems that might be revealed by the title and this can help smooth the passage of the transaction as a whole.

Although the seller's reasons for investigating title are different from those of the buyer, the method that he will use to do so will be identical to that undertaken by a buyer's solicitor.

14.2.2   Buyer's investigation of title

When the seller has supplied the buyer with evidence of his title, the buyer's task is twofold. First, to ensure that the seller is able to transfer what he has contracted to sell. Secondly, to identify whether there are any defects in, or problems raised by, the title which would adversely affect the interests of the buyer. Any matters which are unclear or unsatisfactory on the face of the documentary evidence supplied by the seller may be raised as queries (requisitions) with the seller.

Modern practice is for title to be deduced and investigated before exchange of contracts and for any issues that arise from this process to be resolved before that point. If this is the case, as the buyer will already have had his opportunity to raise any queries and will have entered into the contract with full knowledge of what the title contains, it is usual to find that the contract will contain a provision preventing the buyer raising requisitions on some or all aspects of the title once exchange has taken place (see SC 4.2.1 and SCPC 6.2.1). If, exceptionally, title is deduced after exchange, the contract will usually contain a timetable for the raising of, and responding to, requisitions (see SC4.3 and SCPC6.3).

14.2.3   Lender's investigation of title

If a lender is lending money in the form of a mortgage to help finance the acquisition of a property, it will be concerned to ensure that the property is worth the money that has been advanced. If the borrower defaults on the mortgage, the lender may ultimately need to exercise its power to sell the property to recover the loan, but this power will be of limited value if defects or problems on the title reduce the market value of the property so that the lender is unable to recover the money owed to it. Any lender will therefore want to ensure that the title is investigated to protect its position.

Where the same solicitor is acting for both the buyer and his lender in a simultaneous transaction, investigation is carried out only once, but will be done on behalf of both the borrower and lender client, taking into account the particular interests of each. Where the lender is separately represented, the solicitor acting for the lender may undertake his own investigation of title. However, in commercial property transactions the borrower's solicitor may be required instead to provide the lender with a 'Certificate of Title'. This is a certificate signed by the borrower's solicitors certifying that the borrower has a 'good and marketable' title to the property. This certificate will be relied on by the lender in lieu of its own investigation of title. Special care should be taken in giving such certificates as the lender will be able to sue the borrower's solicitors should there in fact be any problem with the title. The City of London Law Society has produced a standard form of certificate which is in widespread use.

14.3   Investigating title in registered land

The buyer's investigation of title will involve two main elements. Title will be deduced by the seller in the form of official copies of the entries on the register and the title plan and, so, first, a thorough examination of these must be undertaken. Secondly, the buyer needs to carry out investigations to discover if there are any overriding interests affecting the property, as such interests will bind the buyer even though the register contains no mention of them. Information in this respect will come from a variety of sources, the detail of which is considered at **14.3.4**.

Having carried out his investigation of title, the buyer will need to carry out certain checks before completion to update the information revealed and to ensure that no changes have taken place since the investigation of title was carried out. These checks are considered in **Chapter 28**. Part of this process involves carrying out a search at Land Registry to confirm that no new entries have been added to the register since the official copies were issued. Land Registry will not perform this search on official copies that are more than 12 months old and so, when title is deduced, a buyer should not accept official copies that are outside this time limit.

14.3.1 Points to look out for on the official copies and title plan

The following are the particular issues that the solicitor should look out for when examining the official copies and title plan.

14.3.1.1 The property register

(a)   Does the description of the land agree with the contract description?

(b)   Does the title number match the one given in the contract?

(c)   Is the estate freehold or leasehold? Does this accord with expectations from the contract?

(d)   Which easements are enjoyed by the property? Do these match the needs of the client?

14.3.1.2 The proprietorship register

(a)   Is the class of title correct?

(b)   Is the seller the registered proprietor? If not, who has the ability to transfer the land?

(c)   Are there any other entries? What is their effect?

14.3.1.3 The charges register

(a)   Are there any incumbrances?

(b)   How do these affect the buyer?

(c)   Which of them will be removed or discharged on completion?

(d)   Have you agreed in the contract to buy subject to the incumbrances which remain?

14.3.1.4 The title plan

(a)   Is the land being bought included within the title?

(b)   Are there any colourings/hatchings which may indicate rights of way, the extent of covenants or land which has been removed from the title?

14.3.2 Adverse entries

Any adverse entries revealed by a reading of the official copies will need to be considered carefully and a full report made to the buyer and lender client. Any problems that are identified should be resolved before exchange of contracts. It should be remembered that rights can be protected in a variety of ways in registered land, depending on the nature of the interest involved. The practitioner should be familiar with, and be able to anticipate and deal with, issues arising from all of these different methods. For more detail on how third party interests can be protected on the register see **4.8.5**.

14.3.3 Documents referred to on the register

Sometimes, documents or plans are filed with the title at Land Registry and will be referred to as such in the official copies. Where this is the case, a copy of any such items should be obtained and examined in the same way as the official copies themselves.

14.3.4 Overriding interests

The existence of most overriding interests can be discovered through:

(a)   disclosure by the seller in the contract;

(b)   pre-contract enquiries of the seller under which the seller will normally be asked to reveal details of adverse interests and occupiers' rights;

(c)   a local land charges search (local land charges are overriding interests);

(d)   inspection of the property before exchange which may reveal evidence of such matters as non-owning occupiers, easements and adverse possession.

14.4 Unregistered land

Investigation of title to unregistered land comprises:

(a)   An Index Map search at Land Registry, which should be made in all cases when dealing with interest in unregistered land. Application is made to the Land Registry Office for the area in which the land is situated on Form SIM, accompanied by a large-scale plan of the property and the fee. The search result will reveal whether the land is already registered, or is subject to a pending application or caution against first registration. In residential cases, the result of this search should be included in the HIP.

(b)   An examination of the documents supplied in the abstract or epitome to check that:

(i)   the root document is as provided for by the contract – if the wrong document has been supplied, the buyer is entitled to insist on the correct document being supplied in its place;

(ii)   there is an unbroken chain of ownership beginning with the seller in the root document and ending with the present seller, ie, the documents show the progression of the title from A to B, from B to C, from C to D and so on, with no apparent breaks in the chain; and

(iii) there are no defects in the title which will adversely affect the buyer's title or the interests of his lender.

(c)   Verification, ie, inspection of the original deeds (in practice this is frequently postponed until completion and not carried out at this stage of the transaction).

(d)   Checking for evidence of occupiers (this is normally done by inspection of the property).

(e)   Pre-completion searches (see **Chapter 28**).

14.4.1 Events triggering first registration

One crucial question that should be borne in mind throughout an investigation of unregistered title is whether any transaction in the title's history should have triggered first registration. The detail of the events that trigger first registration and the conveyancing consequences of not doing so are dealt with at **4.3**. When turning to each document in the title in turn, it is sensible to begin consideration of it by dealing with this question.

14.4.2   Method of investigation of an unregistered title

In unregistered land, title will be deduced in the form of an abstract or epitome of title. Whilst a systematic approach and the taking of notes is needed in any investigation of title, it is particularly important when investigating a title that is unregistered. Unlike registered land (where the title is in the format of user-friendly official copies), an unregistered title can be made up of many documents, presenting the person investigating it with a significant challenge in terms of document management. The following is suggested as an approach that has proven to work well and is followed in the worked example that appears at the end of this chapter. It is based around a mnemonic: RLSDIES.

Begin by reading over the title to get a broad overview of the history of the property and what has happened to it over the years. Having done that, identify the document that is to form the root of title for this property. This forms the foundation for the title and the investigation should proceed from the date of the root to the present day. Having identified the root, it is then necessary to work through each document in turn, starting with the root itself. The key is to be systematic and to subject each document to the same standard scrutiny. It is with this that the mnemonic above is designed to assist.

The abbreviation RLSDIES stands for:

(a)   root of title;

(b)   links in the chain;

(c)   stamp duties;

(d)   description;

(e)   incumbrances;

(f)   execution; and

(g)   searches.

Each element will now be considered in turn.

14.4.2.1   Root of title

Check that the epitome begins with the root of title specified in the contract. Ideally this should be a 'good' root of title for the purposes of s 44 of the LPA 1925 (see **13.5.2**) for the reasons explained at **13.5.2.2**.

The contract should specify what document is to form the root of title and, generally, it is not possible (or necessary) to require evidence of title prior to the root (LPA 1925, s 45). It is possible, however, in the following circumstances:

(a)   when an abstracted document is executed by an attorney, the buyer is always entitled to a certified copy of the power, whenever that might be dated;

(b)   when the property is described by reference to a plan in a pre-root document, the buyer is entitled to see that plan; and

(c)   when the property is sold subject to or together with matters contained in a pre-root document (eg, the land is sold subject to pre-root covenants), the buyer is entitled to a copy of those matters.

14.4.2.2   Links in the chain

There should be an unbroken chain of ownership from the root of title up to the present seller. Legal estates can be transferred only by means of some form of document (usually a deed), so there should be documentary evidence of every change of ownership. There should be a chain of ownership which shows the transfer from A to B and then from B to C and so on, up to the present seller.

Any changes in the names of owners should also be evidenced, for example a marriage certificate if a name was changed on marriage.

14.4.2.3   Stamp duties

For documents dated prior to 1 December 2003, it is necessary to ensure that the requirements for the payment of stamp duty were complied with. (Stamp duty was replaced with respect to most documents as from 1 December 2003 by stamp duty land tax, to which different considerations apply.) Unstamped or incorrectly stamped documents are neither good roots of title nor good links in the chain. They cannot be produced in evidence in civil proceedings, nor will they be accepted by Land Registry on an application to register the title. The buyer must, therefore, check that all the title deeds have been correctly stamped. The payment of duty is evidenced by an embossed stamp (or stamps) being placed on the deed, usually in the top margin. If stamping defects are discovered, the buyer is entitled to insist that the seller remedies the deficiency at his own expense. Interest and a penalty are usually charged if stamp duty is not paid at the correct time. Any contractual provision requiring the buyer to meet the cost of putting the defect right will be void (Stamp Act 1891, s 117).

The following points should be considered:

(a)   Ad valorem duty. A conveyance on sale is liable to an ad valorem duty, ie, a duty varying according to the amount of the consideration. Rates of duty have changed over the years and in practice a table of stamp duties should be used to check the applicable rates for a particular document. For some lower value properties a reduced rate or total exemption from duty was possible if the consideration was below a certain threshold; again this has changed over the course of time. However, the reduced rates could be claimed only if a certificate of value was included in the conveyance. The wording of the certificate is:

> It is hereby certified that the transaction hereby effected does not form part of a larger transaction or of a series of transactions in respect of which the amount or value or the aggregate amount or value of the consideration exceeds .... pounds.

Therefore, a conveyance on sale which does not have a certificate of value in it and does not bear an ad valorem stamp has not been correctly stamped.

(b)   Stamp duty does not have to be paid on mortgages executed after 1971.

(c)   A conveyance or transfer by way of gift executed after 30 April 1987 is exempt from stamp duty, provided it contains a certificate that it is an instrument within one of the categories of exempt documents under the Stamp Duty (Exempt Instruments) Regulations 1987 (SI 1987/516). This is an example of such a certificate:

> The Donor certifies that this deed falls within category B in the Schedule to the Stamp Duty (Exempt Instruments) Regulations 1987.

The category differs according to the circumstances of the transaction, which should be checked with the Regulations. Category B shown in the example relates to transfers to a beneficiary under a will.

(d)   A power of attorney is not liable for stamp duty (Finance Act 1985, s 85).

(e)   Particulars delivered stamp. The Finance Act 1931 provided that certain documents must be produced to the Inland Revenue (now HMRC), together with a form giving particulars of the documents and any consideration received. The form was kept by the Inland Revenue (it provided useful information for the assessment of the value of the land) and the document was stamped with a stamp (generally called the 'PD stamp') as proof of its production. Without the PD stamp the document was not properly stamped and the person who failed in his responsibility to produce it (ie, the original buyer) could be fined. The document had to be produced irrespective of whether any ad valorem duty was payable. The documents that needed a PD stamp were:

(i)   a conveyance on sale of the freehold;

(ii)   a grant of a lease for seven years or more; and

(iii)   the transfer on sale of a lease of seven years or more.

14.4.2.4   Description

The buyer should check that the description of the property corresponds with the contract and is consistent throughout the epitome, ie, that the ownership of the land presently being sold is included in the deeds. Particular care should be taken where the deeds show that part of the land included in the root document has been sold off separately. Copies of any plans referred to should be obtained, even if they are pre-root.

14.4.2.5   Incumbrances

Particular care should be taken with incumbrances. The solicitor should check to ensure that there are none disclosed by the deeds other than those disclosed in the contract. Copies of all covenants, easements and other burdens affecting the land should be supplied, even if they are pre-root. Burdens should be checked to ensure that have not been breached and they will not impede the client's proposed use for the property. If they appear to do so, the solicitor should consider whether they will in fact bind the client if he buys the land, applying normal land law principles. So, for example, in the case of a restrictive covenant, the solicitor should check if it has been registered as a Class D(ii) land charge; it will not be binding on a purchaser otherwise.

14.4.2.6   Execution

The solicitor should check that all deeds and documents in the title have been properly executed. If a seller did not execute then the legal estate would not have passed to the buyer and there will be a break in the chain of ownership.

The detailed law on execution of documents can be found at **14.5.9**.

14.4.2.7   Searches

Although not essential, a seller should supply with the epitome copies of all previous land charges and company searches made against the previous owners of the land. These would have been made prior to previous dispositions of the land. If the Protocol is being used, a search against the seller should also be produced. Before he can safely buy the land, a buyer needs clear, correctly made searches against the names of all the estate owners revealed by the epitome. However, he need not repeat searches that have been previously made (with the exception of the seller, who must be searched against again), if they have been correctly made. The following matters should, therefore, be checked carefully:

(a)   Was the search made against the correct name of the person as set out in the deeds? The full name must be searched against and the spelling must be correct.

(b)   Was the search made for the full period of the person's ownership? The years of ownership searched against are set out on the search result, and whether it is the correct period can be checked from the epitome.

(c)   Was the transaction which followed the search completed within the priority period of the search? The priority period is set out on the result of the search and this should be compared with the date on the appropriate deed.

(d)   In the case of changes of name (eg, on marriage), is there a search against both old and new versions of the name?

If the above checks reveal any problems, for example a transaction not completed within the priority period, there is a danger that other entries could have been on the register which would not have been revealed by the search but which would be binding on a buyer. It will therefore be necessary to repeat any such searches to ensure that there are no problems.

The approach to note taking adopted in the worked example at the end of this chapter is designed to assist in the task of checking central land charge searches for suitability by closely following the format of the search result for that particular system.

14.5 Particular problem areas

Whilst studying the official copies (in registered land) or the abstract or epitome (in unregistered land), it is necessary to be on the look out for certain issues or situations which can cause particular difficulties. It is these that are considered in this part of the chapter. The points raised apply to both registered and unregistered land, unless otherwise stated.

14.5.1 Conveyance by trustees to themselves

In the case of a conveyance by trustees or personal representatives to one of themselves, enquiry must be made into the circumstances of the transaction because, on the face of it, such a conveyance is in breach of trust and is voidable by the beneficiaries. Such a transaction can be justified if one of the following situations exists:

(a)   there is proof of a pre-existing contract in favour of the trustee or personal representative;

(b)   the personal representative was a beneficiary under the will or intestacy of the deceased;

(c)   the consent of all the legally competent (ie, adult and sane) beneficiaries was obtained to the transaction;

(d)   the conveyance was made under an order of the court;

(e)   the transaction was sanctioned by the trust instrument.

14.5.2 Trustees of land

14.5.2.1 Registered land

In registered land, a restriction may be entered on the proprietorship register which will indicate to the buyer what must be done to overreach the beneficiaries' interests. Provided the terms of the restriction are complied with, the buyer will get good title. In all cases, the disposition must be made by all the trustees, being at least two in number, or a trust corporation.

14.5.2.2 Unregistered land

Since 1 January 1997, trustees of land (including trustees for sale) have the same powers of disposition as a sole beneficial owner, unless the trust deed varies these or imposes a requirement for consents to be obtained. If the trust deed indicates that consents are required to a sale, a buyer is not concerned to see that the consents of more than two persons are obtained and is never concerned with the consent of a person under mental incapacity. Where the person whose consent is required is not of full age, the consent of the minor's parent or guardian must be obtained. A buyer must pay his money to all the trustees, being at least two individuals or a trust corporation, to take the land free from the equitable interests of the beneficiaries (see LPA 1925, ss 2 and 27). A sale by trustees for sale prior to 1 January 1997 will be subject to similar rules, but the provisions of the LPA 1925, ss 26–28 should be checked in transactions other than a sale, or where consents are required.

14.5.2.3 Appointing a further trustee

If there is only one trustee then the buyer must insist that a second trustee is appointed in order to overreach the interests of the beneficiaries. The appointment will usually be made by the surviving trustee (although the trust deed can confer the power of appointment on someone else). The appointment can be made prior to the contract for sale being entered into. In this case, the new trustee will thus be a party to the contract and bound by its terms. This is particularly useful where the new trustee is also in occupation of the property (see **19.4.3**). Alternatively, the sole trustee can enter into the contract on his own and then appoint a further trustee prior to completion in order to receive the purchase price and thus ensure overreaching takes place. A special condition can be included in the contract requiring the seller to appoint the further trustee, although he would be under an obligation to do so anyway in order to comply with the duty to make good title.

14.5.3 Personal representatives

14.5.3.1 Registered land

On production of the grant, personal representatives may become registered as proprietors of the land, in which case, provided the buyer deals with the registered proprietors and complies with any restriction on the register, he will get good title. Personal representatives would not normally register themselves as proprietors unless they intended to hold on to the land without disposing of it for some period of time, for example, during the minority of a beneficiary. In other cases, the personal representatives will produce their grant of representation to the buyer as proof of their authority to deal with the land. Provided the buyer takes a transfer from all the proving personal representatives and submits an office copy or certified copy of the grant with his application for registration, he will obtain a good title. An assent made by personal representatives to a beneficiary must be in the form prescribed under the Land Registration Rules 2003 (SI 2003/1417). Unlike unregistered land (see **14.5.3.2**), there is no danger of the same piece being mistakenly disposed of twice.

14.5.3.2 Unregistered land

Powers of personal representatives

Personal representatives enjoy the same wide powers as trustees of land. If there is only one proving personal representative, he has all the powers of two or more personal representatives and consequently (unlike a sole individual trustee) can convey the land on his own and give a valid receipt for the proceeds of sale. If, however, the grant is made to two or more personal representatives, they must all join in the assent or conveyance. A buyer must therefore call for the grant to see who has or have been appointed as personal representative(s), and must insist that all the personal representatives named in the grant join in the assent or conveyance, or call for evidence of the death of any personal representative who will not be a party to the purchase deed.

Assents

An assent made by personal representatives must be in writing in order to pass the legal estate in the land to the beneficiary. The beneficiary who is to take the land must be named in the document, which must be signed by the personal representatives. If the document contains covenants given by the beneficiary (eg, indemnity in respect of existing restrictive covenants), it must be by deed. Even where the beneficiary is also the sole personal representative (eg, where a widow is her deceased husband's sole personal representative and sole beneficiary) a written assent is required (*In re King's Will Trusts; Assheton v Boyne* [1964] Ch 542). Where there is an assent on the title, it is essential to check that a memorandum of that assent was endorsed on the grant of representation. Otherwise there is a danger that a later sale by the personal representatives will deprive the assentee of the legal ownership; see 'Section 36 statement', below.

Section 36 statement

The purpose of s 36 of the Administration of Estates Act 1925 is to provide protection for a buyer who purchases from personal representatives. It is based on the premise that personal representatives, not dealing with their own property, and perhaps dealing with a large, complicated estate, may be more likely than other owners of land to attempt (mistakenly) to dispose of the same property twice. A buyer will take good title from personal representatives, even if there has been a prior disposition by them, provided that:

(a)   the conveyance to the buyer contains a statement given by the personal representatives that they have not made any previous assent or conveyance of the same land; and

(b)   no memorandum of a previous conveyance or assent of the land is endorsed on the grant; and

(c)   there has been no earlier conveyance of the land.

This last provision means that an assentee is at risk of losing title to a later purchaser who relies on the section, whereas a buyer is not. To prevent this happening, the assentee should have insisted that a memorandum of the assent was endorsed on the grant of representation. A subsequent assentee is not able to rely on the provisions of s 36; it only benefits a 'purchaser', ie, a person who has given value.

Where, as now, the transaction induces first registration, an endorsement on the grant is not required. The need for registration of any disposition will prevent any land being disposed of twice.

Acknowledgement for grant

A disposition by personal representatives should contain an acknowledgement of the right to production of their grant of representation, because this is a document of title the inspection of which may be required by subsequent buyers of the land. The grant should be inspected to check for endorsements which have been made on it.

Naming the beneficiary

An assent or conveyance by personal representatives of a legal estate is sufficient evidence in favour of a buyer that the person in whose favour it is made is the person entitled to have the legal estate conveyed to him, unless there is a memorandum of a previous assent or conveyance on the grant. In effect, this means that a buyer from an assentee of land, having checked the grant and found no adverse endorsements, does not have to look at the deceased's will to check that the assentee was entitled to the land, but this provision will not protect the buyer if it is apparent from some other source (eg, the assent itself) that it was made in favour of the wrong person (see the Administration of Estates Act 1925, s 36).

Investigation of title points

The result of all the above is that, when investigating an unregistered title, the following points should be checked:

(a)   On a sale by personal representatives:
    (i)   inspect grant to check authority of personal representatives;
    (ii)   ensure all proving personal representatives joined in conveyance;
    (iii) check grant contains no memorandum of a prior disposition of the land;
    (iv)   check conveyance contains a s 36 statement;
    (v)   check conveyance contains an acknowledgement for production of the grant.

(b)   On an assent by personal representatives:
    (i)   inspect grant to check authority of personal representatives;
    (ii)   ensure all proving personal representatives joined in assent;
    (iii) check grant contains no memorandum of a prior disposition of the land;
    (iv)   check grant does contain a memorandum of the assent;
    (v)   check assent contains an acknowledgement for production of the grant.

14.5.4   Co-owners

Co-owners hold land on a trust of land, and the remarks relating to trustees in 14.5.2 apply.

14.5.4.1 Registered land

Tenants in common

If the co-owners are tenants in common in equity, a restriction will be entered on the proprietorship register. In the event of death of one or more of the co-owners, so that at the time of sale there is only one surviving trustee, the restriction ensures that a second trustee is appointed to join with the survivor in the transfer. This is the preferred and safest method of dealing with this situation. Alternatively, the buyer can deal with the survivor alone, provided that the restriction is removed from the register. Proof of death of the deceased must also be provided.

The wording of the restriction in use as from 13 October 2003 is:

> No disposition by a sole proprietor of the registered estate (except a trust corporation) under which capital money arises is to be registered unless authorised by an order of the court.

Note, however, that the previous version of this restriction may well still be encountered with regard to registrations made prior to 13 October 2003:

> No disposition by a sole proprietor of the land (not being a trust corporation) under which capital money arises is to be registered except under an order of the registrar or the court.

Joint tenants

If the co-owners are joint tenants in equity, no restriction is placed on the register and a buyer may deal with the survivor of them on proof of the death of the deceased co-owner.

14.5.4.2 Unregistered land

The conveyance under which the co-owners bought the land should be inspected to see whether they held as joint tenants or tenants in common in equity.

Tenants in common

The sole survivor of tenants in common does not automatically become entitled to the whole legal and equitable estate in the land, because a tenancy in common is capable of passing by will or on intestacy, so the trust still subsists. A buyer from the survivor should, therefore, insist on taking a conveyance only from two trustees in order to overreach any beneficial interests which may subsist under the trust. This is the safest and preferred method of dealing with the survivor of tenants in common. Alternatively, if the survivor has become solely and beneficially entitled to the whole legal and equitable interest in the land, he may convey alone as sole owner on proof to the buyer of this fact. Such proof would consist of the death certificate of the deceased, a certified copy or office copy of the grant of representation and an assent made in favour of the survivor.

Joint tenants

The survivor of beneficial joint tenants becomes entitled to the whole legal and equitable interest in the land, but a buyer from him will accept a conveyance from the survivor alone only if he can be satisfied that he will benefit from the protection of the Law of Property (Joint Tenants) Act 1964. The problem is that the joint tenancy could have been severed, turning it into a tenancy in common.

This Act (which is retrospectively effective to 1925) allows the buyer to assume that no severance of the joint tenancy had occurred before the death of the deceased joint tenant. To gain the protection of the Act, the following three conditions must all be satisfied:

(a) there must be no memorandum of severance endorsed on the conveyance under which the joint tenants bought the property;

(b) there must be no bankruptcy proceedings registered against the names of either of the joint tenants at Land Charges Registry;

(c) the conveyance by the survivor must contain a statement that the survivor is solely and beneficially entitled to the land.

If any of the above conditions is not met, the survivor must be treated as a surviving tenant in common and the procedure (above) relating to tenants in common must be followed.

Should it be necessary to appoint a further trustee, the procedure outlined in 14.5.2 should be followed.

14.5.5 Disposing lenders

14.5.5.1 Existence of the power of sale

Section 101 of the LPA 1925 gives a power to sell the legal estate vested in the borrower, subject to prior incumbrances but discharged from subsequent ones, to every lender whose mortgage is made by deed. Thus, unless expressly excluded, the power is available to a lender under a legal mortgage. In relation to registered land, only the proprietor of a registered charge has a power of sale. Where a lender sells in exercise of his power of sale, the mortgage deed will not bear a receipt, but the buyer nevertheless will take free from it and from subsequent mortgages.

14.5.5.2 Power of sale arises

The power of sale arises when the mortgage money becomes due under the mortgage, ie on the legal date for redemption, which is usually set at an early date in the mortgage term. The power becomes exercisable by the lender only as provided for in the mortgage deed, or when one of the events specified in s 103 of the LPA 1925 has occurred. These events are:

(a) a demand has been made for the principal sum outstanding on the mortgage and this demand is unpaid for three months; or

(b) any interest due under the mortgage is in arrears for two months; or

(c) there is breach of any other covenant in the mortgage.

A buyer from the lender must check (by looking at the mortgage deed) that the power of sale has arisen, but need not enquire whether the power has become exercisable.

14.5.6 Attorneys

14.5.6.1 Powers of attorney

A power of attorney is a deed under which the donor appoints someone (the attorney or donee) to carry out certain actions on his behalf. In the context of conveyancing, it might be necessary for a seller to give someone a power of attorney to execute documents on the seller's behalf because the seller was going abroad and would not be available when the documents needed to be signed.

14.5.6.2 Types of power

There are five types of power of attorney:

(a)   a general power, under s 10 of the Powers of Attorney Act 1971, entitles the attorney to deal with all of the donor's assets;

(b)   a special power, which permits the attorney to deal only with certain specified assets or categories of assets;

(c)   a trustee power, which is used where property is held on trust;

(d)   an enduring power, which is made under the Enduring Powers of Attorney Act 1985. This type of power endures through the donor's mental incapacity (subject to registration of the power);

(e)   a lasting power, which has replaced the enduring power as from 1 October 2007.

14.5.6.3 Revocation

Subject as below, a power of attorney can be revoked expressly by the donor or will be revoked automatically on the donor's death, mental incapacity, or bankruptcy. Once registered, enduring powers are irrevocable except by order of the court.

A person who buys from an attorney (and subsequent buyers) will get good title if the power:

(a)   authorises the transaction which is to take place between the attorney and the buyer; and

(b)   is valid and subsisting at the date of completion of the transaction.

The buyer is therefore concerned to ensure that the power had not been revoked at the date of completion of his purchase from the attorney. A summary of the protection given to the buyer by the Powers of Attorney Act 1971 is set out below.

14.5.6.4 Copy of power

The buyer is entitled to a certified copy of any power of attorney which affects the title (even if the transaction involves land which is unregistered and the power is dated earlier than the root of title).

14.5.6.5 Terms of the power

By checking the terms of the power itself the buyer should ensure that the transaction was authorised by the power. A general power of attorney under s 10 of the Powers of Attorney Act 1971 entitles the attorney to take any action the donor could have taken with regard to any of the donor's property. Other types of power should be checked carefully to ensure that they authorise the particular transaction in relation to the particular property concerned.

14.5.6.6 Registered land

The original or a certified copy of the power must be submitted when an application is made to register a disposition made in exercise of the power. If the transaction between the attorney and the buyer is not made within 12 months of the grant of the power, a statutory declaration made by the buyer to the effect that he had no knowledge of the revocation of the power should be obtained. For Land Registry purposes, a certified copy of a power of attorney must be certified on every page.

14.5.6.7   Unregistered land

Non-enduring powers

A person who buys directly from an attorney holding any type of non-enduring power of attorney will take good title under s 5(2) of the Powers of Attorney Act 1971, provided he buys in good faith without knowledge of the revocation of the power. Death revokes such a power, thus the buyer cannot take good title if he is aware of the death of the donor. A subsequent buyer (a person who buys from the person who bought from the attorney, in this paragraph referred to as 'C') obtains the protection of s 5(4) of the Powers of Attorney Act 1971 if either:

(a)   the dealing between the attorney and his immediate purchaser (P) took place within 12 months of the grant of the power; or

(b)   the person (P) who buys directly from the attorney makes a statutory declaration within three months of completion of the sale between P and C to the effect that he (P) had no knowledge of the revocation of the power.

Enduring and lasting powers

An enduring power of attorney under the Enduring Powers of Attorney Act 1985 must be in the form prescribed by that Act. Until the incapacity of the donor, the power takes effect as an ordinary power and the Act contains provisions to protect buyers which are similar to those outlined above. On the incapacity of the donor, the attorney's authority to act becomes limited to such acts as are necessary for the protection of the donor and his estate until such time as the power is registered with the Court of Protection. Once registered, the power is incapable of revocation and the attorney's full authority to act is restored.

Where a person is buying from an attorney who holds an enduring power, he should make a search at the Court of Protection to ensure that no application for registration of the power is pending. If the power has already been registered, the attorney should produce the registration certificate to the buyer. An office copy of the power can be produced as evidence both of the contents of the power and of its registration.

The Mental Capacity Act 2005 (in force 1 October 2007) replaces enduring powers with a new form of power called a lasting power. Existing enduring powers (whether registered or not) will continue to be valid and operate as above. Lasting powers will give an attorney power to deal with the donor's personal welfare and/ or his property and affairs, including authority to deal with such matters when the donor no longer has capacity. As with enduring powers, the lasting power is required to be in a prescribed form but, unlike enduring powers, comes into effect only when registered with the Public Guardian. The Public Guardian is a Government-appointed individual responsible for dealing with various matters in respect of persons who lack mental capacity. As from 1 October 2007, the Public Guardian is also responsible for the registration of enduring powers.

14.5.6.8   Trustees – The Trustee Delegation Act 1999

The law regarding the use of powers of attorney by trustees was changed, non-retrospectively, as from 1 March 2000.

In the case of powers of attorney created prior to that date (even if exercised after it), trustees could not use a general power. They had to use a trustee power under s 25 of the Trustee Act 1925. However, this permitted delegation for a maximum of 12 months only and could not be used to delegate in favour of a sole human co-trustee. This had profound implications in relation to co-owners, who hold the land under an implied trust. Take the case of a husband and wife who were co-owners. They could not use a general power; and if using a trustee power could not appoint the other as attorney – a stranger would have to be appointed.

However, due to the wording of s 3 of the Enduring Powers of Attorney Act 1985, one co-owner could validly appoint the other as attorney if an enduring power was used.

Powers created prior to 1 March 2000

The rules set out above continue to apply. However, any enduring powers created prior to 1 March in favour of a sole human co-trustee will cease to be effective in relation to the trust property on registration of the power with the Court of Protection or on 28 February 2001, whichever is the earlier, unless the donor has a beneficial interest in the land. In such a case, the power will continue to be effective in relation to the trust property. Thus an enduring power made by one co-owner in favour of the other in (say) 1999 can still be used today, as the donor has a beneficial interest under the implied trust under which the co-owners hold the land.

Powers created on or after 1 March 2000

Trustees can now use a general power provided the donor of the power has a beneficial interest in the land. In favour of a purchaser, this is to be taken conclusively if the donee of the power, ie the attorney, makes a statement to that effect either at the time of the disposition by him, or within three months afterwards.

Section 25 of the Trustee Act 1925 has been rewritten to provide for a new general trustee power of attorney. This still allows delegation only for a maximum period of 12 months. Such a power can be an enduring power.

Co-owners can thus use either an ordinary general power or a general trustee power, and can in both cases validly appoint a sole co-owner as attorney. The 1999 Act makes it clear, however, that a person acting both as trustee and as attorney for the other trustee, cannot give a valid receipt for capital money; remember that the receipt of two trustees is required to overreach the beneficial interests under a trust.

So, the end result of these complicated provisions is that if one of two co-owners wishes to appoint an attorney to execute a deed selling the land, the co-trustee cannot be appointed as such co-trustee will not be able to give a valid receipt. In such a case, a stranger will need to be appointed and this rule cannot be evaded by using an enduring power.

14.5.7 Discharged mortgages

14.5.7.1 Registered land

A mortgage over registered land which has been discharged will be deleted from the charges register of the title and is thus of no further concern to the buyer. As far as the seller's existing mortgage is concerned, the buyer should raise a requisition requiring this to be removed on or before completion. Discharge of a mortgage of registered land is effected by filing a completed Form DS1 at Land Registry or by use of the Electronic Notification of Discharge (END) system; see **31.3.5**.

14.5.7.2 Unregistered land

Discharged legal mortgages should be abstracted by the seller and checked by the buyer's solicitor to ensure that the discharge was validly effected.

Where a lender has sold the property in exercise of his power of sale, the mortgage deed will not bear a receipt.

Building society mortgages

Provided that the receipt (usually endorsed on the mortgage deed) is in the form of wording prescribed by the Building Societies Act 1986 and is signed by a person authorised by the particular society, the receipt may be treated as a proper discharge of the mortgage without further enquiry being made.

Other mortgages

By s 115 of the LPA 1925, a receipt endorsed on the mortgage deed operates to discharge the mortgage, provided it is signed by the lender and names the person making repayment. However, where the money appears to have been paid by a person not entitled to the immediate equity of redemption, the receipt will usually operate as a transfer of the mortgage. Thus, if the person making repayment is not the borrower named in the mortgage, or a personal representative or trustee acting on his behalf, the receipt should make it expressly clear that the receipt is to operate as such and is not intended to be a transfer of the mortgage to the person making payment.

14.5.8 Voluntary dispositions

When a voluntary disposition is presented as a link in the chain of title, or when acting for the donee taking a voluntary conveyance from a donor, care needs to be exercised, since the transaction could be set aside by the donor's trustee in bankruptcy under the Insolvency Act 1986 (as amended by the Insolvency (No 2) Act 1994) at any time until five years have elapsed from the date of the voluntary transaction.

The rules relating to voluntary dispositions apply to any transaction at an undervalue, and this includes pure gifts, assents, inter-spouse transfers on marriage breakdown (including those made by court order) and any inter vivos transaction where the full market value consideration is not paid for the property.

14.5.8.1 Disposition by an individual within the past two years

A disposition by an individual within the two years immediately preceding the current transaction may be set aside by the trustee in bankruptcy if the donor is made bankrupt. It is therefore unsafe to proceed with the current transaction until at least two years have elapsed since the date of the voluntary disposition.

14.5.8.2 Disposition by an individual between two and five years ago

In the case where a buyer knows of a voluntary disposition from A to B between two and five years ago, is it safe for a buyer to buy from B, or is there a danger that, if A becomes insolvent, the trustee in bankruptcy could claim against the buyer? The basic principle is that a buyer from B is protected provided that he has acquired in good faith and for value. The buyer is presumed not to be in good faith in either of the following cases:

(a) when the buyer acquired the property, he had notice of the bankruptcy proceedings and that the disposition to B was at an undervalue; or

(b)   the buyer was an associate of either A or B. 'Associate' is widely defined to include a person's spouse or ex-spouse, members of his family and his spouse's family, his partner and his partner's family, and his employees.

Registration of bankruptcy proceedings will amount to notice, so a buyer will need to make a bankruptcy search against A not just for the period of A's ownership, but also up until the date of his own acquisition. This is to ensure that he is not presumed to be lacking in good faith under (a) above. If the search reveals bankruptcy entries against A then the purchase cannot proceed. Similarly, if the buyer is an associate of either A or B then the sale cannot proceed even if the bankruptcy search is clear; in the case of A becoming bankrupt after the purchase, the buyer will be deemed not to be in good faith because he is an associate, even though he had no notice of the bankruptcy when he bought.

14.5.8.3   Disposition by an individual more than five years ago

No problems arise with a disposition made by an individual more than five years before the date of the present transaction, unless the donor went bankrupt within five years of the voluntary disposition. It will therefore be necessary to conduct a Land Charges Department search against the name of the donor from the date when the donor acquired the property until five years after the date of the voluntary disposition.

14.5.8.4   Disposition by a company within the past two years

If a disposition made by a company within the two years preceding the date of the current transaction was to a person connected with the company, it may be set aside by the liquidator on the company's subsequent insolvency. The current transaction cannot therefore proceed until at least two years have elapsed since the voluntary disposition. A 'person connected' is defined by ss 249 and 435 of the Insolvency Act 1986 as a director of the company and any associate (as defined at **14.5.8.2**) of a director and associates of the company.

If the disposition was made within the past two years to someone not connected with the company, the liquidator's power to set the transaction aside on the company's subsequent insolvency applies only if the present buyer has notice of the insolvency proceedings and of the undervalue transaction. These rules also apply to a transfer of property between two companies in the same group.

14.5.8.5   Disposition by a company more than two years earlier

Where a disposition was made by a company more than two years earlier, no problems arise unless the company went into liquidation or became subject to an administration order within two years of the disposition. A company search should be made against the donor company to ensure that no liquidation or administration proceedings were commenced within the two years following the date of the voluntary disposition.

14.5.8.6   Registered land

In the case of dispositions registered on or after 1 April 2000, the register includes details of the price paid by the proprietor. If this appears to be nil or something of no monetary value, then the provisions of the Act should be borne in mind. Where first registration is based on a voluntary disposition, a note will be added in the proprietorship register to the effect that the title is subject to the provisions of the Insolvency Act 1986. Where such a note appears, a buyer from that proprietor will need to consider the effect of the Insolvency Act 1986 as outlined above.

14.5.8.7 Summary

A buyer who buys for value and in good faith will generally now be protected under the Insolvency Act 1986 (as amended by the Insolvency (No 2) Act 1994). However, some lenders are reluctant to lend on property where there has been a voluntary disposition within the past five years unless an insurance policy is obtained covering the possibility of the donor's insolvency within this period.

14.5.9 Execution of deeds

A solicitor should check that all deeds and documents in the title have been properly executed. In order to transfer a legal estate in land, it is usually necessary to do so by deed and this part of the chapter considers the requirements necessary to ensure that a deed has been properly executed as such.

14.5.9.1 Registered land

In the case of registered land, title is updated by Land Registry whenever there is a dealing in respect of that title. As part of this process, Land Registry will scrutinise the execution of the document giving effect to that dealing before recording its effect on the register. Accordingly, it should not be necessary for a solicitor to scrutinise the execution of historic documents in respect of registered land.

14.5.9.2 Unregistered land

In the case of unregistered land, title is proven by title deeds and each document needs to be scrutinised in turn to ensure that it satisfies the relevant formalities for its valid execution.

14.5.9.3 Execution of deeds by an individual

The formalities for execution of a deed changed on 31 July 1990. For deeds executed on or after 31 July 1990, the following rules apply. When made by an individual, a document will be a deed only if:

(a) it is signed by its maker;

(b) that signature is witnessed and attested. This means that the signing of the deed by a party must be witnessed by another person who then also signs the deed to signify that he was present when the deed was so signed. There is no need for the same person to witness all of the signatures;

(c) it is clear that the document is intended to be a deed. That intention can be made clear either by describing the document as a deed (eg, 'This Deed of Conveyance is made 1 September 1993 ...'), or because the document is expressed to be executed or signed as a deed (eg, the attestation clause might say 'signed by the seller as his deed in the presence of ...'); and

(d) the document is delivered as a deed.

A deed is delivered by a seller when it is signed by him with the intention that he will be bound by it. In the case of a transaction involving the disposition or creation of an interest in land, where a solicitor, notary public or licensed conveyancer purports to deliver a document on behalf of a party to the document, a purchaser is conclusively entitled to presume that the solicitor etc has authority to deliver that document.

It is possible for an individual to direct another person to sign a deed on his behalf, provided that the signature is made in his presence and there are two attesting witnesses.

As regards deeds executed before 31 July 1990, the rule was that the document had to be signed and sealed by its maker, and delivered as his deed. The seal was usually only a red, self-adhesive circular piece of paper. However, it was still essential that a seal was placed on the conveyance before the maker signed. If a document purporting to be a deed does not bear a seal, evidence is needed that a seal (or something representing a seal, such as a printed circle) was in position at the time of execution. If a seal was never there then the document is not a deed, and could not have conveyed a legal estate.

The delivery of the deed was a matter of intention. A deed was delivered when it was signed by the maker with the intention that he was to be bound by it. If a person signed and sealed a deed, it was inferred from this that the deed was also delivered, so no evidence that a deed was delivered should be required.

14.5.9.4 Execution by a company

As with individuals, the rules relating to the execution of deeds by a company underwent significant change on 31 July 1990. Other changes were introduced for documents executed on or after 15 September 2005 (as indicated). Further changes were introduced by s 44 of the Companies Act 2006 as from 6 April 2008.

In the case of deeds executed by a company on or after 31 July 1990, the following rules apply. A document can be executed in one of three ways.

(a) *By the affixing of the company seal.* It must be clear on the face of the document that is intended to be a deed. If this method of execution is used, the document is deemed, in favour of a purchaser, to have been duly executed provided that the seal purports to have been affixed in the presence of and attested by two members of the board of directors or a director and the secretary. For deeds executed prior to 15 September 2005, this protection only applied where the seal was affixed and attested in front of a director and secretary.

The following is an example of an attestation clause that would comply with the above conditions and would be accepted by Land Registry:

Executed as a deed by affixing the common seal of *(insert name of company)* in the presence of:

Common seal of company

Signature of director

Signature of [director][secretary]

(b) *By being signed by a director and the secretary, or by two directors of the company, provided that the document is expressed to be executed by the company.* In other words, it must be clear that the signatures amount to execution by the company, rather than execution by the directors personally. If this method of execution is used, the document is deemed, in favour of a purchaser, to have been duly executed provided that it purports to be signed by a director and the secretary or by two directors.

The following is an example of an attestation clause that would comply with the above conditions and would be accepted by Land Registry:

Signed as a deed by *(name of company)* acting by [a director and its secretary] [two directors}

| Signature |
| |
| director |
| Signature |
| |
| [secretary] [director] |

(c)   For documents executed on or after 6 April 2008 only, a third method is available. *A deed can be executed by being signed by a single director in the presence of a witness who then attests that signature.*

The following is an example of an attestation clause that would comply with these conditions and would be acceptable to Land Registry:

Signed as a deed by *(name of company)* acting by a director

In the presence of

Signature of witness

| Signature |
| |
| director |

Name (in BLOCK CAPITALS)

Address

In addition to being *executed* as a deed, the document must also be *delivered* as such. A document which makes it clear on its face that it is intended to be a deed is presumed to have been delivered on execution: this presumption can be rebutted by a contrary intention. Note that for deeds executed prior to 15 September 2005, in favour of a purchaser, if the deed was executed by being signed by a director and secretary (or two directors), it would seem that this presumption of delivery is irrebuttable.

As regards deeds executed by a limited company before 31 July 1990, the execution was valid if the conveyance was executed in accordance with the company's articles of association. By s 74 of the LPA 1925, if the company seal had been affixed in the presence of the secretary and director, the deed was deemed to have been duly executed, even if in fact the articles demanded different formalities. Further, a buyer could assume that the deed had been executed so as to satisfy s 74 if there was on the deed a seal that purported to be the company seal, and signatures that purported to be those of secretary and director.

14.5.9.5   Land Registry Practice Guide

Land Registry publishes a number of forms of advice and Land Registry Practice Guide 8, which can be accessed from Land Registry website (www.landregistry.gov.uk), contains detailed information on Land Registy's current requirements.

14.6 Verification of title

Verification of title consists of checking the evidence of title supplied by the seller against the original deeds. In registered land, the true state of the register can be confirmed by the buyer when making his pre-completion search at Land Registry.

In unregistered land, the abstract or epitome should be checked against the seller's original deeds. In most cases, where the title is not complex, the buyer's solicitor postpones his verification until actual completion. If he then finds an error on the title which had not previously been disclosed by the seller, although SC 4.3.1 (SCPC 6.3.1) allows a further period of six working days to raise further requisitions, there will inevitably be a delay in completion. However, where photocopies of the original deeds have been supplied with the epitome, verification will normally be a formality.

Standard Condition 4.1.3 (SCPC 6.1.3) requires the seller, at his own expense, to produce to the buyer the original of every document within the title or, if the original is not available, an abstract, epitome or copy with an original marking by a solicitor of examination either against the original, or against an examined abstract or against an examined copy.

14.7 Raising requisitions

If the buyer's solicitor's investigation of title reveals any problem then the buyer should raise a 'requisition on title' of the seller's solicitor. A requisition is a question asked about the problem which requires a remedy from the seller.

If the seller ultimately cannot show good title then the buyer may consider whether defective title indemnity insurance is available (perhaps at the seller's cost) in order to protect him should he decide to proceed and accept the defect. If such insurance is unavailable, or the defect is such that it may affect the buyer's enjoyment of the property, the buyer is unlikely to proceed.

The buyer (and the buyer's lender) should be advised of any defects in title as soon as they become apparent.

Traditionally, title was deduced by the seller only following exchange. In such a situation, the seller's inability to make good title would have constituted a breach of contract entitling the buyer to withdraw from the contract and/or claim damages. Where requisitions are raised prior to exchange, a buyer will have no remedy should he choose to withdraw because of defects in title as there is no contract between the parties. Equally, of course, the seller would have no remedy if the buyer chose to withdraw for no good reason.

Standard Condition 4.3.1 (SCPC 6.3.1) requires the buyer to raise requisitions within six working days of the later of exchange or the delivery of the epitome. It is usual in modern practice for the title to be deduced prior to exchange (see **14.2.2**) and in such cases both sets of conditions of sale (SC 4.2.1 and SCPC 6.2.1) prohibit the raising of requisitions after exchange. However, these prohibitions only apply to matters disclosed by the seller prior to exchange. So if the buyer discovers a title problem after exchange which had not been previously disclosed, he can still raise requisitions in the usual way. He must do so within six working days of the particular matter coming to his attention (see SC 4.2.2 and SCPC 6.2.2).

14.8 Worked examples of investigation of title

The chapter ends with two worked examples of how to investigate title which offer a suggestion as to how the task may be approached. The first is in respect of a registered title and the second in respect of an unregistered title. As investigation of title is a skill, you may find it useful to attempt the investigations yourself before looking at the worked examples to see how many issues you were able to identify.

The first worked example picks up on the case study introduced at **7.6**. You act for Roger Evans who is selling his current property, 47, Queens' Road Loamster and buying a new home, 10, Bladen Road, Overton. Official copies for 47, Queens' Road are shown at **4.7**. This is the property being sold by Roger Evans and so, as the solicitor acting on the sale of this property, it will be necessary for you to investigate this title for the reasons set out in **14.2.1**. In fact, the title to 47, Queens' Road does not reveal any particular problems and so the major reason for carrying out the investigation will be in order to draft the contract for sale. A worked example of this contract will be considered in **Chapter 15**. The worked example that follows assumes that the official copies for 10, Bladen Road (the property Roger Evans is buying) have now been received and need to be investigated from a buyer's perspective (see **14.2.2**). The title to this property may prove more problematic. If you wish to use this title to practise investigation of title in registered land, you will find that it is important to re-read the instructions taken at the end of **Chapter 7** before you do so.

The second worked example involves the investigation of an unregistered title and is a free-standing exercise. In unregistered land, title could be deduced in the form of an abstract or an epitome. In the example, the epitome format has been used as this is the format that is most commonly met in practice.

In both cases, the worked examples merely suggest one way of approaching the task and other, equally valid approaches exist. Whichever is taken, however, it should be in writing and equally systematic.

14.8.1 Investigation of a registered title – 10, Bladen Road, Overton, Cornshire

14.8.1.1 The official copies

OFFICIAL COPY OF REGISTER ENTRIES

This official copy shows the entries subsisting on the register on 14 September 2007 at 10:55:50.
This date must be quoted as the 'search from date' in any official search application based on this copy.
Under s.67 of the Land Registration Act 2002 this copy is admissible in evidence to the same extent as the original.

Issued on 15 September 2008.

This title is administered by the **Humberside District Land Registry**.

LAND REGISTRY
TITLE NUMBER: LM 6042
Edition date: 18 December 1990

A: Property Register
This register describes the land and estate comprised in the title.

COUNTY	DISTRICT
CORNSHIRE	OVERTON

1. (18 December 1990) The freehold land shown edged with red on the plan of the above title filed at the Registry and being 10, Bladen Road, Overton, Cornshire, CS1 6AU.

2. (18 December 1990) The property has the benefit of a right of way granted by deed of grant dated 19 April 1969 and made between (1) Ivan Walton and (2) Jonathan Hartley.

    NOTE: Copy filed

B: Proprietorship Register
This register specifies the class of title and identifies the owner. It contains any entries that affect the right of disposal.

Title absolute

1. (18 December 1990) PROPRIETOR(S): NEIL STUART AND ANITA STUART of 10, Bladen Road, Overton, Cornshire, CS1 6AU.

2. (18 December 1990) RESTRICTION: No disposition by a sole proprietor of the registered estate (except a trust corporation) under which capital money arises is to be registered unless authorised by an order of the court.

C: Charges Register
This register contains any charges and other matters that affect the land.

1. (18 December 1990) A conveyance of the land in this title dated 1 April 1968 and made between (1) Ivan Walton and (2) Jonathan Hartley contains the following covenants:

    "The Purchaser with the intent and so as to bind the property hereby conveyed and to benefit and protect the retained land of the Vendor lying to the west of the land hereby conveyed hereby covenants with the Vendor that he and his successors in title will at all times observe and perform the stipulations and conditions set out in the schedule hereto."

    THE SCHEDULE ABOVE REFERRED TO

    "1. Not to use the property other than as a single private dwelling house; and

> 2. Not to build or allow to be built any new building on the property nor alter or allow to be altered any building currently erected on the property without the written consent of the Vendor or his successors in title."

2. (18 December 1990) CHARGE dated 30 November 1990 to secure the monies including the further advances therein mentioned.

3. (18 December 1990) PROPRIETOR - NORTHERN WEST BUILDING SOCIETY of 54 Maine Road, Manchester, M2 3ER.

4. (30 April 2002) CHARGE dated 14 April 2002 to secure the monies including the further advances therein mentioned.

5. (30 April 2002) PROPRIETOR - HOME IMPROVEMENT LOANS LIMITED, 12 Hanging Lane, Liverpool Street, London, EC1 2MM.

END OF REGISTER

Note: A date at the beginning of an entry is the date on which the entry was made in the Register

Authors' note: These official copies should be accompanied by an official copy of the title plan. This has not been reproduced for the purposes of this worked example.

14.8.1.2 Worked example of investigation of title as revealed by official copies

	NOTES
Date of Official Copies	*14 September 2008*[1]
Title Number	*LM6042*[2]
Property Register	
Address:	*10, Bladen Road, Overton, Cornshire, CS1 6AU.*[2]
Entries:	*Note: Entry 2: Benefit of right of way. Copy filed – request from seller.*[3]
Proprietorship Register	
Class of Title:	*Absolute*[4]
Registered Proprietor(s):	*Neil Stuart and Anita Stuart*[5]
Entries:	*Note: Entry 2. NS and AS held property as tenants in common. AS is deceased. Request death certificate. Will need to appoint second trustee to overreach. Ensure this is done before exchange or insert special condition requiring appointment before completion.*[6]

Charges Register

Entries:

Note: Entry 1. Property subject to covenants. Residential user only. No building or alterations without consent. Instructions indicate extension built in 2002. Request evidence of consent. Will need to check planning and building regulations.[7]

Note: Entries 2-5. Two registered charges.[8]

14.8.1.3 Commentary

The notes are laid out in a structured format which follows the layout of the official copies themselves: the right-hand column has space for the solicitor acting for Roger Evans to make notes on the title. These notes will enable the solicitor to consider (and, if necessary, amend) the contract for the sale of 10, Bladen Road and also to identify any problems with the title that need following up.

The following footnotes expand upon the comments made in the worked example.

(1) This is relevant as Land Registry will not permit a pre-completion search to be made for a period exceeding 12 months (see **28.5.1**).

(2) This information is necessary for checking the contract when received from the seller.

(3) The property benefits from a right of way, details of which are contained in a copy of the deed of grant that has been filed with the title. It will be necessary to obtain a copy in order to find out the exact route of this easement. It may well be the path down to the river referred to in Roger Evans's instructions.

(4) This information is necessary for checking the contract. Title is absolute, which is the best class obtainable, but if the title were registered with a lesser class, this would need to be investigated and the buyer client advised accordingly (see **4.6**).

(5) & (6) Anita Stuart has recently died, as indicated in Roger Evans's instructions. The restriction indicates that Anita and Neil Stuart were tenants in common and so her share will pass to her estate. It will be necessary to appoint a second trustee in order to overreach the trust of land. A note has been made of the necessary steps here (see **14.5.2** and **14.5.4** for more detail).

(7) Roger Evans's instructions indicate that the property has been recently extended and the covenants referred to in Entry 1 on the Charges Register indicate that consent for this should have been obtained. Steps will need to be taken to resolve this (see **19.4** for more detail). In addition, consideration needs to be given to the need for planning permission and building regulations consent (see **Chapter 17**).

(8) The final four entries in the Charges Register indicate that there are two mortgages on the property (the second may well have been taken out to finance the extension mentioned above). These will need to be discharged and the solicitor acting for Roger Evans will need to ensure that the contract sells 10, Bladen Road free from both of them.

14.8.2 Investigation of an unregistered title – 15, Mill Street, Torridge, Huntshire

In this worked example, the title concerns 15, Mill Street, Torridge, Huntshire. The property is being bought by first time buyers, David Ecclestone and Nadia Sutcliffe, as their home, from Jennifer Dawes. Jennifer has lived in the property since 1995 when she was given the property by her step-parents.

14.8.2.1 The epitome of title

EPITOME OF TITLE

of freehold premises known as

15, Mill Street, Torridge, Huntshire

No. of Doc.	Date	Description of document including parties or event	Evidence now supplied	Whether original will be handed over on completion
1	21.8.1960	Conveyance by David Henderson to Bryan Tyndal	Photocopy	Yes
2	8.12.1987	Central Land Charges Search	Photocopy	Yes
3	10.12.1987	Conveyance by Danielle Popham to Bernard Holmes and Catherine Eden	Photocopy	Yes
4	10.12.1987	Mortgage by Bernard Holmes and Catherine Eden to Huntshire Building Society	Photocopy	Yes
5	16.12.1995	Deed of Gift by Bernard Holmes and Catherine Eden to Jennifer Dawes	Photocopy	Yes

┌─────────────────────┐   ┌─────────────┐
│ INLAND REVENUE   │   │   │
│ PRODUCED   │   │   £50   │
│   │   │   │
└─────────────────────┘   └─────────────┘

THIS CONVEYANCE is made the 21st August 1960 BETWEEN DAVID HENDERSON of 15, Mill Street, Torridge in the county of Huntshire (hereafter referred to as "the Vendor") of the one part and BRYAN TYNDAL of 17 Roland Street, Redenhill in the County of Cornshire (hereafter referred to as "the Purchaser") of the other part

WHEREAS the Vendor is seised of the property hereby assured for an estate in fee simple in possession subject as hereinafter mentioned but otherwise free from incumbrances

AND WHEREAS the Vendor has agreed to sell the said property to the Purchaser for the sum of Five thousand pounds

NOW THIS DEED WITNESSETH as follows:

1.   In consideration of the sum of Five thousand pounds (£5,000) paid by the Purchaser to the Vendor (the receipt of which the Vendor hereby acknowledges) the Vendor as BENEFICIAL OWNER HEREBY CONVEYS unto the Purchaser ALL THAT piece or parcel of land with the dwelling house erected thereon known as 15 Mill Street, Torridge in the County of Huntshire TO HOLD unto the Purchaser in fee simple SUBJECT to the restrictive covenants referred to in a conveyance dated 25th February 1955 and made between Thomas Terry of the one part and the Vendor of the other part.

2.   THE PURCHASER (with the object of affording to the Vendor a full indemnity in respect of any breach of the said restrictive covenants but not further or otherwise) HEREBY COVENANTS with the Vendor that the Purchaser and the persons deriving title under him will at all times hereafter perform and observe such restrictive covenants and keep the Vendor and his estate and effects indemnified against all actions claims demands and liabilities in respect thereof so far as the same affect the property hereby conveyed and are still subsisting and capable of being enforced

      IN WITNESS whereof the parties hereto have set their respective hands and seals the day and year first before written

SIGNED SEALED and DELIVERED   ⎫
by the said DAVID HENDERSON   ⎬   *David Henderson*   ◯
in the presence of: ⎭

Hilary Miller
Torridge
Secretary

SIGNED SEALED and DELIVERED   ⎫   ◯
by the said BRYAN TYNDAL   ⎬   *Bryan Tyndal*
in the presence of: ⎭   ◯

Damian Noble
Torridge
Builder

FORM K18

CERTIFICATE OF THE RESULT OF SEARCH

CERTIFICATE NO. 2220398	CERTIFICATE DATE 8th December 1987	PROTECTION ENDS ON 31st December 1987

It is hereby certified that an official search in respect of the undermentioned particulars has been made in the index to the registers which are kept pursuant to the Land Charges Act 1972. The results of the search is shown below.

PARTICULARS SEARCHED					
COUNTY OR COUNTIES: HUNTSHIRE					
NAME(S): Particulars of Charge				PERIOD	FEES £
THOMAS TERRY* No subsisting entry				1926–1955	.50p
DAVID HENDERSON* (1) D(ii) No. 0198 Dated 3/3/1955 (2) 15, Mill Street (3) Torridge (4) Huntshire				1955–1960	.50p
BRIAN TYNDAL* No subsisting entry				1960–1987	.50p
DANIELLE POPHAM No subsisting entry				1960–1987	.50p
APPLICANT'S REFERENCE: JP	Ternant & Co	APPLICANT'S KEY NUMBER	56456	AMOUNT DEBITED	£2.00
Ternant and Co 8 London Road Torridge Hunts HT1 6DR				Any enquiries concerning this certificate to be addressed to: The Superintendent Land Charges Department Burrington Way Plymouth PL5 3LP	
				IMPORTANT: PLEASE READ THE NOTES OVERLEAF	

INLAND REVENUE PRODUCED	£550

THIS CONVEYANCE is made the 10th day of December 1987 BETWEEN DANIELLE POPHAM of 15, Mill Street, Torridge in the county of Huntshire (hereinafter called "the Vendor") of the one part and BERNARD HOLMES AND CATHERINE EDEN of 45, Mayer Crescent, Godhall in the County of Huntshire (hereinafter called "the Purchasers") of the second part

WHEREAS the Vendor is seised of the property hereinafter described for an estate in fee simple in possession and has agreed to sell the same to the Purchasers for the sum of Fifty-five thousand pounds AND WHEREAS the Vendor is solely and beneficially entitled to the said property

NOW THIS DEED WITNESSETH as follows:

1   IN consideration of the sum of Fifty-five thousand pounds (£55,000) paid by the Purchasers to the Vendor (the receipt whereof the Vendor hereby acknowledges) the Vendor as BENEFICIAL OWNER HEREBY CONVEYS unto the Purchasers ALL THAT piece or parcel of land with the dwelling house erected thereon known as 15, Mill Street, Torridge in the county of Huntshire TO HOLD the same unto the Purchasers in fee simple as beneficial joint tenants SUBJECT TO the covenants referred to in a conveyance of the property herein conveyed dated the 21st day of August 1960 and made between David Henderson and Bryan Tyndal.

2   THE PURCHASERS (with the object of affording to the Vendor a full indemnity in respect of any breach of the said restrictive covenants but not further or otherwise) HEREBY JOINTLY AND SEVERALLY COVENANT with the Vendor that the Purchasers and any person deriving title under them will at all times hereafter perform and observe such restrictive covenants and keep the Vendor and her estate and effects indemnified against all actions claims demands and liabilities in respect thereof so far as the same affect the property hereby conveyed and are still subsisting and capable of being enforced.

IN WITNESS whereof the parties hereto have set their respective hands and seals the day and year first before written

SIGNED SEALED and DELIVERED
on behalf of the above named
DANIELLE POPHAM by her attorney   }   *Albert Pardew*   ◯
Albert Pardew in the presence of:

Colin Scales
Fernhill
Clerk

SIGNED SEALED and
DELIVERED by the said
BERNARD HOLMES and   }   *Bernard Holmes*   ◯
CATHERINE EDEN in the   *Catherine Eden*
presence of:

Kevin Knowles
Fernhill
Musician

Huntshire Building Society

MORTGAGE DEED

Account Number:	Hol/EDE.1576	Date: 10 December 1987
Society:	**HUNTSHIRE BUILDING SOCIETY**	
Mortgage Conditions:	Huntshire Building Society Mortgage Conditions 1987	
Borrower:	BERNARD HOLMES AND CATHERINE EDEN 15, Mill Street, Torridge, Huntshire	
Property:	15, Mill Street, Torridge, Huntshire	
Title No:	N/A	

1. This Mortgage Deed incorporates the Mortgage Conditions a copy of which has been received by the Borrowers.

2. The Borrowers as beneficial owners charge the Property by way of legal mortgage with payment of all moneys payable by the Borrowers to the Society under the Mortgage Conditions.

3. This Mortgage Deed is made for securing further advances.

Signed sealed and delivered by the Borrowers in the presence of the Witness.

Borrowers:		Witness (signature, name and address)
Bernard Holmes	○	Kevin Knowles, Fernhill, Musician
Catherine Eden	○	Kevin Knowles, Fernhill, Musician

RECEIPT

The Huntshire Building Society hereby acknowledges receipt of the loan secured by this mortgage.

IN WITNESS whereof the Common Seal of the Society has been affixed this 20th day of June 1990 in the presence of:

John Crouch
_____
DIRECTOR

Lee Bell
_____
SECRETARY

○

Huntshire B.S.

Document 5

THIS DEED OF GIFT is made the 16th December 1995 between (1) BERNARD HOLMES and CATHERINE EDEN both of 14, Steed Mews, Cleveland Street, London W9 1HB ('the Donors') and (2) JENNIFER DAWES of Carshalton Mansions, Hawarden Street, London, W9 1NL ('the Donee')

WHEREAS the Donors are seised of the property hereinafter described for an estate in fee simple in possession and out of natural love and affection have decided to convey the same to the Donee.

NOW THIS DEED WITNESSETH as follows:

1   IN consideration of natural love and affection, the Vendors as TRUSTEES HEREBY CONVEY unto the Donee ALL THAT piece or parcel of land together with the dwelling house erected thereon known as 15, Mill Street, Torridge in the county of Huntshire TO HOLD the same unto the Donee in fee simple SUBJECT TO the covenants referred to in a conveyance dated the 21st August 1960 and made between David Henderson and Bryan Tyndal.

2.   THE DONEE (with the object of affording to the Donors a full indemnity in respect of any breach of the said restrictive covenants but not further or otherwise) HEREBY COVENANTS with the Donors that the Donee and any person deriving title under her will at all times hereafter perform and observe such covenants and keep the Donors and their estates and effects indemnified against all actions claims demands and liabilities in respect thereof so far as the same affect the property hereby conveyed and are still subsisting and capable of being enforced.

3.   The Donor certifies that this deed falls within category L in the Schedule to the Stamp Duty (Exempt Instruments) Regulations 1987.

Signed as a deed and delivered by
BERNARD HOLMES and   *Bernard Holmes*
CATHERINE EDEN in the
presence of: *Catherine Eden*

Matthew Pleasance
Trainee Solicitor
London

Signed as a deed and delivered by
JENNIFER DAWES   *Jennifer Dawes*
in the presence of:

Petra McNulty,
Managing Director
Torridge

14.8.2.2   Worked example of investigation of title as revealed by epitome of title

Dates	Parties	Notes
	Compulsory registration: December 1990[1]	
1960–1987	Danielle Popham	Refers to covenants in 1960 conveyance. Obtain copy of conveyance. [2]
		Seller executes by attorney. Need to see power of attorney.[3]
		BH and CE buy as joint tenants.[4]
		BH and CE give indemnity covenant. [5]
1987–1995	Bernard Holmes and Catherine Eden	1987. BH and CE buy with aid of mortgage. Receipted 1990 and so discharged. [6]
1995–date	Jennifer Dawes	Deed of gift. Do search against BH and CE to ensure no bankruptcy. [7]
		JD gives indemnity covenant. [8]
	Pre-root	
1926 – 1955	Thomas Terry	
1955 - *1960*	David Henderson	1960 conveyance refers to plan and covenants in 1955 conveyance. Obtain copy. [9]
		Buyer gives indemnity covenant. [10]
		CLCR Search reveals D(ii) against David Henderson (see below). [11]
1960 - *1987*	Bryan Tyndal	
	Central Land Charges Searches[12]	
~~1926–1955~~	~~Thomas Terry~~	
~~1955–1960~~	~~David Henderson~~	D(ii) registered. 1955 covenants?
1960–1987	Bryan Tyndal	Name misspelt in 1987 search. Re-do search.
1960–1987	~~Danielle Popham~~	
1987–2000	Bernard Holmes and Catherine Eden	Check to 2000 for insolvency due to gift in 1995.
1995– date	Jennifer Dawes	

14.8.2.3   Commentary on investigation of title

The history of 15, Mill Street is broadly as follows. In 1955, Thomas Terry sold the property to David Henderson and imposed new covenants on the buyer in that conveyance (it is possible that this was a sale of part of a bigger plot of land at this stage). In order to ensure that the negative covenants bound successive owners of 15, Mill Street, Thomas Terry registered them as D(ii) land charges against the buyer's name. David Henderson then owned the property for about five years before selling it in 1960 to Bryan Tyndal. It is not entirely clear who owned the property between 1960 and 1987, but what we do know is that sometime between 1960 and 1987 Bryan Tyndal sold the property and Danielle Popham bought it. We do not know who owned it in the meantime, but that does not matter: this took place pre-root and there is no need to trace an unbroken chain of ownership pre-root.

In 1987, in what should form the good root of title, Danielle Popham sold the property to Bernard Holmes and Catherine Eden. Danielle, Bernard and Catherine form the first links in the chain that needs to be built up from the owners in the good root of title to the seller. Bernard and Catherine bought with the aid of a mortgage to Huntshire Building Society, but this was paid off in 1990 as evidenced by the receipt to be found attached to the mortgage itself.

In 1995, Bernard and Catherine gave 15, Mill Street to Jennifer Dawes, completing the chain of ownership from the seller in the root of title, Danielle Popham, down to present day. The fact that the property was given to Danielle raises issues relating to setting aside gifts in the event of bankruptcy and it will be necessary to check that neither Bernard nor Catherine became insolvent in the five years following the gift.

14.8.2.4   Specific points on the worked example

(1)   It is necessary to check when registration became compulsory for the area in which the property is situated in case any of the dispositions revealed by the epitome mean that title should have already been registered (see **4.3**). The area became subject to compulsory registration in 1990.

(2)–(5)   The 1987 conveyance from Danielle Popham forms the root of title and, subject to what follows, should satisfy the definition of a good root (see **13.5.2**). It is from the seller in this document that an unbroken chain of ownership needs to be traced.

(2)   The 1987 conveyance refers to covenants in a 1960 conveyance, which in turn refers to covenants in a 1955 conveyance, and so this pre-root document needs to be requested (see **14.4.2.1**).

(3)   As revealed by the attestation clause, the 1987 conveyance was executed by the seller under a power of attorney. A copy of this will need to be obtained and checked for the issues raised in **14.5.6**. If this is unavailable or the execution of the 1987 conveyance is called into question, the conveyance will not be a good root and, further, represents a serious flaw in the title.

(4)   Bernard Holmes and Catherine Eden buy as joint tenants: should one of them die, this is important information affecting how the title would then devolve.

(5)   As buyers, Bernard and Catherine gave an indemnity covenant. This indicates the presence of a chain of indemnities which

means the current buyers, David Ecclestone and Nadia Sutcliffe, will be expected to give such a covenant themselves.

(6)   Bernard Holmes and Catherine Eden bought with the aid of a mortgage. This was paid off in 1990 and so is not an issue: but any mortgage on the title should be checked to ensure that a receipt is indeed present.

(7)   In 1995, Bernard and Catherine give the property to Jennifer Dawes. An unbroken chain from the seller in the good root to the current owner is made out, but care must be taken because of the fact this was a gift. In the event of insolvency within five years of the gift, it can be set aside (see **14.5.8**). A Central Land Charges Search will need to be done to cover this period (ie, up to 2000) to check that Bernard and Catherine did not become insolvent.

(8)   Jennifer gave an indemnity covenant, continuing the chain down to the present day. See item (5) above for the consequences to the current buyers.

Having investigated title from the good root to the present day, it is now necessary to consider the pre-root documents. Although, generally, a buyer is not entitled to see pre-root documents, in certain circumstances this is not the case (see **14.4.2.1**).

(9)   The 1960 conveyance (in which David Henderson sells to Bryan Tyndal) has been provided as the good root of title states that there are covenants referred to in it. Unfortunately, these covenants are not actually contained in the 1960 conveyance, merely referred to (as is a plan of 15, Mill Street). So, in turn, the 1955 conveyance (between a Thomas Terry and David Henderson, the seller in 1960), containing both the covenants and the plan, should be obtained.

(10)   An indemnity covenant is given. See item (5) above for the consequences of this.

(11)   The Central Land Charges search reveals that a D(ii) land charge has been registered against David Henderson. This will almost certainly relate to the covenants that he gave when he bought the property in 1955. Official copies of the entries should be obtained. The consequence is that such covenants will bind the land and, so, if David Ecclestone and Nadia Sutcliffe acquire 15, Mill Street, they will take subject to them.

(12)   Central Land Charges searches will need to be done against the names of all owners revealed by the title for the period during which they owned the property. This will include the names of individuals revealed in pre-root documents.

Where it is unclear when an individual acquired or disposed of the property, the dates should deal with this uncertainty by covering all possibilities. Thus, although we know Bryan Tyndal bought the property in 1960, we do not know when he sold it, but it must have been sometime in or before 1987 at the latest as Danielle Popham owned it by then. Hence a search will need to be done against Bryan Tyndal's name from 1960 to 1987. Where the solicitor has had to approximate periods of ownership in this way, he has done so by indicating this in italics.

If a Central Land Charges search has been provided as part of the epitome, this may mean that certain searches do not need to be repeated. As such, the names of Thomas Terry, David Henderson and

Danielle Popham have been crossed through as satisfactory searches have been provided in respect of their names. The search against Bryan Tyndal is not acceptable, as the search was done against an incorrect spelling of his name. As you will see, the layout of the solicitor's notes into 'date' and 'parties' columns, replicates the format of the Central Land Charges search to facilitate the process of checking old searches.

The search against Bernard and Catherine will need to be carried out not merely for the periods during which they owned the property, but for a further five years after that, due to the insolvency issues surrounding the gift to Jennifer, and so the search against their names will need to be from 1987 to 2000.

Chapter 15

The Draft Contract

15.1 Purpose of the contract

The purpose of the contract is to define the extent of the land to be sold and to set out the terms on which the seller is prepared to sell. It is the seller's right and duty to draft the contract, since only he will know precisely what he is prepared to sell and on what terms (eg, as to price). Drafting the contract is the most important task which the seller's solicitor has to perform. It is arguably the most important task in the whole transaction since, if the terms of the contract are well drafted, the transaction will usually proceed smoothly to completion. Conversely, a badly drafted contract may give rise to problems. It is vital, therefore, that the utmost care is exercised in drafting the contract.

Although it is the seller's prerogative to dictate the terms on which he is prepared to sell, this does not necessarily mean that he is entitled to draft a contract which is entirely in his own favour and which contains terms prejudicial to the intending buyer. The contract terms are open to negotiation with the buyer and, unless the bargaining strength of the seller is very strong (caused perhaps by the state of the property market generally or, in some cases, by the nature of the property being sold), the seller must be prepared to concede some points in the buyer's favour.

Ultimately, contract drafting is an exercise in the art of compromise. The seller's solicitor must ensure that the terms of the contract adequately protect his own client's interests, but at the same time provide a sufficiently attractive package to persuade the buyer to proceed with the purchase.

Two identical contracts are prepared by the seller's solicitor, both of which are sent to the buyer's solicitor with the pre-contract documentation for his approval. This chapter outlines the legal formalities and contents of a contract for the sale of land, but does not discuss drafting techniques. These are explained in *Skills for Lawyers*.

15.2 Investigation of title

Having obtained official copies of the register of title (registered land) or the seller's title deeds or a copy of them (unregistered land), the seller's solicitor should investigate title before drafting the contract for sale. The method of investigation is dealt with in **Chapter 14**.

15.2.1 Reasons for investigation

Investigation of the title by the seller's solicitor at this stage of the transaction is a precautionary measure to ensure that:

(a) the seller is the owner of, or is otherwise entitled to sell, the whole of the estate which he intends to sell;

(b) any incumbrances on the title can be disclosed in the draft contract in order to satisfy the seller's duty of disclosure (see **15.7**);

(c) any defects in the title are discovered and appropriate steps taken to correct them before exchange of contracts;

(d) any consents which may be necessary from third parties can be obtained;

(e) any queries relating to the title by the buyer can be anticipated.

15.2.2 Capacity

While investigating the seller's title, it is necessary to check that the seller is entitled to sell the whole of the estate in the land which he intends to sell. The following circumstances should be considered.

15.2.2.1 Sole owner

A sole owner, who owns the whole of the legal and equitable interest for his own benefit (a 'beneficial owner'), will normally have unlimited powers of disposal.

15.2.2.2 Trustees (including co-owners)

Where land is held on a trust of land (including a trust arising through co-ownership), any conveyance or transfer of the land must be made by all the trustees, being at least two individuals or a trust corporation, in order to overreach the equitable interests of the beneficiaries. The trustees are normally under a duty to consult with the beneficiaries before selling the land, but a buyer is not bound to enquire whether this has been done (Trusts of Land and Appointment of Trustees Act 1996, s 16).

Trustees of land have the same powers of disposal as a beneficial owner, unless these have been restricted by the terms of the trust. The trust may, for example, require the consent of named persons before a sale takes place, and the sellers must ensure that they obtain all such consents. In registered land, any such limitations on the powers of disposal will be indicated by a restriction on the proprietorship register.

15.2.2.3 Personal representatives

Personal representatives have all the powers of trustees of land but are only entitled to exercise those powers during the administration (Administration of Estates Act 1925, s 39). Their powers are joint as to land, whether freehold or leasehold, therefore if a grant of representation has been made in favour of more than one person, they all must be parties to the contract and the purchase deed. However, a grant of representation can be validly made in favour of a single person and in such a case he can act on his own — there is no need for a second personal representative to be appointed. The usual principles of overreaching apply to a sale by personal representatives.

15.2.2.4 Mortgagees

In order to sell the property, the lender must have an express or implied power of sale, and that power must have arisen and become exercisable. A power of sale is implied in every mortgage made by deed unless expressly excluded (LPA 1925, s 101). A legal mortgage must be made by deed (LPA 1925, s 85). It therefore follows that a legal lender will always have a power of sale unless (exceptionally) that power has been expressly excluded. A lender who is exercising his power of sale must ensure that:

(a)   his power of sale exists;

(b)   the power has arisen; and

(c)   the power has become exercisable.

The power of sale arises on the legal date for redemption. This will be specified in the mortgage and is usually a date early on in the mortgage term (eg, one month after the money was advanced). This is so even if the loan is to be repaid over (say) 25 years.

The lender's power becomes exercisable in the circumstances set out in the mortgage deed. If there are no such terms, then it is exercisable if one of the three conditions set out in s 103 of the LPA 1925 is met:

(a)   notice requiring payment of the principal money has been served on the borrower and default has been made in payment of the principal money for three months; or

(b)   some interest under the mortgage is in arrear and unpaid for two months after becoming due; or

(c)   there has been breach of some other provision contained in the mortgage deed or the LPA 1925.

15.2.2.5 Companies

A company which is regulated by the Companies Acts may deal with land, provided the transaction is within the scope of the objects clause of its memorandum of association (one of its constitutional documents). It would be unusual for a normal trading company to lack the power to hold or dispose of an estate in land, although restrictions on granting mortgages may be encountered. In the case of registered land, if the company's powers are limited, an appropriate restriction will be entered on the proprietorship register.

15.2.2.6 Persons suffering from mental disability

A contract for the sale or purchase of land entered into by a person who is suffering from mental incapacity sufficient to deprive him of understanding of the nature of the transaction is voidable at the option of the incapacitated party, provided he can prove that, at the time of the transaction, the other contracting party was aware of the disability (*Broughton v Snook* [1938] Ch 505).

Once a receiver is appointed under s 99 of the Mental Health Act 1983, the patient loses all contractual capacity and any purported inter vivos disposition by him is void. The receiver has power, subject to the court's approval, to deal with the patient's property (see the Mental Health Act 1983, ss 95 and 96).

15.2.3 Breach of a restrictive covenant or other defect in title

If investigation of the title reveals a breach of a restrictive covenant which cannot be remedied (eg, by obtaining retrospective consent from the person with the benefit of the covenant), consideration should be given to obtaining restrictive covenant indemnity insurance to cover the breach. Insurance is not available for all breaches of covenant.

Other defects or problems with the title which can be corrected (eg, by the appointment of a new trustee) should be rectified as soon as possible. Defects which are irremediable will have to be revealed in the draft contract. It must be anticipated that the buyer will require these matters to be remedied before agreeing to purchase the property. Defective title insurance may also be available to cover certain defects.

15.2.4 Planning

Although not strictly a matter of title, the seller's solicitor should check at this stage that any necessary planning or building regulation consents have been obtained and complied with (see **Chapter 17**). Copies of such consents should be obtained from the local authority for the buyer's use. It must be anticipated that the buyer will request sight of these if they are not provided. Indemnity insurance may be available if copies cannot be obtained.

15.3 The anatomy of a contract

A contract for the sale of land usually comprises three distinct parts:

(a)   the particulars of sale;

(b)   the conditions of sale; and

(c)   the memorandum of agreement.

The particulars describe the estate in and physical extent of the land being sold, sometimes by reference to a plan attached to the contract (see **15.5**). The conditions will set out the terms on which the land is agreed to be sold (see **15.6** and **15.7**). The memorandum states that the seller agrees to sell the property and the buyer to buy it at a specified price, and contains the signatures of the parties.

15.3.1 Terms of the contract

The terms of the contract are dictated by the following.

15.3.1.1 Open contract rules

The open contract rules represent the general law on any particular point connected with a contract for sale of land. Some of the rules are based on the common law and some derive from statute (eg, LPA 1925).

The rules imply conditions into a contract where nothing is expressly stated with regard to a particular matter, ie, where the contract is 'open' on that point.

Some of the rules operate adequately, but others are not satisfactory and are invariably altered by express provision in the contract. Even the rules which do not cause a problem are usually repeated expressly in the contract in the interests of certainty. As most matters are dealt with expressly, the open contract rules have little significance in modern conveyancing.

15.3.1.2 Standard conditions of sale

As many matters relevant to the sale of land are common to all transactions, standard sets of conditions exist which can be incorporated into a contract of sale. Standard conditions sometimes follow the open contract position, but in other cases operate to clarify or amend that position.

15.3.1.3 **Special conditions**

Special conditions are conditions expressly included by the parties because of the circumstances of the transaction or its particular requirements. They are usually used to supplement standard conditions and in some cases will refine or vary the standard condition position.

15.4 Standard forms of contract

A solicitor will usually draft a contract either by using a standard form of contract purchased from a law stationers, or by incorporating a standard set of conditions into a contract generated from his word-processing system. Many of the conditions of sale which are needed in the contract are common to all transactions, so it is advantageous to the solicitor to make use of a standard set of these conditions, which have been drafted by experts and which will be familiar to the buyer's solicitor who will in due course need to look at the terms of the contract very carefully from his own client's point of view.

Many contracts for the sale of land are currently drafted by reference to the Standard Conditions of Sale (The Law Society and Oyez), 4th edn. These conditions are referred to in context throughout this book. An example of the front and back pages of the Standard Conditions of Sale form is set out at **15.11**. The centre pages of this document contain the 'small print' of the agreement and are set out in full in **Appendix 2**.

As an alternative to using the standard form contract purchased from law stationers, the solicitor may produce his own version of the contract on his own word processor, but will then need to include in that document a clause which states that 'the contract is deemed to include the Standard Conditions of Sale, 4th Edition'. This phrase is necessary to incorporate the text of the Standard Conditions within the typed contract, and to ensure that all the terms of the contract are incorporated in writing as required by the Law of Property (Miscellaneous Provisions) Act 1989, s 2. Use of the Standard Conditions of Sale is encouraged in Protocol cases.

Although the use of the Standard Conditions was widespread in residential transactions, they were not designed for, nor entirely suitable for, commercial transactions. Therefore, The Law Society and Oyez produced the **Standard Commercial Property Conditions** for use in high value commercial transactions. These are set out in **Appendix 3**. Although they are based on the residential Standard Conditions, there are many differences to meet the differing needs of a commercial transaction. Most solicitors dealing with sales of commercial property will not use the printed form of contract but will produce their own word-processed version incorporating one or other set of Standard Conditions. The word-processed version will normally include numerous variations and additions to the Standard Conditions.

15.5 The particulars of sale

The particulars of sale describe the estate in land which is being sold, ie whether it is freehold or leasehold, and the physical extent of that land. They may also contain a reference to easements and covenants which benefit the land (eg, the benefit of a right of way). The aim of the particulars is to give a clear and concise description of the property. Where the land being sold can be identified by a regular postal address and has clearly marked boundaries, describing it by reference to its postal address and, in the case of registered land, its title number will suffice. In other cases, for example the sale of agricultural land or on a sale of part only of the seller's property, a fuller description will be needed and reference must be made to a plan attached to the contract showing the precise delineation of the land to be sold. The existing description of the land as contained in the property register (registered land) or title deeds (unregistered land) can be used as the starting-point for drafting a suitable description in such cases.

15.5.1   Plans

A plan must be used on a sale of part of land (which includes the grant of leases of flats) and may be desirable in other cases, for example where the boundaries of the property are not self-evident, but is generally not necessary for the sale of the whole of a freehold registered title. Whatever type of plan is used, it must be of sufficient size and scale to enable the boundaries and other features of the property to be identified readily (see *Scarfe v Adams* [1981] 1 All ER 843). A plan on a scale of 1:1,250 will be adequate in most cases, but a larger scale will usually be required for sales of flats or the division of buildings into separate units.

15.5.1.1   Boundaries

Boundaries shown on plans prepared by Land Registry are general boundaries only and may not show the precise line of the boundaries of the property (LRA 2002, s 60). A Land Registry plan may not therefore be reliable for use as a contract plan.

15.5.1.2   Scale plans

The use of a scale plan is preferable, but it must be entirely accurate and should show the scale used on the plan itself. A hand-drawn plan which is not to scale may be adequate in simple transactions (eg, the sale of part of a garden), but is inappropriate for use in a sale of flats or of a commercial property. Measurements must be shown in metric units.

15.5.1.3   Drawing a plan

An existing plan in the title deeds may be used as the starting-point for the preparation of the plan, but should not be photocopied and reused because photocopying distorts the plan and may make it inaccurate. A title plan obtained with official copy entries may not be drawn on a sufficiently large scale to enable it to be used. Large-scale Ordnance Survey maps can be obtained from HMSO, but a licence is needed to photocopy these maps. Where the value or complexity of the transaction justifies the expense, an architect or surveyor may be instructed to prepare a plan. If there is any doubt as to the size or extent of the property, an inspection should be carried out and measurements taken. The seller usually bears the cost of the preparation of the plan.

15.5.1.4   Showing features on the plan

The wording of the contract and of the purchase deed will need to make reference to the plan and its various features, and this point should be borne in mind when the plan is drawn (eg, a right of way can be more easily described in words in the contract if its beginning and end points are marked 'A' and 'B' on a plan which also shows the demarcation of the route). Markings on the plan should be clear and precise.

The land to be sold should be outlined or coloured in red, and any land to be retained by the seller should be outlined or coloured in blue. Other land referred to should be coloured or hatched in distinct colours other than red or blue. The ownership of boundaries should be indicated by 'T' marks. The stem of the 'T' should rest on the relevant boundary, the 'T' being on the side of the boundary which is responsible for the maintenance. Rights of way and routes of services should be marked with broken or dotted lines of a distinct colour, with each end of the route being identified with separate capital letters.

Where the plan is to scale, the scale should be shown. If the plan is not to scale, metric measurements should be shown along each boundary. A compass point indicating the direction of north should be shown. A key should be included to explain the meaning of the various colours and lines used on the plan.

15.5.1.5   Referring to the contract plan

Care must be taken to ensure that there is no discrepancy between the verbal description of the property and the plan. If there is, it will be a question of construction as to whether the verbal description or the plan will prevail. The contract (and subsequent purchase deed) may refer to the plan as being 'for identification purposes only', or may describe the land as being 'more particularly delineated on the plan'. These two phrases are mutually exclusive and a combination of the two serves no useful purpose *(Neilson v Poole* (1969) 20 P & CR 909).

'Identification purposes only'

Where there is a discrepancy between the land shown on the plan and the contract description, and the plan has been described as being for identification purposes only, the verbal description of the land will normally prevail over the plan. This type of plan is unacceptable for use in connection with registered land and will be returned by Land Registry.

'More particularly delineated'

In the event of a discrepancy between the verbal description of the land and the plan, the plan will prevail over the words where the phrase 'more particularly delineated' has been used. This phrase should not be used unless the plan is to scale.

Note, however, that in many cases there will be no verbal description as such. So, for example, the land being sold may be described as 'All that land edged in red on the plan ... and forming part of property known as ...'. Here the only means of identifying the property is the plan itself and so there can be no question of a discrepancy between the verbal description and the plan.

15.5.2   Easements and rights benefiting the property

The seller's investigation of title will have revealed whether or not the property has the benefit of easements or other rights. These may be included in the particulars of sale, although this is not essential as the benefit of them will pass to the buyer in any event under s 62 of the LPA 1925. On a sale of part of land, new rights (eg, a right to lay a new water pipe) may be granted to the buyer (see **Chapter 40**).

15.5.3   Errors in the particulars

A mistake in the particulars of sale, for example describing a freehold property as leasehold, or describing the extent of the land as 5 hectares when in fact it is only

3 hectares, may give the buyer a remedy in misdescription or misrepresentation. These remedies are both explained in **Chapter 33**.

15.6 The conditions of sale

There are two types of conditions: general conditions and special conditions. General conditions are those which apply in every transaction, such as the Standard Conditions of Sale. Special conditions are those terms which are specially drafted to fit the circumstances of the transaction in hand.

15.6.1 Drafting conditions of sale

It is assumed that the seller's solicitor will be using the Standard Conditions of Sale as the foundation of his contract. On this basis, and having considered which matters need to be dealt with by special conditions (see **15.7**), drafting involves the following process.

(a) Look at the relevant Standard Condition of Sale on the point. Does this deal with the matter in a way acceptable to the needs of the client?

(b) If it does not, a special condition will have to be drafted and included in the contract.

The Standard Conditions are in almost universal use in residential transactions. They are not as widely used in commercial transactions, and, where they are so used, they will need amendment to meet the different circumstances of a commercial sale. The more important of the amendments necessary will be mentioned when the relevant part of the contract is discussed. The Standard Commercial Property Conditions are now available for use in commercial transactions.

15.6.2 Altering the Standard Conditions of Sale

Where it is necessary to modify one of the Standard Conditions of Sale to meet the requirements of a particular transaction, this can be done by including as a special condition in the contract a clause which contains provisions contrary to or different from those contained in the Standard Conditions themselves. It is not necessary to include a special condition which expressly excludes the Standard Condition which is being amended because SC 1.1.4 (SCPC 1.1.4(a)) provides that the Standard Conditions apply 'except as varied or excluded by the contract' so ensuring that where there is a conflict the individually negotiated terms prevail over the Standard Conditions. However, in practice, the Standard Condition in question will often be expressly stated to be excluded in the interests of certainty. An amendment to the Standard Conditions must be made by special condition on the reverse of the contract form. It is not sufficient merely to strike out or alter the offending condition in the centre pages of the contract form.

15.7 Matters commonly dealt with by special conditions

15.7.1 The seller's duty of disclosure

The open contract rule provides that the seller is selling a freehold estate free from incumbrances. This is rarely the case since many properties are subject to restrictive covenants which will continue to bind the land after completion of the sale to the buyer. It is therefore necessary to alter this rule in the contract itself, and this is done by SC 3 (SCPC 3) which amends the open contract rules.

15.7.1.1 Standard Condition 3 (SCPC 3)

Under both sets of Conditions, the seller is deemed to be selling the property free from incumbrances other than those mentioned in SC 3.1.2 (SCPC 3.1.2). Under both sets of Conditions, Condition 3.1.2 is divided into paragraphs lettered (a) to (e) setting out the incumbrances subject to which the property is to be sold. Both sets of Conditions are identical, with the exception of paragraph (d).

Those mentioned in the contract (3.1.2(a))

This is the most important category. Because of the primary implication that the land is being sold free from incumbrances, it is essential that the seller's solicitor investigates his title thoroughly before drafting the contract and includes in the contract details of any and all incumbrances so discovered that will be binding on the buyer after completion. Failure to disclose incumbrances that do not come within one of the remaining paragraphs of SC 3.1.2 (SCPC 3.1.2) may give the buyer the right to rescind the contract and/or claim damages. The remedies for non-disclosure are discussed in Chapter 33.

Those discoverable by an inspection of the property before the contract (3.1.2(b))

Often easements (and some other incumbrances) affecting the land can be discovered by an inspection. If this is the case they are deemed to be patent, ie obvious defects, and need not be expressly disclosed. However, to avoid any dispute as to whether a matter is or is not discoverable by an inspection, it is usual to disclose all incumbrances in the contract, whether or not they could be discovered by an inspection.

If the incumbrance is not discoverable by an inspection, it is irrelevant under SC 3 that the buyer might already know of the existence of an incumbrance, for example because it is on the register in registered land. Such an incumbrance must be included in the contract to comply with the Condition.

Those the seller does not and could not reasonably know about (3.1.2(c))

This is necessary to counteract the strictness of the rule that the property is being sold free from all incumbrances. Apart from this provision, a seller would be in breach of the contractual term that the land was free from incumbrances if it was later discovered to be subject to an incumbrance unknown to the seller. Note that, to come within this provision, it is not enough that the seller did not know about the incumbrance; he must also show that he could not reasonably know of it. However, in reality, it is most unlikely that there would be any incumbrances which the seller both did not know about and could not have known about had the seller's solicitor investigated title properly.

Entries made before the date of the contract in any public register except Land Registry or Land Charges Registry or kept at Companies House (SC 3.1.2(d))

This means that any incumbrances registered at Companies House, or entered on the register in registered land or registered as land charges in unregistered land, must be expressly mentioned in the contract (unless they are discoverable by an inspection) in order to satisfy the disclosure requirements of SC 3. It is not sufficient that they are registered and could be discovered by the appropriate search, or are already known to the buyer. On the other hand, matters entered in other public registers, eg, the Local Land Charges Register (see **Chapter 18**), need not be expressly disclosed in the contract.

SCPC 3.1.2(d))

This condition is much wider than the equivalent in the residential Standard Conditions. It makes the sale subject to matters which 'would have been disclosed by the searches and enquiries which a prudent buyer would have made before entering into the contract'. The only exceptions to this are 'monetary charges or incumbrances', eg, an existing mortgage. This provision does mean, therefore, that the sale would be subject to all entries on the title at Land Registry even if not specifically mentioned in the contract. SC 3.1.2(d) specifically excludes entries made at Land Registry.

Public requirements (3.1.2(e))

These are defined in SC 1.1.1(j) (SCPC 1.1.1(l)) as being any notice order or proposal given or made by a body acting on statutory authority. This would therefore include matters likely to be revealed by the Enquiries of the Local Authority, for example a public right of way affecting the land (see **Chapter 18**). Therefore, these need not be expressly disclosed to the buyer in the contract.

15.7.1.2   Defects in title

The open contract implication that the seller is selling the fee simple free from incumbrances also implies that there are no other flaws or defects in the title itself. For example, details of some old covenants may be missing, or there may be some other defect in the documents proving ownership (see **Chapter 14** on Investigation of Title for details of other possible defects). If these defects are not patent (ie, something that is visible to the eye on inspecting the property) then the buyer might again have remedies against the seller for non-disclosure (see **Chapter 33**). Standard Condition 3 (SCPC 3) does not change the open contract rules with regard to these defects in title, which, therefore, must be disclosed.

15.7.1.3   Matters which will not bind the buyer

These are not defects in title and the seller does not need to disclose them. They would include, for example, the interests of the beneficiaries under a trust of land which will be overreached on a sale by two trustees.

15.7.1.4   Physical defects

These need not be disclosed (see SC 3.2.1 and SCPC 3.2.1) and hence the need for the buyer to commission a survey. However, if the seller deliberately conceals a physical defect (eg, 'papering over the cracks'), this may give rise to a claim in the tort of deceit.

15.7.1.5   Dealing with disclosure in the contract

The seller should make a full disclosure of all incumbrances and defects in title in the contract. He does not want to be faced with an objection that a particular non-disclosed incumbrance or defect was not apparent on an inspection. If an incumbrance is disclosed in the contract, the buyer has agreed to buy subject to it by virtue of SC 3.1.2(a) (SCPC 3.1.2(a)).

As far as other defects in title are concerned, the disclosure of them will probably give rise to an implication that the buyer has agreed to buy subject to them. However, if the defect is capable of being remedied, the buyer will be entitled to request ('raise a requisition') that the seller does in fact remedy it. In practice, the seller may not be able or willing to do so. It is, therefore, necessary to include an express provision in the contract preventing the buyer from objecting to it. For example, if the defect in question is an imperfectly executed conveyance, the clause to be inserted in the agreement might be as follows:

> The Buyer shall assume that the conveyance dated .... is correctly executed and shall raise no requisition or objection in relation to it.

Note, however, that clauses like this do not become operative until contracts are exchanged. The buyer is free to raise queries about the problem up until that time (although the seller is under no obligation to answer them). It does mean, though, that the buyer is able to consider the risk posed by buying the land subject to this defect and, if he considers it too great, he can withdraw from the transaction without any penalty.

15.7.2   Barring requisitions

Standard Condition 4.2.2 (SCPC 6.2.2) allows the buyer to raise requisitions at any time within six working days after contracts have been exchanged. However, it is usual in modern conveyancing practice for title to be deduced in the pre-contract package prior to exchange. In recognition of this, SC 4.2.1 (SCPC 6.2.1) provides that if title has been deduced before exchange then no requisitions can be raised on it.

Note also, however, that this kind of special condition only prevents the buyer raising objections to the title as presented to him by the seller. If, after exchange, he discovered an undisclosed incumbrance or other defect which ought to have been known to the seller, he would still be able to require the problem to be remedied or assert his remedies for non-disclosure (see **Chapter 33**). Standard Condition 4.2.2 (SCPC 6.2.2) provides that in such a case, the buyer has six working days from when the matter came to his attention to raise requisitions.

15.7.3   Proof of the seller's title

The contract must tell the buyer how the seller intends to prove his legal ownership of the property. This is normally done by showing the buyer documentary evidence of the seller's ownership, the precise nature of which varies depending on whether the property is freehold or leasehold, registered or unregistered. The following sub-paragraphs deal only with freehold land. The relevant leasehold provisions are dealt with in **Chapters 35** and **36**.

15.7.3.1   Registered freehold transaction

Standard Condition 4.1 (SCPC 6.1) provides that the seller is to provide the buyer with official copies of the register and any title plan referred to in it, and of any document referred to in the register and kept by the Registrar, except if it is to be overridden or discharged on or before completion. This exception would thus obviate the need for the seller to provide a copy of any mortgage which was going to be paid off on completion.

15.7.3.2   Unregistered freehold title

Where the sale comprises an unregistered freehold interest, s 44 of the LPA 1925 (as amended) contains the relevant open contract principles. This section provides that the seller must show a good root of title which at the date of the contract is at least 15 years old, and all subsequent dealings from that instrument to the present day. This provision is universally regarded as being satisfactory and is rarely departed from. See **13.5.2** for the definition of a good root.

The forms of agreement incorporating both sets of Standard Conditions require the seller to insert on the front page what the root of title document will be. It is possible to contract out of the open contract implications, so that, for example, a root could be specified which did not fulfil the open contract definition of a root, or was not at least 15 years old. However, the buyer would almost certainly not accept anything less than the open contract position, and the root document specified should comply with the open contract rules.

A seller will normally, therefore, look for and insert on the front of the contract a conveyance or mortgage which satisfies the open contract requirements.

Only in extremely unusual circumstances will the seller not be able to comply with the requirements of s 44, and a clause which offers a root which is less than the minimum 15 years in length would be regarded with suspicion by the buyer.

15.7.3.3   Proving title by adverse possession

A seller can establish that he has a good right to sell by proving 12 years' adverse possession under the Limitation Act 1980. However, under an open contract, he has to establish not only that he has (together with his predecessors in title, if necessary) been in possession for at least 12 years, but also that the possession has extinguished the title of the true owner. Twelve years' possession on its own might not do this if, for example, the land is subject to a long lease. Twelve years' possession will extinguish the title of the leaseholder, but time will not begin to run against the freeholder until the end of the lease. So it will be necessary to deduce the title of the original owner to the buyer to show that this has been extinguished by the adverse possession. If the original owner's title is registered, this would be possible as the register is open to public inspection, but it is most unlikely to be possible if the land is unregistered. In such a case, therefore, it will be necessary for a special condition to be inserted in the contract setting out how the seller intends to prove his title. This will normally be in the form of statutory declarations by the seller and others, declaring that the seller (and his predecessors if that is the case) have been in sole undisputed possession for the number of years that they claim to have been in possession. The buyer will then be required by the condition to accept this as proof of title and not to raise any objections or requisitions. It is then for the buyer to consider the proof offered and decide, prior to exchange, whether or not to accept the risk. Once contracts have been exchanged, the buyer will then not be able to object to the title offered.

Note also that the LRA 2002 contains provisions which make it unwise in most circumstances for a buyer to accept title to registered land based on adverse possession (see **4.11**).

15.7.4   Covenants for title

By including 'key words' in the purchase deed it is possible to give the buyer the benefit of certain implied covenants under the Law of Property (Miscellaneous Provisions) Act 1994. It is usual to specify in the contract which (if any) of the implied covenants the seller is prepared to give. The inclusion of the statement 'the seller sells with full title guarantee' (or its Welsh equivalent) will give the buyer the benefit of the full range of covenants implied by the 1994 Act (see 'Full title guarantee' at **15.7.4.1**). A more limited set of covenants is implied if the seller uses the expression 'the seller sells with limited title guarantee' (or the equivalent Welsh expression) (see 'Limited title guarantee' at **15.7.4.1**). Where the contract is silent and makes no reference to title guarantee, both sets of Standard Conditions provide that the seller will sell with full title guarantee (SC 4.6.2 and SCPC 6.6.2). Note that the implied covenants for title are implied into the purchase deed and not the contract. The sole purpose of putting the provision into the contract is to tell the buyer what covenants will be included in the purchase deed when that is executed.

15.7.4.1 Details of the covenants

In the following paragraphs:

'disposition'   includes a transfer of land for value, a gift of land, and the grant of a lease;

'seller'   includes a person who sells, gives away, or grants a lease of land;

'buyer'   includes a person who buys for value, a donee, or a person who is granted a lease.

Full title guarantee

Disposition of freehold land

The following covenants are implied into the disposition:

(a)   (i)   A covenant that the seller has the right to dispose of the land as he purports to. This amounts to a promise that he *can* do what the disposition says he *does* do (eg, transfer ownership or grant a leasehold term).

(ii)   A covenant that he will do all he reasonably can to transfer the title he purports to give. This amounts to a promise that if title is not successfully given to the buyer, the seller will, at his own expense, give reasonable assistance to perfect the buyer's title. This includes assisting the buyer in an application for registration of title under the LRA 1925.

(b)   A covenant that the land is disposed of free from incumbrances, other than those the seller does not know about and could not reasonably know about.

Disposition of leasehold land

If the land disposed of is leasehold land, a third covenant is implied:

(c)   That the lease is subsisting at the time it is disposed of, and that there is no breach of covenant making the lease liable to forfeiture.

Limited title guarantee

Disposition of freehold land

If the seller is expressed to dispose of land 'with limited title guarantee', the following covenants are implied:

(a)   (i)   That the seller has the right to dispose of the land as he purports to (see above).

(ii)   That the seller will do all that he reasonably can to transfer the title he purports to give (see above).

(b)   That the seller has not himself incumbered the land, and also that the seller is not aware that anyone else has done so since the last disposition for value. This means, for example, that if a donee of land later disposes of it with limited title guarantee, the donee covenants that *he* has not incumbered the land, and he also covenants that he is not aware of the donor having incumbered the land.

Disposition of leasehold land

(c)   A third covenant is added, that the lease is subsisting at the time it is disposed of and that there is no breach of covenant making the lease liable to forfeiture.

Note:

(a)   The seller is not in breach of the implied covenants in respect of any matters:

(i)   to which the disposition is expressly made subject (s 6). This means that if the land is expressly conveyed 'subject to a restrictive covenant contained in a deed dated 1 January 1950 between AB(1) and CD(2)', the seller cannot be sued under the covenants for title in respect of that incumbrance; or

(ii)   that the buyer knows about at the time of the disposition (s 6). This means that a buyer of registered title could not sue the seller in respect of an overriding interest, if the buyer knew at the time of the transfer that the overriding interest existed.

(b)   The seller can modify the effect of any of the covenants by a clause in the disposition (s 8).

15.7.4.2   Drafting the agreement for sale

When drafting the agreement on behalf of the seller, it must be decided whether the seller will promise to dispose of the land with 'full title guarantee' or with 'limited title guarantee', or refuse to give any title guarantee at all.

If the seller promises, for example, a 'full title guarantee', that phrase will appear in the subsequent transfer, ie 'the Seller transfers to the Buyer with full title guarantee ...'. The inclusion of the phrase in the transfer will imply the covenants for title into the transfer. Which kind of title guarantee is chosen will depend upon the circumstances of the seller and the state of his title to the land.

15.7.4.3   Title guarantee

Remember that the seller makes certain promises in the agreement about his title, ie:

(a)   the implied promise that he has a good title to the land; and

(b)   the express promise, by virtue of SC 3 (SCPC 3), that he is selling free from incumbrances other than, for example, those mentioned in the agreement and those that the seller does not know about.

He also states what, if any, guarantee of title he will give in the transfer.

The seller's title will be investigated before the agreement is drafted. If the client has, and can prove, a good title, the implied contractual promise that the seller has good title does not need to be amended. Equally, the seller has no reason to refuse to promise a full guarantee, as the covenants implied into the transfer by the 1994 Act will be no wider than the promises about title the seller gives in the agreement.

On the other hand, if the client has no title to the land, or a questionable title (eg, title might be based on adverse possession under the Limitation Acts), a special condition will be inserted in the agreement to negative the implied promise that the seller has a good title. Equally, the seller will not want to give any title guarantee in the transfer. So the contract should make it clear on the front page that no title guarantee is to be given.

15.7.4.4 Sale by trustees holding on trust for people other than themselves

When drafting the agreement for sale on behalf of the trustees, it must be decided whether or not they should give any title guarantee. If there is satisfactory evidence of title, the trustees should be able to give a guarantee to the buyer. In other words, they should not refuse to give a guarantee simply because they are trustees and not absolute owners. However, they may prefer to give a limited title guarantee. If they give a full title guarantee, they will be promising that there are no incumbrances. If they give a limited title guarantee, they will promise only that they did not create any incumbrances, and that they are not aware of any previous trustees or the settlor having done so.

15.7.4.5 Sale by a personal representative

Whether or not a personal representative is prepared to give a guarantee of title will depend on his knowledge, and the evidence that he has, of the title. A personal representative is likely to give a limited guarantee rather than a full title guarantee.

If he gives a limited title guarantee, he will be promising that he has not created any incumbrances, and that he is not aware that the deceased created any.

15.7.4.6 Gifts and assents

If a donor makes a deed of gift, or a personal representative assents with a title guarantee, the covenants can be implied. It is not usual, however, for title guarantee to be given in a gift.

15.7.4.7 Mortgages

If a borrower mortgages with a title guarantee, the covenants for title will be implied. When acting for the lender, the lender's instructions must be checked to see if the lender requires a full title guarantee in the mortgage, or is willing to accept a limited title guarantee. Usually, full guarantee is required.

15.7.4.8 Sales by mortgagees

When a lender sells under his power of sale, there seems no reason why limited guarantee cannot be given; however, in practice, it is common for no title guarantee to be given.

15.7.4.9 Assignment of a lease

If the seller assigns the lease with either full or limited title guarantee, he promises that there is no breach of a tenant's covenant, and that there is nothing that would make the lease liable for forfeiture. Standard Condition 3.2.2 (SCPC 3.2.2), however, says that the lease is sold subject to any breach of a tenant's covenant relating to the physical state of the property which renders the lease liable to forfeiture.

An express clause should be added to the transfer of the lease to give effect to SC 3.2.2 (SCPC 3.2.2); see **36.6.3**.

15.7.4.10   Grant of a lease

If a landlord grants a lease with full or limited title guarantee, the covenants for title will be implied into the lease. A tenant who is taking a long-term residential lease and paying a substantial premium is likely to ask for a guarantee to be given. Title guarantee is not usual in a short-term lease.

15.7.4.11   Commercial property

On a sale by a large company, where knowledge of matters affecting the property may be scattered amongst many staff in many different departments, it may be wisest for the seller to give only limited title guarantee. In the case of a small company (eg, a 'one person' company), there seems no reason why full title guarantee should not be given in the usual way. In practice, however, even large companies will normally give full title guarantee.

15.7.5   Vacant possession

Under the open contract rules, vacant possession of the property is to be given on completion. This provision is reflected in both sets of Standard Conditions of Sale, where a special condition on the back page of the contract form provides: 'The property is sold with vacant possession on completion'. An alternative version of this condition is also printed on the form and the inapplicable version should be deleted ('The property is sold subject to the following leases or tenancies'). Copies of any leases or tenancy agreements should be supplied to the buyer with the draft contract so that he can see the terms of those agreements.

Schedule 4 to the Family Law Act 1996 implies a term that the seller will secure the cancellation of any rights of occupation enjoyed by a spouse and will give vacant possession on completion. This section needs to be borne in mind in situations where legal title to the property is held by a sole married owner.

15.7.6   Date and time for completion

Instructions will have been obtained from the client as to his desired date for completion, but it is not usually possible at this stage of the transaction to insert a definite date for completion in the contract. The actual date for completion agreed between the parties will be inserted in the contract on exchange of contracts, in the space provided for this information on the front page of the contract form. Until that time, this space is left blank. Many factors, including the progress of the client's related purchase transaction, affect the timing of completion and, at the stage when the contract is drafted, it is too early to make a positive decision on the actual date for completion.

If no completion date is inserted in the contract, SC 6.1.1 (SCPC 8.1.1) sets completion at 20 working days after the date of the contract. This provision is a variation on the unsatisfactory open contract provision which provides that completion shall take place within a reasonable time after exchange of contracts.

Standard Condition 6.1.1 (SCPC 8.1.1) also provides that time is not to be of the essence as regards the completion date except where a notice to complete has been served. Where time is not of the essence, a delay in completion beyond the contractual date will not automatically allow the party not in default to repudiate the contract. Although time can be made of the essence by varying this Condition by special condition, this is not usually desirable in a residential transaction and the condition should be left unamended. Problems relating to time being of the essence and to notices to complete are discussed in **Chapter 32**.

Both sets of Standard Conditions do not deal with the precise time on the day of completion by which the transfer must be completed. It is desirable, especially in chain transactions, for this matter to be dealt with by express special conditions in the contract, for example 'completion shall take place by 2 pm'. This is to ensure that there is sufficient time on the day of completion for the seller to use the funds to complete his dependent purchase. Standard Condition 6.1.2 (SCPC 8.1.2), which refers to the time of completion, relates only to the payment of compensation for late completion and does not impose a time limit on completion itself.

15.7.7 Compensation for delayed completion

The contract normally provides for compensation to be paid by one party to the other in the event of completion being delayed beyond the contractual date.

Standard Condition 7.3 (SCPC 9.3) contains provisions for the payment of compensation for late completion, and states that the amount of such payment shall be assessed at the 'contract rate' as defined. According to Condition 1.1.1(e) of both sets of Standard Conditions, the contract rate, unless altered by special condition, is: 'The Law Society's interest rate from time to time in force'. The Law Society's interest rate is published weekly in the *Law Society's Gazette* and is set at 4% above the base lending rate of Barclays Bank plc.

The object of inserting an interest rate is both to provide an incentive to complete on the due date and to provide monetary compensation to the innocent party for any financial losses caused by the delay in completion. In practice, in residential transactions an interest rate of between 3% and 5% above the base lending rate of a major bank is accepted as being normal. The Form of Agreement for both sets of Standard Conditions contains a space on the front page in which the contract rate can be inserted. If it is wished to rely on Condition 1.1.1(e), this can be left blank. However, it is often used to state expressly that The Law Society's interest rate is to be used. Alternatively, many solicitors will substitute a rate of their own choosing, usually linked to the base rate of their own bankers. Providing for a fixed interest rate (eg, 'the contract rate shall be 14% pa') is not normally considered to be desirable in case rates of interest change radically between the time when the contract is drafted and the time when the interest becomes payable. The seller is protected against such fluctuations in interest rates if the contract rate is set to float with a named bank's base rate.

15.7.8 Deposit

Although not required by law, it is customary for the buyer to pay a deposit of 10% of the purchase price on exchange of contracts. This acts both as part-payment of the price and as a guarantee of performance by the buyer, since he cannot usually afford to lose this amount of money. If the buyer subsequently defaulted on the contract, the seller would have the right to forfeit that deposit. Standard Condition 2.2 (SCPC 2.2) provides for payment of a 10% deposit to be held by the seller's solicitor in the capacity of stakeholder. A special condition relating to the deposit is needed only if it is desired to vary the capacity in which the deposit is to be held. The amount of the deposit is inserted in the space provided for this towards the bottom of the front page of the contract form. There is no need for a special condition to change the amount of the deposit.

Provisions relating to the deposit and the capacity in which it should be held are discussed fully in **Chapter 21**.

15.7.9 Indemnity covenants

If the seller entered into a covenant, whether positive or negative, he will remain liable on that covenant even after he has disposed of the land, unless the wording of the covenant makes it clear that he is not to be bound after he has sold. Where he remains bound, it means that if the buyer breaks the covenant, there is a risk of the seller being sued in respect of that breach. To protect himself, therefore, the seller needs to take an indemnity covenant from the buyer in the purchase deed. However, like other matters, the indemnity can be included in the purchase deed only if this is provided for in the contract. Standard Condition 4.6.4 (SCPC 6.6.4) makes satisfactory provision for such an indemnity. It is, however, considered to be good practice to deal expressly with indemnity by special condition in the contract in order to draw this matter specifically to the attention of the buyer. This can be done by including an express indemnity clause in similar wording to that contained in the Standard Conditions.

15.7.10 Fixtures and fittings

Fittings (eg, carpets and curtains) which are to be included in the sale must be specifically identified in the contract, either by special condition, or by making use of a printed special condition, which refers to the chattels which are itemised on a list attached to the contract. In Protocol cases, the Fixtures Fittings and Contents Form can be used for this purpose. Any separate consideration for the chattels must be expressly stated. Fixtures (items which are attached to the land, eg, the central heating system) automatically pass with the land unless a special condition is included giving the seller the right to remove them. Fixtures and fittings are dealt with in detail in **Chapter 10**.

15.8 Void conditions

Certain conditions are rendered void by statute if they are included in a contract for the sale of land. Some examples are given below.

15.8.1 Title made with the concurrence of beneficiaries

It is theoretically possible to conduct a sale of land held on trust by obtaining the consent to the sale of all the beneficiaries. The buyer cannot be required to accept such a situation and can insist that the sale is effected by a minimum of two trustees of the legal estate (LPA 1925, s 42).

15.8.2 Improperly stamped documents

If, unusually, in unregistered land, one or more of the documents which form part of the seller's title does not bear the correct amount of stamp duty, the seller is under an obligation to correct this at his own expense and cannot include a contractual condition requiring the buyer to bear the cost of putting this defect right (Stamp Act 1891, s 117). The checking of stamp duties is discussed at **14.6.5**.

15.8.3 Restricting buyer's choice of solicitor

Any provision which seeks to restrict the buyer's choice of solicitor is rendered void by s 48 of the LPA 1925. Such a provision would also offend against the Solicitors' Code of Conduct.

15.9   Contract races

From time to time a seller will ask his solicitor to deal with more than one buyer at the same time. This practice, known as a 'contract race', is strictly controlled by r 10.06 of the Solicitors' Code of Conduct and is discussed at **5.5**.

15.10   Auctions

Ordinary residential property is not usually sold at auction, except in the case of mortgage repossessions. Investment property, property which is unique or difficult to value, and agricultural land may, however, be sold by auction rather than privately or through an estate agent. An auction contract is usually prepared by the seller's solicitor in collaboration with the auctioneer. The latter will prepare the particulars of sale, while the solicitor will draft the conditions of sale. The conditions will usually make reference to the incorporation of a standard set of contractual conditions such as the Standard Conditions. Standard Condition 2.3 (SCPC 2.3) contains provisions which are needed in order to comply with the Sale of Land by Auction Act 1867.

15.11   Contract drafting: a worked example

Drafting any document is a skill that develops and improves over time. One good idea is to build up a 'precedent bank' made up of documents commonly encountered in practice with guidance on how they should be completed. In this section these are examples of the front and rear pages of both the Standard Conditions of Sale (4th edn) and the Standard Commercial Property Conditions (2nd edn), demonstrating an approach that could be adopted in this regard and showing the fundamental points to cover in each. Transaction-specific amendments have not been included. Some firms or practitioners make 'standard' amendments to the SCS and SCPC but, for reasons of space, these are not considered in these examples.

Having considered the example template or precedent documents, you might like to return to the specimen attendance note at **7.6** and the official copies at **4.7**, and attempt to draft the contract for the sale of 47 Queens' Road. At the end of this chapter is a worked example of how this contract would look and you may like to compare your attempt with this suggestion. Note that the example concerns a registered title but that the precedents shown below also contain examples of the wording you should use if the title were unregistered.

15.11.1   Standard Conditions of Sale: front page

CONTRACT
Incorporating the Standard Conditions of Sale (Fourth Edition)

Date :

Seller : Insert full name and address of (each) seller(s)

Buyer : Insert full name and address of (each) buyer(s)

Property (freehold/leasehold :
1. Delete leasehold or freehold on left as appropriate
2. Insert existing description of property taken from official copies (reg land) or title deeds (unreg land) (if boundary unclear or sale of part refer to plan which should then be affixed to the contract)

Title number/root of title :
1. Delete title number/root of title on left as appropriate
2. (Reg land) Insert title number and class of title; or
3. (Unreg'd) Insert root by document, date & parties eg "The Conveyance dated [ ] made between (1) [Seller] & (2) [Buyer]"

Specified incumbrances :
(1) List all incumbrances that will bind the buyer (exclude mortgages to be redeemed on sale)
(2) (Reg land) Identity by incumbrance + register + entry eg "The [easements] referred to in entry number [4] of the [Charges] Register"
(3) (Unreg) Identify by incumbrance and document eg "The [covenants] referred to in a conveyance dated [ ] between [ ] & [ ]"

Title guarantee (full/limited) : Full or limited

Completion date :

Contract rate : Insert specific contract rate or leave blank and rely on SC 1.1.1(e)

Purchase price : Insert purchase price <u>for land only</u>

Deposit : 10% of <u>purchase price PLUS chattels</u> or as agreed (if different)

Chattels price (if separate) : Insert agreed price for chattels

Balance : Purchase price + chattels price - deposit = balance

The seller will sell and the buyer will buy the property for the purchase price.

WARNING	Signed
This is a formal document, designed to create legal rights and legal obligations. Take advice before using it.	Seller/Buyer

15.11.2   Standard Conditions of Sale: rear page

SPECIAL CONDITIONS

1. (a) This contract incorporates the Standard Conditions of Sale (Fourth Edition).

   (b) The terms used in this contract have the same meaning when used in the Conditions.

2. Subject to the terms of this contract and to the Standard Conditions of Sale, the seller is to transfer the property with either full title guarantee or limited title guarantee, as specified on the front page.

3. The chattels which are on the property and are set out on any attached list are included in the sale and the buyer is to pay the chattels price for them.

4. The property is sold with vacant possession.

(or) 4. The property is sold subject to the following leases or tenancies.

   Spec Cond 3 - Add list if chattels to be sold.

   Spec Cond 4 - Delete second alternative where selling with vacant possession. If selling subject to leases, delete first and list leases here.

Seller's conveyancers*:

Buyer's conveyancers*:

* Adding an e-mail address authorises service by e-mail: see condition 1.3.3(b)

15.11.3 Standard Commercial Property Conditions: front page

CONTRACT
Incorporating the Standard Commercial Property Conditions (Second Edition)

Date	:	
Seller	:	Insert full name and address of (each) seller(s)
Buyer	:	Insert full name and address of (each) buyer(s)
Property (freehold/leasehold	:	1. Delete leasehold or freehold on left as appropriate 2. Insert existing description of property taken from official copies (reg land) or title deeds (unreg land) (if boundary unclear or sale of part refer to plan which should then be affixed to the contract)
Title number/root of title	:	1. Delete title number/root of title on left as appropriate 2. (Reg land) Insert title number and class of title; or 3.(Unreg'd) Insert root by document, date & parties eg "The Conveyance dated [ ] made between (1) [Seller] & (2) [Buyer]"
Specified incumbrances	:	(1) List all incumbrances that will bind the buyer (exclude mortgages to be redeemed on sale) (2) (Reg land) Identity by incumbrance + register + entry eg "The [easements] referred to in entry [4] of the [Charges] Register" (3)(Unreg) Identify by incumbrance and document eg "The [covenants] referred to in a conveyance dated [ ] between (1) [ ] & (2) [ ]"
Completion date	:	
Contract rate	:	Insert specific contract rate or leave blank and rely on SC 1.1.1(e)
Purchase price	:	Insert purchase price for land and chattels
Deposit	:	10% of purchase price for land and chattels or as agreed (if different)

The seller will sell and the buyer will buy:

(a) the property, and

(b) any chattels which, under the special conditions, are

included in the sale

for the purchase price.

WARNING	Signed
This is a formal document, designed to create legal rights and legal obligations. Take advice before using it.	Seller/Buyer

15.11.4 Standard Commercial Property Conditions: rear page

SPECIAL CONDITIONS

---

1. This contract incorporates the Standard Commercial Property Conditions (Second Edition).

2. The property is sold with vacant possession.

(or) 2. The property is sold subject to the leases or tenancies set out on the attached list but otherwise with vacant possession on completion.

3. The chattels at the Property and set out on the attached list are included in the sale. [The amount of the purchase price apportioned to those chattels is £   ].

4. The conditions in Part 2 shown against the boxes ticked below are included in the contract:

☐ Condition A1 (VAT: standard rate)

[or] ☐ Condition A2 (VAT: transfer of a going concern)

☐ Condition B (capital allowances). The amount of the purchase price apportioned to plant and machinery at the property for the purposes of the Capital Allowances Act 2001 is £

☐ Condition C1 (flats: no tenants' rights of first refusal)

[or] ☐ Condition C2 (flats: with tenants' rights of first refusal)

Special Condition 2- Delete second alternative if selling with vacant possession. If selling subject to leases, delete first and list leases here.

Special Condition 3 - Add list if chattels to be sold and insert price apportioned to them.

Special Condition 4

Box 1 - Leave blank if not VATable transaction. Tick if VATable (standard rated or Seller to elect before completion)

[Boxes 2-5 are additional boxes dealing with other matters relating to transfers of going concerns, capital allowances and tenant's rights of first refusal under the Landlord and Tenant Act 1987. These are specialist issues and are outside the scope of this example]

Seller's conveyancers*:

Buyer's conveyancers*:

---

* Adding an e-mail address authorises service by e-mail: see condition 1.3.3(b)

15.11.5   Worked example of the contract

CONTRACT
Incorporating the Standard Conditions of Sale (Fourth Edition)

Date

Seller	:	ROGER EVANS of 47, Queens' Road, Loamster, Maradon, Cornshire, CS1 5TY
Buyer	:	CATHERINE READE and JOANNE READE both of 24, Leeming Road, Bridgeton, Cornshire, CS3 4DD
Property (freehold/~~leasehold~~)	:	47, Queens' Road, Loamster, Maradon, Cornshire CS1 5TY
Title number ~~XXXXXXXXX~~	:	LM 12037 (Absolute Title)
Specified incumbrances	:	The covenants referred to in entry No. 1 of the Charges Register
Title guarantee (full/limited)	:	Full
Completion date	:	
Contract rate	:	The Law Society's Interest rate from time to time
Purchase price	:	£350,000
Deposit	:	£20,000
Chattels price (if separate)	:	£500
Balance	:	£330,500

The seller will sell and the buyer will buy the property for the purchase price.

WARNING	Signed
This is a formal document, designed to create legal rights and legal obligations. Take advice before using it.	Seller/Buyer

SPECIAL CONDITIONS

1. (a) This contract incorporates the Standard Conditions of Sale (Fourth Edition).

    (b) The terms used in this contract have the same meaning when used in the Conditions.

2. Subject to the terms of this contract and to the Standard Conditions of Sale, the seller is to transfer the property with either full title guarantee or limited title guarantee, as specified on the front page.

3. The chattels which are on the property and are set out on any attached list are included in the sale and the buyer is to pay the chattels price for them.[1]

4. The property is sold with vacant possession.

(or) 4. ~~The property is sold subject to the following leases or tenancies.~~

Seller's conveyancers*:   *Buck & Co*

Buyer's conveyancers*:   *SLT Solicitors*

* Adding an e-mail address authorises service by e-mail: see condition 1.3.3(b)

[1] *Author's note*: Not attached for the purposes of this example.

The following comments may be made on the worked example of the contract.

15.11.5.1   Date

The contract is left undated at the draft stage. The date is inserted on actual exchange of contracts.

15.11.5.2   Parties

The full names and addresses of the parties, as they will later appear on the purchase deed, should be inserted. The seller's solicitor may not at this stage know the full names of the buyer and, if necessary, this information can be supplied later by the buyer's solicitor. Note the inclusion of postcodes in the parties' addresses.

15.11.5.3   Property

The property is freehold, so the word 'leasehold' can be deleted. Since the property is registered with an absolute title and is a suburban property with well-defined boundaries, it will suffice to describe it merely by its postal address. This constitutes the 'particulars' of the contract. No plan is needed in this case. Note the inclusion of the postcode in the description of the property; it is Land Registry practice to include this on the register.

15.11.5.4   Title

The property is registered, therefore the reference to 'Root of title' is irrelevant and can be deleted. The title number and confirmation that the class of title is absolute should be inserted here.

15.11.5.5   Incumbrances

As the mortgage is to be discharged on completion, this need not be mentioned. The restrictive covenants must be stated to comply with SC 3. There is no need, however, to set out the covenants verbatim as long as a copy is provided; in this case as it is registered land, official copy entries will be supplied in any event.

15.11.5.6   Title guarantee

The seller is a sole owner and will give full title guarantee. It is customary to insert this on the front page of the contract form, even though in this case the words inserted repeat SC 4.6.2.

15.11.5.7   Completion date

The completion date is left blank at this stage and inserted on actual exchange.

15.11.5.8   Contract rate

Even though it is not intended to vary SC 1.1.1(e), confirmation of that fact is included on the front page of the contract form. Unless there are special circumstances, the solicitor would normally decide on the rate of interest to be included in the contract and this is not a matter on which the client's instructions are sought.

15.11.5.9   Price

The price, amount of deposit, amount (if any) payable for chattels (fittings) and balance due on completion are inserted in the appropriate space towards the bottom of the front page of the contract form. Note that the deposit is calculated as being 10% of the price for the property plus the price payable for the chattels. This is in order to comply with SC 2.2.1. However, here the instructions at **7.6** indicate that a deposit of £20,000 has been agreed.

15.11.5.10 Agreement for sale

The words 'The seller will sell and the buyer will buy the property for the purchase price' above the two boxes at the bottom of the front page of the contract form constitute the agreement for sale. A box is provided for the seller/buyer to sign. This is left blank at this stage and will be signed by the client close to exchange.

15.11.5.11 Printed Special Condition 1

Printed Special Condition 1 incorporates the text of the Standard Conditions of Sale (4th edition) from the centre pages of the contract form. These pages are not reproduced in this example. This Condition should not be deleted, since to remove it is to remove the effect of the Standard Conditions.

15.11.5.12 Printed Special Condition 2

This Condition refers to the implied covenants which are given to the buyer under the Law of Property (Miscellaneous Provisions) Act 1994. In this case, the seller is selling with full title guarantee and this fact is included on the front page of the contract form.

15.11.5.13 Printed Special Condition 3

This is necessary to ensure the chattels are included in the sale. A list of the relevant items needs to be attached.

15.11.5.14 Printed Special Condition 4

This Condition provides two alternatives, depending whether the property is to be sold with vacant possession (as here) or is subject to tenancies. In the latter case the details of the tenancies would be given in the condition.

15.11.5.15 Conveyancers

The names (and if desired the addresses and references) of the parties' conveyancers are inserted at the foot of the back page of the contract form.

15.12 Action after drafting the contract

Two copies of the draft contract should be prepared and both are sent to the buyer's solicitor with the remainder of the pre-contract package. A further copy of the contract should be retained by the seller's solicitor so that he has a copy in his file and can deal with any amendments proposed by the buyer.

Consideration of the contract by the buyer is discussed in **Chapter 19.**

Chapter 16

Conditional Contracts and Options

16.1 Use of conditional contracts

Conditional contracts are generally not desirable since they leave an element of doubt as to the existence and validity of the contractual obligations between the parties.

Most of the situations in which conditional contracts are used benefit the buyer more than the seller (eg, 'subject to planning permission'), and the seller should refrain from entering a conditional contract if at all possible.

Conditional contracts carry with them some risks and uncertainties which make them inappropriate for everyday use, but they may be considered for use in the following circumstances:

(a)   where the buyer has not had the opportunity before exchange of contracts to make searches and enquiries, or to conduct a survey, or where his mortgage arrangements have not been finalised;

(b)   where the contract is dependent on planning permission being obtained for the property;

(c)   where the sale is dependent on permission being obtained from a third party (eg, landlord's consent).

16.1.1 Chain transactions

Conditional contracts should never be used where one or both of the parties has an unconditional sale or purchase contract which is dependent on the conditional contract. In this situation, if the conditional contract was rescinded for non-fulfilment of the condition, this would give rise to great difficulties in the fulfilment of the linked unconditional contract and could result in a breach of that contract.

16.1.2 Alternative solutions

Before agreeing to enter a conditional contract, the seller should consider whether there are any alternative solutions which could be used in preference to the conditional contract. For example, it may be preferable to delay exchange until the matter which was the subject of the condition has been resolved. An alternative solution may be to grant the buyer an option to purchase the property to be exercised within a stated period (see **16.5**).

16.2   Requirements for a valid conditional contract

16.2.1   Certainty

The terms of the condition must be clear and certain. In *Lee-Parker v Izzett (No 2)* [1972] 2 All ER 800, an agreement to sell a freehold house 'subject to the buyer obtaining a satisfactory mortgage' was held to be void because the word 'satisfactory' was too vague and there was, therefore, no certainty regarding the circumstances in which the buyer would validly be able to withdraw from the contract. Not all 'subject to mortgage' clauses will suffer the same fate. Provided that the condition is drafted to make it clear that 'satisfactory' mortgage offer means an offer satisfactory to the buyer acting as a reasonable person, then the condition is likely to be valid. There is now an objective standard by which any mortgage offer received can be judged.

The need for certainty must also be borne in mind with regard to other common conditions. So, a contract subject to 'satisfactory searches' will again need a reasonableness provision inserting to prevent its being void. See **16.4.1** as to drafting contracts 'subject to planning permission.

If the condition is void for uncertainty then the whole contract between the parties will also fail.

16.2.2   Time for performance

It was held in *Aberfoyle Plantations Ltd v Cheng* [1960] AC 115, that the time for performance of the condition is of the essence and cannot be extended either by agreement between the parties or by the court. The same case also laid down the rules relating to the time for performance of the condition, which are summarised as follows:

(a)   Where the contract contains a completion date, the condition must be fulfilled by that date, irrespective of whether time was of the essence of the contractual completion date.

(b)   If a time is stated for the fulfilment of the condition, that time limit must be complied with or the contract will fail.

(c)   If no time limit is specified the condition must be fulfilled within a reasonable time. This provision is clearly unsatisfactory since it leaves room for argument about what is a reasonable time, and so a time limit should always be stated.

16.3   Withdrawal from the contract

Only the party with the benefit of the condition may withdraw from the contract, and only for reasons connected with the condition. No other reason will justify withdrawal, although there is no obligation on the resiling party to prove that he is being reasonable in exercising his rights to withdraw.

It is a question of construction of the condition itself as to whether a party may withdraw before performance of the condition (see, eg, *Tesco Stores Ltd v William Gibson and Co Ltd* (1970) 214 EG 835).

16.4   Drafting

The drafting of a condition requires extreme care to ensure that the requirements outlined in **16.2** have been satisfied. No such provision is included in either set of

Standard Conditions, although a contract to assign a lease may be conditional on the landlord's consent being obtained under SC 8.3 (SCPC 10.3).

The following guidelines should be borne in mind:

(a) Consider the precise event(s) on which the contract is to be made conditional.

(b) By what time must the condition be fulfilled? (The specified time limit cannot be extended.)

(c) Consider the precise terms on which the party with the benefit of the condition will be able to rescind.

(d) Make sure that there are no loopholes which would enable one party to escape from the contract other than for the non-fulfilment of the event(s) contemplated in (a) above.

(e) Use an established precedent, adapting it to fit the exact requirements of the client's circumstances.

16.4.1 'Subject to planning permission'

Where a contract is to be made 'subject to the buyer obtaining planning permission', the following matters should be dealt with in the drafting of the condition:

(a) the form of the application to be agreed by both parties;

(b) if conditions are attached to the consent, the type of conditions that would entitle the buyer to rescind;

(c) who should pay the fee for the application;

(d) whether the buyer can rescind if the local planning authority does not grant permission within a stated period;

(e) the seller should agree not to oppose the buyer's application;

(f) whether the application is to be for detailed or outline consent;

(g) whether the buyer is entitled to rescind if the planning application is never submitted.

16.5 Options

16.5.1 What is an option?

An option is a right given to a prospective buyer which allows him to insist on the seller selling the land to him if the buyer wishes to buy within a specified period. There is no obligation on the buyer to buy, but if he does choose to do so, the seller is obliged to sell. Options are common in commercial transactions, but less so in residential transactions.

16.5.2 Duration

The option agreement will state the time limit within which it must be exercised if the seller is to be obliged to sell. The maximum permitted period is 21 years under the Perpetuities and Accumulations Act 1964, but shorter periods (eg, 12 months) are much more common.

16.5.3 Formalities

An option must comply with the normal requirements for a valid contract – offer, acceptance, consideration, etc. Although the consideration can be a nominal amount (and can be dispensed with altogether if the option is granted by deed), it is common to find that the seller will require a not insubstantial amount to commit himself in this way. The option will also have to provide how the actual sale price of the land is to be arrived at if the buyer exercises the option. If the option is exercisable only for a short period, a fixed price can be specified in the option. In an option exercisable over a period longer than (say) 12 months, the effects of inflation, etc, must be considered and a new price will have to be arrived at. In such a case, the requirements of certainty must be considered, so some formula will need laying down so that the price can be ascertained if the parties are unable to reach agreement. An appointment of a valuer whose decision is final is common. The buyer may wish the consideration for the option itself to be set off against the purchase price; this will need stating expressly.

In addition to the normal contractual rules, as this is a land contract, the provisions of s 2 of the Law of Property (Miscellaneous Provisions) Act 1989 will also need to be taken into account. This requires that the contract is in writing, must incorporate all the agreed terms and be signed by both parties. When the option is exercised, the contract to buy the land comes into existence at that moment. The exercise of the option does not need the signature of both parties.

As the contract for sale comes into existence on the exercise of the option, the terms of that sale contract need considering in the usual way and will need providing for in the option contract. Otherwise, an open contract will be created, which will be unsatisfactory for both buyer and seller. So the option agreement should state that the sale contract will be subject to (for example) the Standard Conditions of Sale, how title will be deduced, what incumbrances the land will be sold subject to, what special conditions will apply, etc, in the same way as if the seller were drafting an ordinary sale contract. The buyer will also need to consider these as he would any other contract.

16.5.4 Protection of the option

In order to make the option binding on a subsequent buyer of the land, it should be protected by registration. This will be a C(iv) in unregistered land and a notice in registered land.

Chapter 17

Town and Country Planning, Building Regulations and Related Matters

17.1 Town and country planning

17.1.1 Outline of the planning system

The planning system exists to ensure that development of land is carried out in a planned and appropriate fashion. Responsibility for town and country planning vests in the local planning authority ('LPA'), usually the district, unitary or London borough council for that area. The LPA is responsible, amongst other things, for the grant or refusal of planning permission and taking enforcement action in respect of breaches of planning control.

In carrying out many of these functions, the LPA will be guided by a variety of central and local government policies. This will include the 'development plan' for the area. The development plan is usually made up of two documents, the 'structure plan' (normally prepared by the county planning authority and which details the broad, strategic development policy for the regional area) and the 'local' plan' (prepared by the district planning authority and which contains more detailed policies for the specific area of that district). In the case of unitary authorities, the structure plan and development plan elements are combined into a single document called the 'unitary development plan'. In addition to the development plan, the central government department responsible for planning control, the Department for Communities and Local Government ('DCLG'), also publishes important policy guidance (in a variety of forms) to which the LPA will need to have regard.

17.1.2 Legislation

The principal legislation is the Town and Country Planning Act 1990 ('TCPA 1990'), as amended. Much of the detail of the system, however, is to be found under various statutory instruments brought into force under this Act. The Planning and Compulsory Purchase Act 2004, which seeks to make the planning system speedier and more predictable, will additionally bring in a variety of changes to the planning system over the coming years.

This chapter draws attention to the principles of planning law only in so far as it affects the normal conveyancing transaction and is not a comprehensive guide to the topic.

17.1.3   Relevance of planning to the transaction

Planning is being dealt with in this book at this point as it is at this stage (particularly when carrying out searches and enquiries) that planning and related issues are most often revealed. As an example, various planning matters are raised as questions on the local search (LLC1) and the standard form of enquiries of a local authority (CON29). Planning issues can also be revealed by the seller's replies to enquiries. An understanding of the principles of planning and related issues is therefore required for the correct interpretation of the answers given to these enquries.

Planning law affects whether a building can be built, altered or extended, and also specifies the particular use to which a property can be put. It is, therefore, important for a buyer to be satisfied that the building which he is buying has permission to be on the site where it has been built, and also that it is being used for its authorised purpose. Heavy fines can be imposed for breach of planning control and, since planning matters (both permission granted and breaches committed) usually run with the land, action for any breach which is outstanding at completion could be brought against the buyer after completion, even though the breach was committed by a predecessor in title.

In addition, it may be the case that the buyer himself intends to carry out works to, or change the use of, the property after he has bought it. Such activity may require planning permission and the buyer's solicitor needs to advise his client on this before exchange of contracts. If planning permission is indeed needed, consideration needs to be given either to ensuring that planning permission is obtained before exchange or to making the contract conditional upon obtaining that permission.

17.1.4   When is planning permission neded?

17.1.4.1   Planning permission required for the carrying out of 'development'

In basic terms, planning permission is needed in respect of any activity which constitutes 'development'. 'Development' is defined in s 55 of the TCPA 1990 as follows:

> the carrying out of building, engineering, mining or other operations in, on, over or under land, or the making of any material change in the use of any buildings or other land.

This definition includes the erection of new buildings, the demolition of and alteration to existing buildings and/or the making of a material change of use to a property. Note that provided any one of these elements is present, the possibility of the need for planning permission needs to be considered. It is possible for there to be building works but not a change of use and, equally, for there to be a change of use without building works: in both cases, the proposals may amount to development and so require planning permission. As regards change of use, only a *material* change in use requires permission. 'Material' is not defined and is a question of fact and degree in each particular case.

17.1.4.2   Matters which do not constitute 'development'

Certain matters which would otherwise fall within the definition of development (and so require planning permission) are specifically excluded from that definition by the TCPA 1990 and statutory instruments made under it. In a typical conveyancing transaction, the most commonly encountered situations where permission is not required either by the statute or by regulation are as follows:

(a)   Works for the maintenance, improvement or other alteration of a building which affect only the interior or do not materially affect the external appearance of a building.

(b)   The use of buildings or land within the curtilage of a dwelling house for any purpose incidental to the use of the dwelling house (eg, using an existing garage as a playroom). The 'curtilage' of a dwelling house is the land immediately surrounding the house and, except where the grounds are extensive, will normally encompass the whole of the garden area.

(c)   Change of use within the same use class as specified by the Town and Country Planning (Use Classes) Order 1987 (SI 1987/764) ('UCO'). The UCO contains lists of uses grouped together into 13 different use classes, each identified by a letter and a number (thus, A1, A2 and B1 are each separate use classes.). A change of use from one use within a given class to another within the same class will not require planning permission. As an example, a change of use from a newsagent to an ironmonger (both uses within use class A1) will not therefore require planning permission. A more detailed planning text book should be consulted for the specifics of the UCO, but the following are the use classes most commonly encountered in a typical conveyancing transaction:

- **A1**   Broadly, this covers use as a retail shop. It does not include, however, use for the sale of hot food except in the case of an internet cafe.

- **A2**   This covers use of premises for professional and financial services and other services which would be found in a shopping area.

- **A3**   This covers use for the sale of food or drink for consumption on the premises.

- **A4**   This covers use as a public house or wine bar.

- **A5**   This covers the sale of hot food for consumption off the premises (ie, hot food takeaways).

- **B1**   This covers offices other than those in A2 (eg, administrative offices of a business) and also light industrial use.

- **B2**   This covers other industrial uses.

- **B8**   This covers use as a storage or distribution centre.

(Please note that these are the use classes applicable in England; in Wales they are slightly different. Please also note that although the basics of the planning system are the same in England and Wales, since planning matters became the responsibility of the Welsh Assembly, some differences between the two countries have crept in.)

Whilst changing uses *within* a use class does not amount to development, a change of use *between* use classes is likely to amount to a material change of use and so will require permission. In addition, it should be noted that the TCPA 1990 expressly provides that changing a single dwelling house into two or more dwelling houses constitutes a material change of use and so is within the definition of development and will require consent.

17.1.4.3   Matters which do not require *express* planning permission

The Town and Country Planning (General Permitted Development) Order 1995 (SI 1995/418) ('GPDO') automatically grants planning permission to 'development' which falls within its scope without the need for an express application. This does not mean that planning permission is not needed: merely that there is no need to make an express application for it to the LPA. The GPDO contains a list of 33 different categories of development for which planning permission is granted in this way. The categories most commonly encountered in a typical conveyancing transaction are as follows:

(a)   *Development within the curtilage of a dwelling house*   This permits a variety of forms of development including the erection of extensions and porches to the dwelling house itself and the laying down of a hard surface such as a car port.

(b)   *Minor operations*   This permits a variety of minor operations including the erection of fences and gates and the painting of the exterior of a building.

(c)   *Changes of use*   This category permits a variety of changes of use based around the use classes set out in the UCO. It includes change from a use within Class A2 to a use within A1, B2 to B1, A3 to A1 and A3 to A2.

Care must be taken with the GPDO and, when advising a client where the GPDO is an issue, the following points should be considered before any advice can be considered to be complete. First, each category of development permitted by the GPDO has conditions attached to it within the GPDO itself (the GPDO sets out what development is permitted and then the conditions). These conditions must be strictly observed and, if they cannot be complied with, express permission for the development is needed. For example, volume and height restrictions apply to any extension to a dwelling house permitted under item (a) above. Equally, height and location restrictions apply to the erection of fences and gates under item (b) above. Secondly, the rights granted by the GPDO are suspended or varied in certain cases, such as in the case of land in an area of outstanding natural beauty. Finally, the LPA has power to restrict the GPDO in whole or in part in relation to its area. This is done by the LPA passing an order under art 4 of the GPDO known as an 'Article 4 Direction'. The existence of any Article 4 Direction can be discovered by making a local search (see **Chapter 18**).

In addition, as of 10 May 2006, LPAs have the power to issue 'local development orders'. These operate like permitted development under the GPDO and can be site specific or cover the whole or part of the LPA's area. There are limitations on the types of development that can be permitted under local development orders, and the LPA must also consult with interested bodies (such as English Nature and the Mayor of London in the case of a London Borough) as appropriate before the order can be confirmed.

17.1.5   Obtaining planning permission

17.1.5.1   General

If an express application for planning permission is required, this should be made to the relevant LPA on a form supplied by that authority. A fee is payable, which is calculated using regulations made under the TCPA 1990. It is not necessary for the applicant to be the owner of the freehold of the land over which permission is sought but, if the applicant is not the landowner, he is required to notify the owner of the application. Regulations made under the TCPA 1990 also impose requirements relating to the content of the application (from 10 August 2006 most applications will need to have a 'design and access statement') and also to consultation and publicity (such as the posting of notices on the site in question).

17.1.5.2 Full or outline?

In most cases, the application will be for full planning permission and will deal with all aspects of a given development proposal. However, where permission is required for the erection of a building, it is possible in the first instance to apply for 'outline' permission only. This will grant permission in principle for the development but require a further application to be made at a later stage for approval of the detailed plans. These detailed plans are known as 'reserved matters' and approval for them will need to be obtained before the development can proceed. The advantage of an outline permission is that an application is less expensive to prepare than for a full permission. Where land has development potential, an outline permission granted for development will often enhance the value of the land and where this is the case, a seller should consider obtaining such permission before attempting to sell it.

17.1.5.3 The LPA's decision

The LPA can refuse the application or grant planning permission which will usually be subject to detailed conditions. In making this decision (including considering what conditions to impose), the LPA must have regard to the development plan, central government advice and other planning-related factors specific to the proposal. Although the LPA can restrict a permission to a named individual, or limit it in time, most planning permissions are not so limited and can therefore be sold with the land.

The LPA must make its decision within certain time limits (depending on the nature of the development), and failure to do so gives the applicant the right to appeal.

17.1.5.4 Duration of planning permission

Once planning permission has been granted, development must be started within a certain time limit. This is usually dealt with expressly in the permission. An ordinary (ie, full) permission is now normally subject to a condition that development must be started within three years (and if the permission is silent on a time limit, this period will be implied by the TCPA 1990). An outline permission is usually subject to conditions that an application for approval of reserved matters must be made within three years and that development must be begun within two years of the approval of the reserved matters. Note that different time limits may apply to permissions granted before 24 August 2005 and care should be taken to check the time limits for such permissions.

Although there is a time limit within which the development must be *commenced*, there is no time limit within which it must be *completed*. However, if the development has not been completed within a reasonable time, the LPA has the power to issue a 'completion notice' specifying a time limit within which this must be done. If it is not, the planning consent is treated as being withdrawn.

17.1.6 Enforcement

17.1.6.1 Time limits

If there has been a breach of planning control, there are time limits within which the LPA must take enforcement action. Enforcement action in respect of building works and for changing the use of a building to use as a single dwelling house must be started within four years of the alleged breach. In all other cases, the time limit is 10 years.

17.1.6.2   The LPA's enforcement powers

The LPA has a wide variety of enforcement powers available to it, including:

(a)   *Enforcement notice*   The notice must state the matters alleged to constitute the breach, the steps required to remedy the breach and the time within which these must be taken. These might be, for example, the removal of buildings or the cessation of any activity on the property. A recipient can appeal against the service of an enforcement notice which is then suspended pending the outcome of the appeal.

(b)   *Stop notice*   This can be only be served in conjunction with an enforcement notice and will stop the activity stated in it pending the outcome of any appeal against the enforcement notice by the recipient.

(c)   *Temporary stop notice*   This is a comparatively new power and allows the LPA to prevent activity stated in the notice whilst it considers whether further, more permanent action should be taken.

(d)   *Breach of condition notice*   This can be served in respect of a breach of a condition attached to a consent. Unlike an enforcement notice, the recipient cannot appeal against its service.

(e)   *Injunction.*

Non-compliance with an operative enforcement or other notice is a criminal offence which can carry heavy penalties.

17.2   Listed buildings and conservation areas

Additional controls exist in respect of listed buildings and conservation areas.

Where it is considered that a building is of outstanding historic or architectural interest, it may be 'listed'. Responsibility for this rests with the Department for Culture, Media and Sport and English Heritage (in England), and the Welsh Assembly and Cadw (in Wales). The effect of the listing depends on which grade of listing is given. Part only of a building may be subject to listing (eg, an Adam fireplace). The consequences of listing are, principally, that tighter controls are exercised over development than is the case with an unlisted building and that, in general, the exceptions from development (examples of which are considered at **17.1.4.2**) do not apply. Listed building consent must be obtained for development affecting such a building. There are criminal sanctions for non-compliance and no time limits for bringing enforcement proceedings.

In addition to the above, the LPA may designate as a conservation area any part of its area which is of special architectural or historic interest, the character or appearance of which it is desirable to preserve or enhance. As a general rule, any non-listed building in a conservation area cannot be demolished without conservation area consent. There may also be other restrictions on development.

17.3   Restrictive covenants and planning

When considering a planning matter, the LPA is not concerned with private controls on the land such as restrictive covenants. An important consequence flows from this which is that it is perfectly possible for planning permission to be granted for a given development, but for that development to contravene a valid restrictive covenant over the land. The contravention of the covenant will need to be dealt with as a separate issue even though the planning issues have been resolved. Various options are available in this respect and are dealt with in more detail at **19.4**.

17.4 Building regulation control

As a separate issue from the need to obtain planning permission, the need to obtain building regulation consent from the local authority must be considered whenever building works are to be undertaken. Building regulation control is concerned with the health and safety aspects of the building to be erected or altered, and regulates the types of materials and construction methods used in carrying out the work. Building regulation consent may be required irrespective of whether the works constitute development for the purposes of planning control. It is not always realised that many 'home improvement' schemes will require consent. So replacement windows, new electrical installations (eg a new plug socket), certain drainage and plumbing alterations, will all need consent. On completion of building works for which consent is required, a 'final certificate' can be obtained from the local authority. This should be kept safe along with other documents relating to the property as evidence of compliance with building regulation control. Several 'self-certification' schemes have been established to enable competent contractors to self-certify their own work, eg the FENSA (Fenestration Self Assessment) scheme in relation to replacement windows/ double glazing and the like. These schemes are regulated by the trade's own governing body, which sets and tests the competency of installers and their understanding of the building regulations specific to their trade or profession. A self-certification certificate is issued by the contractor at the completion of the work and the relevant governing body then sends a notification of the works to the local authority.

Care must be taken by the buyer whenever the seller is unable to produce proof of compliance with building regulations. First, the local authority has enforcement powers in respect of breaches of building regulation control. Prosecutions may only be brought within one year of the alleged breach but other enforcement options, including injunctions, can be still be used after this date (see *Cottingham v Attey Bower* [2000] Lloyd's Rep PN 591). Secondly, a buyer who proceeds with his purchase with knowledge of breach must be advised that, in view of this, there is no guarantee of the safety of the structure of the building, which may therefore require expensive repairs or remedial work. A solicitor acting for a buyer should strongly advise his client to consider obtaining a full structural survey to assess the potential cost of such work. Insurance can be obtained in cases where proof of building regulation consent is not forthcoming, but this will usually only cover the cost of compliance with the regulations should the local authority bring enforcement proceedings. It will not cover personal injuries or loss of trade caused by the defective buildings.

The buyer's lender must also be informed of any breach and may be reluctant to lend on a property where such breach exists, or may impose conditions on the terms of the loan to ensure that the building work is brought up to standard. A lender may insist on a full survey being undertaken.

17.5 Transactional matters

17.5.1 Acting for the seller

Although planning and related matters do not necessarily fall within the seller's duty of disclosure, the buyer's solicitor will be reluctant to proceed with the transaction unless he is satisfied that the buildings and use of the property comply with current planning and other regulations. It is therefore sensible for the seller's solicitor to satisfy himself as to these matters at an early stage so as to be able to anticipate any problems which might otherwise arise. Accordingly, the seller's solicitor should check the following and consider the implications for the transaction:

(a)   The date when the property was first built and the use to which it has been put since then.

(b)   Whether any additions, alterations or extensions have been made to the property or within its grounds since it was first built and, if so, the date of each addition, etc.

(c)   If any activity has been carried out that could potentially have required planning permission, that either planning consent was obtained (either expressly or by virtue of the GPDO) or that such consent was not required. Any conditions attached to the planning consent (or GPDO) should be checked to ensure that they have been complied with.

(d)   Whether any alterations, changes of use etc, have taken place in breach of any covenants which affect the title. If the property is leasehold, this will involve consideration not only of the covenants that bind the freehold, but also consideration of any covenants controlling development contained in the lease.

(e)   Whether the property is a listed building or in a conservation area.

(f)   Where alterations or additions to the property have been made, whether building regulation control has been complied with. A 'final certificate' issued by the local authority will show compliance with these provisions.

17.5.2   Acting for the buyer

The matters itemised in **17.5.1**, if not disclosed by the SPIF (where used), should be raised as pre-contract enquiries with the seller, and the answers to the planning questions on the local search and enquiries of local authority should also be carefully analysed. Any irregularity revealed by the answers should either be corrected at the seller's expense or, depending on the nature of the breach, an indemnity should be taken from the seller in the contract.

The above will identify any problems arising out of the seller's use of the property. In addition, instructions should be obtained from the buyer in respect of his plans for the property following acquisition. If the buyer proposes to carry out works to the property or change the use, it will be necessary to consider if planning permission will be needed. Consideration should be given to obtaining this before exchange of contracts or making the contract conditional upon it being obtained. In addition, issues relating to restrictive covenants and building regulations should be considered.

17.6   Environmental issues

17.6.1   General

Liability for environmental issues can arise from a number of sources. Detailed consideration of this area of practice is outside the scope of this book which will concentrate instead on the impact of environmental controls on a typical transaction. In terms of statutory controls, the main source of liability arises in the context of the 'contaminated land' regime under under the Environmental Protection Act 1990 ('EPA 1990') as amended. This can impose responsibility for polluting substances on land upon the owner or occupier for the time being (including a lender who is in possession of land). Civil liability may also exist in tort (see *Scott-Whitehead v National Coal Board* (1987) 53 P & CR 263; cf *Cambridge Water Co v Eastern Counties Leather plc* [1994] 1 All ER 53).

17.6.2   Consequences of contamination

The presence of contaminants in land can have very serious consequences on a sale: the site may be 'blighted', making it difficult to sell or mortgage and the use of the land for certain proposed uses may be impossible without extensive (and expensive) clean-up works being undertaken. If the buyer fails to detect contamination, this could potentially lead to liability under the EPA 1990 or at common law. The Law Society has issued a Warning Card to solicitors reminding them of the need in every transaction (whether a purchase, a mortgage or a lease, and whether residential or commercial) to consider whether contamination is an issue and to advise clients of the potential liabilities associated with it.

17.6.3   Enforcement

Control of contaminated land falls on the Environment Agency and local authorities. Under ss 78A–78Y, of the EPA 1990, the local authority has the prime responsibility. Each local authority is under a duty to inspect its area for contaminated sites. Once a site has been identified as contaminated, the local authority must then serve a remediation notice on the 'appropriate person'. This will specify the steps necessary to clean up the site so that it is suitable for its intended use. 'Appropriate person', is defined by s 78F. This is essentially the original polluter, ie, the person who caused or knowingly permitted all or some of the contaminating materials to be present in, on or under the land. If such a person cannot be identified after reasonable inspection, then liability falls on the current owner or occupier. It is this last provision which could result in a buyer becoming liable for remediation costs.

17.6.4   Searches and enquiries and other investigations

Until recently, it was not thought necessary to make enquiries with regard to potential contamination when buying residential property. However, after several cases where land on which new houses had been built was found to be contaminated, the need to make enquiries about environmental matters should be considered in every case. A useful and inexpensive method of doing this is to make use of Homecheck Professional (see the website at www.homecheck.co.uk) This provides a wide range of environmental information about the property and the surrounding area from information gathered by the Landmark Information Group.

In the case of new houses, the cover given by the NHBC has been extended to include the cost of cleaning up contamination of the site, should this be subsequently discovered. This applies, however, only to houses registered with the NHBC on and after 1 April 1999. There is no protection in the case of other houses.

The standard form of enquiries of the local authority (see **18.6**) now includes questions to ascertain whether the council has served or resolved to serve any notices relating to contamination in respect of the property. The optional enquiries in Part II of the standard form of enquiries of the local authority also contain questions relating to environmental issues and should be considered where appropriate.

In commercial transactions, and particularly when contemplating the purchase of a previously undeveloped ('green field') or recycled ('brown field') site for development, it will always be necessary to undertake certain checks and enquiries to ensure that the land which is being acquired is clean or, if not, that the steps needed to clean up the land are clearly understood by the client. 'SiteCheck' (see the website at www.sitecheck.co.uk), which also uses information from the Landmark Information Group, provides an easy method of obtaining information about past land use and other environmental matters.

In addition to the above, information can be obtained from the following:

(a)   enquiries of the local authority (see above) and the Environment Agency:

(b)   title deeds which may reveal the history of the site back to the stage where the land was a green field site;

(c)   archive information such as old Ordnance Survey maps, local newspaper and local history archives, and old trade directories;

(d)   a 'desk-top study' or 'Phase 1 Audit'. An environmnental consultant would be engaged to perform such a study. It involves obtaining information from a variety of sources to establish current and former land usage;

(e)   the purchase of environmental data from a commercial search agency;

(f)   the raising of specific pre-contract enquiries of the seller relating to his use of the land.

If these enquiries indicate previous potentially contaminative uses, it will be necessary to establish if the site is actually contaminated and, if so, to what extent. This will involve instructing environmental consultants to undertake a physical survey of the land. Samples of the soil will be taken on a systematic basis using established techniques and then tested in order to discover the extent and nature of the contamination.

If the land proves to be contaminated, the costs of remediation to the standard necessary for the proposed use will have to be considered. Remediation can be very expensive, depending upon the nature and extent of the contamination. It might consist of excavating and then safely disposing of the contaminated soil, or encapsulating it so that the contaminants cannot escape.

17.6.5   Planning and contaminated land

It should not be forgotten that before a proposed development can go ahead, it is likely that planning permission will be required. If there are environmental issues conerning the site, the LPA is likely to impose conditions which require the site to be cleaned up before development can take place, or which require investigations to be made to ascertain the full extent of any potential contamination.

17.7   Radon

Radon is a naturally occurring gas which is present in the ground and is found at low levels in all buildings. In some high-level areas ('Affected Areas' as defined by the National Radiological Protection Board), the Board may recommend that remedial measures are taken in buildings to reduce the radon levels which can cause cancer in human beings. Radon affects both residential and commercial buildings and, in the Affected Areas, a buyer should raise specific pre-contract enquiries of the seller to ask whether a radon survey has been carried out by the Board and whether remedial measures have been recommended or undertaken. In Affected Areas the Board will measure radon levels for the owner of property, but the Board will not release the results of a survey to a prospective buyer. Enquiry 3.13 of the enquiries of local authorities search form will give information as to whether a property is in an Affected Area. Special requirements under building regulations are also in force for new homes built in Affected Areas.

Chapter 18

Searches and Enquiries Before Contract

18.1 Reasons for making searches

It is the responsibility of the buyer's solicitor to find out as much as possible about the property before allowing his client to enter into a binding contract to buy. At this stage the buyer can freely withdraw from the transaction if he discovers something about the property he does not like; if something was discovered after exchange which might lead the buyer to wish to withdraw, he may well not be able to do so without incurring liability for breach of contract. As we have seen (at **15.7.1**), when drafting the contract the seller has only a very limited duty to disclose certain matters affecting the title to the property. He does not have to disclose physical defects, hence the need for a structural survey (see **Chapter 11**), nor matters such as the authorised use of the property for planning purposes, or whether a new motorway is to be built just over the back hedge. The buyer's solicitor must, therefore, as far as possible take steps to ensure that the property is suitable for the buyer's purpose.

Failure by the buyer's solicitor to make these searches may give rise to liability in negligence to the buyer client if, as a result, the buyer suffers loss (see *Cooper v Stephenson* (1852) 21 LJQB 292).

It is, of course, not sufficient just to make the searches; the buyer's solicitor must ensure that the buyer is fully advised of the information discovered and its implications for his proposed purchase.

18.2 Who should make the searches and enquiries?

Since the risk of buying the property subject to undiscovered defects rests with the buyer, it is for the buyer to ensure that all necessary pre-contract searches have been made and that the results are satisfactory.

In residential property, the provision of a HIP does not change the responsibility of the buyer's solicitor to check the results of the searches included in the Pack and ensure that the property is suitable for the client's needs. If the searches in the HIP are more than (say) two months old, it will be necessary to repeat them, as it is unsafe to rely on out-of-date searches. The CML *Lenders' Handbook* requires, when acting for a mortgage lender, that all searches be no more than six months old at the date of completion (*Lenders' Handbook*, para 5.2.3), but many conveyancers would regard this as being too out of date to be acceptable to a buyer. As all the necessary searches may not be included in the Pack, it will still be necessary for the buyer's solicitor to consider what other searches might need to be made.

18.3 National Land Information Service

The buyer's solicitor should make search applications as soon as firm instructions to proceed are received from his client. Search applications should always be submitted without delay, since some authorities take a long time to reply to them. In order to reduce delays in obtaining results of searches (and as part of the transition to e-conveyancing) the National Land Information Service (NLIS) has now been expanded nationwide. It became operational early in 2001 and is intended as a one-stop shop for conveyancers (and others) enabling electronic access to a wide range of information, in particular offering the facility to make searches electronically. There is a central 'hub' with access to the information being provided by three commercial 'channels'. The hub is managed by The Council for the National Land (and Property) Information Service, a not-for-profit community interest company.

The three channels currently licensed are TM Search, Jordans and Searchflow. However, the NLIS is currently actively encouraging more commercial organisations to apply to become licensed channels. At the time of writing, the system has undertaken over 14 million searches. The channels are also able to provide searches and other information from Land Registry such as official copies and priority searches.

The system works by a conveyancer ordering searches through one of the channels. The channel then contacts the hub, which then directs the search to the appropriate data provider. The results are then sent from the data provider to the hub, from the hub to the channel and from the channel to the solicitor. Although this sounds complicated, as everything take place electronically, the whole process can take as little as two minutes, depending upon the nature of the search.

The NLIS system thus allows all searches that a conveyancer might wish to make in a transaction to be requested electronically by ticking a few boxes on a computer screen. This saves the time and expense of making separate, paper-based searches. Ultimately, all search results will be provided electronically. One cloud on the horizon, however, is the extremely slow progress of local authorities in electronically connecting to the NLIS. Without this many local searches still come back through the post weeks after being requisitioned. Over 6,000 conveyancing practitioners have used the NLIS to order online searches. For more details, see www.nlis.org.uk.

18.4 Which searches should be made?

18.4.1 All transactions

The following searches are regarded as 'usual' and should be undertaken in every transaction:

(a) search of the local land charges register;

(b) enquiries of the local authority and, if appropriate, additional enquiries;

(c) pre-contract enquiries of the seller;

(d) water and drainage enquiries.

These searches should be made whether the property being purchased is residential or commercial.

18.4.2 Additional searches

Depending on the circumstances of the transaction, the following searches may need to be made:

(a) commons registration search;

(b) mining search;

(c) Index Map search, if dealing with unregistered land;

(d) a Land Charges Department search against the seller's name (for insolvency) and in unregistered land also against other previous owners of the land (to discover incumbrances);

(e) environmental matters;

(f) a company search;

(g) any of the less usual searches which may be applicable in the circumstances (see **18.13**).

18.4.3 Less usual searches

This chapter summarises only the main searches which are relevant to a normal conveyancing transaction. For a detailed explanation of the contents of the various search forms and of the less usual searches, reference should be made to a specialist work such as Russell Hewitson, *Conveyancing Searches and Enquiries: A Conveyancer's Guide* (Jordans, 2006).

18.5 Local land charges search

A local authority is bound by statute to keep a register of certain matters. This register, which is open to public inspection, is called the Local Land Charges Register. It is divided into the 12 parts which are listed on the reverse of the search application form (Form LLC1).

18.5.1 Making the search

A local land charges search should be made in every transaction by submitting Form LLC1 to the unitary, district or London borough council in which the property is situated.

Where the application is made by post, the form should be completed in duplicate. A plan of the land (also in duplicate) must be submitted if the land cannot clearly be identified from its postal address. A fee is payable for the search. A search should be made in all parts of the register.

18.5.2 The search result

The search result is given by way of certificate, signed by an officer of the council, which shows whether any, and if so how many, entries are revealed by the search. This certificate is accompanied by a schedule which contains a summary of the relevant entries. Further details of the entries can be obtained either by attending at the council offices to inspect documents, or by obtaining office copies of documents from the council. A fee is payable for copies of documents.

18.5.3 What the search reveals

The search result will reveal any entries kept by the council under the statutory obligations mentioned above. Such matters might include the following:

(a)   financial charges (eg, for adoption of estate roads; see **41.2.4**);

(b)   tree preservation orders. These prevent the protected tree(s) being felled without permission;

(c)   smoke control orders. These restrict the use of non-smokeless fuels in domestic fireplaces;

(d)   some compulsory purchase orders;

(e)   planning permissions granted;

(f)   any restrictions on permitted development (eg, Article 4 Direction: see **17.1.4.3**);

(g)   orders revoking or modifying planning permissions.

The buyer should be advised of the entries affecting the property and their significance – for example, in the case of a tree preservation order, that the tree in question cannot be felled or lopped without permission. Consideration should also be given as to how the entries will affect the buyer's proposed use for the property. If financial charges are revealed, the seller should be requested to discharge these prior to completion, or to reduce the purchase price accordingly.

18.5.4 Liability

Where a person suffers as a result of an error in an official certificate of search, compensation may be payable under s 10 of the Local Land Charges Act 1975.

18.6 Enquiries of local authority

18.6.1 Making the search

The enquiries of the local authority search should be made in every transaction by submitting Form CON29 to the appropriate unitary, district or London borough council in which the property is situated. Where the search is made by post, two copies of the form are required. Some local authorities now accept electronic requests for search applications via computer link (but see **18.3**). The local authority may insist on submission of a plan with the search application, even in cases where the land can clearly be identified from its postal address. The fee for this search varies from authority to authority.

The form is divided into two parts. The CON29R enquiries are relevant to every transaction and are covered by the authority's quoted fee. The CON29O enquiries are more specialised in nature and not all the questions will be relevant in every transaction. It should always be considered which, if any, of the CON29O enquiries should be raised in each transaction, and those enquiries which are raised should then be indicated by placing a tick in the box against the relevant question number at the foot of the front page of the search form. A separate fee is chargeable for each CON29O enquiry raised.

If it is necessary to raise additional enquiries covering matters which are not dealt with by the printed questions, such additional questions should be typed on a separate sheet of paper and submitted in duplicate with the search application. An additional fee is chargeable for each supplementary question raised. Some local authorities refuse to answer questions other than those on the printed form.

18.6.2 What the search reveals

A local authority keeps records of a great quantity of information relating to a large number of different matters, extending beyond the limited confines of the local land charges register. It is this enormous quantity of non-statutory information which the search application is designed to reveal. The information revealed by this search will assist the buyer to build up a complete picture of the property he is proposing to buy and is essential to his decision as to whether or not to proceed with the purchase. Examples of the type of entry which might be revealed are as follows:

(a) whether the roads serving the property are maintained at the public expense;

(b) roads and railways proposed within 200 metres of the property;

(c) planning applications made (including those refused);

(d) enforcement and stop notices served and whether they have been complied with (see **17.1.6.2**);

(e) proposed enforcement and stop notices;

(f) proposed tree preservation orders;

(g) proposed restrictions on permitted development;

(h) proposed compulsory purchase orders;

(i) whether any notices have been served in relation to remediation of contaminated land.

The Part II (optional enquiries) include the following:

(a) whether the property is crossed by a public path or bridleway;

(b) whether there are any proposals for permanently stopping up roads or footpaths, or putting any other traffic schemes into operation, for example one-way streets, parking restrictions etc;

(c) commons registration (see **18.13.2**).

As with the local search, the replies should be considered carefully and the client advised accordingly. If the roads and sewers are not maintained at the public expense, the client should be warned of the potential expense should the local authority subsequently decide to 'adopt' the road. However, as long as the enquiries reveal that there is a Highways Act 1980 Section 38 Agreement and bond (for the roads) and a Water Industry Act 1991 Section 104 Agreement and bond (for the sewers), there will be no such problem. See **41.2.4** and **41.2.5** for details of these.

The client should also be advised that, generally, both the local search and enquiries merely reveal matters directly affecting the land being bought; they will not reveal matters relating to adjoining land which may indirectly affect the property. So if a new supermarket is planned for the field at the rear of the house, this will not be revealed. The main exceptions to this are new roads and railways. Those planned within 200 metres of the property will be revealed. However, a new motorway 300 metres away would not be revealed and might still cause disturbance to the occupiers of the property.

'Plansearch', available from Jordans Ltd, can provide information on:

(a) applications for planning consent made within the previous five years in respect of land within 250 metres of the property;

(b)   Local Authority Development Plans (see **17.1.1**) in respect of land within 500 metres;

(c)   whether the property is within a natural river or coastal floodplain.

18.6.3   Liability

Subject to the validity of the exclusion clause printed on the front sheet of the search application form, a local authority could be sued in negligence for an erroneous reply to the printed enquiries.

18.6.4   Differences between Forms LLC1 and CON29

In practice, the two search applications are submitted simultaneously to the same authority with one cheque covering both fees. It is unusual to do one search without the other and, for that reason, the two searches are often treated as being indistinguishable and are together referred to as 'the local search'. In fact they are two totally separate and distinct searches having different functions. Their differences are summarised below:

(a)   Form LLC1 will only reveal matters which fall within the statutory definition of a local land charge (eg, planning permissions granted); Form CON29 covers a wider range of subject matter and is not restricted to land charges (eg, planning applications made, including refusals).

(b)   The liability of the local authority for errors is different (see **18.5.4** and **18.6.3**). For the enquiries, negligence has to be established; this is not necessary for the local search.

(c)   Form LLC1 is restricted to information which is on the register at the moment the search is made; Form CON29 may reveal information which has affected the property in the past (eg, history of planning applications made on the property) or will do so in the future (eg, a compulsory purchase order which is pending but which has not yet been registered as a local land charge).

18.6.5   Personal searches

Due to delays in the return of local searches and enquiries there has been increasing use in recent years of personal search providers. These are agents who will (for a fee) attend personally at the offices of the appropriate local authority and make the search personally.

A slightly different approach is taken by organisations such as OneSearch Direct. This particular organisation maintains its own database of the information that would be revealed by a local search and offers a speedy service at a set fee.

In any case where an official search is not made, it will be necessary to ensure that the personal search is acceptable to any mortgage lender which is advancing money on security of the property. Some mortgage lenders will not accept personal searches, or state that they will do so only at the solicitor's own risk. Where a personal search is to be used (or has been provided in a HIP), the solicitor must ensure that it has been made by a properly trained person and that the results are backed by adequate insurance. A Search Code has been sponsored by the Council of Property Search Organisations (COPSO) to ensure adequate consumer protection. The Search Code will be monitored and enforced by the independent Property Codes Compliance Board.

18.6.6 Home Information Packs (HIPs)

The result of the local search and enquiries will be included in the HIP. However, the buyer's solicitor will still need to check the results and consider whether any of the Part II enquiries need to be raised. In addition, the buyer's solicitor will need to check:

(a) the date of the search. The CML *Lenders' Handbook* requires all searches to be no more than six months old as at completion. Many conveyancers would not advise relying on a search more than two months old. It may well be necessary to make a fresh search;

(b) whether it is necessary to make any of the additional enquiries on Form CON29. If so, then these enquiries should be made without delay; and

(c) if a personal search has been included (see **18.6.5**).

18.7 Pre-contract enquiries of the seller: the Seller's Property Information Form

18.7.1 Purpose of the search

Pre-contract enquiries of the seller are the third of the 'usual' searches and are made in every transaction. The purpose of this search is to elicit from the seller information, mainly relating to the physical aspects of the property, which he is not bound by law to disclose (see **15.7.1**). The information obtained should enable the buyer to gain a complete picture of the property which he is proposing to buy, and can thus be influential in his making the decision whether or not to proceed with the purchase.

Since the object of the exercise is to obtain information which the seller is not by law bound to disclose, it follows that the seller could refuse to answer the buyer's enquiries altogether. Such a refusal would, however, be unusual and would serve no useful purpose, since it would make the buyer suspicious and would, at best, hinder the speedy progress of the transaction or, at worst, cause the buyer to abort his purchase.

Where a HIP has been provided, this should be checked to see if it contains answers to pre-contractual enquiries. If it does not, then the seller should be requested to complete it or a Seller's Property Information Form (see **18.7.2**). If answers to enquiries are provided in the HIP, the seller's solicitor should be required to confirm that the information remains correct.

18.7.2 Protocol cases

In cases where the Protocol is used, the seller's solicitor should ask his client to complete the Seller's Property Information Form (SPIF). This contains various questions about the property, phrased in layman's language so that the average client should be able to complete this form with minimal help from his solicitor. However, The Law Society recommend that the solicitor should then go through the answers with the client to ensure that the questions have been answered correctly.

An erroneous or misleading reply to these questions could give rise to liability in misrepresentation. So, for example, in *Doe v Skegg* [2006] PLSCS 213, a seller who incorrectly answered the question regarding disputes was held liable for fraudulent misrepresentation when sued by the buyer for damages of £150,000. See also **18.7.6**.

The form is then submitted to the buyer's solicitor as part of the pre-contract package.

The Seller's Leasehold Information Form contains additional questions which are relevant in leasehold transactions.

18.7.3 Non-Protocol cases

The buyer should ask similar questions to those included on the SPIF. Law stationers produce a standard form of pre-contract enquiries and many solicitors have their own version. In such a case, two copies of the form should be sent to the seller's solicitor (with any enquiries which are not relevant to the transaction in hand deleted from the forms). The form should be submitted to the seller's solicitor as soon as possible after firm instructions are received from the buyer although, in practice, many solicitors will not send the form until they have received the draft contract from the seller's solicitor, so that any queries arising out of that document can be raised as additional enquiries.

In order to try to bring some uniformity to preliminary enquiries, the Commercial Property Standard Enquiries (CPSE) have been drafted for use in commercial transactions. The CPSE have been endorsed by the British Property Federation. Supplementary enquiries are available for use where the property is tenanted or is leasehold.

The CPSE Form 1, which should be used in every transaction, includes questions on the following areas:

(a)   boundaries;

(b)   adverse rights;

(c)   access to the property;

(d)   fire safety;

(e)   compliance with planning and building regulations;

(f)   VAT status of the transaction.

Other CPSE forms are available for use in addition to CPSE 1:

(a)   CPSE 2 for use on the sale of property subject to tenancies;

(b)   CPSE 3 for use on the grant of a new lease;

(c)   CPSE 4 for use on the assignment of a lease.

These forms are updated regularly. The latest versions (together with guidance notes) can be obtained at http://property.practicallaw.com/0-103-2123.

18.7.4 Supplementary enquiries

Where there are genuine areas of enquiry which are not covered by the questions on the standard forms, but which are relevant to the buyer's situation, these should be raised as supplementary enquiries either on the space at the bottom of the printed form, or on a separate sheet (in duplicate). Additional enquiries may extend to queries arising out of the provisions of the draft contract, or from the evidence of title supplied by the seller.

Additional enquiries should, in any event, be confined to those matters to which an answer cannot be obtained from reading the documentation supplied by the seller, from the estate agent's particulars, or from a survey or physical inspection of the property. The submission of a large number of irrelevant supplementary enquiries may irritate the seller's solicitor who may decline to answer them.

18.7.5 Summary of information to be obtained from search

The following enquiries should be made as a minimum in every case:

(a)   whether there are any disputes with neighbouring owners/occupiers;

(b)   who is in occupation of the property;

(c)   whether there have been any alterations or other building work carried out on the property and, if so, whether planning permission/building regulation consent was obtained;

(d)   whether there has been any change in the use of the property;

(e)   whether services (eg, water) to the property pass through adjoining land;

(f)   whether services to other properties pass through the land to be sold.

The replies should be studied carefully and the client advised of any which will affect his proposed use of the property. For the kind of problems which can be revealed, see **18.14**.

18.7.6 Liability

An incorrect reply to pre-contract enquiries may lead to liability in misrepresentation. Any exclusion clause purporting to avoid or minimise liability for misrepresentation will be subject to the reasonableness test in s 11 of the Unfair Contract Terms Act 1977, and cannot therefore be guaranteed to afford protection to the seller (see SC 7.1.3 (SCPC 9.1.3) and *Walker v Boyle* [1982] 1 All ER 634). Some forms of pre-contract enquiries also contain an exclusion clause.

Where the erroneous reply stems from the seller's solicitor's negligence, he will be liable to his own client (*CEMP Properties (UK) Ltd v Dentsply Research and Development Corporation (No 1)* (1989) 2 EGLR 192), but in this respect he does not owe a duty directly to the buyer (see *Gran Gelato v Richcliffe (Group)* [1992] 1 All ER 865).

It is common for the seller's solicitor to answer enquiries as vaguely as possible with the intent of avoiding any possible liability for misrepresentation. So answers such as 'Not so far as we are aware' or 'Not so far as the seller is aware' are common. However, it should be noted that the effect of *William Sindall plc v Cambridgeshire CC* [1994] 1 WLR 1016 is that such a reply indicates not only that the seller has no actual knowledge of a matter, but also that he has undertaken all reasonable enquiries that a prudent conveyancer should have made.

Some conveyancers try to avoid the need to make such enquiries by inserting a condition in the contract to the effect that such replies are not to be taken to mean that extra enquiries have been made. The effectiveness of such a condition is unclear.

18.8 Water and drainage enquiries

Information about water and sewerage matters is no longer available from local authorities, so drainage and water enquiries should now be made using Form CON29DW. This should be submitted, with the appropriate fee, to the water service company serving the property. These enquiries should be made in every transaction. The enquiry will reveal (inter alia) the following:

(a)   whether the property has foul water drainage to the public sewer;

(b)   whether the property has surface water drainage to the public sewer;

(c)   whether there is a water main within the boundaries of the property;

(d)   whether the property is connected to the public water supply.

The result of this enquiry will be included in the HIP. However, the buyer's solicitor will still need to check the results. In addition, the buyer's solicitor will need to check the date of the search. The CML *Lenders' Handbook* requires all searches to be no more than six months old as at completion.

18.9   Land Charges Department search

A Land Charges Department search should be made in all cases when dealing with unregistered land. Although this search is often undertaken at a later stage of the transaction, it is sensible to make the search prior to exchange so that any problems which do emerge can be dealt with in good time before completion is due. Even with registered land, it is sensible for the seller's solicitor to make a search against his own client's name to ensure that there are no bankruptcy proceedings pending. The search is made by submitting either Form K15 (full search) or Form K16 (bankruptcy only) to the Land Charges Department at Plymouth, or it can be made by telephone. In Protocol cases, the seller should provide searches against the seller and all previous estate owners within the title.

The register comprises a list of names of proprietors of land, and a fee is payable for each name searched against. A search should be made against the names of all previous estate owners revealed by the epitome. The search is therefore made not against the land itself but against the names of the previous owners. Although the seller has a duty of disclosure, under SC 3 but not under SCPC 3 (see **15.7.1**), and should therefore reveal to the buyer any matters which are the subject of registered entries at the Land Charges Department, it is nevertheless sensible for the buyer to undertake this search before contracts are exchanged if only to obtain an early warning of potential problems (eg, the seller's bankruptcy, Family Law Act 1996 rights, estate contracts). If the seller supplies correctly made searches with the epitome (see **14.4.2.7**), the buyer need not repeat searches against these names. Unless completion takes place within 15 working days of the issue of the search certificate (the protection period afforded by an official search) the search, at least against the seller's name, will need to be repeated before completion (see **Chapter 28**).

This search is particularly important where the Standard Commercial Property Conditions are in use. Under SCPC 3.1.2(d) the property is expressed to be sold subject to 'matters . . . which would have been disclosed by the searches and enquiries which a prudent buyer would have made before entering into the contract'. So the seller is under no duty expressly to disclose matters registered as land charges but the sale is still subject to any that do exist. It is thus essential that the buyer's solicitor makes such searches in order to ascertain whether there are any land charges affecting the property and which would thus be binding upon the buyer.

The register is maintained by computer which will, basically, search only against the version of the name as shown on the application form. It is essential to ensure, therefore, that the search is made against the full name of the owner as revealed by the deeds and that the spelling of that name is correct. It is necessary to indicate on the search application the period of years for which the search should be made. This should be the period for which that person was the owner of the land. For further information on Land Charges Registry searches see **28.6**.

If the buyer's solicitor is also acting for the lender, it will be necessary at some time, whether the land is registered or unregistered, to make a bankruptcy search against the borrower to ensure that there are no bankruptcy orders or proceedings affecting him. If the result of the search reveals an entry against the name of the borrower, the lender will not advance the money unless the solicitor is prepared to certify that the entries do not relate to the actual borrower but to someone else with the same name. It is usual to make this search immediately before completion (see **28.7**); however, if any entries are revealed, completion will inevitably be delayed due to the time necessary to resolve the matter. Some conveyancers therefore recommend making this search prior to exchange, when there is more time to resolve any problems. If it were to be made at this stage, however, it would still be necessary to repeat the search prior to completion to guard against any last-minute entries.

18.10 Company search

When the seller is a company, a company search should be made to check that the company:

(a)   exists;

(b)   has power to buy and sell land (although these powers are normally implied by law);

(c)   has no undisclosed fixed or floating charge which affects the land being purchased; and

(d)   is not in administration, receivership or liquidation.

Although the company search is conventionally undertaken at a later stage in the transaction, it is sensible to make the search before exchange so that any problems which do emerge from the search result can be dealt with in good time before completion is due. If required, a search made before exchange can be updated just before completion. There is no official search procedure for this search.

The solicitor or his agent (there are specialist firms who offer company search services) should apply to Companies House in London or Cardiff for a search to be made. A form of application is supplied by Companies House and a charge is made for the search. The search can also be made online at Companies House website, at www.companies-house.gov.uk. The search result, which confers no protection or priority on the applicant, provides copies of all the documents which the company has lodged at Companies House. These will include its memorandum and articles of association (constitutional documents), details of its officers (directors and secretary), filed accounts and details of mortgages.

18.11 Index Map search

A search of the Index Map should have been done as part of the investigation of an unregistered title (see **14.4**).

18.12 Environmental matters

People have become much more aware of environmental issues in recent years and these are matters which ought to be considered on a purchase of land. One obvious problem is the possibility of the land being contaminated – see **17.6**. Apart from the potential expense of clean-up liabilities, the dangers posed by the contamination to the owners and occupiers must also be considered. The Law Society has issued a Warning Card to solicitors reminding them of the need to consider the potential problems posed by contaminated land in every property transaction. The advice to be given to clients is considered at **17.6**.

But other environmental matters might also affect the potential buyer's decision whether or not to proceed. Is the property near a landfill site, or are there factories in the area discharging hazardous substances? Because of issues such as these, it is now regarded as best practice to obtain an environmental report in all property transactions. A useful and inexpensive method of doing this in residential purchases is to make use of Homecheck Professional (see www.homecheck.co.uk). This makes use of environmental information gathered by the Landmark Information Group. More detailed information in relation to commercial properties can be obtained using 'Sitecheck' (see www.sitecheck.co.uk).

Note also that the cover given by the NHBC in relation to new houses has now been extended to cover contaminated land (see **41.2.3**). However, this extended cover applies only to houses registered with the NHBC after 1 April 1999; there is no cover in relation to other properties.

18.13   Less usual searches

The buyer's solicitor should be aware of any features of the property or its location which indicate that one of the less usual searches may be appropriate to the situation. The buyer will usually be bound by any incumbrances which exist over the property, whether or not a search was made. A solicitor who fails to carry out a less usual search in circumstances where he should have done so may be liable in negligence to his client (see *G & K Ladenbau (UK) Ltd v Crawley and De Reya* [1978] 1 All ER 682).

Examples of some of the less usual searches appear below.

18.13.1   Coal mining search

This search should be made whenever the property is situated in an area where there are or have in the past been coal mining operations. The Law Society's Coal Mining Directory (published by Oyez) will indicate whether or not the parish in which the property is situated is in an area where a coal mining search is recommended. This information is also available on the Coal Authority's website at www.coal.gov.uk.

An application for a search should be made on Form CON29M, accompanied by the fee and a large-scale plan of the property, to the Coal Authority. The result of the search will reveal whether the property is in an area where mining has taken place in the past or is likely to take place in the future, the existence of underground workings which may cause problems with subsidence, and whether compensation for subsidence damage has been paid in the past or any claim is pending. No protection is given to the buyer by the search result. Although this search only covers coal mining activities, similar search schemes are available in areas potentially affected by other types of mining, eg, tin and china clay in Cornwall and salt in Cheshire. The Coal Authority is also responsible for Cheshire brine searches, but not the other mining searches.

18.13.2   Commons Registration search

A Commons Registration search should be made in any case where the property to be purchased abuts a village green or common land, where property is to be built on previously undeveloped land, or where a verge strip, not owned by the property, separates the property from the public highway. This search is made by ticking the appropriate box in the Enquiries of the Local Authority Form CON29O.

The search result will show whether any land is registered under the Commons Registration Act 1965 as common land or a village green. Where land has been registered under the 1965 Act it is difficult to remove that land from the register and not possible to obtain planning permission for development over the land. Third parties may have rights over the land which is registered (eg, rights to graze cattle). No protection is given by the official search result and no personal search facilities exist.

18.13.3 Flooding

The Environment Agency states that two million homes and businesses are at risk of flooding in England and Wales. This can easily be checked on the Agency's website at www.environment-agency.gov.uk. This information can also be obtained using 'Plansearch' from Jordans Ltd.

18.13.4 Land adjoining rivers, streams or canals

Enquiries should be made of the water authority to check on responsibility for maintenance of riverbanks. In the case of a canal, enquiry should be made of British Waterways.

18.13.5 Railways

In the case of properties adjoining a railway line, it used to be possible in the days of (nationalised) British Rail to make enquiries (inter alia) as to whether there were any obligations on the property owner to maintain the boundary walls and fences separating the land from the railway. However, nowadays (nationalised) Network Rail will no longer answer such enquiries. It is therefore necessary to raise such issues with the seller as additional pre-contract enquiries. The buyer should also be advised that Network Rail has a statutory right of access onto the adjoining land in order to undertake repairs to railway property. Searches are available in relation to other railway undertakings, eg Docklands Light Railway, London Underground and the Newcastle Metro.

18.13.6 Chancel repairs

For historical reasons, certain properties in certain parishes could be under an obligation to pay the cost of repairing the chancel of the parish church. Parishes where such liability might occur are those with a medieval church with a vicar. The obligation is an overriding interest, but will cease to override in October 2013. As a result there is some evidence that some Church of England dioceses are actively identifying liable property with the object of entering the repairing liability on the register. A cheap (£17.63) screening search (ChancelCheck) can now be made to ascertain whether the property is within a liable parish (see www.clsl.co.uk). If so, a personal search can be made at National Archives in Kew to ascertain whether the particular property is liable – the vast majority will not be. It will usually be cheaper, however, to obtain insurance cover against liability. Note that properties may be liable even if they are some distance from the church. Because of the potential risk, and potential negligence claims, many solicitors are now making the screening search in relation to every property, both residential and commercial.

18.14 Results of searches

On receiving the results of searches, the buyer's solicitor must check the answers given to ensure that the information supplied complies with his client's instructions. Any reply which is unclear must be pursued with the appropriate authority (or seller in the case of pre-contract enquiries) until a satisfactory explanation is received. Failure to pursue an unsatisfactory reply which results in loss being suffered by the client may result in the buyer's solicitor being liable to his own client in negligence (*Computastaff Ltd v Ingledew Brown Bennison & Garrett* (1983) 7 ILR 156).

Any reply which is for any reason not satisfactory must be referred to the client for further instructions. Contracts should not be exchanged until satisfactory results of all searches have been received. A summary of the information received from the searches should be communicated to the buyer by his solicitor. The individual searches should not be looked at in isolation; rather the information from each should be correlated and considered in the light of the particular circumstances of the case. The following scenarios are commonly encountered and need special care.

18.14.1   Property built within last 10 years

(a)   Check that you have copies of NHBC (or similar) documentation. (This provides insurance cover against many structural defects; see **41.2.3**.) Revealed by SPIF.

(b)   Check that there is planning permission and you have copies (see **17.1.6** for enforcement of planning matters). Revealed by SPIF and local search.

(c)   Check that the conditions attached to the planning permission have been complied with. Enforcement revealed by enquiries of local authority (see **17.1.6**).

(d)   Check that building regulation consent was obtained and a copy provided (see **41.2.2**). Revealed by SPIF; proceedings for breach revealed by enquiries of local authority.

(e)   Check that the roads and drains are adopted, or that agreements and bonds exist (see **18.6.2**). Copies should be provided. Revealed by enquiries of local authority.

(f)   If the roads, etc are not adopted, check that adequate easements exist for access. Check title documents.

If no agreements and bonds exist, consider whether a retention should be made from the purchase price until they are adopted.

18.14.2   Access to property or services to property across neighbouring land

(a)   Revealed by pre-contract enquiries. Check title to ensure that there are easements for access, etc. If no express easements exist, will they be implied or presumed by long user? Can seller get a deed of grant now from neighbouring owners?

(b)   What are the arrangements for maintenance and repair? Are there express arrangements in title documents or any informal arrangements?

Unless the property has been recently built, adoption by the local authority will be unlikely.

18.14.3   Occupiers

(a)   Revealed by pre-contract enquiries.

(b)   Do the occupiers claim an equitable interest?

(c) If so, ensure that they will sign agreement to give up rights and leave on completion (see **19.4.3**).

(d) In the case of a non-owning spouse, have rights of occupation under the Family Law Act 1996 been registered? Whether or not such rights have already been registered, the spouse should be required to agree to leave and remove any registration prior to completion (see **19.4.3**).

18.14.4 Extension or alterations carried out by previous owner

(a) Are there any guarantees for work? (See pre-contract enquiries.)

(b) Was planning permission required/obtained for works? (See **17.1**.)

(c) Are works within GPDO or were permissions withdrawn? (See **17.1.4.3**.)

(d) Copies of planning permission required?

(e) Have any covenants on title been complied with, for example consents for work?

(f) If consent required but not obtained, can it be obtained now, or insurance cover obtained?

(g) Was building regulation consent obtained? (See **17.4**.)

(h) Is a survey even more desirable in such cases to ensure work carried out to a proper standard?

18.15 Imputed knowledge

Knowledge acquired by the solicitor while acting on his client's behalf is imputed to the client (regardless of whether the client had actual knowledge of the matter in question). Thus, a seller may be liable in misrepresentation to the buyer for a statement made by his solicitor without his knowledge. In such a case, indemnity against the seller's liability could be sought from the seller's solicitors (see *Strover v Harrington* [1988] Ch 390).

18.16 Relying on searches made by a third party

The results of searches are not personal to the searcher, thus their benefit may be transferred to a third party. Where the seller makes pre-contract searches and passes their results to the buyer, the buyer and his lender may take the benefit of the results. The buyer must check that the seller has undertaken all the searches and enquiries which the buyer deems necessary for the transaction in hand and, if not, he must carry out the additional searches himself. If the buyer is not satisfied with the results of the searches made by the seller because, for example, he considers that insufficient questions have been raised, he should repeat the search himself. Similarly, a lender may rely on searches made by a buyer's solicitor.

18.17 Inspection of the property

Inspection of the property should be undertaken by the client in all cases. There is no obligation on the solicitor, either in law or conduct, to carry out an inspection in every transaction, but he should do so if his client so requests or if matters reported by the client's inspection give rise to suspicion on the part of the buyer's solicitor. The client should be advised to look for (and to report their existence to his solicitor) any of the following matters:

(a) a discrepancy or uncertainty over the identity of or boundaries to the property;

(b)   evidence of easements which adversely affect the property (eg, evidence suggesting that a right of way over the property exists);

(c)   the existence and status of non-owning occupiers;

(d)   a discrepancy between the fixtures and fittings which the client understood to belong to the property and those actually existing.

18.18   Conclusion

The results of these searches and enquiries provide valuable information about the property being bought, and thus about the viability of the transaction and the buyer's proposals for it. The search results should be studied carefully and the buyer kept fully informed about them and their implications. The buyer should not be allowed to exchange contracts until all outstanding queries have been resolved to his satisfaction. The solicitor should also remember that if he is acting for the buyer's lender as well as the buyer, he should keep the lender client informed about any matters affecting the value or saleability of the property, or which otherwise might affect the lender's decision to lend on the security of the property.

Chapter 19

Looking at the Contract from the Buyer's Point of View

19.1 The pre-contract package

The buyer's solicitor will be supplied with two copies of the draft contract by the seller's solicitor. He should also receive copies of any documents referred to in the contract (eg, a conveyance imposing restrictive covenants) and the remainder of the pre-contract package, which should include such items as copies of planning consents, copies of an insurance policy against structural defects, and the seller's evidence of title.

Except where the buyer is purchasing a plot on a building estate (a new house in the course of construction), the terms of the contract will usually be open to negotiation between the parties, and the buyer's solicitor should therefore consider the terms of the draft contract in the light of his instructions and of the information revealed by the other documents in the pre-contract package.

Style of drafting is to an extent a matter of individual taste, and the buyer's solicitor should not seek to amend the contract simply because it is drafted in a style which he does not like.

19.2 Amending the contract

Amendments should be made only where they are both necessary and relevant to the particular transaction. The primary questions in looking at the contract from the buyer's point of view are as follows:

(a) Does the clause accord with the client's instructions?

(b) Does the clause do what it is intended to do?

If the answers to these questions are 'yes', leave the wording alone. If not, alter the clause until it does meet the above criteria.

19.2.1 How to amend the contract

Amendments should be inserted clearly on both copies of the draft contract in a distinctive colour. One copy of the amended contract can then be returned to the seller's solicitor for his consideration of the alterations made by the buyer's solicitor. The copy returned to the seller's solicitor should be marked 'amended in (red) on (date)'. Further amendments (by either party) should follow the same procedure and should be made in distinctive colours not previously used, so that it is possible to identify each layer of changes. Traditionally, first amendments are made in red ink and second amendments in green, but it is not obligatory to follow this sequence of colours.

When final agreement is reached over the contents of the contract, one copy should be returned by the buyer's solicitor to the seller's solicitor marked 'Approved as drawn' (where no amendments have been made) or 'Approved as amended in (green)' (where amendments have been made). In many cases, few amendments, other than inadvertent typographical errors, are needed, and minor amendments can be agreed by the parties' solicitors over the phone, cutting out the need for the contract formally to be sent to and from the respective solicitors. A document which does pass back and forth between the parties for amendment is often referred to as a 'travelling draft'.

In complex transactions, where amendments to a draft contract can be anticipated, it is advisable to send an electronic copy of the draft. Most word processing packages (eg, Microsoft Word) have a 'tracking' facility enabling amendments and additions to be made and then clearly shown when the other party reviews the document. This, together with the use of e-mail, will speed up the process of agreeing the final version of the document.

19.3   What to look for when considering the draft contract

The following are particular matters which the buyer's solicitor should bear in mind when considering the draft contract:

(a)   Are the full names and addresses of the parties correctly included?

(b)   Does the description of the property tie in with that on the register or in the deeds?

(c)   Does the property have the benefit of all the easements necessary for the use to which the buyer intends to put the property or any other reasonable use?

(d)   Is the estate being sold (freehold or leasehold) correctly stated?

(e)   Is the class of title stated (registered land)?

(f)   Is the root of title a 'good root' (unregistered land)? (See 15.7.3.)

(g)   Is the title number correctly stated (registered land)?

(h)   Are the incumbrances stated in the contract the only ones which the deeds/official copies/searches reveal the land is subject to?

(i)   Will the incumbrances restrict the buyer's proposed use of the property in any way?

(j)   Is full title guarantee being offered? If not, why not?

(k)   Is the contract rate more than The Law Society's rate (ie, more than 4% above base rate)?

(l)   Is the purchase price as agreed?

(m)   Is the amount of the deposit as agreed?

(n)   Is the amount payable for chattels and the identity of the chattels as agreed?

(o)   Is the balance correct?

(p)   Is vacant possession to be given on completion? If not, was this agreed?

(q)   Have requisitions been barred out? If so title must be investigated prior to exchange.

(r)   Have any of the Standard Conditions been amended/made inapplicable by a special condition? If so, will this adversely affect the buyer?

(s)   In particular, has SC 5 been amended so that the buyer will need to insure on exchange?

19.4 Restrictive covenants

Many properties are subject to restrictive covenants imposed on a previous sale of the land. In most cases, the nature of the covenants is consistent with the type of property being sold. It is common, for example, to find covenants imposed on residential property which restrict the use of the property to a private dwelling house in the occupation of a single family, which prevent alterations from being made to the property without the consent of a named third party, and which prohibit the keeping of animals other than ordinary domestic pets. In such cases, provided that they will not seriously impede the buyer's intended use of the property, no further action need be taken other than informing the buyer of the extent of the covenants and telling him that he has a liability for breach of the covenants.

19.4.1 Problematical covenants

Instructions may reveal that the buyer's intended use of the property after completion will cause a breach of existing covenants. For example, if there is a restrictive covenant which prevents use of the property except as a single private dwelling house and the client wants to convert the property into flats, a breach of covenant will occur.

The first step to be taken in such cases is to check to see whether the covenants are registered. Post-1925 covenants which are not registered either on the charges register of a registered title or as Class D(ii) entries in unregistered land are unenforceable. Usually the covenants are registered. Next, look at the wording of the covenants to see whether they have been annexed effectively to the land and are prima facie binding. Unless it is very clear on the face of the covenants that they are invalid, it is safest to assume that they are enforceable and to consider whether it is possible to obtain an insurance policy which will cover liability for the future breach of covenant. An insurance company will need the following information or documents when considering whether or not to issue a policy:

(a)   A copy of the document imposing the covenant or, if this is not available, a copy of the exact wording of the covenant.

(b)   The exact nature of the breach which has occurred, or details of the action which is contemplated which will cause the breach.

(c)   The date when the covenant was imposed.

(d)   Whether or not the covenant is registered.

(e)   The nature of other properties in the immediate neighbourhood. This is to enable the insurance company to assess the risk of enforcement of the covenant. Taking the example given above of a potential breach being caused by a conversion of a dwelling into flats, if many of the neighbouring properties have already been converted into flats, the likelihood of this particular covenant being enforced if breached is more remote than if the surrounding properties remain in single ownership. A plan which shows the property in the context of the surrounding locality is often useful.

(f)   A copy of any planning permission which permits the development to be undertaken by the client.

(g)   What steps have been taken (if any) to trace the person(s) with the benefit of the covenant and the results of those enquiries.

If a policy is issued, it is normally a single premium policy (a single sum is paid on the issue of the policy). The benefit of the policy can be passed on to successors in title. The buyer's lender should be consulted about the proposed breach of covenant and his approval obtained to the terms of the insurance policy. In arranging such a policy on behalf of a client, the solicitor is technically acting as an insurance intermediary and so is bound by FSA regulations. This means that he must issue the client with a 'demands and needs' statement, setting out why the policy is required and why the policy recommended satisfies the client's needs.

19.4.2 Other methods of dealing with covenants

If no policy can be obtained (the risk of enforcement might cause the insurance company to charge a prohibitive premium), consideration might be given to one of the solutions suggested below. If, however, it appears that valid and enforceable covenants will impede the client's proposed use of the land and that no viable solution to this problem can be achieved, the client should be advised not to proceed with his proposed purchase.

19.4.2.1 Obtaining the consent of the person with the benefit of the covenant

Obtaining the consent of the person with the benefit of the covenant is rarely a viable option. If the covenant was imposed many years ago, it will be difficult to trace the person with the benefit (unless the covenant was imposed by the owner of a large estate such as the Duke of Westminster). If the covenant has been imposed during the last 20 or so years, it may be possible to trace the person with the benefit, but the price for granting a release or modification of the covenant may be prohibitive.

The person with the benefit will be the present owner of the land for the benefit of which the covenant was taken. Remember also that, if the covenant was taken for the benefit of a piece of land which has now been divided between several owners, you will need to obtain the consent of all the present owners of that land.

19.4.2.2 Application to the Lands Tribunal

The Lands Tribunal has power in certain circumstances under the LPA 1925, s 84 to grant a modification or discharge of a restrictive covenant, but this solution may not be quick or cheap to pursue. The county court enjoys a similar, but more limited, jurisdiction.

19.4.3 Occupiers

If the SPIF, or the buyer's inspection, reveals that someone other than the seller is occupying the property, it will be necessary to ensure that they will vacate the property on or before completion. Even if the sale is to be made by two trustees (which would thus overreach the equitable interest of the occupier) it is still necessary to get a written agreement by the occupier to leave. Although the occupier's rights may be overreached and so not binding on a buyer, there is a risk of the buyer turning up on completion and finding the occupier still in possession. He may have no defence to a court action by the buyer for possession, but the buyer would have much preferred not to have had to go to court in order to obtain possession. By asking the occupier to confirm in writing that he will leave, this should ensure that any potential problems will be revealed at an early stage of the transaction by the occupier refusing to sign such an agreement.

19.4.3.1 Suggested form of wording for release of rights

In consideration of the Buyer entering into this Agreement, I .... [name of occupier] ...... agree:

(1)   to the sale of the Property on the terms of this Agreement; and

(2)   not to register any rights I may have in relation to the Property (whether under the Family Law Act 1996 or otherwise); and

(3)   to remove any registrations made by me in relation to these rights before completion; and

(4)   to give vacant possession of the Property on completion.

This form of wording is appropriate for inclusion in the contract; alternatively, it could be amended slightly and set out as a separate document. If the occupier is not the seller's spouse or civil partner, the reference to the Family Law Act 1996 should be deleted.

An alternative solution, if the occupier is claiming an equitable interest in the property, is to appoint the occupier as a second trustee of the property. The appointment should be made prior to exchange so that the occupier is a party to the contract and is thus bound by the contractual terms as to selling free from incumbrances and giving vacant possession on completion.

Chapter 20

Mortgage Offers

20.1 Acceptance of offer

Where the buyer is purchasing a property with the assistance of mortgage finance, his solicitor must ensure that the client has received and accepted a satisfactory offer before advising the client to exchange contracts. Advice given to the client about the terms of a mortgage offer may be 'investment business' within the terms of the Financial Services and Markets Act 2000. The types of mortgage available to the client are discussed in **Chapter 8**.

20.2 Terms of offer

A mortgage offer made by an institutional lender in respect of a loan to be made for the purchase of residential property will normally deal with some or all of the matters listed below:

(a) A description of the property which is to be mortgaged, its purchase price and tenure (ie, freehold or leasehold).

(b) The amount of the advance (loan) and period of the mortgage (eg, 25 years).

(c) The interest rate applicable to the loan. Unless the mortgage is a 'fixed rate' mortgage, this rate may from time to time be altered in line with changes in bank base rates.

(d) The amount of the borrower's initial monthly repayments to the lender. This sum is subject to fluctuation if the interest rate charged under the mortgage is altered.

(e) Whether the mortgage is to be repayment or endowment. In the case of the latter, the offer will usually stipulate the details of the life policy which is to be taken out over the borrower's life and the time by which this must be done (eg, by completion date).

(f) Where the lender is to insure the property, the amount of cover and when that cover will start. The solicitor must ensure that the time when the lender's policy is to come into force coincides with the contractual provisions relating to insurance (see **Chapter 22**). The amount of cover taken out by the lender is usually index-linked and may appear to be for an amount in excess of the current purchase price. This is because the insurance is to cover the cost of rebuilding the property in the event of its total destruction and, where the property is not detached, must also cover the cost of repairs to any adjoining or neighbouring property which is damaged by the accident.

(g) Details of any repair works which the lender requires to be carried out to the property, including the time limit by which these works must be done.

Where repairs are required, the lender may also decide to hold back a part of the loan until he is satisfied that the repairs have been completed. This 'retention' from the mortgage advance will cause a shortfall in the money available on completion and a recalculation of the client's finances will be necessary to ensure that sufficient funds will be available both to complete the transaction and to carry out the necessary repairs.

(h)   The amount of any 'guarantee premium' which is payable by the borrower. Where the lender is agreeing to lend a larger sum than he feels is advisable in the circumstances of the case, some lenders insist that an insurance policy is taken out to insure against the risk of the borrower defaulting on the mortgage and the lender not being able to recover the full amount owing on resale of the property. A single premium is payable for this insurance. The cost is usually borne by the borrower (see **8.2.2**).

(i)   It is usually a term of a mortgage offer for a first mortgage over property that any existing mortgage which the client has (eg, over his present house) should be discharged on or before completion of the new loan. The buyer's solicitor must ensure that his client is aware of and can comply with this condition.

20.3   Conditions attached to offer

Before accepting the offer or committing his client to the purchase, the buyer's solicitor should ensure that his client understands the conditions and terms attached to the mortgage offer and will be able to comply with them. Conditions may be general (eg, a condition that the property must not be let to a tenant without the lender's consent) or special, having application to this offer only (eg, a condition that the buyer carries out certain repairs to the property). The solicitor should check the offer to see whether or not the lender requires a formal acceptance of the offer. If a formal acceptance is required, the client must be advised to do this within the time limit stipulated by the lender. Failure to accept a formal offer (where required) will result in the mortgage funds not being available to complete the transaction.

20.4   Instructions to act

At the same time as a mortgage offer is sent to the client, the lender will instruct solicitors to act for him in connection with the grant of the new mortgage. These solicitors will receive a number of documents from the lender, including instructions to act (which contain similar information to the mortgage offer sent to the borrower), blank mortgage deeds and any other documents relevant to the transaction. In many cases, the solicitor who is instructed to act for the lender will be the same solicitor who is acting for the borrower. The objectives of these two clients coincide in that both seek a property which is structurally sound and has a good safe legal title; the risk of conflict of interests nevertheless exists and the solicitor must always bear in mind that he owes a duty to both clients (see *Mortgage Express v Bowerman & Partners (A Firm)* [1996] 2 All ER 836). Acting for both clients in this way has advantages in terms of time and costs, since the same solicitor can do the work required for both clients at the same time.

20.4.1   The *Lenders' Handbook*

If a solicitor is to act for both lender and borrower, then the conditions laid down by the Solicitors' Code of Conduct must be complied with – see **5.3**. Most lenders have adopted the *Lenders' Handbook* promulgated by the Council of Mortgage

Lenders. This is a set of standardised mortgage instructions, written in plain English, and use of it guarantees compliance with the requirements of the Solicitors' Code. The instructions in the *Handbook* are in two parts. Part 1 applies to all lenders using the *Handbook*; Part 2 sets out the requirements of each individual lender in cases where they differ from Part 1. Part 1 of the *Lenders' Handbook* is set out in **Appendix 7**. It should be noted, however, that the *Handbook* is liable to change and that a printed version should not be relied upon. An up-to-date version can be obtained from the Council of Mortgage Lenders' website at www.cml.org.uk, as can copies of Part 2 for any particular lender.

The solicitor must ensure that he carries out his lender client's instructions as set out in both parts of the *Lenders' Handbook*.

20.5   Conflict of interests

Where some of the conditions attached to the mortgage offer are unacceptable or prejudicial to the buyer client, and where the buyer's solicitor has also been instructed to act for the lender, a conflict arises between the interests of the buyer client and the lender client. Unless the conflict can be resolved to the satisfaction of both clients, the solicitor cannot continue to act for either. If it comes to the notice of the solicitor that the buyer client will be in breach of the terms of the mortgage offer (eg, where the purchase price for the property has been misrepresented to the lender), the lender must be informed of the breach (but see 20.5.1).

20.5.1   Duty of confidentiality

Where a conflict of interests exists between the buyer client and the lender client, the solicitor, acting in his capacity of adviser to the buyer, may disclose the nature of the conflict to the lender only with the consent of the buyer client (see *Halifax Mortgage Services v Stepsky* [1996] 1 FLR 620). Disclosure of information without the buyer client's consent will be a breach of the solicitor's duty of confidentiality. In such a case the CML *Lenders' Handbook* (para. 1.15) requires the solicitor to cease acting for the lender.

Chapter 21

The Deposit

21.1 Need for deposit

It is customary for a buyer, on exchange of contracts, to pay to the seller a deposit of 10% of the purchase price. Standard contractual conditions (such as SC 2.2) reflect this practice. In law, a deposit is unnecessary, and neither common law nor statute provides for any deposit to be payable.

21.1.1 Purpose of deposit

The payment of a deposit acts as part payment of the purchase price, demonstrates the buyer's good intentions of completing the contract and gives the seller leverage to ensure the fulfilment of the contract, since he is usually able to forfeit the deposit if the buyer defaults.

21.2 Preliminary deposits

Neither party needs to pay a preliminary deposit since neither is committed to the sale and purchase until contracts have been exchanged. An estate agent will frequently ask a prospective buyer to pay a preliminary deposit as an indication of the buyer's good intentions to proceed with negotiations. If a preliminary deposit is paid, the buyer should ensure that the agent has the seller's authority to receive the deposit. In the absence of the seller's authority, the buyer has no recourse against the seller if the agent misappropriates the money (see *Sorrell v Finch* [1977] AC 728). A preliminary deposit is normally fully refundable to the buyer if the transaction does not proceed.

21.2.1 Buying a newly built house

A seller who is a builder or developer will invariably require a prospective buyer to pay a preliminary deposit. Since this type of preliminary deposit often buys an option to purchase a numbered plot at a stated price, it is not unusual to find that the deposit is not returnable to the buyer in any circumstances, although it will be credited as part of the purchase price if the matter proceeds.

21.3 Amount of deposit

No deposit at all is payable unless the contract expressly makes provision for one. A deposit of 10% of the purchase price has until recently been standard practice and is the figure provided by SC 2.2 (SCPC 2.2) in both sets of Standard Conditions unless specifically amended. Deposits of less than 10% are not uncommon.

21.3.1 Reduced deposit

It is clearly to the seller's advantage to demand a 10% deposit. If, however, he is asked by the buyer to accept a reduced amount, the following matters should be considered by the seller's solicitor:

(a)   The risk of the sale going off, with the consequent need to forfeit the deposit to compensate for loss.

(b)   The amount of the buyer's mortgage offer. (It may be reasonable to accept a less than 10% deposit from a buyer who has a firm offer of advance for the whole of the balance of the purchase price, taking into account the amount of the reduced deposit.)

(c)   The likely amount of loss which the seller would suffer if the buyer were to default (eg, the cost of bridging finance or interest needed to complete a related purchase, the length of time which will be taken to effect a resale and the costs of such a resale).

21.3.2 Seller's solicitor's duty

The seller's solicitor must explain the consequences of taking a reduced deposit to his client and obtain his client's express authority before agreeing to accept a reduced deposit. *Morris v Duke-Cohan & Co* (1975) 119 SJ 826 suggests that it may be professional negligence for a solicitor to accept a reduced deposit without the client's express authority.

21.3.3 No deposit payable

Only in exceptional circumstances should the transaction proceed without any deposit being taken. Examples might include family transactions, or sales to sitting tenants. However, in commercial transactions, some major institutions will refuse to pay a deposit on the basis that they are of such standing that there is no risk of loss to the buyer.

21.3.4 Calculating the deposit

The amount of the deposit actually payable on exchange should take into account any preliminary deposit already paid. Under SC 2.2.1 it is calculated as 10% of the total of the purchase price and the price payable for any chattels included in the sale. Under SCPC 2.2.1 the deposit is 10% of the 'purchase price'. Whether the 'purchase price' includes any chattels will depend upon the special conditions.

21.4 Funding the deposit

Instructions should be obtained from the buyer client as to how he proposes to fund the deposit. When initial instructions are taken from the client, it is best to assume that the seller will require payment of a full 10% deposit. If the buyer wishes to pay a reduced deposit, the matter will have to be raised during negotiations with the seller's solicitor.

21.4.1 From an investment account

Where the buyer intends to fund the deposit from money in an investment account held by him, the length of notice which the buyer needs to give to withdraw his funds without losing a significant amount of interest should be borne in mind.

21.4.2 Bridging finance

Bridging finance from a bank or other lender may be needed in a situation where the purchase is dependent on a related sale. Bridging finance will be required in the situation where the buyer will have sufficient funds for all of the purchase price on completion (eg, because of a related sale), but does not have sufficient funds at exchange of contracts to fund the deposit. A loan will then be required to 'bridge the gap' between when the money is needed (exchange) and when it will be available (completion of the sale). It should be apparent at an early stage in the transaction that bridging finance will be required and arrangements should be made as soon as possible, so that the money is immediately available when required on exchange. An undertaking to repay the bridging loan out of the proceeds of sale of the client's existing property will often be required from the solicitor.

The client should be advised about the costs and risks of bridging finance, such as the high interest rate which will be payable over an uncertain period if the sale goes off, and the arrangement fees charged by the lender for negotiating the loan. If the client has a high cash flow passing through his current account, it may be more cost effective for him to take advantage of the lower interest rates payable on an overdraft on current account.

21.4.3 Deposit guarantees

A deposit guarantee, obtainable from some insurance companies, is an insurance policy which is bought by the buyer and tendered to the seller on exchange in place of payment of a money deposit. If the buyer wishes to fund the deposit in this way, the seller's consent must be obtained and the contract amended to provide for payment by way of the guarantee. The guarantee should be taken out in the sum required as deposit (ie, normally 10% of the purchase price). The seller will be able to enforce the guarantee against the insurance company, and so recover the deposit in cash in the event of the buyer defaulting on completion. Although guarantees which can be moved up through a chain of transactions can be obtained (ie, their benefit can be assigned), they are not popular with sellers and are not commonly used.

21.4.4 Use of deposit from related sale

If the buyer is also selling his existing house, he will be receiving a deposit on that sale. Can that money be used to fund (or partly fund) the deposit on the purchase? Standard Condition 2.2.5 permits this in certain circumstances (see **21.6.1**). If, as is likely, the deposit received on the sale is less than the deposit required on the purchase, the balance can be funded in one of the ways previously mentioned. Alternatively, it may be possible to persuade the seller to accept a reduced deposit, ie, to try to get the deposit reduced to the amount being received by the buyer on the sale of his present house.

Such a provision is obviously inapplicable in a commercial transaction and so the Standard Commercial Property Conditions do not include a similar provision.

21.5   Clearing funds

The buyer's solicitor must ensure that he receives the amount of the deposit from his own client in sufficient time to allow the client's cheque to be cleared through the solicitor's client account before drawing the cheque in favour of the seller.

21.6   Capacity in which deposit is held

The deposit can be held in one of the three capacities listed below:

(a)   agent for the seller;

(b)   agent for the buyer;

(c)   stakeholder.

Most deposits are paid to the seller's solicitor in the capacity of stakeholder.

21.6.1   Capacity implied by law

In the absence of contrary agreement, solicitors and estate agents hold in the capacity of agent for the seller, but an auctioneer holds as stakeholder (see *Edgell v Day* (1865) LR 1 CP 80; *Ryan v Pilkington* [1959] 1 All ER 689). This general rule may be varied by express contractual condition. Both sets of Standard Conditions of Sale (SC 2.2 and SCPC 2.2) generally provide for the deposit to be held as stakeholder. However, SC 2.2.5 allows the seller to use the deposit as deposit on his related purchase of a house for his own occupation, provided that in such related purchase it will be held on the same terms as the Standard Condition. This is a very important provision as it allows the seller to use the deposit to fund his own deposit on a related purchase without the need for the express permission of the buyer. It is widely taken advantage of in practice. Such a provision is inapplicable in a commercial transaction and so the Standard Commercial Property Conditions do not include a similar provision.

21.6.2   Agent for the buyer

The capacity of agent for the buyer is rarely used, since in most situations the seller will be reluctant to agree to the deposit being held in this way. It may, however, be necessary to use this capacity where the seller is represented by an unqualified person.

21.6.3   Agent for the seller

If the deposit is held as agent for the seller, the agent may hand the money over to the seller before completion. This capacity is advantageous to the seller who can, if he wishes, use the money immediately for any purpose he wishes. Where this occurs, the buyer may have difficulty in recovering the money if the seller defaults on completion, because the money will have passed into the hands of a third party who may be unknown to the buyer and with whom the buyer has no contractual relationship. If either set of the Standard Conditions is being used, a special condition will be required to state that this capacity is to apply if the deposit is to be held by the seller's solicitor. However, in the case of auction sales, Condition 2.3.6 of both sets of Standard Conditions provides for the deposit to be held by the auctioneer as agent for the seller. It is also usual on the purchase of a new house from a builder to find that the deposit is to be held as agent. This is to allow the builder to use the money to fund the building work. The risk here is that the builder may become insolvent, but any loss in such a situation would be fully recoverable as long as the builder is selling the house with NHBC or similar insurance cover (see **41.2.3**).

21.6.4 Stakeholder

A stakeholder is a middleman standing between both parties and, where this capacity is used, the money cannot generally be handed to either party without the consent of the other. This capacity is disadvantageous to the seller (because he cannot use the money), but advantageous to the buyer who knows that the money is safe in the solicitor's bank account and will therefore be recoverable in the event of the sale going off due to the seller's default. However, SC 2.2.5 mitigates this disadvantage to the seller by allowing him to use the deposit on a related purchase of a house for his own occupation, provided that in such purchase the deposit will be held on the same terms as SC 2.2.5 and 2.2.6. So, even if the deposit is passed along a chain of related purchases, it will ultimately be held by a solicitor as stakeholder.

21.7 Methods of payment of deposit

Except in the case of an auction sale, SC 2.2.4 requires the deposit to be paid either by a direct credit to the seller's solicitor's bank account or by a cheque drawn on a solicitor's or licensed conveyancer's client bank account. SCPC 2.2.2 requires the deposit to be payable by a direct credit, again with an exception in the case of auction sales. These provisions are designed to avoid problems with the payment of cheques drawn on the buyer's personal bank account which might be dishonoured when presented for payment. Both sets of Standard Conditions do allow payment by a personal cheque in the case of auction sales, but this is often varied by a special condition to provide for a more secure form of payment.

21.8 The deposit cheque bounces

If a cheque taken in payment of the deposit bounces, this constitutes a fundamental breach of contract which gives the seller the option either of keeping the contract alive, or of treating the contract as discharged by the breach, and in either event of suing for damages (*Millichamp v Jones* [1983] 1 All ER 267). A separate cause of action arises out of the cheque itself. The contract should be drafted to indicate precisely what the rights of the parties are in the event of the dishonour of the deposit cheque. Standard Condition 2.2.2 (SCPC 2.3.7) allows the seller to give notice to the buyer that the contract has been discharged by his breach, provided that he does so within seven working days of his being informed of the cheque being dishonoured.

The option of treating the contract as discharged is of little consolation to a seller who, on the strength of his sale contract, has exchanged contracts for the purchase of another property. Provision is therefore made in the contract to ensure that the deposit is payable by a method which will be honoured on presentation (see SC 2.2.4, which requires payment to be made by direct credit or solicitor's or licensed conveyancer's cheque and SCPC 2.2.2, which requires payment to be made by a direct credit to be held by the seller's conveyancer as stakeholder). The seller should insist on compliance with these conditions.

21.9 Interest on the deposit

Where the deposit is held by a solicitor, irrespective of the capacity in which the money is held, interest may be payable under r 24 of the Solicitors' Accounts Rules 1998. Standard Condition 2.2.6 (SCPC 2.2.2) provides that where the deposit, or part of it, is held in the capacity of stakeholder, interest on the deposit will be payable to the seller on completion. If the buyer negotiates an agreement that he is to be credited with interest on the deposit, a special condition must be inserted in the contract to that effect.

21.9.1 The Solicitors' Accounts Rules 1998

The Solicitors' Accounts Rules 1998 apply to all money held by a solicitor on behalf of a client, including a deposit held by a solicitor as agent or stakeholder in a conveyancing transaction. Where the rules apply, interest must be paid to the client irrespective of whether the money was held on deposit or current account.

Where clients' money is held in a separate designated account, the solicitor must account to the client for the interest actually earned on that account. A separate designated account must be a deposit account. If the money is held in a general client account, the duty to pay interest depends on the amount of money held and the period for which it is held. Interest must be paid when the money is held for as long as or longer than the number of weeks set out in the table below and the minimum balance held during that period equals or exceeds the amounts set out in the table.

No of weeks	Minimum balance (£)
8	1,000
4	2,000
2	10,000
1	20,000

If a sum exceeding £20,000 is held for less than one week and it is fair and reasonable to do so, the solicitor must pay interest on that sum to the client.

21.9.2 Rate of interest

The rate of interest for money not held in a separate designated account is the rate currently payable on small deposits by the bank or building society where the money is held. Where money is held in a separate designated account (which should be a deposit account with a building society or major clearing bank), the amount of interest payable is the sum actually earned on that money while on deposit.

21.10 Buyer's lien

From the moment when he pays the deposit to the seller in the capacity of agent (but not stakeholder), the buyer has a lien over the property for the amount of the deposit. The lien is enforceable only by a court order for sale of the property and may be protected as a notice (registered land) or Class C(iii) land charge (unregistered land). If the buyer is in occupation, his lien may be an overriding interest in registered land under the LRA 2002. It is not usual to register the lien unless problems arise in the transaction.

Chapter 22

Insurance

22.1 Risk in the property

At common law, and unless the contract provides otherwise, the risk of accidental damage to the property passes to the buyer from the moment of exchange of contracts. The buyer bears the risk of loss or damage, except where it can be shown that the loss or damage is attributable to the seller's lack of proper care (*Clarke v Ramuz* [1891] 2 QB 456; *Phillips v Lamdin* [1949] 2 KB 33). The buyer should therefore normally insure the property from exchange of contracts onwards. A solicitor who fails to advise his client of the consequences of failure to insure, or who fails to carry out his client's instructions to insure the property, will be liable in negligence if the client suffers loss as a result of the lack of insurance.

Although the seller is under no obligation to insure the property, he will normally maintain his existing insurance policy until completion (if the seller has a mortgage, he will be under an obligation to do so). In such a case there will be two insurance policies covering the property and a risk that, on a claim being made, the buyer's insurers would reduce the amount payable because of the existence of the other policy (if you have two insurance policies over a property, you cannot claim the full value twice). Buyers should, therefore, include a special condition in the contract to the same effect as SCPC 7.1.4(b) (see **22.3.3**).

22.2 Insuring the property

It is essential that the buyer's insurance arrangements have been made in advance of actual exchange so that the policy will be effective immediately upon exchange. Insurance is generally effected by one of the following methods:

(a) By noting the property on a block policy held by the buyer's solicitor which covers all properties currently being handled by the firm.

(b) Where the buyer is financing his purchase with the assistance of a mortgage, the lender will normally insure the property on being requested to do so by the buyer's solicitor. The lender's standing instructions to solicitors should be checked to ensure that:

    (i) the amount of cover will be adequate both in terms of the value of the property and the type of risks covered;

    (ii) the property will be put on cover from the time of exchange;

    (iii) the lender's insurance requirements do not conflict with the terms of the contract or of any lease to which the property is subject.

(c) By the buyer taking out a policy which will cover the property from exchange.

22.3 Property at seller's risk

In some cases, and commonly with new property which is in the course of construction, the contract will provide that the property is to remain at the seller's risk until completion.

22.3.1 Standard Condition 5.1

Standard Condition 5.1 provides for the seller to bear the risk in the property until completion, and permits rescission if the property is substantially damaged between exchange and completion. Except in certain cases applicable to the sale of leaseholds, the seller is not obliged by the condition to maintain his own insurance policy after exchange. Where the risk in the property remains with the seller, the buyer need not take out his own policy until completion.

Standard Condition 5.1 is sometimes expressly excluded by special condition, in which case the insurance position under the contract reverts to the common law principles, ie the buyer takes the risk from exchange and therefore must insure from that time. Irrespective of the terms of the contract, the buyer's lender will frequently insist that the property is insured in the buyer's name from the date of exchange. The lender's instructions must therefore be checked to ensure that they do not conflict with the provisions of the contract.

22.3.2 The Law of Property Act 1925, s 47

Standard Condition 5.1 excludes the LPA 1925, s 47, which would otherwise give the buyer the right, in certain circumstances, to claim off the seller's policy in the event of damage to the property.

22.3.3 The Standard Commercial Property Conditions

Standard Commercial Property Condition 7 takes a completely different approach from the Residential Standard Conditions. It does not change the common law position that the risk passes to the buyer on exchange. SCPC 7.1.4(a) provides that the seller is under no obligation to insure the property, except where required by the terms of any lease or the contract of sale. It is, therefore, essential for a buyer to take out his own policy of insurance as from exchange.

However, in practice, it is likely that the seller will keep up his policy until completion, and SCPC 7.1.4(b) deals with such a case of dual insurance. Where there are two policies on the same property, there is a danger that, on a claim being made, an insurance company would reduce the amount it was prepared to pay out because of the existence of the other policy. SCPC 7.1.4(b) thus provides that where there is a reduction in any payment made to the buyer because of the existence of the seller's policy, the purchase price is to be reduced accordingly. The seller could then claim that reduction from his insurers.

The Commercial Conditions also envisage the possibility of a condition being included in the sale contract requiring the seller to maintain his insurance until completion. If such a special condition is included, SCPC 7.1.2 requires the seller (inter alia) to maintain the policy until completion. If, before completion, the property suffers damage, the seller must pay to the buyer all policy monies received, or assign to the buyer all rights under the policy. Similar provisions apply if the seller is obliged to insure the property under the terms of a lease. This might be the case where the property being sold is leasehold, and the seller, as tenant is obliged to insure under the terms of the lease, or where freehold property is being sold subject to a lease and the seller, as landlord, is similarly obliged to insure.

22.4   Maintenance of seller's policy

Except where the seller is required by a condition of the contract of sale or his mortgage or lease to maintain his policy, he could cancel his insurance policy on exchange of contracts but, in practice, he would be unwise to do so (eg, in case the buyer failed to complete). The seller should also be advised not to cancel his contents or other policies until completion.

22.5   Other types of insurance

In appropriate cases, the buyer should be advised to take out insurance to cover other risks (eg, life insurance). These policies should be taken out immediately after exchange of contracts, so that their proceeds would be available to the buyer's personal representatives in the unlikely event of the buyer dying before completion takes place. If the buyer did die at this stage of the transaction the personal representatives could be forced to complete the sale, and without the proceeds of a life policy they would not have the funds to do so since the buyer's mortgage offer would have been revoked by his death. Advice given by the solicitor to his client about the terms of a life insurance policy will in most cases be subject to the provisions of the Financial Services and Markets Act 2000. A house contents policy does not need to be taken out until the buyer moves his furniture into the property (ie, normally on completion day).

Chapter 23

Preparing to Exchange

23.1 Introduction

A binding contract will come into existence on exchange of contracts, after which time neither party will normally be able to withdraw from the contract without incurring liability for breach. It is therefore essential to check that all outstanding queries have been dealt with and that all financial arrangements are in order before the client is advised to commit himself to the contract.

23.2 Matters to be checked

Consideration should be given to the following matters before exchange takes place. The matters marked with an asterisk in the lists concern both seller and buyer; the unmarked items are mainly of concern to a buyer client.

23.2.1 Searches

(a)   Have all necessary searches and enquiries been made?

(b)   Have all the replies to searches and enquiries been received?

(c)   Have all search and enquiry replies been checked carefully to ensure that the replies to individual questions are satisfactory and accord with the client's instructions?

(d)* Have all outstanding queries been resolved?

(e)   Has a survey of the property been undertaken and, if so, is the result satisfactory?

23.2.2 Financial arrangements

(a)   Has a satisfactory mortgage offer been made and (where necessary) accepted by the client?

(b)   Are arrangements in hand to comply with any conditions attached to the advance (eg, obtaining estimates for repairs to the property)?

(c)   Taking into account the deposit, the mortgage advance (less any retention) and the costs of the transaction (including disbursements), is there sufficient money for the client to proceed with the purchase?

(d)* Have arrangements been made to discharge the seller's existing mortgage(s) or, on a sale of part, to release the part being sold from the mortgage?

23.2.3 Deposit

(a)* How much (if any) preliminary deposit has been paid?

(b)* How much money is needed to fund the deposit required on exchange?

(c)   Has a suitable undertaking been given in relation to bridging finance?

(d)* To whom is the deposit to be paid?

(e)   Have the deposit funds been obtained from the client and cleared through clients' account?

23.2.4 The contract

(a)* Have all outstanding queries been satisfactorily resolved?

(b)* Have all agreed amendments been incorporated clearly in both parts of the contract?

(c)* Has the approved draft been returned to the seller?

(d)* Is a clean copy of the contract available for signature by the client?

(e)* Have the terms of the contract been explained to the client?

(f)* Has the list of fixtures and fittings been agreed between the parties?

23.2.5 Insurance

(a)   Have steps been taken to insure the property immediately on exchange?

(b)   Have steps been taken to obtain any life policy required under the terms of the buyer's mortgage offer?

23.2.6 Completion date

*   Has a completion date been agreed?

23.2.7 Method of exchange

(a)* Which method of exchange is most suitable to be used in this transaction?

(b)* Where the client requires a simultaneous exchange on both sale and purchase contracts, are both transactions and all related transactions in the chain also ready to proceed?

23.2.8 Signature of contract

*   Has the client signed the contract?

23.2.9 Occupiers

*   Has the consent of all non-owning occupiers been obtained?

23.3 Reporting to client

When the buyer's solicitor has completed his searches and enquiries, and the form of the draft contract has been agreed, he should report to his client in writing, explaining the results of his investigations and the terms of the contract and mortgage offer to the client. Some firms prepare a 'Buyer's Report' for this purpose.

23.4 Signature of contract

Both parties must sign the contract (or each must sign one of two identical copies) in order to satisfy s 2 of the Law of Property (Miscellaneous Provisions) Act 1989. The signature need not be witnessed. Signature by a duly authorised agent is sufficient.

23.4.1 Signature by the client

Signature by the client in the presence of his solicitor, the solicitor first having ensured that the client understands and agrees with the terms of the contract, is desirable but is not always practicable. Where the contract is to be sent to the client for signature, the accompanying letter should clearly explain where and how the client is required to sign the document. If not already done, the letter should also explain the terms of the contract in language appropriate to the client's level of understanding, and request a cheque for the deposit indicating by which date the solicitor needs to be in receipt of cleared funds.

23.4.2 Signature by solicitor on behalf of client

A solicitor needs his client's express authority to sign the contract on behalf of the client (*Suleman v Shahsavari* [1989] 2 All ER 460). Unless the solicitor holds a valid power of attorney, it is recommended that such authority should be obtained from the client in writing, after the client has been informed of the legal consequences of giving such authority (ie, signature implies authority to proceed to exchange, and exchange creates a binding contract). Failure to obtain authority may render the solicitor liable in damages for breach of warranty of authority (*Suleman v Shahsavari* (above)).

23.4.3 Companies

Provided that the transaction has been authorised by the company, an officer of the company (usually a director or the secretary) may be authorised to sign on behalf of the company.

23.4.4 Client's authority

Before exchanging contracts, the solicitor should ensure that the client's authority to exchange has been obtained. Clients should be made aware of the consequences of exchange, ie, that they can no longer withdraw from the transaction. In order to emphasise the importance of exchange, some firms require instructions to exchange to be given in writing.

Chapter 24

Exchange of Contracts

24.1 The practice of exchange

The physical exchange of contracts between the parties is not a legal requirement for a contract for the sale of land, but where a contract is drawn up by solicitors acting for the parties it is usual for the contract to be prepared in two identical parts, one being signed by the seller, the other by the buyer. When the two parts are physically exchanged, so that the buyer receives the part of the contract signed by the seller and vice versa, a binding contract comes into existence. The actual time when the contract comes into being depends on the method which has been used to effect the exchange.

Since exchange is not a legal necessity, it is possible for the contract to comprise a single document which is signed by both parties. In such a case, the contract becomes binding and enforceable as soon as the second signature has been put on the document (*Smith v Mansi* [1962] 3 All ER 857). This situation is uncommon because the same solicitor is usually forbidden to act for both parties by r 3.07 of the Solicitors' Code of Conduct.

24.2 Authority to exchange

A solicitor who exchanges contracts without his client's express or implied authority to do so will be liable to the client in negligence. In *Domb v Isoz* [1980] 1 All ER 942, it was held that once the solicitor has his client's authority to exchange he has the authority to effect the exchange by whichever method the solicitor thinks most appropriate to the situation.

24.3 Methods of exchange

Whichever method is chosen, the exchange is usually initiated by the buyer indicating to the seller that he is now ready to commit himself to a binding contract. Once contracts have been exchanged, neither party will be able to withdraw from the contract. It is therefore essential that the parties' solicitors have checked that all necessary arrangements are in order before proceeding to exchange. Also, in residential transactions, where the purchase of one property is dependent on the sale of another, the solicitor must ensure that the exchange of contracts and completion dates on both properties are synchronised to avoid leaving his client either owning two houses or being homeless. Failure to synchronise the exchange where the client has instructed that his sale and purchase transactions are interdependent constitutes professional negligence. The solicitor must ensure, therefore, that he either exchanges on both the sale and the purchase or exchanges on neither; he does not want to be in the position of exchanging on one transaction, only to find that the other party to the dependent transaction has decided to withdraw. Ideally, the exchange on the two transactions should take place simultaneously in order to avoid this danger, but this is not practical. The best that the solicitor can do is to ensure that there is as little time delay as is practically possible between exchanging on one transaction and on the other.

24.3.1 Telephone

Exchange by telephone is now the most common method of effecting an exchange of contracts. Legal recognition of the practice was given by the Court of Appeal in *Domb v Isoz* [1980] 1 All ER 942. With the exception of personal exchange, this method represents the quickest way of securing an exchange of contracts and is particularly useful in a chain of transactions.

The method is not free of risk. Where exchange is effected by telephone, the contract between the parties becomes effective as soon as the parties' solicitors agree in the course of a telephone conversation that exchange has taken place. The telephone conversation is followed by a physical exchange of documents through the post, but the existence of the contract is not dependent on this physical exchange, the contract already exists by virtue of the telephone conversation. If one party were subsequently to change his mind about the contract, it would be easy to dispute or deny the contents of the telephone conversation and thus the existence of the contract itself. The problems arising out of a telephonic exchange are as follows:

(a)   neither party is able to check that the other's contract has been signed;

(b)   neither party is able to check that the other's contract is in the agreed form and incorporates all agreed amendments.

If one part of the contract has not been signed, or if the two parts are not identical, then there can be no contract, even if the parties purport to exchange. The seller may also be exchanging without having received a deposit. This would be professional negligence on the part of his solicitors.

To avoid the uncertainties arising out of this method of exchange, the parties' solicitors must agree prior to exchange that the telephonic exchange will be governed by one of The Law Society's formulae which were drawn up by the Society in response to the decision in *Domb v Isoz* (above). An accurate attendance note recording the telephone conversation must also be made as soon as possible. The formulae rely on the use of solicitor's undertakings to overcome these problems.

24.3.2 Use of the formulae for exchange

There are three Law Society formulae:

(a)   Formula A: this is used where one solicitor (usually the seller's solicitor) already holds both parts of the contract before the exchange is initiated;

(b)   Formula B: this is used where at the time of the telephone exchange each party's solicitor is still in possession of his own client's signed contract;

(c)   Formula C: this is designed to be used in chain transactions.

The wording of the formulae is set out in **Appendix 4**. Whichever formula is used, the client's express authority to exchange must be obtained before the procedure to exchange is commenced. If any variation to a formula is to be made, that variation must be expressly agreed and noted in writing by all the solicitors involved before exchange takes place. Subject to agreed variations, the conditions attached to the formula in use must be strictly adhered to.

24.3.2.1 Formula A

This is little used in practice. The buyer will have sent his part of the contract, together with the deposit cheque, to the seller, with an instruction to hold both of these to his order. When ready to exchange, the buyer will telephone the seller and a completion date will be agreed. The seller will then confirm that he holds his client's part of the contract duly signed by the seller and that this is in the agreed form. It will then be agreed that exchange takes place as at that moment. The seller then undertakes to send his client's part of the contract to the buyer on the same day.

In practice, Formula A is the safest of the three formulae to use because, before actual exchange takes place, the seller's solicitor has the opportunity of seeing the buyer's signed part of the contract and can check that it is identical to his own client's part. He is also usually in possession of the buyer's deposit cheque, which will have been sent to him with the buyer's part of the contract. Although the seller cannot bank the cheque until exchange has taken place, he is secure in the knowledge that the deposit will be paid.

24.3.2.2 Formula B

This is the most commonly used of the formulae. Each solicitor still holds his own client's part of the contract. In the telephone conversation, both will confirm that their respective parts of the contract are signed and in the agreed form. After the exchange has taken place each undertakes to hold their signed part of the contract to the other's order. Then both parties undertake to send their respective parts of the contract to the other, the buyer also undertaking to send the deposit. Although not specifically designed for use in chain transactions, it is frequently used in such situations.

Imagine a chain of transactions in which A is selling to B, who, in turn, is selling to C. We act for B, who thus has a dependent sale (to C) and purchase (from A). Before exchanging with C, we will check with A that he is ready to exchange and agree a completion date. We will then exchange with C, with completion fixed for the same day. (Agreeing the same completion date for both transactions may in reality need further telephone calls.) Having exchanged with C, we will then immediately telephone A and exchange with him. There is, of course, a risk that since first speaking to A, his client may have decided to withdraw, but this is often thought an acceptable risk as long as contracts can be exchanged on the same day as the initial assurance was received. The other main problem comes if we (B) wish to use the deposit received from C as the deposit on our purchase from A. When we exchange with A we will not have then received the money from C and so will not be able to give the Formula B undertaking that we will send it 'that day'. Prior to exchanging on either transaction, therefore, we will have had to obtain A's approval to an amendment to the formula. We could either undertake to get C to send the money direct to A, or alternatively undertake that we have exchanged with C and will send the money on as soon as it is received by us.

24.3.2.3 Formula C

This is specifically designed for use in chain transactions and will avoid any risk of a client exchanging on one transaction without also exchanging on the dependent transaction. It also makes provision for the seller using the buyer's deposit towards the deposit he will need to pay on his dependent purchase. It is, however, somewhat complex and thus little used in practice in many areas of the country. Formula C consists of two parts. Under Part I, the parties will initially agree that they each hold signed parts of the contract (as in Formula B). Exchange does not take place at that time, however, but each party undertakes that they will exchange, provided that the other party contacts them by a specified time later that day. This thus gives time for both buyer and seller to enter into any dependent contract, secure in the knowledge that this first transaction will become binding provided that contact is made by the specified time. Part II of Formula C is activated later when contact is made by the specified time. Under this there is the usual undertaking as to exchange taking place, but also provision for buyer and seller to make use of a deposit due under a dependent sale. So the undertaking is that the buyer will either send the deposit 'that day' or 'arrange' for it to be sent. So a buyer can arrange for the buyer on his own sale to send it. And it is to be sent either to the seller or to such other solicitor as the seller nominates, so allowing the seller to use that same money as deposit on his own related purchase. Note, however, that before using Formula C, we will need to have obtained our client's express permission to use that formula.

24.3.3 Personal exchange

By this method, the solicitors for the parties meet, usually at the seller's solicitor's office, and the two contracts are physically exchanged. A contract exists from the moment of exchange. Although this type of exchange represents the safest and most instantaneous method of exchange, it is frequently not practical to use personal exchange because the physical distance between the offices of the respective solicitors makes it impractical to do so. Personal exchange is infrequently used in residential transactions, but is still used in high-value commercial contracts. This method has two benefits: it is instantaneous, thus leaving no uncertainty over the timing of the creation of the contract; and it enables both parties to see the other party's part of the contract before exchange actually takes place, so that both can check that the parts of the contract are identical in form and have been properly signed. The seller can also ensure that he is in receipt of the deposit before exchanging.

24.3.4 Postal exchange

Where exchange is to take place by post, the buyer's solicitor will send his client's signed contract and the deposit cheque to the seller's solicitor who, on receipt of these documents, will post his client's signed contract back to the buyer.

Generally, a contract does not come into being until the buyer has received the seller's contract. Exchange of contracts by post forms an exception to this rule and the contract is made when the seller posts his part of the contract to the buyer (*Adams v Lindsell* (1818) 1 B and Ald 6813). It follows from the above that a contract will be formed even if the seller's part of the contract is lost in the post and never received by the buyer.

Using the post as a method of exchange is reasonably satisfactory when dealing with a single sale or purchase which is not dependent on another related transaction, but even in this situation there will inevitably be a delay between the buyer sending his contract to the seller and the seller posting his part back, during which time the buyer is uncertain of whether he has secured the contract. There is also no guarantee that the seller will complete the exchange by posting his part of the contract back to the buyer. Until he actually does so, he is free to change his mind and withdraw from the transaction. Although these risks are small where a single sale or purchase is being undertaken, they assume a much greater significance where a chain of transactions is involved and the use of postal exchange is not advised in linked transactions.

24.3.5 Document exchange

A document exchange, or DX, is a private postal system not under the control of the Post Office. Most solicitors belong to a document exchange. A document exchange can be used to effect an exchange of contracts in a similar way to the normal postal service and is subject to the same risks. The court has approved the use of document exchanges for the service and delivery of documents in non-contentious matters in *John Wilmott Homes v Reed* (1986) 51 P & CR 90. The rules on postal acceptance do not apply to document exchanges and, unless the contract contains a contrary provision, the contract will come into existence when the seller's part of the contract is received by the buyer. Where either set of Standard Conditions is used, Condition 2 provides that the contract is made when the last copy of the contract is deposited at the document exchange. If the Standard Conditions of Sale do not form the basis of the contract, the contract probably comes into existence when the last part of the contract is placed in the recipient's box at the document exchange, but there is no decided case in this area.

24.3.6 Fax

The main use of fax in the context of exchange of contracts is to transmit the messages which activate the Law Society formulae. Fax is merely a substitute for using the telephone. Condition 1.3.3 in both sets of Standard Conditions does not permit fax to be used as a valid method of service of a document where delivery of the original document is essential (as it is with the contract), thus effectively ruling out an exchange by faxing copies of the signed contract. Further, an exchange of faxes is not a valid exchange of contracts under s 2 of the Law of Property (Miscellaneous Provisions) Act 1989 (*Commissioner for the New Towns v Cooper (Great Britain) Ltd* [1995] Ch 259).

24.3.7 E-mail

At the moment, contracts for the sale of land must be in writing so cannot be entered into electronically via e-mail or the Internet. However, e-mail can be used to transmit the messages activating The Law Society formulae.

The Government's proposals for electronic conveyancing would allow contracts to be made electronically. There would then be only one copy of the contract which would be stored and 'signed' electronically. Thus there would no longer be exchange of contracts; instead the contract, once 'signed' by both parties, would come into existence at a time agreed between the parties. An electronic 'signature' will consist of the transmission of an encrypted message which is certified as coming only from the person transmitting it.

24.4 Standard Conditions of Sale

Standard Condition 2.1 and SCPC 2.1 govern the making of the contract and allow contracts to be exchanged by document exchange, post, or by telephone using the Law Society formulae.

24.5 Insurance

If the buyer is to insure the property from exchange (see **Chapter 22**), the buyer's solicitor should immediately after exchange put in hand the previously decided arrangements. So, for example, if the buyer's lender is to effect the insurance, the lender should be telephoned immediately and informed that contracts have been exchanged and that the property should be placed on risk. Written or faxed confirmation of the telephone call should also be given.

Parts II and III Summary – Taking Instructions to Exchange of Contract

Sub-section heading	Summary
Taking instructions	The transaction will begin when the buyer makes an offer to buy the property for an agreed price. The seller and buyer then need to instruct a legal practitioner to act on their behalf. Save in exceptional circumstances, they will need to be separately represented.
	In both cases, detailed instructions should be taken. Key points include obtaining details of the following:
	• the property;
	• the parties;
	• the agreed sale price; and
	• the timetable to which the parties are working and whether the clients have a related sale or purchase which must be co-ordinated.
	In the case of a buyer, the following additional points are also key:
	• **Finances** It is important to check that the buyer can afford to buy the property. This will include not only the purchase price but additional expenses such as any SDLT payable.
	Details of any mortgage being raised need to be obtained. It is usual, in residential transactions, for the solicitor also to act for the lender, and this needs to be confirmed.
	As an additional issue, it needs to be confirmed how the buyer is going to fund any deposit payable on exchange, as any mortgage advance will not normally be available to help fund this.
	• **Co-owners** Where there are joint buyers, the ways in which the beneficial interest can be held – joint tenancy and tenancy in common – need to be explained and a decision made by the clients as to how they are to hold the property.
Searches and enquiries	This section deals with three separate issues: searches and enquiries; investigation of title; and surveys.
	The buyer will need to carry out detailed investigations to find out about the property he has agreed to buy. This is referred to as carrying out searches and enquiries. In the case of residential property, some of this information will be provided in the Home Information Pack by the seller.

Sub-section heading	Summary
	Precisely what searches and enquiries need doing will vary from transaction to transaction, and geographical and physical location are important factors in decided what needs to be done. The following are regarded as being necessary in a typical transaction:
	• **'Local Search'** This is made up of two elements: a search of the local land charges register; and enquiries of the local authority. In combination, these will reveal a lot of important information such as details of planning permissions granted and whether roads serving the property are maintainable at the public expense.
	• **Drainage and Water enquiries** This will confirm details of whether the property has foul and surface drainage to the public sewer, and whether it is connected to the public water mains.
	• **Enquiries of the seller** The seller will be able to provide a wealth of valuable information about the property. Although the enquiries can take any format, in the case of residential transactions, it is usual to adopt the forms made available under The Law Society's Protocol scheme. In commercial transactions, many practitioners use the Commercial Property Standard Enquiries, drafted by a working party of representatives of the property industry.
Investigation of title	The buyer's solicitor will need to investigate title. In the case of registered land, this will be provided by the seller in the form of official copies of the title and the title plan. In the case of unregistered land, title is usually provided in the form of an epitome of title – a copy of the title deeds together with an index showing its contents.
	The buyer's solicitor will need to check that the seller has title to sell the property, and that the covenants and easements affecting the property provide adequate protection and rights for the buyer but do not impose burdens which are going to be problematic.
Survey	The seller makes no promise about the physical state of the property and will not generally be liable after sale for any defects that are revealed. The buyer must therefore consider commissioning a survey before exchange of contracts. If problems are revealed, the buyer may need to approach the seller to negotiate a reduction in the purchase price.
	It is desirable to obtain a full survey in all cases, but the cost of obtaining the appropriate level of survey will be a factor that may influence the ultimate decision by the client in this respect.

Sub-section heading	Summary
The contract	The contract is the document which will bind the seller to sell and the buyer to buy the property. It is drafted by the seller's solicitor and, once agreed, in order to be binding, must be in writing, signed by all the parties and contain all the terms of the contract, either because the terms are all printed in the contract itself or by reference to some other document.
	The precise form the contract takes can vary. Standard form printed contracts are available, but many practitioners now use word-processed versions tailored to reflect the needs of their practice. Whatever format is used, the contract will contain details of the following:
	• the property;
	• the seller and buyer;
	• incumbrances that bind the property, such as covenants and easements. Usually, this should not include any mortgage currently over the property as this will be discharged by the seller from the proceeds of sale;
	• the amount of the deposit; and
	• whether any chattels are included in the sale.
	In addition, the contracts will also incorporate detailed provisions to govern the relationship between the parties, such as what happens if completion is delayed. These are generally known as standard conditions and two versions are commonly in use: the Standard Conditions of Sale 4th Edition and the Standard Commercial Property Condition 2nd Edition. The former is used in most residential transactions and can also be used in commercial transactions. The latter is designed to be more tailored to the needs of a commercial transaction. Whichever version is used, it will need to be incorporated expressly into the contract.
	The standard form printed contracts reproduce the standard contracts as part of the contract itself.
Exchange of contracts	Exchange of contracts is the point at which the parties become legally bound to each other. It is therefore essential to ensure that all outstanding matters are settled before this date, including the buyer's finances. Where a party has a related sale and purchase, it is important to synchronise exchange on both transactions.
	On exchange, it is usual for the buyer to pay a deposit, as provided in the contract. The buyer's solicitor should check that funds are available for this, ready for exchange.

Sub-section heading	Summary
	Exchange can be carried out in person, but it is now more usual for it to be done by telephone. The Law Society has devised formulae, labelled A, B and C, in order to ensure this happens satisfactorily. Formula A is used when one party's solicitor holds both signed contracts. Formula B, the most commonly used, applies where each party holds their client's signed contracts. Formula C was designed for use where there is a long chain of dependent sales and purchases, but it is complex and, in practice, little used.
	The formulae rely on the giving of undertakings. If each side holds their client's signed part copy of the contract, they must undertake to forward this to the other side. The buyer's solicitor will also need to undertake to forward the deposit to the seller's solicitor. In the light of the undertakings being given and the significance of exchange, a detailed written note should be taken.
	The contract may provide for the buyer to take over responsibility for insurance of the property from exchange. Where this is the case, appropriate cover should have been arranged in advance and be ready to be put into effect following exchange. The contract should be checked carefully to determine the precise position in this respect.

Part IV
AFTER EXCHANGE

Chapter 25

The Consequences of Exchange

25.1 The effects of exchange

Following exchange a binding contract exists from which normally neither party may withdraw without incurring liability for breach. At common law, the beneficial ownership in the property passes to the buyer, who becomes entitled to any increase in value of the property but also bears the risk of any loss or damage; hence the need to ensure that insurance of the property is effective from the moment of exchange.

The seller retains the legal title to the property until completion, but holds the beneficial interest on behalf of the buyer. During this period, the seller is entitled to remain in possession of the property and to the rents and profits (unless otherwise agreed). He must also pay the outgoings (eg, water rates) until completion. He owes a duty of care to the buyer and will be liable to the buyer in damages if loss is caused to the property through neglect or wanton destruction (*Clarke v Ramuz* [1891] 2 QB 456; *Phillips v Lamdin* [1949] 2 KB 33). This duty continues as long as the seller is entitled to possession of the property, and does not terminate because the seller vacates the property before completion.

25.2 After exchange

25.2.1 The seller

The seller's solicitor should inform the client and estate agent that exchange has taken place and enter the completion date in his diary or file-prompt system. Where exchange has taken place by telephone, the copy of the contract signed by the seller should immediately be sent to the buyer's solicitor to fulfil any undertaking given in the course of an exchange by telephone, having first checked that the contract is dated and contains the agreed completion date. Any deposit received must immediately be paid into an interest-bearing clients' deposit account.

25.2.2 The buyer

The buyer's solicitor should inform the client and his lender that exchange has taken place and enter the completion date in his diary or file-prompt system. Where exchange has taken place by telephone, he should immediately send to the seller (or as directed by him) the signed contract and deposit cheque in accordance with the undertaking given, having first checked that the contract is dated and contains the agreed completion date. Where appropriate, the contract should be protected by registration. Where the buyer is to insure (see **Chapter 22**), the buyer's solicitor should immediately put in hand the insurance arrangements previously decided upon.

25.3 Registration of the contract

25.3.1 Registered land

The contract constitutes a minor interest which, in order to bind future buyers of an interest in the land, needs to be protected by entry of a notice on the register of the title. A buyer who is in occupation of the property may have an overriding interest within the LRA 2002, in which case protection of the contract by registration is not necessary.

25.3.2 Unregistered land

The contract is an estate contract within the Class C(iv) category of land charge and will be void against a buyer of the legal estate for money or money's worth if not registered. Registration must be made against the name of the legal estate owner for the time being.

25.4 When to register the contract

Since completion of most contracts occurs within a very short period following exchange, in practice registration of the contract is uncommon.

However, the contract should always be registered if any of the circumstances listed below apply:

(a)   there is to be a long interval (eg, more than two months) between contract and completion;

(b)   there is reason to doubt the seller's good faith;

(c)   a dispute arises between the seller and buyer;

(d)   the seller delays completion beyond the contractual date.

25.5 Death of a contracting party

The death of one of the contracting parties between contract and completion does not affect the validity of the contract; the benefit and burden of the contract passes to the deceased's personal representatives who are bound to complete.

If completion does not take place on the contractual completion date, a breach of contract will occur (irrespective of whether time was of the essence of the completion date) and remedies (eg, compensation, damages) will be available to the innocent party.

If time was not originally of the essence of the completion date, it can be made so by service of a notice to complete addressed to the deceased and the executor(s) named in the seller's will. A copy of the notice must be sent to the Public Trustee. If the deceased died intestate, notice can be served on the Public Trustee.

25.5.1   Death of one co-seller

Property owned by beneficial co-owners is held on a trust of land, and all the trustees must join in any conveyance of the legal estate. The death of one trustee between contract and completion does not, however, affect the validity of the contract. Where following the death there still remain at least two trustees of the legal estate, the transaction can proceed to completion without delay. In other cases, another trustee may have to be appointed so that the minimum number of two trustees is accomplished. This will depend upon whether the co-owners held the land as beneficial joint tenants or tenants in common (see **14.5.4**). It will be necessary to produce the death certificate of the deceased in order to provide the buyer with evidence of the death, and the purchase deed will need to be redrawn to reflect the change of parties to the transaction.

25.5.2   Death of buyer

The personal representatives step into the shoes of the deceased and will be bound to complete the contract. Some delay in completion may occur because the purchase deed will have to be redrafted to reflect the change in parties and the personal representatives cannot complete until they obtain the grant of representation. Where the purchase was due to be financed by a mortgage, the death of the buyer will usually mean that the offer of mortgage is revoked and the personal representatives may find themselves with insufficient funds to complete unless an alternative source of finance can be found, eg the proceeds of a life policy.

The survivor of joint buyers remains bound by the contract and can be forced to complete. Finance may have to be rearranged and a new mortgage deed prepared. Some delay will be inevitable, and the seller will have a claim against the buyer for loss caused by the delay.

25.6   Bankruptcy

25.6.1   Bankruptcy of seller

A buyer will be affected by the bankruptcy of the seller only if there is a bankruptcy entry shown on the result of his official search or on official copy entries. On the bankruptcy of an individual, the legal estate in property owned by him passes to his trustee in bankruptcy and the buyer must from that time deal only with the trustee and not the seller. The trustee may complete the sale subject to his right to disclaim onerous property. Property is defined as 'any unprofitable contract'. However, the trustee is not allowed to disclaim the contract just because he could raise more money by selling to someone else. The trustee will thus normally proceed with the sale.

However, a trustee also has powers to apply to court to set aside transactions at an undervalue. There will be such a transaction if the consideration provided by the buyer is 'significantly' less than the value of the property being sold.

Where the matter proceeds to completion, the purchase deed will have to be redrafted to show the trustee as the seller. The bankrupt is not a party to the deed. Some delay may occur pending appointment of the trustee and while the purchase deed is redrafted and re-executed.

The legal estate in property held by co-owners does not vest in a bankrupt's trustee, but one co-owner's beneficial interest will do so on the latter's bankruptcy. Therefore, on the bankruptcy of one co-owner, the legal estate is unaffected and completion may proceed, the trustee joining in the purchase deed to give his consent to the sale of the beneficial interest.

25.6.2 Bankruptcy of buyer

If the buyer goes bankrupt, the benefit of the contract passes to the buyer's trustee in bankruptcy who may complete the transaction, subject to his right to disclaim onerous contracts. Where the transaction was to be financed by a mortgage, the buyer's mortgage offer will have been revoked by the bankruptcy, and there will obviously be no other available funds to complete the purchase. Some delay is inevitable pending the appointment of the trustee and while waiting for his decision whether or not to disclaim.

Where one of two or more co-purchasers goes bankrupt, the bankrupt's equitable interest will pass to his trustee. The remaining buyer(s) may have difficulty in completing on the contractual completion date, or at all, since a joint mortgage offer may have been vitiated by the co-purchaser's bankruptcy.

25.7 Appointment of liquidator

Every disposition of a company's property after presentation of a winding-up petition to the court is void unless sanctioned by the court. The presentation of a petition for the compulsory winding-up of a company thus freezes the transaction until a liquidator is appointed. On a voluntary liquidation, the directors' powers cease on appointment of the liquidator. The liquidator can complete a sale transaction on behalf of the company and can (with the consent of the court) bring proceedings to force the buyer to complete. Where a seller company goes into liquidation the liquidator will normally complete the transaction. The company normally remains as 'seller', the liquidator attesting the deed on the company's behalf. The liquidator will be the 'seller' in the purchase deed only if an order vesting the legal estate in him has been made by the court. Such an order is rare in practice.

A copy of the liquidator's deed of appointment should be supplied on completion. Where the liquidator is appointed to a company which is buying land, the liquidator has power to complete or to disclaim onerous contracts, but lack of money may present practical problems in proceeding to completion. Some delay is inevitable in this situation, for which the innocent party may seek compensation by claiming in the liquidation.

25.8 The buyer in possession

In many cases, the seller will be in physical occupation of the property until completion and the question of the buyer taking possession before completion does not arise. The seller is entitled to retain possession until completion unless he agrees to do otherwise. The buyer's request to enter and occupy the premises before completion should be regarded with caution by the seller, because once the buyer takes up occupation he may lose his incentive to complete on the contractual completion date and if, ultimately, he does not complete the transaction at all, it may be difficult for the seller to regain possession of the property. Where the seller has a subsisting mortgage on the property, his lender's consent must be obtained before the buyer is allowed into occupation.

25.8.1 Occupation as licensee

In order to avoid problems relating to security of tenure arising from the buyer's occupation, it is essential to ensure that the buyer's occupation is as licensee and not as tenant. Standard Condition 5.2 expressly states that the buyer's occupation is to be construed as a licence, and this statement will probably be effective in most circumstances to prevent an inadvertent tenancy from arising. Even where a licence is granted, a court order will always be necessary to remove a residential occupier who does not voluntarily vacate the property (see the Protection from Eviction Act 1977, s 2) and may be necessary in non-residential cases where the tenant will not peaceably surrender his occupation.

25.8.2 Conditions of the buyer's occupation

25.8.2.1 Standard Conditions of Sale

Where the seller agrees to allow the buyer into possession, some restrictions or conditions should be attached to the buyer's occupancy. Standard Condition 5.2.2 sets out that the terms of the licence are that the buyer:

(a)   cannot transfer it;

(b)   may permit members of his household to occupy;

(c)   is to pay for or indemnify the seller against all outgoings;

(d)   is to pay the seller a fee calculated at the contract rate on the balance of the purchase price;

(e)   is entitled to the rents and profits from the property;

(f)   is to keep the property in as good a state of repair as it was when he took possession and not to make any alterations;

(g)   is to insure the property for not less than the purchase price and assume the risk of damage to the property;

(h)   is to quit the property when the licence ends.

Either party can terminate the licence on five working days' notice.

The buyer may wish to renegotiate some of these terms. He may wish, for example, to take possession for the purpose of carrying out building works for alterations, improvements, etc, which is not permitted under the Standard Condition. In deciding whether to agree to possession for this purpose, the seller should bear in mind that if the contract fails for some reason he may be left with a property severely damaged because of half-finished works of alteration or improvement. Standard Condition 5.2.4 provides that the buyer is not deemed to be in occupation for the purposes of this condition if he is merely allowed access to carry out work agreed by the seller. Accordingly, if the seller does allow the buyer access for such purposes, express provision will need to be made as to termination of the licence, making good any damage caused, etc.

As an alternative solution, the seller may consider granting the buyer a licence for access only (eg, for measuring up for carpets and curtains, or to obtain estimates for alterations to be made to the property after completion).

25.8.2.2 Standard Commercial Property Conditions

These contain no provisions allowing the buyer to take possession prior to completion, nor any provisions regulating such occupation. Such matters will thus need negotiating individually between the parties. Similar factors as those mentioned above would need to be considered.

25.9 Tenanted property

The Standard Commercial Property Conditions do contain extensive provisions dealing with tenanted property, both where the leasehold interest is being sold and where the freehold is being sold subject to tenancies. Thus SCPC 4.2 deals with general management issues, and SCPC 5 with rent reviews, which might arise between exchange and completion. These recognise that the buyer is concerned as to the outcome of such matters. So under SCPC 4.2.6, the seller is not to give or formally withhold any licence or approval under the lease without the buyer's consent. Similarly under SCPC 5.5 neither party is to agree a new rent figure unless the other agrees.

25.10 Pre-completion steps

Traditionally, the major task to be undertaken between exchange and completion was the deduction of title by the seller and its investigation by the buyer. Nowadays it is almost universal practice for proof of title to be dealt with at the pre-contract stage of the transaction. Thus, once contracts have been exchanged, most of the legal work in the conveyancing transaction has already been done by the parties' solicitors, and the interval between exchange and completion is used to tidy up outstanding matters and to prepare for completion itself. There are, however, four important matters which must be dealt with at this stage:

(a) preparation of the purchase deed;

(b) dealing with redemption of the seller's mortgage and the creation of the buyer's mortgage;

(c) pre-completion searches made by the buyer; and

(d) ensuring that the financial aspects of the transaction are in order.

25.11 The interval between exchange and completion

The interval between exchange and completion in residential transactions was conventionally a four-week period, giving ample time for the above tasks to be undertaken. In many cases, however, the clients will want completion to follow more quickly after exchange, a completion date which is 14 days or less after exchange being commonly encountered. In such a case, the solicitors will need to plan their timetable of pre-completion steps carefully to ensure that all necessary matters can be accomplished within the available time. Alternatively, in order to save time at this stage of the transaction, some of the pre-completion steps may be brought forward and dealt with at the pre-contract stage of the transaction. Pre-completion searches should be made as close to the date of actual completion as possible (see **Chapter 28**) because of the protection period given to the buyer with the result of an official search. There is no reason, however, why the preparation of the purchase deed should not be undertaken as soon as the contents of the contract have been agreed between the parties. It is sometimes the case that exchange and completion take place on the same day.

Chapter 26

Requisitions on Title

26.1 Purpose of requisitions

The purpose of requisitions on title is to require the seller's solicitor to clarify and, if necessary, to rectify matters on the title supplied which the buyer's solicitor finds unsatisfactory. In practice, they are commonly used also to resolve administrative queries relating to the arrangements for completion.

26.2 Time for raising requisitions

By SC 4.3.1 and SCPC 6.3.1, written requisitions on the title supplied must be raised within six working days after either the date of the contract or the day of delivery of the seller's evidence of title, whichever is the later. The buyer will lose his right to raise requisitions if he does not do so within the time limits prescribed by this condition.

26.2.1 Evidence of title supplied before exchange

In most cases, the seller's evidence of title will be supplied to the buyer before exchange of contracts, and the contract will contain a clause excluding the buyer's right to raise requisitions once contracts have been exchanged (see SC 4.2.1 and SCPC 6.2.1). The time limits contained in the Standard Conditions (or other form of contract used) allowing the buyer to raise requisitions also become irrelevant and, unless requisitions are raised before exchange of contracts, the buyer will be unable to query the title. Note, however, that such a special condition only prevents the buyer raising requisitions on the title as presented to him by the seller. If, after exchange, he discovers an undisclosed incumbrance or other defect, he will still be able to require it to be remedied or assert his remedies for non-disclosure (see **Chapter 33**). Standard Condition 4.2.2 (SCPC 6.2.2) requires the buyer to raise any further requisitions within six working days of any further matter coming to his attention.

26.3 Standard form requisitions

Most law stationers produce a standard form of requisitions on title which include many commonly asked questions (eg, confirmation that the seller's mortgage on the property will be discharged on or before completion). In addition, the printed questions frequently deal with the administrative arrangements for completion itself (eg, method of payment of money, the time and place for completion, whether completion can take place by post, etc). Queries which are specific to the title under consideration may either be added to the end of the standard form, or be typed on a separate sheet. Where title has been investigated before exchange, the only question relating to title is to ask the seller to confirm that nothing has altered since the date of exchange. The buyer's solicitor should send two copies of the form to the seller's solicitor, who will return one copy with his answers, keeping the other copy on his own file for reference. In Protocol cases, use of the Completion Information and Requisitions on Title Form is recommended. This form, as well as asking for the usual information, also contains a request for confirmation that existing mortgages will be discharged on completion. The answer to this question takes effect as an undertaking to discharge the mortgages referred to and avoids the need for such an undertaking to be handed over on completion. Note, however, that if the lender intends to make use of the Electronic Notification of Discharge (END) system, then this undertaking will need modifying: see **30.7.1.10**.

26.3.1 Replies to requisitions

Standard Condition 4.3.1 (SCPC 6.3.1) requires the seller's solicitor to reply to requisitions four working days after receiving them from the buyer's solicitor. This time limit does not apply to requisitions which are raised before exchange of contracts.

26.3.2 Further queries

The buyer's solicitor should ensure that the answers given to his requisitions are satisfactory in relation both to the title and to the client's interests. Any replies which are unsatisfactory should be taken up with the seller's solicitor and further written queries raised until the matter is resolved. Standard Condition 4.3.1 (SCPC 6.3.1) governs the time limits for raising further queries.

Chapter 27

The Purchase Deed

27.1 Who prepares the deed?

It is normally the buyer's duty to prepare the purchase deed, but the seller may, by s 48(1) of the LPA 1925, reserve the right by contractual condition to prepare the deed himself. This right is usually used only in sales of new houses where the seller will supply an engrossment (top copy) of the purchase deed after attaching a draft of this deed to the contract.

27.2 Time for preparation of the deed

Traditionally the purchase deed was prepared after the buyer has completed his investigation of title, but in practice the deed is usually prepared shortly after exchange of contracts and sent to the seller for his approval with the buyer's requisitions on title. At common law, the buyer is deemed to have accepted the seller's title when he submits the purchase deed for approval, and so the submission of the purchase deed at the same time as requisitions are raised would preclude the buyer's right to raise requisitions on the seller's title. This problem is resolved by SC 4.6.1 (SCPC 6.6.1), which preserves the buyer's right to raise requisitions in such circumstances, subject to any express condition in the contract barring out requisitions. By SC 4.3.2 (SCPC 6.3.2), the buyer is required to submit the draft purchase deed to the seller at least 12 working days before contractual completion date. Under the Protocol, the buyer's solicitor is required to submit the draft purchase deed simultaneously with his requisitions on title, as soon as possible after exchange of contracts and in any case within the time limits specified in the contract.

27.3 Form of the deed

The purchase deed must be a deed in order to transfer the legal estate in the land to the buyer (LPA 1925, s 52). The purchase deed puts into effect the terms of the contract and so must reflect its terms. The form of the deed varies depending on whether the land concerned is registered or unregistered, freehold or leasehold. This chapter concentrates on the form of the purchase deed in freehold transactions. Leaseholds are dealt with in **Chapters 35** and **36**. Under the system of electronic conveyancing soon to be introduced, an electronic version of the purchase deed will be used. This will be deemed to be a deed, even though it does not satisfy the formal requirements.

27.3.1 Registered land

Where the property being transferred is registered land, the form of the purchase deed is prescribed by rules made under the LRA 2002 and, subject to permitted variations, the prescribed form of wording must be used. Many of the standard Land Registry forms are reproduced by law stationers and in straightforward transactions these can be used as the basis of the purchase deed. In more complex cases, it will be necessary to produce an individually drafted deed, but in either case the form of wording prescribed by the rules should be followed as closely as circumstances permit. A traditional conveyance cannot be used to transfer registered land. The same form of transfer is used whether the registered estate is freehold or leasehold.

27.3.2 Unregistered land

No prescribed form of wording exists for a conveyance of unregistered land. The buyer is thus free to choose his own wording, subject to the seller's approval and provided that it accurately reflects the terms of the contract. As the transaction will lead to an application for first registration of title after completion, instead of using a traditional conveyance the buyer may prepare his purchase deed as a Land Registry transfer.

27.4 Drafting the deed

When drafting the purchase deed the buyer's solicitor needs to have access to:

(a) the contract, because the purchase deed must reflect the terms of the contract;

(b) the official copy entries/title deeds, because the contract may refer to matters on the title which need to be repeated or reflected in the purchase deed; and

(c) except in straightforward cases, a precedent on which to base the deed under preparation.

27.5 Seller's approval of the draft deed

When the draft has been prepared, two copies should be sent to the seller's solicitor for his approval. A further copy of the draft should be kept by the buyer's solicitor so that amendments can be agreed over the telephone if required.

On receipt of the draft, the seller's solicitor should check it carefully to ensure that the document accurately reflects the terms of the contract. Amendments should be restricted to those which are necessary for the fulfilment of the document's legal purpose, bearing in mind that the choice of style and wording is the buyer's prerogative. Small amendments may be agreed with the buyer's solicitor by telephone in order to save time. More substantial amendments should be clearly marked in a distinct colour on both copies of the draft, one copy being returned to the buyer's solicitor for his consideration, the other being retained in the seller's solicitor's file for reference. Under both sets of Standard Conditions, the seller's solicitor is to approve or return the revised draft document four working days after delivery of the draft transfer by the buyer's solicitor (SC 4.3.2 and SCPC 6.3.2).

27.6   Engrossment

When amendments (if any) to the draft deed have been finalised, the buyer's solicitor should prepare an engrossment (clean copy) of the deed. The engrossment must be checked carefully to ensure that all agreed amendments have been incorporated. A copy of the engrossment should be kept on the buyer's solicitor's file for reference. The completed engrossment should then be sent to the seller's solicitor for execution (signature) by his client.

Where the buyer is required to execute the deed, it is common practice for him to do so before it is sent to the seller for his signature. By SC 4.3.2 (SCPC 6.3.2), the buyer must deliver the engrossment of the purchase deed to the seller at least five working days before completion.

27.7   Execution

To be valid in law a deed must:

(a)   indicate clearly that it is a deed (eg, by containing the words 'This deed');
(b)   be signed by the necessary parties in the presence of a witness; and
(c)   be delivered (Law of Property (Miscellaneous Provisions) Act 1989, s 1). (See also Land Registration (Execution of Deeds) Rules 1990 (SI 1990/1010).)

Signature by the seller is always required in order to transfer the legal estate (LPA 1925, s 52). The buyer is required to execute the deed if it contains a covenant or declaration on his behalf. Execution by the buyer will be needed where the document contains an indemnity covenant in respect of existing covenants, or a declaration by the buyers relating to the trusts on which they hold the property. Where other parties are joined in the deed (eg, a lender to release the property from a mortgage), they should also sign the document. The provisions relating to execution of deeds are further explained in **14.5.9**.

27.7.1   Signature by an individual

Signature by an individual must be made by him in person, preferably in ink. Where an individual is incapable of signing the document himself (eg, because he is blind or illiterate), another person may execute it on his behalf. In such a situation the document should be read over to the individual, or its contents clearly explained to him, before signature. Two witnesses are required to the signature in these circumstances (Law of Property (Miscellaneous Provisions) Act 1989, s 1).

27.7.2   Attorneys

A person who holds a power of attorney on behalf of another can execute a deed on that person's behalf. The attorney may sign either in his own name, or in that of the person on behalf of whom he is acting (eg, 'A by his attorney B' or 'B as attorney on behalf of A').

27.7.3   Companies

The requirements for execution of a deed by a company are set out at **14.5.9.4**.

27.7.4   Witnesses

Any responsible adult person may be a witness to the signature of an individual. There is no legal restriction on one party to a document being a witness to the other party's signature, nor on one spouse being a witness to the signature of the other spouse, but an independent witness is preferable because, if the validity of the document was ever challenged in court, the independent witness would provide a stronger testimony. The witness should sign his name and add, underneath the signature, his address and occupation. It is sensible to ask the witness also to write his full name in block capitals after his signature.

27.7.5 Delivery

In addition to being signed, a deed must be delivered, ie the parties must intend to be bound by it. A deed takes effect on its delivery. When the buyer delivers the engrossment to the seller for execution by him, he does not normally intend the deed to become effective at that time. It is therefore common practice for the buyer to deliver the deed to the seller 'in escrow', ie conditionally, so that the operation of the deed is postponed until completion. In the case of a company, delivery is presumed at the date of execution unless the contrary is proved (Companies Act 1985, s 36A).

27.8 Explaining the document to the client

A solicitor should always ensure before submitting a document for signature that the client understands the nature and contents of the document. Where the solicitor invites his client to sign the purchase deed in the solicitor's presence, the deed can be explained to the client before signature and may actually be signed in the presence of the solicitor who can then act as a witness to the signature. If this is not possible, the purchase deed may be sent to the client for signature and return. The letter which accompanies the purchase deed should:

(a)   explain the purpose and contents of the document;

(b)   contain clear instructions relating to the execution of the deed;

(c)   tell the client when the signed document must be returned to the solicitor; and

(d)   ask the client not to date the document (it is dated on actual completion).

27.9 Plans

If the contract provides for the use of a plan, the purchase deed will also refer to the plan. In other cases, the buyer is not entitled to demand that a plan is used with the purchase deed unless the description of the property as afforded by the contract and title deeds is inadequate without one. If the buyer wishes to use a plan in circumstances where he is not entitled to demand one, he may do so with the seller's consent, but he will have to pay for its preparation.

Where the sale is of the whole of the seller's property, use of a plan is not normally considered necessary. On a sale of part (including flats and office suites), a plan is highly desirable and, where the land is registered, generally must be used. The plan(s) to be used with the purchase deed should be checked for accuracy, including all necessary colourings and markings, and firmly bound into the engrossment of the deed, which should in its wording refer to the use of the plan(s). In registered land cases, all parties who execute the deed must also sign the plan as an acknowledgement of its inclusion as an integral part of the document. In unregistered land cases, signature of the plan is not compulsory but is highly desirable. Signatures on a plan need not be witnessed. Where a company seals the purchase deed, it should also seal the plan.

The preparation and use of plans are discussed at **15.5.1**.

27.10 Parties

Anyone whose consent is necessary in order to transfer the legal estate, or who is to give a valid receipt for capital money arising out of the transaction, must be joined as a party to the deed. The seller and buyer will usually be the only parties to the deed, but it may be necessary to join, for example, a receiver or liquidator, where a selling company is insolvent, or a non-owning occupier who will release his or her rights in the property. Where the seller is bankrupt, his trustee in bankruptcy will transfer the property so the seller is not a party to the deed. If the seller is a company which is in liquidation or under receivership, the company itself transfers the property, with the receiver or liquidator joining in the deed to give a receipt for the purchase price. In such a case, the liquidator actually executes the deed.

27.11 Transfer of whole

A transfer of the whole of a registered title will usually follow Land Registry Form TR1. A copy of this form is set out in **Appendix 8**. It is divided into a number of boxes and is designed so that it can be reproduced on a word processor. The following paragraphs discuss completion of these boxes in further detail.

27.11.1 Stamp duty

It was formerly necessary to complete Box 1 to comply with the requirements for paying stamp duty. However, following the introduction of stamp duty land tax as from 1 December 2003, this box can now be left blank.

27.11.2 Title number and property

Boxes 2 and 3 contain spaces for the title number and a description of the property. All of this information can be obtained from the official copy entries supplied by the seller. The description should include the postcode.

27.11.3 Date

The date will be left blank until completion (box 4).

27.11.4 Transferor

Box 5 contains space for the name of the transferor to be entered. If the transferor is a company, the registered number should be included. There is no need to include the transferor's address. Note that Form TR1 uses the terms 'transferor' and 'transferee'. If preferred, these can be changed to 'seller' and 'buyer'.

27.11.5 Transferee

The transferee's name and address (including postcode) should then be inserted in boxes 6 and 7. Again, a company's registration number should be included. The address will be the one which is entered on the register and is intended as an address at which any notices concerning the property can be served. It should, therefore, be the address which will be relevant after the purchase, ie, in the case of a house purchase, it will normally be the address of the property being purchased, assuming that the buyers do intend to reside there. Note that up to three addresses for service can be stated including an e-mail address, to ensure that any notices from Land Registry do come to the proprietor's attention.

27.11.6   Operative words and consideration

The operative words, ie, 'the transferor transfers the property to the transferee', are printed in box 8 and need no amendment. The amount of consideration must be expressly stated in box 9 and should be set out in both words and figures. The amount stated should be the total amount payable for the property (ie, not just the balance due on completion) but should exclude any amount payable in respect of chattels. Where VAT is payable, the amount stated should include VAT. It is on this amount that the liability to stamp duty land tax will be calculated. There is a pre-printed receipt clause which renders unnecessary the need for any other receipt and is authority for the buyer to pay the money over to the seller's solicitor. Note that if chattels are being purchased for an additional sum, a separate receipt will need to be prepared for this amount.

27.11.7   Title guarantee

On the reverse of the form, box 10 requires an X to be inserted to indicate whether the transfer is with full or limited title guarantee. There is also space to include any modifications to the covenants which may have been agreed in the contract.

27.11.8   Declaration of trust

Where there is more than one transferee, box 11 requires the buyers to declare whether they will hold the land as joint tenants or tenants in common. If they are to hold as tenants in common, it is necessary for the precise shares to be set out. If the trusts are complicated, they should be continued onto the prescribed continuation sheet (form CS). Alternatively, a separate deed of trust can be drafted. This may be preferable as any document sent to Land Registry is open to public inspection and it may well be that the buyer will not want details of the trust to be open to public view. If a separate deed is used, this need not be sent to Land Registry, the TR1 simply declaring that the property is held on the trusts declared by that deed.

27.11.9   Additional provisions

There is then a box (box 12) in which any other agreed clauses can be inserted. The most common will be an indemnity covenant. Remember, that additional clauses can be included only if they were agreed in the contract. Where the sale is subject to any obligation on which the seller will remain liable after the sale, SC 4.6.4 and SCPC 6.6.4 will provide that the buyer should enter into an indemnity covenant. A typical form of wording to comply with the Standard Condition would be as follows:

> The transferees jointly and severally covenant to observe and perform the covenants referred to in Entry No 1 on the charges register and to indemnify the transferor against any future liability for their breach or non-observance.

27.11.10   Execution

The form then ends with space for the execution by the parties (box 13). The seller must always execute; a buyer need only execute if he is entering into covenants or making some form of declaration in the transfer. Due to the inclusion of the declaration of trust for co-owners, co-owners will always need to execute the deed. The form of execution is laid down by the Land Registration Rules 2003 and will vary depending upon the identity of the signatory, but a witness will always be required.

27.12 Conveyance

As a conveyance of unregistered land will lead to first registration, it is possible to use the usual form of Land Registry transfer, ie, Form TR1 (see **27.11** and **Appendix 8**). This is very commonly used in practice. The only amendments required to the printed form will be the omission of the title number in box 2 – as the land is not registered there will not be one – and the need to include a fuller description of the property in box 3. This need contain only a reference to another document in the title which contains a full description. This might read, for example:

> 10, Coronation Street, Weatherfield, GM4 8YY, as is more particularly described in a conveyance dated 4 February 1962 and made between.....

It will also be necessary to include reference (in box 12) to the incumbrances subject to which the property has been sold.

Where a traditional conveyance is to be used, it will contain the same information as in Form TR1, but in a different format.

An example of a conveyance drafted in a modern style is given below.

27.12.1 Specimen modern form: conveyance

This Conveyance is made on

between FREDERICK ALBERT BROWN and CLAIRE BROWN both of Brookside, 73A Manor Grove Avenue, Newton, Blankshire ('the Sellers') and LEONARD ARTHUR JOHNSON and JENNIFER JOHNSON both of 27 Albert Road, Newton, Blankshire ('the Buyers').

1. In consideration of ninety-nine thousand eight hundred pounds (£99,800) paid by the Buyers to the Sellers (the receipt of which the Sellers acknowledge) the Sellers convey to the Buyers with full title guarantee the freehold property known as Brookside 73A Manor Grove Avenue, Newton, Blankshire described in a Conveyance dated 18th November 1970 and made between John Edward Smith and the Sellers ('the Property') subject to the matters in that Conveyance so far as they affect the Property and are still effective.

2. The Buyers hold the Property on trust for themselves as joint tenants.

3. The Buyers jointly and severally covenant with the Sellers to observe and perform the restrictions covenants and conditions contained in a conveyance dated 23rd April 1938 and made between Hedley Verity of the one part and Wilfred Rhodes of the other and to indemnify the Seller against any future breach or non-observance.

Signed as a deed and delivered by   )
Frederick Albert Brown
and Claire Brown   }
in the presence of:)

Signed as a deed and delivered by   )
Leonard Arthur Johnson
and Jennifer Johnson   }
in the presence of:)

Chapter 28

Pre-completion Searches

28.1 Who makes the searches?

It is the buyer's solicitor's responsibility to ensure that such pre-completion searches as are relevant to the transaction are carried out, and that their results are satisfactory to his client. The buyer's lender also has an interest in the soundness of the title to the property and the solvency of the borrower, so searches will need making on the lender's behalf also.

28.2 Reason for making searches

The main reason for making pre-completion searches is for the buyer's solicitor to confirm that information obtained about the property before exchange remains correct.

28.3 When to make searches

The searches must be made in sufficient time to guarantee that the results are received by the buyer's solicitor in time for completion to take place on the contractual completion date. Pre-completion searches should generally be made about seven days before the contractual completion date, but may be left until closer to completion date if, for example, a telephone, computer or fax search is to be made.

28.4 Which searches to make

The following searches should be made:

(a) for registered land, search against title number at the Land Registry (see **28.5**);

(b) for unregistered land, including an unregistered reversion to a lease, search at the Land Charges Department against names of estate owners of the land (see **28.6**);

(c)   if acting for a lender, a bankruptcy search against the name of the borrower (see **28.7**);

(d)   such other of the searches listed in **28.8–28.13** as are relevant to the transaction.

28.5   Land Registry search

Registered Land

When buying registered land, a pre-completion search should be made at the appropriate Land Registry Office. The object of the search is to ascertain whether any further entries have been made on the register of title to the property since the date of the official copies supplied prior to exchange. A fee is payable. Fees can be paid by cheque or credit account, provided in the case of the latter that the applicant's solicitor's key number is quoted on the application form. Prescribed forms of wording should be followed when requesting a search by telex or fax. The Land Registry Direct Service and NLIS now enable solicitors to make searches via the Internet, but they can also be made by post or telephone.

28.5.1   Search of whole title

Where the interest being purchased, leased or mortgaged concerns the whole of a registered title, the search application should be made on Form OS1 (see **Appendix 8**). The application will give details of the title number of the property to be searched, a brief description of its situation, ie, postal address, county and district, and the names of the registered proprietors. The applicant's name must also be given, together with his reason for making the search, ie, he intends to purchase/lease/take a charge on the land.

Where a solicitor is acting both for a buyer and his lender, the search application should be completed in the name of the lender client. If this is done, the buyer can take the benefit and protection of the search and a separate search in the buyer's name is unnecessary. However, a search made on behalf of the buyer will not protect a lender.

The search application form asks the registrar to supply information relating to any fresh entries which have been made on the register since a stated date, which will usually be the date of the official copy entries given to the buyer and must be a date no earlier than 12 months before the date of the search application. An official certificate of search made on this form confers on the searcher a priority period of 30 working days from the date of the certificate. This provides protection to the buyer (and lender, if the search was made on his behalf) against any subsequent entries which may be placed on the register after the date of the search but before the buyer is registered as proprietor. The buyer will take free from any such entries, provided that he submits his application for registration within the priority period.

Unregistered land.

28.6   Land Charges Department search

This search is only of relevance to unregistered land and is made by submitting Form K15 to the Land Charges Department at Plymouth with the appropriate fee. Fees can be paid by credit account, provided the applicant's solicitor's key number is stated on the application form. An official certificate of result of search confers a priority period of 15 working days on the applicant. This protects the buyer against any entries which may be made on the register after the date of the search but before he completes the purchase. Provided that he completes the transaction within the 15 working days priority period, the buyer will take free from such entries. The search application can be made by post, telephone, telex or fax by a credit account holder. Where title was deduced prior to exchange, and this search was carried out at the pre-contract stage of the transaction, the search need only now be made against the current seller's name. This is to ensure that no further entries have been made against the seller's name since the date of the previous search. No further entries can validly be made against the names of previous estate owners once they have disposed of the land, so these need not be searched against again.

28.6.1 Form of the register

The register comprises a list of the names of estate owners of land, with details of charges registered against those names. The search is therefore made not against the land itself but against the names of the estate owners. A fee is payable for each name searched. The search must be made against the names of all the estate owners whose names appear on the abstract or epitome of title supplied by the seller, including those who are merely referred to in the bodies of deeds (as opposed to being parties to the deeds themselves) or in schedules attached to deeds which form part of the title. There is no need to repeat searches where a proper search certificate made against previous estate owners has been supplied with the abstract of title.

The register is maintained on a computer which will search only against the exact version of the name as shown on the application form. It is therefore important to check that the name inserted on the application form is identical to that shown on the title deeds and that, if any variations of that name appear in the deeds, for example if Samuel Smith is variously referred to as 'Sam Smith', 'Samuel James Smith' and 'Samuel Smyth', all the given variations of the name are separately entered on the search form and a separate fee paid in respect of each. Guidance on filling in the application form, together with a list of accepted abbreviations and variations which the computer will search against, is given in Land Registry Practice Guide 63.

28.6.2 Period to be searched against

It is generally only possible for an effective entry to be made against a name in relation to that person's (or company's) period of estate ownership of the land in question. It is therefore usually only necessary to search against a name for the period during which the estate owner owned the land and for the period between his death and the date of the appointment of personal representatives. For the purposes of the search form, periods of ownership must be stated in whole years and can be ascertained by looking at the abstract or epitome of title supplied by the seller. If the estate owner's period of ownership is not known, as will be the case when searching against the name of the person who was the seller in the document forming the root of title, the search is, in practice, made from 1926 (the year when the register was opened). Where there is a voluntary disposition in the title which is, at the date of the contract, less than five years old, it is necessary to search against the donor's name for a period up to and including the current year to ensure that no bankruptcy of the donor occurred during this period. The bankruptcy of the donor during this period could lead to the disposition being set aside by the trustee in bankruptcy (see **14.5.8**).

28.6.3 Description of the land

Unless a description of the land is inserted on the search application form, the computer will produce entries relating to every person of the given name in the whole of the county or counties specified. In order to avoid having to read through and then reject multiple search entries revealed by the certificate of search, a brief description of the land, sufficient to identify it clearly, should be included on the application form. Although the intention of describing the land is to curtail the number of irrelevant entries produced by the computer, care should be taken in supplying the description, because an inaccurate description of the land may result in a relevant entry not being revealed by the search.

Particular care is needed when the abstract shows that the land formerly was part of a larger piece of land (eg, when buying one plot on a building estate where the estate is being built on land which was previously part of a farm), because the land may previously have been known by a description other than its current postal address. If the search is limited to the present postal address, entries registered against its former description will not be revealed by the search. In such a case, both the present address and former description of the land should be entered on the search application form.

There is a possibility that because of local government reorganisation the land was formerly situated in a different administrative county from that in which it is now. For the reasons given above, both the present and former county must be included in the description of the land given on the search application form. Where the postal address of the property differs from its actual address (eg, the village of Rogate is in the administrative county of West Sussex, but its postal address is Hampshire), the search must be made against the actual address of the property, not its postal address.

28.6.4 Pre-root estate owners

The buyer does not need to search against estate owners who held the land prior to the date of the root of title supplied to him, except in so far as the names of such persons have been revealed to him in documents supplied by the seller.

28.6.5 Official certificate of search

An official certificate of search is conclusive in favour of the searcher, provided that the search has been correctly made, ie it extends over the whole period of the title supplied by the seller and has been made:

(a) against the correct names of the estate owners for this period;

(b) against the correct county or former county; and

(c) for the correct periods of ownership of each estate owner.

In order to ensure that the buyer gains the protection afforded by the search and the accompanying priority period, it is vital to check that the search application form is accurately completed.

28.6.6 Search certificates supplied by the seller

Where the seller provides previous search certificates as part of the evidence of title, it is not necessary to repeat a search against a former estate owner provided that the search certificate supplied by the seller reveals no adverse entries and:

(a) was made against the correct name of the estate owner as shown in the deeds;

(b) was made for the correct period of ownership as shown in the title deeds;

(c) was made against the correct description of the property as shown in the deeds; and

(d)   the next disposition in the chain of title took place within the priority period afforded by the search certificate.

If any of the conditions outlined above is not met, a further search against the previous estate owner must be made.

28.7   Bankruptcy search

Irrespective of whether the transaction relates to registered or unregistered land, a lender will require a clear bankruptcy search against the name of the buyer before releasing the mortgage funds. Unless a full search of the register has been made on Form K15 (which includes a bankruptcy search) (see **28.6**), the lender's solicitor should submit Form K16 to the Land Charges Department, completed with the full and correct names of the borrower(s). A search certificate will be returned by the Department. In the unusual event of there being an adverse entry revealed by the search, the lender's instructions must be obtained immediately. Paragraph 5.12.2 of the CML *Lenders' Handbook* makes it clear that the lender will not proceed to advance the loan unless the solicitor certifies that the entry does not relate to the borrower, ie, that it relates to someone else with the same name. If a solicitor certifies a search entry as not relating to his client, this certification is construed as an undertaking. Obviously, a solicitor must take great care in giving such a certificate. The Insolvency Service website (www.insolvency.gov.uk) enables a free instant search of current bankruptcies to be made which will reveal the date of birth of the person against whom a bankruptcy order has been made. This can then be compared with the client's birth details on the document used to prove identity. In case of any doubt, the matter must be reported to the lender which will make its own enquiries. However, a delay in completion will be inevitable and the lender may decide not to proceed with the loan. It is for this reason that it is suggested that this search should be made prior to exchange (see **18.9**). It will need repeating prior to completion to cover the possibility that the buyer has become bankrupt since the date of the previous search (although the chances of this are very slight) and it will ensure that many potential problems can be resolved at a time where they will not cause a delay in completion.

28.8   Company search

A company search may be done as one of the pre-contract searches and the information updated at this stage of the transaction. The procedure for making a company search is discussed at **18.10**.

28.8.1   Registered land

When buying registered land from a company, it is prima facie unnecessary to make a company search in addition to a Land Registry search. However, floating charges and impending insolvency will not generally be revealed by a Land Registry search and it is suggested that a company search (which will reveal these things) should still be made, even in the case of registered land. A floating charge is a type of mortgage which can be created by a company but not by an individual. The charge 'floats' over all the assets of the company so that the company is free to deal with its assets without the lender's consent, perhaps selling some, free of the charge, to a third party and buying others, which become subject to the charge as soon as they are acquired by the company. The charge fixes and attaches to particular assets of the company (which then cannot be dealt with without the lender's consent) only when it crystallises. Crystallisation occurs when a specified event happens which makes the sum due under the mortgage payable (eg, default in payment of an instalment). A certificate of non-crystallisation given in a letter signed by the lender may be needed where a floating charge subsists.

28.8.2   Unregistered land

When buying unregistered land from a company, or where the title reveals that a company had previously owned the land, a company search ought to be undertaken in order to ensure that there are no adverse entries which would affect the buyer. Adverse entries would include such matters as fixed or floating charges, or the appointment of a receiver or liquidator.

28.9   Enduring powers of attorney

Where the purchase deed is to be executed by a person who is acting under the authority of an enduring power of attorney, a search should be made with the Office of the Public Guardian to check whether or not registration of the power has been effected or is pending. If no registration has been made or is pending, the transaction may proceed to completion. If the power has been registered, the attorney may deal with the land and thus, provided the donor is still alive, completion may proceed, because the power is no longer capable of revocation without notification to the Public Guardian. While registration is pending, the transaction may proceed only if it is within one of the limited categories permitted by the Enduring Powers of Attorney Act 1985.

28.10   Local land charges search and enquiries

These searches are invariably made before exchange of contracts and are discussed in **Chapter 18**. Although the local land charges search shows only the state of the register at the time of issue of the search certificate, and neither search confers a priority period on the buyer, a repeat of these searches before completion is not normally considered to be necessary, provided that completion takes place within a short time after receipt of the search results. Delay in receipt of the replies to these searches sometimes makes it impracticable for them to be repeated at this stage of the transaction. These searches should nevertheless be repeated prior to completion if:

(a)   there is to be a period of two months or more between exchange of contracts and completion, and the search has not been covered by insurance or replaced by insurance; or

(b)   information received by the buyer's solicitor suggests a further search may be advisable in order to guard against a recently entered adverse entry on the register; or

(c)   the contract was conditional on the satisfactory results of later searches.

The discovery of a late entry on such a search is not a matter of title and will not entitle the buyer either to raise requisitions about the entry, or to refuse to complete, unless the contract was made conditional on the satisfactory result of searches. It is still, however, best for the client to be advised of any further entries so that he understands the position he will be in once the purchase has been completed.

Although clause 5.2.3 of the CML *Lenders' Handbook* requires that all searches should be not more than six months old at the date of completion, many conveyancers consider that repeating the searches after two months is preferable. Some lenders will, however, accept search insurance in such a situation which will provide insurance indemnity against late entries.

28.11   Inspection of the property

Inspection or re-inspection of the property may be necessary just before completion. Such a step is advisable in the case of the purchase of a house which is in the course of construction (and may be done by the buyer's lender's surveyor in such cases), or where there has been a problem with non-owning occupiers. Inspection of the property is dealt with at **18.17**.

28.12   Results of searches

Completion cannot proceed until the search results have been received and are deemed to be satisfactory to the interests of the client. In the majority of cases, the results of searches will either show no subsisting entries or merely confirm information already known, such as an entry on the register protecting existing restrictive covenants. In such circumstances, no further action on the search results is required from the buyer's solicitor. If an unexpected entry (other than a Class D(ii) entry protecting restrictive covenants, which cannot generally be removed) is revealed by the search result, the buyer's solicitor should:

(a)   find out exactly what the entry relates to;

(b)   if the entry appears adversely to affect the property, contact the seller's solicitor as soon as possible to seek his confirmation that the entry will be removed on or before completion;

(c)   in the case of a Land Charges Department search, apply for an official copy of the entry using Form K19 (the official copy consists of a copy of the application form which was submitted when the charge was registered and will reveal the name and address of the person with the benefit of the charge who may have to be contacted to seek his consent to its removal);

(d)   keep the client, his lender and, subject to the duty of confidentiality, other solicitors involved in the chain of transactions informed of the situation, since negotiations for the removal of the charge may cause a delay in completion. Any such delay will give rise to contractual remedies for breach of contract. Further, if the seller is unable or unwilling to remove an entry which the contract did not make the sale subject to, this will also be a breach of contract. For remedies for breach of contract, see **Chapter 33**.

28.12.1   Removing an entry from the register

An application form for the removal of an entry from the register in either registered or unregistered land will be accepted by the Chief Land Registrar only if it is signed by the person with the benefit of the charge or a person acting on his behalf. An application form signed by the seller's solicitors, or an undertaking given by them on completion to secure the removal of the charge may not, therefore, suffice, unless the seller is the person with the benefit of the charge (see *Holmes v Kennard (H) and Son (A Firm)* (1985) 49 P & CR 202). The court has a discretion to remove entries which are redundant but which cannot be removed from the register because the person with their benefit either will not consent to their removal or cannot be contacted. Entries protecting a spouse's rights under the Family Law Act 1996 can be removed on production of the death certificate of the spouse or a decree absolute of divorce. In the absence of these items, the charge can be removed only with the consent of the spouse who has the benefit of the charge.

28.12.2   Irrelevant land charges entries

Charges which are registered at the Land Charges Department can only validly be entered against the name of an estate owner in relation to the period during which he was the owner of the land in question. Thus, an entry which was made before or after this time cannot prejudice the buyer. The computerised system which is used to process these searches will sometimes throw up entries which are clearly irrelevant to the transaction in hand, particularly where the name searched against is a very common one such as John Jones. Having checked that the entry is irrelevant, it may either be disregarded or, at completion, the seller's solicitor may be asked to certify the entry as being inapplicable to the transaction. A solicitor's certificate is construed as an undertaking and should therefore only be given where the solicitor is sure that the entry is irrelevant. Particular care is needed in relation to bankruptcy entries.

28.12.3   Official certificates of search

28.12.3.1   Registered land

An official certificate of search issued by Land Registry is not conclusive in favour of the searcher, who will thus take his interest in the land subject to whatever entries are on the register, irrespective of whether or not they were revealed by the search certificate (see *Parkash v Irani Finance Ltd* [1970] Ch 101). However, where a person suffers loss as a result of an error in an official certificate of search, he may be able to claim compensation under the LRA 2002.

28.12.3.2   Unregistered land

An official certificate of search issued by the Land Charges Department is conclusive in favour of the searcher, who will thus take his interest in the land free of any entries which are on the register but which were not revealed by the search certificate. Where a person suffers loss as a result of an error in an official certificate of search, he may be able to claim compensation from the Chief Land Registrar, but there is no statutory right to compensation in these circumstances. No liability will attach to the solicitor who made the search, provided that a correctly submitted official search was made (Land Charges Act 1972, s 12).

28.13   Priority periods

28.13.1   Registered land

An official certificate of search issued by Land Registry following a search made on Form OS1 gives a priority period to the searcher of 30 working days from the date of the search. A buyer will also take advantage of this protection where a search was made on his behalf in the name of his lender. The searcher will take priority over any entry made during the priority period, provided that completion takes place and a correct application for registration of the transaction is received by the appropriate Land Registry Office by 9.30 am on the day when the priority period given by the search expires.

28.13.2   Unregistered land

An official certificate of search issued by the Land Charges Department gives a priority period of up to 15 working days from the date of the certificate, during which time the searcher will take free of any entries made on the register between the date of the search and the date of completion, provided that completion takes place during the priority period given by the search.

28.13.3 Date of expiry of priority period

The date of expiry of the priority period is shown on the search certificate. It should be marked on the outside of the client's file and entered in the solicitor's diary or file-prompt system to ensure that it is not overlooked. The priority period given by these searches cannot be extended, so if completion is delayed and cannot take place within the priority period given by the search, a new search application will have to be made. The new search certificate will give another priority period, but does not extend the original priority period from the first search. This means that entries made in the intervening period may be binding.

28.14 Comparison of local and central land charges searches

	Local	*Central*
Form:	LLC1	K15
When to make:	in every transaction	unregistered land only
Time to make:	before exchange	part of investigation of title
Send to:	district council	Plymouth
Search against:	description of land	owners' names
Information revealed:	mainly public incumbrances	mainly private incumbrances
Protection of search:	none	priority for 15 working days

28.15 Comparison of Land Registry and Land Charges Department searches

	Land Registry	*Land Charges Department*
Form:	OS1 or OS2	K15
When to use:	registered land	unregistered land
Search against:	title number	owners' names
Protection given:	search not conclusive	conclusive in favour of searcher
Fee:	standard fee for each search	fee for each name searched
Priority period:	30 working days	15 working days

Chapter 29

Preparing for Completion

29.1 Introduction

Both parties need to carry out a number of preparatory steps to ensure that completion proceeds smoothly. Most of these steps have been explained in other chapters of this book. This chapter contains a summary of the matters to be dealt with at this stage of the transaction by way of checklists, with some additional commentary.

29.2 Seller's checklist

(1) Check that purchase deed has been approved and requisitions answered.

(2) Receive engrossed purchase deed from buyer. Has buyer executed the deed (where appropriate) and plan (if used)?

(3) Obtain seller's signature (and witness) to purchase deed in time for completion.

(4) Obtain redemption figure(s) for seller's mortgage(s).

(5) Obtain last receipts, etc (eg, rent receipts for leasehold property) where apportionments are to be made on completion.

(6) Prepare completion statement (ie, statement of amount due on completion) and send two copies to buyer in good time before completion.

(7) Remind client to organise final readings of meters at the property.

(8) Prepare forms for discharge of land charges where necessary (unregistered land).

(9) Prepare any undertaking which needs to be given on completion (eg, for discharge of seller's mortgage if also acting for the lender).

(10) Contact lender to confirm final arrangements for discharge of seller's mortgage, method of payment, etc.

(11) Check through file to ensure all outstanding queries have been dealt with.

(12) Prepare list of matters to be dealt with on actual completion.

(13) Locate deeds and documents which will need to be inspected or handed over on completion and prepare certified copies for the buyer of those documents which are not being handed to the buyer on completion.

(14) Prepare two copies of schedule of deeds to be handed to buyer on completion.

(15) Prepare inventory of and receipt for money payable for chattels.

(16) Check arrangements for vacant possession and handing over keys.

(17) Receive instructions from buyer's solicitor to act as his agent on completion and clarify instructions with him if necessary.

(18) Make final arrangements with buyer's solicitor for time and place of completion.

(19) Inform estate agents of completion arrangements.

(20) Prepare bill for submission to client.

29.3 Buyer's checklist

(1) Ensure purchase deed has been approved and requisitions satisfactorily answered.

(2) Engross purchase and mortgage deeds.

(3) Get buyer to execute mortgage deed, purchase deed and plan (if necessary) and return it to solicitor.

(4) Send (executed) purchase deed to seller's solicitor for his client's execution in time for completion.

(5) Make pre-completion searches and ensure their results are satisfactory.

(6) Make report on title to lender and request mortgage advance in time for completion.

(7) Receive completion statement (where necessary) and copies of last receipts in support of apportionments and check they are correct.

(8) Remind client of arrangements for completion.

(9) Prepare and agree the form of wording of any undertaking which needs to be given or received on completion (eg, in relation to the discharge of the seller's mortgage).

(10) Contact lender to confirm final arrangements for completion.

(11) Ensure that any life policy required by the lender has been obtained and check with client that any other insurances required for the property (eg, house contents insurance) have been taken out.

(12) Check through file to ensure all outstanding queries have been dealt with.

(13) Prepare statement of account and bill for client and submit, together with a copy of the completion statement, requesting balance due from client to be paid in sufficient time for the funds to be cleared before completion.

(14) Receive mortgage advance from lender and balance of funds from buyer. Pay into client account and clear funds before completion.

(15) Arrange for final inspection of property by lender's valuer if necessary.

(16) Prepare list of matters to be dealt with on actual completion.

(17) Check arrangements for vacant possession and handing over keys.

(18) Instruct seller's solicitor to act as agent on completion if completion not to be by personal attendance.

(19) Make final arrangements with seller's solicitor for time and place of completion.

(20) Ensure estate agents are aware of completion arrangements.

(21) Make arrangements to send completion money to seller's solicitor (or as he has directed).

(22) Ensure relevant SDLT forms completed and signed.

29.4   The client's mortgage

29.4.1   The seller

The seller's solicitor must ensure that he has obtained from the seller's lender(s) a statement, known as 'a redemption statement', which shows the exact amount required to discharge the seller's mortgage(s), on the day of completion. The lender will usually also indicate the daily rate which applies to the seller's mortgage so that the redemption figure can be adjusted if completion takes place earlier or later than anticipated.

The form of discharge of the mortgage must be prepared for signature by the lender. Form DS1 is used for this purpose when dealing with registered land (see **Appendix 8**). Some lenders are now making use of an Electronic Notification of Discharge (END) system. Where this is in use, Land Registry will accept an electronic message from the lender notifying the discharge of the loan in place of Form DS1. In such a case, the seller's solicitor will need to draft Form END 1 requesting the lender to send the discharge message to the Registry. This is then sent to the lender instead of Form DS1. A receipt endorsed on the reverse of the mortgage deed is commonly used in unregistered land.

29.4.2   The buyer

Once he has completed his investigation of title and is satisfied as to it, the solicitor acting for the buyer's lender will report to the lender that the title to the property is safe, marketable and acceptable as security for the loan. Rule 3.20 of The Solicitors' Code of Conduct requires that, in a residential transaction, the form of certificate of title appended to the rule must be used. This cannot be amended without the consent of the lender (CML *Lenders' Handbook*, para 10.1). In commercial transactions the City of London Law Society's form of certificate is often used. Any problems or queries relating to the title should have been clarified with the lender before this stage of the transaction is reached.

It will also be necessary for the solicitor acting for the buyer's lender to make a formal request for the advance money from the lender. Depending on the practice of the particular lender, this request may form part of the report on title form or may be made on a separate form.

The mortgage deed should be prepared for signature by the borrowers. Many lenders insist that the mortgage deed is executed by the borrowers in the presence of their solicitor.

29.5   Apportionments

Where completion does not take place on a date when outgoings (eg, rent or water rates) on the property fall due, outgoings which attach to the land can be split between the parties on completion. The calculations of the apportioned sums are shown on the completion statement.

Council tax and water rates can be apportioned, but it is normally considered better practice to inform the relevant authority after completion of the change of ownership and request it to send apportioned accounts to seller and buyer.

Standard Condition 6.3 deals with apportionments and allows a provisional apportionment to be made where exact figures are not available at completion (eg, in respect of service charges). The seller must be asked to produce the last demands or receipts for all sums which are to be apportioned so that the calculations of the amounts due or to be allowed on completion may be made. Copies of these receipts should be sent to the buyer with the completion statement to allow him to check the accuracy of the calculation.

Standard Commercial Property Condition 8.3 is similar, but includes more comprehensive provisions dealing with apportionments when the property is being sold subject to a lease. Note also that under the residential Standard Conditions, the *seller* is deemed to own the property for the whole of the day of completion, whereas under the Commercial Conditions the *buyer* is deemed to own the property for the whole of that day.

29.6 Completion statement

A completion statement is prepared by the seller's solicitor which shows the amount of money required to complete the transaction and how that figure is calculated. The statement will be requested by the buyer when he sends his requisitions on title to the seller. It is necessary to provide the buyer with a completion statement only where the sum due on completion includes apportionments or other sums in excess of the balance of the purchase price (*Carne v De Bono* [1988] 3 All ER 485). Two copies of the completion statement should be sent to the buyer, together with copies of any receipts or demands relating to apportionments so that the buyer's solicitor can check the accuracy of the calculations.

The statement should show clearly the total amount due on completion, and how that total sum is made up. Depending on the circumstances, it may be necessary to deal with some or all of the following items:

(a)   the purchase price, giving credit for any deposit paid;
(b)   apportionments of outgoings;
(c)   money payable for chattels;
(d)   compensation if completion is delayed;
(e)   a licence fee if the buyer has been in occupation of the property.

Often in a residential transaction only the balance of the purchase price will be payable and a completion statement will not be required.

29.7 Land transaction returns

After completion it will be necessary to make a land transaction return to HMRC giving details about the transaction and the buyer (see **31.7**). This is normally the case whether or not any SDLT is payable. Form SDLT 1 (and often Form SDLT 4) will need completing. Form SDLT 1 is very lengthy, and should be completed and signed by the client before completion to avoid delays after completion. Many solicitors charge an extra fee for completing and submitting these forms due to the amount of work involved.

If the buyer's solicitor is also acting for a lender, it is essential that the land transaction return is completed and approved by the buyer before the loan is used to finance the purchase. Otherwise, if the loan is used and the buyer subsequently refuses to co-operate in filing the return, it will not be possible for the transaction – including the mortgage – to be registered at Land Registry. The lender will thus have no security for its loan – and the solicitor could be held liable for any loss suffered. See CML *Lenders' Handbook*, **Appendix 7**.

29.8 Statement to client

The buyer's solicitor should prepare and send to his client a financial statement which shows clearly the total sum due from him on completion and how that sum is calculated. In addition to the matters dealt with on the completion statement, the financial statement should also take account of such of the following matters as are relevant to the transaction:

(a) the mortgage advance and any costs and/or retentions made in respect of it;

(b) disbursements (eg, stamp duty land tax and Land Registry fees);

(c) the solicitor's costs.

The financial statement, together with a copy of the completion statement and the solicitor's properly drawn bill, should be sent to the client in sufficient time before completion to allow the client to forward the required balance of funds to the solicitor so that those funds can be cleared by completion.

29.9 Money

As soon as the buyer's solicitor is informed of the amount required to complete, he should check the figures for accuracy. Any discrepancies must be clarified with the seller's solicitor. If at this stage it appears that there is any shortfall in the buyer's funds, the client must immediately be informed and steps must be taken to remedy the shortfall. If bridging finance or a further loan are necessary in order to complete the transaction, arrangements to secure these funds must be made, otherwise a delay in completion may occur. The buyer's mortgage advance and balance of funds received from the client should be obtained in sufficient time to allow the funds to be cleared through client account before completion. A breach of the Solicitors' Accounts Rules 1998 may occur if uncleared funds are taken from client account.

A solicitor may be guilty of a criminal offence if he assists someone who is known or suspected to be laundering money generated by serious crime. The solicitor must therefore exercise caution in circumstances where the buyer client settles a large property transaction in cash or where payment for the property is made through a third party who is unknown to the solicitor. Reference should be made to The Law Society's guidance on money laundering. See **5.11**.

On the day of completion, arrangements must be made to send the amount due to the seller's solicitor in accordance with his instructions.

29.10 Completion checklist

When preparing for completion, the solicitor should make a checklist of the matters which need to be dealt with on actual completion to ensure that nothing is overlooked. Where the buyer instructs a person to act as his agent on completion, he should, when instructing the agent, send him a copy of the checklist so that the agent is aware of the matters which need to be dealt with.

Some or all of the items in the following checklist will need to be attended to on actual completion.

The list should contain an itemised list of the documents which need to be inspected, marked, handed over or received at completion.

(1) Documents to be available at completion:

    (a) contract;

        (b)   evidence of title;

        (c)   copy purchase deed;

        (d)   answers to requisitions;

        (e)   completion statement.

(2)   Documents to be inspected by buyer:

        (a)   title deeds, where in unregistered land these are not to be handed over on completion (eg, on a sale of part);

        (b)   power(s) of attorney;

        (c)   grant of administration;

        (d)   receipts/demands for apportionments if not previously supplied.

(3)   Documents, etc, to be handed to buyer on completion:

        (a)   title deeds;

        (b)   original lease (on purchase of a lease);

        (c)   executed purchase deed;

        (d)   schedule of deeds;

        (e)   Form DS1/discharged mortgage or undertaking in respect of discharge of mortgage(s);

        (f)   receipt for money paid for chattels;

        (g)   keys of the property (if these are not available the seller's solicitor should be asked to telephone the key holder to request the release of the keys);

        (h)   certified copy of any memorandum endorsed on retained deeds.

(4)   Documents, etc, to be handed to seller on completion:

        (a)   executed duplicate purchase deed/counterpart lease (where appropriate);

        (b)   receipted schedule of deeds received from seller;

        (c)   release of deposit if held by third party in capacity of stakeholder.

(5)   Endorsements on documents (if required by buyer):

        (a)   endorsement of sale on most recently dated retained document of title (sale of part of unregistered land);

        (b)   abstract or epitome to be marked up as compared with the original deeds (unregistered land in respect of any document the original of which is not handed over on completion).

Part V
COMPLETION AND POST-COMPLETION

Chapter 30

Completion

30.1 Purpose and effect of completion

For the client, completion is the culmination and climax of the transaction. It is the day on which he moves into his new home, or takes possession of his new factory unit. It is also the day on which the balance of the purchase price has to be paid to the seller in return for the title deeds to the property.

For the modern solicitor, completion is a paperwork transaction frequently conducted via the telephone and postal service from the solicitor's own office. It represents the climax of the past few weeks' work, but not the end of the transaction, since several matters will still need to be attended to by the solicitor even after the client has physically moved into his property (see **Chapter 31**).

The drama and excitement attached by the client to his house move is not always shared by the solicitor, for whom this client's completion is just one of many which will be carried out by the solicitor on every working day. The drama of completion affects the solicitor only when things go wrong, for example if the money is not received by the seller and he will not allow the buyer into possession, or if the seller's mother-in-law refuses to move out of the property and the buyer's removal van is standing outside the gate waiting to unload its contents. An understanding of what happens at completion and why it happens, and careful planning of what appears to be a mundane event (until it goes wrong), will avoid most of the foreseeable problems attached to completion.

30.1.1 Effect of completion

The effect of completion differs according to whether the land concerned is registered or unregistered. In unregistered land, legal title to the property passes to the buyer at completion. In registered land, title does not pass to the buyer until the buyer becomes registered at Land Registry as proprietor of the land.

On completion, the contract merges with the purchase deed in so far as the contract and purchase deed cover the same ground, so that after completion it is not generally possible to bring a claim which arises out of one of the terms of the contract, unless that provision has been expressly left extant by a term of the contract itself. For this reason the contract usually contains a non-merger clause (see SC 7.4 and SCPC 9.4), which will preserve the right to sue on the contract even though completion has taken place. Claims not based on the contract (eg, in tort or for misrepresentation) are not affected by this rule (see **Chapter 33**).

30.2   Date of completion

The date of completion will be agreed between the parties' solicitors (after discussion with their respective clients) shortly before exchange of contracts. Where the buyer's purchase is dependent on his sale of another property, the completion dates in both contracts must be synchronised. It follows that the completion dates in all transactions in a chain of transactions must also be synchronised if the chain is not to break. In residential transactions, a completion date 14 days or less from the date of exchange is common. Sufficient time must be allowed between exchange and completion for the pre-completion steps in the transaction to be carried out. If the parties want to complete very quickly after exchange, arrangements can usually be made for some of the pre-completion steps, such as preparation of the purchase deed, to be done before exchange.

30.2.1   Standard Condition 6.1 (SCPC 8.1)

In the absence of express agreement, SC 6.1 (SCPC 8.1) provides that completion shall take place on the twentieth working day after exchange. Time is not 'of the essence' of the completion date. This means that the stipulation as to time merely has the status of a contractual warranty and not a condition, so that although a delay in completion beyond the date fixed in the contract would give the innocent party the right to bring a claim in damages and would activate the compensation provisions of SC 7.3 (SCPC 9.3) (see **Chapter 32**), the delay would not of itself entitle the innocent party to withdraw from the contract at that stage.

Since delay in completion can occur for reasons beyond the control of the contracting parties (eg, postal delays), it is not generally a good idea to make time of the essence of the completion date. If the parties do want to make time of the essence (this would be very unusual in a residential transaction), an express provision to this effect can be inserted in the contract (eg, by adding the words 'as to which time shall be of the essence' alongside the insertion of the contractual completion date in the contract).

30.3   Time of completion

Where a buyer's purchase is dependent on the receipt of money from a related sale transaction, the solicitor must ensure that arrangements for completion day are made so that the sale transaction will be completed before the purchase transaction (otherwise there will be insufficient funds available to complete the purchase), and with a sufficient interval between the two transactions (eg, a minimum of an hour) to allow the money received from the sale to be transferred to and used in the purchase transaction. These arrangements will be made when final completion arrangements are made shortly before the day fixed for completion. Where the transaction is part of a long chain, the arrangements may be complex since, inevitably, the transaction at the bottom of the chain (which will usually involve a buyer who is not selling in a related transaction) must complete first, the money then progressing upwards through the chain. Note that many banks will not accept instructions for same day transmission of funds later than 3 pm. Such a transaction will frequently have to be completed early in the morning of completion day to allow all the subsequent transactions to take place within the same working day. A completion time earlier than 10 am is often difficult to comply with unless the money is sent to the seller on the previous day, because of restrictions on banking hours.

Even where a seller has no related purchase, he should ensure that the completion time agreed allows sufficient time for the proceeds of sale to be banked on the day of completion. If the money is not banked or sent to the lender (to discharge the seller's existing mortgage) until the following working day, the seller will suffer loss of interest on his money. For these reasons, a completion time later than 2.30 pm is inadvisable.

30.3.1 Standard Condition 6.1.2 (SCPC 8.1.2)

In the absence of contrary provision, these Conditions provide that if completion does not take place by 2 pm on the day of completion, interest for late completion becomes payable, ie, completion is 'deemed' to have taken place on the next working day. Non-compliance with this condition is a deemed late completion which invokes the compensation provisions of SC 7.3 (SCPC 9.3), requiring payment of compensation at the contractual interest rate for the delay. Standard Condition 6.1.2 (SCPC 8.1.2) does not apply where the sale is with vacant possession and the seller has not vacated the property by 2 pm on the date of actual completion. These Conditions affect only the payment of compensation for late completion. They do not make it a term of the contract that completion shall take place by a specified time. If it is desired to make it a term of the contract that completion takes place by a specified time on contractual completion day, a special condition to this effect must be added to the contract.

30.4 Place of completion

By SC 6.2 (SCPC 8.2), completion is to take place in England and Wales, either at the seller's solicitor's office or at some other place which the seller reasonably specifies. If completion is not to take place at the seller's solicitor's office, he should give the buyer's solicitor sufficient notice of the chosen venue to allow the buyer's solicitor to make his arrangements for attendance at completion and/or transmission of funds. If possible, the buyer's solicitor should be informed of the venue for completion in the answers given to his requisitions on title.

Where the seller has an undischarged mortgage over the property and the seller's solicitor is not also acting for the lender, completion may have to take place at the offices of the seller's lender's solicitors.

30.4.1 Chain transactions

Where there is a long chain of transactions, it may sometimes be convenient for some or all of the solicitors for the parties involved in the chain to meet at a mutually convenient location in order to complete several of the transactions in the chain within a very short interval.

30.4.2 Completion by post

Although traditionally the buyer's solicitor attends the seller's solicitor's office in person to effect completion, it is common today (especially in residential transactions) for completion to be effected by using The Law Society's Code for Completion by Post. In such cases, the actual place of completion is of little significance to the transaction as long as both parties' solicitors are able to contact each other by telephone or fax to confirm the transmission and receipt of funds on the day of completion itself (see **30.8** for completion by post).

30.5 The money

30.5.1 Method of payment

Both sets of Standard Conditions provide for payment to be made only by a direct credit to a bank account and an unconditional release of a deposit held by a stakeholder. (See SC 6.7 and SCPC 8.7.)

The banks' computerised money transfer system allows funds to be transmitted direct from one bank account to another on a same-day basis, even if with a different bank. This is frequently referred to in practice as a 'telegraphic transfer' (or 'TT'), reflecting methods of money transfer in the pre-computer age. The seller's solicitor should inform the buyer's solicitor of the amount needed to complete the transaction and of the details of the account to which the funds are to be sent. This information is normally given in answer to the buyer's requisitions on title and is a standard enquiry on the Completion Information and Requisitions on Title Form used in Protocol transactions.

The buyer's solicitor will then instruct his bank to remit a specific sum from the buyer's solicitor's client account to the account nominated by the seller's solicitor. The bank will charge a fee for this service. Instructions to the bank must be given sufficiently early on the day of completion to ensure that the funds arrive at their destination before the time limit for receipt of funds, as specified in the contract, expires. Some delay in the transmission of funds may be experienced where the funds are to be transmitted from one bank to another as opposed to transfers between different branches of the same bank. The seller's bank should be asked to telephone the seller's solicitor to inform him of the receipt of the funds immediately they arrive. Completion can proceed as soon as the seller's solicitor is satisfied about the arrival of the funds in his client account. The transmission of funds can be facilitated by the solicitor having a direct computer link with his bank. This will enable him to effect the transmission of funds himself, rather than having to rely on a telephone call or personal visit to the bank and then waiting for a clerk to effect the transfer.

30.5.2 Cleared funds

In order to avoid breach of the Solicitors' Accounts Rules 1998, payment of completion money must be made only from cleared funds in client account. This means that the buyer's solicitor must be put in funds by his client in sufficient time for the money to clear through client account before it becomes necessary to draw against them.

30.5.3 Discharge of seller's mortgage

The seller's existing mortgage over the property being sold will often be discharged immediately after completion of the sale using part of the proceeds of sale to make payment to the lender. Where payment is to be made by telegraphic transfer and the lender is represented by a different solicitor from the solicitor acting for the seller, the seller's solicitor may request that a direct transfer is made to the lender's solicitor, and a second transfer for the balance of funds due is made to the seller's solicitor.

30.5.4 Release of deposit

A deposit which is held in the capacity of agent for the seller belongs to the seller and does not need to be released expressly to his use on completion. Where a deposit is held by some person in the capacity of stakeholder, the buyer's solicitor should, on completion, provide the seller's solicitor with a written release addressed to the stakeholder, authorising payment of the deposit to the seller or as he directs.

Where the deposit is being held by the seller's solicitor as stakeholder, a written release is often neither asked for nor provided, the release being given orally once completion has taken place. If the deposit is being held by a third party (eg, an estate agent in the capacity of stakeholder) a written release will be required. This can be done by letter addressed by the buyer's solicitor to the stakeholder, informing the stakeholder that completion has taken place and that the funds are now released to the seller's hands.

30.6 Method of completion

Completion may take place by personal attendance by the buyer's solicitor or his agent, or through the post using The Law Society's Code for Completion by Post. The method of completion will usually have been agreed by the parties' solicitors at the requisitions on title stage of the transaction.

30.7 Completion by personal attendance

Personal attendance by the buyer's solicitor on the seller's solicitor or seller's lender's solicitor is the traditional method by which completion takes place, but it is not commonly used in uncomplicated transactions where, particularly in residential conveyancing, it is now more common for completion to take place through the post.

30.7.1 What happens at completion

30.7.1.1 Appointment for completion

A few days before the date arranged for completion, the buyer's solicitor should telephone the seller's solicitor to arrange a mutually convenient appointment for completion.

30.7.1.2 Transfer of funds

The buyer's solicitor should arrange with the bank to transmit the balance of the purchase price to the bank account(s) nominated by the seller's solicitor. The amount required will have been notified to the buyer's solicitor on the replies to requisitions on title.

30.7.1.3 Documents to be taken to completion

The representative from the buyer's solicitors who is to attend completion (often a trainee) should take with him to the seller's solicitor's office the following items:

(a) the contract (queries which arise at completion can sometimes be resolved by checking the terms of the contract);

(b) evidence of title (in order to verify the title);

(c) a copy of the approved draft purchase deed and of any other document which is to be executed by the seller and handed over on completion (in case there is any query over the engrossments);

(d) answers to requisitions on title (some queries which arise (eg, over who has the keys) can be resolved by the answers supplied to requisitions on title);

(e) the completion checklist and completion statement (see **Chapter 29**);

(f)   any documents which are required to be handed over to the seller's solicitor on completion (eg, release of deposit held by a stakeholder).

30.7.1.4   Verifying title

Verification is the process of comparing the original deeds with the abstract or epitome provided to ensure that the abstract is a true copy of the original. It is usually left until completion and, if photocopies of the original documents have been provided with the epitome, is very much a formality. If discrepancies are discovered, the buyer would not be precluded from objecting to these by the usual clause preventing the raising of requisitions as this prevents only requisitions on matters discoverable from the abstract as presented by the seller. There would inevitably be a delay in the transaction however. In the case of registered land, verification is unnecessary since the official copies supplied by the seller's solicitor will show the true, up-to-date position of the register.

30.7.1.5   Title documents

When the buyer's solicitor is satisfied as to the title, he should ask the seller's solicitor to hand over the documents necessary to complete the transaction. These documents will include the title deeds (in unregistered land) and will have been agreed previously in a list drawn up between the parties and itemised on the completion checklist. Except where these documents have recently been checked by verification, the buyer's solicitor should check each document to ensure it is as he expects to find it, and tick each off on his list as he receives it. Although land and charge certificates are no longer issued after 13 October 2003, existing certificates may well be still handed over on completion – the seller will have no need for them. However, it is no longer necessary for these to be handed over and they will not be required when an application to register the transaction is made at Land Registry. Also to be handed over will be any other documents requested during the transaction that have not already been sent to the buyer. These may include planning consents, building regulation approval and indemnity insurance policies in relation to title defects.

30.7.1.6   Purchase deed

The purchase deed will be among the documents to be received by the buyer's solicitor and should be dated at completion, after being checked by the buyer's solicitor to ensure that it has been validly executed and has not been altered since the buyer last saw the document.

30.7.1.7   Schedule of deeds

The seller's solicitor will have prepared a schedule of deeds in duplicate. One copy should be handed to the buyer's solicitor to keep, the other should be signed by the buyer's solicitor when he is satisfied that he has received all the documents listed on it and returned to the seller's solicitor as evidence for his file of the handing over of the deeds.

30.7.1.8   Inspection of receipts

It may be necessary for the buyer's solicitor to inspect receipts where, for example, the last payments of outgoings have been apportioned on the completion statement. Copies of these receipts should have been supplied to the buyer's solicitor with the completion statement in order to allow him to check the amount of the apportionments.

30.7.1.9 Chattels

Where the sale includes fittings or chattels, a separate receipt for the money paid for those items should be signed by the seller's solicitor and handed to the buyer's solicitor. A copy of the receipt should be retained by the seller's solicitor. The receipt clause on the purchase deed only operates as a receipt for the money paid for the land, therefore a separate receipt for the money paid for chattels is necessary.

30.7.1.10 Discharge of seller's mortgage

Arrangements for the discharge of the seller's mortgage(s) over the property will have been agreed between the parties at the requisitions on title stage of the transaction. Where the mortgage is a first mortgage of the property in favour of a building society lender, the parties will frequently have agreed to permit the seller to discharge his mortgage after actual completion by using part of the proceeds of sale to make payment to the lender. In such a case, it will often have been agreed that the seller's lender's solicitor should hand to the buyer's solicitor, on completion, an undertaking, in the form of wording recommended by The Law Society, to discharge the mortgage and to forward the receipted deed or Form DS1 to the buyer's solicitor as soon as this is received from the lender. An undertaking to discharge the seller's mortgage should be accepted only from a solicitor or licensed conveyancer because of the difficulties of enforcement of undertakings against unqualified persons. The undertaking should also be in the form of wording approved by The Law Society as follows:

> In consideration of you today completing the purchase of [insert description of property] we hereby undertake to pay over to [insert name of lender] the money required to discharge the mortgage/legal charge dated [insert date of charge] and to forward the receipted mortgage/Form DS1 to you as soon as it is received by us from [insert name of lender].

In Protocol cases, this undertaking is given on the Completion Information and Requisitions on Title Form.

Increasingly, lenders are making use of the Electronic Notification of Discharge (END) system as a means of discharging registered charges. This consists of the lender sending an electronic message to the Registry as evidence of the discharge of the mortgage instead of Form DS1. The solicitor acting for the borrower will pay off the loan in the normal way, but instead of sending Form DS1 to the lender he will send Form END 1 requesting the lender to discharge the charge by sending the END to Land Registry. Lenders using the END system have agreed that they will send the END within 21 working days of receiving Form END 1, or tell the solicitor sending Form END 1 why the END cannot be transmitted, for example because the money sent was insufficient to discharge the loan.

Where the END system is in use, the form of undertaking given above will be inappropriate. Land Registry has suggested use of the following:

> In consideration of your today completing the purchase of [insert description of property] we hereby undertake forthwith to pay over to the lender the money required to discharge the legal charge dated [insert date of charge] and to forward to it a completed Form END 1, to deal promptly with any queries raised by the lender within the 21 day period, and, at the end of that period, if asked to do so by the buyer's conveyancer, to take such steps as may reasonably be required to ensure that the lender transmits the END to the Land Registry.

An extension of the END system that is likely to become increasingly prevalent (it has already been successfully piloted) is the Electronic Discharge (or ED). In this system, the lender's electronic message to Land Registry actually removes the charge from the register; under the END system, the charge still has to be deleted from the register by a Land Registry official on receipt of the message.

30.7.1.11   Documents to be handed to seller's solicitor

When the buyer's solicitor is satisfied with the documents received from the seller's solicitor and those which he has inspected, he should hand to the seller's solicitor any documents which the seller's solicitor requires in accordance with the list agreed prior to completion (eg, release of deposit held by an estate agent), and a banker's draft for the amount specified on the completion statement or otherwise notified to the buyer's solicitor by the seller's solicitor.

30.7.1.12   Copy documents

In some cases the buyer will be entitled to have only copies of documents relating to the seller's title and not the originals. This will mainly happen on a sale of part of unregistered land where the seller is entitled to keep the title deeds which relate to the land retained by him. Other examples include purchases from personal representatives where they are entitled to retain the original grant, and purchases from attorneys who hold a general or enduring power. Where a power is a special power, relating only to the sale of this property, the buyer is entitled to the original power.

In any case where an original document relevant to the title is not being handed over, the buyer's solicitor should call for the original document and examine his copy against the original. The copy should then be marked to show that it has been examined against the original and is a true copy of the original document. On a sale of part of unregistered land, all the documents contained in the abstract or epitome of title will have to be so marked, and each examined document should bear the wording:

> examined against the original at the offices of [insert name of seller's solicitors or as appropriate] signed [by buyer's solicitor's representative either in his own name or in the name of the firm] and dated [insert date of examination].

Where a certified copy of a document will be required (eg, by Land Registry of a grant of representation), the certification should be carried out by a qualified solicitor by writing on the document clearly and in a conspicuous position the words:

> I certify this to be a true copy of the [insert type of document] dated [insert date of document being certified] signed [signature of solicitor] and dated [insert date of certification].

30.8   Completion through the post

In many cases, particularly with simple residential transactions, the buyer's solicitor will not want to attend completion personally. In such a case, arrangements can be made with the seller's solicitor to complete the transaction through the post. These arrangements should be made, at the latest, at the requisitions on title stage of the transaction.

30.8.1   The Law Society's Code for Completion by Post

The Law Society's Code for Completion by Post should be used. The text of the code is set out in **Appendix 5**. The buyer's solicitor should agree any variations to the code in writing with the seller's solicitor well before completion is due to take place. He should also send written instructions to the seller's solicitor, specifying precisely what the buyer's solicitor requires the seller's solicitor to do on the buyer's solicitor's behalf at completion, and agreeing a time on the day of completion itself when completion will take place.

30.8.2   The money

The buyer's solicitor must remit the necessary funds by telegraphic transfer to the seller's solicitor's nominated bank account to arrive there in time for completion to take place at the agreed time.

30.8.3   The seller's solicitor's role

The seller's solicitor will act as the buyer's solicitor's agent for the purpose of carrying out the completion procedure. The instructions given by the buyer's solicitor should cover such of the matters detailed in **30.7** as the buyer's solicitor would have carried out had he attended personally at completion. On being satisfied as to the proper payment of the completion money, either by draft or telegraphic transfer (see **30.5.1**), the seller's solicitor must carry out the buyer's instructions and effect completion on his behalf. He should then immediately telephone (or fax) the buyer's solicitor to inform him that completion has taken place and post to the buyer's solicitor, by first-class post or document exchange, the documents which the buyer is entitled to receive on completion. Where documents are required to be marked, certified or endorsed, the seller's solicitor will carry out these operations on behalf of the absent buyer's solicitor. Under the Code, the seller's solicitor is not entitled to make a charge to the buyer's solicitor for acting as his agent in carrying out completion.

30.9   Using an agent

If the buyer's solicitor is unable to attend personally at completion and does not wish to complete through the post, he can appoint another solicitor to act as his agent. The agent will attend completion in person and will carry out the same procedures that the buyer's solicitor would have done had he been present. This is not common in residential transactions.

30.10   Lender's requirements

The buyer's solicitor will often also be acting for the buyer's lender. In such a case, the buyer's solicitor should check the lender's requirements for completion when he is preparing his own checklist and making arrangements for completion. In most cases the lender's requirements will be identical to the buyer's solicitor's own requirements, but a check on the lender's instructions should always be made to ensure that nothing is overlooked.

Chapter 31

After Completion

31.1 Introduction

The solicitor's role in the transaction does not end when completion has taken place; a number of matters still need to be attended to by both parties, some of which have stringent time limits attached to them. The steps outlined below should therefore be taken as soon as possible after completion has occurred.

31.2 Reporting to the client

Whichever party the solicitor is acting for, the client is entitled to be informed that completion of his sale or purchase has taken place. The solicitor should therefore contact his client as soon as possible after completion (eg, by phone) to inform him of the successful outcome of the transaction. Where the solicitor is also acting for the client's lender, the lender should be informed of completion. A letter sent by first-class post on the day of completion will suffice in this case.

31.3 Acting for the seller

Not all of the steps listed below will be relevant in every transaction. Those which are relevant to the circumstances of the case should be carried out promptly.

31.3.1 Contact the buyer's solicitor

Where completion has taken place by post, telephone the buyer's solicitor to inform him that completion has taken place.

31.3.2 Contact the estate agent

Telephone the estate agent to inform him of completion and to ask him to release the keys of the property to the buyer.

31.3.3 Send documents to buyer's solicitor

Where completion has taken place by post, send the purchase deed, title deeds and other relevant documents to the buyer's solicitor by first-class post or document exchange.

31.3.4 Deal with the proceeds of sale

If part of the proceeds of sale is to be used towards the purchase of another property on the same day, arrangements should be made for the transmission of these funds in accordance with instructions received. Where the client is undertaking simultaneous sale and purchase transactions, the interval between the time of completion of the sale and the proposed time of completion of the purchase may be as short as an hour. The funds for the purchase must, therefore, be dealt with as a matter of urgency. If instructed to do so, pay the estate agent's commission and obtain a receipt for the payment. Account to the seller's bank for the proceeds of sale in accordance with any undertaking given to them. Account to the client for the balance (if any) of the proceeds of sale in accordance with his instructions.

31.3.5   Discharge the seller's mortgage(s)

Deal with the discharge of the seller's existing mortgage(s) by sending a client account cheque for the amount required (as per redemption statement previously obtained) to the lender, together with the engrossment of the Form DS1 requesting him to discharge the mortgage and return the receipted Form DS1 as quickly as possible. If the mortgage is over unregistered land, the lender will complete the receipt clause on the reverse of the mortgage deed and forward the receipted deed to the seller's solicitor instead of using a Form DS1. Where necessary, the benefit of a life policy which was assigned to the lender as collateral security in an endowment mortgage should be reassigned to the seller. A lender who has insured the property will also need to be told to cancel the property insurance cover. On receipt of the completed Form DS1 or receipted mortgage from the lender, check it to ensure that it is correct, then send it to the buyer's solicitor and ask to be discharged from the undertaking given on completion.

If the END system is being used (see **30.7.1.10**), Form DS1 will not be used. Instead, Form END 1 will be sent to the lender, requesting the lender to transmit the END to Land Registry to discharge the charge. There will thus be a saving of work and time in that the notification of the discharge is sent directly by the lender to Land Registry instead of the lender completing Form DS1 and sending it to the seller's solicitors, who have to check it and then send it to the buyer, who then has to send it to Land Registry. Electronic discharges (whereby lenders are able to remove mortgages from the register by means of a direct computer link) have been piloted and may become more common during 2008.

31.3.6   Send bill to the client

If not already done, a bill of costs should be drafted and sent to the client. Money which is being held by the solicitor on account of costs may be transferred to office account, provided that the client has expressly or impliedly agreed to this being done.

31.3.7   Letter to client

The client should be reminded to notify the local authority and water undertaker of the change of ownership of the property and to cancel insurance cover over the property and its contents. In appropriate cases, the client may also be reminded about his liability to capital gains tax.

31.3.8   Custody of deeds

Deal with the custody of deeds in accordance with the client's instructions. Most, if not all, original deeds will have passed to the buyer's solicitor on actual completion, but the seller will have retained custody of the deeds on a sale of part, or may have such documents as an original grant of representation or power of attorney.

31.3.9 Check file for outstanding matters

Check through the file to ensure that all outstanding matters have been dealt with before sending the file for storage.

31.4 Acting for the buyer

Where relevant to the transaction, the following steps should be taken by the buyer's solicitor as soon as possible after completion has taken place.

31.4.1 Complete mortgage deed

Complete the mortgage deed by insertion of the date and any other information which still has to be completed (eg, date when first repayment is due).

31.4.2 Complete file copies of documents

Complete file copies of the mortgage, purchase deed and other relevant documents. These are spare copies of the documents which will remain in the file for future reference or, in some cases, will be used as duplicate copies to send to Land Registry.

31.4.3 Stamp documents

Submit the land transaction return (see **29.7**) and attend to payment of SDLT on the purchase deed and other appropriate documents (see **31.7**).

31.4.4 Account for bridging finance

Account to the buyer's bank for any bridging finance in accordance with any undertaking given to it, and ask to be released from that undertaking.

31.4.5 Send bill to client

If not already done, draft and send a bill of costs to the client. Where money is being held by the solicitor on account of costs, it can be transferred to office account provided that the client has expressly or impliedly agreed to this being done.

31.4.6 Discharged mortgage

On receipt of the completed Form DS1 (if END is not being used) or receipted mortgage from the seller's lender's solicitor, check it to make sure it is correct, acknowledge its receipt and release the sender from the undertaking given on completion.

31.4.7 Make copies of documents

Make copies of all documents which are to be sent to Land Registry to ensure that file copies exist, in case requisitions are raised by the Registry or the documents are lost or damaged before registration is complete. Make copies of any documents of which Land Registry requires copies (eg, the buyer's mortgage, a transfer or conveyance of part which imposes new restrictive covenants). Certify copy documents which are to be sent to Land Registry. Certification is effected by writing or typing on the document (in the margin, or at the foot of the document):

I/We certify this to be a true copy of the [type of document] dated [insert date] [signed XYZ and Co].

The certification, which can be signed in the name of an individual or of a firm, can be carried out only by a solicitor who holds a current practising certificate. Except in the case of powers of attorney, which need to be separately certified on each page, one certificate on the reverse of a document will cover the whole document.

31.4.8   Register the title

Make application for registration of title using Form AP1 within the relevant priority period (land already registered) or within two months of completion (application for first registration) (see **31.8** and **Appendix 8**).

31.4.9   Register company charges

Register any charge created by a company at Companies House within 21 days of its creation, in accordance with the Companies Acts requirements. A fee is payable and must accompany the application. This time limit is absolute and cannot be extended without an order of the court. Failure to register within the time limit may prejudice the lender's security. The requirement to register under the Companies Acts is separate and additional to the requirement to register the charge at Land Registry.

31.4.10   Diary entry for registration to be effected

Make a diary or file-prompt entry recording the approximate date when registration is expected to be effected (as notified by Land Registry) and send a reminder to the Registry if confirmation is not received by that time.

31.4.11   Discharge entries protecting the contract

Where an entry was lodged to protect the contract (notice or Class C(iv)), an application should now be made for the discharge of that entry which, completion having taken place, is now redundant.

31.4.12   Check register entries

Once the transaction has been registered, Land Registry will send a copy of the register to the solicitor lodging the application. The entries should be checked carefully, and if they do not appear to be accurate the solicitor should advise the Registry and ask for errors to be corrected.

31.4.13   Custody of deeds

The question of the custody of the deeds and other title documents needs to be addressed. Once land has been registered, there are no title deeds as such; Land Registry no longer issues Land or Charge Certificates and the register itself is proof of ownership, but there may well be various other documents that will need to be produced on a subsequent sale. So there may well be planning consents, building regulation approvals, defective title insurance polices, guarantees for building work etc which will need safe keeping. Where there is a mortgage on the property, the lender is entitled to these and the lender's instructions must be complied with. However, in the case of residential property, most lenders no longer wish to take custody of these documents due to the administrative expenses of receiving, storing and producing such documents when they are required for a subsequent sale. In such a case, or where there is no mortgage, the buyer's instructions on these should be obtained. The buyer may wish to retain custody of these himself, or may wish them to be sent to his bank or kept by the solicitor. These last two options will generally result in a storage fee being payable by the client. However, if the buyer wishes to keep the documents himself, it must be emphasised that these must be kept safely as they will be required on a subsequent sale.

31.4.14 Check file for outstanding matters

Check through the file to ensure that all outstanding matters have been dealt with before sending the file for storage.

31.5 The lender's solicitor

Where a separate solicitor has been instructed to act for the buyer's lender, the lender's solicitor will normally have taken custody of the purchase deed and other title deeds on completion, and he will deal with the stamping and registration of the documents instead of the buyer's solicitor.

31.6 Undertakings

Any undertaking given must be honoured and any obligations accepted must be fulfilled without delay. A solicitor who has performed his undertaking (eg, to discharge the seller's mortgage) should formally ask the recipient to release the giver from his undertaking, so that the giver has written evidence of the fulfilment of the undertaking. The recipient may either acknowledge the giver's release by letter, or return the original undertaking to the giver. In either case, the evidence of release is to be kept on the giver's file.

31.7 Land transaction returns and SDLT

Certain documents attract SDLT, payable to HMRC within 30 days of completion. Tax is payable on the value of land, but not on chattels. Non-payment or evasion of tax gives rise to fines and penalties, for which the client and his solicitor may face prosecution. Stamp duty land tax replaced stamp duty for most conveyancing documents as from 1 December 2003. There is no longer any need for a deed to bear an embossed stamp to prove the payment of duty/tax. A land transaction return in Form SDLT 1 must be submitted for each transaction, containing details of the transaction and the parties to it. The buyer is personally responsible for completing this tax return – just as he would be for an income tax return – but it is normally completed by the buyer's solicitor. It must, however, be signed personally by the buyer(s); it cannot be signed by the solicitor, except under a power of attorney.

Form SDLT 1, together with the payment of any tax, is submitted to HMRC's Rapid Data Capture Centre in Netherton, Liverpool. The deed itself should not be submitted. The form is then scanned and a certificate issued in Form SDLT 5 to prove that the return has been submitted and any tax necessary paid. Without this certificate the transaction will not be accepted for registration by Land Registry.

The land transaction return can also be submitted online at www.hmrc.gov.uk/so/online. This system also permits the solicitor immediately to print off Form SDLT 5. If the return is submitted by post, SDLT 5 will be returned in the same way and this may cause a delay before the transaction can be registered. Where it is submitted online, the solicitor must certify that the form has been approved by the buyer before submission. Although this approval can be in any medium as far as HMRC is concerned, it will be sensible for the solicitor to obtain approval in writing. For reasons for obtaining this approval before completion, see **29.7**. The actual payment of the SDLT due can also be made online, or a cheque may be sent through the post in the usual way.

31.7.1   Purchase of freehold property for value

The transfer of freehold property for full value will attract SDLT at the following rates, depending upon the purchase price:

(a)   purchase price not exceeding £125,000 (£150,000 for commercial property), no tax payable;

(b)   purchase price exceeding £125,000 but not exceeding £250,000, tax payable at 1% of the purchase price;

(c)   purchase price exceeding £250,000 but not exceeding £500,000, tax payable at 3% of the purchase price;

(d)   purchase price exceeding £500,000, tax payable at 4% of the purchase price.

Note that in each case the tax is payable at the stated rate on the full amount of the purchase price. As far as residential property is concerned, the threshold for payment of tax is £150,000 in specified disadvantaged areas. A solicitor should always check whether property is in a disadvantaged area, as this relief from tax has to be specifically claimed. However, if it is not claimed, HMRC will normally, on submission of the land transaction return, write back and enquire whether you wish to claim the relief. The areas which qualify as disadvantaged can be checked on HMRC's website by searching against the post code of the property.

31.8   Registration of title

It is essential that the relevant time limits for submission of an application for registration of a client's title are complied with. The time limits, and the effect of non-compliance with them, differ according to whether it is a first registration of land previously unregistered or whether it is a registration of a dealing with land already registered. Failure to make an application for first registration within two months of completion results in the transfer of the legal estate becoming void. Failure to make an application for registration of a dealing within the priority period of 30 working days given by a pre-completion Land Registry search may have the consequence of the client's interest losing priority to another application.

31.8.1   Registration of dealings

Where registered land is transferred, an application for registration of the dealing must be made on the appropriate application form, accompanied by the correct documentation and fee, and must be received by the Land Registry Office for the area within the priority period of 30 working days given by the land registry search made before completion. The application must be received by the Land Registry Office by 9.30 am on the day on which protection under the applicant's search expires, in order to preserve the applicant's priority over the registration of other interests. The period of protection under the search cannot be extended (although a second search conferring a separate priority period can be made) and failure to lodge the client's application within the priority period may result in his interest ceding priority to another application.

31.8.2 Transfer of whole

The following points apply to any transfer of the whole of the seller's registered title, regardless of whether the interest transferred is freehold or leasehold. Application for registration of the dealing on Form AP1 (see **Appendix 8**), accompanied by the following documents, should be lodged within 30 working days of the date of issue of the applicant's pre-completion official search certificate:

(a)   the transfer (generally no copy of this document is required);

(b)   the appropriate fee unless to be paid by credit account.

In addition, such of the documents listed below as are appropriate to the circumstances of the transaction should be submitted with the application:

(c)   completed Form DS1 (to show the discharge of the seller's mortgage) (if the lender is using the END system (see **30.7.1.10**) there is no need for this form);

(d)   mortgage deed relating to the buyer's new mortgage and certified copy;

(e)   office copy or certified copy grant of representation where the seller was personal representative of the deceased proprietor;

(f)   original power of attorney if transfer has been executed under a special power which is limited to the disposal of this property;

(g)   certified copy power of attorney if the transfer has been executed under a power of attorney other than as in (f) above;

(h)   SDLT certificate;

(i)   Form DI (see **31.8.5**).

31.8.3 First registration of title

An application for first registration of title (freehold or leasehold) must be made within two months of completion of the transaction which induces the registration on Form FR1 (see **Appendix 10**).

The application form and fee (unless being paid by credit account), accompanied by the documents listed below, should be sent to the Land Registry Office for the area. Documents accompanying the application must be listed in duplicate on Form DL. One copy of this form will be returned to the applicant's solicitor in acknowledgement of receipt of the application. The acknowledgement copy will also give an estimate of the likely time which the Registry expects to take to deal with the application. This anticipated time should be noted in the solicitor's diary or file-prompt system, and a reminder should be sent to the Registry if the Title Information Document has not been received within that period.

31.8.4 Documents to be submitted on application for first registration of title

The Registrar needs to investigate title on an application for first registration in order to decide which class of title can be allocated to the title. He therefore needs to have access to all the documents which formed the evidence of title supplied to the applicant by the seller's solicitor. These documents should be individually numbered in chronological sequence and listed in the same sequence on Form DL. Such of the following documents as are relevant to the transaction should be submitted to the Registry:

(a)   all the documents which formed the evidence of title supplied by the seller's solicitor;

(b)   all the buyer's pre-contract searches and enquiries relating to the title with their replies (including any variations or further information contained in relevant correspondence);

(c)   the contract;

(d)   requisitions on title with their replies;

(e)   all pre-completion search certificates;

(f)   the purchase deed with a certified copy;

(g)   the seller's mortgage, duly receipted;

(h)   the buyer's mortgage with a certified copy;

(i)   where the property is leasehold, the original lease and a certified copy;

(j)   SDLT certificate;

(k)   cheque for fee (unless paid by credit account);

(l)   Form DI (see **31.8.5**).

31.8.5 Disclosing overriding interests

As part of the policy to reduce the number of overriding interests, an applicant for registration must complete Form DI (see **Appendix 8**) setting out any overriding interests affecting the title. These will then be entered on the register and thus cease to be overriding.

Part VI
DELAY AND REMEDIES

Chapter 32

Late Completion

32.1 Introduction

There are many reasons why completion may be delayed and does not take place on the contractual date. Common examples of causes of delay in completion are the buyer not being in receipt of funds from his lender, or the seller's solicitor not managing to get the purchase deed signed by his client. Where the transaction forms part of a chain of transactions, all the transactions in the chain may be delayed if there is a problem with one of the links in the chain. In the majority of cases, the delay in completion is merely a temporary hitch in the transaction, causing practical difficulties both to the solicitor and, particularly, to his client, who may not be able to move house on the date when he wished to do so and may now have to alter his removal arrangements. Where the delay is caused by, for example, the buyer not having received his mortgage advance from his lender, there is generally no doubt that completion will occur, even if it takes place a few days later than the anticipated date stipulated in the contract. The provisions for payment of compensation for late completion contained in most contracts (see SC 7.3) are designed to compensate the innocent party for the losses suffered as a result of minor delays in completion. The provisions relating to delays in completion in the Standard Commercial Property Conditions are somewhat different from those in the residential Standard Conditions. These are, therefore, dealt with separately at **32.6**.

32.2 Breach of contract

Any delay in completion beyond the contractual date will be a breach of contract entitling the innocent party to damages for his loss, but will not entitle him immediately to terminate the contract unless time was of the essence of the completion date (*Raineri v Miles* [1981] AC 1050).

32.2.1 Time of the essence

Standard Condition 6.1 provides that time is not of the essence of the contract (but it can be made so by express contractual condition), unless a notice to complete has been served.

32.3 Related transactions

Delay in completing one transaction may affect the client's ability to complete a related sale or purchase. If, for example, completion of the client's sale is delayed, he will not have the money (from the proceeds of sale) with which to complete his synchronised purchase transaction, and failure to complete that purchase on the contractual date for completion will be a breach of contract.

Although the solicitor should try to ensure that no breach of contract occurs (eg, by arranging bridging finance in order to complete the purchase transaction on time), he is also under a duty to act in his own client's best interests and, in these circumstances, completion of the purchase with the assistance of bridging finance may not necessarily be the best course of action for the client to take. For example, in the situation outlined above, where the client's sale transaction is delayed, if the client does go ahead with completion of his purchase not only will he incur a heavy charge in interest on the bridging finance used to complete the purchase, but he will also be in the position of owning two houses until the sale is completed and, if the sale transaction is not completed within a short space of time, this too will represent an onerous commitment for the client. The reason for the delay on the sale transaction and its likely duration must be taken into account when advising the client whether to complete the purchase on time, or to delay completion of the purchase and commit a breach of that contract.

In the converse situation, where the sale can proceed but the purchase is delayed, completion of the sale transaction on the contract date will result in the client becoming homeless for a potentially indefinite length of time with resultant problems relating to alternative accommodation for the period of the delay and storage of furniture.

32.4 Compensation for delay

Damages are payable under normal contractual principles (see **33.2.6**) for delayed completion. In addition, at common law, there are rules dealing with the payment of interest as compensation for late completion. However, these are generally considered inadequate and are replaced in the Standard Conditions of sale by SC 7.3. This requires the payment of compensation for delayed completion irrespective of whether the innocent party has suffered any loss. Where loss has been suffered in excess of the amount payable under SC 7.3 (eg, the cost of alternative accommodation), this can still be recovered in a claim for breach of contract. However, any compensation paid under SC 7.3 must be taken into account in a claim for breach of contract.

32.4.1 Standard Condition 7.3

Standard Condition 7.3 provides for the payment of compensation at the 'contract rate', which is defined by SC 1.1.1(e) as being 'The Law Society's interest rate from time to time in force' (as published weekly in *The Law Society's Gazette*), although the parties may substitute a different rate by special condition if they wish. Interest is payable on the purchase price, or, where the buyer is the paying party, on the purchase price less the deposit paid. Under SC 7.3, compensation is assessed using the 'concept of relative fault', so that whoever is most at fault for the delay pays the compensation; it is not simply a matter of the party who delayed in actual completion being liable to pay compensation.

32.4.2 Calculating compensation

To calculate the liability for compensation, it is necessary to refer back to the timetable of events contained in SC 4.3.1 and 4.3.2 in order to establish whether the delay in completion has been caused by a delay in carrying out a procedural step earlier in the transaction. Delay occurring before completion is assessed by reference to the definition of a 'working day' contained in SC 1.1.1(m), but this definition ceases to apply once the completion date has passed, after which every day's delay counts towards the liability for compensation. Having apportioned the delay between the parties, the party who is most at fault for the delay pays compensation to the other for the period by which his delay exceeds the delay of the other party, or for the actual period of delay in completion, if this is shorter. Compensation under this provision is neither additional to nor in substitution for common law damages, but merely on account.

Example

The seller was three days late in delivering his evidence of title under SC 4.3.1; the buyer was then five days late in delivering his requisitions on title and a further four days late in delivering his draft purchase deed, but completion itself was delayed two days because of the seller's fault.

To assess who is liable for compensation, it is necessary to add up the total periods of default of each party. Here the seller's total default amounts to five days, but the buyer's to nine days. The buyer's default therefore exceeds that of the seller by four days and, in this example, the buyer would be liable to pay up to four days' compensation to the seller for the delay, even though the delay in actual completion was not his fault; however, since the actual delay was only two days, his liability is limited to two days' compensation.

The calculation of the delay under SC 7.3 is thus rather complicated, but does have the merit of recognising that the delay might not be the fault of the party who is actually unable to complete on time. His delay might be the knock-on effect of the other party's delay earlier in the transaction. The complications of SC 7.3 are further exacerbated by the fact that the timetable laid down in SC 4.3.1 is based on the traditional practice of title being deduced after exchange, which rarely happens in modern practice, and by the fact that the timetable is based on a minimum period of 15 working days (ie, three weeks) between exchange and completion. Where, as is usual, completion is to take place earlier than 15 working days after exchange, the time limits laid down have to be reduced accordingly.

32.4.3 Deemed late completion

By SC 6.1.2 and 6.1.3, where the sale is with vacant possession and the money due on completion is not paid by 2 pm on the day of actual completion (or such other time as may have been agreed by the parties), for the purposes of the compensation provisions only, completion is deemed to have taken place on the next following working day, unless the seller had not vacated the property by 2 pm (or other agreed time). If this time limit is not complied with, the buyer may find himself liable to pay compensation to the seller under SC 7.3. If, for example, completion was due on a Friday, and the buyer's money did not arrive until 2.15 pm, the seller would be able to treat completion as not having taken place until the following Monday and, subject to the application of SC 7.3, recover compensation for the delay (irrespective of his actual loss). Since the 'working day' definition contained in SC 1.1.1(m) ceases to apply once completion has taken place, the seller in this example would be able to charge interest for three days, ie, Saturday and Sunday are included in the calculation.

32.5 Service of a notice to complete

Where it appears that the delay in completion is not likely to be resolved quickly (or at all), consideration may be given to the service of a notice to complete, which will have the effect of making time of the essence of the contract so that, if completion does not take place on the new completion date specified in the notice, the aggrieved party may then terminate the contract immediately, forfeit or recover his deposit (as the case may be) with accrued interest and commence a claim for damages to recover his loss. This then gives the aggrieved party the certainty of knowing that on a stated date he can make a definite decision, either to look for a new property to purchase (if a buyer) or to resell the property elsewhere (as a seller).

Making time of the essence imposes a condition which binds both parties. If, therefore, unforeseen events occur between the date of service of the notice and the new date for completion as specified by the notice, which result in the previously aggrieved party being unable to complete on the new date, the previously defaulting party could turn round and terminate the contract, leaving the aggrieved party in breach of contract himself. For this reason a notice to complete should never be served as an idle threat. The server must be sure that he will be able to comply with the new completion date himself before serving the notice.

32.5.1 Standard Condition 6.8

Although permitted at common law, the contract normally contains a provision relating to the service of a notice to complete. Standard Condition 6.8 provides that, on service of a notice to complete, completion must take place within 10 working days (exclusive of the date of service) and makes time of the essence of the contract. Standard Condition 6.8.3 requires a buyer who has paid less than a 10% deposit to pay the balance of the full 10% immediately on receipt of a notice to complete.

The parties' rights and obligations where a valid notice has been served but not complied with are governed by SC 7.5 and 7.6. Once served, a notice to complete cannot be withdrawn.

32.5.2 Non-compliance with a notice to complete

Non-compliance with a notice to complete gives the aggrieved party the right to terminate the contract, but is not in itself an automatic termination of the contract.

32.5.2.1 Buyer's failure to comply with a notice to complete

Standard Condition 7.5 provides that, in addition to rescinding the contract, the seller may:

(a) forfeit and keep the deposit and any accrued interest;
(b) resell the property and any chattels included in the contract; and
(c) claim damages.

The seller is expressly stated to retain his other rights and remedies and so would be able to issue a claim for specific performance should he so wish.

32.5.2.2 Seller's failure to comply with a notice to complete

Standard Condition 7.6 provides that, in addition to rescinding the contract, the buyer is entitled to the return of the deposit and accrued interest. He also keeps his other rights and remedies, so he would be able to issue a claim for specific performance or damages if he wished.

32.6 Standard Commercial Property Conditions

The provisions of the Standard Commercial Property Conditions relating to time not being of the essence (SCPC 8.1.1), deemed late completion (SCPC 8.1.2) and service of a notice to complete (SCPC 8.8) are the same as under the residential Standard Conditions. Failure to comply with a notice to complete is dealt with by SCPC 9.5 and 9.6. The provisions are the same as under the Standard Conditions. However, SCPC 9.3, which deals with compensation for delays in completion, is much changed from the equivalent residential Standard Condition. The concept of relative fault in the residential Standard Conditions (see **32.4**) is not adopted. Instead, a contractual entitlement to compensation is given to the seller where the buyer has defaulted in some way and completion is delayed. If the seller defaults and completion is delayed, there is no contractual right to compensation given to the buyer, who would have to bring a claim for damages for breach of contract.

Chapter 33

Remedies

33.1 Introduction

A contract for the sale of land is subject to the general principles of the law of contract, and remedies for breach of that contract follow normal contractual principles. This chapter contains only a summary of the application of those principles to sale of land transactions, together with a brief reminder of some other remedies which might be available in a sale of land transaction. Contractual remedies need be considered, however, only in the case of a failure to comply with a notice to complete and/or where compensation payable under SC 7.3 (or SCPC 9.3) is inadequate (see **Chapter 32**).

33.2 Breach of contract

Remedies for breach of contract depend on whether the breach is of a condition in the contract, entitling the aggrieved party to terminate the contract and/or claim damages, or of a warranty, entitling the aggrieved party to claim damages only.

33.2.1 Conditions and warranties

A term of the contract will be a 'condition' if it is a major or fundamental term. Minor terms are classified as 'warranties'.

In some cases, it is not possible to classify a term as specifically falling into one or other of these categories until the consequences of the breach can be seen. Where the consequences are serious or far-reaching, the unclassified term will be treated as a condition; otherwise, it will be treated as a warranty. In conveyancing contracts, all terms are usually called 'conditions', but in law some of those terms will only have the status of warranties. The classification attached to a term by the parties is not necessarily conclusive as to its status.

A defect in title, for example an undisclosed incumbrance, will normally amount to a breach of condition entitling the buyer to treat the contract as discharged by breach. The buyer will also be able to reclaim his deposit and claim damages for any further loss he suffers. Where the Standard Conditions apply, SC 7.1 (SCPC 9.1) amends the common law position; see **33.2.4**.

33.2.2 Limitation periods

A claim on a contract not made by deed has a limitation period under the Limitation Act 1980 of six years, running from the date of the breach. A limitation period of 12 years applies where the contract was made by deed.

33.2.3 Merger

On completion, the terms of the contract merge with the purchase deed in so far as the two documents cover the same ground, and a claim on the contract is no longer sustainable after completion except where it is based on a contract term which remains extant despite completion taking place. For this to happen the contract would generally have to contain a non-merger clause (such as SC 7.4 or SCPC 9.4) which expressly allows a particular clause or clauses to remain alive after completion.

33.2.4 Exclusion clauses

Standard Condition 7.1 (SCPC 9.1) restricts the remedies available for a breach of contract. The buyer is only entitled to damages if there is a material difference in the tenure or value of the property. In addition, he is entitled to treat the contract as at an end only if the error or omission results from fraud or recklessness, or where he would otherwise be obliged to accept property differing substantially in quality, quantity or tenure from what he had been led to expect. Thus, in the case of an undisclosed incumbrance, the buyer would be entitled to damages only if this caused a material difference in the value of the land. Similarly, he would be able to treat the contract as at an end only if there was fraud or recklessness on the seller's part, or if the value of the property was substantially reduced because of the incumbrance. Obviously, a covenant preventing building on land otherwise suitable for development, would have a much greater effect on its value than a covenant restricting a dwelling house to use as a house. Note, however, that if there is fraud or recklessness on the seller's part, the buyer will always be entitled to rescind no matter what the effect on the value of the property.

Exclusion clauses contained in contracts for the sale of land (except those relating to the exclusion of liability for misrepresentation) are not subject to the reasonableness test in the Unfair Contract Terms Act 1977.

33.2.5 Delayed completion

Unless time was of the essence of the completion date, or had been made so by service of a notice to complete, a delay in completion will be a breach of warranty entitling the aggrieved party to recover damages for any loss suffered as a result of the delay (*Raineri v Miles* [1981] AC 1050). For details of compensation payable for delayed completion under SC 7.3, see **32.4**, and under SCPC 9.3, see **32.6**.

33.2.6 Damages for breach

Damages for breach of a contract for the sale of land are assessed under the normal contractual principles established in *Hadley v Baxendale* (1854) 9 Exch 341. Subject to establishing causation, damages for losses naturally flowing from the breach may be claimed, as may damages for reasonably foreseeable consequential loss.

33.2.6.1 Quantum

The quantum of damages under the consequential loss head is limited to loss which was reasonably foreseeable by the defaulting party in the light of the facts known by him (or by his agent) at the date when the contract was made (not at

the date of the breach of contract). The starting point for damages for breach of a contract for the sale of land is the difference between the contract price and the market price of the property at the date of the breach. To this may be added actual financial loss suffered as a result of the breach, such as wasted conveyancing costs, legal costs involved in the purchase of another property, interest payable on a mortgage or bridging loan, costs of removal or storage of furniture, and/or costs of alternative accommodation pending purchase of another property (see *Beard v Porter* [1948] 1 KB 321).

33.2.6.2 Loss of development profit

Loss of development profit, or loss of profit on a sub-sale, can be claimed only if the defendant was aware of the claimant's proposals for the property at the time the contract was made (see *Diamond v Campbell Jones* [1961] Ch 22; cf *Cottrill v Steyning and Littlehampton Building Society* [1966] 2 All ER 295).

33.2.6.3 Resale by seller

Where the buyer defaults and the seller makes a loss on the resale, that loss can be claimed as damages; but if the seller makes a profit on the resale he would have to give credit for the amount of the profit in his claim, because he is entitled only to recover his financial loss and is not entitled to benefit from the buyer's breach. The purpose of contractual damages is to place the parties in the position in which they would have been had the contract been duly performed, not to punish the guilty party.

33.2.6.4 Mental distress

As a general principle of contractual damages, it is possible to recover for financial loss only, and no claim can be made in respect of mental distress suffered as a result of the defendant's breach. The practice of awarding a nominal sum in respect of damages for mental distress established by *Jarvis v Swans Tours* [1973] 1 QB 233 seems to be confined to holiday contracts and contracts for leisure activities. (See also *Bliss v South East Thames Regional Health Authority* [1987] ICR 700.)

33.2.6.5 Pre-contract losses

Damages can normally be claimed only in respect of losses which have occurred since the contract was made, thus there is generally no possibility of recovering expenses incurred at the pre-contract stage of the transaction (eg, for a wasted survey); but, in *Lloyd v Stanbury* [1971] 1 WLR 535, pre-contract expenditure including money spent on repairs to the property was recovered.

33.2.6.6 Mitigation

The claimant must have attempted to mitigate his loss, for example by trying to purchase another similar property (as disappointed buyer) or by attempting to resell the property (as disappointed seller). If no attempt to mitigate is made, the award of damages may be reduced because of the failure to mitigate. If the claimant attempts to mitigate and, in so doing, increases his loss, the defendant will be liable for the increased loss.

33.2.6.7 Giving credit for money received

Credit must be given in the claim for damages for any compensation received under SC 7.3 or SCPC 9.3, or for any deposit forfeited by the seller.

33.3   Rescission

In this chapter the word 'rescission' is used in the context of contracts which involve a vitiating element such as misrepresentation, fraud or mistake, and refers to the remedy which is available in those circumstances.

Rescission entails the restoration of the parties to their pre-contract position by 'undoing' the contract and balancing the position of the parties with the payment of compensation by one party to the other. Damages in the conventional sense of that word are not payable, because there will have been no breach of contract. Since rescission is an equitable remedy, its operation is subject to the general equitable bars (eg, lapse of time).

33.3.1   Contractual right to rescind

A right to rescind may be given by a specific contractual condition which sets out the circumstances in which the right is to operate and the parties' rights and obligations in the event of rescission taking place. Such a clause might be included where, for example, the contract is conditional on the fulfilment of a condition. Under both sets of Standard Conditions of Sale, the right to rescind is available in the following situations:

(a)   where risk in the property remains with the seller and the property is rendered unusable between contract and completion (SC 5.1);

(b)   for misrepresentation (SC 7.1; SCPC 9.1);

(c)   where a licence to assign is not forthcoming in leasehold transactions (SC 8.3; SCPC 10.3);

(d)   where either the buyer or the seller has failed to comply with a notice to complete (SC 7.5 and 7.6; SCPC 9.5 and 9.6).

Where the right to rescind is exercised under one of the above Conditions, the parties' rights on rescission are governed by SC 7.2 or SCPC 9.2, which provide for the repayment of the deposit to the buyer with accrued interest, the return of documents to the seller and the cancellation of any registration of the contract at the buyer's expense.

33.3.2   Limitation periods

Where the right to rescind arises out of a contractual provision, it must be exercised within the time limits given within the condition or, if no time is specified, within a reasonable time. A claim based on a contractual rescission clause is subject to the normal six-year limitation period under the Limitation Act 1980 (unless the contract was by deed, when a 12-year limitation period would be available). Claims for rescission arising out of the general law principles (eg, for misrepresentation) are subject to the equitable doctrine of laches (lapse of time).

33.4   Misrepresentation

33.4.1   Definition

A misrepresentation is an untrue statement of fact made by one contracting party which is relied on by the aggrieved party, which induces him to enter the contract, and as a result of which he suffers loss. The statement must be of fact, not law (see *Solle v Butcher* [1950] 1 KB 671). A statement of opinion is not actionable unless it can be proved that the opinion was never genuinely held (*Edgington v Fitzmaurice* (1885) 29 Ch D 459). A misrepresentation may be fraudulent (ie, deliberately dishonest) within the definition of fraud laid down in *Derry v Peek* (1889) 14 App Cas 337, negligent (ie, made carelessly without having checked the facts, but not necessarily negligent within the tortious meaning of that word), or innocent (ie, a genuine and innocently made mistake).

33.4.2 Fraudulent misrepresentation

Where the misrepresentation has been made fraudulently, the aggrieved party may issue a claim in tort for deceit, which may result in rescission of the contract and damages. The party who alleges fraud must prove fraud. This places a very onerous burden of proof on the claimant and, except where there is clear evidence of fraud, it is more usual to treat the misrepresentation as having been made negligently and to pursue a remedy under the Misrepresentation Act 1967.

33.4.3 Claims under the Misrepresentation Act 1967

The claimant must show that he has an actionable misrepresentation, after which the burden of proof shifts to the defendant who has to disprove negligence. A misrepresentation is negligent if the defendant cannot prove that he had reasonable grounds for believing and did believe the statement he made was true up to the time the contract was made. There is therefore a duty to correct a statement which, although being true at the time when it was made, subsequently becomes untrue.

The remedies for a negligent misrepresentation are rescission of the contract and damages. If the defendant successfully establishes the defence of grounds and belief, thus showing that the misrepresentation was truly innocent, rescission is available, but not damages.

33.4.4 Rescission

The award of rescission lies within the equitable jurisdiction of the court and is thus discretionary and subject to the equitable bars. If none of the equitable bars applies but, nevertheless, the court decides not to grant rescission, it may instead award damages in lieu of rescission to the claimant under s 2(1) of the Misrepresentation Act 1967. Rescission is likely to be awarded only where the result of the misrepresentation is substantially to deprive the claimant of his bargain (see *Gosling v Anderson* (1972) *The Times*, 6 February, cf *Museprime Properties Ltd v Adhill Properties Ltd* (1990) 36 EG 114). Rescission is available even after completion, although this is subject to the usual equitable rules and so may not be possible where a third party (eg, a lender) has acquired an interest in the land.

33.4.5 Damages

Damages under the Misrepresentation Act 1967 are awarded on a tortious basis (*Chesneau v Interhome Ltd* (1983) *The Times*, 9 June). An award of damages can be made both as an award in lieu of rescission and as an award to compensate the claimant for his loss, subject to the overriding principle that the claimant cannot recover more than his actual loss, thus the awards under s 2(1) and (2) of the Misrepresentation Act 1967 are not cumulative.

33.4.6 Limitation period

A claim in misrepresentation does not arise out of the contract nor out of tort. The limitation periods prescribed by the Limitation Act 1980 do not therefore apply in this situation, and it seems that the limitation period for a claim based on misrepresentation relies on the equitable doctrine of laches.

33.4.7   Incorporation as a term of the contract

Where a misrepresentation has become incorporated as a term of the contract it is possible, by s 1 of the Misrepresentation Act 1967 to treat the statement as a representation and to pursue a remedy under the Misrepresentation Act 1967. This option gives the claimant the right to ask for rescission of the contract as well as damages. If the claim was confined to breach of a minor contractual term, the only available remedy would be damages.

33.4.8   Imputed knowledge

Knowledge gained by a solicitor in the course of a transaction is deemed to be known by the solicitor's client, whether or not this is in fact the case. Thus where a solicitor gives an incorrect reply to pre-contract enquiries, the solicitor's knowledge, and also his misstatement, is attributable to the client who will be liable to the buyer in misrepresentation (*CEMP Properties (UK) Ltd v Dentsply Research and Development Corporation (No 1)* (1989) 2 EGLR 192). In such a situation, the solicitor would be liable to his own client in negligence. Similarly, if the seller makes a misrepresentation to the buyer personally but the misrepresentation is later corrected in correspondence between the seller's solicitors and the buyer's solicitors, the buyer is deemed to know of the correction (even if not actually told by his solicitor) and would not in such circumstances be able to bring a claim for misrepresentation against the seller (*Strover v Harrington* [1988] Ch 390).

33.4.9   Exclusion clauses

By s 3 of the Misrepresentation Act 1967, as substituted by s 8 of the Unfair Contract Terms Act 1977, any clause which purports to limit or exclude liability for misrepresentation is valid only in so far as it satisfies the reasonableness test laid down in s 11 of and Sch 2 to the Unfair Contract Terms Act 1977. The reasonableness test is applied subjectively, in the light of the circumstances which were known to the parties at the time when the contract was made. It therefore depends on the circumstances of each particular case as to whether the exclusion clause is valid in that situation.

There is no guarantee that any given form of wording will satisfy the test. Standard Condition 7.1 (SCPC 9.1) purports to limit the seller's liability for (inter alia) misrepresentation. Under the condition, damages are payable for a misrepresentation only if there is a material difference between the property as represented and as it really is. Similarly, rescission is available only where there is fraud or recklessness, or where the innocent party would be obliged to accept something differing substantially (in quality, quantity or tenure) from what he had been led to expect. The validity of this clause is subject to its satisfying the reasonableness test on the facts of each particular case.

Some standard forms of pre-contract enquiries (but not the Seller's Property Information Form used in Protocol transactions) have an exclusion clause printed on them. This exclusion clause is also subject to the reasonableness test (see *Walker v Boyle* [1982] 1 All ER 634, where an exclusion clause contained in a then current edition of a standard form of pre-contract enquiries failed the test).

33.5   Misdescription

Misdescription occurs when an error is made in the particulars of sale of the contract, for example, misdescribing the tenure of the property as freehold when it is in fact leasehold, or wrongly describing the physical extent of the land to be sold. Standard Condition 7.1 (SCPC 9.1) (see **33.4.9**) controls the remedies available for misdescription as well as for misrepresentation, in cases where the Standard Conditions are in use.

33.6   Non-disclosure

Non-disclosure arises out of the seller's failure to comply with his duty of disclosure (see **15.7.1**). Where the Standard Conditions of Sale is in use, the remedies for non-disclosure are again governed by SC 7.1 (SCPC 9.1).

33.7   Specific performance

Although specific performance is an equitable remedy which is granted at the discretion of the court, an order for specific performance is not uncommon in sale of land cases where, since no two pieces of land are identical, an award of damages would be inadequate compensation for the injured party's loss. The claim can be made either on its own, or in conjunction with a claim for damages or rescission, depending on the circumstances.

33.7.1   General bars to the award

The award of a decree of specific performance is subject to the usual principles of equity. It will not therefore be awarded where (inter alia):

(a)   an award of damages would adequately compensate for the loss sustained by the breach;

(b)   the contract contains a vitiating element such as mistake, fraud or illegality;

(c)   a third party has acquired an interest for value in the property;

(d)   the seller cannot make good title.

33.7.2   Delay

The doctrine of laches (lapse of time) applies to equitable remedies. The remedy may therefore be barred if the innocent party delays in seeking an award.

33.7.3   Damages in lieu

If, in a situation where specific performance would otherwise be available to the injured party, the court decides not to make such an order, it can award damages in lieu of specific performance under the Supreme Court Act 1981, s 50. These damages are assessed using normal contractual principles as outlined in **33.2**. Where an award of specific performance has been made but has not been complied with, the injured party may return to the court asking the court to withdraw the order and to substitute the decree of specific performance with an award of damages (*Johnson v Agnew* [1980] AC 367).

33.8   Return of deposit

Where the buyer defaults on completion the seller will want to forfeit the deposit, but s 49(2) of the LPA 1925, gives the court an absolute discretion to order the return of the deposit to the buyer. Where the seller retains the deposit, this must be taken into account in any assessment of damages for breach of contract.

Where the seller defaults on completion, the buyer will have a right to the return of the deposit under SC 7.6 (SCPC 9.6).

33.9   Rectification

33.9.1   Rectification of the contract

Where the parties have reached agreement over a particular matter but that matter is either omitted from the written contract in error, or is wrongly recorded in the written agreement, an application for rectification of the contract to correct the error can be made. Under s 2(4) of the Law of Property (Miscellaneous Provisions) Act 1989, where rectification is ordered, the court has a discretion to determine the date on which the contract comes into operation.

33.9.2   Rectification of the purchase deed

Where a term of the contract is either omitted from or inaccurately represented in the purchase deed, an application for rectification of the deed may be made to the court.

33.10   Covenants for title

Certain covenants for title will be implied into the purchase deed, the nature of those covenants depending on whether the seller has sold with full or limited title guarantee (or none at all) (see **15.7.4**). Because of the principle of merger of the contract with the conveyance on completion, a claim arising out of the contract is not generally possible after completion has taken place and the primary post-completion remedy available to the buyer is a claim for breach of the implied covenants for title. However, SC 7.4 (SCPC 9.4) preserves the right to sue on the contract even after completion, subject to the normal six-year limitation period.

33.10.1   Enforcement of the covenants

In the case of unregistered land, liability on the covenants is strict. The limitation period of 12 years runs from the date of completion in the case of the 'right to dispose of the property' covenant, and usually from the date of actual breach in other cases. The covenants for title have equal application to registered land (except that liability is not strict), but the State guarantee of a registered title means that, in practice, claims on the covenants are less likely to occur with the transfer of registered land.

Parts IV, V and VI Summary – From Exchange of Contract to Completion and Beyond

Sub-section heading	Summary
Pre-completion searches	The buyer will need to carry out certain pre-completion searches. What searches need doing will depend on the specifics of a given transaction, but in the case of the purchase of a registered title, the following will normally be required: • **Land Registry search** This search is done to confirm that the details shown in the official copy of the title provided by the seller earlier in the transaction remain unchanged. The search is done on Form OS1 and will give the buyer a 30 working-day priority period within which to submit the application to be registered as the new owner at Land Registry. • **Bankruptcy search** If the buyer is buying with the aid of a mortgage and the buyer's solicitor also acts for the lender, a search needs to be done to confirm that the buyer is not bankrupt. • **Company search** This needs to be done where the seller is a company, and will confirm a number of important points, including that the company exists and has not become insolvent. Different searches are needed if title to the land being bought is unregistered.
The purchase deed	The purchase – or transfer – deed is the document that actually transfers title from the seller to the buyer. Its terms will be fixed by the contract and it is drafted by the buyer's solicitor to give effect to this. In registered land, there is a prescribed form of deed called a TR1. In unregistered land, a traditional form of conveyance can still be used, but it is also possible to use a TR1, and this is what many practitioners use. The following three key points should be noted about the TR1: • **Purchase price** The TR1 has a space for inserting the purchase price. Note that the sum to be inserted is the amount being paid for the land only. Any separate sum for chattels also being bought should not be mentioned. • **Title guarantee** The title guarantee is a promise given by the seller in the purchase deed about the title he is giving to the buyer. In essence, it replaces the similar promises made in the contract. It is necessary as, on completion, the contract is deemed to merge with the transfer. The title guarantee to be given is determined by what was agreed in the contract.

Sub-section heading	Summary
	• **Indemnity covenant** If there are covenants affecting the title, the seller will usually seek an indemnity from the buyer against the possibility of the buyer breaching these covenants following completion. The indemnity will be given in the purchase deed, but will be inserted only if the contract provides for one to be given. Both the Standard Conditions of Sale and Standard Commercial Property Conditions contain provisions providing for one to be given. Similar points would apply if a traditional form of conveyance were to be used.
	The purchase deed needs to be executed in time for completion. It must always be executed by the seller. It must also be executed by the buyer if the buyer is 'doing something' in the purchase deed. This could include giving an indemnity covenant, or declaring how the property is to be held in the case of co-owners.
Completion	It is rare for completion to be carried out face-to-face by the parties' solicitors. The Law Society has produced a Code for Completion by Post which the parties can adopt to ensure that completion takes place satisfactorily. The seller's solicitor acts as agent for the buyer, completing on the buyer's behalf as instructed.
	On the day of completion itself, the buyer's solicitor will transfer the balance of the purchase price to the seller's solicitor and, on receipt of the money, the purchase deed will be dated and completion will have taken place.
	The seller's solicitor should contact his client to confirm that completion has taken place. He should also contact the estate agent to inform the agent that the keys to the property can now be released to the buyer.
	The buyer's solicitor should date the mortgage deed. He should also inform his buyer client that completion has taken place and that the property is now his.
Post-completion The seller	The buyer now owns the property and so the seller will need to forward the transfer deed to him, as well as other documentation relating to the property that the buyer will now need. This could include any guarantees or service contract documentation relating to the structure of the property or services such as central heating within it. If title to the land is unregistered, the seller should also now forward the original title deeds.

Sub-section heading	Summary
The buyer	If there was a mortgage over the property prior to sale, this will need to be discharged from the proceeds of sale, and proof of discharge should be forwarded to the buyer as soon as it is available. The seller's solicitor will usually have been expected to have given an undertaking to do this and so should seek confirmation from the buyer's solicitor that this has now been discharged once done.
	The buyer's solicitor should check that the correct documentation has been received from the seller.
	A SDLT return must be submitted to HM Revenue and Customs within 30 days of completion together with payment of any SDLT due. On the sale of freehold residential land, it is payable at the following rates:
	• Up to £125,000 = 0%
	• Over £125,000–250,000 = 1%
	• Over £250,000–500,000 = 3%
	• Over £500,000 = 4%
	The £125,000 threshold changes to £150,000 for residential property in certain designated disadvantaged areas, and for commercial property.
	If title to the property is registered, the transaction must then be registered at Land Registry. This will include registering the removal of any mortgage the seller had over the property as well as the transfer to the new owner. The application should be made before the expiry of the priority period of the buyer's OS1 search.
	If title is unregistered, the transaction will trigger first registration, and an application to register the title should be made within two months of completion.
	In either case, the results of the application should be checked carefully when returned by Land Registry. If the owner has correctly been registered as the new proprietor and all other matters are satisfactory, the buyer's solicitor can close the file on the transaction.

Part VII
LEASEHOLDS

Chapter 34

Introduction to Leasehold Property

34.1 Introduction

So far, this book has concentrated on the law and practice involved in the outright sale and purchase of freehold land. This part of the book will move on to consider the law and practice relating to the grant and assignment of leases.

Leasehold land is encountered for a number of reasons. First, there can be a ready market for leasehold property, such as that for the short-term letting of residential premises. Secondly, for reasons explained below, where a property forms part of a building rather than the whole, it is usual to find that each unit within the building will be held under a lease rather than being sold freehold. This can apply to both commercial property, such as an office suite, and residential property, such as a flat. Further, in some parts of England and Wales, for reasons which are largely historic in origin, it is not uncommon to find residential property being sold leasehold rather than freehold.

34.2 Advantages and disadvantages of leaseholds

34.2.1 Advantages

There can be advantages to both parties in leasing property. First, although the term of a lease must be fixed once granted, the length of the actual term chosen can, theoretically, be of any duration. This gives parties flexibility to meet their mutual needs. The example of the short-term residential letting market has been mentioned in **34.1** above. Such lettings give tenants a place to live whilst, say, saving for a deposit to buy a home of their own, but also provide landlords with income from the rent paid by the tenants. Further, from a landlord's perspective, not only does he enjoy the benefit of a steady income from the property, he also retains an interest (ie, the freehold estate) which is a saleable capital asset in its own right, which can be disposed of separately from the leasehold interest.

Another advantage is that the parties are more easily able to enforce covenants than is the case with freehold land. In freehold land, positive covenants (eg, a covenant to repair) are not enforceable against future owners of the land. In the case of leasehold land, almost all covenants, both positive and negative, are enforceable against such successors in title. Where the enforcement of both positive as well as negative covenants is of particular importance in respect of a given property, it is therefore common to find that leases are used. Thus, where a property forms part of a larger building, it is usual to find that each unit within the building is let rather than being sold freehold. This meets the needs of the landlord, in that the landlord can enforce positive covenants such as repair on the tenants of each unit, but it also meets the needs of the tenants as they can ensure that common parts retained by the landlord are also maintained as appropriate. As regards this latter point, in practice the way this is dealt with is that one individual (normally the landlord or a management company) will be responsible for the maintenance of the common parts but will recover the costs incurred by way of a 'service charge' levied on the tenants of the individual units within the building. This obligation to pay the service charge is itself a positive covenant, the enforcement of which could present problems in the case of freehold land.

34.2.2 Disadvantages

The disadvantages of leasehold property are mainly on the tenant's side. First, as a lease is granted for a fixed period of time, it will eventually expire. Should the tenant wish to remain in the property in this event, he will have to approach the landlord for a renewal, which the landlord may not be willing to give. Further, if the lease has a capital value, the lease is in effect a wasting asset in the tenant's hands. This difficulty is alleviated to a degree, as some tenants have statutory rights to renew or extend the term in certain circumstances. The most important examples of these rights are considered in **Chapters 38** and **39.** The fundamental problem remains, however, especially where such rights are not available.

An additional disadvantage for tenants relates to covenants. Leases often impose considerable burdens on tenants, including covenants relating to repair, obligations to contribute towards the cost of maintaining the building of which the property let forms part, and restrictions on the tenant's ability to assign or otherwise deal with the property. This is compounded by the remedies available to the landlord to ensure compliance with these obligations (see **Chapter 3** at **3.11** for more details). Ultimately, the landlord can forfeit the lease, bringing it to an end. This remedy is dramatic, particularly if the lease has a capital value, as this capital value will be lost along with the lease itself.

From the landlord's point of view, the main disadvantage of granting a lease rather than selling the property outright is that, together with the rights which he retains in the property, he may also retain various obligations in relation to matters such as repairs and insurance. The burden of these obligations must, however, be set against the benefit of the income received from the rent of the property and the covenants agreed to be performed by the tenant.

34.3 Common illustrations of leasehold property

34.3.1 The residential market

34.3.1.1 Short-term residential lettings

The market for the short-term letting of residential property has already been mentioned. Such leases are usually granted for a period of, say, a year at the full open market rent (or 'rack rent') for the property. The lease will therefore have no capital value in the hands of the tenant. The procedure on the grant of a short-term lease is normally very informal. Such lettings are often handled by letting agents. It is likely that neither party will be legally represented and the tenant will make no searches or enquiries at all about the property. The landlord will be most concerned about the status of the tenant rather than legal matters (ie, whether the tenant will be a 'good' tenant or not; whether he will pay the rent regularly and not damage the property). Further, it is usual for the lease to provide that the lease cannot be assigned by the tenant and so the only 'dealing' with the lease is when it is originally granted.

Given the comparatively 'informal' nature of such transactions, the usual conveyancing procedures seen in this book do not, in effect, apply, and for the remainder of this part of the book this will be assumed to be the case. Such lettings can, however, give rise to certain statutory rights and protections in favour of tenants, and these are considered in outline in **Chapter 39**.

34.3.1.2 The residential long lease

Historically, the units on many housing estates were sold on long leases rather than as freeholds. Whilst this is comparatively rare today, long residential leases are still routinely encountered where the units being disposed of form part of a larger building, such as units in a block of flats or maisonettes. Such units are disposed of using a leasehold arrangement due to the greater ability to enforce both positive and negative covenants as discussed at **34.2.1** above. In either case, the lease will usually be granted for a lengthy term (say 125 years) in return for a lump sum payment (a 'premium') and a low 'ground rent' (often no more than £100 or so).

Such leases thus have a capital value and, unlike short-term residential lettings, there are usually few controls on the tenant's ability to dispose of the property by way of assignment (although there may be more controls on a tenant's freedom to assign part – as opposed to the whole – and to sub-let). Such leases can therefore be bought and sold like freehold land. Indeed, if it were not for the need to ensure the effective enforcement of positive and negative covenants, the leasehold route would probably not need to be used in such cases at all.

The conveyancing aspects of long residential leaseholds in many ways therefore mirror the procedure for the sale of a freehold. This is the case both on the grant of the original lease and in the event of the subsequent assignment of that lease. On grant, the developer will charge a purchase price, just as it would on the sale of a house, and, when the buyer tenant in turn comes to sell, he too will sell the lease for a capital sum. As such, the original tenant (in the case of the grant of a lease) or a purchaser from the tenant (in the case of a subsequent assignment) will need to investigate title and carry out searches and enquiries in the usual way, and will need to consider how to fund the acquisition, often with the aid of a mortgage. In addition, the freehold model of exchanging contracts before subsequently completing is also usually followed.

Given the length of such leases and the low yield provided in the form of rent, ownership of the freehold in such circumstances is not viewed as a particularly attractive investment. This is compounded by the fact that tenants of such properties have various statutory rights to extend the terms of their leases (the detail of which is considered in **Chapter 39**), so landlords are unlikely to be able regain vacant possession of the land and re-let. In the light of this, the developer landlord will often dispose of the freehold of the common parts to a management company (owned through its shares by the tenants of the individual units) rather than retain any interest in the development following completion of it.

34.3.2 The commercial property market

It is less usual for commercial occupiers to own the freehold to their premises, and instead most commercial property is occupied under leases. There are a number of reasons for this. First, businesses can be attracted by the flexibility a lease provides. To take an example of a new start-up business, this might prosper and so wish to move to larger premises. Alternatively, the business might not be such a success, and a move to smaller, cheaper premises might be desired. A short-term lease allows greater flexibility in this context. Secondly, the cost of buying a freehold will often be prohibitively expensive and, in any case, most businesses will simply not want to tie up capital in this way even if the money were available. Lastly, where the premises form part of a building, the same issue relating to the effective enforcement of both positive and negative covenants applies as discussed above.

The willingness of businesses to rent property creates a market for landlords to supply that need. In fact, commercial property plays an important part of the investment portfolios of institutions such as insurance companies, pension funds and the like. It has given rise to the development of what is often referred to as the 'institutional lease'. The landlord will seek to pass the day-to-day operational cost for occupying the property to the tenants, leaving the rent as pure profit in the hands of the landlord.

Historically, leases for periods of five to 21 years were common, but in recent years the trend has been towards shorter terms, and now periods of between five and 15 years are more usual. Whilst it is possible for a capital sum to be payable (both on the grant of a commercial lease and any subsequent assignment of it), this is less usual than is the case for the grant or assignment of a long residential lease. Instead, the 'cost' to the tenant comes in the form of the payment of a market rent, much higher relatively than the rent which is payable under a long residential lease. Further, the rent is usually subject to review every few years under a term to this effect in the lease. A consequence of this is that leases of commercial property, whatever the length, usually contain detailed controls on the tenant's freedom to assign or otherwise deal with the property, as the landlord will be keen to ensure that any assignee, for example, is at least as able as the current tenant to meet the liabilities due under the lease.

The terms of commercial leases are often the subject of detailed negotiation between the parties on grant. Partly in response to Government pressure for greater flexibility, the property industry has developed a guidance code, the latest edition of which, the Code for Leasing Business Premises in England and Wales 2007, was recently published and can be found at www.leasingbusinesspremises. co.uk. It must be understood that the Code is voluntary and consists in the main part of guidance and suggestions as to the options available to the parties. The detail of the negotiations and the terms that will be agreed by the parties will turn on the specifics of each case. It is nonetheless a valuable resource, particularly to small businesses, providing access to information about the obligations that may be assumed by the parties, in clear English.

In terms of procedure, it is less usual for the parties to exchange contracts, and instead the transaction will often simply proceed straight to completion. This is because it is less usual to need to synchronise a chain of transactions than is the case in the residential context. Subject to this, the steps that make up the procedure for granting or assigning a lease broadly follow those for the sale of freehold land. It should be noted, however, that for shorter terms, a prospective tenant or assignee may choose not to carry out some of the more usual steps, such as investigating title. This is a commercial decision for the client. The following chapters will work on the basis that the client does not wish to omit any of these steps.

34.4 Key terminology – grant, assignment and sub-letting

It is important to understand the terminology in respect of dealings with leases. This is perhaps best explained by the diagram which follows:

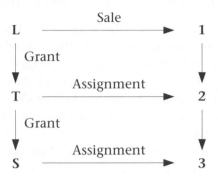

When a lease is brought into being, the transaction is known as a 'grant'. Thus, in the diagram, when the owner of the freehold (L) creates a lease in favour of the tenant (T), this is said to be the grant of that lease. This lease is the head-lease, because the only superior title above it is the freehold (also known as the freehold reversion). Just as the landlord is able to carve a lease out of his freehold, T can do the same out of his lease and so, in turn, when T grants a lease to S, this is called the grant of a sub-lease.

The effect of this is that there are now three legal estates in existence over the land: the freehold; the head-leasehold; and the sub-leasehold. Each of these estates can be bought and sold in its own right. Thus, L can transfer the freehold to 1, T can transfer the head-lease to 2, and S can transfer the sub-lease to 3. To distinguish between transfers of freeholds, on the one hand, and leaseholds on the other, it is usual to refer to the transfer of a leasehold as an 'assignment'.

It is important to distinguish between 'grant' and 'assignment' as they are distinct and separate types of transaction, as will be shown in **Chapters 35** and **36**. In particular, it is important to understand that the grant of a lease creates the lease for the first time (and the document giving effect to the transaction will be the lease itself), whilst an assignment transfers the remainder of such a lease once it has been created (and the document giving effect to the transaction will be a deed of assignment).

Two final points need to be made. First, when a tenant grants a sub-lease, the term of the sub-lease must be for a period that is shorter than the head-lease itself. If the tenant purports to grant a sub-lease for a term equal to or greater than the head-lease, this transaction will be treated, instead, as being an assignment of the tenant's lease. Secondly, in the example above, it has been assumed that there are no restrictions on either T's or S's freedom to dispose of their respective leasehold interests. In practice, it is common to find restrictions on a tenant's freedom to assign or sub-let. It is important to check the terms of any lease at an early stage of a transaction for any such restrictions.

34.5 Underlying law – liability on covenants in leases

As has been seen, one of the major advantages of creating a lease relates to the enforcement of covenants between the parties. This section contains an outline of the underlying principles in this respect.

34.5.1 Leases granted on or after 1 January 1996

The Landlord and Tenant (Covenants) Act 1995 applies to leases granted on or after 1 January 1996. Note that it is the date of the *grant* of the lease, not any subsequent assignment, that determines this.

The original landlord (who granted the lease) and original tenant will be bound by all covenants in the lease while the tenant remains as tenant, but when the tenant lawfully assigns the lease he is automatically released from future liability under the lease covenants unless he has agreed to enter into an 'authorised guarantee agreement' (AGA). The AGA is an agreement entered into by the outgoing tenant with his landlord in which the outgoing tenant guarantees the performance of the lease covenants by his immediate successor in title. Note that the guarantee contained in the AGA extends to the performance of covenants by the immediate successor in title only, and will not extend to subsequent tenants. The outgoing tenant remains liable, however, for any breaches of covenant which were committed before the date of the assignment.

An assignee of a lease is bound by all the tenant's covenants in the lease, except those expressly stated to be 'personal' to the original tenant. On a subsequent assignment, the assignee remains liable for any breaches committed before the date of the assignment, but is released from liability for any future breaches, unless he too has been required to give an AGA to guarantee the performance of the lease covenants by *his* immediate successor.

Two final points should be noted about a tenant's liability. First, the automatic release provisions considered above do not apply if the assignment is in breach of a covenant in the lease, nor if it occurs by operation of the law (eg, on the death of the tenant where the lease passes to his personal representatives). Secondly, where a former tenant remains liable under an AGA, he should seek protection in the form of an indemnity covenant from his successor in title. This must be given expressly, as the law does not imply one.

As regards landlords, the original landlord (and any subsequent assignee of the landlord's interest) is not automatically released from his covenants when he sells the reversion, but can apply to the tenant for the time being to be released from future liability before or within four weeks of the date of the assignment of the reversion.

34.5.2 Leases granted before 1 January 1996

34.5.2.1 Liability of tenants

The Landlord and Tenant (Covenants) Act 1995 generally does not apply to these leases.

The basic principle is that the original tenant remains bound by the covenants in the lease for the whole of the contractual term under the doctrine of privity of contract. This liability continues even after assignment, unless the landlord expressly agrees to release him. The significance of this is worth emphasising: unless released by the landlord, the original tenant is liable on all the express covenants in the lease for breaches committed at any time during the term of the lease, ie he is liable not only for breaches which he commits himself, but also for those committed by his successors in title.

In addition to the liability of the original tenant, any assignee will also be liable for breaches committed whilst ownership of the lease is vested in that assignee in respect of covenants which 'touch and concern' the land. In essence, covenants which 'touch and concern' are those which would be entered into between parties as landowners, rather than in their capacity as mere individuals. This is under the doctrine of privity of estate.

Thus the landlord can potentially seek redress against either the original tenant or the assignee who committed the breach. Whilst the landlord cannot claim double compensation, this is nonetheless an advantage to the landlord as it gives him a choice as to whom he can sue. This is particularly attractive if the assignee is in financial difficulties and so not worth suing. It should be noted that where the original landlord transfers the reversion, the right to sue passes to the transferee of that reversion (and any subsequent landlord for the time being), because on a transfer of the reversion all rights of action attached to the reversion pass to the transferee, including the right to sue for an existing breach of covenant (LPA 1925, s 141; and see *In re King (deceased); Robinson v Gray* [1963] Ch 459).

In the light of the above, an assignee of a lease will usually be required to indemnify his assignor in respect of any breach of covenant committed after the date of the assignment to him, regardless of whether he has parted with the lease. On the transfer of a registered lease, such an indemnity covenant is implied by Sch 12, para 20 to the LRA 2002 (preserving the effect of LRA 1925, s 24), whether or not value was given for the assignment. A similar indemnity provision is implied by s 77 of the LPA 1925 on the assignment of an unregistered lease, but only where value has been given for the assignment. Where, in unregistered land, there is to be no valuable consideration for the assignment, an express indemnity covenant will be required by the assignor. Standard Condition 4.6.4 and SCPC 6.6.4 require the purchase deed to contain an express indemnity covenant, except where one is implied by law.

One final point remains to be made. If the lease contains a requirement to obtain the landlord's consent before any assignment takes place, the landlord may, in appropriate circumstances, insist that any assignee enter into a direct contractual relationship with him. This is usually contained in the same document in which the landlord gives his consent to the assignment, known as a licence to assign. This has the effect of imposing on any assignee the same liability under privity of contract as is faced by the original tenant.

34.5.2.2 Liability of landlords

The original landlord remains contractually bound to the original tenant throughout the term of the lease under the doctrine of privity of contract. If an original landlord is unable through his own act or default (eg, by transferring the reversion to a third party) to carry out an obligation imposed on him by the lease, the landlord may be liable in damages to the tenant. See, for example, *Eagon v Dent* [1965] 2 All ER 334, where a landlord sold the reversion to a third party and the original tenant, who failed in his attempt to exercise an unregistered option against the buyer of the reversion, recovered damages from the original landlord for breach of covenant.

In addition to the original landlord, any transferee of the reversion for the time being will also be liable in respect of breaches of covenant which touch and concern the land which are committed whilst the reversion is vested in them. Again, this is under the doctrine of privity of estate.

34.5.3 Default notices – liability of former tenants

As can be seen from the above, former tenants can remain liable for breaches of covenants by assignees; in the case of leases granted before 1 January 1996, under the doctrine of privity of contract, and for leases granted on or after that date, where the outgoing tenant has given an AGA. In order to afford some protection to former tenants in respect of arrears of fixed sums such as rent, s 17 of the Landlord and Tenant (Covenants) Act 1995 provides that a landord can pursue a former tenant only if he first serves what is known as a 'default notice' on the former tenant. This must be served within six months of the sum falling due. If the notice is not served, the landlord cannot pursue the former tenant. This protection applies to leases whether created before or after the Landlord and Tenant (Covenants) Act 1995 came into force.

The recent case *Scottish & Newcastle v Raguz* [2006] EWHC 821 has highlighted a specific issue for landlords where the lease in question contains a rent review clause. The detail of the drafting and operation of rent review clauses is considered in **Chapter 37**. For the moment it is sufficient to understand that rent review provisions typically fix a date upon which the reviewed rent becomes payable (the 'rent review date'), and if the amount of that rent has not been determined by that date, as can happen, the lease will provide for the tenant to pay a balancing sum on determination. In *Raguz*, the court held that for the purposes of s 17, the date on which the rent becomes due is the rent review date rather than the date that the new rent is determined. The effect of this is that, in order to preserve their position in these circumstances, landlords should serve s 17 notices on former tenants within six months of each rent review date (and each subsequent rent payment date) even if the current tenant is not in default. This adds a significant burden on landlords, especially where the landlord has a large portfolio of commercial properties.

34.6 Liability between head-landlord and sub-tenant

No privity of estate exists between a head-landlord and a sub-tenant, although a contractual relationship will exist between them if the sub-tenant has entered into direct covenants with the head-landlord (eg, where the head-landlord has insisted on this as a precondition to allowing the sub-letting). The sub-tenant will in any event be directly liable to the head-landlord on restrictive covenants in the head-lease of which the former had notice when he took his sub-lease. Irrespective of direct contractual liability, if the sub-tenant breaches a covenant in the head-lease, the head-landlord will have the right to forfeit the head-lease, and this will mean that the sub-lease which is derived out of the head-lease will also terminate.

34.7 Commonhold

The Government has introduced a new form of land ownership called 'commonhold', which is designed to overcome some of the disadvantages of leases in dispositions of units in interdependent premises, for example flats, office blocks and shopping centres. Each unit is held freehold, and the common parts held by a Commonhold Association, which will be responsible for repairs, etc to the common parts. The Commonhold Association is a private limited company of which the unit owners will be members. A Commonhold Community Statement sets out the obligations of each unit holder, including the obligation to pay a service charge. These obligations, whether positive or negative, will be binding on successors in title.

As each flat or other unit will be held freehold, the problem of leases being a wasting asset will disappear. Also, the fact that a company owned by the tenants will own the common parts will avoid the problem that can sometimes arise in blocks of flats, of landlords charging excessive service charges. Commonhold is available both for new developments and for existing developments. The conversion of existing blocks will be possible, however, only at the request of the landlord and with the consent of all the tenants.

Chapter 35

The Grant of a Lease

35.1 Introduction

This chapter considers the procedure for the grant of a lease.

In the case of a short-term letting of residential premises, the procedure will be informal and will, in effect, usually consist of not much more than the landlord taking references (such as from the tenant's bank) and presenting the lease to the tenant for signature on a 'take it or leave it' basis. The procedure considered in this chapter would not therefore apply to such transactions. Instead, this chapter considers the procedure that is adopted in the following two contexts:

(a) *The grant of a long residential lease.* The conveyancing procedure employed in this type of transaction is similar to that used on a freehold sale and purchase. This chapter deals only with those matters where the procedure for the grant of a lease differs from that used in a freehold transaction.

The landlord grants the lease to the tenant on terms stipulated by the landlord (whose duty it is to draft the lease). The draft lease will be annexed to the draft contract and is then open to negotiation with the tenant. The Protocol is expressed to apply to both freehold and leasehold transactions, but makes no express reference to the procedure on the grant of a lease.

(b) *The grant of a lease of commercial property.* The procedure on the grant of a commercial lease will follow a similar pattern to the above. However, it is less usual for a contract to be drawn up. Instead, the parties will agree the terms of the lease and then proceed directly to grant. As this is a commercial situation, the terms of the lease are often the subject of detailed negotiation between the prospective landlord and tenant.

Where a commercial lease is for a comparatively short term, a prospective tenant may choose not to carry out some of the more usual steps, such as investigating title. This is a commercial decision for the client. This chapter will work on the basis that the client does not wish to omit any of these steps.

35.2 Taking instructions from the landlord

Much of the information required by the landlord's solicitor from his client will be similar to that required from the seller in the case of a freehold transaction, which is discussed in **Chapter 7**. In addition, instructions need to be obtained from the client (and advice given to him) relating to such matters as the length of the term to be granted, the rent to be charged to the tenant, who is to be responsible for the repair and insurance of the property, and various other matters which will need to be dealt with in the lease itself. These matters are considered in **Chapter 37**.

Before drafting the lease, the landlord's solicitor should investigate his own client's title. This needs to be done for a number of reasons. Investigation of title must be carried out to ensure that the client is entitled to grant the lease and to anticipate any problems with the title, such as covenants which prevent the use proposed under the lease. In addition, the landlord's solicitor will need to investigate title in order to be able to draft the contract (where there is one). The investigation is done in exactly the same way as if the solicitor was acting for a seller in a freehold transaction (see **Chapter 14**).

Particular consideration needs to be given to any mortgage over the property. Where the property is subject to an existing mortgage, the mortgage will frequently contain a provision which prohibits or restricts the borrower/landlord's ability to grant a lease of the property. In such a case, the lender must be contacted and his permission to grant the lease obtained before the matter proceeds.

35.3 Drafting the lease

The landlord's solicitor will draft the lease. This will then be sent to the prospective tenant's solicitor for negotiation and approval. Some of the most usual terms to be included in a lease are examined in **Chapter 37**.

A lease for a term of over three years must be granted by deed to vest the legal estate in the tenant. A lease for three years or less, taking effect in possession at the best rent without a fine, may be granted orally or in writing (LPA 1925, ss 52–54, as amended).

35.4 Drafting the contract

Where a contract for the grant of the lease is to be entered into, such as is usually the case with the purchase for a premium of a long-term residential lease, this will also need to be drafted. It is drafted by the landlord's solicitor in the same way that the seller's solicitor will draft the contract in the case of the sale of a freehold. The particulars of sale must state that the property is leasehold and give details of the term to be vested in the tenant. Incumbrances affecting the freehold title must be disclosed (as these will affect the tenant in the same way as they would affect a buyer of the freehold) and the contract should provide for an indemnity to be given in the transfer in respect of future breaches of any covenants affecting the title. In other respects, the contract will be similar to that prepared on a freehold transaction.

Except where the lease is to be for a term not exceeding three years, taking effect in possession and with no premium payable for its grant, the contract for the lease must satisfy s 2 of the Law of Property (Miscellaneous Provisions) Act 1989.

Standard Condition 8.2 (SCPC 10.2) provides for the lease to be in the form annexed to the draft contract, and for the landlord to engross the lease and supply the tenant with the engrossment at least five working days before completion date.

35.5 Title

A lender will not accept a lease of residential property as security for a loan unless the freehold title has been satisfactorily deduced. The absence of the freehold title will usually prevent the tenant and his successors from obtaining an absolute leasehold title on the subsequent registration of the lease unless the freehold is already registered. Under an open contract, the tenant is not entitled to call for deduction of the freehold reversionary title on the grant of a lease (LPA 1925, s 44(2)). This rule is unsatisfactory where a premium is to be paid for the grant of the lease, or where a tenant is paying a significant rent for commercial premises. However, as from 13 October 2003, this rule has been disapplied to grants of leases for more than seven years by Sch 11 to the LRA 2002. The intending tenant will thus be able to insist on the deduction of the freehold title and so obtain registration with absolute leasehold title.

Where the lease will exceed seven years, SC 8.2.4 (SCPC 10.2.4) requires the landlord to deduce such title as would enable the tenant to obtain registration with an absolute title at Land Registry. This, in effect, means that the landlord must deduce the freehold and all other superior titles to the lease being granted, for example title to any head-lease.

35.5.1 Sub-leases

In the case of the grant of a sub-lease out of an unregistered head-lease, the sub-tenant is entitled to call for the head-lease out of which his sub-lease is to be derived and all subsequent assignments under which the lease has been held for the last 15 years. However, s 44 of the LPA 1925 provides that he is not entitled to call for production of the freehold title.

This rule is again unsatisfactory where a premium is to be paid on the grant, or where the tenant is paying a significant amount by way of rent. However, Sch 11 to the LRA 2002 amends s 44 so that, as from 13 October 2003, this provision does not apply to the grant of a sub-lease for more than seven years. The prospective tenant will thus be able to insist on the production of title to the head-lease and the freehold. Standard Condition 8.2.4 (SCPC 10.2.4) also applies to the grant of a sub-lease.

This requirement to provide details of the freehold title, whether under SC 8.2.4 (SCPC 10.2.4) or the LRA 2002, may cause problems to a head tenant wanting to grant the sub-lease when he did not call for the deduction of the freehold title when he took the head-lease. He may not be able to comply and so will need to exclude this requirement by a special condition in the contract.

The Sch 11 amendments to s 44 will also apply if the title to the head-lease is registered with its own title. If the head-lease is registered with absolute title, there will be no need to see the title to the freehold.

In any event, if the title to the reversion is registered, the open Registry rules will always allow the prospective tenant to inspect that reversion.

35.6 The pre-contract package

35.6.1 General principles

As a matter of general principle, the landlord's solicitor should provide the tenant's solicitor with at least the following documents:

(a)   draft contract (if applicable);

(b)   draft lease;

(c)   evidence of the freehold title;

(d)   copies of any relevant planning consents; and

(e)   evidence of the lender's consent to the grant of the lease (where relevant).

Where the Protocol applies, the landlord's solicitor will need to comply with the terms of that scheme in the same way as would be the case for the sale of freehold land. This will include providing the tenant's solicitor with a PIF and a Fittings and Contents Form as part of the pre-contract package.

In addition to the above, in the case of the grant of a flat lease where there is going to be a management company providing the services, the company will need incorporating and share certificates (if relevant) and company documents will need to be prepared before the completion of the sale of the first flat. Details of the company should be included in the pre-contract package.

35.6.2   Home Information Packs

The Home Information Pack Regulations 2007 apply to transactions involving the grant of a lease of residential premises where the term granted exceeds 21 years. Fundamentally, the HIP must contain the same prescribed information and in the same manner as for the sale of a freehold, and the sale statement must be completed as if the leasehold interest had already been created. In addition to this, the HIP must contain information about the following:

(a)   the terms of the draft lease; and

(b)   estimates of the contributions likely to be required of the tenant, within 12 months of completion of the lease, in respect of the following:

  (i)   service charge;

  (ii)   ground rent;

  (iii)   insurance for the building in which the property is situated; and

  (iv)   occupiers' liability insurance for the building in which the property is situated (where not covered in the service charge).

As is the case for the sale of freehold residential property, the Regulations also make provision for information and documentation that the landlord can choose (but is not obliged) to provide as part of the HIP. An example of such information would be details of the membership and existence of any management company, and the HIP could also include an HCR.

If the Protocol applies, Form TA3 (Required Leasehold Information Form) and Form TA7 have been designed to facilitate the assembly of HIPs to cover these issues.

35.6.3   Energy Performance Certificates

These certificates form part of the compulsory contents of a HIP where one is required. In addition, EPCs will be required as from 6 April 2008 on the sale or letting of buildings, other than dwellings, with a floor area over 10,000 m^2. As from 1 July 2008 they will be required for the construction, sale or rent of buildings, other than dwellings, with a floor area over 2,500 m^2, and as from 1 October 2008 they will be required on the rent of all remaining dwellings and on the construction, sale or rent of all remaining buildings other than dwellings. This means that as from 1 October 2008 (at the latest), EPCs will be required in all commercial and residential sales and lettings. Except where a HIP is required on a sale of a dwelling, the EPC will last for 10 years before a new one needs to be obtained.

There are transitional arrangements for buildings already on the market at 6 April. Any building which is on the market before then and remains on the market afterwards will need an EPC by 1 October 2008 at the latest. If it is sold or rented out in the meantime, an EPC must be commissioned and then handed over as soon as reasonably practicable. This is intended to make it easier for owners and landlords of large buildings to comply with the legislation. Similar provisions will apply for the introduction of EPCs on buildings over 2,500 m^2 in July 2008, expiring also on 1 October 2008.

35.7 Acting for the tenant

The information required by the tenant's solicitor from his client will be similar to that required in a freehold purchase transaction (see **Chapter 7**).

35.7.1 The draft contract and draft lease

Where the parties are to enter into a contract before grant, the terms of the contract must be agreed before exchange, as is the case in the context of the sale of freehold land. The contract will normally require the tenant to accept the draft lease in the form annexed to the contract (see, eg, SC 8.2.3 or SCPC 10.2.3), and therefore the terms of the lease must also be settled so that the agreed version can be annexed to the contract ready for exchange. If the parties intend to proceed straight to the grant of the lease (as is often the case with leases of commercial property), the terms of the lease need to be agreed prior to grant.

In either case, even where the lease appears to contain 'usual' clauses appropriate to the particular transaction in hand, the document must be carefully examined by the tenant's solicitor to ensure that it contains provisions which are adequate to protect his client's interests and no onerous clauses.

The particular points to look out for when checking the draft lease are considered in **Chapter 37**.

35.7.2 Searches

The tenant's solicitor will want to undertake the same searches and enquiries (both before and after exchange) as if he were buying the freehold (see **Chapters 18** and **28**). As with a freehold transaction, some of these searches may be undertaken by the landlord's solicitor and their results supplied to the tenant's solicitor as part of the pre-contract package or HIP where one is required.

As has been discussed, where a lease is for a shorter term, it is not usual for searches and enquiries to be made, since the low risk attached to these lettings does not justify the expense of making the searches.

35.7.3 Lender's requirements

Where the tenant is acquiring the lease with the aid of a mortgage, the tenant's lender's requirements, contained in the instructions given to the solicitors acting for the lender, must be observed.

The *Lenders' Handbook* requires compliance with the following conditions:

(a)   the consent of the landlord's lender has been obtained to the transaction (where relevant);

(b)   the length of the term to be granted provides adequate security for the loan (terms of less than 60 years are often unacceptable for mortgage purposes in the case of residential leases);

(c)   the lease contains adequate insurance provisions relating both to the premises themselves and (where relevant) to common parts of the building, and the insurance provisions coincide with the lender's own requirements for insurance;

(d)   title to the freehold reversion is deduced, enabling the lease itself to be registered with an absolute title at Land Registry;

(e)   the lease contains proper repairing covenants in respect both of the property itself and (where relevant) the common parts of the building;

(f)   in the case of residential leases, that there is no provision for forfeiture on the insolvency of the tenant.

35.7.4   Advising the client

The tenant's obligations under the lease, which are often complex and extensive, should be explained clearly to him. In particular, the tenant should be warned of the danger of losing the lease through forfeiture for breach of covenant.

35.8   Engrossment and execution of the lease

The lease is normally prepared in two identical parts, the lease and counterpart. The lease is executed by the landlord and the counterpart by the tenant. On completion, these are exchanged so that each party has a copy of the lease signed by the other in case of subsequent dispute.

As with the purchase deed in the case of the sale of freehold land, a top copy (or engrossment) of the lease and counterpart will need to be made and it is these that the parties will sign. Standard Condition 8.2.5 (SCPC 10.2.5) provides that it is for the landlord's solicitor to prepare the engrossments. If the landlord requires the tenant to pay a fee for the preparation of the engrossment, this must be dealt with by special condition in the contract. The landlord will sign the lease itself in readiness for completion, and the counterpart should be sent to the tenant's solicitor at least five working days before contractual completion date (SC 8.2.5 and SCPC 10.2.5) for execution by the tenant. The requirements for execution of a deed are dealt with in 27.7.

35.9   Apportionment of rent

Unless completion takes place on a day when rent under the lease falls due, a proportionate amount of rent calculated from the date of completion until the next rent payment day will be payable by the tenant on completion. This applies where the rent reserved by the lease is payable in advance, not in arrears. The apportionment should be shown on the completion statement supplied by the landlord. Neither set of Standard Conditions provides for the apportionment of rent on completion of the grant of a lease, therefore an express special condition is required to deal with this matter, unless, as is usually the case, it is dealt with in the lease itself.

35.10   Completion

On completion, in addition to or in substitution for the matters relevant to a freehold transaction, the landlord will receive:

(a)   the counterpart lease executed by the tenant;

(b)   any premium payable for the grant (less any deposit paid on exchange of contracts);

(c) an apportioned sum representing rent payable in advance under the lease (see **35.9**).

The landlord should give to the tenant:

(a) the lease executed by him;

(b) if not already done, properly marked or certified copies of the freehold title deeds (unregistered land);

(c) where relevant and if not already done, a certified copy of the consent of the landlord's lender to the transaction.

In the case of a flat lease where a management company is to provide the services, the tenant's share certificate in the company (or an undertaking for it) will be handed over on completion. Frequently, however, the company will be limited by guarantee, not shares, so the flat buyer will have been required to become a member of the company, but there will be no share certificate to hand over.

35.11 After completion

35.11.1 Registration

35.11.1.1 Short leases

A lease for seven years or less is not capable of being registered with its own title at Land Registry but will take effect as an overriding interest under the LRA 2002, whether or not the tenant is in actual occupation of the land. It is possible voluntarily to note leases of over three years in length.

In unregistered land, a legal lease is binding on all subsequent owners of the land, irrespective of notice.

35.11.1.2 Registrable leases

The grant of a lease for a term which exceeds seven years is registrable in its own right after completion, irrespective of whether the freehold title is itself registered. It will be registered with its own separate title and title number, and will also be noted against the landlord's title (see **35.11.2**).

35.11.2 The tenant

35.11.2.1 Stamp duty land tax

A land transaction return must be submitted to HMRC on the grant of a lease in the usual way. In the case of the *grant* of a lease, SDLT is potentially chargeable both on any capital sum being paid (referred to as a 'premium') and on the amount of the rent.

In terms of SDLT payable on any premium, this is essentially calculated using the same bands and rates as for the consideration on the sale of freehold land (see **31.7**). If, however, the annual rent exceeds £600, the lower thresholds under which no SDLT is chargeable do not apply. Instead, SDLT will be payable on the whole of the premium at the appropriate rate.

In terms of SDLT on any rental element, a complex formula is used to identify the Net Present Value ('NPV') of the rent and SDLT is then calculated using this figure. Calculating the NPV consists of working out how much rent is payable in total over the term of the lease and then discounting rental payments to be made in future years by 3.5% per annum. The HMRC website contains a calculator for ascertaining the NPV. Once the NPV has been calculated, duty is then payable at 1% on the amount of the NPV in excess of £125,000 (£150,000 for commercial property), ie, duty is never chargeable on the first £125,000 (or £150,000) of NPV. There are special provisions for dealing with the situation where the lease provides for rent increases during the term.

35.11.2.2   Registration of the lease

Where applicable, the lease must be registered at Land Registry within the relevant priority period or, on first registration, within two months of completion of the grant of the lease. If the freehold is unregistered, the tenant's application is for first registration. If the freehold is itself registered, the tenant's application is for registration of a dealing. Where the landlord's title is registered, the lease will be noted against the reversionary title.

35.11.2.3   Notice to landlord

Where the tenant is, as usual, obliged by the lease to give notice of dealings to the landlord, this covenant may (depending on its wording) include the obligation to give notice of a mortgage created by the tenant. In any event, para 5.10.11 of the *Lender's Handbook* requires notice of a mortgage to be served on the landlord and the management company (if any). Notice should be given by sending two copies of the notice, together with a cheque for the appropriate fee, to the landlord's solicitor or other person named in the covenant. The landlord should be asked to sign one copy of the notice and to return it to the tenant, so that the receipted notice may be kept with the tenant's title deeds as evidence of compliance with this requirement.

35.11.3   The landlord

After completion, the landlord may receive notice in duplicate from the tenant, in accordance with the tenant's covenant in the lease, of the tenant's mortgage of the property. One copy of the notice should be placed with the landlord's title deeds, the other should be receipted on behalf of the landlord and returned to the tenant's solicitor.

Chapter 36

The Assignment of a Lease

36.1 Introduction

An assignment is the transfer of an existing lease by the tenant (the 'assignor' or 'seller') to a third party (the 'assignee' or 'buyer'). It will arise chiefly in the following two contexts:

(a) *Residential.* Assignment of short-term residential lettings is usually prohibited in the lease. The procedure considered in this chapter would not therefore apply to such transactions. Instead, in the residential context, assignment will take place in the case of a long lease of a house or flat, which, as has been seen, will have a capital value which translates into a purchase price on the market. The house or flat will be sold by a seller to a buyer for this price in the same way as a freehold property is also sold for its price.

(b) *Commercial.* Leases of commercial premises are usually capable of assignment. In the commercial context, however, as the tenant will be paying the market rent for the property, the lease is unlikely to have any capital value. In such a case, therefore, no 'purchase price' will be paid by the assignee to the assignor on the assignment (or if, unusually, one is payable, it will usually be for a comparatively small sum). Assignment is usually only allowed subject to the fulfilment of specified conditions, the detail of which will be considered later in this chapter.

For the sake of clarity, in the remainder of this chapter, the term 'seller' is used to denote the assignor and 'buyer' to denote the assignee, whether or not any consideration is actually being paid on the assignment.

It is important to understand the precise nature of the transaction into which the seller and buyer are entering. In the same way that a seller of freehold land is selling the freehold that he owns, in the case of an assignment of a lease, the seller is selling his lease (or however much of the term granted by it now remains). The buyer will be acquiring that unexpired term together with the benefits, but subject to the burdens, that go with that lease. The terms of the lease are not open to negotiation by the buyer, because the lease is already in existence and the buyer must take it or leave it as it stands. The only way in which the buyer can obtain an alteration to the lease terms is by negotiating a deed of variation of the lease with the owner of the reversion (the landlord).

The procedure on an assignment is similar to that used in a sale and purchase of freehold land. This chapter deals only with those areas which differ from a freehold transaction.

36.2 Pre-contract matters: the seller's solicitor

On taking instructions, the information required by the seller's solicitor will be similar to that needed in a freehold transaction (see **Chapter 7**), with the addition of details of the lease to be sold.

The seller's solicitor should investigate title in the same way as for the sale of a freehold. The superior freehold title should be checked as part of this process, as it should be remembered that any covenants or easements affecting the freehold will also bind the leasehold interest. Any potential problems should be identified and all relevant incumbrances will need to be disclosed in the contract.

Investigation of title should include checking the terms of the lease being assigned to anticipate any problems that may arise with the lease itself. Of particular importance is the question of whether the landlord's consent to the transaction will be required (see **36.5**). The length of the residue of the term should also be checked. Where the buyer is buying with the aid of a mortgage (as will usually be the case with the assignment of a long residential lease), his lender will usually require that a minimum stated length of the term remains unexpired at the date of acquisition of the buyer's interest in order to provide adequate security for the loan. A lease which has only a short length of its original term left to run may, unless the term is extended, be difficult to sell. For the rights of certain tenants to insist on an extension, see **Chapter 39**.

Once title has been investigated, the seller's solicitor should be in a position to draft the contract for submission to the buyer's solicitor for amendment or approval.

36.3 The pre-contract package

36.3.1 General principles

As a matter of general principle, the landlord's solicitor should provide the tenant's solicitor with at least the following documents:

(a)   draft contract;

(b)   copy lease;

(c)   evidence of title (see **36.6**);

(d)   any licence permitting assignment to the current and previous tenants;

(e)   the insurance policy relating to the property and receipt for the last premium due;

(f)   receipts for the last payments of rent and service charge on the property; and

(g)   where there is a management company providing services, details of that company.

Where the Protocol applies, the seller's solicitor will need to comply with the terms of that scheme in the same way as would be the case for the sale of freehold land. This will include providing the buyer with a PIF and a Fittings and Contents Form as part of the pre-contract package. In addition, Forms TA3 (Required Leasehold Information Form) and TA7 (Leasehold Information Form) should be completed and contain information about relevant matters, such as details of the current landlord and who is responsible for repairing the property.

36.3.2 Home Information Packs

The Home Information Pack Regulations 2007 apply to transactions involving the assignment of leases of residential premises where the term originally granted under the lease exceeds 21 years. Fundamentally, the HIP must contain the same prescribed information in the same manner as for the sale of a freehold. There are issues which are peculiar to assignment, though, as follows.

36.3.2.1 Required documents

The HIP must contain the following documents:

(a) the lease;

(b) any regulations concerning the management of the property;

(c) details of service charges in respect of the property relating to the 36 months preceding the first point of marketing; and

(d) the most recent demands for (where applicable) service charge, ground rent, buildings insurance and occupiers' liability insurance relating to the 12 months preceeding the first point of marketing.

36.3.2.2 Required information

The information that seller must provide includes the following information:

(a) the names and addresses of the lessor, and those of any managing agents or such other persons who manage the property; and

(b) details of any proposed amendments to the lease or regulations governing the management of the property.

36.3.2.3 Additional leasehold information

As is the case for the sale of freehold residential property, the Regulations also make provision for information and documentation that the landlord can choose (but is not obliged) to provide as part of the HIP. An example of such information would be details of the membership and existence of any management company, and the HIP could additionally also include an HCR.

In Protocol cases, Forms TA3 and TA7 (see **36.3.1**) have been designed to facilitate the assembly of HIPs to cover these issues.

36.3.3 Energy Performance Certificates

These certificates form part of the compulsory contents of a HIP where one is required. In addition, EPCs will be required as from 6 April 2008 on the sale or letting of buildings, other than dwellings, with a floor area over 10,000 m^2. As from 1 July 2008 they will be required for the construction, sale or rent of buildings, other than dwellings, with a floor area over 2,500 m^2, and as from 1 October 2008 they will be required on the rent of all remaining dwellings and on the construction, sale or rent of all remaining buildings other than dwellings. This means that as from 1 October 2008 (at the latest), EPCs will be required in all commercial and residential sales and lettings. Except where a HIP is required on a sale of a dwelling, the EPC will last for 10 years before a new one needs to be obtained.

36.4 Pre-contract matters: the buyer's solicitor

The steps carried out by the buyer's solicitor on assignment of lease are, like those undertaken by the seller's solicitor, similar to those taken in the case of the sale of freehold land. The buyer's solicitor will need to investigate title and consider the terms of the draft contract supplied to him. The seller's solicitor will have supplied a copy of the lease, and the buyer's solicitor should check this carefully and identify and, if necessary, deal with any problems revealed. He should advise his client about his responsibility under the various covenants in the lease. The terms of the lease should be checked to ensure that they will be acceptable to the buyer's lender (see **Chapter 35**).

The buyer's solicitor should make the same searches, and for the same reasons, as on a purchase of a freehold (see **Chapter 18**). It may be the case, in the context of a commercial lease where the lease has only a short period left unexpired, that the buyer may choose not to carry out some or all searches, as the risk does not justify the cost involved.

As with a freehold transaction, some of these searches and enquiries may be provided by the landlord's solicitor and their results supplied to the tenant's solicitor as part of the pre-contract package or HIP where one is required.

36.5 Landlord's consent

36.5.1 General

Commercial leases usually provide for the landlord's consent to be obtained before any assignment can take place. The need for the landlord's consent is not usual in long residential leases, except, perhaps, in the last few years of the term, or in the case of high-value properties. In both cases, where consent is required, this must be obtained and will, in all likelihood, involve both the seller and buyer in order to obtain it. The following points should be considered. As discussed above, these issues predominantly relate to the assignment of commercial property.

Covenants controlling the tenant's freedom to assign usually also contain controls on other forms of dealing (or 'alienation') such as sub-letting or charging the property. This chapter concentrates on controls on assignment.

36.5.2 References

Where the lease requires the seller to obtain his landlord's consent to the transfer, the landlord will want to take up references on the prospective buyer to ensure that he is a solvent and trustworthy individual. The buyer should be asked to supply his solicitor with the names and addresses of potential referees so that this information may be passed on to the landlord's solicitor via the seller's solicitor as quickly as possible, in order to avoid any delay in obtaining the consent. References are commonly required from all or some of the following sources:

(a)   a current landlord;

(b)   the buyer's bankers;

(c)   the buyer's employer;

(d)   a professional person such as an accountant or solicitor;

(e)   a person or company with whom the buyer regularly trades; and

(f)   three years' audited accounts in the case of a company or self-employed person.

36.5.3 Surety

The landlord may also require a surety (guarantor) to the lease as a condition of the grant of his consent. On the assignment of a commercial lease, the landlord may require the assignor to enter into an AGA to guarantee the performance of the tenant's covenants by the assignee (see **34.5**). The landlord may have inserted the need for an AGA in the lease as a pre-condition of his giving consent (see **36.5.5**). In this case, he can always insist on the assignor entering into the AGA whether or not it is reasonable. In the absence of the provision in the lease, the landlord can insist on the AGA only if it is reasonable to do so.

36.5.4   Types of covenant – absolute covenants

If the covenant against alienation in the lease is absolute (eg, 'the tenant shall not assign or part with possession of the property'), any assignment (or other dealing depending on the wording of the restriction), although effective, will be a breach of covenant by the tenant and may lead to forfeiture of the lease. An absolute covenant is not subject to any statutory restrictions on its operation, except those imposed by the Sex Discrimination Act 1975 and the Race Relations Act 1976. Where an absolute covenant exists, the tenant may ask the landlord's permission to grant him a variation of the lease to permit assignment, but there is no obligation on the landlord to give consent, nor to give reasons for his refusal. Absolute bars on assignment are never acceptable in long-term residential leases and would not be acceptable to a prospective lender. The landlord may waive the covenant and give consent to this transaction, but there is no guarantee that he would consent to any other disposition and so a buyer runs the risk that the lease would be unsaleable.

36.5.5   Types of covenant – qualified covenants

A qualified covenant permits the tenant to assign (or part with possession, as the case may be), provided that the tenant obtains the prior consent of the landlord to the dealing. Section 19 of the Landlord and Tenant Act 1927 adds to the covenant the non-excludable proviso that consent must not be withheld unreasonably by the landlord. If the landlord does refuse consent, the prospective buyer is unlikely to wish to proceed with the transaction, because he runs the risk of the lease being forfeited against him.

The Landlord and Tenant Act 1988 provides that the landlord must, after having received a written request for consent, give his consent within a reasonable time unless it is reasonable for him to withhold his consent. He must serve written notice of his decision on the tenant within a reasonable time, stating what conditions (if any) are attached to the consent or, if consent is refused, stating his reasons for withholding his consent. Breach of the landlord's duty under the 1988 Act is actionable in tort as a breach of statutory duty, giving a remedy to the tenant in damages.

In leases of commercial property granted on or after 1 January 1996 the lease may provide for the circumstances in which the landlord would withhold his consent to an assignment and any conditions subject to which such consent will be granted (Landlord and Tenant (Covenants) Act 1995). A landlord will not be withholding his consent unreasonably if he insists on compliance with these conditions, so both buyer and seller should check them carefully and ensure that they can be complied with. See further **Chapter 37** as to the kind of conditions commonly imposed.

In an old commercial lease (ie, granted prior to 1 January 1996) it is common to find a requirement for the assignee to enter into a direct covenant with the landlord to comply with the covenants in the lease. This should be explained to the client, as it will mean that the assignee will remain liable on the covenants in the lease even after a subsequent disposition by him.

36.5.6 Demanding a premium for consent

Unless (unusually) the lease specifically allows the landlord to charge a premium for giving his consent, the landlord may not require a premium to be paid by the tenant as a condition of the grant of consent.

36.5.7 Undertaking for landlord's costs

The landlord is entitled to ask the tenant to pay the landlord's solicitor's reasonable charges in connection with the preparation of the deed of consent (licence to assign). On the assignment of a commercial lease, it is usual for the landlord's solicitors to require an undertaking from the assignor's solicitors for the payment of the costs, although it is not clear whether it is reasonable to insist on such an undertaking. The assignor's solicitor should first seek his client's authority to give the undertaking, the the undertaking should be limited to the reasonable costs incurred and the assignee's solicitors could also seek a cap on such costs.

36.5.8 Standard Conditions of Sale

Standard Condition 8.3 requires the seller to apply for the landlord's consent at his own expense and to use all reasonable efforts to obtain such consent, the buyer providing all information and references reasonably required. Unless in breach of these obligations, either party may rescind the contract by notice if the consent has not been given three working days before completion date, or if, by that time, consent has been given subject to a condition to which the buyer reasonably objects. Although the existence of SC 8.3 allows contracts to be exchanged before the landlord's consent is obtained, it still gives rise to uncertainty as to whether the transaction is to proceed, as this will depend upon the consent being forthcoming.

In a transaction where timing of completion is important (eg, in the context of a residential transaction where there is often a dependent sale and purchase), it is safest not to exchange until the landlord's consent has been obtained. Otherwise this transaction may fall through when the landlord refuses his consent, whereas the dependent transaction would still be binding.

36.5.9 Standard Commercial Property Conditions

The Commercial Conditions contain much more comprehensive provisions dealing with the situation where consent is needed from a landlord or superior landlord to an assignment or sub-letting. Standard Commercial Property Condition 10.3.3 requires the seller to enter into an AGA, if it is lawfully required. Standard Commercial Property Condition 10.3.5 further provides that if the landlord's consent has not been obtained by the completion date, completion is postponed until five working days after the seller notifies the buyer that consent has been given, or until four months after the original completion date, whichever is the earlier. Again, if timing of completion is important, it is safest not to exchange until the landlord's consent has been obtained.

36.6 Title

36.6.1 Lease registered with absolute title

Both sets of Standard Conditions (SC 4.1.1; SCPC 6.1.1) require the seller/assignor to provide the buyer/assignee with official copies of the register and title plan in the usual way. A copy of the lease must also be provided, and the buyer is then to be treated as entering into the contract knowing and fully accepting the lease terms (SC 8.1.2; SCPC 10.1.2). In any event, due to the open Registry rules, the buyer can always inspect the seller's title. Since the title to the lease is guaranteed by Land Registry there is no need for the buyer to investigate the title to the freehold or superior leases.

36.6.2   Lease registered with good leasehold title

Both sets of Standard Conditions require the seller to provide the buyer with official copies of the register and title plan in the usual way. A copy of the lease must also be provided, and the buyer is then to be treated as entering into the contract knowing and fully accepting the lease terms (see **36.6.1**). Registration with a good leasehold title provides no guarantee of the soundness of the title to the freehold reversion and thus, although not entitled under the general law to do so, the buyer should insist on deduction of the superior title to him. The provision for deduction of the reversionary title must be dealt with by special condition in the contract, because neither set of Standard Conditions deals with this point.

Without deduction of the reversionary title the lease may be unacceptable to the buyer and/or his lender (see para 5.4.2 of the *Lenders' Handbook* in **Appendix 8**). The reversionary title will be deduced by the appropriate method applicable to unregistered land (see **13.5**). The registers of title at Land Registry are open to public inspection, so that a buyer could make a search and obtain details of the reversionary title (assuming it is registered) if the seller was unable or unwilling to deduce it.

36.6.3   Unregistered lease

Under the general law contained in s 44 of the LPA 1925, the buyer is entitled to call for the lease or sub-lease which he is buying and all assignments under which that lease or sub-lease has been held during the last 15 years, but is not entitled to call for evidence of any superior title. Without deduction of the superior title, unless the reversion is already registered with absolute title, the buyer, on registration of the lease at Land Registry following completion, would obtain only a good leasehold title, which may be unacceptable to him and/or to his lender. Unless the contract contains a special condition requiring the seller to deduce the reversionary title, the buyer has no right under either the general law or the Standard Conditions of Sale to call for evidence of the reversionary title. Where title is deduced, the buyer will want to see deduction of the freehold title from a good root of title which was at least 15 years old at the date of the grant of the lease (see **13.5**).

36.7   The purchase deed

36.7.1   Registered land

An assignment of an existing registered lease, irrespective of how long it has left to run, is the transfer of a registered estate and the purchase deed will be a Land Registry transfer form. The form prescribed under the Land Registration Rules 2003 (SI 2003/1417) for the transfer of a leasehold is the same as for the transfer of a freehold (Form TR1) (see **Appendix 8**).

36.7.2   Unregistered land

The assignment of a lease exceeding seven years in length will lead to compulsory first registration and so Land Registry Form TR1 will normally be used. In the case of the assignment of a shorter lease (which will not be registrable), a deed of assignment will be used. This is similar in format to a conveyance of unregistered land.

36.7.3 Covenants for title

If a seller is in breach of a repairing covenant in the lease, the lack of repair could involve him in liability to the buyer after completion under the covenants for title which will be implied in the purchase deed (see **15.7.4**). This is because, where the seller sells with full or limited title guarantee, the covenants for title include a promise that the seller has complied with the tenant's covenants in the lease, including repair. However, the principle of *caveat emptor* (see **11.2)** makes it the buyer's responsibility to satisfy himself as to the physical state of the property and the seller should not be expected to make any promises in this respect.

Clearly, therefore, there is a conflict here between the promise implied by the covenants for title and *caveat emptor*. It is resolved by modifying the covenants for title to bring them into line with *caveat emptor* (see SC 3.2.2 and SCPC 3.2.2) by excluding references to repair.

This type of contractual condition must be reflected by an express modification of the covenants in the purchase deed itself. A suggested form of wording is as follows:

> The covenants for title implied by s 4 of the Law of Property (Miscellaneous Provisions) Act 1994 shall not be deemed to imply that any of the covenants contained in the lease on the part of the tenant for repair or decoration have been performed.

Panel 10 of Form TR1 contains space to insert this wording which could, alternatively, be inserted in panel 12 (additional provisions).

36.7.4 Indemnity

In relation to the assignment of leases granted before 1 January 1996, an indemnity covenant from the assignee to the assignor is implied except where, in unregistered land, value is not given by the assignee for the transaction (LPA 1925, s 77). In such a case, an express indemnity covenant will be inserted if required by the contract (see SC 4.6.4 and SCPC 6.6.4).

In relation to the assignment of leases granted on or after 1 January 1996, the assignor will usually automatically be released for future liability on the assignment and so will not require indemnity. If, however, the assignor is to remain liable (eg, under the terms of an AGA) an express indemnity covenant between the assignee and the assignor must be included in the purchase deed because no implied covenant exists in this situation. Again, SC 4.6.4 and SCPC 6.6.4 entitle the seller to insert an indemnity in such circumstances.

36.8 Preparing for completion

36.8.1 The purchase deed

The purchase deed will be prepared by the buyer's solicitor. The form and contents of this document are discussed in **36.7**.

36.8.2 Pre-completion searches

Where the lease is registered with an absolute title, the buyer will make a pre-completion search at Land Registry in the same way as if he was buying the freehold. Any other searches which would be appropriate to the purchase of a registered freehold should also be undertaken (see **Chapter 28**). Where the title to the lease is unregistered, a Land Charges Department search against the names of the estate owners of the leasehold title should be made. Where a company is the landlord (or a former tenant in the case of unregistered land) then a company search will also be required. Where the freehold or other reversionary title has been deduced, the names revealed through investigation of that title should also be included in the land charges search application. If the lease is registered with a good leasehold title, a search at Land Registry must be made in respect of the registered title and a Land Charges Department search must be made against the estate owners of the unregistered reversion.

36.8.3 Landlord's consent

The landlord's solicitor will supply the engrossment (or 'top copy') of the licence, which must be by deed if it is to contain covenants. Where the buyer is to give direct covenants to the landlord, the licence is usually drawn up in two parts, the landlord executing the original licence which will be given to the seller on completion for onwards transmission to the buyer, the buyer executing the counterpart which will be given to the landlord on completion.

36.8.4 Apportionments

Unless completion takes place on a day when rent and other outgoings become due under the lease, it will be necessary for these sums to be apportioned on completion, and the seller should supply the buyer with a completion statement which shows the amounts due and explains how they have been calculated. Copies of the receipts or demands on which the apportionments are based should be supplied to the buyer with the completion statement, so that the buyer can check the apportioned sums. In many cases, it will not be possible to make an exact apportionment of outgoings such as service charges, since the figures required in order to make this calculation will not be available. In such a case, a provisional apportionment of the sum should be made on a 'best estimate' basis, in accordance with SC 6.3.5 (SCPC 8.3.5).

36.9 Completion

The procedure on completion follows closely that in a freehold transaction (see Chapter 30). The buyer will pay the seller the balance of the purchase price (where one is to be paid) and any other sums due, including any apportionment as considered in **36.8.4** above.

36.9.1 Documents to be handed over by the seller

The seller will hand to the buyer such of the following documents as are relevant to the transaction in hand:

(a)   the lease/sub-lease;

(b)   the purchase deed (TR1 or deed of assignment, as appropriate);

(c)   the landlord's licence to assign;

(d)   marked abstract or other evidence of superior titles in accordance with the contract (lease not registered or not registered with absolute title);

(e)   evidence of discharge of the seller's mortgage;

(f)   copies of duplicate notices served by the seller and his predecessors on the landlord in accordance with a covenant in the lease requiring the landlord to be notified of any dispositions;

(g)   insurance policy (or copy if insurance is effected by the landlord) and receipt (or copy) relating to the last premium due;

(h)   receipts for rent and other outgoings; and

(i)   share certificate/stock transfer form for management company.

36.9.2   Items to be handed over by the buyer

The buyer should hand to the seller such of the following items as are appropriate to the transaction:

(a)   money due in accordance with the completion statement;

(b)   duly executed counterpart licence to assign; and

(c)   a release of deposit.

36.9.3   Rent receipts

Section 45(2) of the LPA 1925 provides that, on production of the receipt for the last rent due under the lease or sub-lease which he is buying, a buyer must assume, unless the contrary appears, that the rent has been paid and the covenants performed under that and all superior leases. The buyer's solicitor should inspect the receipts on completion and also, where appropriate, receipts for payment of other apportioned outgoings. Standard Condition 6.6 (SCPC 8.6) requires a buyer to assume that the correct person gave the receipt.

36.10   After completion

36.10.1   Stamp duty land tax

On the grant of a lease, SDLT is potentially payable both on any premium and on the rent. The position is different in the case of an assignment. In this case, SDLT is payable only on any purchase price charged by the seller, and is due at the same rates as for the sale of freehold land. The same procedure for payment is also followed. No SLDT will be charged on the rent.

36.10.2   Notice of assignment

Where, following completion, notice has to be given to a landlord of an assignment or mortgage, such notice should be given in duplicate accompanied by the appropriate fee set out in the lease. The CML *Lenders' Handbook* requires notice of a mortgage to be given to the landlord whether or not this is required by the lease. An example of a notice of assignment is set out overleaf. The recipient of the notice should be asked to sign one copy of the notice in acknowledgement of its receipt, and to return the receipted copy to the sender. The receipted copy will then be kept with the title deeds as evidence of compliance with this requirement.

36.10.3   Registered lease

Where the lease is already registered at Land Registry with separate title, an application for registration of the transfer to the buyer should be made within the priority period given by the buyer's pre-completion search.

36.10.4   Unregistered lease

An unregistered lease or sub-lease which, at the date of the transfer to the buyer, still has over seven years unexpired will need to be registered at Land Registry within two months of the assignment. An application for registration with absolute title can be made where the buyer can produce to the Registry satisfactory evidence relating to the superior title(s). In other cases, only good leasehold title can be obtained. An application for first registration of title should therefore be made within this time limit.

If the title to the reversion is already registered, the lease will be noted against the superior title. In other cases, the buyer may consider lodging a caution against first registration against the freehold title, in order to protect his interests against a subsequent buyer of the reversion. If the lease has seven years or less unexpired, it is incapable of registration with separate title, but will take effect as an overriding interest against a superior title which is itself registered.

36.10.5 Outstanding apportioned sums

As soon as the figures are available, the parties' solicitors should make an adjustment of the provisional apportionments which were made on completion. By SC 6.3.5 (SCPC 8.3.5), payment must be made within 10 working days of notification by one party to the other of the adjusted figures.

36.10.6 Example Notice of Assignment

Notice of Assignment

To: Jackson Properties Ltd,
   15 Mount Street,
   Weyford,
   Blankshire ('the Landlord')

TAKE NOTICE that by an assignment dated the 6th day of July 2008 made between (1) JAMES BLISS ('the Seller') and (2) GRAHAM MARTIN WENTWORTH and SARAH JANE WENTWORTH ('the Buyer') the property known as 25, Mackintosh Way, Marshfield, Greatshire comprised in a lease dated 10th August 1981 and made between (1) the Landlord and (2) Mark John Green and Susan Margaret Green was assigned by the Seller to the Buyer for all the unexpired residue of the term

Dated 12 July 2008

Lytham and Co,
40 St Bede's Road,
Marshfield,
Greatshire

Solicitors for the Buyer

WE ACKNOWLEDGE receipt of a duplicate of this notice with a fee of £15 plus VAT
this [   ] day of [   ] 2008

Signed   Solicitors for the Landlord

Chapter 37

Drafting Leases

37.1 Why use a lease?

The basic legal and practical considerations behind granting a lease of property rather than selling the freehold have already been discussed in **Chapter 34**, and you may wish to re-read **34.1** to **34.3** in particular to remind yourself of these issues.

37.2 Drafting leases

37.2.1 Why are precedent leases so long?

When you first look at a lease of an office or a long lease of a flat you will probably be horrified at its length. Forty pages is common; 100 pages not unknown! But this is again due to the nature of the premises. There will need to be extensive provisions defining precisely what is let, who is responsible for repairs and services, and setting out how these are to be paid for. There will be the need for lengthy provisions granting each tenant various easements over the rest of the block. There will also be numerous covenants designed to ensure that the value of the individual offices and flats (and of the landlord's reversion) is not affected by the conduct of one irresponsible tenant. Leases of self-contained premises, for example a lock-up shop, will not have to deal with as many problem areas and may well therefore be somewhat shorter.

37.2.2 How to draft a lease – landlord's solicitor

37.2.2.1 Use of precedents

It is inevitable that when you draft a lease you will start with an established precedent. Many firms will have their own precedents, developed over the years, on word processor. Other firms will rely on a favourite set of published precedents, which again is likely to be available in a word-processable form. The latter can also prove a valuable resource when the specifics of a development mean that a 'general' precedent does not do what is required.

However, bringing up on screen a precedent headed 'Flat Lease', for example, is only the start of the drafting, not the end. Just because you have retrieved what appears to be an appropriate precedent does not mean that you can use it as it stands. You will need to check the content carefully to ensure that it meets the needs of, and instructions you have received from, your landlord client. Quite frequently, you will find that you will need to combine parts of one precedent with clauses from another in order to meet your instructions. At the same time, it is important to bear in mind the need not to draft the lease so strongly in the landlord's favour that it will be unacceptable to a prospective tenant. Harsh terms can also have a negative effect on rent review (see **37.4.10**).

You should also check the drafting of the precedent. Just because a precedent appears in a well-known and respected published series does not necessarily mean that it is free from errors or inconsistencies. Recent legislation or case law developments may not yet have been addressed.

37.2.2.2   Particular problem areas

The following are the matters to which you should pay particular attention:

(a)   the description of the premises to be let;

(b)   the easements to be granted and reserved;

(c)   the arrangements for repair, maintenance and other services;

(d)   the provisions for payment of the service charge (if any);

(e)   the insurance arrangements;

(f)   the restrictions on the use to which the premises may be put;

(g)   any restrictions on assignment and sub-letting;

(h)   any restrictions on the making of alterations and improvements;

(i)   enforcement of covenants; and

(j)   the provisions for rent and rent review.

Some of these matters will be of more significance to a commercial tenant (eg, user), and others of more relevance in the case of a flat (eg, the management scheme), but all must be considered in turn. What you should look out for in relation to each particular topic will be considered later in this chapter.

37.2.2.3   Style of drafting

You will soon develop your own style of drafting, but initially you might have problems when combining clauses from two (or more) different precedents. You should ensure that the lease is a coherent whole and that it is in a consistent style. As an example, you need to ensure that defined terms from official documents are made to match (eg, when taking a clause referring to 'lessee' from one document into another where the word 'tenant' is used).

Check also that it is in a modern, easy-to-understand style. Remember that this lease is going to govern the day-to-day relationship of landlord and tenant for many years. If any disputes or problems arise, it will be the lease that is the starting point for finding a solution. It may well need to be referred to at frequent intervals. It should, therefore, be drafted in plain, modern English, using short sentences and proper punctuation. Archaic terms and legal jargon should be avoided. It should be drafted in such a way that both landlord and tenant can understand what it means.

37.2.3   Land Registry prescribed clauses leases

The LRA 2002 empowered Land Registry to prescribe a form of lease which would have to be used in all cases where the lease was registrable. This was necessary to facilitate the registration of the lease and also because of the proposed introduction of electronic conveyancing. After consultation, Land Registry decided against a prescribed form of lease as such. However, the Land Registration

(Amendment) (No 2) Rules 2005 (SI 2005/1982) provide that certain leases must contain prescribed clauses.

Use of the prescribed clauses is compulsory for leases that are dated on or after 19 June 2006, which are granted out of registered land and are compulsorily registrable. These leases will be known as 'prescribed clauses leases'.

A lease will not, however, be a prescribed clauses lease if it arises out of a variation of a lease which is a deemed surrender and re-grant, or if it is granted in a form expressly required by any of the following:

(a)   an agreement entered into before 19 June 2006;

(b)   a court order;

(c)   an enactment; and

(d)   a necessary consent or licence for the grant of the lease given before 19 June 2006.

If an applicant claims that a lease is not a prescribed clauses lease due to one of these exceptions, a conveyancer's certificate or other evidence must be supplied with the application for registration.

37.2.3.1   Required wording

The wording required in a prescribed clauses lease must appear at the beginning of the lease or immediately after any front cover sheet and/or front contents page. A new Sch 1A is inserted into the Land Registration Rules 2003 (SI 2003/1417) which sets out the required wording and gives instructions as to how the prescribed clauses must be completed. Land Registry Practice Guide 64 gives detailed guidance on use of the clauses. This and other guidance may be accessed at www.landreg.gov.uk.

The following is required in the prescribed clauses in a prescribed clauses lease (Sch 1A to the 2003 Rules).

* *All words in italicised text and inapplicable alternative wording in a clause may be omitted or deleted.*

* *Clause LR13 may be omitted or deleted.*

* *Clause LR14 may be omitted or deleted where the Tenant is one person.*

* *Otherwise, do not omit or delete any words in bold text unless italicised.*

* *Side-headings may appear as headings if this is preferred.*

* *Vertical or horizontal lines, or both, may be omitted.*

LR1. Date of lease	
LR2. Title number(s)	**LR2.1 Landlord's title number(s)**
	Title number(s) out of which this lease is granted. Leave blank if not registered.
	LR2.2 Other title numbers
	Existing title number(s) against which entries of matters referred to in LR9, LR10, LR11 and LR13 are to be made.

LR3. Parties to this lease	Landlord
Give full names, addresses and company's registered number, if any, of each of the parties. For Scottish companies use a SC prefix and for limited liability partnerships use an OC prefix. For foreign companies give territory in which incorporated.	Tenant *Other parties* *Specify capacity of each party, for example "management company", "guarantor", etc.*
LR4. Property *Insert a full description of the land being leased* *or* *Refer to the clause, schedule or paragraph of a schedule in this lease in which the land being leased is more fully described.* *Where there is a letting of part of a registered title, a plan must be attached to this lease and any floor levels must be specified.*	**In the case of a conflict between this clause and the remainder of this lease then, for the purposes of registration, this clause shall prevail.**
LR5. Prescribed statements etc. *If this lease includes a statement falling within LR5.1, insert under that sub-clause the relevant statement or refer to the clause, schedule or paragraph of a schedule in this lease which contains the statement.* *In LR5.2, omit or delete those Acts which do not apply to this lease.*	*LR5.1 Statements prescribed under rules 179 (dispositions in favour of a charity), 180 (dispositions by a charity) or 196 (leases under the Leasehold Reform, Housing and Urban Development Act 1993) of the Land Registration Rules 2003.* *LR5.2 This lease is made under, or by reference to, provisions of:* *Leasehold Reform Act 1967* *Housing Act 1985* *Housing Act 1988* *Housing Act 1996*

LR6. Term for which the Property is leased
 	
Include only the appropriate statement (duly completed) from the three options.
 	
NOTE: The information you provide, or refer to, here will be used as part of the particulars to identify the lease under rule 6 of the Land Registration Rules 2003.
	From and including
	To and including
	  OR
	The term as specified in this lease at clause/schedule/paragraph
	  OR
	The term is as follows:

LR7. Premium *Specify the total premium, inclusive of any VAT where payable.*	
LR8. Prohibitions or restrictions on disposing of this lease *Include whichever of the two statements is appropriate.* *Do not set out here the wording of the provision.*	This lease does not contain a provision that prohibits or restricts dispositions. OR This lease contains a provision that prohibits or restricts dispositions.

LR9. Rights of acquisition etc. *Insert the relevant provisions in the sub-clauses or refer to the clause, schedule or paragraph of a schedule in this lease which contains the provisions.*	**LR9.1 Tenant's contractual rights to renew this lease, to acquire the reversion or another lease of the Property, or to acquire an interest in other land** **LR9.2 Tenant's covenant to (or offer to) surrender this lease** **LR9.3 Landlord's contractual rights to acquire this lease**
LR10. Restrictive covenants given in this lease by the Landlord in respect of land other than the Property *Insert the relevant provisions or refer to the clause, schedule or paragraph of a schedule in this lease which contains the provisions.*	
LR11. Easements *Refer here only to the clause, schedule or paragraph of a schedule in this lease which sets out the easements.*	**LR11.1 Easements granted by this lease for the benefit of the Property** **LR11.2 Easements granted or reserved by this lease over the Property for the benefit of other property**
LR12. Estate rentcharge burdening the Property *Refer here only to the clause, schedule or paragraph of a schedule in this lease which sets out the rentcharge.*	
LR13. Application for standard form of restriction *Set out the full text of the standard form of restriction and the title against which it is to be entered. If you wish to apply for more than one standard form of restriction use this clause to apply for each of them, tell us who is applying against which title and set out the full text of the restriction you are applying for.* *Standard forms of restriction are set out in Schedule 4 to the Land Registration Rules 2003.*	The Parties to this lease apply to enter the following standard form of restriction [against the title of the Property] *or* [against title number]

LR14. Declaration of trust where there is more than one person comprising the Tenant	The Tenant is more than one person. They are to hold the Property on trust for themselves as joint tenants.
If the Tenant is one person, omit or delete all the alternative statements.	*OR*
If the Tenant is more than one person, complete this clause by omitting or deleting all inapplicable alternative statements.	The Tenant is more than one person. They are to hold the Property on trust for themselves as tenants in common in equal shares.
	OR
	The Tenant is more than one person. They are to hold the Property on trust *Complete as necessary*

37.3 Approving the draft lease – tenant's solicitor

37.3.1 Read, read and read again!

Assuming that you are acting for a prospective tenant and are looking at the lease for the first time, you must accept the fact that you are going to have to read through the lease several times in order to see if it is acceptable from the tenant's point of view.

Just because others have not spotted problems does not necessarily mean that there is none. Further, just because a lease is acceptable for the purposes of one client does not mean that it will be acceptable for the particular client for whom you are now acting. This is especially the case with regard to commercial leases, where the requirements of one commercial tenant may well be very different from those of the tenant in the next-door unit. The Code for Leasing Business Premises in England and Wales 2007 contains useful guidance in this regard.

37.3.2 Particular problem areas

The matters which you should particularly check are the same as those mentioned from the point of view of the landlord in **37.2.2.2** and will be considered in turn in **37.4** below. Indeed, in many cases you will see that the landlord's and the tenant's concerns will be the same, for example that the building will be properly maintained. Often, however, they will differ, for example on whether alienation is allowed.

37.4 The contents of the lease

37.4.1 Commencement

The lease starts with the words 'This lease', followed by the date of its grant (this date will be the date of completion of the transaction and is inserted on actual completion), and the names and addresses of the parties. Where the lease is created out of a registered title, the document will carry the usual Land Registry heading (county and district, landlord's title number, brief description of the property, and date) at the top of its first page.

37.4.2 Payment of premium and receipt

Where the landlord is to grant a long lease of residential premises (ie, over 21 years) he will usually charge a capital sum, or premium, for its grant. This is broadly equivalent to the price which a buyer pays on purchase of freehold premises, and consideration and receipt clauses, which have the same effect as those included in a freehold purchase deed, are included in the lease. In addition to the premium, the tenant's consideration for the grant also comprises the payment of rent and the promise to perform various obligations under the lease (covenants), and these are mentioned as being part of the consideration (eg, 'IN CONSIDERATION of the sum of forty thousand pounds (receipt of which the Landlord acknowledges) and of the rent reserved and of the covenants by the Tenant contained in this lease ...').

37.4.3 Operative words

The operative words in the lease were traditionally 'hereby demises', but in more modern leases 'grants', or 'lets' or 'leases' are more commonly used.

37.4.4 Title guarantee

The landlord may give the tenant the benefit of full or limited title guarantee covenants in the same way as on a transfer of freehold land (see **Chapter 15**). The appropriate words 'with full title guarantee' or 'with limited title guarantee', together with any express modifications of the covenants, will be included in the document after the operative words.

37.4.5 Term

The length (term) of the lease, including its starting date, must be set out. Care should be taken with the commencement date of the term as often other matters are tied to it. For example, rent review is usually to occur on specified anniversaries of the commencement date. It is not unusual to find that the date specified is before the actual signature of the lease. So a lease entered into on 1 January 2006 might be stated to commence on 1 October 2005. This is common in lettings of offices and flats where the landlord wants all of the leases in the block to come to an end on the same day. When specifying a commencement date, it should be made clear whether or not the date specified is to be included in the term. So if a lease is stated to run for five years, from 1 November 2007, it will, in fact, probably commence on 2 November and so expire at midnight on 1 November 2012. The use of the word 'from' probably excludes the day stated. It should be made clear by stating 'on and from' or 'from and including'.

37.4.6 The parcels clause – the description of the premises to be let

37.4.6.1 Certainty

The precise extent of what is to be transferred must be clearly and exactly stated. This is always the case in any conveyancing document, but is particularly relevant in the case of offices and flats as the letting is likely to be of only part of a larger building. It must be possible to say with absolute precision what is and is not being let.

It is necessary to define precisely where one unit ends and another begins. Think of the wall which separates one office from another: where in that wall is the boundary between the two offices going to be? Similarly with the floor and ceiling which divide the premises to be let from those below and above it: where is the boundary going to be situated in the floor and ceiling? Often the tenants' repairing obligations are co-extensive with ownership, ie if a tenant owns a wall (or floor or ceiling) he has to repair it, so who owns what becomes especially important.

Often it will not be sensible to provide that the whole of a particular wall or floor belongs to one unit; the boundary will have to be somewhere within the wall or floor. Precisely where will depend upon the method of construction of the particular building. It will obviously be meaningless nonsense to talk of floor boards and wooden joists in a modern building constructed with concrete beams.

37.4.6.2   Top floor and ground floor units

Particular care should be taken with top floor and ground floor/basement lettings. In the case of a top floor letting, is it intended to include the roof and the air space above it in the letting? If these are included, this will enable the tenant to extend upwards, which may not be the landlord's intention. The responsibility for repairing the roof may also be affected by such an inclusion. In the case of the ground floor or basement (if there is one), the same problems arise, but allowing a downwards extension rather than upwards.

37.4.6.3   Garage/car parking

Sometimes the letting of a unit (and particularly a flat) will also include a garage and/or car parking space.

Car parking may be underground or in the surrounding grounds. If a specific car parking space or garage is allocated, this should be included in the property let to the tenant. If the lease merely gives a right to park a car somewhere in a car park, this will be an easement. You should inform the client precisely which arrangement exists in each particular case. Numerous arguments can arise over car parking.

37.4.7   Easements to be granted

37.4.7.1   Access and services

As well as the precise definition of what is being let, you should also look closely at the ancillary rights which benefit the property. In a letting of part, the tenant should be granted all necessary easements over the remainder of the block and the surrounding grounds. This not only involves rights of way – on foot over the entrance lobby, hallways, stairways and lifts inside the block, and by car and on foot from the street and over the surrounding grounds – but also easements for the various essential services to reach the office or flat. These may include water, gas, electricity, drains and telephone, depending upon the circumstances. In an office building the need for the tenant to have direct computer links with other premises should be provided for. Do not forget either that the flat tenant will want to watch television. You should check the arrangements for access to a suitable aerial or similar facilities. Is a communal aerial to be provided – and if so, a right to run a cable to it? And can the tenant install his own satellite dish, or is there to be a communal one? Or is there an easement allowing each tenant to fix his own aerial? In office lettings television may be irrelevant, but you will need to think about the erection of microwave/satellite dishes and aerials and the connecting cables.

37.4.7.2   Access for repair, etc

An easement just to use these pipes and cables is not enough on its own. Rights of access are necessary in order to inspect and to repair and replace them as required. You should check that these are granted as well.

37.4.7.3 New rights

In a lease that will run for some years, it is also sensible to make provision for the possible need to install new cables and facilities in addition to those already there on the grant of the lease. Technology makes great advances very quickly and it would be unfortunate if a lease did not allow the installation of some major new development into the block.

37.4.7.4 Use of toilets, etc

In office blocks (particularly older ones) it is sometimes the case that each office does not have its own separate toilet facilities. There are communal toilets located elsewhere in the block. In this kind of situation, it will be necessary for easements to be granted for the use of these facilities. The cost of maintaining and cleaning them will then be included in the service charge.

37.4.7.5 Rubbish

The question of disposal of rubbish will also have to be addressed. When acting for the landlord, you will have to find out whether there is to be a communal bin or whether each unit is to have its own, and if so, where. Rights will have to be given for the use of communal facilities or for the placing of individual bins.

37.4.8 Easements to be reserved

As well as the benefit of easements over the rest of the block, you must also ensure that corresponding reservations are made in favour of the landlord and the other tenants in the block. Remember that one tenant's grant of an easement will be the next-door tenant's reservation. Each unit let will have to be made subject to similar rights to those granted to it. Each lease should, therefore, expressly reserve such rights. If it does not, it is likely that the rights granted will not have been reserved over the rest of the block and thus could be ineffective. Therefore, something you should check is whether you are acting for a landlord or for a tenant.

37.4.9 Rent and rent review – flat leases

In the case of a flat lease, the annual rent will be comparatively low. After all, the tenant will have paid a large premium to 'buy' his flat and therefore cannot be expected to pay a large rent as well. So you will find that the rent will perhaps be in the region of £200 per year. The lease should make it clear what the rent payment date is and whether the rent is to be paid in advance or in arrears. Often, the rent is payable half-yearly rather than in one lump sum.

It is usual in a long lease to find some provision dealing with increases in rent. A rent fixed at the start of a 99-year term will very rapidly have its value eroded by inflation. If you are acting for a landlord, you should take instructions on this. The landlord will probably want to be able to increase the rent in order to compensate for this. However, the dictates of the market must be borne in mind. Tenants (and their mortgagees) are not going to find a lease acceptable which gives a landlord an unfettered right to increase the rent. Remember that a substantial premium has already been paid and a tenant (or mortgagee) will wish to recoup this on a subsequent assignment. This will not be possible if the landlord has imposed a large increase in the rent.

So it is usual in a flat lease to find that the rent increases are agreed in advance and set out in the lease. You might, for example, find that the rent for the first 20 years of the term is (say) £200, and then for the next 20 years £300, and so on. When acting for a tenant you should check the rent provisions and explain these to the client, particularly the provisions for increase.

37.4.9.1   VAT

The grant of a residential lease is zero rated, so no special provisions are required to deal with the payment of VAT on the rent. However, where the tenant is to be liable for the landlord's legal and other costs, the lease should make clear that the tenant is to pay these plus VAT.

37.4.10   Rent and rent review – commercial leases

As with flat leases, the lease should make clear what the rental payment dates are and whether the rent is payable in advance or arrears; advance is usual. In all types of commercial lease, the amount of the rent will be a prime consideration for both landlord and tenant. Often this will be separately negotiated by surveyors acting on behalf of the landlord and the tenant. The provisions for reviewing the rent to take account of inflation are, however, a legal matter and will be the concern of the landlord's and the tenant's solicitors.

37.4.11   The need for review in commercial leases

If the lease is granted for anything longer than about five years, the parties will have to address their minds to the question of whether provision should be made in the lease for varying the annual rent at intervals during the term.

37.4.12   Regularity of review in commercial leases

Reviews are commonly programmed to occur at three- or five-year intervals during the term. In, say, a modern 15-year 'institutional' letting, reviews will be programmed to occur at every fifth anniversary of the term.

It is suggested that computation of the review dates in the lease is best achieved by reference to anniversaries of the term commencement date. However, if this method is adopted, the tenant should check that the term commencement date has not been significantly backdated by the landlord, as this would have the effect of advancing the first review date (eg, if the term runs from 29 September 2005, but the lease is completed only on 1 November 2006, the fifth anniversary of the term is now less than four years away). Instead of calculating the dates as anniversaries of the start of the term, some leases set out the exact review dates in the lease. This, however, ought to be avoided since it can create valuation problems at review if the rent review clause in the lease (with its specific review dates) is incorporated as a term of the hypothetical letting (as to which, see **37.4.15**).

Landlords may attempt to insert a rent review date on the penultimate day of the term. At first sight this might seem illogical since the term is about to end, but of course the tenant is likely to enjoy a statutory continuation of his tenancy under s 24(1) of the Landlord and Tenant Act 1954, whereby his tenancy will continue beyond the expiry date at the rent then payable. Where the tenant enjoys the benefit of a statutory continuation, the landlord may be able to apply to the court under s 24A of the Landlord and Tenant Act 1954 for an interim rent to be fixed (see **38.9**) in order to increase the rent payable by the tenant during the continuation. However, many landlords are not content to rely on the provisions of s 24A, preferring instead to achieve a rental uplift by implementing a contractual rent review clause on the penultimate day of the contractual term (ie, just before the statutory continuation is due to begin). In practice, because the contractual method of assessment in the rent review clause may differ from the statutory basis of assessment adopted by the court, a penultimate day rent review can secure a greater increase in rent and therefore ensures that the rent payable during the statutory continuation is greater than would be the case under the interim rent provisions.

The tenant ought to resist a penultimate day rent review for the obvious reason that s 24A may give him a better deal.

37.4.13 Types of rent review clauses

There are various ways in which rent can be varied during the term of a commercial lease.

37.4.13.1 Fixed increases

The lease could provide, for example, that in a lease for a 10-year term, the rent is set at £10,000 for the first three years of the term, £15,000 for the next three years, and £20,000 for the remainder of the term. This sort of clause would be very rare, since the parties to the lease would be placing their faith in the fixed increases proving to be realistic.

37.4.13.2 Index-linked clauses

Some of the early forms of rent review clauses required the rent to be periodically reassessed by linking the rent to an index recording supposed changes in the value of money. Indexes such as the General Index of Retail Prices and the Producer Price Index can be used in order to revise the rent either at the review dates, or at every rent payment date. Reference should be made to one of the standard works on landlord and tenant law for information as to how such clauses work in practice.

37.4.13.3 Turnover and sub-lease rents

A turnover rent is one which is geared to the turnover of the tenant's business, and can therefore be considered by the landlord only where turnover is generated at the premises. A turnover rent would be impractical in the case of office or warehouse premises, but could be considered, for example, in the case of a shop. The tenant's rent (or at least a proportion of it) is worked out as a percentage of the turnover. If a turnover rent clause is to be used, thought will have to be given in the lease to the definition of the turnover of the business (eg, whether credit sales are to be included with cash sales as part of the turnover, or whether Internet sales are to be included). The impact of VAT should also be dealt with, ie, is the turnover to be taken as excluding or including VAT? Other considerations include whether access will be given to the landlord to inspect the tenant's books, how turnover is to be apportioned if it is generated at the demised premises and other premises, and whether the tenant is to be obliged in the lease to continue trading from the premises in order to generate turnover. Reference should be made to one of the standard works on landlord and tenant law for further details of the operation of turnover rent clauses.

37.4.13.4 Open market revaluation review clauses

An open market revaluation review (OMRV) requires the rent to be revised in accordance with changes in the property market.

The most common form of rent review clause will provide that at every rent review date (eg, every fifth anniversary of the term) the parties should seek to agree upon a figure that equates to what is then the current open market rent for a letting of the tenant's premises. The aim of the exercise is to find out how much a tenant in the open market would be prepared to pay, in terms of rent per annum, if the tenant's premises were available to let in the open market of the relevant review date. This agreement is achieved either by some form of informal negotiated process between the landlord and the tenant, or, more rarely, by the service of notices and counter-notices which specify proposals and counter-proposals as to the revised rent. If agreement cannot be reached, the clause should provide for the appointment of an independent valuer who will determine the revised rent. The valuer will be directed by the review clause to take certain matters into account in conducting his valuation, and to disregard others, and he will call upon evidence of rental valuations of other comparable leasehold interests in the locality.

A clause which provides for an open market revaluation is the type of review clause most frequently encountered in practice, and is the one upon which the remainder of this section will concentrate.

Historically, such reviews usually operated on an 'upwards only' basis; in other words, on review, the rent would be the higher of the rent currently being paid or that determined on review. In this way, rent could never decrease and instead could be expected to rise for the duration of the term of the lease. It is now becoming more common to encounter provisions which allow for rent to decrease on review if the OMRV has fallen, which is sometimes referred to an 'upwards and downwards' rent review.

37.4.14   Open market revaluations

In conducting the valuation on review, it should be understood what the valuer is assessing. This will not only be the value of the physical premises and their geographical location, but also the length of the term for which the premises are let and also the terms of the lease under which they are held, as these elements can have just as important an impact on the level of rent as the state and location of the premises.

Having established that it is not the premises but an interest in the premises which has to be valued at each review date, it must also be understood that it is not the tenant's own interest that will be valued but a hypothetical interest in the premises as the premises are not actually being made available on the market given that the current tenant is in occupation of the premises under the terms of his existing lease. Given the artificiality of this exercise, it is necessary to build in certain adjustments to the valuation exercise to prevent unfairness and uncertainty between the parties. For example, consider the position of the tenant who, in breach of his obligations under the lease, has allowed the premises to fall into disrepair, which has had the effect of reducing the open market rental valuation (OMRV) of the premises. Is it fair that the landlord should suffer at rent review by having the rent depressed on account of the tenant's breach of covenant? Equally, from a tenant's perspective, consider the position of a tenant who, in the fourth year of the term, at his own expense, voluntarily made improvements to the premises which had the effect of increasing the OMRV of his interest in the premises. Is it fair that the tenant should suffer at rent review by having to pay an increased rent which reflects in part the rental value attributable to his improvements?

These are just two of the many problems inherent in a valuation of the tenant's actual lease. As a result of these difficulties and injustices connected with such a valuation, it is accepted that the valuer should be instructed by the rent review clause to ascertain the OMRV of a hypothetical interest in the premises. He should be directed by the clause to calculate how much rent per annum a hypothetical willing tenant would be prepared to pay for a letting of the premises, with vacant possession, for a hypothetical term. He is directed by the lease to make certain assumptions about the terms of the letting, and to disregard certain matters which might otherwise distort the OMRV, in order to overcome the difficulties and eradicate the injustices referred to above.

37.4.15   The hypothetical letting

It is important that the parties ensure that the terms and circumstances of the hypothetical letting (which will form the basis of valuation at review) are clearly stated in the lease, and achieve a fair balance between the parties without departing too far from the reality of the tenant's existing letting.

The lease should make it clear that the date of valuation, when the OMRV is assessed, is the review date itself. A negotiated agreement as to the revised rent between the landlord and the tenant, or a determination by an independent valuer, may occur several months before or after the relevant review date, although the new rent is usually stated to be payable from the review date itself.

Irrespective of the date of assessment, the tenant should not allow the valuation date to be capable of variation; it should be fixed at the relevant review date. Any clause which purports to allow the valuation date to be fixed by the service of a notice by the landlord is to be resisted for the simple reason that, in a falling market, the landlord would serve his notice early to secure a higher rent, whilst in a rising market he would serve his notice late at a time when the market was at its peak, safe in the knowledge that the revised rent would be backdated and payable from the review date.

In a similar way, any clause which defines the valuation date as the day upon which agreement is reached or the third party determination is to be made is to be resisted, as it might encourage the landlord to protract the review process to get the benefit of a later valuation date.

37.4.15.1   The aim of the exercise

The valuer will be directed by the lease to ascertain the open market rental value of a hypothetical letting of the premises at each review date. Different phrases are used by different clauses to define the rent to be ascertained. Some leases will require the valuer to find a 'reasonable rent' for a letting of the premises, or a 'fair rent', or a 'market rent', or a 'rack rent' or 'the open market rent'. It is submitted that the last clause is the preferred phrase to adopt, as it is the one most commonly used in practice, and is therefore a phrase with which professional valuers are familiar. Other phrases are less common, and are open to adverse interpretations by valuers and the court.

Most tenants would want to avoid the use of the expression 'the best rent at which the premises might be let', since this might allow the valuer to consider the possibility of what is known as a special purchaser's bid. If, by chance, the market for a hypothetical letting of the premises contains a potential bidder who would be prepared to bid in excess of what would ordinarily be considered to be the market rent, the 'best' rent would be the rent which the special bidder would be prepared to pay. For example, if the premises which are the subject matter of the hypothetical letting are situated next to premises occupied by a business which is desperate to expand, the 'best' rent might be the rent which that business would be willing to pay.

37.4.15.2   The circumstances of the letting

To enable the valuer to do his job, the rent review clause must clearly indicate the circumstances in which a hypothetical letting of the premises is to be contemplated. For example, he must be able to establish which premises are to be the subject matter of the letting, whether there is a market for such a letting, whether the premises would be available with or without vacant possession, and what the terms of the letting would be. It is common for the clause to require the valuer to find the open market rent of a letting of the tenant's vacant premises, for a specified duration, on the assumption that there is a market for the letting which will be granted without the payment or receipt of a premium, and subject only to the terms of the actual lease (except as to the amount of the annual rent).

The premises

Usually, the valuer is required to ascertain the rental value of a hypothetical letting of the premises actually demised by the tenant's lease. The draftsman should therefore ensure that the demised premises are clearly defined by the parcels clause in the lease (see **37.4.6**), and that they enjoy the benefit of all necessary rights and easements to enable them to be used for their permitted purpose.

A valuer uses comparables as evidence in his valuation of a letting of the premises. He draws upon evidence of rents currently being paid by tenants of comparable buildings, let in comparable circumstances, on comparable terms. If the actual premises demised to the tenant are unique or exceptional (eg, an over-sized warehouse) there may be no comparables in the area for the valuer to use. In that case, the lease ought to require the valuer to adopt a different approach to his valuation, perhaps by directing him to take account of rental values of other premises which would not ordinarily count as comparables. This in itself may lead to valuation problems as, for example, in *Dukeminster (Ebbgate House One) Ltd v Somerfield Properties Co Ltd* [1997] 40 EG 157.

The market

As the hypothetical letting is an artificial creation, and since leasehold valuations cannot be carried out in the abstract, an artificial market has to be created. If the rent review clause does not create a well-balanced hypothetical market in which the letting can be contemplated, it would be open for the tenant (in appropriate cases) to argue at review that no market exists for a letting of the tenant's premises, and that therefore an 'open market' rent for the premises would be merely nominal, or a peppercorn. An example of this could occur if the tenant was occupying premises which were now outdated to such an extent that they were impractical for modern use, or that the premises were so exceptional that only the tenant himself would contemplate occupying them. Only the actual tenant would be in the hypothetical market for such premises, and even he might not be in the market if he can show that he has actively been trying to dispose of his lease. The market might truly be dead.

To create a market, the rent review clause usually requires the valuer to assume that the hypothetical letting is taking place in the open market and being granted by a 'willing landlord' to a 'willing tenant'. In *FR Evans (Leeds) Ltd v English Electric Co Ltd* (1977) 245 EG 657 it was held that where such phrases are used, it means that the valuer must assume that there are two hypothetical people who are prepared to enter into the arrangement, neither of whom is being forced to do so, and neither of whom is affected by any personal difficulties (eg, a landlord with cash-flow problems, or a tenant who has just lost his old premises) which would prejudice their position in open market negotiations. A willing landlord is an abstract person, but is someone who has the right to grant a lease of the premises; and a willing tenant, again an abstraction, is someone who is actively seeking premises to fulfil a need that these premises would fulfil. It is implicit in the use of these phrases that there is at least one willing tenant in the market, and that there is a rent upon which they will agree.

Even if the lease is silent as to whether there is assumed to be a willing tenant, the Court of Appeal has held in *Dennis & Robinson Ltd v Kiossos Establishment* [1987] 1 EGLR 133 that such a creature is in any case to be assumed, since a rent review clause which asks for an open market valuation by its nature requires there to be at least one willing tenant in the market. This means that for rent review purposes, where an open market valuation is required, there will always be someone in the hypothetical market who would be prepared to take a letting of the premises, and therefore the tenant cannot argue that the market is completely dead. However, quite how much a willing tenant would be willing to pay is for the valuer to decide. If the market is well and truly dead, the landlord's only protection is an upwards only rent review clause.

The consideration

Any consideration moving between the parties at the time of the grant is likely to have a bearing on the amount of rent to be paid by the tenant. Such movements are not uncommon in the open market. For example, a landlord may seek to induce a tenant to take the lease at a certain level of rent by offering him a reverse premium (ie, a sum of money payable by the landlord to the tenant to induce him to take the lease), without which the tenant might only be prepared to pay rent at a lower level. A rent-free period may be offered by a landlord, either as a straightforward inducement as above, or to compensate a tenant for the costs that he will incur in fitting out the premises at the start of the term. Without the rent-free period, the tenant might only be prepared to pay a lower rent. If the tenant pays a premium to the landlord at the outset, this may be reflected in the tenant paying a rent lower than he would otherwise pay.

As far as the hypothetical letting is concerned, it is common for the rent review clause to assume that no consideration (in the form of a premium) will be moving between the parties on the grant of the hypothetical letting. As seen above, such payments can distort the amount of initial rent payable by a tenant. Therefore, to get the clearest indication of what the market rent for the letting would be, it ought to be assumed that no premium is to be paid on the grant of the hypothetical letting. Furthermore, the landlord may seek to include a provision which states that no inducement in the form of a rent-free period will be given to the hypothetical tenant on the grant of the hypothetical lease.

This is an attempt by the landlord to deprive the tenant of the effect of such concessions granted in the market place (thereby keeping the level of rent, on review, artificially high). The landlord is trying to achieve a headline rent rather than an effective rent. For example, if the tenant agrees to take a lease at £100,000 per annum for a term of five years, but is to receive a 12-month rent-free period, whilst the headline rent (the rent stated to be payable under the lease) remains at £100,000 per annum, the annual rent effectively payable (the 'effective' rent) is only £80,000. At review, therefore, the landlord would argue that the effect of disregarding any rent-free period which might be available in the open market, is that the new rent payable from review should be a headline rent not an effective rent. The tenant would argue that, since the hypothetical tenant is not getting the benefit of a rent-free period, therefore the revised rent should be discounted to compensate the hypothetical tenant for a benefit he has not received. There have been several cases on the effect of these types of provisions.

The Court of Appeal in *Broadgate Square plc v Lehman Brothers Ltd* [1995] 01 EG 111, applying the purposive approach to the interpretation of the relevant clause said that '... the court will lean against a construction which would require payment of rent upon an assumption that the tenant has received the benefit of a rent-free period, which he has not in fact received ...' (*per* Leggatt LJ). However, such an approach cannot be adopted in the face of clear, unambiguous language. According to Hoffmann LJ, '... if upon its true construction the clause deems the market rent to be whatever is the headline rent after a rent-free period granted ... the tenant cannot complain because in changed market conditions it is more onerous than anyone would have foreseen'. The presence of such a clause in the hypothetical letting may itself be an onerous provision which justifies a reduction in the OMRV (possibly to the extent that it negates the effect of the landlord's clever drafting).

Possession

As the valuer is assessing the rental value of the tenant's existing premises, is he to assume that the tenant is still there (in which case rent to be paid by a hypothetical bidder would be very low), or is he to assume that the tenant has vacated? Naturally, he must assume that the tenant has moved out, and therefore most rent review clauses of this type include an assumption that vacant possession is available for the hypothetical letting.

Care must be taken in making this assumption, because in certain cases it can give rise to problems:

(a) If the tenant has sub-let all or part of the premises, an assumption that vacant possession is to be available will mean that the effect on rent of the presence of the sub-tenant will have to be disregarded. If the sub-tenant occupies for valuable business purposes (eg, the premises in question are high street offices where the ground floor has been sub-let as a high class shop), the presence of the sub-tenancy would ordinarily increase the rental value of the head leasehold interest since the head tenant would expect to receive lucrative sub-lease rents. The assumption of vacant possession would deny the landlord the opportunity to bring a valuable sub-letting into account at review. If the sub-tenancy was for residential purposes yielding precious little in terms of sub-lease rents, the assumption of vacant possession would allow the landlord to have the sub-letting disregarded and, depending on the other terms of the hypothetical letting, enable the premises to be valued as a whole for the permitted business purpose.

(b) The assumption of vacant possession means that the tenant is deemed to have moved out of the premises and, as all vacating tenants would do, he is deemed to have removed and taken his fixtures with him. In respect of shop premises, this might mean that all of the shop fittings must be assumed to have been removed, leaving nothing remaining but a shell. (Of course, in reality, the premises are still fully fitted out, but for hypothetical valuation purposes, the tenant's fixtures are assumed to have gone.) If a hypothetical tenant were to bid in the open market for these premises then, depending upon market forces prevalent at the time, he might demand a rent-free period in order to compensate him for the time it will take for him to carry out a notional fitting out of the premises (ie, to restore the fittings that have notionally been removed). Since the revised rent has to be a consistent figure payable throughout the period until the next review date, this notional rent-free period would have to be spread out during the review period, or possibly over the rest of the term, thereby reducing the general level of rent (eg, the valuer finds that the rent for the next five years should be £10,000 per annum, but that an incoming tenant would obtain a rent-free period of 12 months; by spreading the notional rent-free period over the five-year review period the rent would be £8,000 per annum). The landlord can counter this problem by including an assumption that, notwithstanding vacant possession, the premises are fully fitted out for occupation (see **37.4.15.3**).

The terms

The valuer, in ascertaining the OMRV of a leasehold interest, must look at all of the proposed terms of the lease. The more onerous the lease terms, the less attractive the lease becomes from a tenant's point of view, and therefore the lower the OMRV of the interest. If the rent review clause is silent, the hypothetical letting will be assumed to be granted upon the terms of the tenant's existing lease, since the court does not like to stray too far away from reality, and there is a general preference by the court to construe rent review clauses in such a way as to ensure that the tenant does not end up paying in terms of rent for something that he is not actually getting. Usually, however, the clause directs the valuer to assume that the letting is to be made upon the terms of the tenant's actual letting, as varied from time to time. The fact that the valuer must take account of variations means that it is imperative that, when conducting the review, the valuer checks the terms of all deeds of variation entered into, and all licences granted since the date of the lease, to see if the terms of the actual lease have been changed.

Each of the terms of the lease will be analysed by the valuer at review to see if they will have any effect on the rental value. If either party, with sufficient foresight, feels that a particular term will have a detrimental effect on the rental value (because the term is too wide, or too narrow, or too onerous) that party may seek to have the term excluded from the hypothetical letting, by use of an assumption or a disregard (see **37.4.15.3**).

The valuer will look closely at all of the terms of the lease, but in particular at the following.

The alienation covenant

If the alienation covenant in the actual lease is too restrictive (eg, by prohibiting all forms of alienation), its incorporation as a term of the hypothetical letting will lead to a decrease in the OMRV of that interest. Similarly, if the actual lease allows only the named tenant to occupy the premises (or only companies within the same group of companies as the tenant), this will have a negative impact on the OMRV. In these cases it will be advisable for the landlord to exclude the excessive restrictions on alienation from the terms of the hypothetical letting. The tenant might consider this to be unfair and, perhaps, a compromise would be to widen the alienation covenant in the actual lease.

The user covenant

If the actual lease narrowly defines the permitted use of the premises and allows little or no scope for the tenant to alter that use, a tenant bidding for the lease in the open market is likely to reduce his rental bid to reflect the fact that he would be severely hindered should he wish to dispose of the premises during the term, or change the nature of his business. According to *Plinth Property Investments Ltd v Mott, Hay & Anderson* [1979] 1 EGLR 17, the possibility of the landlord agreeing to waive a breach of covenant (eg, by allowing a wider use of the premises than the covenant already permits) has to be ignored. This principle is not just applicable to user covenants (although the *Plinth* case specifically concerned a user covenant) but to all covenants where the landlord is freely able to withhold his consent to a change. It is not open to the landlord at review to disregard the detrimental effect on rent of a restrictive clause which has been incorporated into the hypothetical letting by saying that he is or might be prepared to waive the restriction. Further, a landlord cannot unilaterally vary the terms of the lease (see *C & A Pensions Trustees Ltd v British Vita Investments Ltd* (1984) 272 EG 63). If the landlord is intent on tightly restricting the tenant in the user clause in the actual lease, but wants to maximise the rental value of the hypothetical letting at review and is concerned that the incorporation of the restrictive clause into the hypothetical letting will harm the OMRV, he should draft the review clause so that the actual user covenant is to be disregarded and an alternative permitted use is to be assumed. Obviously, the tenant should strongly resist such an approach, since he would find himself paying a rent from review assessed on the basis of a freedom that he does not in fact possess. Again, a compromise might be to widen the user covenant in the actual lease.

If the lease allows only the named tenant to use the premises for a named business (ie, a very restrictive user covenant), the landlord should try to have the user covenant disregarded at review. If he fails to do so, the court might be prepared to step in to assist the landlord, as in *Sterling Land Office Developments Ltd v Lloyds Bank plc* (1984) 271 EG 894, where a covenant not to use the premises other than as a branch of Lloyds Bank plc was incorporated into the hypothetical letting, but with the name and business left blank, to be completed when the name and business of the hypothetical tenant were known.

Rent and rent review

The review clause will state that the hypothetical letting is to be granted upon the same terms as the actual lease save as to the amount of rent. As the aim of the review exercise is to vary the amount of rent, it is clear that the rent initially reserved by the lease must not be incorporated into the hypothetical letting. However, the tenant must be alert to guard against any form of wording which has the effect of excluding from the hypothetical letting not only the amount of rent reserved, but also the rent review clause itself.

It is a commonly-held view that a tenant bidding for a medium- or long-term letting of premises in the open market, where the annual rent cannot be increased during the term, is likely to pay more than if the letting contained a rent review clause. The tenant would pay a rent in excess of the current market rent in return for a guarantee that the rent will not rise but would be fixed at the initial rent for the entire duration of the term. A long series of cases followed the decision in *National Westminster Bank plc v Arthur Young McClelland Moores & Co* [1985] 1 WLR 1123, where the provisions of a rent review clause were interpreted in such a way as to exclude from the hypothetical letting the rent review provisions. This alone led to the annual rent being increased from £800,000 to £1.209 million, instead of £1.003 million if the rent review clause had been incorporated. Courts today tend to shy away from interpreting a rent review clause in such a way as to exclude a provision for review from the hypothetical letting. In the absence of clear words directing the rent review clause to be disregarded, the court will give effect to the underlying purpose of the clause and will assume that the hypothetical letting contains provisions for the review of rent. However, the tenant must always check carefully that the review clause is not expressly excluded from the hypothetical letting, since the court would be bound to give effect to such clear words. Ideally, the hypothetical letting should be '... upon the terms of this lease, other than the amount of rent'.

The length of term

Whether the lease is for a short term or a long term will affect how much rent a tenant is prepared to pay. Whilst a landlord often needs to guarantee rental income by granting a long-term lease, in times of uncertain trading tenants often prefer short-term lettings in order to retain a degree of flexibility and to avoid long-term liability in the event of business failure. If a short-term letting is more attractive to tenants in the current market, it follows that a tenant would be prepared to bid more in terms of rent per annum for such a letting than if a longer term was proposed. On the other hand, other tenants with long-term business plans and a desire for stability and security would be prepared to increase their rental bid in return for a longer letting. The rent review clause must define the length of the hypothetical letting. The landlord will want to maximise the rental value of the hypothetical letting by specifying as the hypothetical term a length which is currently preferred in the market by prospective tenants of premises of the type in question. The landlord will have to ask his surveyor for advice in this regard, since the term to be adopted is purely a matter of valuation, which will differ from lease to lease.

When the valuer makes his valuation, he is allowed to take into account the prospect of the term being renewed under the Landlord and Tenant Act 1954 (see *Secretary of State for Employment v Pivot Properties Limited* (1980) 256 EG 1176). Obviously, the rent will turn out to be higher if there is a strong possibility of renewal. In the *Pivot* case, that possibility led to an uplift in the rent of £850,000 per annum.

37.4.15.3 Assumptions to be made

Several assumptions have already been considered in respect of the circumstances of the hypothetical letting. Certain other assumptions are also commonly made.

Premises fitted out and ready for occupation and use

An assumption is made that the premises are fully fitted out and ready for immediate occupation and use by the incoming tenant. An assumption of vacant possession necessarily leads to an assumption that the tenant has moved out and taken all his fixtures with him. The assumption that the premises are fully fitted out attempts to counter the deemed removal of fixtures by assuming that the hypothetical tenant would be able to move straight into the premises without asking for a rent-free period in which he could carry out his notional fitting out works. Hence the assumption removes any discount the tenant would claim at review in respect of the rent-free period that the hypothetical tenant might have claimed. The phrase 'fit for occupation' does not appear to go as far as 'fully fitted out', since the former assumption anticipates a stage where the premises are simply ready to be occupied for fitting-out purposes, in which case the hypothetical tenant might still demand a rent-free period (see *Pontsarn Investments Ltd v Kansallis-Osake-Pankki* [1992] 22 EG 103). Some solicitors prefer to deal with this problem in a different way by including an assumption that '...

no reduction is to be made to take account of any rental concession which on a new letting with vacant possession might be granted to the incoming tenant for a period within which its fitting-out works would take place'.

Covenants performed

An assumption is made that the covenants have been performed. Most rent review clauses include an assumption that the tenant has complied with his covenants under the lease. In the absence of such a provision, a court is willing to imply one in any case, since it is a general principle that a party to a transaction should not be allowed to profit from its own wrongdoing (see *Family Management v Grey* (1979) 253 EG 369). This is particularly important when considering the tenant's repairing obligation. Clearly the hypothetical tenant can be expected to pay more in terms of rent if the premises are in good repair and, conversely, less if they are in a poor condition (for whatever reason). A tenant should not be allowed to argue in reduction of the rent at review that the premises are in a poor condition, if it is through his own default that the disrepair has come about – hence the reason for the assumption under consideration.

The landlord may try to include an assumption in respect of his own covenants (ie, that the landlord has performed his covenants). The tenant ought to resist this, especially where the landlord will be taking on significant obligations in the actual lease. For example, in a lease of part of the landlord's premises, the landlord may be entering into covenants to perform services, and to repair and maintain the structure, exterior and common parts of the building. If the landlord fails to perform his covenants, the likely result is that the rental value of an interest in the building will decrease, since the building will be less attractive to tenants in the market. Accordingly, the rent at review would be adjusted to reflect this. However, an assumption that the landlord has performed his covenants enables the landlord to have the review conducted on the basis that the building is fully in repair (without regard to his own default), which means that the tenant would be paying for something at review (ie, a lease of premises in a building which is in first-rate condition) that he does not in fact have. Such an assumption should be resisted by the tenant.

However, the landlord will not concede the tenant's argument easily. Landlords will argue that, without it, the valuer will assess the new rent at a lower level, even though immediately afterwards the tenant might bring proceedings against the landlord in respect of the landlord's breach of covenant, forcing the landlord to put the building into repair. Landlords will argue that it is unfair that the rent will be set at a low level for the entire review period on the basis of a temporary breach of covenant, which the landlord might soon be required to remedy. The tenant's counter-argument is that a claim for breach of covenant is no substitute for a dilapidated building.

Recovery of value added tax

If the landlord has waived the VAT exemption in respect of the premises, so that VAT is payable in addition to the rent, this will negatively affect a tenant who has an adverse VAT status. Organisations such as banks, building societies and insurance companies make exempt supplies in the course of their business and therefore do not receive any output tax which can be set off against the input tax to be paid on the rent. These organisations have to bear the VAT on the rent as an overhead of the business. Arguably, such tenants in the market would reduce their bids in order to compensate for the VAT overhead that they will have to absorb. Some landlords counter this by including an assumption that the hypothetical tenant will be able to recover its VAT in full (thereby removing the need for the hypothetical tenant to ask for a discount on rent to cover his VAT overhead), or by ensuring that the hypothetical letting includes a covenant by the landlord not to waive the exemption for VAT purposes. Tenants ought to try to resist such a provision, leaving the valuer to value the lease on the basis of the reality of the actual letting.

37.4.15.4 Matters to be disregarded

In order to be fair to the tenant, the landlord usually drafts the review clause so that certain matters which would otherwise increase the OMRV of a letting of the premises are disregarded.

Goodwill

A letting of premises will be more attractive in the open market if there is existing goodwill at the premises, in the shape of a regular flow of clients or customers, or the benefit of a good reputation. The letting would command a higher rent than could otherwise be expected, as tenants will be eager to obtain possession of the premises in order to take advantage of the goodwill. However, it is the tenant who generates such goodwill, and so it is only fair that any effect on rent of that goodwill ought to be disregarded at review.

Occupation

The fact that the tenant, his predecessors or his sub-tenants have been in occupation of the premises is usually disregarded. It is accepted that, if the tenant was bidding for a letting of his own premises, he would bid more than most others in the market in order to avoid the expense of having to move to other premises. The rental effect of occupation should therefore be disregarded. In appropriate cases, where the tenant also occupies adjoining premises, his occupation of those premises should also be disregarded, to avoid the argument that the tenant would increase his bid for the demised premises to secure a letting of premises which are adjacent to his other premises.

If the rent review clause requires occupation by the tenant to be disregarded but makes no similar requirement as regards his goodwill (see above), the valuer should nevertheless disregard the rental effect of the tenant's goodwill, since goodwill must necessarily be the product of the tenant's occupation (see *Prudential Assurance Co Ltd v Grand Metropolitan Estate Ltd* [1993] 32 EG 74).

Improvements

If the tenant improves the premises then he usually does so at his own expense, but the result will inevitably be that the rental value of an interest in the premises will increase. It is unfair for the landlord to ask that the rent be increased at review to reflect the increase in rental value brought about by the tenant's improvements. If improvements were to be taken into account, the tenant would be paying for his improvements twice over (once on making them, and once again when the revised rent becomes payable). The landlord usually drafts the rent review clause so that the effect on rent of most of the tenant's improvements is disregarded.

It does not follow, however, that all improvements should be disregarded. The tenant will want to make sure that the effect on rent of all improvements that have been voluntarily carried out either by him or by his sub-tenants or his predecessors in title is disregarded, whether they were carried out during the term, during some earlier lease or during a period of occupation before the grant of the lease (eg, during a pre-letting fitting-out period). He will also want to have disregarded the effect on rent of improvements executed by the landlord but which were carried out at the tenant's expense. The landlord, however, will want to make sure that any improvements that the tenant was obliged to make are taken into account. These will include improvements made under the lease granted in consideration of the tenant carrying out works to the premises, or improvements the tenant was obliged to carry out under some other document, such as an agreement for lease, or by virtue of a statutory provision requiring the tenant to carry out work (eg, the installation of a fire escape and doors). An obligation in a licence to alter to execute the permitted works in accordance with agreed drawings, or by a stipulated time, is not an obligation in itself to do the works in a particular way (see *Historic Houses Hotels Ltd v Cadogan Estates* [1997] AC 70).

User, alienation and improvements

It is possible that for his own benefit the landlord might try to have disregarded some of the more restrictive covenants contained in the actual lease, such as user, alienation and improvements. This is unfair to the tenant, who ought to be advised to resist such a disregard.

37.4.16   The mechanics of the commercial rent review

There are two principal ways in which the review process can be conducted:

(a)   (the most commonly encountered method) by negotiations between the parties, but in default of agreement, by reference to an independent third party for determination (see **37.4.16.2**);

(b)   (the less commonly encountered method, but still seen in some older leases) by the service of trigger notices and counter-notices in an attempt to agree the revised rent, but in default, by reference to a third party (see **37.4.16.3**).

Whichever method is to be adopted, the first consideration to be dealt with is whether time is to be of the essence in respect of any time limits contained in the clause, or in respect of the rent review dates.

37.4.16.1   Is time of the essence?

As a general rule, if time is of the essence of a particular clause, a party who fails to act by the time limit specified loses the right given by that clause. If time is of the essence of the whole rent review clause, the slightest delay will mean that the landlord will be denied the opportunity to increase the rent until the next review date (or, indeed, the tenant will be denied the opportunity to decrease the rent until the next review date if the clause permits downward reviews).

The House of Lords in *United Scientific Holdings Ltd v Burnley Borough Council* [1977] 2 All ER 62 held that, in the absence of any contrary indications in the express wording of the clause, or in the interrelation of the rent review clause with other clauses in the lease, there is a presumption that time is not of the essence of the clause and that the review can still be implemented and pursued, even though specific dates have passed (see, eg, *McDonald's Property Co Ltd v HSBC Bank plc* [2001] 36 EG 181). It follows from this decision that there are three situations where time will be of the essence either of the whole clause, or in respect of certain steps in the review procedure.

An express stipulation

Time will be of the essence in respect of all or any of the time limits in the review clause if the lease expressly says so.

Any other contrary indication

The phrase 'time is of the essence' may not have been used in the lease, but there are cases where other forms of wording used by the draftsman have been sufficient to indicate an intention to rebut the usual presumption. In *First Property Growth Partnership v Royal & Sun Alliance Services Ltd* [2002] 22 EG 140, the clause required the landlord to serve notice of intention to review upon the tenant 12 months before the relevant review date 'but not at any other time'. This was held to make time of the essence, and thus the landlord's notice served after the relevant review date was invalid. In *Starmark Enterprises Ltd v CPL Distribution Ltd* [2001] 32 EG 89 (CS), the lease provided for service of a trigger notice by the landlord specifying the amount of rent payable for the following period, but went on to provide that if the tenant failed to serve a counter-notice within one month the tenant would be 'deemed to have agreed to pay the increased rent specified in that notice'. The Court of Appeal held that time was of the essence; the 'deeming' provision was a sufficient contra-indication to rebut the usual presumption. Reference should be made to one of the standard works on landlord and tenant law for further consideration of the many cases dealing with this issue.

The interrelation of the review clause with other clauses in the lease

The usual way in which a clause might interrelate with the review clause in such a way as to make time of the essence is if the tenant is given an option to break the term on or shortly after each review date. The inference in such an interrelation is that if the tenant cannot afford to pay the revised rent, or, where the level of rent is not yet known, he does not envy the prospect of an increase, he is given an opportunity to terminate the lease by exercising the break clause. Since time is usually of the essence in respect of the exercise of a break clause, time may also be construed to be of the essence of the rent review clause. It does not matter that the review clause and the option are separate clauses in the lease; the court simply has to be able to infer a sufficient interrelation. Nor, apparently, does it matter that the option to break is mutual and linked to only one of several rent review dates (*Central Estates Ltd v Secretary of State for the Environment* [1997] 1 EGLR 239).

Unless a rigid timetable for conducting the review is required by either party, it is not often that time will be made of the essence, because of the fatal consequences arising from a delay. It might be advisable to state expressly that time is not of the essence. However, in most leases the timetable is so flexibly drafted that the parties do not feel the need to make express declaration that time is not of the essence, preferring instead to rely upon the usual presumption (but see *Barclays Bank plc v Savile Estates Ltd* [2002] 24 EG 152). If any time clauses are intended to be mandatory, the lease should clearly say so.

37.4.16.2   The negotiated revision

The negotiated approach to arriving at a revised rent usually provides for the new rent to be agreed between the parties at any time (whether before or after the relevant review date) but that if agreement has not been reached by the review date, either or both of the parties will be allowed by the clause to refer the matter to an independent third party for him to make a determination as to the new rent. If such an approach is adopted, the tenant should ensure that the rent review clause does not reserve the right to make the reference to the third party exclusively to the landlord. The tenant must ensure that he also has the ability to make the reference. Even though the rent review clause may permit upward only revisions, it may be in the tenant's interests to have a quick resolution of the review, particularly if he is anxious to assign his lease or sell his business. In exceptional cases (eg, *Royal Bank of Scotland plc v Jennings and Others* [1997] 19 EG 152) the court might be prepared to imply an obligation upon the landlord to refer a review to the third party to give business efficacy to the clause.

37.4.16.3   Trigger notices

The service of a trigger notice usually requires the parties to follow a rigid timetable for the service of notices. One party sets the review in motion by the service of a trigger notice, specifying his proposal for the revised rent, and the other party responds by the service of a counter-notice. A typical clause might provide for the landlord to implement the review by the service on the tenant of a trigger notice, between 12 and 6 months before the relevant review date, in which the landlord specifies a rent that he considers to be the current market rent for the premises. The tenant should be given the right to dispute the landlord's proposal by serving a counter-notice within, say, three months of the service of the trigger notice. The parties would then be required to negotiate; but in default of agreement within, say, three months of the service of the counter-notice, either or both parties may be given the right to make a reference to a third party for a determination. Time may be stated to be of the essence in respect of all or part of the timetable.

Great care must be taken with this more rigid style of approach, particularly if time is of the essence (see **37.4.16.1**). Problems can easily arise, as follows:

(a)   There is no requirement for the landlord to be reasonable when he specifies his proposal for the revised rent in his trigger notice (see *Amalgamated Estates Ltd v Joystretch Manufacturing Ltd* (1980) 257 EG 489). This is very dangerous for the tenant where time is of the essence in respect of the service of the tenant's counter-notice. If the tenant fails to respond within the time limit required by the lease, he will be bound by the rent specified in the landlord's notice. A well-advised tenant should avoid such a clause.

(b)   There has been much litigation surrounding the question of whether a particular form of communication, often in the form of a letter between the parties' advisers, suffices as a notice for the purposes of the review clause. If a communication is to take effect as a notice it ought to be clear and unequivocal, and must be worded in such a way as to make it clear to the recipient that the sender is purporting to take a formal step, or exercise some right under the review clause. Phrases such as 'subject to contract' and 'without prejudice', although not necessarily fatal to the notice, are to be avoided.

(c)   For the same reasons stated in connection with negotiated reviews, the tenant must ensure that the review timetable allows him to implement the review and to refer the rent revision for determination by the third party. These rights must not be left exclusively with the landlord.

Unless there is some compelling reason to the contrary, the negotiated approach is to be preferred and is the one almost invariably encountered in modern commercial leases.

37.4.16.4   The third party

A surveyor usually acts as the independent third party. The lease will provide for the parties to agree upon a surveyor, failing which one or both of the parties will be allowed to make an application to the President of the Royal Institution of Chartered Surveyors (RICS) for the appointment of a surveyor to determine the revised rent. The RICS operates a procedure to deal efficiently with such applications, and will appoint a surveyor with knowledge and experience of similar lettings in the area. It is important that the lease makes it clear in which capacity the surveyor is to act: as an arbitrator between the parties, or as an expert. There are considerable differences between the two:

(a) An arbitrator seeks to resolve a dispute by some quasi-judicial process, whereas an expert imposes his own expert valuation on the parties.

(b) The arbitrator is bound by the procedure under the Arbitration Act 1996, which deals with hearings, submission of evidence and the calling of witnesses. An expert is not subject to such external controls, and is not bound to hear the evidence of the parties. Whilst an arbitrator decides on the basis of the evidence put before him, an expert simply uses his own skill and judgment.

(c) There is a limited right of appeal to the High Court on a point of law against an arbitrator's award, whereas an expert's decision is final and binding unless it appears that he failed to perform the task required of him.

(d) An arbitrator is immune from suit in negligence, whereas an expert is not. Using an expert tends to be quicker and cheaper and is, therefore, often provided for in lettings of conventional properties at modest rents. Where there is something unorthodox about the property, which might make it difficult to value, or where there is a good deal of money at stake in the outcome of the review, an arbitrator is to be preferred so that a fully argued case can be put. Alternatively, the review clause could leave the capacity of the third party open, to be determined by the party who makes the reference at the time the reference is made.

37.4.17   Ancillary provisions – commercial leases

The landlord invariably includes additional provisions to deal with:

(a) payment of the revised rent where the review is implemented after the review date;

(b) recording a note of the revised rent.

37.4.17.1   The late review

If time has not been made of the essence of the rent review date, the landlord can attempt to increase the rent by implementing the clause after the date for review has passed. To deal with this possibility, the review clause is usually drafted to include the following types of provisions:

(a) that the existing rent (the old rent) continues to be payable on account of the new rent until the new rent has been ascertained;

(b) that the new rent, once ascertained, becomes payable from, and is backdated to, the rent review date;

(c) that as soon as the new rent has been ascertained, the tenant is to pay to the landlord the amount by which the old rent paid on account of the new rent since the review date actually falls short of the new rent; and because the landlord has been denied the benefit of this shortfall pending the outcome of the review, the tenant is to pay it with interest calculated from the rent review date until the date of payment.

The tenant should check the operation of these provisions. If the rent review clause permits both upward and downward reviews, he should ensure that there is some equivalent provision for the landlord to pay any shortfall (with interest) to the tenant if the new rent turns out to be lower than the old rent (although in *Royal Bank of Scotland v Jennings* (see **37.4.16.2**) the court was prepared to imply such a term in any case). He should also check that the rate of interest at which the shortfall is to be paid is not set at the usual interest rate under the lease (4% or 5% above base rate). The usual rate is intended to operate on the occasion of tenant default, whereas in the case of a late rent review, the fault may lie with a delaying landlord as much as with a delaying tenant. The interest rate should be set at base rate itself or, perhaps, 1% or 2% above base rate. Finally, the tenant should check that the review clause allows the tenant to instigate the review process, and to force negotiations or the third party reference, since the tenant might prefer a speedy settlement of the review as an alternative to facing a future lump sum payment of a shortfall with interest.

For a potential difficulty where there is a late review in the event of tenant default in paying rent, see **34.5.3**.

37.4.17.2   Recording the review

It is good practice to attach memoranda of the revised rent to the lease and counterpart as evidence for all persons concerned with the lease of the agreement or determination. The rent review clause usually obliges both parties to sign and attach identical memoranda to their respective parts of the lease. It is usual for both parties to bear their own costs in this regard.

37.4.18   VAT – commercial leases

The grant of a commercial lease is an exempt supply, but subject to the landlord's right to elect to waive the exemption and charge VAT. See **6.5.2** as to the purpose of this option to tax. If the landlord decides to elect to tax, it is essential that he should be able to add the VAT onto the agreed amount of rent. However, the effect of s 89 of the VATA 1994 is that if the landlord elects before the grant of the lease, he will only be able to add VAT to the rent if the lease contains a provision permitting this; see **6.5.6**. In every lease, therefore, there should be such a provision.

37.4.19   Rent suspension

The lease will continue to run and the rent will continue to be payable even if the property is rendered unusable, for example because of a fire. If the block is totally destroyed, it will only be in exceptional circumstances that the doctrine of frustration will apply and the lease will be terminated (see *National Carriers Ltd v Panalpina (Northern) Ltd* [1981] AC 675).

However, it is usual to include a provision in the lease suspending the rental payments whilst the premises are unusable. Usually, landlords will wish to limit this to cases where the damage, etc has been caused by an insured risk. This means that if you are acting for a tenant, you must look vary carefully at what the insured risks are to make sure that all potential dangers are covered. Otherwise, if damage is caused by a non-insured risk, the rent will continue to be payable – and there will be no insurance money with which to rebuild the block.

37.4.20 Alterations and improvements

At common law, the tenant's ability to make alterations or improvements is somewhat unclear. It all depends upon the centuries-old doctrine of 'waste'. It is best, therefore, for these matters to be dealt with expressly in the lease.

A landlord will usually want to exercise some form of control over what can and cannot be done on his premises. Whilst some alterations may well increase the value of the office and the reversion, some may not. He will be concerned, particularly in comparatively short commercial leases, lest any alterations carried out by a particular tenant will decrease the letting value of the premises when he comes to re-let. This will be less of a problem in a 99-year lease of a flat, for example, but alterations may still affect the value of the reversion. There are also safety aspects: tenants cannot be allowed to remove or interfere with structural walls and the like, otherwise the whole block might collapse.

In a short-term lease, the landlord may wish to prohibit all alterations and so will impose an absolute covenant. Prospective tenants should consider this carefully. Are the premises, as they are now, definitely going to be adequate for the tenant's needs throughout the lease and any possible renewal? It is true to say that the landlord could still grant permission for a particular alteration, despite the absolute prohibition, but, of course, he does not have to. The tenant will be at the landlord's mercy. However, in an office or flat lease, bearing in mind the nature of the premises, an absolute prohibition on structural alterations would be acceptable.

A qualified covenant would be preferable with regard to other alterations. This prohibits alterations without the landlord's prior consent. Under s 19(2) of the Landlord and Tenant Act 1927, a term is implied into a qualified covenant against making improvements that the landlord cannot unreasonably withhold his consent. That term cannot be excluded. This provision will thus apply to a covenant against making alterations to the extent that the alteration in question amounts to an improvement. According to *Lambert v FW Woolworth & Co Ltd* [1938] Ch 883, whether an alteration amounts to an improvement for these purposes, must be looked at purely from the point of view of the tenant. If the works in question will increase the value or usefulness of the premises to the tenant then it will be an improvement, even if it will result in the reduction in the value of the landlord's reversionary interest. In relation to improvements, therefore, the landlord will not be able to withhold his consent unreasonably; in relation to other alterations, he can be as awkward as he likes.

Although the *Woolworth* case is beneficial to tenants, they would often prefer a fully qualified covenant, one that makes it clear on the face of it that the landlord cannot withhold his consent unreasonably to an alteration, whether or not it amounts to an improvement. Landlords must think very carefully before agreeing to concede any kind of qualified covenant.

37.4.21 Insurance

37.4.21.1 General

It is clearly important, from both a landlord's and a tenant's perspective, to ensure that adequate provisions are in place to insure the property against damage by fire, flood, etc. From a landlord's perspective, the building forms the physical basis of his investment, and so he will want it to be reinstated in the event of damage.

Equally, the tenant will want the building to be reinstated so that he can continue to occupy the let premises as intended under the lease.

In the case of a letting of whole, the tenant could be made solely responsible for insurance. Alternatively, the landlord could take out the insurance and charge the tenant for the cost through a service charge, which has the advantage of giving the landlord the comfort that insurance is actually in place.

In the case of lettings of part, there are two basic options:

(a)   Each tenant could insure his own premises and the landlord insure the common parts. This may not be the most attractive arrangement for the landlord, for a number of reasons. First, the landlord has to check that the tenants have complied with the covenants. Secondly, each tenant needs to rely on every other tenant complying with the insurance covenant. Checking this will be practically impossible, and if a tenant has not insured, it may well mean that the proceeds from the various policies will not be enough to rebuild. There is also the problem of ensuring that those who have insured actually use the proceeds to make good any damage caused and do not just pocket them and walk away. Lastly, although the lease could require all the policies to be taken out with the same company, there will still be a multiplicity of claims should one need to be made.

(b)   The alternative (and the most commonly adopted approach) is for the landlord or management company to insure the whole block, with the cost being passed on to the tenants through the service charge. Sometimes the insurance company to be used will be specified, but more usually the choice is left to the landlord. When acting for the landlord you should ensure that he can recover the premium through the service charge when drafting the lease. You should also ensure that the landlord will be able to keep any discounts or commissions he may receive from the insurance company. Otherwise the landlord may have to account for these to the tenants.

Whether the letting is of whole or part, the following matters should always be checked from both the landlord's and the tenant's perspective:

(a)   risks insured against;

(b)   amount of cover;

(c)   application of policy monies.

37.4.21.2   Risks covered

An obligation 'to insure' is not sufficient – to insure against what? The risks insured against should be stated expressly. There is often an inclusive list of the risks which the landlord must insure against, for example 'fire, storm, flood, etc'. The problem with this, though, is that the landlord may continue to insure against unlikely or expensive risks, and if new risks arise (eg, terrorist violence), these may not be covered.

You should inspect the policy itself (and not just rely on the covenant) and ascertain what risks are covered. If an important risk is not covered, it would, in theory, be possible for an individual tenant to arrange extra cover for that risk or renegotiate the clause, but this would probably not be possible in practice.

The following suggested clause covers most foreseeable risks:

subject to the reasonable availability of cover, fire, explosion, lightning, tempest, storm, flood, burst pipes, landslip, subsidence, riot, civil commotion, industrial unrest, impact by vehicles, aircraft and other aerial devices and articles dropped therefrom, acts of malicious persons and vandals and such other risks as the landlord may reasonably require or the tenant may reasonably request.

37.4.21.3 Amount of cover

You must ensure that the property is insured to its full reinstatement value, otherwise if the property is totally destroyed there will not be enough money to pay for its rebuilding. Full reinstatement value will include:

(a)   costs of demolition and site clearance;

(b)   professional fees (eg, architects, surveyors, etc);

(c)   an allowance for inflation.

A professional valuation or index linking is advisable.

37.4.21.4 Application of policy monies

There should be at the very least a covenant by the landlord to use the proceeds to reinstate the premises. Ideally, a tenant would like this extended to include an obligation for the landlord to make good any shortfall in the proceeds out of his own pocket.

You should also check whether there is any provision to deal with the possibility of reinstatement being impossible. Should this provide for the monies to be retained by the landlord, whose building it is, or to be passed over to the tenants who have been paying the premiums? It is probably fairest for the proceeds to be shared between landlord and tenant proportionate to the values of their respective interests.

37.4.22 Permitted user

At common law, a tenant can use premises for whatever purposes he wishes – subject, of course, to planning laws and any covenants on the superior title. This may well not be acceptable to the landlord who will want to be able to exercise some control as to the use to which 'his' premises are put. He will want this control both for financial and for estate management reasons.

When you are acting for a tenant, you should consider the user provisions carefully, to ensure that they are not going to cause your client any problems in his occupation of the unit, or if he should wish to assign the lease.

37.4.22.1 Flats

In the case of a lease of a flat, the landlord will usually want to ensure that the block is used solely for residential purposes. This is to preserve the value of the reversion. If one or more flats start to be used for commercial purposes, this may well make the other flats in the block less desirable residences and so more difficult to dispose of. This possibility of non-residential use might influence potential tenants into declining to take the leases when the block is being first developed. Illegal and immoral use will also be prohibited.

So, both landlords and tenants will have the same concerns and a covenant limiting the use to residential only will be acceptable to both. (Sometimes you will find that certain professional uses are permitted, eg, doctor, solicitor, presumably on the basis that this kind of use would not affect the value of the other flats adversely.)

37.4.22.2   Commercial leases

Use is much more of a problem in commercial leases. In lettings of shops, for example, the landlord may need to prevent competition with other premises of his, or may wish to ensure a good mix of retail units to make the development attractive to the shopping public. This may cause problems for a tenant who cannot change from an unprofitable shop use to one more profitable.

In a letting of an office block both landlord and tenants will again have a common interest in ensuring that it is all just used for office purposes. Use for (say) a manufacturing purpose would not be acceptable to the other tenants. This would almost certainly cause noise and other forms of pollution which would adversely affect the other tenants. Tenants would leave, offices could not be re-let, and the landlord would thus suffer financially.

The parties need to agree upon the way in which the permitted use is to be defined in the lease. Whether you are acting for landlord or tenant, you should bear in mind that a user clause can have an effect on the rent when it comes to rent review. A very restrictive user clause will inevitably have the effect of reducing the rent that would otherwise be payable; a very wide user clause will tend to increase the rent.

One common way to define user is to make use of the categories set out in the Use Classes Order 1987 (see **17.1.4.2**). Thus, in the case of public house/wine bar premises, user could be limited to use within Class A4. Alternatively, the landlord may decide not to use the Use Classes Order and instead restrict the use to a stated purpose, for example office use for marketing consultants. This may suit the present tenant in his current business, but inhibits any change (or expansion) of business and limits the class of persons who might be interested in taking an assignment. It is for this reason that such a clause would almost certainly result in a lower rent at review than a wider user clause based on the Use Classes Order. A possible compromise is to have a specific use but allow changes to other uses within the same use class as the permitted user, but only with the landlord's consent. Thus, a lease might permit use as a warehouse 'or such other use within Class B8 of the Use Classes Order 1987 as the landlord shall permit'.

In light of the above, it should therefore be understood that the user covenant may be an absolute prohibition on other uses, or it may be qualified, ie provide that a change to another use can be made, but with the landlord's prior consent. In the latter case, there is no implication that the landlord's consent cannot be unreasonably withheld, but s 19(3) of the Landlord and Tenant Act 1927 does provide that the landlord cannot charge a fine or an increased rent as a condition of his giving consent, provided no structural alteration is involved.

37.4.23   Assignment and sub-letting

At common law, a tenant is free to dispose of his lease, whether by an outright assignment or by a sub-lease. But a landlord may well want to exercise close control over who will be in occupation of his property.

37.4.23.1   Flat leases

In long-term flat leases you will recall that the tenant will have paid a substantial premium on the grant of the lease. He will not want his freedom to dispose of the lease, and so recoup this premium, to be substantially restricted. Equally, the landlord must accept that the lease must be acceptable to any prospective mortgagee.

The mortgagee will want to be able to sell in exercise of its power of sale without any limitations being imposed. It is usual, therefore, in a long flat lease to find that assignment is freely permitted. There may, however, be restrictions on the assignment or sub-letting of part. Further, controls on assignment are sometimes found being imposed in respect of assignments in the final few years of the term.

Even where dealings are freely permitted, the landlord will obviously want to know the identity of the new tenants, and so you will find that there will be a covenant by the tenant to register any dealings with the landlord and pay a fee.

37.4.23.2 Commercial leases

Much stricter controls are usual in office and other commercial leases. Such leases are usually for a much shorter term at a much higher rent. The identity and status of the occupier is of much greater significance than in a long flat lease with a low ground rent. An unsatisfactory tenant could greatly damage the value of the landlord's reversion, either by not paying rent or by damaging the property which the landlord has then to try to re-let.

The landlord will wish to control sub-letting as well as assignment. In some circumstances, a sub-tenant can become the direct tenant of the head landlord, and so again the landlord could be faced with an unsatisfactory tenant causing financial damage to his interests.

37.4.23.3 Absolute prohibition

An absolute prohibition on assignment, etc would probably not be acceptable to a tenant, except perhaps in a very short-term letting. Although the landlord could waive the covenant in any given case, the tenant would be completely at the landlord's mercy with regard to this.

37.4.23.4 A qualified prohibition

A qualified covenant on assignment, etc prohibits alienation by the tenant without the landlord's consent. Sometimes the covenant will go further and state that the landlord's consent is not to be unreasonably withheld. This is known as a fully qualified covenant. Such a covenant gives a tenant considerable leeway when seeking licence to assign.

Section 19(1)(a) of the Landlord and Tenant Act 1927 provides that, notwithstanding any contrary provision, a covenant not to assign, underlet, charge or part with possession of the demised premises or any part thereof without the landlord's licence or consent, is subject to a proviso that such licence or consent is not to be unreasonably withheld. In other words, a qualified covenant can be converted into a fully qualified covenant by the operation of s 19(1)(a). As a general rule, a landlord will be acting unreasonably unless his reasons for refusal relate to the status of the proposed assignee, or the use to which the assignee proposes to put the premises.

The Landlord and Tenant Act 1988 further strengthened the position of a tenant seeking consent to assign, sub-let, or part with possession. The Act applies where the lease contains a qualified covenant against alienation (whether or not the proviso that the landlord's consent is not to be unreasonably withheld is express or implied by statute). When the tenant has made written application for consent, the landlord owes a duty, within a reasonable time, to give consent, unless it is reasonable not to do so (the giving of consent subject to an unreasonable condition will be a breach of this duty). In addition, the landlord must serve on the tenant written notice of his decision whether or not to give consent, specifying in addition the conditions he is imposing, or the reasons why he is withholding consent. The burden of proving the reasonableness of any refusal or any conditions imposed is on the landlord.

37.4.23.5 Special rules for covenants against assigning commercial leases

Under s 19(1A) of the Landlord and Tenant Act 1927 (inserted by s 22 of the Landlord and Tenant (Covenants) Act 1995), special rules apply in relation to covenants against assigning contained in commercial leases granted on or after 1 January 1996. These rules enable the landlord and tenant to agree in advance (ie, in the covenant against assigning) specified circumstances in which the landlord may withhold his consent to an assignment and specified conditions subject to which consent to assignment may be given.

If the landlord withholds consent because any of those specified circumstances exist, or imposes any of those specified conditions on his consent, he will not be taken to be acting unreasonably. Hence, by careful use of s 19(1A) in the drafting of the lease, the landlord can provide himself with cast-iron reasonable grounds for withholding consent to an assignment.

The provisions permitted under s 19(1A) may be either of a factual nature (eg, whether the assignee is a company quoted on the London Stock Exchange), or discretionary (eg, whether in the landlord's opinion the assignee is capable of performing the tenant covenants of the lease). Where the provision involves an exercise of discretion, then s 19(1A) requires either:

(a) that the provision states that discretion is to be exercised reasonably (eg, 'if in the landlord's reasonable opinion the assignee is capable of performing the tenant covenants of the lease'); or

(b) that the tenant is given an unrestricted right to have the exercise of the discretion reviewed by an independent third party whose identity is ascertainable from the provision (eg, 'if in the landlord's opinion the assignee is capable of performing the tenant covenants of the lease, but if the tenant disagrees with the landlord's opinion, the tenant may apply to an expert appointed in accordance with the terms of the lease for a second opinion').

37.4.23.6 Sub-lettings

Sub-lettings of the whole of the premises are usually subject to the same kinds of restrictions as assignments. However, in the case of sub-lettings of part, the lease provisions are usually considerably stricter. Sub-letting of part is often subject to an absolute prohibition. A landlord who let premises to one tenant does not want to find sometime in the future that he now has to deal with a multi-tenanted block.

Section 19(1)(a) of the Landlord and Tenant Act 1927 and the Landlord and Tenant Act 1988 apply to covenants against assignment, sub-letting or parting with possession. However, s 19(1A) of the Landlord and Tenant Act 1927 applies only to assignments.

A similar result to s 19(1)(A) can nevertheless be achieved by careful drafting of the alienation provisions, by imposing conditions precedent to the landlord giving consent. Thus, for example, a requirement that the tenant first offer to surrender the lease without any consideration before assignment was held not to contravene s 19(1)(a) (*Bocardo SA v S & M Hotels* [1980] 1 WLR 17). The position is different if the lease seeks to exclude the right of the court to decide whether the landlord is acting reasonably (*Re Smith's Lease* [1951] 1 TLR 254). This will be a matter for the court to decide and so the position is less certain than is the case if s 19(1)(A) applies.

37.4.24   The arrangements for repair, maintenance and other services

You will appreciate by now that, due to the nature of a block of offices or flats, it is essential from the point of view of both the landlord and the tenant that every part of the block is covered by a repairing obligation in order to preserve the value of their respective interests. When he was setting up the development, the landlord will have decided whether he wanted to retain responsibility for some or all of the repairs himself, or whether he preferred to drop out of the picture – and the hassle of responsibility – and impose the obligation on someone else. For details of the various management schemes available, see **37.5**.

37.4.24.1   The landlord's concerns

The landlord is concerned to ensure that the whole block will be properly maintained in order to preserve its value.

Each tenant may have assumed responsibility for the repair of his particular unit, either the whole of the unit, or possibly only non-structural parts. It must be appreciated, however, that specific performance is not likely to be available against a tenant, and that due to the restrictions placed on forfeiture of leases for breaches of repairing covenants by the Leasehold Property (Repairs) Act 1938, forfeiture will be possible only in the case of serious lack of repair. So the only real remedy against a defaulting tenant may be damages. But these will not get the necessary repairs done. You should therefore ensure that there is some form of back-up provision which allows the landlord to enter and effect any repairs which have not been done by a tenant, and then to charge the tenant with the cost.

The landlord must consider the repair of any part of the block not covered by a tenant's covenant. He may decide to accept responsibility himself, or use some form of management company. Whichever management scheme is chosen, he will need to ensure that a right of access is reserved in order to do the repairs and to ascertain what repairs need doing.

He will need to ensure that the service charge provisions enable him to recoup the full amount of the expenditure from the tenants. For details of service charge provisions, see **37.6**.

37.4.24.2   The tenant's concerns

The tenant (and any prospective mortgagee, in the case of a flat) will also be concerned to ensure that the whole of the block will be properly maintained in order to preserve the value of their respective interests. A business tenant will also think of the effect on his business of having premises in a potentially run-down building. So, not only must the premises let to the tenant be properly maintained, but so also must the other flats and offices and the common parts: lifts, hallways, stairways, etc.

When checking the lease, you must ensure that there are covenants to repair from the landlord or others responsible so that repair can be enforced should the need arise.

You will often find that obligations to repair are placed on someone other than the tenant's immediate landlord. This is particularly common in flat leases when a management company is often used. If enforcement is not possible under normal landlord and tenant or privity of contract grounds, you will need to ensure that there is some other way in which the tenant will be able to enforce those obligations, should the need arise. Where the obligation to repair the structure and common parts is imposed on a management company, you should check that the management scheme used enables such enforcement (see **37.7**). Sometimes, repairing obligations are imposed on other tenants. In this case, you should check to see that there is a covenant from the landlord that the landlord will enforce them against the other tenants on request, or that the provisions of the Contracts (Rights of Third Parties) Act 1999 are complied with. For details of enforcement of covenants between tenants, see **37.7**.

If, as is often the case with flats, the repairs are to be undertaken by a management company specially set up for that purpose, consideration should be given as to the worth of such a covenant and, if necessary (and possible), a guarantee should be obtained from the landlord. The danger here is that the management company may become insolvent and thus unable to carry out its repairing obligations. A guarantee from the landlord will not be implied by the courts.

37.4.24.3   Who does what?

The express obligations must cover every part of the building; repairing obligations will not normally be implied against either landlords or tenants. Often the landlord will covenant to repair the main structure and exterior of the block, with the individual tenants covenanting to carry out the internal repairs and decoration to their own particular units. Whatever scheme is adopted, you must ensure that there is a clear division of responsibility between the various parties. It must be made certain that every part of the building is covered by a repairing obligation, and clear also as to whose responsibility it is to repair each and every part. There must be no grey areas where responsibility is unclear; no black holes where no one has responsibility and no overlaps where two persons are apparently responsible and can then start squabbling as to who will actually have to do the work.

37.4.24.4   Operative words

As in any other covenant, the party responsible for the repairs can be obliged to do only what he has agreed to do. You should ensure, therefore, that the operative words of the clause are sufficient to cover all foreseeable repair activities (eg, 'to repair maintain cleanse paint decorate ...'). A covenant to 'repair' only would not oblige the covenantor to decorate, for example. And if a service charge was being paid by the tenants, if the landlord did in fact decorate the tenants could not be obliged to pay for this where they had promised to pay for 'repairs' alone.

Is the repairing covenant intended to include renewal and/or improvement? Many arguments arise in practice over this simple point. Replacement of defective window frames, for example, is within the ambit of a covenant to 'repair', but what if the old frame is to be replaced with improved double glazed units? This is probably not a repair but an improvement, and so is not within the obligation imposed by a covenant to 'repair'. As above, if the landlord did install double glazed units, the tenants would not be obliged to pay for them through the service charge where they had agreed to pay only for 'repairs'.

If the covenant does include improvements, is this acceptable to the tenants? Do the tenants not want the property improved, you may ask? But bear in mind that the tenants will be expected to pay for any work done through the service charge.

There is a risk that the landlord/management company could decide to carry out large-scale improvements, which the tenants do not want or need, all at the tenants' expense.

Consider a clause 'to improve and renew to the extent such renewals or improvements are necessary or desirable to keep the Building in good and substantial repair ...' as a fair compromise.

In the case of inherent defects in design or construction of the building, you should appreciate that remedying these will normally be within the obligations imposed by a repairing covenant, and so again the ultimate cost will fall on the tenants through the service charge.

37.4.24.5 Notice of breaches

When a landlord enters into a repairing covenant, there will be no breach unless and until he has notice (no matter from what source) of the lack of repair. Even though he may reserve a right of entry to view the state of repair, he is under no obligation to do so and you should advise the tenant to inform the landlord of any lack of repair as soon as it is known.

When acting for a landlord, you should include a tenant's covenant to notify the landlord of the need to repair. If the tenant fails to do this, he will also be in breach of covenant and liable to the landlord for damages (ie, any extra cost incurred by reason of the delay in reporting it).

However, if the part of the property in question is in the control of the landlord, for example the common parts, then the landlord's liability does not depend upon his having received notice of the disrepair.

37.4.24.6 Occupiers' liability

If the landlord is in occupation of the common parts, he will owe the common duty of care to visitors under the Occupiers' Liability Act 1957. You should look out for clauses which require the tenant to indemnify the landlord against any such claim made by the tenant's visitors.

37.5 Flat management schemes

37.5.1 Introduction

In the case of an office block, the landlord will commonly provide the services himself, either directly or through the use of agents who will manage the block on his behalf. Because of the high rental income and investment value of the reversion, the landlord will have a close personal interest in the management of the block.

In the case of a block of flats, however, the landlord will very often want to rid himself of the responsibility for providing the services – and also the hassle of dealing with complaining tenants. So, some form of management company will often be used. There needs to be some scheme in existence which allows the tenants to enforce the provision of services against the company and enables the company to enforce payment of the service charge against the tenants.

37.5.2 Objectives

37.5.2.1 For the landlord

The objective for the landlord is to relieve himself of all responsibility for the maintenance of the block, yet provide a system of maintenance which will be acceptable to prospective tenants and their mortgagees. The landlord will also often require a system which preserves for him the rental income and investment value of the reversion to the block and will ensure that the service charge contributions are recoverable from successors in title to the original tenant. Remember the problems of enforcing positive covenants.

37.5.2.2   For the tenant

The objective for the tenant is to be able to enforce the maintenance and repairing obligations both as against the landlord and against his successors in title. In the larger schemes, it is usual for a management company to take over the landlord's responsibilities, and special problems can then arise.

37.5.2.3   For the mortgagee

It is usual for an institutional mortgagee to insist that there should be a satisfactory scheme for enforcing landlord's covenants and that a copy of a management company's memorandum and articles of association, together with the tenant's share certificate, should be deposited with the title deeds.

37.5.3   Types of scheme

37.5.3.1   Direct management by landlord

Here, the landlord has responsibility for providing the services personally because of his covenant to do so. He will recoup the cost through the service charge. The tenants will then covenant to pay the service charge. The obligations will then be enforceable by and against successors in title under normal landlord and tenant principles.

37.5.3.2   Management by agent

In this case, as above, the landlord is responsible for the repairs, etc, but he discharges that responsibility by employing agents ('managing agents') to take day-to-day charge of matters. As the ultimate responsibility is the landlord's and the service charge is payable to the landlord, enforceability is as in **37.5.3.1**.

37.5.3.3   Use of a management company

The use of a management company has great attractions for both landlords and tenants. The landlord fulfils his objectives; he is free from the responsibility of running the block. The scheme is normally that the management company will be owned and controlled by the flat owners themselves, and so the tenants have the bonus of being in control of the maintenance of the block. They will thus be able to ensure that the block is properly maintained and that the service charges are not excessive.

However, the company has to be run. Someone will need to look after the accounts, make the necessary returns to Companies House, and arrange for the provision of the services and repairs themselves. Is there someone willing to take on this often thankless job? Is the person who is willing actually able to do the job? Many blocks of flats with tenants' management companies work very well; but some of the most badly maintained are run by tenants' companies, where agreement to undertake work, which some tenants do not think necessary, can never be found.

There are various alternative schemes which make use of a management company.

Transfer of freehold

Here, the landlord transfers the reversion to the management company. The management company then becomes the tenants' landlord and the covenants are enforceable against and by it under normal landlord and tenant principles. This has the disadvantage to a landlord that he loses his investment in the ownership of the freehold reversion.

Concurrent lease

Here, having granted leases of the individual flats, the landlord then grants a concurrent lease of the reversion in the whole of the block to the management company. This concurrent lease takes effect at the same time as and subject to the leases of the individual flats. It thus has the effect of making the management company the flat owners' landlord for the duration of the concurrent lease. (This will usually be perhaps one or two days shorter in length than the flat leases themselves.) In this way, the repairing obligations and the obligation to pay the service charge are enforceable under normal landlord and tenant principles.

Variations

Management company joins in the flat leases

The landlord grants the leases of the flats in the usual way, but the management company joins in those leases to covenant to provide the services. The tenants then covenant to pay the service charge to the management company.

However, there is a problem here. The covenants between the management company and tenants are not covenants between landlord and tenant and so are not enforceable by and against successors in title to the tenant and the management company. However, such schemes may become more popular for 'new leases' (ie, those granted on or after 1 January 1996) because of s 12 of the Landlord and Tenant (Covenants) Act 1995. This provides that a covenant in a lease with a management company in these circumstances will be enforceable in the same way as covenants between landlord and tenant. Use of this provision will avoid the need for the complications (and slight extra expense) of the concurrent lease. However, where the management company has no legal estate in the common parts then it is necessary to ensure that it is given adequate rights of access to the building in order to enable it to carry out the repair and maintenance obligations.

Service charge directed to be paid to management company

In this scheme, the landlord grants the leases of the flats and covenants with the tenants to provide the services in the usual way. The management company joins in the leases and the landlord directs payment of the service charge to it, in consideration of it agreeing to provide the services. The covenants are then enforceable between the landlord and the tenants in the normal way. But if the management company defaults, the landlord has to provide the services. This is not good for the landlord, but it is a worthwhile reassurance for the tenants.

The *Lenders' Handbook* (see **Appendix 7**) sets out in para 5.11 detailed requirements as to what management arrangements are acceptable for mortgage purposes.

37.6   Service charge provisions

37.6.1   Introduction

Although the landlord/management company will usually be responsible for the repairs to the major parts of the block, including the structure and the common parts, the cost of all this will be passed on to the tenants by means of a service charge. The total expenditure in a year will be divided up between the various tenants in the block in proportions set out in the lease. In addition to repairs, the service charge payments will also usually cover other matters such as the painting and decoration of the block and the cleaning and maintenance of the hallways, stairs, lifts, gardens, car parks, toilets, etc.

Many of the problems which arise as between landlord and tenant stem from service charge disputes. This is particularly so in residential leases. Tenants frequently complain of work not being done to proper standards, or of costs being too high – or both! Particular care should therefore be taken in drafting or approving this clause.

37.6.2   Contents of the clause

37.6.2.1   General principle

Tenants are obliged to pay only for matters which have been agreed in the lease. You should therefore take care in drafting the lease to ensure that all necessary expenditure on the building can be recovered from the tenants. When acting for a prospective tenant, you should also check precisely what the tenant will be agreeing to pay for if he enters into the lease. You should also check carefully as to what services the landlord/management company is actually *obliged* to provide.

37.6.2.2   Obligatory and discretionary services

It is usual to provide that the landlord will be obliged to provide the essential services, for example repairs, and then provide that if the landlord provides various ancillary matters, for example an entry phone system in residential flats, or the employment of security guards in a commercial block, then the tenants will be obliged to pay for it if the landlord actually does provide that facility. You should ensure that there is an obligation to provide all essential services, not just repairs, but also cleaning and maintenance of the common parts. Also, you should check to see what optional items are included and warn the client if there is a potential for considerable extra expense in respect of non-essential items which the landlord might decide to provide.

37.6.2.3   Landlord's obligations

The landlord's obligations should include:

(a)   repairs and decoration;

(b)   insurance;

(c)   any payments under a head lease;

(d)   furnishing, cleaning and lighting the common parts;

(e)   car park/garden and grounds maintenance; and

(f)   maintenance of lifts.

37.6.2.4   Discretionary services

The optional items may include:

(a)   establishing a reserve or sinking fund;

(b)   improvements;

(c)   entry phone system;

(d)   resident caretaker; and

(e)   security staff/other enhanced security arrangements.

37.6.2.5   Other expenditure

The landlord will probably have to incur other items of expenditure in providing the services. You should make sure that these are expressly made recoverable, for example:

(a)   bank interest and bank charges;

(b)   legal expenses and other professional fees;

(c)   management charge; and

(d)   costs of enforcing the obligations under the lease, for example to pay the rent and service charge.

Otherwise, the landlord would have to bear the cost of these personally.

37.6.3   Methods of apportioning the cost

There are various formulae which you will find used to apportion the cost amongst the various flat and office tenants. Which one is appropriate in any given situation will depend upon the full circumstances of each particular case. When drafting a lease you should discuss the formula to be chosen with the landlord and the landlord's surveyors at an early stage so that the appropriate formula can be included in the draft lease.

The following is a selection of those you are most likely to come across.

37.6.3.1   Proportionate to rateable value

This is common in older developments, the principle being that larger offices and flats (with larger rateable values) should pay a larger share than the smaller ones. With the ending of domestic rates, this method is no longer possible for new flat developments.

37.6.3.2   Proportionate to floor area

This is another way of ensuring that larger premises pay a higher proportion for services than smaller.

37.6.3.3   Equally between the tenants

This is only sensible in a block where all the premises are the same size and will make the same use of the services.

37.6.3.4   A 'fair proportion'

This allows variations to be made to take into account the fact that different offices and flats may make differing amounts of use of the various services provided. It also allows changes to be made during the term of the lease to take into account differing uses or circumstances, for example an extension of the block. Such a vague provision may, however, lead to disputes with tenants as to what is in fact 'fair'.

37.6.3.5   A stated proportion of each of the various expenses

This proportion will vary depending upon the situation and size of the office or flat concerned. This may be the same proportion of *all* the expenses, or it may allow almost infinite flexibility to apportion different elements of the service charge costs in different proportions amongst the various tenants. For example, why should ground-floor tenants have to contribute towards the (often large) cost of maintaining the lift? Care should be taken when you are drafting the leases to ensure that all the different proportions to be paid by the various tenants add up to 100%!

37.6.3.6   Unlet units

Both landlords' and tenants' advisers should think carefully as to what is to be done about the contributions due in respect of any offices or flats which are unlet.

If no one is making up the contributions from unlet units, this could have serious implications. It is likely to be the case that the cost of providing the services will still be the same, even though one or more units are unlet. Without the contributions due from those premises, the landlord/management company may well not be able to afford to provide all the services. This may affect the value and enjoyment of the let units. In the case of a new development, tenants will expect to find that the landlord will covenant to make up these payments until all the units have been sold, and the landlord will have little choice other than to go along with this.

37.6.4   Reserve and sinking funds

37.6.4.1   Purpose and effect

Although normally the idea behind a service charge is that all expenditure incurred in one year will be covered by the payments made in that year, you will sometimes find that the landlord/management company will set up a reserve or sinking fund to deal with unexpected expenditure which might arise during a year, or to cover anticipated major expenditure. For example, every few years the outside of the block will need painting, an expensive task. Similarly, eventually the lifts will need replacing – a very expensive item to be paid for out of one year's service charges.

A large increase in the amounts demanded by way of service charge in one year when compared with the previous year could pose serious financial difficulties for the tenants and, if some are unable or refuse to pay, for the landlord/management company itself and the other tenants. It is often thought sensible, therefore, to build up a fund by small contributions every year so that this can be used in years of expected or unexpectedly high expenditure to even out the amount of the service charge contributions.

Apart from evening out the bills in this way, a sinking fund may also be seen to be fairer when changes in the identity of the tenants are considered. For example, someone buying a flat in the year in which the lift was going to be replaced would have to pay a very large service charge that year to pay for it, whereas the previous owners who had used (and worn out) the lift would have had to pay nothing towards its replacement.

37.6.4.2   Express provisions required

In order to recover contributions to such a fund, express provision is required in the lease. The lease should declare that the fund is to be held on trust. This is to protect the fund against it, being seized by the landlord's creditors should the landlord become insolvent.

37.6.4.3 When can the fund be used?

When drafting or approving a clause dealing with a reserve or sinking fund, careful thought needs to be given as to when recourse to the fund may or must be made by the landlord. You must appreciate that everything depends upon the wording of the lease itself.

The landlord will not wish to be too tied down or restricted by the terms of the lease. On the other hand, the tenant will want to limit the landlord's discretion.

Is there a danger that when a major item of expenditure falls due, the landlord simply charges it to that year's service charge in the normal way and does not make use of the sinking fund? Equally, is there a risk that the landlord uses the reserve fund for items of a recurring nature, for example cleaning bills, rather than the unexpected items for which it is really intended? Perhaps a fair compromise is a provision obliging the landlord to charge at least 50% of the cost of stated major items to the fund, for example painting the exterior, replacing lifts, etc.

37.6.4.4 Unlet units

As with the service charge itself, there is again the problem of unlet units. Is the landlord required to make the contributions in respect of these? Often he will not wish to do so, and the terms of the lease should make it clear whether the landlord's obligation to make the service charge contributions in respect of unlet units includes the contributions to the sinking fund or not.

37.6.4.5 Assignments of the lease

A tenant assigning his lease may wish to be reimbursed by the assignee with the amount of his unexpended contributions to the fund. After all, the incoming tenant will reap the benefit of these in reduced service charge contributions in the future. This will only be possible, however, if the landlord is obliged by the lease to provide information about the size, etc, of the fund. The landlord will probably not wish to agree to this because of the work involved in providing the information.

37.6.5 Certificate of amount due

37.6.5.1 Who is to prepare the certificate?

The lease should state who is to prepare the accounts and certify the amount due from each tenant. It is usual to state that this certificate is conclusive. It would obviously be inconvenient for the landlord if such a certificate were to be open to challenge. Tenants should be warned that apparently, at common law, if you agree to such a clause then it will be conclusive on matters of law, ie, as to the construction of the service charge clause, as well as matters of fact, ie, the costs incurred.

37.6.5.2 Can an employee be used?

When acting for a tenant, you should check carefully who is to prepare this certificate. It should be someone independent of the landlord and not an employee of the landlord or an associated company.

If the landlord wishes an employee to be able to prepare the certificate, this must be clearly stated. However, if it is clearly stated then this will be binding upon the tenant. Would you be prepared to accept this on behalf of a client?

In any event, under s 21 of the Landlord and Tenant Act 1985, a residential tenant is entitled to request a written summary of the costs incurred. If the service charges are payable by more than four tenants then those costs must be certified by a qualified accountant, defined to exclude an employee of the landlord or the landlord's managing agents. When the provisions of the Commonhold and Leasehold Reform Act 2002 are brought into force, expected to be sometime in 2006, the landlord will be placed under an obligation to supply tenants, without being requested, with full details of the service charge accounts, certified by a qualified accountant. If this information is not provided, the tenant may withhold payment of the service charge.

37.6.6   Methods of recouping costs

37.6.6.1   Payments in advance essential

Provision for advance payments will be essential to ensure that the landlord has sufficient funds in hand to finance the necessary works. The method of calculating the amount of the advance payment must also be specified in the lease. You will find several alternatives in use in precedents.

(a)   The previous year's expenditure. This is obviously not going to be practical in the first year of a new development; special provision should be made for the first year. In any event, however, it should be borne in mind that expenditure in the previous year might not accurately reflect the expected expenditure in the following year. For example, one year's accounts may include the cost of decoration which would not need to be repeated in the following year.

(b)   A fixed sum. There is a danger, however, that this, if it cannot be changed by the terms of the lease, will rapidly become ineffective due to inflation.

(c)   An estimate of probable expenditure. This is often the most sensible, as expenditure can vary greatly from year to year due to non-recurring items of expenditure.

37.6.6.2   Payment/refund of balance

There must be provision for a final balance to be paid when the actual costs for the year are known. Any underpayment will then be payable as a lump sum.

What is to happen to any overpayment? Is this to be repaid to the tenant, or credited towards the next year's account? Usually, the landlord will require it to be credited to the next year's account.

37.7   Mutual enforcement of covenants

37.7.1   Why the need?

When checking the lease on behalf of a prospective tenant of a flat you will need to ensure that there is some effective scheme for the enforcement of covenants between the tenants. When drafting the lease on behalf of a landlord, therefore, you should ensure that such a scheme is set up.

It is unlikely that this will be necessary with regard to payment of the service charge provisions as the landlord/management company will be able – and anxious – to recover this. But due to the close proximity of flat tenants, it is usual to find that the tenants are subject to a wide range of covenants controlling their use of the units. So there will be covenants against business use and against causing a nuisance to the neighbours, for example, by noise. If these are to be enforced it will be a matter for the flat owners themselves as they are the ones affected by any breach.

37.7.2   What to look for

You should check the following:

(a)   There should be a covenant by the landlord in the lease that he will impose the same covenants in all the flat leases.

(b)   There should then be a covenant by the landlord to enforce all the covenants in the lease against another flat owner on the request of another tenant. This will, of course, be at the requesting tenant's expense. There is often a proviso that the landlord is obliged to commence proceedings only if counsel's advice is produced recommending such a course of action. The advantage of this kind of clause is that it will enable the enforcement of both negative and positive covenants.

(c)   Another method of enforcement is a scheme of development, often in freehold land referred to as a 'building scheme', which works in the same way in leasehold flats as well. This will enable any flat owner to sue any other directly, ie, without the landlord's assistance. This only works, though, in relation to negative (restrictive) covenants, for example those restricting the use of the property. You should check to ensure that the basic requirements of such a scheme are present, ie, that the lease contains statements that it is intended to impose the same covenants on all the flats and that it is the intention of the parties that they should be mutually enforceable.

Another possibility is to make use of the provisions of the Contracts (Rights of Third Parties) Act 1999. This allows someone who is not a party to a contract to sue on it, provided that it purports to confer a benefit on him. The third party must be expressly identified, either by name, or as a member of a class, or as answering a particular description, but need not be in existence when the contract is entered into. Thus, if the covenant purports to benefit 'the Tenants for the time being of the other flats in the Building', this would allow both present and future tenants to enforce the covenant.

37.8   Forfeiture clause

A proviso for a re-entry or forfeiture clause is an essential part of a fixed-term lease. It enables the landlord to terminate the lease because of the tenant's breach of covenant. An express forfeiture provision is essential; without such a clause a landlord would be unable to remove a tenant until the end of the fixed term even though he was not complying with the covenants in the lease. The clause should give the landlord the right to forfeit if the rent is a specified number of days in arrears (eg, 21 days) and for breach of any other covenant. However, despite the existence of the clause, a landlord will not be able to forfeit for covenants other than non-payment of rent unless he has previously served a notice on the tenant under s 146 of the LPA 1925. A court order will be required if possession cannot be acquired peaceably, and is always necessary in the case of residential property. The Commonhold and Leasehold Reform Act 2002 has introduced severe restrictions on a landlord's right to forfeit residential leases. No forfeiture is possible in the case of non-payment of sums of money not exceeding £350 unless the sum has been outstanding for more than three years. For all other breaches, the landlord cannot forfeit unless the tenant has either admitted the breach, or a court or the Leasehold Valuation Tribunal has determined that there is in fact a breach of covenant.

In addition to being able to forfeit for breaches of the lease, it is common to find in leases of commercial premises, that the landlord is entitled to forfeit the lease in the event of the tenant becoming insolvent. Given that the tenant will be paying an open market rent for the property, the landlord's concern is obvious: it is likely that the tenant will be unable to pay the rent on the next occasion it falls due, and the landlord may not want to have to wait until this date arrives to begin the process of forfeiting the lease. In the case of residential long leases, however, such a provision should be resisted. The tenant is likely to be paying a comparatively small sum in rent and so the landlord's concerns (above) do not apply. Furthermore, the lease will represent a valuable capital asset for the tenant which he will not want to lose, especially if in financial difficulties.

37.9   Unfair Terms in Consumer Contracts Regulations 1999

As explained at **3.12.2**, the Unfair Terms in Consumer Contracts Regulations 1999 (SI 1999/2083) apply to leases made between someone acting in the course of a business (eg, a builder or professional landlord) and a consumer (ie, a private individual). They do not apply to commercial leases. The Regulations require the lease to be drafted in plain English, and there must not be a significant imbalance in the parties' rights and obligations to the disadvantage of the consumer. Any term which is held to be unfair will be void and unenforceable, although the rest of the document will remain valid. This must be borne in mind when drafting any lease to which the Regulations apply.

The Office of Fair Trading has published guidelines with regard to the drafting of short-term residential leases. The guidelines suggest that the following terms may well be void if contained in a short-term tenancy agreement:

(a)   absolute prohibitions on both assignment and sub-letting;

(b)   absolute prohibitions on keeping pets;

(c)   a traditional forfeiture clause; and

(d)   requirements to keep the premises clean and tidy.

Chapter 38

The Landlord and Tenant Act 1954, Part II

38.1 Introduction

'Security of tenure' is a generic phrase given to statutory rights granted to tenants to protect their interest under their leases. This could include, amongst other things, the right to renew or extend an existing tenancy. The exact nature of the protection given depends on the type of tenancy (there are, for example, separate regimes in respect of agricultural land or residential premises). This chapter is concerned with the protections made available to tenants of business premises which are contained in the Landlord and Tenant Act 1954 ('the Act').

The Act gives security of tenure to tenants who occupy premises for business purposes. A business tenancy will not come to an end at the expiry of a fixed term, nor can a periodic tenancy be terminated by an ordinary notice to quit. Instead, the tenancy will continue after the contractual termination date until it is ended in one of the ways specified by the Act. When it is terminated under the Act, the tenant has the right to apply to the court for a new lease to be granted and the landlord can oppose this new lease only on the grounds laid down in the Act. Any such new tenancy will also be protected under the Act. If the tenant has to vacate the premises, he may be entitled to compensation.

The Government has reformed various key aspects of the Act using the procedure laid down by the Regulatory Reform Act 2001. These changes came into force on 1 June 2004.

38.2 When does the Act apply?

Section 23(1) provides that:

> ... this Act applies to any tenancy where the property comprised in the tenancy is or includes premises which are occupied by the tenant and are so occupied for the purpose of a business carried on by him or for those and other purposes.

The various parts of this provision must be looked at separately.

38.2.1 There must be a 'tenancy'

In order for the Act to apply, the person claiming security of tenure must occupy under the terms of a 'tenancy' (or 'lease'). For the purposes of the Act, the definition of tenancy includes an agreement for a lease and an underlease. Security of tenure will not be available if the person seeking to claim such rights merely occupies under a licence.

Deciding whether a particular arrangement has given rise to a lease or a licence will be a question of fact in each case. In the light of case law, the basic position is that a lease will be held to have been granted if the occupier has been given exclusive possession of the property for a fixed period of time and is paying a rent (see **3.10** for more details). This is a test of substance and not form and so even if a document calls itself a licence, the courts may still hold that what the parties have created is a lease.

Certain tenancies are specifically excluded from the protection of the Act (see **38.2.4**).

38.2.2   The premises must be occupied by the tenant

Whether a tenant is in occupation is a question of fact. Occupation can be by the tenant personally, or through the medium of an agent or manager, or by a company owned by the tenant.

In the case of sub-lettings, if there is a sub-tenant in occupation of the whole of the premises originally let to the head-tenant, the head-tenant will not benefit from security of tenure as, by definition, he will not be in occupation. Instead, it will be the sub-tenant who will enjoy the benefit of these rights, provided the other qualifying conditions required by the Act are also satisfied. Equally, in the case of a sub-letting of part only of those premises, the head-tenant will be protected in relation to the part he still occupies for business purposes and the sub-tenant will be protected in respect of the part the sub-tenant occupies.

38.2.3   Occupied for business purposes

The tenant must be occupying for the purposes of a business carried on by him. 'Business' is widely defined and includes 'a trade, profession or employment and in the case of a 'body of persons' any activity carried on by them. 'Any activity' means just that; it need not be a business or commercial activity. So, running a tennis club or running a hospital have both amounted to a business use under the final part of this definition, when carried on by a body of persons.

The business user need not be the sole purpose of occupation. The Act will still apply as long as the business user is the main purpose and not merely incidental to a residential or other purpose. So a shop with a flat above will be within the Act; but if a residential tenant occasionally brings work home with him, this would not result in his tenancy coming within the Act.

38.2.4   Excluded tenancies

Various tenancies are excluded from protection under the Act. Amongst others, this includes the following:

38.2.4.1   Tenancies at will

A tenancy at will is a tenancy that can be terminated by either the landlord or tenant at any time. Such tenancies can arise both expressly and impliedly. A common example of when a tenancy at will can arise impliedly is where an individual is let into occupation before a formal tenancy is granted, pending the outcome of negotiations for the formal term.

38.2.4.2 Fixed-term tenancies not exceeding six months

These are excluded unless the tenancy contains any provision for renewing or extending the term beyond six months. Further, as an anti-avoidance measure, this exception will not apply if a tenant has already been in occupation for a period exceeding 12 months when the lease comes to be granted.

38.2.4.3 'Contracted-out' tenancies

Although contracting out of the Act is generally forbidden, s 38(4) allows the parties to agree that security of tenure under the Act should not apply to a given tenancy. This is only possible, however, in the case of fixed-term lettings. It is not possible to contract out in respect of a periodic tenancy.

For leases granted prior to 1 June 2004, the approval of the court to contract out had to be obtained prior to the grant of the lease. In the case of such leases, it is therefore important to check whether the necessary court order was indeed obtained.

For leases granted on or after 1 June 2004, a court order is no longer required and, instead, a notice procedure has to be complied with. The detail of this is as follows:

(a) the procedure must be completed either before the lease is granted or, if earlier, before the tenant becomes contractually bound to take the lease;

(b) the landlord must give the tenant notice in a prescribed form which contains a 'health warning', warning the tenant of the fact that he is agreeing to a lease without security of tenure and advising him to obtain professional advice;

(c) the tenant must then make a declaration (again in a prescribed form) that he has received the notice and agrees that the lease should be contracted out. If the tenant is given the notice less than 14 days before the grant of the lease (or, as the case may be, is given the notice less than 14 days before he becomes contractually bound to take the lease), the tenant's declaration must be made in the form of a statutory declaration before an independent solicitor;

(d) a reference to the service of the notice and the tenant's declaration must be contained or endorsed on the document creating the lease.

38.3 Continuation tenancies

A business tenancy within the Act will not come to an end on the expiry of the fixed term, but will continue on the same terms by virtue of s 24. Although it will continue at the same rent, the landlord is able to apply to the court under s 24A for an interim rent to apply until a new tenancy is granted (see **38.9**).

38.4 Termination under the Act

A business tenancy can be terminated only in one of the ways laid down by the Act:

(a) by the service of a landlord's notice under s 25;

(b) by the service of a tenant's request for a new tenancy under s 26;

(c) forfeiture;

(d) surrender;

(e) in the case of a periodic tenancy, by the tenant giving the landlord a notice to quit;

(f)   in the case of a fixed-term lease, by the tenant serving three months' written notice on the landlord under s 27. This cannot expire before the contractual expiry date;

(g)   in the case of a fixed-term lease, by the tenant ceasing to be in occupation for business purposes at the end of the lease. In such a situation, the tenant need give no notice or warning to the landlord: see *Esselte AB v Pearl Assurance plc* [1997] 1 WLR 891.

Note that a business lease can still be forfeited for breach of covenant in the usual way. Apart from forfeiture, the usual methods of termination are the s 25 notice (see **38.6**) and the s 26 request (see **38.7**).

38.5   The competent landlord

The Act provides that the conduct of the various procedures under it (such as, for example, serving a s 25 or s 26 notice) must be carried out between the tenant and the tenant's 'competent landlord'. In the case of a lease granted straight out of a freehold, the position is simple: the competent landlord will be the freeholder. The position is more complicated in the case of a sub-lease and is best illustrated by a diagram and explanation:

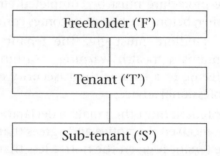

Under s 44 of the Act, a sub-tenant's competent landlord is defined as the person who has a superior tenancy which will not come to an end within 14 months or, if there is no such person, the freeholder.

Applying this to the diagram above, what this means is that if T does not enjoy security of tenure under the Act (say, for example, T has sub-let the whole of the premises to S and so is no longer in occupation for the purposes of the Act), whether T will be S's competent landlord is simply determined by how long T's lease has left to run. If the lease has more than 14 months left to run, T will be S's competent landlord but, if less than that, T will not be S's competent landlord and instead it will be F.

The position is different if T's lease does enjoy security of tenure (say, for example, T has only sub-let part of the premises to S and so remains in occupation for the purposes of the Act). If no steps have been taken to terminate T's lease, T will be S's competent landlord and this is the case even if T's *contractual* term has 14 months or less to run: the operation of the Act means that this lease will automatically be continued when it ends. However, once a s 25 or s 26 notice to terminate T's lease has been served, T's lease will (as will be seen at **38.6** and **38.7**) terminate within 14 months and so T will cease to be S's competent landlord and instead it will be F.

Mechanisms exist under the Act to allow the parties to determine who is the competent landlord at any given time.

38.6   The section 25 notice

The usual way for a landlord to begin the process of terminating a lease is by serving notice on the tenant under s 25 of the Act.

38.6.1   The prescribed form

The notice must be in the prescribed form and must be given not less than 6 months, nor more than 12 months, prior to the date of termination specified in it. The date of termination specified cannot be before the contractual termination date of the lease but can be, and often is, after it. Apart from this, there is no requirement for the notice to expire on any particular day, as long as it is of the correct length.

The notice must also state whether or not the landlord will oppose an application by the tenant to the court for a new tenancy, and, if so, on which of the statutory grounds he will rely. The tenant has the right to apply for a new lease, but the landlord can oppose that application on one of seven grounds set out in s 30 of the Act (see **38.8**). The landlord is only able to rely on the grounds of opposition stated in his s 25 notice. However, commonly, the landlord will be willing to grant a new lease. He will be ending the current lease so that a new tenancy can be granted on different terms, usually a higher rent. The landlord must indicate his proposals as to the terms of the new lease in the s 25 notice.

38.6.2   The application to the court

If the landlord has indicated in his s 25 notice that he will not oppose the grant of a new tenancy, the parties will now enter into negotiations for the grant of a new lease. But there is still a danger to the tenant. Unless he applies to the court before the expiry of the s 25 notice, he will lose his rights under the Act. The application is usually made to the county court. This time limit can be extended by agreement between the parties – eg, where they are near to agreement on the terms of a new lease and wish to avoid the expense, etc of court proceedings. It is also possible for the landlord to make the application to the court for a new lease to be granted – eg, where the tenant is thought to be unreasonably dragging out the negotiations. Where the landlord is not opposing the grant of a new tenancy, it is unusual for applications to proceed to a hearing, the parties usually reaching agreement as to terms.

If the landlord has indicated that he will oppose the grant of a new tenancy, the tenant's only chance of obtaining a new lease is to apply to the court within the time limits stated above. As an alternative, the landlord can pre-empt this by applying for an order to terminate the lease on the grounds stated in his s 25 notice (but not if an application has already been made by the tenant asking for the lease to be renewed).

38.7   The section 26 request

Rather than wait for the landlord to serve a s 25 notice, the tenant can often take the initiative and serve a request for a new tenancy under s 26. However, this procedure is not available to periodic tenants, or those for a fixed term of one year or less. The s 26 notice must again be in a prescribed form. It must state the proposed terms of the new tenancy and the date on which it is to begin. This date must be not less than 6 months before nor more than 12 months after service and cannot be before the contractual termination date.

If the landlord wishes to oppose the grant of a new tenancy, he must serve a counter-notice on the tenant within two months of the service of the tenant's s 26 request. He must also state his s 30 ground(s) of opposition. If the landlord does this, the tenant must ensure that he applies to court for a new lease or he will lose his rights under the Act. The tenant must make this application prior to the commencement date of the new tenancy specified by him in his s 26 request (unless the landlord agrees an extension of this time limit). As an alternative, the landlord can pre-empt this by applying for an order to terminate the lease on the grounds stated in his counter-notice (but not if an application has already been made by the tenant asking for the lease to be renewed).

If the landlord does not wish to oppose the grant of a new tenancy, he need not serve a counter-notice. The parties will then negotiate the terms of the new lease. However, as with s 25 notices, the tenant must ensure that, if negotiations drag on, an application to court is made before the commencement date of the new tenancy specified by him in his s 26 request or lose his rights under the Act. Again, the parties can agree to extend this time limit and if negotiations are continuing satisfactorily, this is the most sensible method of proceeding.

Although normally a tenant will be best advised not to serve a s 26 request (the sooner he gets a new lease, the sooner the rent will go up), there are circumstances where this may be advisable. For example, if the tenant has plans to sell the lease, he might find it more marketable if he has already been granted a new fixed term. Equally, if the rent in the open market is less than that presently payable under the lease, he may want a new lease as soon as possible at a new, lower market rent.

38.8 The landlord's grounds for opposition under section 30

When the landlord serves his s 25 notice, or his counter-notice to a tenant's s 26 request, if he wishes to oppose the grant of a new lease he must specify his grounds of opposition. Section 30 sets out seven grounds of opposition. The landlord can rely only on the grounds stated in his notice or counter-notice; no later amendment is possible. The grounds are as follows.

Ground (a)   Tenant's failure to repair

Ground (b)   Persistent delay in paying rent

Ground (c)   Substantial breaches of other obligations

All of these first three grounds are discretionary grounds. It is not sufficient for the landlord just to establish the ground; he also has to show that the tenant ought not to be granted a new tenancy in view of the facts giving rise to the ground.

Ground (d)   Alternative accommodation

This must be suitable to the tenant's needs and on reasonable terms.

Ground (e)   Sub-letting of part where higher rent can be obtained by single letting of whole building

This is little used, as the necessary requirements are seldom fulfilled. It applies only where the tenancy was created by the sub-letting of part of premises comprised in a superior tenancy and the head-landlord wishes to obtain possession so that he can let the whole as the combined rents from the sub-lettings are substantially less than can be obtained on a letting of the whole. Like grounds (a) to (c), this ground is also discretionary.

Ground (f)   The landlord intends to demolish or reconstruct and could not reasonably do so without obtaining possession

This is the most frequently used ground. The landlord must show that, on the termination of the tenancy:

(a)   he has a firm and settled intention to carry out the relevant work. This is a question of fact in each case, but the landlord's position will be strengthened if he can show, eg, that he has obtained the necessary planning permission and that his financial arrangements are in position; and

(b)   he intends to demolish or reconstruct the premises (or a substantial part of them), or to carry out substantial works of construction on the holding or a part of it; and

(c)   that he cannot reasonably carry out the work without obtaining possession. This again is a question of fact, but the landlord will not succeed if the tenant will agree to terms which allow the landlord access to carry out the work, which can then be reasonably carried out without obtaining possession and without substantially interfering with the tenant's use.

Ground (g)   Landlord's intention to occupy the holding for his own business or a residence

This is also a frequently used ground; again the landlord must have a firm and settled intention. There is, however, an important restriction on the use of this ground. A landlord cannot rely on it if his interest was purchased or created within five years before the ending of the current tenancy. The object of this provision is to prevent a landlord buying the reversion cheaply within five years of the end of the lease and then acquiring vacant possession using this ground. It is important to note, however, that the ground will be available to a landlord who buys property with vacant possession, lets it and then seeks possession within five years of buying it.

38.9   Interim rent

Where a tenant has applied to the court for a new tenancy, his current tenancy will not end on the expiry of the s 25 notice or s 26 request. Instead it will be continued, at the same rent, until three months after the conclusion of the proceedings. It is possible, however, for either landlord or tenant to apply for an interim rent to apply pending the outcome of the proceedings.

The interim rent will normally be the rent payable under the new lease, as calculated according to the rules set out in **38.10.3**. However, this will not be the case if the landlord is opposing the grant of a new tenancy, if the terms of the new lease are substantially different from the old one or rental values have changed significantly in the period before the grant of the new lease. In these cases the interim rent will be set as the market rent for a yearly tenancy of the premises 'having regard' to the rent under the old lease. This formula will generally result in a lower rent being assessed than would otherwise be the case – hence the popularity with landlords of penultimate day rent reviews — see **37.4.12**.

38.10   The terms of the new lease

38.10.1   The premises

The tenant is only entitled to a tenancy of the 'holding'. This means the property comprised in the current tenancy, but excluding any part not occupied by the tenant, ie those parts which the tenant has sub-let. However, the landlord (but not the tenant) has the right to insist that any new tenancy will be a tenancy of the whole of the originally demised premises, ie, including those parts sub-let.

38.10.2 Duration

This will be such as is reasonable in the circumstances but cannot exceed 15 years; it will normally be much less, for example, five or seven years.

38.10.3 The rent

This is the open market rent having regard to the other terms of the tenancy. But in assessing this, the court must disregard.

(a)   the fact that the tenant and his predecessors have been in occupation;

(b)   any goodwill attached to the holding;

(c)   any effect on rent of any improvements voluntarily carried out by the tenant during the tenancy; and

(d)   in the case of licensed premises, any addition in value due to the tenant's licence.

The court can insert a rent review clause in the lease, even though there was not one in the previous tenancy.

38.10.4 Other terms

In the absence of agreement, these will again be fixed by the court, which must have regard to the terms of the current tenancy and all other relevant circumstances. It is likely that the new terms will be much the same as the old. If a party wishes to change the current terms, the case of *City of London Real Property Co Ltd v O'May* [1983] 2 AC 726, establishes that it is for the party wanting a change to justify that change. The change must also be fair and reasonable.

38.10.5 Commencement of the new lease

Any new lease ordered by the court will not commence until three months after the proceedings are 'finally disposed of'. This is when the time limit for appeal has elapsed, ie, four weeks after the order. The new lease will thus commence three months and four weeks after the order.

If the tenant finds the terms of a new lease ordered by the court unacceptable (eg, as to rent), he may apply for the order to be revoked. Note that the landlord has no such right; if he is unhappy with the terms of the new lease, his only remedy is to appeal.

38.11   Compensation for failure to obtain a new lease

38.11.1 Availability

If the tenant does not obtain a new lease, he may be entitled to compensation. It is available only in the following circumstances:

(a)   where the landlord's s 25 notice or counter-notice to a s 26 request specifies only one or more of grounds (e), (f) and (g) (see **38.8**); or

(b)   where the landlord has specified one or more of grounds (e), (f) or (g) along with other grounds, and the court refuses to grant a new tenancy solely on one or more of grounds (e), (f) or (g), ie, the no-fault grounds (see **38.8**).

38.11.2 Amount

The amount of compensation will be equivalent to the rateable value of the holding, unless the tenant and his predecessors in the same business have been in occupation for at least 14 years, when it will be twice the rateable value.

38.11.3 Contracting out

Any agreement restricting or excluding the payment of compensation is void if the tenant or his predecessors in the same business have been in occupation for five years or more. This means that contracting out is permissible in circumstances where the tenant has been in occupation for less than five years.

Chapter 39

The Rights of Residential Occupiers

39.1 Introduction

One major problem for a developer (or, indeed, any other buyer) of the reversion to property let for residential purposes is ascertaining what, if any, security of tenure and other rights the residential tenant may have. The developer will be bound by these rights, and they may prevent him from putting the property to the use which he intended.

The law in this area is both extensive and complicated, the pitfalls many and deep, and the consequences for a buyer (and his legal adviser) very serious. A property lawyer needs to be alert to the problems so that, in appropriate circumstances, he knows to research further into the applicable law. The object of this chapter, therefore, is to provide an outline of the different rights which the occupier may have; it does not purport to provide a comprehensive statement of those rights.

39.2 What kind of rights may a residential tenant have?

The kind of rights that a buyer might find himself subject to may be summarised as follows:

(a) security of tenure, ie a right to remain in occupation even though the contractual tenancy may have ended;

(b) a right not to be evicted without a court order;

(c) a right compulsorily to acquire the freehold reversion (ie, without the landlord's consent);

(d) a right to take an extended lease (again without the landlord's consent);

(e) a right to have the contractually agreed rent reduced;

(f) a right of first refusal, ie, if the landlord wishes to make a disposal of the reversion, a right to compel the landlord to dispose of it to the tenants on the same terms;

(g) a right to have certain parts of the property kept in repair by the landlord, notwithstanding the terms of the tenancy agreement.

You should note that not all tenants will have *all* of these rights; most will have some of them, a few may have none at all.

39.3   Why is the law so complicated?

The protections given to tenants have generally tended to be granted piecemeal over the years as different problems have come to light. Often, legislation has been enacted to deal with a particular problem without any real thought as to how that particular piece of legislation fitted in with earlier legislation or the common law.

Further, social and political attitudes have changed over the years. This has resulted in some rights (particularly security of tenure) changing according to the political complexion of the government of the day. Usually, however, when any such changes are made, people with existing tenancies keep their existing protections, the changes only affecting tenancies granted after a specified date. So both old and new laws continue to be relevant.

39.4   How do I decide which tenants have which rights?

Although there are some rights which nearly all tenants will have, the existence of most rights depends upon the type of lease which the tenant has. Before you can advise as to these rights, you will need to obtain a copy of the lease. In particular, you will then need to find out the following:

(a)   the date of the grant of the lease;

(b)   the length of the lease;

(c)   the rent payable under the lease, both currently and at its commencement.

All of these factors are relevant in ascertaining the various rights which the tenant may have. Each of the various protections available to tenants has its own list of qualifying conditions, each of which must be tested against the particular lease with which you are dealing.

However, the protections given can be very broadly broken down into three categories:

(a)   Category 1: Rights given to most residential tenants, no matter what type of lease they have. These will include protection against harassment and eviction without a court order.

(b)   Category 2: Protections given to tenants of long leases who have bought their house or flat (usually by paying a lump sum 'premium' at the start of the lease) and are just paying a 'ground rent', ie, a comparatively small amount just for the use of the land on which the property is built. You should note, however, that this ground rent may well be more than a nominal amount; it could amount to several hundred pounds a year. The protections given may include rights to have a new lease and to buy the freehold. These are in addition to the rights in Category 1.

(c)   Category 3: Those rights given to tenants with short-term leases who are paying the full open market rent for the use of the accommodation. These may include security of tenure, the right to have the rent reduced, and repairs. Again, these are additional to the Category 1 rights.

Note that these three categories have no legal significance and are designated purely for explanatory purposes. There are, of course, exceptions. Some tenants with long leases may be paying a full occupation rent; equally, some short-term tenants may only be paying a ground rent. In such cases as these, the qualifying conditions of the various statutory protections will need to be carefully studied to ascertain the tenant's rights.

39.5   Is it a long lease?

The length of the lease is a relevant factor in much, but not all, of the legislation.

The basic dividing line between long and short leases is 21 years. If the lease exceeds 21 years in length, it will normally qualify as a long lease within Category 2; if it is for 21 years or less, it will normally be within Category 3.

You should note that when assessing the length of a lease, the deciding factor is the length of the lease when it was originally granted, *not* the length of the lease which remains unexpired. So a lease which has only three years left to run until its expiry date will still be a long lease if, when it was originally granted, it was granted for a term of more than 21 years.

39.6   Category 1: rights given to nearly all residential tenants

39.6.1   Protection from Eviction Act 1977

39.6.1.1   Unlawful eviction

The right not to be evicted without a court order is given to virtually all residential occupiers by s 1 of the Protection from Eviction Act 1977 ('PEA 1977'). Unlawful eviction is a criminal offence under this Act, and anyone so evicted has a right in civil proceedings to seek an injunction to restore them to occupation. Damages would also be payable.

There are various exceptions to this rule. Eviction will not be unlawful if the tenant and the landlord share living accommodation, or in the case of a letting for holiday purposes. It is also a defence for a landlord to establish that he reasonably believed that the tenant no longer lived in the premises.

39.6.1.2   Harassment

It is also a criminal offence to harass a tenant if the landlord knows (or has reasonable cause to believe) that the conduct is likely to cause the tenant to leave the premises (PEA 1977, s 1(3A)).

Civil damages will also be available. Exemplary and/or aggravated damages may well be relevant in cases of harassment. If the harassment actually causes the tenant to leave then substantial damages may be awarded under s 27 of the Housing Act 1988. These will represent the difference between the value of the property to the landlord with the tenant in occupation and the value with vacant possession, ie the damages represent the gain to the landlord rather than the loss to the tenant.

39.6.2   Criminal Law Act 1977 – use of violence to obtain entry

In addition to the prohibitions laid down by the PEA 1977, it is a separate offence under s 6(1) of the Criminal Law Act 1977 to use or threaten violence to secure entry to property if there is someone on the premises who is opposed to that entry.

39.7   Category 2: rights mainly given to tenants with long leases

39.7.1   Landlord and Tenant Act 1987, Pt I – the right of first refusal

Tenants of flats with long leases at low rents have a collective right to 'take over' any proposed disposal of the reversion by the landlord. This right is given by Pt I of the Landlord and Tenant Act 1987.

Exceptionally, the right is also given to statutory and protected tenants under the Rent Act 1977, even though they may not have long leases at low rents.

Prior to making a disposal, a landlord must give the tenants two months' notice. This takes effect as an offer to dispose to them on the same terms. This offer can then be accepted by at least 50% of the qualifying tenants.

Criminal sanctions are imposed if the landlord makes a disposition in breach of these requirements. Such a disposition would be valid to pass the legal estate, but the buyer has to notify the tenants of their rights to acquire from him on the same terms as he obtained the property. This is again backed up by criminal sanctions.

39.7.2 Leasehold Reform, Housing and Urban Development Act 1993

39.7.2.1 Enfranchisement, the right to buy the freehold

Under the Leasehold Reform, Housing and Urban Development Act 1993 ('LRHUDA 1993'), tenants with long leases of flats have a collective right to compel the landlord to sell the freehold to them. This is so whether or not the landlord intends to make a disposal (cf the Landlord and Tenant Act 1987, Pt I, at **39.7.1**).

At least half of the tenants in the block must join in the purchase. So, like the right of first refusal, this is not a right which can be exercised by individual tenants.

39.7.2.2 The right to an extended lease

The LRHUDA 1993 also gives qualifying tenants a right to seek a 90-year extension to their lease. This is an *individual* right which can be exercised by a tenant on his own without the consent or co-operation of the other tenants in the block.

39.7.3 Landlord and Tenant Act 1954, Pt I – security of tenure

You will normally think of security as being relevant only to short-term tenants (see **39.8** below), but thought also has to be given as to what will be the position of the tenant under a long lease when that comes to an end. A lease for 99 years seems to cause no worries about what will happen when it ends – unless it was granted (say) in the year 1910!

Many such long leases will never actually terminate because the tenants will buy the freehold, or will take an extended lease to put off the evil hour of termination for another 90 years. But protection is also given to those tenants who do not (or are unable to afford to) take advantage of such rights.

Protection is given by Pt I of the Landlord and Tenant Act 1954 (as amended). At the end of the tenancy, the tenant is allowed to remain in occupation as an assured tenant under the Housing Act 1988 (see **39.8.2**). He will thus have security of tenure, but will have to pay the full market rent for the house, rather than just a ground rent.

39.7.4 Leasehold Reform Act 1967

This Act gives tenants of long leases of houses (but not flats) the right to acquire the freehold, or to take a 50-year extension of their lease.

39.7.5 Protections in relation to service charges

Tenants with long leases of flats who pay a service charge often experience problems. They frequently complain that the amounts demanded by way of service charge are excessive, or that the services are not provided to an acceptable standard, or both. There are various statutory protections for tenants, amongst which are the following.

39.7.5.1 Restriction on forfeiture for non-payment of service charge (Housing Act 1996, ss 81–82)

A landlord cannot forfeit for failure to pay a service charge unless the amount of the charge has been agreed to by the tenant, or determined by the court or by arbitration.

39.7.5.2 Summary of costs incurred

Under the Landlord and Tenant Act 1985, a tenant is entitled to a summary of the costs incurred by the landlord. If there are more than four flats in the block, this summary must be certified by a qualified accountant.

39.7.5.3 Management audit

Under ss 76–84 of the LRHUDA 1993, tenants can appoint an accountant or a surveyor to conduct a management audit in relation to the provision of services. This will enable the tenant to check whether the landlord is discharging his management obligations effectively and efficiently; and whether the service charge is being applied in an efficient and effective manner.

39.7.5.4 Right to appoint surveyor as adviser

Under s 84 of the Housing Act 1996, a recognised tenants' association may appoint a surveyor to advise it about any matters relating to the payment of a service charge. The surveyor is given extensive rights to inspect the property and of access to documents in the landlord's control to enable him to advise on service charge matters.

39.7.5.5 Restrictions on the landlord's right to recover costs

By ss 18–30 of the Landlord and Tenant Act 1985, costs can be recovered only to the extent that they are reasonably incurred; and where they are incurred in the provision of services or the carrying out of works, only if those services or works are of a reasonable standard.

39.7.5.6 Determination of reasonableness of service charges

Either landlord or tenant can apply to the Leasehold Valuation Tribunal for a determination as to whether costs incurred were incurred reasonably, whether services were to a reasonable standard and as to whether the insurance provided or premiums payable are reasonable.

39.7.5.7 Estimates and consultation

Where costs are to be incurred on works above the limit specified in s 20(3) of the Landlord and Tenant Act 1985, the landlord must obtain at least two estimates for the work and submit these to the tenants and have regard to their observations on them.

39.7.5.8 Appointment of a manager or compulsory acquisition of the freehold

In cases of extreme bad management, the tenants can apply to the Leasehold Valuation Tribunal for a manager to be appointed to run the block, and even for the freehold to be acquired by them. These rights are given by the Landlord and Tenant Act 1987.

39.7.5.9 Commonhold and Leasehold Reform Act 2002

When this is brought fully into force it will greatly extend the protections given in relation to service charges. Tenants of flats will have to be provided with a summary of the service charge costs without request. Tenants also have the right to manage the block as of right without proof of fault on the landlord's part and without any payment.

39.8 Category 3: rights mainly given to short-term tenants

39.8.1 Rent Act 1977

39.8.1.1 Security of tenure

This Act primarily protects tenants of dwelling houses let by private landlords, ie not local authorities, whose tenancies were granted before 15 January 1989. (However, a tenancy granted on or after that date to an existing Rent Act tenant by the person who is then the landlord will, exceptionally, still be within the 1977 Act.)

Tenants are protected only if the rent payable is more than two-thirds of the rateable value of the property.

Security is given to tenants no matter what the length of the lease, but only if and so long as the tenant occupies the property as a home. At the end of a contractual tenancy the tenant can remain in possession as a 'statutory tenant'. The landlord will then be able to obtain possession only if he can prove one of the various grounds. Many of these are based on the tenant's default, eg, non-payment of rent.

39.8.1.2 Rent control

During both a contractual tenancy and a statutory tenancy, the agreed rent can be overridden by the tenant making an application for a 'fair rent'. The application is made to the rent officer (employed by the local authority), who must fix a rent according to a formula laid down by the Act. This is basically the open market rent, but reduced to remove the effects of scarcity.

39.8.1.3 Right of first refusal

Exceptionally, this right is also given to statutory and protected tenants under the Rent Act 1977 even though they do not have long leases at low rents. See Category 2 (**39.7**) for more details of this right.

39.8.2 Housing Act 1988 (as amended)

39.8.2.1 Security of tenure

This Act applies to lettings of dwelling houses by private landlords on or after 15 January 1989 (except those to existing Rent Act tenants by their present landlord). It introduces two types of tenancy: the assured tenancy (sometimes referred to as an 'ordinary' assured tenancy), and the assured shorthold tenancy, which is often just referred to as a 'shorthold'.

39.8.2.2   Assured tenancies

These offer wide-ranging security of tenure, much the same as under the Rent Act 1977. So, a landlord cannot obtain possession unless he can prove a ground for possession, even though the contractual tenancy has ended. This Act applies, however, only if and so long as the tenant occupies the property as his only or main home. There are various other conditions which must be fulfilled, for example the rent must be over £250 per year (£1,000 in Greater London), but not exceeding £25,000 per year.

39.8.2.3   Assured shorthold tenancies

This is a type of assured tenancy, but offering a tenant no security of tenure; the landlord is guaranteed possession. However, the landlord does need to give the tenant two months' notice before possession can be obtained.

For lettings entered into before 28 February 1997, a landlord could create a shorthold only if the letting complied with the following conditions:

(a)   the letting was preceded by the landlord giving the tenant a warning notice in the prescribed form;

(b)   the letting was for a fixed term (ie, not periodic);

(c)   the letting was for a minimum of six months; and

(d)   the letting contained no power for the landlord to bring it to an end during the first six months. However, a normal forfeiture clause would not fall foul of this requirement.

For lettings on or after 28 February 1997, all lettings otherwise within the Act are shortholds (ie, there is no need to comply with any of the above provisions) unless the landlord serves a notice stating that the letting is not to be a shorthold. Lettings after that date to existing ordinary assured tenants by their then landlord will, however, remain ordinary assured tenancies unless the tenant serves a notice stating that he wants the new letting to be a shorthold.

39.8.2.4   Rent control

There are no restrictions on the amount of the rent which a landlord can charge for an ordinary assured tenancy. The rent will be governed entirely by the terms of the agreement between the parties. However, if, in the case of a periodic tenancy, the agreement makes no provision for the landlord to increase the rent, the landlord can increase the rent only if he follows the correct statutory procedure.

There is a limited degree of rent control in relation to shortholds. If the tenant considers the rent to be excessive, he can refer it to the Rent Assessment Committee.

For tenancies entered into on or after 28 February 1997, the tenant can refer the rent to the Rent Assessment Committee only during the first six months of the letting.

39.8.2.5   Tenancy deposit protection

For assured shorthold tenancies granted on or after 6 April 2007 (including renewals for a fixed term of existing assured shortholds), any deposits paid to landlords or agents will be subject to new deposit protection legislation introduced under the Housing Act 2004. Any deposits must be paid either to the landlord's agent (backed by an insurance scheme), or into a separate custodial scheme. In either case, if there is a dispute about the deposit, each scheme contains dispute resolution mechanisms to resolve such difficulties.

39.8.3 Landlord and Tenant Act 1985 – repairs

By ss 11–14 of the Landlord and Tenant Act 1985, repairing obligations are imposed on landlords of certain short leases. The provisions apply to any lease of a dwelling house granted on or after 24 October 1961, provided that the term is for less than seven years. Periodic tenancies will be within the Act, even though they may have subsisted for longer than seven years.

In such leases there is an implied covenant by the landlord to repair the structure and exterior of the dwelling, and to keep in repair and proper working order the installations in the dwelling for the supply of water, gas, electricity, sanitation and for space and water heating.

These obligations can be contracted out of only with the consent of the court. Such consent is rarely sought.

Part VII Summary – Leases and Leasehold Conveyancing

Sub-section heading	Summary
Reasons for leasing	There are a number of reasons why parties prefer to lease property, whether as landlord or tenant, rather than selling or buying the freehold.
	First, the burden of both positive and restrictive covenants can be enforced against successors in title to the landlord or tenant. If a unit forms part of a building, where it is important that both types of covenant can be enforced, a lease is usually used as a result.
	Secondly, the length of a lease allows the parties flexibility. An individual may, for example, want to occupy premises only for a short period and therefore not commit to buying a freehold.
	Thirdly, a lease is a useful investment structure. A landlord can let out the property, enjoying income from the rent whilst retaining the capital asset in the form of the freehold. This can also suit a tenant, who may be able to pay rent but cannot afford the cost of buying the freehold.
The grant of a lease	This is the transaction undertaken to create the lease in the first place.
	In many cases, the procedure will broadly follow that for the sale of a freehold. The tenant will need to carry out searches and enquiries. The tenant will also need to investigate title: he can be bound by any matters affecting the freehold title just as if he were buying that freehold.
	The major additional step that needs to be taken is agreeing the terms of the lease that the parties will enter into. If the parties exchange contracts before the grant of the lease, the contract will have a copy of the agreed version of the lease annexed. The contract will commit the parties to enter into the lease in this form on completion.
	Following the grant of the lease, SDLT may need to be paid. In the case of the *grant* of a lease, SDLT can be charged both on any capital sum paid by the tenant and on the rent.
	If the lease is for a term in excess of 7 years, it will need to be registered at Land Registry.
The assignment of a lease	Should the tenant want to sell the lease once it has been granted, this is called 'assignment'. What the tenant will be selling will be the lease itself, in other words, what remains of the term originally granted, subject to all the other terms of the lease.
	In many cases, the procedure for the sale of a lease will broadly follow that used for the sale of a freehold. Any restrictions on the tenant's freedom to assign the lease should be checked and complied with.

Sub-section heading	Summary
	The lease will be transferred by a deed of assignment. If the lease is registered, this deed will be in the form of a TR1 just as for the sale of a freehold.
	Following assignment of the lease, SLDT may be payable on any purchase price charged to the assignee but not on the rent. This is payable at the same rates as for the sale of a freehold.
	If the leasehold title is registered, the assignee will need to be recorded as the new registered proprietor. The assignment of any unregistered lease which still has more than 7 years left to run will trigger first registration.
The contents of a lease – seven key points	The precise contents of a lease will depend on the given needs of the property. The following are seven key points to look for:
	• **The parties** The original landlord and tenant will inevitably be parties, but if the tenant has been required to supply a guarantor, the guarantor too will need to be a party.
	• **Term** A lease must be granted for a fixed period: the precise beginning and end of this should be checked. In addition, check for any break clause allowing a party to terminate the lease before the end of the term.
	• **Rent** This should state the level of rent and how and when it is payable. Unless the lease contains a provisions for review, the original rent stated is payable throughout the term.
	• **Covenants** These can be imposed on both the landlord and tenant. Check that they are not unduly onerous but also give each party the protection they need.
	• **Easements** In a sale of part, check that all necessary easements have been given to both parties.
	• **Alienation** An 'alienation clause' controls the tenant's freedom to assign or otherwise deal with the lease after it is granted. Check that the controls are appropriate for the situation in which the lease is being granted. For example, in a long residential lease, it is unusual to find much control on the tenant's freedom to assign the whole of the lease. Greater control on assignment can be expected in a commercial lease.
	• **Forfeiture** This is the right for the landlord to terminate the lease in the event of breach by the tenant of the terms of the lease. All well-drafted leases contain such provisions. A tenant's solicitor should ensure that the clause is not too onerous. If, at a later date, the landlord needs to exercise the right to forfeit, he must ensure that he complies with the terms of this clause in order to do so successfully.

Sub-section heading	*Summary*
Security of tenure under the Landlord and Tenant Act 1954	The Landlord and Tenant Act 1954 (the Act) grants important rights to tenants of business premises. The Act applies if three conditions are met: • there is a lease (as opposed to a licence) of the property; • the tenant is in occupation; and • that occupation is for business purposes. In addition, certain exceptions exist under the Act and none of these must apply. If the Act applies, the lease does not automatically end on the contractual determination date. Instead, the lease can be brought to an end only as permitted under the Act. The tenant can apply for a renewal of the lease, which can be opposed by the landlord only if it can prove certain grounds. Additionally, the tenant may be entitled compensation if unsuccessful in its application to renew the lease. The landlord has three options if it wants to bring the lease to an end. It can: • forfeit the lease if the tenant is in breach; • negotiate a surrender (if the tenant is willing); or • serve notice under s 25 of the Act. This must specify the grounds on which the landlord intends to rely to oppose the tenant's right to renew. The notice must state a date on which the current lease will end, which cannot be earlier than the contractual termination date of the lease but can be later. It must be served not less than six nor more than 12 months before the termination date specified in it. The tenant must apply to court for a new lease, if one has not already been agreed before the termination date specified, or it will lose its rights under the Act.

Part VIII

SALES OF PART AND NEW PROPERTIES

Chapter 40

Sales of Part

40.1 Introduction

A sale of part is a more complex transaction than the sale of the whole of the seller's interest in a particular piece of land, and some matters additional to those relevant to a sale of the whole must be considered. This chapter deals only with those matters which are exclusive to sales of part. Reference should also be made to **Chapter 15**, which deals with drafting the contract.

40.2 Describing the land

The description of the land in the seller's existing register of title (or title deeds) must be adapted to provide a new, accurate description of the property which is being sold. It will be necessary to describe the land in the particulars of sale of the contract by reference to a plan which shows clearly the extent of the land being sold and, where relevant, the extent of the land being retained in the seller's ownership. If the plan is not drawn to scale, the measurements of the land should be set out in the verbal description contained in the particulars of sale. For more details on the use of plans, see **15.5.1**.

40.2.1 Retained land

It will usually be necessary to refer to the land which is to remain in the ownership of the seller after the sale (eg, in relation to easements and reservations). Such land must, therefore, be defined verbally in the contract and marked clearly on the plan attached to the contract. The Standard Conditions of Sale contain no adequate definition of retained land.

40.2.2 Form CI

Where the sale comprises a plot on a building estate, the whole of which is registered at Land Registry, the seller will frequently have deposited a site plan at Land Registry and the official copies which are issued will give a certificate in Form CI in lieu of a title plan. This certificate states that the plot lies within the boundaries of the site plan deposited at the Registry but does not specifically identify the plot. It will also indicate whether any of the matters referred to in the charges register (eg, easements or covenants) affect that particular plot.

40.3 Grants and reservations of easements

On a sale of part of land, unless excluded, certain easements can be impliedly granted in favour of a buyer. This includes easements of necessity and common intention. In addition, s 62 of the LPA 1925 and the rule in *Wheeldon v Burrows* (1879) 12 Ch D 31 may give the buyer certain rights over the land retained by the seller for the benefit of the part sold. Section 62 of the LPA 1925 may operate to create easements over retained land where, at the time of sale, the two tenements are in separate occupation. Further, the rule in *Wheeldon v Burrows* will impliedly grant as easements to the buyer all rights which are continuous and apparent and necessary to the reasonable enjoyment of the property sold, and actually in use at the time of the sale. So if, at the time of the sale, a drain from the land being sold passes through the retained land, the right to use this drain will be impliedly granted to the buyer as a legal easement. However, rights that do not already exist cannot be implied under *Wheeldon v Burrows*. So if the land being sold did not already have the benefit of the drain at the time of sale, a right to lay one would not be implied.

Thus, the rule in *Wheeldon v Burrows* will frequently not give the buyer all the easements he needs. On the other hand, it may inadvertently give a buyer more than the seller intends to grant. It is, therefore, considered preferable to exclude the implied grant rules by a special condition in the contract. Such a condition might be worded as follows:

> The transfer will contain a declaration that it will only operate to grant those easements expressly referred to and will not operate or be construed to imply the grant of any other easement.

The question of easements is then dealt with by express conditions in the contract granting specific easements tailored to suit the particular circumstances of the case. In such a case, the buyer should check very carefully to ensure that the property being bought will acquire all the easements necessary for its full use and enjoyment. The following may be relevant, depending upon the circumstances:

(a)   a right of way to gain access to the property. Ensure that this is at all times, for all purposes, and allows access both on foot and by motor vehicles;

(b)   a right for the usual services to reach the property – drains, water, gas, electricity, telephone, etc;

(c)   a right of access to maintain all these;

(d)   a right of light; and

(e)   a right of support. Although there is a natural right for a piece of land to be supported by neighbouring land, there is no such right for the land to be supported where it has the extra weight of a building on it. This must be expressly granted. Although a right of support will normally be implied between terraced and semi-detached houses, if the implied grant rules are excluded, these will also need expressly granting.

If any rights are to be shared by the buyer and seller, for example use of drains or driveway, a covenant to maintain or contribute to the maintenance costs should also be imposed. Rights to enter to effect that maintenance (and make good any damage so caused) may be needed, as appropriate.

Remember that the seller can grant easements only over his own land; if the services, access, etc, are over someone else's land, the seller must either be passing on the benefit of rights already granted to him, or will have to negotiate with the owner of the land for a new deed of grant.

On the sale of, for example, a building plot, it is likely that the drains, etc will not be in existence at the time of the sale so that the easements for laying and using them will arise in the future. So you will be granting a future interest in land which will need to comply with the rule against perpetuities. This basically requires the new easement to come into existence within the perpetuity period of 21 years, so it is often not a problem where the building work, etc is going to be carried out within a much shorter time scale. However, it is thought safest to take advantage of the ability to specify expressly a longer perpetuity period and specify a period of 80 years (the maximum allowed under the Perpetuities and Accumulations Act 1964) within which the rights can arise.

Where easements are being granted (or reserved in favour of the seller), the exact route of the right of way/drain, etc will need indicating clearly on the plan.

40.3.1   Reservations for the seller

Section 62 of the LPA 1925 and the rule in *Wheeldon v Burrows* operate only in the buyer's favour. There is no reciprocal section or case which entitles the seller to easements over the land being sold off (other than easements of necessity and common intention). For this reason it is important to consider what rights the seller will need to exercise over the land being sold (eg, passage of pipelines, drainage, etc) and to reserve these expressly in the contract.

40.3.2   Rights of light and air

Rights of light and air may pass to the buyer either under s 62 of the LPA 1925, or under the rule in *Wheeldon v Burrows*. If the buyer were to acquire rights of light and air, this might enable him at some future time to frustrate the seller's plans to build close to the boundary of the two properties. Thus the gain of rights of light and air by the buyer may be balanced by a consequent loss of amenity value to the seller's land. As the existence and extent of these rights may be difficult to ascertain, since they are not visible to the eye, it is usually considered necessary to exclude the buyer's right to easements of light and air by an express condition in the contract which provides for the insertion of a provision to this effect in the purchase deed. Standard Condition 3.4 (SCPC 3.3) contains a provision to this effect, although many solicitors prefer to state it expressly as a special condition. The specimen clause given in **40.3** would exclude rights of light and air along with all other impliedly granted easements. If all implied grants are not to be excluded, then a condition in the following terms should be used:

> There is not included in the sale any easement of light or air which would or might interfere with or restrict the free use of the retained land for building or any other purpose. The transfer to the buyer must expressly exclude those rights.

40.3.3   Fall-back provisions

Standard Condition 3.4 (SCPC 3.3) provides for the exclusion of rights of light and air and for the mutual grant of easements and reservations on a sale of part, but the rights given by this condition are limited and imprecise and will in most cases be inadequate to deal effectively with the parties' needs on a sale of part of land. This condition should therefore be regarded as a fall-back provision, to be used only in a case where the contract has omitted to deal expressly with these matters.

40.4   Imposition of new covenants

On a sale of part, the seller will frequently wish to impose new covenants on the buyer for the protection of the retained land. All such new covenants will need to be stated expressly in the contract; none will be implied. The seller should consider imposing some or all of the following, depending upon the circumstances of the case:

(a)   restrictions on use, for example use as a single private dwelling house in the occupation of one family only;

(b)   restrictions on building, for example no building without seller's consent; or seller to approve plans; or no building within (say) 10 metres of the boundary line;

(c)   not to cause nuisance or annoyance to the seller and neighbouring owners;

(d)   to erect and maintain boundary fence/wall; the materials, height, time limit for building, etc, must be specified; and

(e)   to contribute to the maintenance of shared facilities, for example drains, rights of way.

In the case of restrictive covenants (ie, all of the above except the fencing covenant, which is positive), care should be taken in the drafting to ensure that both the benefit and the burden will run to future owners of the land. The condition in the contract should state that the covenants, when entered into in the transfer, will be 'given for every part of the Retained Land and that it is intended that the burden of the covenants will run with every part of the Property'.

The seller should be reminded that positive covenants will not be enforceable against the buyer's successors in title (although the existence of a chain of indemnity and the impact of the principle of mutual benefit and burden in *Halsall v Brizell* should be borne in mind – see **3.5.3.1**).

When acting for a buyer, you should ensure that the covenants being imposed are not too onerous.

40.5   Consent of seller's lender

Where the land to be sold consists of part of the land which is mortgaged to the seller's lender, the seller must obtain his lender's consent to the sale at the earliest possible opportunity. The lender should be asked whether the repayment of the whole or any part of the mortgage is required out of the proceeds of the sale of part and, if part, how much. Arrangements must be made for the lender to release the land being sold from the mortgage at or before completion. In registered land, the release will be effected by Form DS3 (see **Appendix 10**) (accompanied by a plan to show the extent of the land being released). Alternatively, the release will be notified to the Registry electronically. In unregistered land, the lender will either give a deed of release, or he may prefer to be joined as a party to the conveyance in order both to release the land being sold and to give a receipt for the money being paid to him. An appropriate undertaking to discharge the mortgage should be obtained.

40.6   The purchase deed

As will be clear from **40.3** and **40.4**, perhaps the major difference between a sale of whole and a sale of part is the need to provide for the imposition of new covenants and easements. These will actually be imposed in the purchase deed, but must be provided for in the contract. This can be done in one of two ways. First, the contract can specify the terms that the purchase deed should contain (see, for example, the wording to exclude implied grant of easements in **40.3**). Alternatively, a copy of the agreed purchase deed containing all the relevant provisions can be annexed to the contract, with a special condition stating that the form of the purchase deed shall be that annexed to the contract. The wording of the provisions will need to be amended accordingly, and so, by way of example, as the exclusion of implied grant now appears in the purchase deed itself, should appear as a straightforward declaration as follows:

> It is hereby declared that this transfer only operates to grant those easements expressly granted and will not operate or be construed to imply the grant of any other easement.

As regards the purchase deed itself, if title is registered, the transfer must be in the form of Land Registry Form TP1 (see **Appendix 8**). This can also be used if the land being sold is unregistered, as the transaction will trigger the need for an application for first registration. Form TP1 is similar to Form TR1, used for a transfer of whole, but contains space for the new easements and covenants that may be required on a sale of part. All of the clauses referred to in **27.11** will be relevant to a sale of part, but the following will also be required, either in addition to or in substitution for the above.

40.6.1   Title number

The seller's existing title number is inserted in the document. A new title number for the part being sold will be allocated by Land Registry on registration of the transaction.

40.6.2   Description of land to be sold

A clear description of the land being sold must be included with reference to the plan annexed to the transfer. The land retained by the seller should be expressly defined and identified on the plan. The land should be described as 'part of title number LM12037' (or as appropriate). The description of the land given in the contract may be adequate for these purposes.

40.6.3   Easements and reservations

Where the contract made provision for the grant of easements to the buyer or reservations in favour of the seller, these contractual provisions must be implemented by insertion expressly into the transfer. The contract will usually provide for the exclusion of the implied grant of easements. A declaration to this effect must be inserted in the transfer to activate this requirement.

40.6.4   New restrictive covenants

New restrictive covenants are frequently imposed in a contract for the sale of part of land, and these must be expressly set out in the transfer. Except where the land forms part of a building scheme, covenants are enforceable against subsequent owners of the land sold only if they are for the benefit of land retained by the seller and the burden of them is annexed to the land sold. Express words should be included to give effect to these principles. Frequently, a short reference only to easements, covenants, etc is made in the body of the deed, the detail of such matters being set out in numbered schedules at the end of the document.

40.6.5   Schedules

Schedules should appear after the main body of the deed, but above the attestation clauses, to ensure that they are incorporated as part of the signed document and that there cannot be any argument about them having been added to it at a later stage.

40.6.6 Building estates

Where the land being sold forms a plot on a building estate, the draft purchase deed will often be prepared by the seller and attached to the draft contract, so that in this situation the buyer has no discretion over its form or contents (see **Chapter 41**).

40.7 Completion and post-completion

40.7.1 Unregistered land

Where the land is presently unregistered, the seller will not be handing over his title deeds to the buyer on completion. The buyer should therefore verify his abstract or epitome against the original deeds and mark his abstract or epitome as examined against the original. Where the Protocol is used, the seller is required to mark the abstract as examined against the original title deeds before sending it to the buyer. The transaction will trigger first registration and so this procedure is necessary so that immediately after completion the buyer can produce proper evidence of the title to Land Registry with his application for first registration.

A note of any restrictive covenants imposed by the conveyance to the buyer (or a copy of that conveyance) should be retained by the seller, otherwise he will not have any evidence of those covenants when he comes to sell his own land at a later stage. New restrictive covenants will automatically be entered on the register of the new title on first registration.

40.7.2 Registered land

Where the seller's title is already registered, it is not necessary to provide for an acknowledgement for production of the deeds, because the buyer will obtain his own title number on registration of the sale of part. New restrictive covenants imposed by the transfer of part will automatically be entered on the charges register of the new title on registration.

Application for the registration of the dealing on Form AP1 (see **Appendix 8**) accompanied by such of the documents listed in **31.8.2** as are relevant to the transaction, must be made within the 30 working days protection period given by the pre-completion search. In the case of a sale of part, the search is submitted on Form OS2. This is essentially the same as Form OS1 used on the sale of whole, but reflects the nature of the transaction by identifying the property by its estate plan plot number (see **40.2.2**) or by a description and plan. Where the transfer imposes fresh restrictive covenants, a certified copy of it must also be supplied with Form AP1.

Chapter 41

New Properties

41.1 Introduction

The sale of a new property is a more complex transaction than the sale of an existing house or building, and some matters additional to those relevant to a sale of an existing house or building must be considered. This chapter contains a summary of the matters which are exclusive to new and recently built properties.

The main characteristics of this type of transaction which make it different from an ordinary sale and purchase are:

(a) it is a sale/purchase of a 'new property', ie, a house or flat being constructed by the seller;

(b) it is a 'sale of part'. The developer usually owns the whole site and is disposing of it in the form of housing plots (or, in the case of a flat development, the developer owns the whole of the block and is disposing of the flats individually). Issues relating to sales of part are considered in **Chapter 40**;

(c) as the developer is disposing of a number of properties, he may adopt a slightly different conveyancing procedure from that normally encountered. All the usual steps will be taken, but not always by the same person as in a normal transaction and sometimes in a different order. The developer adopts this different system for his own convenience (and to save expense) in dealing with a large number of sales simultaneously.

Note that, although this chapter relates to new properties, you should bear the points dealt with in mind not just when buying directly from the developer, but also when buying 'second hand', ie buying a recently constructed house or flat.

41.2 New property

41.2.1 Planning permission

Check whether planning permission has been granted. In particular, check whether any attached conditions have been or will be complied with. Bear in mind that the enforcement period for building works in breach of planning control is four years, so planning matters must be checked in the case of any purchase of a house or flat within four years of its construction. For details of planning control, see **Chapter 17**.

41.2.2 Building regulations consent

Check that building regulations consent was granted.

The Building Regulations control the methods and materials to be used in the construction of a property to ensure that proper standards are maintained in all new properties. Thus, the lack of building regulations consent in a recently constructed property may suggest that it may not have been constructed to the proper standards, and that it may be sensible to advise the client to point this out to his surveyor in order that a proper check on the structure of the property is made.

41.2.3 Structural guarantee

Some form of structural guarantee should be offered. Without this a buyer will not be in a position to secure a mortgage. If any structural defects develop after purchase, the buyer may not be able to obtain compensation from the developer as he may no longer be in business; building companies have a very high failure rate. A structural guarantee from an independent third party is thus essential and will inevitably be a condition of any mortgage offer in relation to a new or recently constructed house or flat.

In the residential context, the NHBC 'Buildmark' scheme is the most widely used. It provides a two-part guarantee. The developer agrees to be responsible to remedy all defects which occur within two years of purchase. In the case of default, the NHBC will itself step in. Similarly, if the developer becomes insolvent before completion of the house, the NHBC will make good any loss to a buyer, for example, in respect of the deposit.

After the first two years, the NHBC provides an insurance-style guarantee that it will rectify specified structural defects arising in the house during the next eight years. Structural defects are defined to exclude, for example, defective plasterwork or decorations. There is thus a 10-year guarantee offered. When buying a house (or flat) constructed within the previous 10 years, ensure that the property is covered by such a guarantee. Although the balance of the NHBC guarantee is sometimes expressly assigned to a subsequent buyer, the NHBC has publicly stated that it will honour its obligations whether or not the benefit has been assigned. Statistically, most defects occur between 5 and 10 years after construction, emphasising the importance of obtaining a structural guarantee even when not buying directly from the developer.

In the case of houses registered with the NHBC after 1 April 1999, the cover will also include the cost of cleaning up any contamination in the land on which the house is built; there is no such cover for houses registered with the NHBC before that date.

On the purchase of a new property, the contract with the developer should include a term that he is registered with the NHBC (and will continue to be so until completion) and that on exchange he will offer to enter into this 10-year guarantee. Despite this contractual term as to membership, the buyer's solicitor should not exchange without checking that the builder is actually registered with the NHBC. This can be done online via the NHBC website. Alternatively, it would be in order to accept an undertaking from the builder's solicitor on exchange that the builder is registered with the NHBC. On exchange, a separate 'offer of cover' (Form BM 1) will be handed over. The acceptance of cover (Form BM 2) should be signed by the client and returned to the NHBC. There is also a comprehensive guidance booklet handed over which the solicitor has to certify that he has given to his client, ie, the buyer. Once the property is completed, the NHBC will undertake a final inspection and, if all is satisfactory, will issue a 'cover note'. This confirms that the NHBC will provide the 10-year insurance cover once the acceptance of cover form has been returned to the NHBC. The builder's solicitor should send the cover note to the buyer's solicitor as soon as it has been received from the builder client. Under para 6.6.2 of the CML *Lenders' Handbook*, the solicitor acting for the lender is not able to submit the Certificate of Title to the lender (and thus request the mortgage advance) until this cover note has been received. In the case of flats, in addition to the 10-year notice in respect of the individual flat being bought, there will be a separate notice in relation to the common parts of the block.

Although the NHBC Buildmark scheme is by far the most common, other similar insurance-backed schemes do exist, for example, the Zurich Mutual Newbuild Scheme. Alternatively, if the building work was supervised by, for example, an architect or surveyor, a certificate to that effect will allow a claim to be brought against such person in the case of structural defects arising out of his negligent supervision. The effectiveness of such action, however, may well be dependent upon his having professional indemnity insurance.

Where the new property is to be bought with the aid of a mortgage loan, the *Lenders' Handbook* contains a requirement that one or other of the above forms of protection is in existence. See para 6.6 of the *Lenders' Handbook*.

Note that subsidence is not generally covered by these schemes and so needs to be covered by the buyer's own insurance.

41.2.4 Estate roads

The new estate roads (being, at present, unadopted private roads) are likely to be 'adopted' (ie, become publicly maintained) at some point in the future (but be aware that sometimes they might not be). As between the developer and the buyer, there should be a clause in the contract that the developer will be responsible for making up the roads to the local authority's standard and keeping them in that condition until they are adopted at no extra cost to the house buyer.

The roads are usually one of the last things a developer will complete when he is building a housing estate, and so there is a risk that if he does become insolvent he will not have completed the roads. In that situation, when the roads are adopted, the properties 'fronting' onto the road might incur road charges if the highway authority has to spend money to 'make up' the road to its standard. The local authority will divide the cost of making up the road between 'frontagers', ie, the owners of the properties 'fronting' on to it. In this context, a house 'fronts' onto a road even if it is at the back of the property which adjoins the road, and even if the property in question has no access on to the road. There is thus a danger that having paid for the roads as part of the price of the house, the buyer will have to pay for them all over again. Obviously, there would be a right of action against the developer, but this will be only an academic right if he is insolvent.

To protect the owners of such properties from these charges, check to see that a Highways Act 1980 Section 38 Agreement has been entered into by the developer with the highway authority. This is an agreement between the developer and the highway authority that the developer will be responsible for the roads. Obviously, on its own it suffers from the same defect as the similar agreement between the developer and buyer, ie if the developer becomes insolvent. This agreement must therefore be supported by a financial bond, issued by a bank or insurance company, in a sufficient amount to cover against the developer defaulting on the Road Agreement. This, in effect, acts as an insurance policy against the developer defaulting and is paid for by the developer. If the developer does default, the bank or insurance company will pay out under the bond and so avoid the risk of the 'frontagers' having to meet the cost of making up the road.

It can take several years for the roads on a new estate to be adopted, particularly if it is a large estate which takes several years to be completed. Therefore, when buying a house or flat 'second hand', always check the results of the enquiries of the local authority carefully to see whether the roads have been adopted yet. If they have not, then the existence of the agreement and bond will still be relevant.

In cases where there is no agreement and bond, a mortgage lender will usually protect itself against the property owner having to pay road charges by making a retention from the advance of the estimated cost of those charges. This retention will be released only when the roads are adopted and may well cause the buyer financial problems on completion.

If an assessment to road charges is made by a local authority against a property, this will be registered as a local land charge. It is unlikely that any subsequent buyer would complete a purchase without this being discharged.

41.2.5 Drains and sewers

Similar problems can arise with regard to the new drains and sewers which will be necessary to serve the property. Check whether the ownership and maintenance of the drains has been or is to be transferred to the water authority. If the water authority were to adopt the drains without their having been constructed to the proper standards, there is a risk that the properties being served might incur charges. To protect the owners, ensure that a Water Industry Act 1991 Section 104 Agreement and Bond has been entered into. This works in a similar way to the Highways Act Agreement (see **41.2.4**).

41.3 Sale of part

41.3.1 Evidence of title

Evidence of title will be supplied in the form of:

(a) *Unregistered title*: abstract/epitome of title in the usual form. However, as the original deeds, etc, will not be handed over on completion because the developer needs them to prove ownership of the remainder of the land, on completion the abstract/epitome, if not already marked, must be marked as a true copy of the original title documents.

(b) *Registered title*: official copies of the whole site, with title plan. With estate development, however, a Land Registry Form CI is often used instead of the title plan. This confirms that the plot being sold is within the developer's registered title, and indicates if any matters (eg, existing covenants in the charges register) affect that plot. The detail of this is considered at **40.2.2**.

41.3.2 Description of the property

Ensure that the contract contains a detailed description of the new property in the form of a verbal description and a professionally prepared plan.

41.3.3 Easements

Check that the contract provides for the grant to the buyer of all necessary easements. These must include:

(a) a right of way over the estate roads until adopted;

(b) a right to use the drains and sewers;

(c) a right to use all the pipes and cables for all the other services, for example gas, electricity, water, telephone, etc;

(d) rights of access to maintain all of these.

41.3.4 Reservations

The contract should also provide for easements to be reserved for the developer's retained land and the other houses/flats in the development, for example the right to run the services of water, gas and electricity across the buyer's property to the developer's adjoining land. The buyer should be told of the easements which will affect the property prior to exchange of contracts, although it is unlikely that the existence of such rights will restrict the client's proposed use of the property, if only because of the covenants that will be entered into restricting development (see **41.3.5** below). However, these easements will include a right of access onto the buyer's property for the purpose of inspection and maintenance of the various services, and the buyer must be made aware of this.

41.3.5 Covenants

New covenants will be created, some of a restrictive nature (eg, to use the property for residential purposes only) and some of a positive nature (eg, maintenance of boundary fences). Check that these are not too onerous and ensure that they are brought to the attention of the client. There is frequently a covenant restricting the use of the property to that of a single private dwelling house, and other restrictions are common, for example prohibiting the parking of caravans or boats, or making any alterations without the developer's consent. All of these could pose problems for a buyer with special plans for the property and should always be discussed with the client before contracts are exchanged.

41.3.6 Existing mortgages

Check to see if the developer's title is mortgaged. If so, the lender's release is required for the sale. This release should be in Form DS3 for a registered title (see **Appendix 8**), or a Deed of Release if the title is unregistered. You should ensure that the appropriate document is available at completion, and that if there is a floating charge in favour of the developer's bank (to finance the development) a certificate of non-crystallisation will be handed over on completion.

41.4 Conveyancing procedures

41.4.1 Contract

The contract will be in the developer's standard form. Although this will normally incorporate the Standard Conditions of Sale, it may not be in familiar form. The developer is usually unwilling to accept amendments to this standard form contract. For his own administrative convenience he will want to ensure that every property in the development is sold on exactly the same terms.

In addition to dealing with the sale of the property, the contract may contain clauses dealing with the construction of the property, for example, clauses requiring that the property is to be built in accordance with plans and specifications, time limits for building, clauses allowing for variations to original plans, etc. (Alternatively, this could be included in a separate building contract.)

41.4.2   Transfer

The draft transfer (and the engrossment of the transfer) is prepared by the developer (at the buyer's cost) in standard form, and is attached to and forms part of the contract. It will contain all of the new covenants and easements being imposed as a result of the sale. As with the contract, the developer will usually be unwilling to accept any amendments to this. The purchase deed will contain the detailed description of the property, easements and covenants.

41.4.3   Pre-contract package

41.4.3.1   General principles

The developer will need to provide the buyer with a bundle of information at the start of the transaction, just as in the case of the sale of the whole of an existing freehold property. In the context of a residential development, although the developer could adopt the National Conveyancing Protocol, it will not usually do so as such, but it will, at the start of the transaction, supply a package of information which is very similar to the Protocol package but in a different form. This will usually include copies of relevant planning permissions, building regulations consents, Highways Act and Water Industry agreements and bonds. In addition, the draft transfer will be included, as it is usually annexed to and forms part of the draft contract. Title will be deduced as stated above, but the standard SPIF will not be used. However, similar information will be given on a printed sheet prepared specifically for that development.

41.4.3.2   Home Information Packs and Energy Performance Certificates

The Home Information Pack Regulations 2007 apply to transactions involving the sale of new residential properties in the same way as for the sale of existing residential properties. The HIP must contain the same prescribed information and in the same manner as for the sale of an existing residential building. Subject to certain transitional provisions, this will need to include an EPC. Where the property in not physically complete at the first point of marketing, a 'Predicted Energy Assessment' must be provided.

It should be noted that, from 6 April 2008, EPCs are needed for the sale or rent of all buildings with a floor area in excess of 500 square metres which are not dwellings, which will include commercial premises.

41.4.4   Completion date

The completion date in the contract will not be a definite fixed date. This is because, when a property is in the course of construction, the developer cannot predict with certainty the precise date when it will be available for occupation. In such cases, the contract will usually provide for completion of the transaction to take place within a specified number of days (eg, 20 days) after the developer certifies that the property is completed and ready for habitation.

This contractual provision could cause further problems for a buyer who has a contract for the sale of his present house. It may prove difficult to synchronise completion of both sale and purchase, as it is unlikely that the buyer's purchaser would be willing to agree to a similar condition in the sale contract. There are various practical solutions. The ideal is to wait until the house is completed before exchanging contracts and thus agreeing a fixed completion date. This is sometimes possible. In other cases, the developer will be able to give an indication as to when the property will be finished, for example 'about the last week in

February'. Having taken the client's instructions and explained the problem to him, it would be possible to exchange on the dependent sale with a completion date of (say) 1 March. Thus if the house were to be completed as estimated, or a week later or even a week earlier, it would still be possible to complete both transactions in accordance with the terms of the respective contracts. The risks must be explained to the client, however, and if there is an exceptionally long delay in the completion of the new property, the danger of having to complete the sale and move into alternative accommodation must be fully discussed. You should ask the client to bear in mind also that in such a case there would be no question of claiming any compensation from the developer for the costs of this alternative accommodation. It has to be said that although this uncertain completion date could potentially lead to all sorts of disasters, it does not normally do so in practice. Developers and their solicitors are fully aware of the problems involved and will usually do their best to assist purchasers.

Part VIII Summary – Sales of Part and New Properties

Sub-section heading	Summary
Sales of part	
Overview	The conveyancing process for selling part, as opposed to the whole, of a property will in most respects be the same as for the sale of the whole. The major difference will be that the parties will need to consider what new covenants and easements will need to be created in order to make the sale of part work satisfactorily for the seller and buyer.
	These covenants and easements will be contained in the deed transferring title to the buyer, and their terms must be finalised before exchange. This can be done in one of two ways:
	• First, the contract could contain provisions which set out the wording of the new covenants and easements, and provide that this wording will be inserted into the purchase deed.
	• Alternatively, the parties can draft the purchase deed with these new covenants and easements already in it, and annex this to the contract. The contract will then provide that the parties will enter into the purchase deed in the form that has been annexed.
Form of transfer	In registered land, a special form of transfer, called a TP1, is used. It is essentially the same as a TR1 but has additional space to insert the new covenants and easements. In unregistered land, a traditional form of conveyance could be used, but in practice, a TP1 is often used instead.
Drafting the transfer	Most lawyers will use precedents to assist with drafting the transfer; but even then, free-hand drafting may be necessary from time to time. The terms of the transfer deed will, of course, depend on the specifics of the transaction, but the following five key points should always be considered:
	• **Definitions** The land being sold and the land being retained should always be clearly defined, usually by reference to a plan, which should also be defined. Other defined terms, such as the roads serving the estate, should also be considered as appropriate.
	• **Covenants** The covenants being given by the seller and buyer should be set out separately. Each section should be further sub-divided into positive and negative covenants, as the practical and legal effect of these are different.
	• **Easements** Those being granted to the buyer and those being reserved by the seller should be set out separately.

Sub-section heading	Summary
	• **Introductory wording for covenants and easements** Covenants and easements are interests in land. It is good practice to have appropriate introductory wording before each set of covenants and easements to make this clear. For example, the dominant and servient tenement should clearly be identified in the case of easements. Most sets of precedents will contain examples of this wording for use as appropriate. • **Exclusion of implied easements** On a sale of part, certain easements can be impliedly created by operation of the law. To avoid uncertainty, it is usual for the seller to provide that only those easements expressly granted in favour of the buyer in the purchase deed are to be created. This prevents the creation of any implied easements in favour of the buyer. The buyer should therefore take extra care to check that the easements granted meet his needs, as none will otherwise be implied in his favour.
New properties	
Structural guarantee	On the sale of an existing property, the buyer has the opportunity to carry out a survey to establish the existence of any physical defects. This is not so easy in the case of new properties, such as units on a new housing estate. The property may not have been completed – or indeed even begun – at exchange. In the context of residential developments, a scheme exists in order to protect buyers against problems that can arise. This is the NHBC Buildmark scheme which is offered by most residential developers. If a developer is a member of the scheme, the buyer will be entitled to cover under it. The scheme provides protection for a period of 10 years. The protection afforded is more extensive during the first two years of cover. A buyer should ensure before exchange of contracts that cover under the Buildmark scheme is to be provided. If it is not, the buyer will need to consider alternative forms of protection and ensure that these are in place.
Infrastructure	In a new development, roads, sewers and drains will be being constructed alongside the units that make up the development. It is usual for the roads, sewers and drains to be adopted when the development is finished. This will mean that they will be maintained at public expense and can be used by the public accordingly.

Sub-section heading	Summary
	A buyer will want to check that an agreement has been entered into between the developer and the relevant authority to ensure that adoption will take place. This should be backed by a bond to guarantee that the work necessary to construct the roads, sewers and drains will be carried out to a suitable standard. In the case of roads, the agreement is made under s 38 of the Highways Act 1980; and in the case of sewers and drains, under s 104 of the Water Industry Act 1991. Pending adoption, the buyer will need to ensure that he has appropriate rights to use the roads, sewers and drains in the meantime. These rights should be included within the transfer deed.

Appendices

Appendix 1

National Protocol for Domestic Freehold and Leasehold Property

© The Law Society of England and Wales

The National Protocol (Fifth Edition)

Acting for the seller

1 *The first step*

The seller should inform the solicitor as soon as it is intended to place the property on the market so that delay may be reduced after a prospective purchaser is found.

2 *Preparing the package: assembling the information*

On receipt of instructions, the solicitor should then immediately take the following steps, at the seller's expense:

2.1 Whenever possible instructions should be obtained from the client in person. The Consumer Protection (Distance Selling) Regulations 2000 should then not apply.

2.2 Check the client's identity if the client is not known to you. Comply with money laundering regulations and any guidance issued by the Law Society.

2.3 Give the client information as to costs, information relating to the name and status of the person who will be carrying out the work and, if that person is not a partner, the name of the partner who has overall responsibility for the matter. Give any other information necessary to comply with Rule 15 of the Solicitors' Practice Rules 1990 and Solicitors' Costs Information and Client Care Code 1999. If given orally this information should be confirmed in writing.

2.4 Give the seller details of whom to contact in the event of a complaint about the firm's services (Rule 15).

2.5 Consider with client whether to make local authority and other searches so that these can be supplied to the buyer's solicitor as soon as an offer is made. If thought appropriate request a payment on account in relation to disbursements.

2.6 Ascertain the whereabouts of the deeds and, if not in the solicitor's custody, obtain them or if registration has taken place after 13 October 2003, apply for an official copy of entries on the register and the title plan.

2.7 Ask the seller to complete the Seller's Property Information Form and on its return remind the seller of the need to notify you of any changes in the information supplied prior to completion.

2.8 Obtain such original guarantees with the accompanying specification, planning decisions, building regulation approvals and certificates of completion as are in the seller's possession and copies of any other planning consents that are with the title deeds or details of any highway and sewerage agreements and bonds or any other relevant certificates relating to the property (eg structural engineer's certificate or an indemnity policy).

2.9   Give the seller the Fixtures, Fittings and Contents Form, with a copy to retain, to complete and return prior to the submission of the draft contract.

2.10   If the title is unregistered make an index map search.

2.11   If so instructed requisition a local authority search and enquiries and any other searches (eg mining or commons registration searches).

2.12   Obtain details of all mortgages and other financial charges of which the seller's solicitor has notice including, where applicable, improvement grants and discounts repayable to a local authority. Redemption figures should be obtained at this stage in respect of all mortgages on the property so that cases of negative equity or penalty redemption interest can be identified at an early stage.

2.13   Ascertain the identity of all people aged 17 or over living in the dwelling and ask about any financial contribution they or anyone else may have made towards its purchase or subsequent improvement. All persons identified in this way should be asked to confirm their consent to the sale proceeding.

2.14   In leasehold cases, ask the seller to complete the Seller's Leasehold Information Form and to produce, if possible:

(1)   A receipt or evidence from the landlord of the last payment of rent.

(2)   The maintenance charge accounts for the last three years, where appropriate, and evidence of payment.

(3)   Details of the buildings insurance policy.

If any of these are lacking, and are necessary for the transaction, the solicitor should obtain them from the landlord. At the same time investigate whether a licence to assign is required and, if so, enquire of the landlord what references or deeds of covenant are necessary and, in the case of some retirement schemes, if a charge is payable to the management company on change of ownership. On receipt of the form back from the seller, remind the seller of the need to notify you of any changes in the information supplied prior to completion.

2.15   In commonhold cases:

(1)   Ask the seller to complete the Seller's Commonhold Information Form, and to produce, if possible:

(i)   Commonhold Association Memorandum and Articles of Association

(ii)   Commonhold Community Statement

(iii) Details of the building insurance policy.

(2)   Make a search at Companies House against the commonhold association.

(3)   Obtain an official copy of commonhold title for the common parts.

(4)   Obtain the account from the commonhold association for the unit and ask if there are:

(i)   any other claims or assessment against the unit;

(ii)   details of the annual budget or estimates;

(iii) any reserve fund; and

(iv)   any restricted use areas

2.16   Check replies given by the seller on the Seller's Property Information Form and, if appropriate, the Seller's Leasehold Information Form and Seller's Commonhold Information Form from the information in your possession (see the guidance from the Law Society's Conveyancing and Land Law Committee [2003] Gazette, 16 October 43).

3 Preparing the package: the draft documents

As soon as the title deeds are available, and the seller has completed the Seller's Property Information Form and, if appropriate, the Seller's Leasehold Information Form, the solicitor shall:

3.1 If the title is unregistered:

(1) Make a land charges search against the seller and any other appropriate names.

(2) Make an index map search in the Land Registry (if not already obtained — see 2.10) in order to verify that the seller's title is unregistered and ensure that there are no interests registered at the Land Registry adverse to the seller's title.

(3) Prepare an epitome of title. Mark copies or abstracts of all deeds which will not he passed to the buyer's solicitor as examined against the original.

(4) Prepare and mark as examined against the originals copies of all deeds, or their abstracts, prior to the root of title containing covenants, easements, etc. affecting the property.

(5) Check that all plans on copied documents are correctly coloured.

3.2 If the title is registered, obtain office copy entries of the register and copy documents incorporated or referred to in the certificate.

3.3 Prepare the draft contract and complete the second section of the Seller's Property Information Form and, if appropriate, the Seller's Leasehold Information Form and the Seller's Commonhold Information Form.

3.4 Check contract package is complete and ready to be sent out to the buyer's solicitor.

3.5 Deal promptly with any queries raised by the estate agent.

4 Buyer's offer accepted

When made aware that a buyer has been found the solicitor shall:

4.1 Check with the seller agreement on the price and, if appropriate, that there has been no change in the information already supplied (Seller's Property Information Form, Seller's Leasehold Information Form, Seller's Commonhold Information Form and Fixtures, Fittings and Contents Form). Also check the seller's position on any related purchase. If any part of the purchase price is being apportioned to chattels, which will be in a separate state of severance at completion, advise the seller that apportionment must be a just and reasonable figure, and if in any doubt professional advice from a valuer should be obtained. If appropriate, supply the seller with a copy of the leaflet issued by the Inland Revenue, 'Fixtures and Chattels – Stamp Duty Land Tax'.

4.2 Inform the buyer's solicitor that the Protocol will be used.

4.3 Ascertain the buyer's position on any related sale and in the light of that reply, ask the seller for a proposed completion date.

4.4 Send to the buyer's solicitor as soon as possible the contract package to include:

(1) Draft contract.

(2) Office copy entries of the registered title (including office copies of all documents mentioned), or the epitome of title (including details of any prior matters referred to hut not disclosed by the documents themselves) and the index map search.

(3) The Seller's Property Information Form with copies of all relevant planning decisions, guarantees, etc.

(4) The completed Fixtures, Fittings and Contents Form. Where this is provided it will form part of the contact and should be attached to it.

(5)   In leasehold cases

    (i)   the Seller's Leasehold Information Form, with all information about maintenance charges and insurance and, if appropriate, the procedure (including references required) for obtaining the landlord's consent to the sale;

    (ii) a copy of the lease.

(6)   In commonhold cases

    (i)   Seller's Commonhold Information Form, with all information obtained under 2.15;

    (ii) A copy of the registered title for the commonhold common parts and a copy of the registered title for the sellers's unit.

(7)   If available, the local authority search and enquiries and any other searches made by the seller's solicitor.

If any of these documents are not available the remaining items should be forwarded to the buyer's solicitor as soon as they are available.

4.5   Inform the estate agent when the draft contract has been submitted to the buyer's solicitor.

4.6   Ask the buyer's solicitor if a 10 per cent deposit will be paid and, if not, what arrangements are proposed.

4.7   If and to the extent that the seller consents to the disclosure, supply information about the position on the seller's own purchase and of any other transactions in the chain above, and thereafter, of any change in circumstances.

4.8   Notify the seller of all information received in response to the above.

4.9   Inform the estate agent of any unexpected delays or difficulties likely to delay exchange of contracts.

Acting for the buyer

5   The first step

On notification of the buyer's purchase the solicitor should then immediately take the following steps, at the buyer's expense:

5.1   Whenever possible instructions should be obtained from the client in person. The Consumer Protection (Distance Selling) Regulations 2000 should then not apply.

5.2   Check the client's identity if the client is not known to you. Comply with money laundering regulations and any guidance issued by the Law Society.

5.3   Give the client information as to costs, information relating to the name and status of the person who will he carrying out the work and, if that person is not a partner, the name of the partner who has overall responsibility for the matter. Give any other information necessary to comply with Rule 15 of the Solicitor's Practice Rules 1990 and Solicitors' Costs Information and Client Care Code 1999. If given orally this information should be confirmed in writing.

5.4   Give the client details of whom to contact in the event of a complaint about the firm's services (Rule 15).

5.5   Request a payment on account in relation to disbursements.

5.6   Confirm to the seller's solicitor that the Protocol will be used.

5.7   Ascertain the buyer's position on any related sale, mortgage arrangements and whether a 10 per cent deposit will he provided.

5.8   If and to the extent that the buyer consents to the disclosure, inform the seller's solicitor about the position on the buyer's own sale, if any, and of any connected transactions, the general nature of the mortgage application, the amount of deposit available and if the seller's target date for completion can be met, and thereafter, of any change in circumstances.

On receipt of the draft contract and other documents:

5.9 Notify the buyer that these documents have been received, check the price and send the client a copy of the Fixtures, Fittings and Contents Form and, if appropriate, a copy of the filed plan for checking. If any part of the purchase price is being apportioned to chattels, which will be in a separate state of severance at completion, advise the seller that apportionment must be a just and reasonable figure, and if in any doubt professional advice from a valuer should be obtained. If appropriate, supply the seller with a copy of the leaflet issued by the Inland Revenue, 'Fixtures and Chattels – Stamp Duty Land Tax'.

5.10 Subject to 5.20 below, make a local authority search with the usual part one enquiries and any additional enquiries relevant to the property.

5.11 Make a commons registration search, if appropriate.

5.12 Make mining enquiries and drainage enquiries if appropriate and consider any other relevant searches, eg environmental searches.

5.13 Check the buyer's position on any related sale and check that the buyer has a satisfactory mortgage offer and all conditions of the mortgage are or can he satisfied.

5.14 Check the buyer understands the nature and effect of the mortgage offer and duty to disclose any relevant matters to the lender.

5.15 Advise the buyer of the need for a survey on the property.

5.16 Check the draft contract to ensure title is satisfactory and add any special conditions necessary to achieve this (eg for the removal of or consents needed under any restrictions or notices revealed on the title).

5.17 Confirm approval of the draft contract and return it approved as soon as possible, having inserted the buyer's full names and address, subject to any outstanding matters.

5.18 At the same time ask only those specific additional enquiries which are required to clarify some point arising out of the documents submitted or which are relevant to the particular nature or location of the property or which the buyer has expressly requested. Any enquiry, including those about the state and condition of the building, which is capable of being ascertained by the buyer's own enquiries or survey or personal inspection should not be raised. Additional duplicated standard forms should not be submitted; if they are, the seller's solicitor is under no obligation to deal with them nor need answer any enquire seeking opinions rather than facts.

5.19 If title has been deduced, check the seller's title to the property and raise any requisitions on the title deduced. (See Standard Conditions of Sale (fourth edition) 4.2.1.) Matters relating to the completion arrangements should not be raised at this stage.

5.20 If a local authority search has been supplied by the seller's solicitors with the draft contract, consider the need to make a local authority search with the usual part one enquiries and any additional enquiries relevant to the property. (The local authority search should not be more than three months' old at exchange of contracts nor six months' old at completion).

5.21 Ensure that buildings insurance arrangements are in place.

5.22 Check the position over any life policies referred to in the lender's offer of mortgage.

5.23   Check with the buyer if property is being purchased in sole name or jointly with another person. If a joint purchase cheek whether as joint tenants or tenants in common and advise on the difference in writing.

Both parties' solicitor

6   *Prior to exchange of contracts*

If acting for the buyer

When all satisfactory replies received to enquiries and searches:

6.1   Prepare and send to the buyer a contract report and invite the buyer to make an appointment to call to raise any queries on the contract report and to sign the contract ideally in the presence of a solicitor.

6.2   When the buyer signs the contract check:

   (1)   Completion date.

   (2)   That the buyer understands and can comply with all the conditions on the mortgage offer if appropriate.

   (3)   That all the necessary funds will be available to complete the purchase.

If acting for the seller

6.3   Advise the seller on the effect of the contract and ask the seller to sign it, ideally in the presence of the solicitor.

6.4   Check the position on any related purchase so that there can be a simultaneous exchange of contracts on both the sale and purchase.

6.5   Check completion date.

7   *Relationship with the buyer's lender*

On receipt of instructions from the buyer's lender:

7.1   Check the mortgage offer complies with Practice Rule 6(3)(c) and (e) and is certified to that effect.

7.2   Cheek any special conditions in the mortgage offer to see if there are additional instructions or conditions not normally required by Practice Rule 6(3)(e).

7.3   Go through any special conditions in the mortgage offer with the buyer.

7.4   Notify the lender if Practice Rule 6(3)(b) or 1.13 or 1.14 of the CML *Lenders' Handbook* ('Lenders' Handbook') are applicable.

7.5   Consider whether there are any conflicts of interest which prevent you accepting instructions to act for the lender.

7.6   If you do not know the borrower and anyone else required to sign the mortgage, charge or other document, check evidence of identity (Practice Rule 6(3)(e)(i)).

7.7   Consider whether there are any circumstances covered by the Law Society's:

   (1)   Green Card on property fraud

   (2)   Blue Card on money laundering

   (3)   Pink Card on undertakings

   (4)   Money Laundering Guidance

7.8   If you do not know the seller's solicitor/licensed conveyancer cheek that they appear in a legal directory or are on the record of their professional body (see Practice Rule 6(3)(c)(i) and the Lenders' Handbook).

7.9   Carry out any other checks required by the lender provided they comply with Practice Rule 6(3)(c).

7.10   Check the lender's requirements as to whether it requires the original mortgage deed to be lodged with it following registration.

7.11   At all times comply with the requirements of Practice Rule 6(3) and the Lenders' Handbook and ensure if a conflict of interest arises you cease to act for the lender.

8   Exchange of contracts

On exchange, the buyer's solicitor shall send or deliver to the seller's solicitor:

8.1   The signed contract with all names, dates and financial information completed.

8.2   The deposit provided in the manner prescribed in the contract. Under the Law Society's Formula C the deposit may have to he sent to another solicitor nominated by the seller's solicitor.

8.3   If contracts are exchanged by telephone the procedures laid down by the Law Society's Formulae A, B or C must be used and both solicitors must ensure (unless otherwise agreed) that the undertakings to send documents and to pay the deposit on that day are strictly observed.

8.4   The seller's solicitor shall, once the buyer's signed contract and deposit are held unconditionally, having ensured that the details of each contract are fully completed and identical, send the seller's signed contract on the day of exchange to the buyer's solicitor in compliance with the undertaking given on exchange.

8.5   Notify the client that contracts have been exchanged.

8.6   Notify the seller's estate agent or property seller of exchange of contracts and the completion date.

9   Between exchange and the day of completion

As soon as possible after exchange and in any ease within the time limits contained in the Standard Conditions of Sale:

9.1   The buyer's solicitor shall send to the seller's solicitor, in duplicate:

(1)   Completion Information Form and include any requisitions on title which are necessary and could not be raised prior to exchange of contracts, or ask seller's solicitor to confirm that there is no variation in any replies given prior to exchange.

(2)   Draft conveyance/transfer or assignment incorporating appropriate provisions for joint purchase.

(3)   Other documents, eg draft receipt for purchase price of fixtures, fittings and contents.

9.2   As soon as possible after receipt of these documents the seller's solicitor shall send to the buyer's solicitor:

(1)   Replies to Completion Information and Requisitions on Title Form.

(2)   Draft conveyance/transfer or assignment approved.

(3)   If appropriate, completion statement supported by photocopy receipts or evidence of payment of apportionments claimed.

(4)   Copy of licence to assign from the landlord if appropriate.

9.3   The buyer's solicitor shall then:

(1)   Engross the approved draft conveyance/transfer or assignment.

(2)   Explain the effect of that document to the buyer and obtain the buyer's signature to it (if necessary).

(3)   Send it to the seller's solicitor in time to enable the seller to sign it before completion without suffering inconvenience.

(4)   If appropriate prepare any separate declaration of trust, advise the buyer on its effect and obtain the buyer's signature to it.

(5)   Advise the buyer on the contents and effect of the mortgage deed and obtain the buyer's signature to that deed. If possible, and in all eases where the

lender so requires, a solicitor should witness the buyer's signature to the mortgage deed.

(6)   Send the certificate of title (complying with Rule 6(3)(d)) to the lender.

(7)   Take any steps necessary to ensure that the amount payable on completion will be available in time for completion including sending to the buyer a completion statement to include legal costs, Land Registry fees and other disbursements and, if appropriate, stamp duty land tax.

(8)   Make the Land Registry and land charges searches and, if appropriate, a company search.

(9)   Ensure that you have by this stage obtained sufficient information from each buyer to complete the relevant land transaction return, including national insurance numbers, and prepare the return. After checking with the buyer that the information on the form is accurate, advise the buyer that an Inland Revenue enquiry is possible within the following nine months which might result in costs and penalties. Ask the buyer to sign the form in black ink and return it immediately as penalties will be charged by the Inland Revenue unless the form is lodged within 30 days of completion.

(10) Explain and discuss with the buyer the need to disclose overriding interests in the property and complete form DI.

9.4   The seller's solicitor shall:

(1)   Request redemption figures for all financial charges on the property revealed by the deeds/office copy entries/land charges search against the seller.

(2)   On receipt of the engrossment of the conveyance/transfer or assignment, after checking the engrossment to ensure accuracy, obtain the seller's signature to it after ascertaining that the seller understands the nature and contents of the document. If the document is not to be signed in the solicitor's presence the letter sending the document for signature should contain an explanation of the nature and effect of the document and clear instructions relating to the execution of it.

(3)   On receipt of the estate agent's or property seller's commission account obtain the seller's instructions to pay the account on the seller's behalf out of the sale proceeds.

(4)   Consider if the consent of any restrictioner (eg a managing agent or management company) who will have a continuing interest is needed and if so, take steps to ensure that such consent will be available on completion.

10   Relationship with the seller's estate agent or property seller

Where the seller has instructed estate agents or property seller, the seller's solicitor shall take the following steps:

10.1 Inform them when the draft contracts are submitted (see 4.5).

10.2 Deal promptly with any queries raised by them.

10.3 Inform them of any unexpected delays or difficulties likely to delay exchange of contracts (see 4.9).

10.4 Inform them when exchange has taken place and the date of completion (see 8.6).

10.5 On receipt of their commission account send a copy to the seller and obtain Instructions as to arrangements for payment (see 9.4(3)).

10.6 Inform them of completion and, if appropriate, authorise release of any keys held by them (see 11.3(1)).

10.7 If so instructed pay the commission (see 9.4(3) and 11.6(2)).

11 *Completion: the day of payment and removals*

11.1   If completion is to be by post, the Law Society's Code for Completion shall be used, unless otherwise agreed.

11.2   As soon as practicable and not later than the morning of completion, the buyer's solicitor shall advise the seller's solicitor of the manner and transmission of the purchase money and of steps taken to despatch it.

11.3   On being satisfied as to the receipt of the balance of the purchase money, the seller's solicitor shall:

(1)   Notify the estate agent or property seller that completion has taken place and authorise release of the keys.

(2)   Notify the buyer's solicitor that completion has taken place and the keys have been released.

(3)   Date and complete the transfer.

(4)   Despatch the deeds including the transfer to the buyer's solicitor with any appropriate undertakings.

11.4   The seller's solicitor shall check that the seller is aware of the need to notify the local and water authorities of the change in ownership.

11.5   After completion, where appropriate, the buyer's solicitor shall give notice of assignment to the lessor.

11.6   Immediately after completion, the seller's solicitor shall:

(1)   Send to the lender the amount required to release the property sold.

(2)   Pay the estate agent s or property seller's commission if so authorised.

(3)   Account to the seller for the balance of the sale proceeds.

11.7   Immediately after completion, the buyer's solicitor shall:

(1)   Date and complete the mortgage document and, if appropriate, give notice of any second or subsequent charge to the first chargee.

(2)   Confirm completion of the purchase and the mortgage to the buyer.

(3)   Lodge Form SDLT with the Inland Revenue and pay any Stamp Duty Land Tax that is due. On receipt of the certificate of notification from the Inland Revenue, hold it to lodge with the Land Registry application.

(4)   Consider the need to register a restriction and, if appropriate, complete Form RX1.

(5)   Deal with the registration of the transfer document and mortgage with the Land Registry within the priority period of the search including lodging with the application form AP1 or FR1, Form DI and, if appropriate, Form RX1.

(6)   If appropriate send a notice of assignment of a life policy to the insurance company.

(7)   On receipt of notification from the Land Registry that registration has been completed and a title information document has been supplied, check its contents carefully and supply a copy of the document to the buyer.

(8)   Send the original mortgage deed and/or title information document to the lender, if appropriate, and deal with any other documents in accordance with its instructions.

(9)   Take the buyer's instructions as to any documents not being held by the lender, and if the documents are to be sent to the buyer or to anyone else to hold on the buyer's behalf, inform the buyer of the need to keep the documents safely so that they will be available on sale of the property.

(10) If the sale was a sale of part of the land in the registered title, then on completion of the registration of the transfer of part, the seller's solicitor shall check that the title certificate and amended registration plan are accurate and send a copy to the seller.

Appendix 2

Standard Conditions of Sale (Fourth Edition)

© The Solicitors Law Stationery Society Limited and the Law Society of England and Wales

(National Conditions of Sale 24th Edition, Law Society's Conditions of Sale 2003)

1. GENERAL

1.1 Definitions

1.1.1 In these conditions:

    (a)   'accrued interest' means:

        (i)   if money has been placed on deposit or in a building society share account, the interest actually earned

        (ii)   otherwise, the interest which might reasonably have been earned by depositing the money at interest on seven days' notice of withdrawal with a clearing bank

        less, in either case, any proper charges for handling the money

    (b)   'chattels price' means any separate amount payable for chattels included in the contract

    (c)   'clearing bank' means a bank which is a shareholder in CHAPS Clearing Co. Limited.

    (d)   'completion dale' has the meaning given in condition 6.1.1

    (e)   'contract rate' means the Law Society's interest rate from time to time in force

    (f)   'conveyancer' means a solicitor, barrister, duly certified notary public, licensed conveyancer or recognised body under sections 9 or 23 of the Administration of Justice Act 1985

    (g)   'direct credit' means a direct transfer of cleared funds to an account nominated by the seller's conveyancer and maintained by a clearing bank

    (h)   'lease' includes sub-lease, tenancy and agreement for a lease or sub-lease

    (i)   'notice to complete' means a notice requiring completion of the contract in accordance with condition 6

    (j)   'public requirement' means any notice, order or proposal given or made (whether before or after the date of the contract) by a body acting on statutory authority

    (k)   'requisition' includes objection

    (l)   'transfer' includes conveyance and assignment

    (m)   'working day' means any day from Monday to Friday (inclusive) which is not Christmas Day, Good Friday or a statutory Bank Holiday.

1.1.2 In these conditions the terms 'absolute title' and 'official copies' have the special meanings given to them by the Land Registration Act 2002.

1.1.3 A party is ready, able and willing to complete:

    (a)   if he could be, but for the default of the other party, and

    (b)   in the case of the seller, even though the property remains subject to a mortgage, if the amount to be paid on completion enables the property to be transferred freed of all mortgages (except any to which the sale is expressly subject).

1.1.4   These conditions apply except as varied or excluded by the contract.

1.2   Joint parties

If there is more than one seller or more than one buyer, the obligations which they undertake can be enforced against them all jointly or against each individually.

1.3   Notices and documents

1.3.1   A notice required or authorised by the contract must be in writing.

1.3.2   Giving a notice or delivering a document to party's conveyancer has the same effect as giving or delivering it to that party.

1.3.3   Where delivery of the original document is not essential, a notice or document is validly given or sent if it is sent:

(a)   by fax, or

(b)   by e-mail to an e-mail address for the intended recipient given in the contract.

1.3.4   Subject to conditions 1.3.5 to 1.3.7, a notice is given and a document is delivered when it is received.

1.3.5   (a)   A notice or document sent through a document exchange is received when it is available for collection

(b)   A notice or document which is received after 4.00pm on a working day, or on a day which is not a working day, is to be treated as having been received on the next working day

(c)   An automated response to a notice or document sent by e-mail that the intended recipient is out of the office is to be treated as proof that the notice or document was not received.

1.3.6   Condition 1.3.7 applies unless there is proof:

(a)   that a notice or document has not been received, or

(b)   of when it was received.

1.3.7   A notice or document sent by the following means is treated as having been received as follows:

(a)	by first-class post:	before 4.00pm on the second working day after posting
(b)	by second-class post:	before 4.00pm on the third working day after posting
(c)	through a document exchange:	before 4.00pm on the first working day after the day on which it would normally be available for collection by the addressee
(d)	by fax:	one hour after despatch
(e)	by e-mail:	before 4.00pm on the first working day after despatch.

1.4   VAT

1.4.1   An obligation to pay money includes an obligation to pay any value added tax chargeable in respect of that payment.

1.4.2   All sums made payable by the contract are exclusive of value added tax.

1.5 **Assignment**

The buyer is not entitled to transfer the benefit of the contract.

2. FORMATION

2.1 Date

2.1.1 If the parties intend to make a contract by exchanging duplicate copies by post or through a document exchange, the contract is made when the last copy is posted or deposited at the document exchange.

2.1.2 If the parties' conveyancers agree to treat exchange as taking place before duplicate copies are actually exchanged, the contract is made as so agreed.

2.2 Deposit

2.2.1 The buyer is to pay or send a deposit of 10 per cent of the total of the purchase price and the chattels price no later than the date of the contract.

2.2.2 If a cheque tendered in payment of all or part of the deposit is dishonoured when first presented, the seller may, within seven working days of being notified that the cheque has been dishonoured, give notice to the buyer that the contract is discharged by the buyer's breach.

2.2.3 Conditions 2.2.4 to 2.2.5 do not apply on a sale by auction.

2.2.4 The deposit is to be paid by direct credit or to the seller's conveyencer by a cheque drawn on a solicitor's or licensed conveyancer's client account.

2.2.5 If before completion date the seller agrees to buy another property in England and Wales for his residence, he may use all or any part of the deposit as a deposit in that transaction to be held on terms to the same effect as this condition and condition 2.2.6.

2.2.6 Any deposit or part of a deposit not being used in accordance with condition 2.2.5 is to be held by the seller's conveyancer as stakeholder on terms that on completion it is paid to the seller with accrued interest.

2.3 Auctions

2.3.1 On a sale by auction the following conditions apply to the property and, if it is sold in lots, to each lot.

2.3.2 The sale is subject to a reserve price.

2.3.3 The seller, or a person on his behalf, may bid up to the reserve price.

2.3.4 The auctioneer may refuse any bid.

2.3.5 If there is a dispute about a bid, the auctioneer may resolve the dispute or restart the auction at the last undisputed bid.

2.3.6 The deposit is to be paid to the auctioneer as agent for the seller.

3. MATTERS AFFECTING THE PROPERTY

3.1 Freedom from incumbrances

3.1.1 The seller is selling the property free from incumbrances, other than those mentioned in condition 3.1.2.

3.1.2 The incumbrances subject to which the property is sold are:
   (a) those specified in the contract
   (b) those discoverable by inspection of the property before the contract

(c)   those the seller does not and could not reasonably know about

(d)   entries made before the date of the contract in any public register except those maintained by HM Land Registry or its Land Charges Department or by Companies House

(e)   public requirements.

3.1.3   After the contract is made, the seller is to give the buyer written details without delay of any new public requirement and of anything in writing which he learns about concerning a matter covered by condition 3.1.2.

3.1.4   The buyer is to bear the cost of complying with any outstanding public requirement and is to indemnify the seller against any liability resulting from a public requirement.

3.2   Physical state

3.2.1   The buyer accepts the property in the physical state it is in at the date of the contract unless the seller is building or converting it.

3.2.2   A leasehold property is sold subject to any subsisting breach of a condition or tenant's obligation relating to the physical state of the property which renders the lease liable to forfeiture.

3.2.3   A sub-lease is granted subject to any subsisting breach of a condition or tenant's obligation relating to the physical state of the property which renders the seller's own lease liable to forfeiture.

3.3   Leases affecting the property

3.3.1   The following provisions apply if any part of the property is sold subject to a lease.

3.3.2   (a)   The seller having provided the buyer with full details of each lease or copies of the documents embodying the lease terms, the buyer is treated as entering into the contract knowing and fully accepting those terms.

(b)   The seller is to inform the buyer without delay if the lease ends or if the seller learns of any application by the tenant in connection with the lease; the seller is then to act as the buyer reasonably directs, and the buyer is to indemnify him against all consequent loss and expense.

(c)   Except with the buyer's consent, the seller is not to agree to any proposal to change the lease terms nor to take any step to end the lease.

(d)   The seller is to inform the buyer without delay of any change to the lease terms which may be proposed or agreed.

(e)   The buyer is to indemnify the seller against all claims arising from the lease after actual completion; this includes claims which are unenforceable against a buyer for want of registration.

(f)   The seller takes no responsibility for what rent is lawfully recoverable, nor for whether or how any legislation effects the lease.

(g)   If the let land is not wholly within the property, the seller may apportion the rent.

3.4   Retained land

Where after the transfer the seller will be retaining land near the property:

(a)   the buyer will have no right of light or air over the retained land, but

(b)   in other respects the seller and the buyer will each have the rights over the land of the other which they would have had if they were two separate buyers to whom the seller had made simultaneous transfers of the property and the retained land.

The transfer is to contain appropriate express terms.

4.   TITLE AND TRANSFER

4.1   Proof of title

4.1.1   Without cost to the buyer, the seller is to provide the buyer with proof of the title to the property and of his ability to transfer it, or to procure its transfer.

4.1.2   Where the property has a registered title the proof is to include official copies of the items referred to in rules 134(1)(a) and (b) and 135(1)(a) of the Land Registration Rules 2003, so far as they are not to be discharged or overridden at or before completion.

4.1.3   Where the property has an unregistered title, the proof is to include:

(a)   an abstract of title or an epitome of title with photocopies of the documents, and

(b)   production of every document or an abstract, epitome or copy of it with an original marking by a conveyancer either against the original or an examined abstract or an examined copy.

4.2   Requisitions

4.2.1   The buyer may not raise requisitions:

(a)   on the title shown by the seller taking the step described in condition 4.1.1 before the contract was made

(b)   in relation to the matters covered by condition 3.1.2.

4.2.2   Notwithstanding condition 4.2.1. the buyer may, within six working days of a matter coming to his attention after the contract was made, raise written requisitions on that matter. In that event, steps 3 and 4 in condition 4.3.1 apply.

4.2.3   On the expiry of the relevant time limit under condition 4.2.2 or condition 4.3.1, the buyer loses his right to raise requisitions or to make observations.

4.3   Timetable

4.3.1   Subject to condition 4.2 and to the extent that the seller did not take the steps described in condition 4.1.1 before the contract was made, the following are the steps for deducing and investigating the title to the property to be taken within the following time limits:

Step		Time Limit
1.	The seller is to comply with condition 4.1.1	Immediately after making the contract
2.	The buyer may raise written requisitions	Six working days after either the date of contract or the date of delivery of the seller's proof of title on which the requisitions are raised, whichever is the later
3.	The seller is to reply in writing to any requisitions raised	Four working days after receiving the requisitions
4.	The buyer may make written observations on the seller's replies	Three working days after receiving the replies

The time limit on the buyer's right to raise requisitions applies even where the seller supplies incomplete evidence of his title, but the buyer may, within six working days from delivery of any further evidence, raise further requisitions resulting from that evidence.

4.3.2 The parties are to take the following steps to prepare and agree the transfer of the property within the following time limits:

Step		Time Limit
A.	The buyer is to send the seller a draft transfer	At least twelve working days before completion date
B.	The seller is to approve or revise that draft and either return it or retain it for use as the actual transfer	Four working days after delivery of the draft transfer
C.	If the draft is returned the buyer is to send an engrossment to the seller	At least five working days before completion date

4.3.3 Periods of time under conditions 4.3.1 and 4.3.2 may run concurrently.

4.3.4 If the period between the date of the contract and completion date is less than 15 working days, the time limits in conditions 4.2.2, 4.3.1 and 4.3.2 are to be reduced by the same proportion as that period bears to the period of 15 working days. Fractions of a working day are to be rounded down except that the time limit to perform any step is not to be less than one working day.

4.4 Defining the property

4.4.1 The seller need not

(a)   prove the exact boundaries of the property

(b)   prove who owns fences, ditches, hedges or walls

(c)   separately identify parts of the property with different titles

further than he may be able to do from information in his possession.

4.4.2 The buyer may, if it is reasonable, require the seller to make or obtain, pay for and hand over a statutory declaration about facts relevant to the matters mentioned in condition 4.4.1. The form of the declaration is be agreed by the buyer, who must not unreasonably withhold his agreement.

4.5 Rents and rent charges

The fact that a rent or rent charge, whether payable or receivable by the owner of the property, has been, or will on completion be, informally apportioned is not to be regarded as a defect in title.

4.6 Transfer

4.6.1 The buyer does not prejudice his right to raise requisitions, or to require replies to any raised, by taking any steps in relation to preparing or agreeing the transfer.

4.6.2 Subject to condition 4.6.3, the seller is to transfer the property with full title guarantee.

4.6.3 The transfer is to have effect as if the disposition is expressly made subject to all matters covered by condition 3.1.2.

4.6.4 If after completion the seller will remain bound by any obligation affecting the property which was disclosed to the buyer before the contract was made, but the law does not imply any covenant by the buyer to indemnify the seller against liability for future breaches of it:

(a)   the buyer is to covenant in the transfer to indemnify the seller against liability for any future breach of the obligation and to perform it from then on, and

(b)   if required by the seller, the buyer is to execute and deliver to the seller on completion a duplicate transfer prepared by the buyer.

4.6.5   The seller is to arrange at his expense that, in relation to every document of title which the buyer does not receive on completion, the buyer is to have the benefit of:

(a)   a written acknowledgement of his right to its production, and

(b)   a written undertaking for its safe custody (except while it is held by a mortgagee or by someone in a fiduciary capacity).

5.   PENDING COMPLETION

5.1   Responsibility for property

5.1.1   The seller will transfer the property in the same physical state as it was at the date of the contract (except for fair wear and tear), which means that the seller retains the risk until completion.

5.1.2   If at any time before completion the physical state of the property makes it unusable for its purpose at the date of the contract:

(a)   the buyer may rescind the contract:

(b)   the seller may rescind the contract where the property has become unusable for that purpose as a result of damage against which the seller could not reasonably have insured, or which it is not legally possible for the seller to make good.

5.1.3   The seller is under no obligation to the buyer to insure the property.

5.1.4   Section 47 of the Law of Property Act 1925 doss not apply.

5.2   Occupation by buyer

5.2.1   If the buyer is not already lawfully in the property, and the seller agrees to let him into occupation, the buyer occupies on the following terms.

5.2.2   The buyer is a licensee and not a tenant. The terms of the licence are that the buyer:

(a)   cannot transfer it

(b)   may permit members of his household to occupy the property

(c)   is to pay or indemnify the seller against all outgoings and other expenses in respect of the property

(d)   is to pay the sellers fee calculated at the contract rate on a sum equal to the purchase price and the chattels price (less any deposit paid) for the period of the licence

(e)   is entitled to any rents and profits from any part of the property which he does not occupy

(f)   is to keep the property in as good a state of repair as it was in when he went into occupation (except for fair wear and tear) and is not to alter it

(g)   is to insure the property in a sum which is not less than the purchase price against all risks in respect of which comparable premises are normally insured

(h)   is to quit the property when the licence ends.

5.2.3   On the creation of the buyer's licence, condition 5.1 ceases to apply, which means that the buyer then assumes the risk until completion.

5.2.4   The buyer is not in occupation for the purposes of this condition if he merely exercises rights of access given solely to do work agreed by the seller.

5.2.5   The buyer's licence ends on the earliest of: completion date, rescission of the contract or when five working days' notice given by one party to the other takes effect.

5.2.6   If the buyer is in occupation of the property after his licence has come to an end and the contract is subsequently completed he is to pay the seller compensation for his continued occupation calculated at the same rate as the fee mentioned in condition 5.2.2(d).

5.2.7   The buyer's right to raise requisitions is unaffected.

6.   COMPLETION

6.1   Date

6.1.1   Completion date is twenty working days after the date of the contract but time is not of the essence of the contract unless a notice to complete has been served.

6.1.2   If the money due on completion is received after 2.00pm, completion is to be treated, for the purposes only of conditions 6.3 and 7.3, as taking place on the next working day as a result of the buyer's default.

6.1.3   Condition 6.1.2 does not apply and the seller is treated as in default if:
(i)   the sale is with vacant possession of the property or any part of it, and
(ii)   the buyer is ready, able and willing to complete but does not pay the money due on completion until after 2.00pm because the seller has not vacated the property or that part by that time.

6.2   Arrangements and place

6.2.1   The buyer's conveyancer and the seller's conveyancer are to co-operate in agreeing arrangements for completing the contract.

6.2.2   Completion is to take place in England and Wales, either at the seller's conveyancer's office or at some other place which the seller reasonably specifies.

6.3   Apportionments

6.3.1   Income and outgoings of the property are to be apportioned between the parties so far as the change of ownership on completion will affect entitlement to receive or liability to pay them.

6.3.2   If the whole property is sold with vacant possession or the seller exercises his option in condition 7.3.4, apportionment is to be made with effect from the date of actual completion; otherwise, it is to be made from completion date.

6.3.3   In apportioning any sum, it is to be assumed that the seller owns the property until the end of the day from which apportionment is made and that the sum accrues from day to day at the rate at which it is payable on that day.

6.3.4   For the purpose of apportioning income and outgoings, it is to be assumed that they accrue at an equal daily rate throughout the year.

6.3.5   When a sum to be apportioned is not known or easily ascertainable at completion, a provisional apportionment is to be made according to the best estimate available. As soon as the amount is known, a final apportionment is to be made and notified to the other party. Any resulting balance is to be paid no more than ten working days later, and if not then paid the balance is to bear interest at the contract rate from then until payment.

6.3.6   Compensation payable under condition 5.2.6 is not to be apportioned.

6.4 **Amount payable**

The amount payable by the buyer on completion is the purchase price and the chattels price (less any deposit already paid to the seller or his agent) adjusted to take account of:

(a) apportionments made under condition 6.3

(b) any compensation to be paid or allowed under condition 7.3.

6.5 **Title deeds**

6.5.1 As soon as the buyer has complied with all his obligations on completion the seller must hand over the documents of title.

6.5.2 Condition 6.5.1 does not apply to any documents of title relating to land being retained by the seller after completion.

6.6 **Rent receipts**

The buyer is to assume that whoever gave any receipt for a payment of rent or service charge which the seller produces was the person or the agent of the person then entitled to that rent or service charge.

6.7 **Means of payment**

The buyer is to pay the money due on completion by direct credit and, if appropriate, an unconditional release of a deposit held by a stakeholder.

6.8 **Notice to complete**

6.8.1 At any time on or after completion date, a party who is ready, able and willing to complete may give the other a notice to complete.

6.8.2 The parties are to complete the contract within ten working days of giving a notice to complete, excluding the day on which the notice is given. For this purpose, time is of the essence of the contract.

6.8.3 On receipt of a notice to complete:

(a) if the buyer paid no deposit, he is forthwith to pay a deposit of 10 per cent

(b) if the buyer paid a deposit of less than 10 per cent, he is forthwith to pay a further deposit equal to the balance of that 10 per cent.

7. **REMEDIES**

7.1 **Errors and omissions**

7.1.1 If any plan or statement in the contract, or in the negotiations leading to it, is or was misleading or inaccurate due to an error or omission, the remedies available are as follows.

7.1.2 When there is a material difference between the description or value of the property, or of any of the chattels included in the contract, as represented and as it is, the buyer is entitled to damages.

7.1.3 An error or omission only entitles the buyer to rescind the contract:

(a) where it results from fraud or recklessness, or

(b) where he would be obliged, to his prejudice, to accept property differing substantially (in quantity, quality or tenure) from what the error or omission had led him to expect.

7.2 **Rescission**

If either party rescinds the contract:

(a) unless the rescission is a result of the buyer's breach of contract the deposit is to be repaid to the buyer with accrued interest

(b)   the buyer is to return any documents he received from the seller and is to cancel any registration of the contract.

7.3   Late completion

7.3.1   If there is default by either or both of the parties in performing their obligations under the contract and completion is delayed, the party whose total period of default is the greater is to pay compensation to the other party.

7.3.2   Compensation is calculated at the contract rate on an amount equal to the purchase price and the chattels price, less (where the buyer is the paying party) any deposit paid, for the period by which the paying party's default exceeds that of the receiving party, or, if shorter, the period between completion date and actual completion.

7.3.3   Any claim for loss resulting from delayed completion is to be reduced by any compensation paid under this contract.

7.3.4   Where the buyer holds the property as tenant of the seller and completion is delayed, the seller may give notice to the buyer, before the date of actual completion, that he intends to take the net income from the property until completion. If he does so, he cannot claim compensation under condition 7.3.1 as well.

7.4   After completion

Completion does not cancel liability to perform any outstanding obligation under this contract.

7.5   Buyer's failure to comply with notice to complete

7.5.1   If the buyer fails to complete in accordance with a notice to complete, the following terms apply.

7.5.2   The seller may rescind the contract, and if he does so:
(a)   he may
(i)   forfeit and keep any deposit and accrued interest
(ii)   resell the property and any chattels included in the contract
(iii)   claim damages
(b)   the buyer is to return any documents he received from the seller and is to cancel any registration of the contract.

7.5.3   The seller retains his other rights and remedies.

7.6   Sellers failure to comply with notice to complete

7.6.1   If the seller fails to complete in accordance with a notice to complete, the following terms apply.

7.6.2   The buyer may rescind the contract, and if he does so:
(a)   the deposit is to be repaid to the buyer with accrued interest
(b)   the buyer is to return any documents he received from the seller and is, at the seller's expense, to cancel any registration of the contract.

7.6.3   The buyer retains his other rights and remedies.

8.   LEASEHOLD PROPERTY

8.1   Existing leases

8.1.1   The following provisions apply to a sale of leasehold land.

8.1.2   The seller having provided the buyer with copies of the documents embodying the lease terms, the buyer is treated as entering into the contract knowing and fully accepting those terms.

8.1.3   The seller is to comply with any lease obligations requiring the tenant to insure the property.

8.2   New leases

8.2.1   The following provisions apply to a contract to grant a new lease.

8.2.2   The conditions apply so that:

'seller' means the proposed landlord

'buyer' means the proposed tenant

'purchase price' means the premium to be paid on the grant of a lease.

8.2.3   The lease is to be in the form of the draft attached to the contract.

8.2.4   If the term of the new lease will exceed seven years, the seller is to deduce a title which will enable the buyer to register the lease at HM Land Registry with an absolute title.

8.2.5   The seller is to engross the lease and a counterpart of it and is to send the counterpart to the buyer at least five working days before completion date.

8.2.6   The buyer is to execute the counterpart and deliver it to the seller on completion.

8.3   Consent

8.3.1   (a)   The following provisions apply if a consent to let, assign or sub-let is required to complete the contract

(b)   In this condition 'consent' means consent in the form which satisfies the requirement to obtain it.

8.3.2   (a)   The seller is to apply for the consent at his expense, and to use all reasonable efforts to obtain it

(b)   The buyer is to provide all information and references reasonably required.

8.3.3   Unless he is in breech of his obligation under condition 8.3.2, either party may rescind the contract by notice to the other party if three working days before completion date (or before a later date on which the parties have agreed to complete the contract):

(a)   the consent has not been given, or

(b)   the consent has been given subject to a condition to which a party reasonably objects. In that case, neither party is to be treated as in breach of contract and condition 7.2 applies.

9.   COMMONHOLD LAND

9.1   Terms used in this condition have the special meanings given to them in Part 1 of the Commonhold and Leasehold Reform Act 2002.

9.2   This condition applies to a disposition of commonhold land.

9.3   The seller having provided the buyer with copies of the current versions of the memorandum and articles of the commonhold association and of the commonhold community statement, the buyer is treated as entering into the contract knowing and fully accepting their terms.

9.4   If the contract is for the sale of property which is or includes part only of a commonhold unit:

(a)   the seller is to apply for the written consent of the commonhold association at his expense and is to use all reasonable efforts to obtain it

(b)   either the seller, unless he is in breach of his obligation under paragraph (a), or the buyer may rescind the contract by notice to the other party if three working days before completion date (or before a later date on which the parties have agreed to complete the contract) the consent has not been given. In that case, neither party is to be treated as in breach of contract and condition 7.2 applies.

10.   CHATTELS

10.1   The following provisions apply to any chattels which are included in the contract, whether or not a separate price is to be paid for them.

10.2   The contract takes effect as a contract for sale of goods.

10.3   The buyer takes the chattels in the physical state they are in at the date of the contract.

10.4   Ownership of the chattels passes to the buyer on actual completion.

Appendix 3

Standard Commercial Property Conditions (Second Edition)

PART 1

1. GENERAL

1.1 Definitions

1.1.1 In these conditions:

(a) 'accrued interest' means:

    (i) 'if money has been placed on deposit or in a building society share account, the interest actually earned

    (ii) otherwise, the interest which might reasonably have been earned by depositing the money at interest on seven days' notice of withdrawal with a clearing bank

    less, in either case, any proper charges for handling the money

(b) 'apportionment day' has the meaning given in condition 8.3.2

(c) 'clearing bank' means a bank which is a shareholder in CHAPS Clearing Co. Limited

(d) 'completion date' has the meaning given in condition 8.1.1

(e) 'contract rate' is the Law Society's interest rate from time to time in force

(f) 'conveyancer' means a solicitor, barrister, duly certified notary public, licensed conveyancer or recognised body under sections 9 or 23 of the Administration of Justice Act 1985

(g) 'direct credit' means a direct transfer of cleared funds to an account nominated by the seller's conveyancer and maintained at a clearing bank

(h) 'election to waive exemption' means an election made under paragraph 2 of Schedule 10 to the Value Added Tax Act 1994

(i) 'lease' includes sub-lease, tenancy and agreement for a lease or sublease

(j) 'notice to complete' means a notice requiring completion of the contract in accordance with condition 8

(k) 'post' includes a service provided by a person licensed under the Postal Services Act 2000

(l) 'public requirement' means any notice, order or proposal given or made (whether before or after the date of the contract) by a body acting on statutory authority

(m) 'requisition' includes objection

(n) 'transfer' includes conveyance and assignment

(o) 'working day' means any day from Monday to Friday (inclusive) which is not Christmas Day, Good Friday or a statutory Bank Holiday.

1.1.2 In these conditions the terms 'absolute title' and 'official copies' have the special meanings given to them by the Land Registration Act 2002.

1.1.3   A party is ready, able and willing to complete:

(a)   if it could be, but for the default of the other party, and

(b)   in the case of the seller, even though a mortgage remains secured on the property, if the amount to be paid on completion enables the property to be transferred freed of all mortgages (except those to which the sale is expressly subject).

1.1.4   (a)   The conditions in Part 1 apply except as varied or excluded by the contract.

(b)   A condition in Part 2 only applies if expressly incorporated into the contract.

1.2   Joint parties

If there is more than one seller or more than one buyer, the obligations which they undertake can be enforced against them all jointly or against each individually.

1.3   Notices and documents

1.3.1   A notice required or authorised by the contract must be in writing.

1.3.2   Giving a notice or delivering a document to a party's conveyancer has the same effect as giving or delivering it to that party.

1.3.3   Where delivery of the original document is not essential, a notice or document is validly given or sent if it is sent:

(a)   by fax, or

(b)   by e-mail to an e-mail address for the intended recipient given in the contract.

1.3.4   Subject to conditions 1.3.5 to 1.3.7. a notice is given and a document delivered when it is received.

1.3.5   (a)   A notice or document sent through the document exchange is received when it is available for collection

(b)   A notice or document which is received after 4.00 pm on a working day, or on a day which is not a working day, is to be treated as having been received on the next working day

(c)   An automated response to a notice or document sent by e-mail that the intended recipient is out of the office is to be treated as proof that the notice or document was not received.

1.3.6   Condition 1.3.7 applies unless there is proof:

(a)   that a notice or document has not been received, or

(b)   of when it was received.

1.3.7   Unless the actual time of receipt is proved, a notice or document sent by the following means is treated as having been received as follows:

(a)   by first class post: before 4.00 pm on the second working day after posting

(b)   by second-class post: before 4.00 pm on the third working day after posting

(c)   through a document exchange: before 4.00 pm on the first working day after the day on which it would normally be available for collection by the addressee

(d)   by fax: one hour after despatch

(e)   by e-mail: before 4.00 pm on the first working day after despatch.

1.3.8   In condition 1.3.7, 'first class post' means a postal service which seeks to deliver posted items no later than the next working day in all or the majority of cases.

1.4   VAT

1.4.1   The seller:

(a)   warrants that the sale of the property does not constitute a supply that is taxable for VAT purposes

(b)   agrees that there will be no exercise of the election to waive exemption in respect of the property, and

(c)   cannot require the buyer to pay any amount in respect of any liability to VAT arising in respect of the sale of the property, unless condition 1.4.2 applies.

1.4.2   If, solely as a result of a change in law made and coming into effect between the date of the contract and completion, the sale of the property will constitute a supply chargeable to VAT, the buyer is to pay to the seller on completion an additional amount equal to that VAT in exchange for a proper VAT invoice from the seller.

1.4.3   The amount payable for the chattels is exclusive of VAT and the buyer is to pay to the seller on completion an additional amount equal to any VAT charged on that supply in exchange for a proper VAT invoice from the seller.

1.5   Assignment and sub-sales

1.5.1   The buyer is not entitled to transfer the benefit of the contract.

1.5.2   The seller may not be required to transfer the property in parts or to any person other than the buyer.

2.   FORMATION

2.1   Date

2.1.1   If the parties intend to make a contract by exchanging duplicate copies by post or through a document exchange, the contract is made when the last copy is posted or deposited at the document exchange.

2.1.2   If the parties' conveyancers agree to treat exchange as taking place before duplicate copies are actually exchanged, the contract is made as so agreed.

2.2   Deposit

2.2.1   The buyer is to pay a deposit of 10 per cent of the purchase price no later than the date of the contract.

2.2.2   Except on a sale by auction the deposit is to be paid by direct credit and is to be held by the seller's conveyancer as stakeholder on terms that on completion it is to be paid to the seller with accrued interest.

2.3   Auctions

2.3.1   On a sale by auction the following conditions apply to the property and, if it is sold in lots, to each lot.

2.3.2   The sale is subject to a reserve price.

2.3.3   The seller, or a person on its behalf, may bid up to the reserve price.

2.3.4   The auctioneer may refuse any bid.

2.3.5   If there is a dispute about a bid, the auctioneer may resolve the dispute or restart the auction at the last undisputed bid.

2.3.6   The auctioneer is to hold the deposit as agent for the seller.

2.3.7   If any cheque tendered in payment of all or part of the deposit is dishonoured when first presented, the seller may, within seven working days of being notified that the cheque has been dishonoured, give notice to the buyer that the contract is discharged by the buyer's breach.

3.   MATTERS AFFECTING THE PROPERTY

3.1   Freedom from incumbrances

3.1.1   The seller is selling the property free from incumbrances, other than those mentioned in condition 3.1.2.

3.1.2   The incumbrances subject to which the property is sold are:

(a)   those specified in the contract

(b)   those discoverable by inspection of the property before the contract

(c)   those the seller does not and could not reasonably know about

(d)   matters, other than monetary charges or incumbrances. disclosed or which would have been disclosed by the searches and enquiries which a prudent buyer would have made before entering into the contract

(e)   public requirements,

3.1.3   After the contract is made, the seller is to give the buyer written details without delay of any new public requirement and of anything in writing which he learns about concerning a matter covered by condition 3.1.2.

3.1.4   The buyer is to bear the cost of complying with any outstanding public requirement and is to indemnify the seller against any liability resulting from a public requirement.

3.2   Physical state

3.2.1   The buyer accepts the property in the physical state it is in at the date of the contract unless the seller is building or converting it.

3.2.2   A leasehold property is sold subject to any subsisting breach of a condition or tenant's obligation relating to the physical state of the property which renders the lease liable to forfeiture.

3.2.3   A sub-lease is granted subject to any subsisting breach of a condition or tenant's obligation relating to the physical state of the property which renders the seller's own lease liable to forfeiture.

3.3   Retained land

Where after the transfer the seller will be retaining land near the property:

(a)   the buyer will have no right of light or air over the retained land, but

(b)   in other respects the seller and the buyer will each have the rights over the land of the other which they would have had if they were two separate buyers to whom the seller had made simultaneous transfers of the property and the retained land.

The transfer is to contain appropriate express terms.

4.   LEASES AFFECTING THE PROPERTY

4.1   General

4.1.1   This condition applies if any part of the property is sold subject to a lease.

4.1.2   The seller having provided the buyer with full details of each lease or copies of documents embodying the lease terms, the buyer is treated as entering into the contract knowing and fully accepting those terms.

4.1.3   The seller is not to serve a notice to end the lease nor to accept a surrender.

4.1.4   The seller is to inform the buyer without delay if the lease ends.

4.1.5   The buyer is to indemnify the seller against all claims arising from the lease after actual completion; this includes claims which are unenforceable against a buyer for want of registration.

4.1.6   If the property does not include all the land let, the seller may apportion the rent and, if the lease is a new tenancy, the buyer may require the seller to apply under section 10 of the Landlord and Tenant (Covenants) Act 1995 for the apportionment to bind the tenant.

4.2 Property management

4.2.1   The seller is promptly to give the buyer full particulars of:

(a)   any court or arbitration proceedings in connection with the lease, and

(b)   any application for a licence, consent or approval under the lease.

4.2.2   Conditions 4.2.3 to 4.2.8 do not apply to a rent review process to which condition 5 applies.

4.2.3   Subject to condition 4.2.4, the seller is to conduct any court or arbitration proceedings in accordance with written directions given by the buyer from time to time (for which the seller is to apply), unless to do so might place the seller in breach of an obligation to the tenant or a statutory duty.

4.2.4   If the seller applies for directions from the buyer in relation to a proposed step in the proceedings and the buyer does not give such directions within 10 working days, the seller may take or refrain from taking that step as it thinks fit.

4.2.5   The buyer is to indemnify the seller against all loss and expense resulting from the seller's following the buyer's directions.

4.2.6   Unless the buyer gives written consent, the seller is not to:

(a)   grant or formally withhold any licence, consent or approval under the lease, or

(b)   serve any notice or take any action (other than action in court or arbitration proceedings) as landlord under the lease.

4.2.7   When the seller applies for the buyer's consent under condition 4.2.6:

(a)   the buyer is not to withhold its consent or attach conditions to the consent where to do so might place the seller in breach of an obligation to the tenant or a statutory duty

(b)   the seller may proceed as if the buyer has consented when:

(i)   in accordance with paragraph (a), the buyer is not entitled to withhold its consent, or

(ii)   the buyer does not refuse its consent within 10 working days.

4.2.8   If the buyer withholds or attaches conditions to its consent, the buyer is to indemnify the seller against all loss and expense.

4.2.9   In all other respects, the seller is to manage the property in accordance with the principles of good estate management until completion.

4.3   Continuing liability

At the request and cost of the seller, the buyer is to support any application by the seller to be released from the landlord covenants in a lease to which the property is sold subject.

5.   RENT REVIEWS

5.1   Subject to condition 5.2, this condition applies if:

(a)   the rent reserved by a lease of all or part of the property is to be reviewed,

(b)   the seller is either the landlord or the tenant,

(c)   the rent review process starts before actual completion, and

(d)   no reviewed rent has been agreed or determined at the date of the contract.

5.2   The seller is to conduct the rent review process until actual completion, after which the buyer is to conduct it.

5.3   Conditions 5.4 and 5.5 cease to apply on actual completion if the reviewed rent will only be payable in respect of a period after that date.

5.4   In the course of the rent review process, the seller and the buyer are each to:

(a)   act promptly with a view to achieving the best result obtainable,

(b)   consult with and have regard to the views of the other,

(c)   provide the other with copies of all material correspondence and papers relating to the process,

(d)   ensure that its representations take account of matters put forward by the other, and

(e)   keep the other informed of the progress of the process.

5.5   Neither the seller nor the buyer is to agree a rent figure unless it has been approved in writing by the other (such approval not to be unreasonably withheld).

5.6   The seller and the buyer are each to bear their own costs of the rent review process.

5.7   Unless the rent review date precedes the apportionment day, the buyer is to pay the costs of a third party appointed to determine the rent.

5.8   Where the rent review date precedes the apportionment day, those costs are to be divided as follows:

(a)   the seller is to pay the proportion that the number of days from the rent review date to the apportionment day bears to the number of days from that rent review date until either the following rent review date or, if none, the expiry of the term, and

(b)   the buyer is to pay the balance.

6.   TITLE AND TRANSFER

6.1   Proof of title

6.1.1   Without cost to the buyer, the seller is to provide the buyer with proof of the title to the property and of his ability to transfer it, or to procure its transfer.

6.1.2   Where the property has a registered title the proof is to include official copies of the items referred to in rules 134(1)(a) and (b) and 135(1)(a) of the Land Registration Rules 2003, so far as they are not to be discharged or overridden at or before completion.

6.1.3   Where the property has an unregistered title, the proof is to include:

(a)   an abstract of title or an epitome of title with photocopies of the documents, and

(b) production of every document or an abstract, epitome or copy of it with an original marking by a conveyancer either against the original or an examined abstract or an examined copy.

6.2 Requisitions

6.2.1 The buyer may not raise requisitions:

(a) on the title shown by the seller taking the steps described in condition 6.1.1 before the contract was made

(b) in relation to the matters covered by condition 3.1.2

6.2.2 Notwithstanding condition 6.2.1, the buyer may, within six working days of a matter coming to his attention after the contract was made, raise written requisitions on that matter. In that event steps 3 and 4 in condition 6.3.1 apply.

6.2.3 On the expiry of the relevant time limit under condition 6.2.2 or condition 6.3.1, the buyer loses his right to raise requisitions or to make observations.

6.3 Timetable

6.3.1 Subject to condition 6.2 and to the extent that the seller did not take the steps described in condition 6.1.1 before the contract was made, the following are the steps for deducing and investigating the title to the property to be taken within the following time limits:

Step		Time limit
1.	The seller is to comply with condition 6.1.1	Immediately after making the contract
2.	The buyer may raise written requisitions	Six working days after either the date of the contract or the date of delivery of the seller's evidence of title on which the requisitions are raised whichever is the later
3.	The seller is to reply in writing to any requisitions raised	Four working days after receiving the requisitions
4.	The buyer may make written observations on the seller's replies	Three working days after receiving the replies

The time limit on the buyer's right to raise requisitions applies even where the seller supplies incomplete evidence of its title, but the buyer may, within six working days from delivery of any further evidence, raise further requisitions resulting from that evidence.

6.3.2 The parties are to take the following steps to prepare and agree the transfer of the property within the following time limits:

Step		Time limit
A.	The buyer is to send the seller a draft transfer	At least twelve working days before completion date
B.	The seller is to approve or revise that draft and either return it or retain it for use as the actual transfer	Four working days after delivery of the draft transfer
C.	If the draft is returned the buyer is to send an engrossment to the seller	At least five working days before completion date

6.3.3 Periods of time under conditions 6.3.1 and 6.3.2 may run concurrently.

6.3.4 If the period between the date of the contract and completion date is less than 15 working days, the time limits in conditions 6.2.2, 6.3.1 and 6.3.2 are to be reduced by the same proportion as that period bears to the period of 15 working days.

Fractions of a working day are to be rounded down except that the time limit to perform any step is not to be less than one working day.

6.4 Defining the property

6.4.1 The seller need not, further than it may be able to do from information in its possession:

    (a)   prove the exact boundaries of the property

    (b)   prove who owns fences, ditches, hedges or walls

    (c)   separately identify parts of the property with different titles.

6.4.2 The buyer may, if to do so is reasonable, require the seller to make or obtain, pay for and hand over a statutory declaration about facts relevant to the matters mentioned in condition 6.4.1. The form of the declaration is to be agreed by the buyer, who must not unreasonably withhold its agreement.

6.5 Rents and rentcharges

The fact that a rent or rentcharge, whether payable or receivable by the owner of the property, has been or will on completion be, informally apportioned is not to be regarded as a defect in title.

6.6 Transfer

6.6.1 The buyer does not prejudice its right to raise requisitions, or to require replies to any raised, by taking steps in relation to the preparation or agreement of the transfer.

6.6.2 Subject to condition 6.6.3, the seller is to transfer the property with full title guarantee.

6.6.3 The transfer is to have effect as if the disposition is expressly made subject to all matters covered by condition 3.1.2.

6.6.4 If after completion the seller will remain bound by any obligation affecting the property and disclosed to the buyer before the contract was made, but the law does not imply any covenant by the buyer to indemnify the seller against liability for future breaches of it:

    (a)   the buyer is to covenant in the transfer to indemnify the seller against liability for any future breach of the obligation and to perform it from then on, and

    (b)   if required by the seller, the buyer is to execute and deliver to the seller on completion a duplicate transfer prepared by the buyer.

6.6.5 The seller is to arrange at its expense that, in relation to every document of title which the buyer does not receive on completion, the buyer is to have the benefit of:

    (a)   a written acknowledgement of the buyer's right to its production, and

    (b)   a written undertaking for its safe custody (except while it is held by a mortgagee or by someone in a fiduciary capacity).

7. INSURANCE

7.1 Responsibility for insuring

7.1.1 Conditions 7.1.2 and 7.1.3 apply if:

    (a)   the contract provides that the policy effected by or for the seller and insuring the property or any part of it against loss or damage should continue in force after the exchange of contracts, or

(b)   the property or any part of it is let on terms under which the seller (whether as landlord or as tenant) is obliged to insure against loss or damage.

7.1.2   The seller is to:

(a)   do everything required to continue to maintain the policy, including the prompt payment of any premium which falls due

(b)   increase the amount or extent of the cover as requested by the buyer, if the insurers agree and the buyer pays the additional premium

(c)   permit the buyer to inspect the policy, or evidence of its terms, at any time

(d)   obtain or consent to an endorsement on the policy of the buyer's interest, at the buyer's expense

(e)   pay to the buyer immediately on receipt, any part of an additional premium which the buyer paid and which is returned by the insurers

(f)   if before completion the property suffers loss or damage:

    (i)   pay to the buyer on completion the amount of policy moneys which the seller has received, so far as not applied in repairing or reinstating the property, and

    (ii)   if no final payment has then been received, assign to the buyer, at the buyer's expense, all rights to claim under the policy in such form as the buyer reasonably requires and pending execution of the assignment, hold any policy moneys received in trust for the buyer

(g)   on completion:

    (i)   cancel the insurance policy

    (ii)   apply for a refund of the premium and pay the buyer, immediately on receipt, any amount received which relates to a part of the premium which was paid or reimbursed by a tenant or third party. The buyer is to hold the money paid subject to the rights of that tenant or third party.

7.1.3   The buyer is to pay the seller a proportionate part of the premium which the seller paid in respect of the period from the date when the contract is made to the date of actual completion, except so far as the seller is entitled to recover it from a tenant.

7.1.4   Unless condition 7.1.2 applies:

(a)   the seller is under no obligation to the buyer to insure the property

(b)   if payment under a policy effected by or for the buyer is reduced, because the property is covered against loss or damage by an insurance policy effected by or for the seller, the purchase price is to be abated by the amount of that reduction.

7.1.5   Section 47 of the Law of Property Act 1925 does not apply.

8.   COMPLETION

8.1   Date

8.1.1   Completion date is twenty working days after the date of the contract but time is not of the essence of the contract unless a notice to complete has been served.

8.1.2   If the money due on completion is received after 2.00 pm, completion is to be treated, for the purposes only of conditions 8.3 and 9.3, as taking place on the next working day as a result of the buyer's default.

8.1.3   Condition 8.1.2 does not apply if:

(a)   the sale is with vacant possession of the property or a part of it, and

(b)   the buyer is ready, willing and able to complete but does not pay the money due on completion until after 2.00 pm because the seller has not vacated the property or that part by that time.

8.2   Place

Completion is to take place in England and Wales, either at the seller's conveyancer's office or at some other place which the seller reasonably specifies.

8.3   Apportionments

8.3.1   Subject to condition 8.3.6 income and outgoings of the property are to be apportioned between the parties so far as the change of ownership on completion will affect entitlement to receive or liability to pay them.

8.3.2   The day from which the apportionment is to be made ('apportionment day') is:

(a)   if the whole property is sold with vacant possession or the seller exercises its option in condition 9.3.4, the date of actual completion, or

(b)   otherwise, completion date.

8.3.3   In apportioning any sum, it is to be assumed that the buyer owns the property from the beginning of the day on which the apportionment is to be made.

8.3.4   A sum to be apportioned is to be treated as:

(a)   payable for the period which it covers, except that if it is an instalment of an annual sum the buyer is to be attributed with an amount equal to 1/365th of the annual sum for each day from and including the apportionment day to the end of the instalment period

(b)   accruing —

(i)   from day to day, and

(ii)   at the rate applicable from time to time.

8.3.5   When a sum to be apportioned, or the rate at which it is to be treated as accruing, is not known or easily ascertainable at completion, a provisional apportionment is to be made according to the best estimate available. As soon as the amount is known, a final apportionment is to be made and notified to the other party. Subject to condition 8.3.8, any resulting balance is to be paid no more than ten working days later, and if not then paid the balance is to bear interest at the contract rate from then until payment.

8.3.6   Where a lease of the property requires the tenant to reimburse the landlord for expenditure on goods or services, on completion:

(a)   the buyer is to pay the seller the amount of any expenditure already incurred by the seller but not yet due from the tenant and in respect of which the seller provides the buyer with the information and vouchers required for its recovery from the tenant, and

(b)   the seller is to credit the buyer with payments already recovered from the tenant but not yet incurred by the seller.

8.3.7   Condition 8.3.8 applies if any part of the property is sold subject to a lease and either:

(a)   (i)   on completion any rent or other sum payable under the lease is due but not paid

(ii)   the contract does not provide that the buyer is to assign to the seller the right to collect any arrears due to the seller under the terms of the contract, and

(iii)   the seller is not entitled to recover any arrears from the tenant, or

(b) (i)   as a result of a rent review to which condition 5 applies a reviewed rent is agreed or determined after actual completion, and

(ii)   an additional sum then becomes payable in respect of a period before the apportionment day.

8.3.8 (a)   The buyer is to seek to collect all sums due in the circumstances referred to in condition 8.3.7 in the ordinary course of management, but need not take legal proceedings or distrain.

(b)   A payment made on account of those sums is to be apportioned between the parties in the ratio of the amounts owed to each, notwithstanding that the tenant exercises its right to appropriate the payment in some other manner.

(c)   Any part of a payment on account received by one party but due to the other is to be paid no more than ten working days after the receipt of cash or cleared funds and, if not then paid, the sum is to bear interest at the contract rate until payment.

8.4 Amount payable

The amount payable by the buyer on completion is the purchase price (less any deposit already paid to the seller or its agent) adjusted to take account of:

(a)   apportionments made under condition 8.3

(b)   any compensation to be paid under condition 9.3

(c)   any sum payable under condition 7.1.2 or 7.1.3.

8.5 Title deeds

8.5.1 As soon as the buyer has complied with all its obligations on completion the seller must hand over the documents of title.

8.5.2 Condition 8.5.1 does not apply to any documents of title relating to land being retained by the seller after completion.

8.6 Rent receipts

The buyer is to assume that whoever gave any receipt for a payment of rent which the seller produces was the person or the agent of the person then entitled to that rent.

8.7 Means of payment

The buyer is to pay the money due on completion by direct credit and, if appropriate, by an unconditional release of a deposit held by a stakeholder.

8.8 Notice to complete

8.8.1 At any time on or after completion date, a party who is ready, able and willing to complete may give the other a notice to complete.

8.8.2 The parties are to complete the contract within ten working days of giving a notice to complete, excluding the day on which the notice is given. For this purpose, time is of the essence of the contract.

9. REMEDIES

9.1 Errors and omissions

9.1.1 If any plan or statement in the contract, or in the negotiations leading to it. is or was misleading or inaccurate due to an error or omission, the remedies available are as follows.

9.1.2 When there is a material difference between the description or value of the property as represented and as it is, the buyer is entitled to damages.

9.1.3   An error or omission only entitles the buyer to rescind the contract:

(a)   where the error or omission results from fraud or recklessness, or

(b)   where the buyer would be obliged, to its prejudice, to accept property differing substantially (in quantity, quality or tenure) from that which the error or omission had led it to expect.

9.2   Rescission

If either party rescinds the contract:

(a)   unless the rescission is a result of the buyer's breach of contract the deposit is to be repaid to the buyer with accrued interest

(b)   the buyer is to return any documents received from the seller and is to cancel any registration of the contract

(c)   the seller's duty to pay any returned premium under condition 7.1.2(e) (whenever received) is not affected.

9.3   Late completion

9.3.1   If the buyer defaults in performing its obligations under the contract and completion is delayed, the buyer is to pay compensation to the seller.

9.3.2   Compensation is calculated at the contract rate on the purchase price (less any deposit paid) for the period between completion date and actual completion, but ignoring any period during which the seller was in default.

9.3.3   Any claim by the seller for loss resulting from delayed completion is to be reduced by any compensation paid under this contract.

9.3.4   Where the sale is not with vacant possession of the whole property and completion is delayed, the seller may give notice to the buyer, before the date of actual completion, that it will take the net income from the property until completion as well as compensation under condition 9.3.1

9.4   After completion

Completion does not cancel liability to perform any outstanding obligation under the contract.

9.5   Buyer's failure to comply with notice to complete

9.5.1   If the buyer fails to complete in accordance with a notice to complete, the following terms apply.

9.5.2   The seller may rescind the contract, and if it does so:

(a)   it may

(i)   forfeit and keep any deposit and accrued interest

(ii)   resell the property

(iii)   claim damages

(b)   the buyer is to return any documents received from the seller and is to cancel any registration of the contract.

9.5.3   The seller retains its other rights and remedies.

9.6   Seller's failure to comply with notice to complete

9.6.1   If the seller fails to complete in accordance with a notice to complete, the following terms apply:

9.6.2   The buyer may rescind the contract, and if it does so:

(a)   the deposit is to be repaid to the buyer with accrued interest

(b)   the buyer is to return any documents it received from the seller and is, at the seller's expense, to cancel any registration of the contract.

9.6.3   The buyer retains its other rights and remedies.

10.   LEASEHOLD PROPERTY

10.1   Existing leases

10.1.1   The following provisions apply to a sale of leasehold land.

10.1.2   The seller having provided the buyer with copies of the documents embodying the lease terms, the buyer is treated as entering into the contract knowing and fully accepting those terms.

10.1.3   The seller is to comply with any lease obligations requiring the tenant to insure the property.

10.2   New leases

10.2.1   The following provisions apply to a contract to grant a new lease.

10.2.2   The conditions apply so that:
'seller' means the proposed landlord
'buyer' means the proposed tenant
'purchase price' means the premium to be paid on the grant of a lease.

10.2.3   The lease is to be in the form of the draft attached to the contract.

10.2.4   If the term of the new lease will exceed seven years, the seller is to deduce a title which will enable the buyer to register the lease at the Land Registry with an absolute title.

10.2.5   The seller is to engross the lease and a counterpart of it and is to send the counterpart to the buyer at least five working days before completion date.

10.2.6   The buyer is to execute the counterpart and deliver it to the seller on completion.

10.3   Consents

10.3.1   (a)   The following provisions apply if a consent to let, assign or sub-let is required to complete the contract
          (b)   In this condition 'consent' means consent in a form which satisfies the requirement to obtain it.

10.3.2   (a)   The seller is to:
                 (i)   apply for the consent at its expense, and to use all reasonable efforts to obtain it
                 (ii)   give the buyer notice forthwith on obtaining the consent
          (b)   The buyer is to comply with all reasonable requirements, including requirements for the provision of information and references.

10.3.3   Where the consent of a reversioner (whether or not immediate) is required to an assignment or sub-letting, then so far as the reversioner lawfully imposes such a condition:
          (a)   the buyer is to:
                 (i)   covenant directly with the reversioner to observe the tenant's covenants and the conditions in the seller's lease
                 (ii)   use reasonable endeavours to provide guarantees of the performance and observance of the tenant's covenants and the conditions in the seller's lease

        (iii)   execute or procure the execution of the licence

    (b)   the seller, in the case of an assignment, is to enter into an authorised guarantee agreement,

10.3.4   Neither party may object to a reversioner's consent given subject to a condition:

    (a)   which under section 19A of the Landlord and Tenant Act 1927 is not regarded as unreasonable, and

    (b)   which is lawfully imposed under an express term of the lease.

10.3.5   If any required consent has not been obtained by the original completion date:

    (a)   the time for completion is to be postponed until five working days after the seller gives written notice to the buyer that the consent has been obtained or four months from the original completion date whichever is the earlier

    (b)   the postponed date is to be treated as the completion date.

10.3.6   At any time after four months from the original completion date, either party may rescind the contract by notice to the other, if:

    (a)   consent has still not been given, and

    (b)   no declaration has been obtained from the court that consent has been unreasonably withheld.

10.3.7   If the contract is rescinded under condition 10.3.6 the seller is to remain liable for any breach of condition 10.3.2(a) or 10.3.3(b) and the buyer is to remain liable for any breach of condition 10.3.2(b) or 10.3.3(a). In all other respects neither party is to be treated as in breach of contract and condition 9.2 applies.

10.3.8   A party in breach of its obligations under condition 10.3.2 or 10.3.3 cannot rescind under condition 10.3.6 for so long as its breach is a cause of the consent's being withheld.

11.   COMMONHOLD

11.1   Terms used in this condition have the special meanings given to them in Part 1 of the Commonhold and Leasehold Reform Act 2002.

11.2   This condition applies to a disposition of commonhold land.

11.3   The seller having provided the buyer with copies of the current versions of the memorandum and articles of the commonhold association and of the commonhold community statement, the buyer is treated as entering into the contract knowing and fully accepting their terms.

11.4   If the contract is for the sale of property which is or includes part only of a commonhold unit:

    (a)   the seller is, at its expense, to apply for the written consent of the commonhold association and is to use all reasonable efforts to obtain it

    (b)   either the seller, unless it is in breach of its obligation under paragraph (a), or the buyer may rescind the contract by notice to the other party if three working days before completion date (or before a later date on which the parties have agreed to complete the contract) the consent has not been given. In that case, neither party is to be treated as in breach of contract and condition 9.2 applies.

12.   CHATTELS

12.1   The following provisions apply to any chattels which are included in the contract.

12.2   The contract takes effect as a contract for the sale of goods.

12.3   The buyer takes the chattels in the physical state they are in at the date of the contract.

12.4   Ownership of the chattels passes to the buyer on actual completion but they are at the buyer's risk from the contract date.

PART 2*

A. **VAT**

A1. **Standard rated supply**

A1.   Conditions 1.4.1 and 1.4.2 do not apply.

A1.2   The seller warrants that the sale of the property will constitute a supply chargeable to VAT at the standard rate.

A1.3   The buyer is to pay to the seller on completion an additional amount equal to the VAT in exchange for a proper VAT invoice from the seller.

A2   **Transfer of a going concern**

A2.1   Condition 1.4 does not apply.

A2.2   In this condition 'TOGC' means a transfer of a business as a going concern treated as neither a supply of goods nor a supply of services by virtue of article 5 of the Value Added Tax (Special Provisions) Order 1995.

A2.3   The seller warrants that it is using the property for the business of letting to produce rental income.

A2.4   The buyer is to make every effort to comply with the conditions to be met by a transferee under article 5(1) and 5(2) for the sale to constitute a TOGC.

A2.5   The buyer will, on or before the earlier of:

(a)   completion date, and

(b)   the earliest date on which a supply of the property could be treated as made by the seller under this contract if the sale does not constitute a TOGC.

notify the seller that paragraph (2B) of article 5 of the VAT (Special Provisions) Order 1995 does not apply to the buyer.

A2.6   The parties are to treat the sale as a TOGC at completion if the buyer provides written evidence to the seller before completion that it is a taxable person and that it has made an election to waive exemption in respect of the property and has given a written notification of the making of such election in conformity with article 5(2) and has given the notification referred to in condition A2.5.

A2.7   The buyer is not to revoke its election to waive exemption in respect of the property at any time.

A2.8   If the parties treat the sale at completion as a TOGC but it is later determined that the sale was not a TOGC, then within five working days of that determination the buyer shall pay to the seller:

(a)   an amount equal to the VAT chargeable in respect of the supply of the property, in exchange for a proper VAT invoice from the seller; and

(b)   except where the sale is not a TOGC because of an act or omission of the seller, an amount equal to any interest or penalty for which the seller is liable to account to HM Customs and Excise in respect of or by reference to that VAT.

A2.9   If the seller obtains the consent of HM Customs and Excise to retain its VAT records relating to the property, it shall make them available to the buyer for inspection and copying at reasonable times on reasonable request during the six years following completion.

B   CAPITAL ALLOWANCES

B1   To enable the buyer to make and substantiate claims under the Capital Allowances Act 2001 in respect of the property, the seller is to use its reasonable endeavours to provide, or to procure that its agents provide:

(a)   copies of all relevant information in its possession or that of its agents, and

(b)   such co-operation and assistance as the buyer may reasonably require.

B2.1   The buyer is only to use information provided under condition B1 for the stated purpose.

B2.2   The buyer is not to disclose, without the consent of the seller, any such information which the seller expressly provides on a confidential basis.

B3.1   On completion, the seller and the buyer are jointly to make an election under section 198 of the Capital Allowances Act 2001 which is consistent with the apportionment in the Special Conditions.

B3.2   The seller and the buyer are each to submit the amount fixed by that election to the Inland Revenue for the purposes of their respective capital allowance computations.

C   REVERSIONARY INTERESTS IN FLATS

C1.   No tenants' rights

C1.1   In this condition, sections refer to sections of the Landlord and Tenant Act 1987 and expressions have the special meanings given to them in that Act.

C1.2   The seller warrants that:

(a)   it gave the notice required by section 5,

(b)   no acceptance notice was served on the landlord or no person was nominated for the purposes of section 6 during the protected period, and

(c)   that period ended less than 12 months before the date of the contract.

C2.   Tenants' right of first refusal

C2.1   In this condition, sections refer to sections of the Landlord and Tenant Act 1987 and expressions have the special meanings given to them in that Act.

C2.2   The seller warrants that:

(a)   it gave the notice required by section 5, and

(b)   it has given the buyer a copy of:

(i)   any acceptance notice served on the landlord and

(ii)   any nomination of a person duly nominated for the purposes of section 6.

C2.3   If the sale is by auction:

(a)   the seller warrants that it has given the buyer a copy of any notice served on the landlord electing that section 8B shall apply,

(b)   condition 8.1.1. applies as if 'thirty working days' were substituted for 'twenty working days',

(c)   the seller is to send a copy of the contract to the nominated person as required by section 8B(3), and

(d)   if the nominated person serves notice under section 8B(4):
  (i)   the seller is to give the buyer a copy of the notice, and
  (ii)   condition 9.2 is to apply as if the contract had been rescinded.

---

*The conditions in Part 2 do not apply unless expressly incorporated. See condition 1.1.4(b).

Appendix 4

The Law Society's Formulae for Exchanging Contracts by Telephone, Fax or Telex

Introduction

It is essential that an agreed memorandum of the details and of any variations of the formula used should be made at the time and retained in the file. This would be very important if any question on the exchange were raised subsequently. Agreed variations should also be confirmed in writing. The serious risks of exchanging contracts without a deposit, unless the full implications are explained to and accepted by the seller client, are demonstrated in *Morris v Duke-Cohan & Co* (1975) 119 SJ 826.

As those persons involved in the exchange will bind their firms to the undertakings in the formula used, solicitors should carefully consider who is to be authorised to exchange contracts by telephone, fax or telex and should ensure that the use of the procedure is restricted to them. Since professional undertakings form the basis of the formulae, they are only recommended for use between firms of solicitors and licensed conveyancers.

Law Society telephone/telex exchange – formula A (1986)

(For use where one solicitor holds both signed parts of the contract.)

A completion date of   20 is agreed.

The solicitor holding both parts of the contract confirms that he or she holds the part signed by his or her client(s), which is identical to the part he or she is also holding signed by the other solicitor's client(s) and will forthwith insert the agreed completion date in each part.

Solicitors mutually agree that exchange shall take place from that moment and the solicitor holding both parts confirms that, as of that moment, he or she holds the part signed by his or her client(s) to the order of the other. He or she undertakes that day by first-class post, or where the other solicitor is a member of a document exchange (as to which the inclusion of a reference thereto in the solicitor's letterhead shall be conclusive evidence) by delivery to that or any other affiliated exchange, or by hand delivery direct to that solicitor's office, to send his or her signed part of the contract to the other solicitor, together, where he or she is the purchaser's solicitor, with a banker's draft or a solicitor's client account cheque for the deposit amounting to £. . . . .

Note

1. A memorandum should be prepared, after use of the formula, recording:
   (a)   date and time of exchange;
   (b)   the formula used and exact wording of agreed variations;
   (c)   the completion date;

(d)   the (balance) deposit to be paid;

(e)   the identities of those involved in any conversation.

Law Society telephone/telex exchange – formula B (1986)

(For use where each solicitor holds his or her own client's signed part of the contract.)

A completion date of   is agreed. Each solicitor confirms to the other that he or she holds a part contract in the agreed form signed by the client(s) and will forthwith insert the agreed completion date.

Each solicitor undertakes to the other thenceforth to hold the signed part of the contract to the other's order, so that contracts are exchanged at that moment. Each solicitor further undertakes that day by first-class post, or, where the other solicitor is a member of a document exchange (as to which the inclusion of a reference thereto in the solicitor's letterhead shall be conclusive evidence) by delivery to that or any other affiliated exchange, or by hand delivery direct to that solicitor's office, to send his or her signed part of the contract to the other together, in the case of a purchaser's solicitor, with a banker's draft or a solicitor's client account cheque for the deposit amounting to £. . . . .

Notes

1.   A memorandum should be prepared, after use of the formula, recording:

(a)   date and time of exchange;

(b)   the formula used and exact wording of agreed variations;

(c)   the completion date;

(d)   the (balance) deposit to be paid; and

(e)   the identities of those involved in any conversation.

2.   Those who are going to effect the exchange must first confirm the details in order to ensure that both parts are identical. This means in particular, that if either part of the contract has been amended since it was originally prepared, the solicitor who holds a part contract with the amendments must disclose them, so that it can be confirmed that the other part is similarly amended.

9 July 1986, revised January 1996

Law Society telephone/fax/telex exchange – formula C (1989)

Part I

The following is agreed:
Final time for exchange: pm
Completion date:
Deposit to be paid to:

Each solicitor confirms that he or she holds a part of the contract in the agreed form signed by his or her client, or, if there is more than one client, by all of them. Each solicitor undertakes to the other that:

(a)   he or she will continue to hold that part of the contract until the final time for exchange on the date the formula is used, and

(b)   if the vendor's solicitor so notifies the purchaser's solicitor by fax, telephone or telex (whichever was previously agreed) by that time, they will both comply with part II of the formula.

The purchaser's solicitor further undertakes that either he or she or some other named person in his or her office will be available up to the final time for exchange to activate part II of the formula on receipt of the telephone call, fax or telex from the vendor's solicitors.

Part II

Each solicitor undertakes to the other henceforth to hold the part of the contract in his or her possession to the other's order, so that contracts are exchanged at that moment, and to despatch it to the other on that day. The purchaser's solicitor further undertakes to the vendor's solicitor to despatch on that day, or to arrange for the despatch on that day of, a banker's draft or a solicitor's client account cheque for the full deposit specified in the agreed form of contract (divided as the vendor's solicitor may have specified) to the vendor's solicitor and/or to some other solicitor whom the vendor's solicitor nominates, to be held on formula C terms.

'To despatch' means to send by first-class post, or, where the other solicitor is a member of a document exchange (as to which the inclusion of a reference thereto in the solicitor's letterhead is to be conclusive evidence) by delivery to that or any other affiliated exchange, or by hand delivery direct to the recipient solicitor's office. 'Formula C terms' means that the deposit is held as stakeholder, or as agent for the vendor with authority to part with it only for the purpose of passing it to another solicitor as deposit in a related property purchase transaction on these terms.

Notes

1.   Two memoranda will be required when using Formula C. One needs to record the use of Part I, and a second needs to record the request of the vendor's solicitor to the purchaser's solicitor to activate Part II.

2.   The first memorandum should record:
    (a)   the date and time when it was agreed to use Formula C;
    (b)   the exact wording of any agreed variations;
    (c)   the final time, later that day, for exchange;
    (d)   the completion date;
    (e)   the name of the solicitor to whom the deposit was to be paid, or details of amounts and names if it was to be split; and
    (f)   the identities of those involved in any conversation.

3.   Formula C assumes the payment of a full contractual deposit (normally 10%).

4.   The contract term relating to the deposit must allow it to be passed on, with payment direct from payer to ultimate recipient, in the way in which the formula contemplates. The deposit must ultimately be held by a solicitor as stakeholder. Whilst some variation in the formula can be agreed this is a term of the formula which must not be varied, unless all the solicitors involved in the chain have agreed.

5.   If a buyer proposes to use a deposit guarantee policy, Formula C will need substantial adaptation.

6.   It is essential prior to agreeing Part I of Formula C that those effecting the exchange ensure that both parts of the contract are identical.

7.   Using Formula C involves a solicitor in giving a number of professional undertakings. These must be performed precisely. Any failure will be a serious breach of professional discipline. One of the undertakings may be to arrange that someone over whom the solicitor has no control will do something (ie to arrange for someone else to despatch the cheque or banker's draft in payment of the deposit). An undertaking is still binding even if it is to do something outside the solicitor's control.

8.   Solicitors do not as a matter of law have an automatic authority to exchange contracts on a Formula C basis, and should always ensure that they have the client's express authority to use Formula C. A suggested form of authority is set out below. It should be adapted to cover any special circumstances:

I/We . . . . understand that my/our sale and purchase of . . . . are both part of a chain of linked property transactions, in which all parties want the security of contracts which become binding on the same day.

I/We agree that you should make arrangements with the other solicitors or licensed conveyancers involved to achieve this.

I/We understand that this involves each property-buyer offering, early on one day, to exchange contracts whenever, later that day, the seller so requests, and that the buyer's offer is on the basis that it cannot be withdrawn or varied during that day.

I/We agree that when I/we authorise you to exchange contracts, you may agree to exchange contracts on the above basis and give any necessary undertakings to the other parties involved in the chain and that my/our authority to you cannot be revoked throughout the day on which the offer to exchange contracts is made.

15 March 1989, revised January 1996

Appendix 5

The Law Society's Code for Completion by Post 1998

Preamble

The Code provides a procedure for postal completion which practising solicitors may adopt by reference. It may also be used by licensed conveyancers.

Before agreeing to adopt this Code, a solicitor must be satisfied that doing so will not be contrary to the interests of the client (including any mortgagee client).

When adopted, the Code applies without variation, unless agreed in writing in advance.

Procedure

General

1. To adopt this Code, all the solicitors must expressly agree, preferably in writing, to use it to complete a specific transaction.
2. On completion, the seller's solicitor acts as the buyer's solicitor's agent without any fee or disbursements.

Before completion

3. The seller's solicitor will specify in writing to the buyer's solicitor before completion the mortgages or charges secured on the property which, on or before completion, will be redeemed or discharged to the extent that they relate to the property.
4. The seller's solicitor undertakes:
   (i) to have the seller's authority to receive the purchase money on completion; and
   (ii) on completion to have the authority of the proprietor of each mortgage or charge specified under paragraph 3 to receive the sum intended to repay it,

   BUT

   if the seller's solicitor does not have all the necessary authorities then:
   (iii) to advise the buyer's solicitor no later than 4.00pm on the working day before the completion date that they do not have all the authorities or immediately if any is withdrawn later; and
   (iv) not to complete until he has the buyer's solicitor's instructions.
5. Before the completion date, the buyer's solicitor will send the seller's solicitor instructions as to any of the following which apply:
   (i) documents to be examined and marked;
   (ii) memoranda to be endorsed;
   (iii) undertakings to be given;

(iv) deeds, documents (including any relevant undertakings) and authorities relating to rents, deposits, keys, etc. to be sent to the buyer's solicitors following completion; and

(v) other relevant matters.

In default of instructions, the seller's solicitor is under no duty to examine, mark or endorse any document.

6.   The buyer's solicitor will remit to the seller's solicitor the sum required to complete, as notified in writing on the seller's solicitor's completion statement or otherwise, or in default of notification as shown by the contract. If the funds are remitted by transfer between banks, the seller's solicitor will instruct the receiving bank to telephone to report immediately the funds have been received. Pending completion, the seller's solicitor will hold the funds to the buyer's solicitor's order.

7.   If by the agreed date and time for completion the seller's solicitor has not received the authorities specified in paragraph 4, instructions under paragraph 5 and the sum specified in paragraph 6, the seller's solicitor will forthwith notify the buyer's solicitor and request further instructions.

Completion

8.   The seller's solicitor will complete forthwith on receiving the sum specified in paragraph 6, or at a later time agreed with the buyer's solicitor.

9.   When completing, the seller's solicitor undertakes:

(i) to comply with the instructions given under paragraph 5; and

(ii) to redeem or obtain discharges for every mortgage or charge so far as it relates to the property specified under paragraph 3 which has not already been redeemed or discharged.

After completion

10.   The seller's solicitor undertakes:

(i) immediately completion has taken place to hold to the buyer's solicitor's order every item referred to in (iv) of paragraph 5 and not to exercise a lien over any such item;

(ii) as soon as possible after completion, and in any event on the same day:

(a) to confirm to the buyer's solicitor by telephone or fax that completion has taken place; and

(b) to send written confirmation and, at the risk of the buyer's solicitor, the items listed in (iv) of paragraph 5 to the buyer's solicitor by first class post or document exchange.

Supplementary

11.   The rights and obligations of the parties, under the contract or otherwise, are not affected by this Code.

12.   (i) References to the seller's solicitor and the buyer's solicitor apply as appropriate to solicitors acting for other parties who adopt the Code.

(ii) When a licensed conveyancer adopts this Code, references to a solicitor include a licensed conveyancer.

13.   A dispute or difference arising between solicitors who adopt this Code (whether or not subject to any variation) relating directly to its application is to be referred to a single arbitrator agreed between the solicitors. If they do

not agree on the appointment within one month, the President of The Law Society may appoint the arbitrator at the request of one of the solicitors.

Notes to the Code:

1. This Code will apply to transactions when the Code is adopted after 1 July 1998.

2. The object of this Code is to provide solicitors with a convenient means for completion on an agency basis when a representative of the buyer's solicitor is not attending at the office of the seller's solicitor.

3. As with The Law Society's formulae for exchange of contracts by telephone and fax, the guide embodies professional undertakings and is only recommended for adoption between solicitors and licensed conveyancers.

4. Paragraph 2 of the Code provides that the seller's solicitors will act as agents for the buyer's solicitors without fee or disbursements. The convenience of not having to make a specific appointment on the day of completion for the buyer's solicitor to attend to complete will offset the agency work that the seller's solicitor has to do and any postage payable in completing under the Code. Most solicitors will from time to time act for both sellers and buyers. If a seller's solicitor does consider that charges and/or disbursements are necessary in a particular case this would represent a variation in the Code and should be agreed in writing before the completion date.

5. In view of the decision in *Edward Wong Finance Company Limited v Johnson, Stokes & Master* [1984] AC 1296, clause 4(ii) of the Code requires the seller's solicitor to undertake on completion to have authority of the proprietor of every mortgage or charge to be redeemed to receive the sum needed to repay such charge.

6. Paragraph 11 of the Code provides that nothing in the Code shall override any rights and obligations of the parties under contract or otherwise.

7. The buyer's solicitor is to inform the seller's solicitor of the mortgages or charges which will be redeemed or discharged (see paragraph 3 above) and is to specify those for which an undertaking will be required on completion (paragraph 5(iii)). The information may be given in reply to requisitions on title. Such a reply may also amount to an undertaking.

8. Care must be taken if there is a sale and sub-sale. The sub-seller's solicitor may not hold the title deeds nor be in a position to receive the funds required to discharge the seller's mortgage on the property. Enquiries should be made to ascertain if the monies or some part of the monies payable on completion should, with either the authority of the sub-seller or the sub-seller's solicitor, be sent direct to the seller's solicitor and not to the sub-seller's solicitor.

9. Care must also be taken if there is a simultaneous resale and completion and enquiries should be made by the ultimate buyer's solicitor of the intermediate seller's solicitor as to the price being paid on that purchase. Having appointed the intermediate seller's solicitor as agent, the buyer's solicitor is fixed with the knowledge of an agent even without having personal knowledge (see Green Card Warning on Property Fraud).

10. If the seller's solicitor has to withdraw from using the Code, the buyer's solicitor should be notified of this not later than 4.00pm on the working day prior to the completion date. If the seller's solicitor's authority to receive the monies is withdrawn later, the buyer's solicitor must be notified immediately.

These notes refer only to some of the points in the Code that practitioners may wish to consider before agreeing to adopt it. Any variation in the Code must be agreed in writing before the completion date.

Appendix 6

Form of Undertaking to Discharge Building Society Mortgages Approved by The Law Society in Conveyancing Matters

In consideration of you today completing the purchase of . . . .

WE HEREBY UNDERTAKE forthwith to pay over to the . . . .

Building Society the money required to redeem the mortgage/legal charge dated
. . . . and to forward the receipted mortgage/legal charge to you as soon as
it is received by us from the . . . . Building Society.

Appendix 7

The CML Lenders' Handbook for England and Wales (Last updated 1 June 2007)

© Council of Mortgage Lenders

Contents

PART 1 – INSTRUCTIONS AND GUIDANCE

Those lenders who instruct using the CML Lenders' Handbook certify that these instructions have been prepared to comply with the requirements of Rule 6 (3) of the Solicitors' Practice Rules 1990 (or when applicable the Solicitors' Code of Conduct 2007).

1. **GENERAL**

1.1   The CML Lenders' Handbook is issued by the Council of Mortgage Lenders. Your instructions from an individual lender will indicate if you are being instructed in accordance with the Lenders' Handbook. If you are, the general provisions in part 1 and any specific requirements in part 2 must be followed.

1.2   References to 'we', 'us' and 'our' means the lender from whom you receive instructions.

1.3   The Lenders' Handbook does not affect any responsibilities you have to us under the general law or any practice rule or guidance issued by your professional body from time to time.

1.4   The standard of care which we expect of you is that of a reasonably competent solicitor or licensed conveyancer acting on behalf of a mortgagee.

1.5   The limitations contained in rule 6(3)(c) and (e) of the Solicitors' Practice Rules 1990 (and when applicable the Solicitors' Code of Conduct 2007) apply to the instructions contained in the Lenders' Handbook and any separate instructions. This does not apply to licensed conveyancers following clause 3B.

1.6   You must also comply with any separate instructions you receive for an individual loan.

1.7   If the borrower and the mortgagor are not one and the same person, all references to 'borrower' shall include the mortgagor. Check part 2 to see if we lend in circumstances where the borrower and the mortgagor are not one and the same

1.8   References to 'borrower' (and, if applicable, 'guarantor' or, expressly or impliedly, the mortgagor) are to each borrower (and guarantor or mortgagor) named in the mortgage instructions/offer (if sent to the conveyancer). This applies to references in the Lenders' Handbook and in the certificate of title.

1.9   References to 'mortgage offer' include any loan agreement, offer of mortgage or any other similar document.

1.10 If you are instructed in connection with any additional loan (including a further advance) then you should treat references to 'mortgage' and 'mortgage offer' as applying to such 'additional loan' and 'additional loan offer' respectively.

1.11 In any transaction during the lifetime of the mortgage when we instruct you, you must use our current standard documents in all cases and must not amend or generate them without our written consent. We will send you all the standard documents necessary to enable you to comply with our instructions, but please let us know if you need any other documents and we will send these to you. Check part 2 to see who you should contact. If you consider that any of the documentation is inappropriate to the particular facts of a transaction, you should write to us (see part 2) with full details and any suggested amendments.

1.12 In order to act on our behalf your firm must be a member of our conveyancing panel. You must also comply with any terms and conditions of your panel appointment.

1.13.1 If you or a member of your immediate family (that is to say, a spouse, civil partner, co-habitee, parent, sibling, child, step-parent, step-child, grandparent, grandchild, parent-in-law, or child-in-law) is the borrower and you are a sole practitioner, you must not act for us.

1.13.2 Your firm or company must not act for us if the partner or fee earner dealing with the transaction or a member of his immediate family is the seller, unless we say your firm may act (see part 2) and a separate fee earner of no less standing or a partner within the firm acts for us.

1.14   Your firm or company must not act for us if the partner or fee earner dealing with the transaction or a member of his immediate family is the borrower, unless we say your firm may act (see part 2) and a separate fee earner of no less standing or a partner within the firm acts for us.

1.15   If there is any conflict of interest, you must not act for us and must return our instructions.

1.16   Nothing in these instructions lessens your duties to the borrower.

1.17   In addition to these definitions any reference to any regulation, legislation or legislative provision shall be construed as a reference to that regulation, legislation or legislative provision as amended, re-enacted or extended at the relevant time.

2.   COMMUNICATION

2.1   All communication between you and us should be in writing quoting the mortgage account or roll number, the surname and initials of the borrower and the property address. You should keep copies of all written communication on your file as evidence of notification and authorisation. If you use PC fax or e-mail, you should retain a copy in readable form.

2.2   If you require deeds or information from us in respect of a borrower or a property then you must first of all have the borrower's authority for such a request. If there is more than one borrower, you must have the authority of all the borrowers.

2.3   If you need to report a matter to us, you must do so as soon as you become aware of it so as to avoid any delay. If you do not believe that a matter is adequately provided for in the Handbook, you should identify the relevant Handbook provision and the extent to which the issue is not covered by it. You should provide a concise summary of the legal risks and your recommendation on how we should protect our interest. After reporting a matter you should not complete the mortgage until you have received our further written instructions. We recommend that you report such matters before exchange of contracts because we may have to withdraw or change the mortgage offer.

3.   SAFEGUARDS

A   This section relates to solicitors and those working in practices regulated by the Solicitors' Regulation Authority only

A3.1.1   You must follow the guidance in the Law Society's Green Card (mortgage fraud) and Pink Card (undertakings)

A3.1.2   You must follow the Law Society's guidance relating to money laundering and comply with the current money laundering regulations and the Proceeds of Crime Act 2002 to the extent that they apply.

A3.2   If you are not familiar with the seller's solicitors or licensed conveyancers, you must verify that they appear in a legal directory or they are currently on record with the Law Society or Council for Licensed Conveyancers as practising at the address shown on their note paper. If the seller does not have legal representation you should check part 2 to see whether or not we need to be notified so that a decision can be made as to whether or not we are prepared to proceed.

A3.3   Unless you personally know the signatory of a document, you must ask the signatory to provide evidence of identity, which you must carefully check. You should check the signatory's identity against one of the documents from list A or two of the documents in list B:

List A

- a valid full passport; or
- a valid H M Forces identity card with the signatory's photograph; or
- a valid UK Photo-card driving licence; or
- any other document listed in the additional list A in part 2.

List B

- a cheque guarantee card, credit card (bearing the Mastercard or Visa logo) American Express or Diners Club card, debit or multi-function card (bearing the Switch or Delta logo) issued in the United Kingdom with an original account statement less than three months old; or
- a firearm and shot gun certificate; or
- a receipted utility bill less than three months old; or
- a council tax bill less than three months old; or
- a council rent book showing the rent paid for the last three months; or
- a mortgage statement from another lender for the mortgage accounting year just ended; or
- any other document listed in the additional list B in part 2.

A3.4   You should check that any document you use to verify a signatory's identity appears to be authentic and current, signed in the relevant place. You should take a copy of it and keep the copy on your file. You should also check that the signatory's signature on any document being used to verify identity matches the signatory's signature on the document we require the signatory to sign and that the address shown on any document used to verify identity is that of the signatory.

B   This section applies to licensed conveyancers practices only

B3.1   You must follow the professional guidance of the Council for Licensed Conveyancers relating to money laundering and comply with the current money laundering regulations and the Proceeds of Crime Act 2002 to the extent that they apply and you must follow all other relevant guidance issued by the Council for Licensed Conveyancers.

B3.2   If you are not familiar with the seller's solicitors or licensed conveyancers, you must verify that they appear in a legal directory or they are currently on record with the Law Society or Council for Licensed Conveyancers as practising at the address shown on their note paper. If the seller does not have legal representation you should check part 2 to see whether or not we need to be notified so that a decision can be made as to whether or not we are prepared to proceed.

B3.3   Unless you personally know the signatory of a document, you must ask the signatory to provide evidence of identity, which you must carefully check. You must satisfy yourself that the person signing the document is the borrower, mortgagor or guarantor (as appropriate). If you have any concerns about the identity of the signatory you should notify us immediately.

B3.4   You should check that any document you use to verify a signatory's identity appears to be authentic and current, signed in the relevant place. You should take a copy of it and keep the copy on your file. You should also check that the signatory's signature on any document being used to verify identity matches the signatory's signature on the document we require the signatory to sign and that the address shown on any document used to verify identity is that of the signatory.

4.   VALUATION OF THE PROPERTY

4.1   Valuation

4.1.1   Check part 2 to see whether we send you a copy of the valuation report or if you must get it from the borrower.

4.1.2   You must take reasonable steps to verify that there are no discrepancies between the description of the property as valued and the title and other documents which a reasonably competent conveyancer should obtain, and, if there are, you must tell us immediately. The requirements in this clause and clause 4.1.3 apply to valuation reports and home condition reports. Where there is both a valuation report and a home condition report the requirements apply to both.

4.1.3   You should take reasonable steps to verify that the assumptions stated by the valuer (and where applicable a home inspector) about the title (for example, its tenure, easements, boundaries and restrictions on its use) in the valuation and home condition report are correct. If they are not, please let us know as soon as possible (see part 2) as it will be necessary for us to check with the valuer whether the valuation needs to be revised. We are not expecting you to assume the role of valuer. We are simply trying to ensure that the valuer has valued the property based on correct information.

4.1.4   When a home condition report is not provided we recommend that you should advise the borrower that there may be defects in the property which are not revealed by the inspection carried out by our valuer and there may be omissions or inaccuracies in the report which do not matter to us but which would matter to the borrower. We recommend that, if we send a copy of a valuation report that we have obtained, you should also advise the borrower that the borrower should not rely on the report in deciding whether to proceed with the purchase and that he obtains his own more detailed report on the condition and value of the property, based on a fuller inspection, to enable him to decide whether the property is suitable for his purposes.

4.2   Re-inspection

Where the mortgage offer states that a final inspection is needed, you must ask for the final inspection at least 10 working days before the advance is required (see part 2). Failure to do so may cause delay in the issue of the advance. Your certificate of title must be sent to us in the usual way (see part 2).

5.   TITLE

5.1   Surrounding Circumstances

5.1.1   Please report to us (see part 2) if the owner or registered proprietor has been registered for less than six months or the person selling to the borrower is not the owner or registered proprietor unless the seller is:

5.1.1.1   a personal representative of the registered proprietor; or

5.1.1.2   an institutional mortgagee exercising its power of sale; or

5.1.1.3   a receiver, trustee-in-bankruptcy or liquidator; or

5.1.1.4   developer or builder selling a property acquired under a part-exchange scheme.

5.1.2   If any matter comes to your attention which you should reasonably expect us to consider important in deciding whether or not to lend to the borrower (such as whether the borrower has given misleading information to us or the information which you might reasonably expect to have been given to us is no longer true) and you are unable to disclose that information to us because of a conflict of interest, you must cease to act for us and return our instructions stating that you consider a conflict of interest has arisen.

5.2 Searches and Reports

5.2.1 In carrying out your investigation, you must ensure that all usual and necessary searches and enquiries have been carried out. You must report any adverse entry to us but we do not want to be sent the search itself. We must be named as the applicant in the Land Registry search.

5.2.2 In addition, you must ensure that any other searches which may be appropriate to the particular property, taking into account its locality and other features are carried out.

5.2.3 All searches except where there is a priority period must not be more than six months old at completion.

5.2.4 You must advise us of any contaminated land entries revealed in the local authority search. Check part 2 to see if we want to receive environmental or contaminated land reports (as opposed to contaminated land entries revealed in the local authority search). If we do not, you do not need to make these enquiries on our behalf.

5.2.5 Check part 2 to see if we accept:

5.2.5.1 personal searches; or

5.2.5.2 search insurance.

5.2.6 If we do accept personal searches or search insurance, check part 2 to see our requirements as to such searches. If no requirements are specified in part 2 you must ensure:

5.2.6.1 a suitably qualified search agent carries out the personal search and has indemnity insurance that adequately protects us; or

5.2.6.2 the search insurance policy adequately protects us.

5.2.7 You must be satisfied that you will be able to certify that the title is good and marketable.

5.3 Planning and Building Regulations

5.3.1 You must by making appropriate searches and enquiries take all reasonable steps (including any further enquiries to clarify any issues which may arise) to ensure the property has the benefit of any necessary planning consents (including listed building consent) and building regulation approval for its construction and any subsequent change to the property (see part 2) or its current use; and

5.3.2 there is no evidence of any breach of the conditions of that or any other consent or certificate affecting the property; and

5.3.3 that no matter is revealed which would preclude the property from being used as a residential property or that the property may be the subject of enforcement action.

5.3.4 If there is such evidence and all outstanding conditions will not be satisfied by completion, then this must be reported to us (see part 2). Check part 2 to see if copies of planning permissions, building regulations and other consents or certificates should be sent to us.

5.3.5   If the property will be subject to any enforceable restrictions, for example under an agreement (such as an agreement under section 106 of the Town and Country Planning Act 1990) or in a planning permission, which, at the time of completion, might reasonably be expected materially to affect its value or its future marketability, you should report this to us (see part 2).

5.4   Good and Marketable Title

5.4.1   The title to the property must be good and marketable free of any restrictions, covenants, easements, charges or encumbrances which, at the time of completion, might reasonably be expected to materially adversely affect the value of the property or its future marketability (but excluding any matters covered by indemnity insurance) and which may be accepted by us for mortgage purposes. Our requirements in respect of indemnity insurance are set out in paragraph 9. You must also take reasonable steps to ensure that, on completion, the property will be vested in the borrower.

5.4.2   Good leasehold title will be acceptable if:

5.4.2.1   a marked abstract of the freehold and any intermediate leasehold title for the statutory period of 15 years before the grant of the lease is provided; or

5.4.2.2   you are prepared to certify that the title is good and marketable when sending your certificate of title (because, for example, the landlord's title is generally accepted in the district where the property is situated); or

5.4.2.3   you arrange indemnity insurance. Our requirements in respect of indemnity insurance are set out in paragraph 9.

5.4.3.1   A title based on adverse possession or possessory title will be acceptable if the seller is or on completion the borrower will be registered at the Land Registry as registered proprietor of a possessory title or there is satisfactory evidence by statutory declaration of adverse possession for a period of at least 12 years. In the case of lost title deeds, the statutory declaration must explain the loss satisfactorily;

5.4.3.2   we will also require indemnity insurance where there are buildings on the part in question or where the land is essential for access or services;

5.4.3.3   we may not need indemnity insurance in cases where such title affects land on which no buildings are erected or which is not essential for access or services. In such cases, you must send a plan of the whole of the land to be mortgaged to us identifying the area of land having possessory title. We will refer the matter to our valuer so that an assessment can be made of the proposed security. We will then notify you of any additional requirements or if a revised mortgage offer is to be made.

5.5   Flying Freeholds, Freehold Flats, other Freehold Arrangements and Commonhold

5.5.1   If any part of the property comprises or is affected by a flying freehold or the property is a freehold flat, check part 2 to see if we will accept it as security.

5.5.2   If we are prepared to accept a title falling within 5.5.1:

5.5.2.1   (unless we tell you not to in part 2) you must report to us that the property is a freehold flat or flying freehold; and

5.5.2.2   the property must have all necessary rights of support, protection, and entry for repair as well as a scheme of enforceable covenants that are also such that subsequent buyers are required to enter into covenants in identical form; and

5.5.2.3   you must be able to certify that the title is good and marketable; and

5.5.2.4   in the case of flying freeholds, you must send us a plan of the property clearly showing the part affected by the flying freehold.

If our requirements in 5.5.2.2 are not satisfied, indemnity must be in place at completion (see paragraph 9).

Other freehold arrangements

5.5.3   Unless we indicate to the contrary (see part 2), we have no objection to a security which comprises a building converted into not more than four flats where the borrower occupies one of those flats and the borrower or another flat owner also owns the freehold of the building and the other flats are subject to long leases.

5.5.3.1   If the borrower occupying one of the flats also owns the freehold, we will require our security to be:

5.5.3.1.1   the freehold of the whole building subject to the long leases of the other flats; and

5.5.3.1.2   any leasehold interest the borrower will have in the flat the borrower is to occupy.

5.5.3.2   If another flat owner owns the freehold of the building, the borrower must have a leasehold interest in the flat the borrower is to occupy and our security must be the borrower's leasehold interest in such flat.

5.5.3.3   The leases of all the flats should contain appropriate covenants by the tenant of each flat to contribute towards the repair, maintenance and insurance of the building. The leases should also grant and reserve all necessary rights and easements. They should not contain any unduly onerous obligations on the landlord.

5.5.4   Where the security will comprise:

5.5.4.1   one of a block of not more than four leasehold flats and the borrower will also own the freehold jointly with one or more of the other flat owners in the building; or

5.5.4.2   one of two leasehold flats in a building where the borrower also owns the freehold reversion of the other flat and the other leaseholder owns the freehold reversion in the borrower's flat;

check part 2 to see if we will accept it as security and if so, what our requirements will be.

Commonhold

5.5.5   If any part of the property comprises of commonhold, check part 2 to see if we will accept it as security.

5.5.6   If we are prepared to accept a title falling within 5.5.5, you must:

5.5.6.1   ensure that the commonhold association has obtained insurance for the common parts which complies with our requirements (see 6.13);

5.5.6.2   obtain a commonhold unit information certificate and ensure that all of the commonhold assessment in respect of the property has been paid up to the date of completion;

5.5.6.3   ensure that the commonhold community statement does not include any material restrictions on occupation or use (see 5.4 and 5.6);

5.5.6.4   ensure that the commonhold community statement provides that in the event of a voluntary termination of the commonhold the termination statement provides that the unit holders will ensure that any mortgage secured on their unit is repaid on termination;

5.5.6.5   make a company search to verify that the commonhold association is in existence and remains registered, and that there is no registered indication that it is to be wound up; and

5.5.6.6   within 14 days of completion, send the notice of transfer of a commonhold unit and notice of the mortgage to the commonhold association.

5.6   Restrictions on Use and Occupation

You must check whether there are any material restrictions on the occupation of the property as a private residence or as specified by us (for example, because of the occupier's employment, age or income), or any material restrictions on its use. If there are any restrictions, you must report details to us (see part 2). In some cases, we may accept a restriction, particularly if this relates to sheltered housing or to first time buyers.

5.7   Restrictive Covenants

5.7.1   You must enquire whether the property has been built, altered or is currently used in breach of a restrictive covenant. We rely on you to check that the covenant is not enforceable. If you are unable to provide an unqualified certificate of title as a result of the risk of enforceability you must ensure (subject to paragraph 5.7.2) that indemnity insurance is in place at completion of our mortgage (see paragraph 9).

5.7.2   We will not insist on indemnity insurance:

5.7.2.1   if you are satisfied that there is no risk to our security; and

5.7.2.2   the breach has continued for more than 20 years; and

5.7.2.3   there is nothing to suggest that any action is being taken or is threatened in respect of the breach.

5.8   First Legal Charge

On completion, we require a fully enforceable first charge by way of legal mortgage over the property executed by all owners of the legal estate. All existing charges must be redeemed on or before completion, unless we agree that an existing charge may be postponed to rank after our mortgage. Our standard deed or form of postponement must be used.

5.9   Other Loans

You must ask the borrower how the balance of the purchase price is being provided. If you become aware that the borrower is not providing the balance of the purchase price from his own funds and/or is proposing to give a second charge over the property, you must report this to us if the borrower agrees (see part 2), failing which you must return our instructions and explain that you are unable to continue to act for us as there is a conflict of interest.

5.10   Leasehold Property

5.10.1   Our requirements on the unexpired term of a lease offered as security are set out in part 2.

5.10.2   There must be no provision for forfeiture on the insolvency of the tenant or any superior tenant.

5.10.3   The only situations where we will accept a restriction on the mortgage or assignment (whether by a tenant or a mortgagee) of the lease is where the person whose consent needs to be obtained cannot unreasonably withhold giving consent. The necessary consent for the particular transaction must be obtained before completion. If the lease requires consent to an assignment or mortgage to be obtained, you must obtain these on or before completion (this is particularly important if the lease is a shared ownership lease). You must not complete without them.

5.10.4   You must take reasonable steps to check that:

5.10.4.1   there are satisfactory legal rights, particularly for access, services, support, shelter and protection; and

5.10.4.2   there are also adequate covenants and arrangements in respect of the following matters, buildings insurance, maintenance and repair of the structure, foundations, main walls, roof, common parts, common services and grounds (the 'common services').

5.10.5   You should ensure that responsibility for the insurance, maintenance and repair of the common services is that of:

5.10.5.1   the landlord; or

5.10.5.2   one or more of the tenants in the building of which the property forms part; or

5.10.5.3   the management company – see paragraph 5.11.

5.10.6   Where the responsibility for the insurance, maintenance and repair of the common services is that of one or more of the tenants;

5.10.6.1   the lease must contain adequate provisions for the enforcement of these obligations by the landlord or management company at the request of the tenant.

5.10.6.2   In the absence of a provision in the lease that all leases of other flats in the block are in, or will be granted in, substantially similar form, you should take reasonable steps to check that the leases of the other flats are in similar form. If you are unable to do so, you should effect indemnity insurance (see paragraph 9). This is not essential if the landlord is responsible for the maintenance and repair of the main structure.

5.10.6.3   We do not require enforceability covenants mutual or otherwise for other tenant covenants.

5.10.7   We have no objection to a lease which contains provision for a periodic increase of the ground rent provided that the amount of the increased ground rent is fixed or can be readily established and is reasonable. If you consider any increase in the ground rent may materially affect the value of the property, you must report this to us (see part 2).

5.10.8   You should enquire whether the landlord or managing agent foresees any significant increase in the level of the service charge in the reasonably foreseeable future and, if there is, you must report to us (see part 2).

5.10.9   If the terms of the lease are unsatisfactory, you must obtain a suitable deed of variation to remedy the defect. We may accept indemnity insurance (see paragraph 9). See part 2 for our requirements.

5.10.10   You must obtain on completion a clear receipt or other appropriate written confirmation for the last payment of ground rent and service charge from the landlord or managing agents on behalf of the landlord. Check part 2 to see if it must be sent to us after completion. If confirmation of payment from the landlord cannot be obtained, we are prepared to proceed provided that you are satisfied that the absence of the landlord is common practice in the district where the property is situated, the seller confirms there are no breaches of the terms of the lease, you are satisfied that our security will not be prejudiced by the absence of such a receipt and you provide us with a clear certificate of title.

5.10.11   Notice of the mortgage must be served on the landlord and any management company immediately following completion, whether or not the lease requires it. If you cannot obtain receipt of the notice then, as a last resort, suitable evidence of the service of the notice on the landlord should be provided. Check part 2 to see if a receipted copy of the notice or evidence of service must be sent to us after completion.

5.10.12   We will accept leases which require the property to be sold on the open market if pre-building or reinstatement is frustrated provided the insurance proceeds and the proceeds of sale are shared between the landlord and tenant in proportion to their respective interests.

5.10.13   You must report to us (see part 2) if it becomes apparent that the landlord is either absent or insolvent. If we are to lend, we may require indemnity insurance (see paragraph 9). See part 2 for our requirements.

5.10.14   If the leasehold title is registered but the lease has been lost, we are prepared to proceed provided you have checked a Land Registry produced copy of the registered lease. Whilst this will not be an official copy of the lease you may accept it as sufficient evidence of the lease and its terms when approving the title for mortgage purposes provided it is, on its face, a complete copy.

5.11   Management Company

5.11.1   In paragraph 5.11 the meanings shall apply:

- 'management company' means the company formed to carry out the maintenance and repair of the common parts;
- 'common parts' means the structure, main walls, roof, foundations, services grounds and any other common areas serving the building or estate of which the property forms part.

If a management company is required to maintain or repair the common parts, the management company should have a legal right to enter the property; if the management company's right to so enter does not arise from a leasehold interest, then the tenants of the building should also be the members of the management company.

If this is not the case, there should be a covenant by the landlord to carry out the obligations of the management company should it fail to do so.

5.11.1.1   For leases granted before 1 September 2000:

If the lease does not satisfy the requirements of paragraph 5.11.1 but:

you are nevertheless satisfied that the existing arrangements affecting the management company and the maintenance and repair of the common parts are sufficient to ensure the adequate maintenance and repair of the common parts; and you are able to provide a clear certificate of title, then we will rely on your professional judgement.

5.11.2 You should make a company search and verify that the company is in existence and registered at Companies House. You should also obtain the management company's last three years' published accounts (or the accounts from inception if the company has only been formed in the past three years). Any apparent problems with the company should be reported to us (see part 2). If the borrower is required to be a shareholder in the management company, check part 2 to see if you must arrange for the share certificate, a blank stock transfer form executed by the borrower and a copy of the memorandum and articles of association to be sent to us after completion (unless we tell you not to). If the management company is limited by guarantee, the borrower (or at least one of them if two or more) must become a member on or before completion.

5.12 Insolvency Considerations

5.12.1 You must obtain a clear bankruptcy search against each borrower (and each mortgagor or guarantor, if any) providing us with protection at the date of completion of the mortgage. You must fully investigate any entries revealed by your bankruptcy search against the borrower (or mortgagor or guarantor) to ensure that they do not relate to them.

5.12.2 Where an entry is revealed against the name of the borrower (or the mortgagor or guarantor):

5.12.2.1 you must certify that the entry does not relate to the borrower (or the mortgagor or guarantor) if you are able to do so from your own knowledge or enquiries; or

5.12.2.2 if, after obtaining office copy entries or making other enquiries of the Official Receiver, you are unable to certify that the entry does not relate to the borrower (or the mortgagor or guarantor) you must report this to us (see part 2). We may as a consequence need to withdraw our mortgage offer.

5.12.3 If you are aware that the title to the property is subject to a deed of gift or a transaction at an apparent undervalue completed within five years of the proposed mortgage then you must be satisfied that we will acquire our interest in good faith and will be protected under the provisions of the Insolvency (No 2) Act 1994 against our security being set aside. If you are unable to give an unqualified certificate of title, you must arrange indemnity insurance (see paragraph 9).

5.12.4 You must also obtain clear bankruptcy searches against all parties to any deed of gift or transaction at an apparent undervalue.

5.13 Powers of Attorney

5.13.1.1 If any document is being executed under power of attorney, you must ensure that the power of attorney is, on its face, properly drawn up, that it appears to be properly executed by the donor and that the attorney knows of no reason why such power of attorney will not be subsisting at completion.

5.13.1.2 Where there are joint borrowers the power should comply with section 25 of the Trustee Act 1925, as amended by section 7 of the Trustee Delegation Act 1999, or with section 1 of the Trustee Delegation Act 1999 with the attorney making an appropriate statement under section 2 of the 1999 Act.

5.13.1.3 In the case of joint borrowers, neither borrower may appoint the other as their attorney.

5.13.2 A power of attorney must not be used in connection with a regulated loan under the Consumer Credit Act 1974.

5.13.3 Check part 2 to see if:

5.13.3.1   the original or a certified copy of the power of attorney must be sent to us after completion;

5.13.3.2   where the power of attorney is a general power of attorney and was completed more than 12 months before the completion of our mortgage, you must send us a statutory declaration confirming that it has not been revoked.

5.14   Title Guarantee

Whilst we recommend that a borrower should try to obtain a full title guarantee from the seller, we do not insist on this. We, however, require the borrower to give us a full title guarantee in the mortgage deed. The mortgage deed must not be amended.

5.15   Affordable Housing: Shared Ownership and Shared Equity

Housing associations, other social landlords and developers sometimes provide schemes under which the borrower will not have 100% ownership of the property and a third party will also own a share or will be a taking a charge over the title. In these cases you must check with us to see if we will lend and what our requirements are unless we have already provided these (see part 2).

6.   THE PROPERTY

6.1   Mortgage Offer and Title Documents

6.1.1   The loan to the borrower will not be made until all relevant conditions of the mortgage offer which need to be satisfied before completion have been complied with and we have received your certificate of title.

6.1.2   You must check your instructions and ensure that there are no discrepancies between them and the title documents and other matters revealed by your investigations.

6.1.3   You should tell us (see part 2) as soon as possible if you have been told that the borrower has decided not to take up the mortgage offer.

6.2   Boundaries

These must be clearly defined by reference to a suitable plan or description. They must also accord with the information given in the valuation report, if this is provided to you. You should check with the borrower that the plan or the description accords with the borrower's understanding of the extent of the property to be mortgaged to us. You must report to us (see part 2), if there are any discrepancies.

6.3   Purchase Price

6.3.1   The purchase price for the property must be the same as set out in our instructions. If it is not, you must tell us (unless we say differently in part 2).

6.3.2   You must tell us (unless we say differently in part 2) if the contract provides for or you become aware of any arrangement in which there is:

6.3.2.1   a cashback to the buyer; or

6.3.2.2   part of the price is being satisfied by a non-cash incentive to the buyer or

6.3.2.3   any indirect incentive (cash or non cash) or rental guarantee

Any such arrangement may lead to the mortgage offer being withdrawn or amended.

6.3.3   You must report to us (see part 2) if you will not have control over the payment of all of the purchase money (for example, if it is proposed that the borrower pays money to the seller direct) other than a deposit held by an estate agent or a reservation fee of not more than £1000 paid to a builder or developer.

6.4   Vacant Possession

Unless otherwise stated in your instructions, it is a term of the loan that vacant possession is obtained. The contract must provide for this. If you doubt that vacant possession will be given, you must not part with the advance and should report the position to us (see part 2).

6.5   Properties Let At Completion

6.5.1   Unless it is clear from the mortgage offer that the property is let or is to be let at completion then you must check with us whether we lend on 'buy to let' properties and that the mortgage is for that purpose (see part 2).

6.5.2   Where the property, or part of it, is already let, or is to be let at completion, then the letting must comply with the details set out in the mortgage offer or any consent to let we issue. If no such details are mentioned, you must report the position to us (see part 2).

6.5.3   Check part 2 for whether counterparts or certified copies of all tenancy agreements and leases in respect of existing tenancies must be sent to us after completion.

6.5.4   Where the property falls within the definition of a house in multiple occupation under the Housing Act 2004 see part 2 as to whether we will accept this as security and if so what our requirements are.

6.6   New Properties – Building Standards Indemnity Schemes

6.6.1   If the property has been built or converted within the past ten years, or is to be occupied for the first time, you must ensure that it was built or converted under a scheme acceptable to us (see part 2 for the list of schemes acceptable to us and our requirements).

6.6.2   Where the cover under a scheme referred to in clause 6.6.1 is not yet in place before you send us the certificate of title, you must obtain a copy of a new home warranty provider's cover note from the developer. The cover note must confirm that the property has received a satisfactory final inspection and that the new home warranty will be in place on or before legal completion. This does not apply to self-build schemes. Check part 2 to see what new home warranty documentation should be sent to us after completion.

6.6.3   We do not insist that notice of assignment of the benefit of the new home warranty agreement be given to the builder in the case of a second and subsequent purchase(s) during the period of the insurance cover. Check part 2 to see if any assignments of building standards indemnity schemes which are available should be sent to us after completion.

6.6.4   Where the property does not have the benefit of a scheme under 6.6.1 and has been built or converted within the past 6 years check part 2 to see if we will proceed and, if so, whether you must satisfy yourself that the building work is being monitored (or where the work is completed was monitored) by a professional consultant. If we do accept monitoring you should ensure that the professional consultant has provided the lender's Professional Consultant's Certificate which forms an appendix to this Handbook or such other form as we may provide. The professional consultant should also confirm to you that he has appropriate experience in the design or monitoring of the construction or conversion of residential buildings and has one or more of the following qualifications:

6.6.4.1   fellow or member of the Royal Institution of Chartered Surveyors (FRICS or MRICS); or

6.6.4.2   fellow or member of the Institution of Structural Engineers (F.I.Struct.E or M.I.Struct.E); or

6.6.4.3   fellow or member of the Chartered Institute of Building (FCIOB or MCIOB); or

6.6.4.4   fellow or member of the Architecture and Surveying Institute (FASI or MASI); or

6.6.4.5   fellow or member of the Association of Building Engineers (FB.Eng or MB.Eng); or

6.6.4.6   member of the British Institute of Architectural Technologists (MBIAT); or

6.6.4.7   architect registered with the Architects Registration Board (ARB). An architect must be registered with the Architects Registration Board, even if also a member of another institution, for example the Royal Institute of British Architects (RIBA); or

6.6.4.8   fellow or member of the Institution of Civil Engineers (FICE or MICE).

6.6.5   At the time he issues his certificate of practical completion, the consultant must have professional indemnity insurance in force for each claim for the greater of either:

6.6.5.1   the value of the property once completed; or

6.6.5.2   £250,000 if employed directly by the borrower or, in any other case, £500,000.

If we require a collateral warranty from any professional adviser, this will be stated specifically in the mortgage instructions.

6.6.6   Check part 2 to see if the consultant's certificate must be sent to us after completion.

6.7   Roads and Sewers

6.7.1   If the roads or sewers immediately serving the property are not adopted or maintained at public expense, there must be an agreement and bond in existence or you must report to us (see part 2 for who you should report to).

6.7.2   If there is any such agreement, it should be secured by bond or deposit as required by the appropriate authority to cover the cost of making up the roads and sewers to adoptable standards, maintaining them thereafter and procuring adoption.

6.7.3   If there is an arrangement between the developer and the lender whereby the lender will not require a retention, you must obtain confirmation from the developer that the arrangement is still in force.

6.7.4   Where roads and sewers are not adopted or to be adopted but are maintained by local residents or a management company this is acceptable providing that in your reasonable opinion appropriate arrangements for maintenance repairs and costs are in place.

6.8   Easements

6.8.1   You must take all reasonable steps to check that the property has the benefit of all easements necessary for its full use and enjoyment. All such rights must be enforceable by the borrower and the borrower's successors in title. If they are not check part 2 for our requirements.

6.8.2   If the borrower owns adjoining land over which the borrower requires access to the property or in respect of which services are provided to the property, this land must also be mortgaged to us.

6.9   Release of Retentions

6.9.1   If we make a retention from an advance (for example, for repairs, improvements or road works) we are not obliged to release that retention, or any part of it, if the borrower is in breach of any of his obligations under the mortgage, or if a condition attached to the retention has not been met or if the loan has been repaid in full. You should, therefore not give an unqualified undertaking to pay the retention to a third party.

6.9.2   Check part 2 to see who we will release the retention to.

6.10   Neighbourhood Changes

The local search or the enquiries of the seller's conveyancer should not reveal that the property is in an area scheduled for redevelopment or in any way affected by road proposals. If it is please report to us (see part 2).

6.11   Rights of Pre-emption and Restrictions on Resale

You must ensure that there are no rights of pre-emption, restrictions on resale, options or similar arrangements in existence at completion which will affect our security. If there are, please report this to us (see part 2).

6.12   Improvement and Repair Grants

Where the property is subject to an improvement or repair grant which will not be discharged or waived on completion, check part 2 to see whether you must report the matter to us.

6.13   Insurance

Where we do not arrange the insurance, you must:

6.13.1   report to us (see part 2) if the property is not insured in accordance with our requirements (one of our requirements, see part 2, will relate to whether the property is insured in the joint names of us and the borrower or whether our interest may be noted);

6.13.2   arrange that the insurance cover starts from no later than completion;

6.13.3   check that the amount of buildings insurance cover is at least the amount referred to in the mortgage offer. If the property is part of a larger building and there is a common insurance policy, the total sum insured for the building must be not less than the total number of flats multiplied by the amount set out in the mortgage offer for the property – check part 2 for our requirements on this;

6.13.4   ensure that the buildings insurance cover is index linked;

6.13.5   ensure that the excess does not exceed the amount set out in part 2;

6.13.6   Check part 2 to see if we require you to confirm that all the following risks are covered in the insurance policy:

6.13.6.1   fire;

6.13.6.2   lightning;

6.13.6.3   aircraft;

6.13.6.4   explosion;

6.13.6.5   earthquake;

6.13.6.6   storm;

6.13.6.7   flood;

6.13.6.8   escape of water or oil;

6.13.6.9   riot;

6.13.6.10   malicious damage;

6.13.6.11   theft or attempted theft;

6.13.6.12   falling trees and branches and aerials;

6.13.6.13   subsidence;

6.13.6.14   heave;

6.13.6.15   landslip;

6.13.6.16   collision;

6.13.6.17   accidental damage to underground services;

6.13.6.18   professional fees, demolition and site clearance costs; and

6.13.6.19   public liability to anyone else.

6.13.7   Check part 2 to see if we require you to obtain before completion the insurer's confirmation that the insurer will notify us if the policy is not renewed or is cancelled or if you do not obtain this, report to us (see part 2).

6.13.8   Check part 2 to see if we require you to send us a copy of the buildings insurance policy and the last premium receipt to us.

7.   OTHER OCCUPIERS

7.1   Rights or interests of persons who are not a party to the mortgage and who are or will be in occupation of the property may affect our rights under the mortgage, for example as overriding interests.

7.2   If your instructions state the name of a person who is to live at the property, you should ask the borrower before completing the mortgage that the information given by us in our mortgage instructions or mortgage offer about occupants is correct and nobody else is to live at the property.

7.3   Unless we state otherwise (see part 2), you must obtain a signed deed or form of consent from all occupants aged 17 or over of whom you are aware who are not a party to the mortgage before completion of the mortgage.

7.4   We recognise that in some cases the information given to us or you by a borrower may be incorrect or misleading. If you have any reason to doubt the accuracy of any information disclosed, you should report it to us (see part 2) provided the borrower agrees; if the borrower does not agree, you should return our instructions.

8.   SEPARATE REPRESENTATION

Unless we otherwise state (see part 2), you must not advise:

8.1.1   any borrower who does not personally benefit from the loan; or

8.1.2   any guarantor; or

8.1.3   anyone intending to occupy the property who is to execute a consent to the mortgage

and you must arrange for them to seek independent legal advice.

8.2   If we do allow you to advise any of these people, you must only do so after recommending in the absence of any other person interested in the transaction that such person obtains independent legal advice. Any advice that you give any of these people must also be given in the absence of any other person interested in the transaction. You should be particularly careful if the matrimonial home or family home is being charged to secure a business debt. Any consent should be signed by the person concerned. A power of attorney is not acceptable.

9.   INDEMNITY INSURANCE

You must effect an indemnity insurance policy whenever the Lenders' Handbook identifies that this is an acceptable or required course to us to ensure that the property has a good and marketable title at completion. This paragraph does not relate to mortgage indemnity insurance. The draft policy should not be sent to us unless we ask for it. Check part 2 to see if the policy must be sent to us after completion. Where indemnity insurance is effected:

9.1   you must approve the terms of the policy on our behalf; and

9.2   the limit of indemnity must meet our requirements (see part 2); and

9.3   the policy must be effected without cost to us; and

9.4   you must disclose to the insurer all relevant information which you have obtained; and

9.5   the policy must not contain conditions which you know would make it void or prejudice our interests; and

9.6   you must provide a copy of the policy to the borrower and explain to the borrower why the policy was effected and that a further policy may be required if there is further lending against the security of the property; and

9.7   you must explain to the borrower that the borrower will need to comply with any conditions of the policy and that the borrower should notify us of any notice or potential claim in respect of the policy; and

9.8   the policy should always be for our benefit and, if possible, for the benefit of the borrower and any subsequent owner or mortgagee. If the borrower will not be covered by the policy, you must advise the borrower of this.

10.   THE LOAN AND CERTIFICATE OF TITLE

10.1   You should not submit your certificate of title unless it is unqualified or we have authorised you in writing to proceed notwithstanding any issues you have raised with us.

10.2   We shall treat the submission by you of the certificate of title as a request for us to release the mortgage advance to you. Check part 2 to see if the mortgage advance will be paid electronically or by cheque and the minimum number of days notice we require. See part 2 for any standard deductions which may be made from the mortgage advance.

10.3.1   You are only authorised to release the loan when you hold sufficient funds to complete the purchase of the property and pay all stamp duty land tax and registration fees to perfect the security as a first legal mortgage or, if you do not have them, you accept responsibility to pay them yourself.

10.3.2   Before releasing the loan when the borrower is purchasing the property you must either hold a properly completed and executed stamp duty land tax form or you must hold an appropriate authority from the borrower allowing you to file the necessary stamp duty land tax return(s) on completion.

10.3.3   You must ensure that all stamp duty land tax returns are completed and submitted to allow registration of the charge to take place in the priority period afforded by the search.

10.3.4   You must hold the loan on trust for us until completion. If completion is delayed, you must return it to us when and how we tell you (see part 2).

10.4   You should note that although your certificate of title will be addressed to us, we may at some time transfer our interest in the mortgage. In those circumstances, our successors in title to the mortgage and persons deriving title under or through the mortgage will also rely on your certificate.

10.5   If, after you have requested the mortgage advance, completion is delayed you must telephone or fax us immediately after you are aware of the delay and you must inform us of the new date for completion (see part 2).

10.6   See part 2 for details of how long you can hold the mortgage advance before returning it to us. If completion is delayed for longer than that period, you must return the mortgage advance to us. If you do not, we reserve the right to require you to pay interest on the amount of the mortgage advance (see part 2).

10.7   If the mortgage advance is not returned within the period set out in part 2, we will assume that the mortgage has been completed, and we will charge the borrower interest under the mortgage.

11.   THE DOCUMENTATION

11.1   The Mortgage

The mortgage incorporates our current mortgage conditions and, where applicable, loan conditions. If the mortgage conditions booklet is supplied to you with your instructions you must give it to the borrower before completion of the mortgage.

11.2   Explanation

You should explain to each borrower (and any other person signing or executing a document) his responsibilities and liabilities under the documents referred to in 11.1 and any documents he is required to sign.

11.3   Signing and Witnessing of Documents

It is considered good practice that the signature of a document that needs to be witnessed is witnessed by a solicitor, legal executive or licensed conveyancer. All documents required at completion must be dated with the date of completion of the loan.

12. INSTALMENT MORTGAGES AND MORTGAGE ADVANCES RELEASED IN INSTALMENTS

12.1 Introduction

12.1.1 If the cost of the building is to be paid by instalments as work progresses (for example, under a building contract) the amount of each instalment which we will be able to release will be based on a valuation made by our valuer at the time. Whilst we will not be bound by the terms of any building contract we will meet the reasonable requirements of the borrower and the builder as far as possible.

12.1.2 The borrower is expected to pay for as much work as possible from his own resources before applying to us for the first instalment. However, we may, if required, consider advancing a nominal sum on receipt of the certificate of title to enable the mortgage to be completed so long as the legal estate in the property is vested in the borrower.

12.1.3 The borrower is responsible for our valuer's fees for interim valuations as well as the first and final valuations.

12.2 Applications for Part of the Advance

As in the case of a normal mortgage account, funds for instalment mortgages may be sent to you. However, instalments (apart from the first which will be sent to you to enable you to complete the mortgage) can be sent directly to the borrower on request. We may make further payments and advances without reference to you.

12.3 Requests for Intermediate Funds

To allow time for a valuation to be carried out, your request should be sent to us (see part 2) at least 10 days before the funds are required.

12.4 Building Contract as Security

We will not lend on the security of a building contract unless we tell you to the contrary. As a result the mortgage must not be completed and no part of the advance released until the title to the legal estate in the property has been vested in the borrower.

13. MORTGAGE INDEMNITY INSURANCE OR HIGHER LENDING CHARGE

You are reminded to tell the borrower that we (and not the borrower) are the insured under any mortgage indemnity or similar form of insurance policy and that the insurer will have a subrogated right to claim against the borrower if it pays us under the policy. Different lenders call the various schemes of this type by different names. They may not involve an insurance policy.

14. AFTER COMPLETION

14.1 Registration

14.1.1.1 You must register our mortgage as a first legal charge at the Land Registry. Before making your Land Registry application for registration, you must place a copy of the results of the Official Search on your file together with certified copies of the transfer, mortgage deed and any discharges or releases from a previous mortgagee.

14.1.1.2 Where the borrower or mortgagor is a company an application to register the charge must be lodged at Companies House within the required time period.

14.1.2 Our mortgage conditions and mortgage deed have been deposited at the Land Registry and it is therefore unnecessary to submit a copy of the mortgage conditions on an application for registration.

14.1.3   Where the loan is to be made in instalments or there is any deferred interest retention or stage release, check part 2 to see whether you must apply to Land Registry on form CH2 for entry of a notice on the register that we are under an obligation to make further advances. If the mortgage deed states that it secures further advances, and that the lender is under an obligation to make them, there is no need to submit a form CH2 provided the mortgage deed also states that application is made to the Registrar for a note to be entered on the register to that effect and the mortgage deed bears a Land Registry MD reference at its foot.

14.1.4   The application for registration must be received by the Land Registry during the priority period afforded by your original Land Registry search made before completion and, in any event, in the case of an application for first registration, within two months of completion. Please check part 2 to see if we require the original mortgage deed to be returned to us.

14.2   Title Deeds

14.2.1   All title deeds, official copies of the register (where these are issued by the Land Registry after registration), searches, enquiries, consents, requisitions and documents relating to the property in your possession must be held to our order and you must not create or exercise any lien over them. Check part 2 for our requirements on what you should do with these documents following registration. If registration at the Land Registry has not been completed within three months from completion you should advise us in writing with a copy of any correspondence with the Land Registry explaining the delay.

14.2.2   You must only send us documents we tell you to (see part 2). You should obtain the borrower's instructions concerning the retention of documents we tell you not to send us.

14.3   Your Mortgage File

14.3.1   For evidential purposes you must keep your file for at least six years from the date of the mortgage before destroying it. Microfiching or data imaging is suitable compliance with this requirement. It is the practice of some fraudsters to demand the conveyancing file on completion in order to destroy evidence that may later be used against them. It is important to retain these documents to protect our interests.

14.3.2   Where you are processing personal data (as defined in the Data Protection Act 1998) on our behalf, you must;

14.3.2.1   take such security measures as are required to enable you to comply with obligations equivalent to those imposed on us by the seventh data protection principle in the 1998 Act; and

14.3.2.2   process such personal data only in accordance with our instructions. In addition, you must allow us to conduct such reasonable audit of your information security measures as we require to ensure your compliance with your obligations in this paragraph.

14.3.4   Subject to any right of lien or any overriding duty of confidentiality, you should treat documents comprising your file as if they are jointly owned by the borrower and us and you should not part with them without the consent of both parties. You should on request supply certified copies of documents on the file or a certified copy of the microfiche to either the borrower or us, and may make a reasonable charge for copying and certification.

15. LEGAL COSTS

Your charges and disbursements are payable by the borrower and should be collected from the borrower on or before completion. You must not allow non-payment of fees or disbursements to delay the payment of stamp duty land tax, the lodging of any stamp duty land tax return and registration of documents. For solicitors the Law Society recommends that your costs for acting on our behalf in connection with the mortgage should, in the interest of transparency, be separately identified to the borrower.

16. TRANSACTIONS DURING THE LIFE OF THE MORTGAGE

16.1 Requests for Title Documents

All requests for title documents should be made in writing and sent to us (see part 2). In making such a request you must have the consent of all of the borrowers to apply for the title documents.

16.2 Further Advances

Our mortgage secures further advances. Consequently, when a further advance is required for alterations or improvements to the property we will not normally instruct a member of our conveyancing panel but if you are instructed the appropriate provisions of this Handbook will apply.

16.3 Transfers of Equity

16.3.1 You must approve the transfer (which should be in the Land Registry's standard form) and, if we require, the deed of covenant on our behalf. Check part 2 to see if we have standard forms of transfer and deed of covenant. When drafting or approving a transfer, you should bear in mind that:

16.3.1.1 although the transfer should state that it is subject to the mortgage (identified by date and parties), it need give no details of the terms of the mortgage;

16.3.1.2 the transfer need not state the amount of the mortgage debt. If it does, the figure should include both principal and interest at the date of completion, which you must check (see part 2 for where to obtain this);

16.3.1.3 there should be no statement that all interest has been paid to date.

16.3.2 You must ensure that every person who will be a borrower after the transfer covenants with us to pay the money secured by the mortgage, except in the case of:

16.3.2.1 an original party to the mortgage (unless the mortgage conditions are being varied); or

16.3.2.2 a person who has previously covenanted to that effect.

16.3.3 Any such covenant will either be in the transfer or in a separate deed of covenant. In a transfer, the wording of the covenant should be as follows, or as close as circumstances permit: 'The new borrower agrees to pay the lender all the money due under the mortgage and will keep to all the terms of the mortgage.' If it is in the transfer, you must place a certified copy of the transfer with the deeds (unless we tell you not to in part 2).

16.3.4 If we have agreed to release a borrower or a guarantor and our standard transfer form (if any) includes no appropriate clause, you must add a simple form of release. The release clause should be as follows, or as close as circumstances permit: 'The lender releases ... from [his/her/their] obligations under the mortgage.' You should check whether a guarantor who is to be released was a party to the mortgage or to a separate guarantee.

16.3.5   You must obtain the consent of every guarantor of whom you are aware to the release of a borrower or, as the case may be, any other guarantor.

16.3.6   You must only submit the transfer to us for execution if it releases a party. All other parties must execute the transfer before it is sent to us. See part 2 for where the transfer should be sent for sealing. Part 2 also gives our approved form of attestation clause.

16.4   Properties To Be Let After Completion (Other than 'Buy to Let')

16.4.1   If after completion the borrower informs you of an intention to let the property you should advise the borrower that any letting of the property is prohibited without our prior consent. If the borrower wishes to let the property after completion then an application for consent should be made to us by the borrower (see part 2). Check part 2 to see whether it is necessary to send to us a copy of the proposed tenancy when making the application.

16.4.2   If the application for our consent is approved and we instruct you to act for us, you must approve the form of tenancy agreement on our behalf in accordance with our instructions.

16.4.3   Please also note that:

16.4.3.1   an administration fee may be payable for our consideration of the application whether or not consent is granted; and

16.4.3.2   the proposed rent should cover the borrower's gross mortgage payments at the time; and

16.4.3.3   You should draw the borrower's attention to the fact that, under the terms of the mortgage, we may reserve the right to charge a higher rate of interest to the borrower or change the terms of the mortgage.

16.5   Deeds of Variation etc

16.5.1   If we consent to any proposal for a deed of variation, rectification, easement or option agreement, we will rely on you to approve the documents on our behalf.

16.5.2   Our consent will usually be forthcoming provided that you first of all confirm in writing to us (see part 2) that our security will not be adversely affected in any way by entering into the deed. If you are able to provide this confirmation then we will not normally need to see a draft of the deed. If you cannot provide confirmation and we need to consider the matter in detail then an additional administration fee is likely to be charged.

16.5.3   Whether we are a party to the deed or give a separate deed or form of consent is a matter for your discretion. It should be sent to us (see part 2) for sealing or signing with a brief explanation of the reason for the document and its effect together with your confirmation that it will not adversely affect our security.

16.6   Deeds of Postponement or Substitution

If we agree to enter into an arrangement with other lenders concerning the order of priority of their mortgages, you will be supplied with our standard form of deed or form of postponement or substitution. We will normally not agree to any amendments to the form. In no cases will we postpone our first charge over the property.

17. REDEMPTION

17.1 Redemption Statement

17.1.1 When requesting a redemption statement you should quote the expected repayment date and whether you are acting for the borrower or have the borrower's authority to request the redemption statement in addition to the information mentioned in paragraph 2.1. You should request this at least five working days before the expected redemption date. You must quote all the borrower's mortgage account or roll numbers of which you are aware when requesting the repayment figure. You must only request a redemption statement if you are acting for the borrower or have the borrower's written authority to request a redemption statement.

17.1.2 To guard against fraud please ensure that if payment is made by cheque then the redemption cheque is made payable to us and you quote the mortgage account number or roll number and name of the borrower.

17.2 Discharge

On the day of completion you should send the discharge and your remittance for the repayment to us (see part 2). Check part 2 to see if we discharge via a DS1 form or direct notification to the Land Registry.

APPENDIX 1 - PROFESSIONAL CONSULTANT'S CERTIFICATE

Return to:
Name of Applicant(s)
Full address of property

I certify that:

1. I have visited the site at appropriate periods from the commencement of construction to the current stage to check generally:
(a) progress, and
(b) conformity with drawings, approved under the building regulations, and
(c) conformity with drawings/instructions properly issued under the building contract.

2. At the stage of my last inspection on _____ , the property had reached the stage of

_____

_____

_____

_____

3. So far as could be determined by each periodic visual inspection, the property has been generally constructed:
(a) to a satisfactory standard, and
(b) in general compliance with the drawings approved under the building regulations.

4. I was originally retained by

_____

_____

who is the applicant/builder/developer in this case
(delete as appropriate).

5. I am aware this certificate is being relied upon by the first purchaser

_____

_____ of the property and also by _____ (name of lender) when making a mortgage advance to that purchaser secured on this property.

6. I confirm that I will remain liable for a period of 6 years from the date of this certificate. Such liability shall be to the first purchasers and their lenders and upon each sale of the property the remaining period shall be transferred to the subsequent purchasers and their lenders.

7. I confirm that I have appropriate experience in the design and/or monitoring of the construction or conversion of residential buildings.

_____

Name of Professional Consultant

_____

Qualifications _____
Address

_____

_____

_____

_____

_____

Telephone No. _____
Fax No. _____

Professional Indemnity Insurer

----

8. The box below shows the minimum amount of professional indemnity insurance the consultant will keep in force to cover his liabilities under this certificate [   ] for any one claim or series of claims arising out of one event.

Signature ---------------------------------

Date------------------------

_____

Appendix 8

Land Registry Forms

Transfer of part
of registered title(s)

Land Registry

TP1

If you need more room than is provided for in a panel, use continuation sheet CS and attach to this form.

1. Stamp Duty

Place "X" in the appropriate box or boxes and complete the appropriate certificate.

☐ It is certified that this instrument falls within category ☐ in the Schedule to the Stamp Duty (Exempt Instruments) Regulations 1987

☐ It is certified that the transaction effected does not form part of a larger transaction or of a series of transactions in respect of which the amount or value or the aggregate amount or value of the consideration exceeds the sum of £ _____

☐ It is certified that this is an instrument on which stamp duty is not chargeable by virtue of the provisions of section 92 of the Finance Act 2001

2. Title number(s) out of which the Property is transferred *Leave blank if not yet registered.*

3. Other title number(s) against which matters contained in this transfer are to be registered, if any

4. Property transferred *Insert address, including postcode, or other description of the property transferred. Any physical exclusions, e.g. mines and minerals, should be defined. Any attached plan must be signed by the transferor.*

The Property is defined: *Place "X" in the appropriate box.*

☐ on the attached plan and shown *State reference e.g. "edged red".*

☐ on the Transferor's title plan and shown *State reference e.g. "edged and numbered 1 in blue".*

5. Date

6. Transferor *Give full name(s) and company's registered number, if any.*

7. Transferee **for entry on the register** *Give full name(s) and company's registered number, if any. For Scottish companies use an SC prefix and for limited liability partnerships use an OC prefix before the registered number, if any. For foreign companies give territory in which incorporated.*

Unless otherwise arranged with Land Registry headquarters, a certified copy of the Transferee's constitution (in English or Welsh) will be required if it is a body corporate but is not a company registered in England and Wales or Scotland under the Companies Acts.

8. Transferee's intended **address(es) for service (including postcode) for entry on the register** *You may give up to three addresses for service **one** of which **must** be a postal address but does not have to be within the UK. The other addresses can be any combination of a postal address, a box number at a UK document exchange or an electronic address.*

9.   The Transferor transfers the Property to the Transferee

10. Consideration *Place "X" in the appropriate box. State clearly the currency unit if other than sterling. If none of the boxes applies, insert an appropriate memorandum in the additional provisions panel.*

☐ The Transferor has received from the Transferee for the Property the sum of *In words and figures.*

☐ *Insert other receipt as appropriate.*

☐ The transfer is not for money or anything which has a monetary value

11. The Transferor transfers with *Place "X" in the appropriate box and add any modifications.*

☐ full title guarantee   ☐ limited title guarantee

12. Declaration of trust *Where there is more than one Transferee, place "X" in the appropriate box.*

☐ The Transferees are to hold the Property on trust for themselves as joint tenants

☐ The Transferees are to hold the Property on trust for themselves as tenants in common in equal shares

☐ The Transferees are to hold the Property *Complete as necessary.*

13. Additional provisions
Use this panel for:
- *definitions of terms not defined above*
- *rights granted or reserved*
- *restrictive covenants*
- *other covenants*
- *agreements and declarations*
- *other agreed provisions.*

The prescribed subheadings may be added to, amended, repositioned or omitted.

Definitions

Rights granted for the benefit of the Property

Rights reserved for the benefit of other land *The land having the benefit should be defined, if necessary by reference to a plan.*

Restrictive covenants by the Transferee *Include words of covenant.*

Restrictive covenants by the Transferor *Include words of covenant.*

14. Execution *The Transferor must execute this transfer as a deed using the space below. If there is more than one Transferor, all must execute. Forms of execution are given in Schedule 9 to the Land Registration Rules 2003. If the transfer contains Transferee's covenants or declarations or contains an application by the Transferee (e.g. for a restriction), it must also be executed by the Transferee (all of them, if there is more than one).*

**Transfer of whole
of registered title(s)**

Land Registry

If you need more room than is provided for in a panel, use continuation sheet CS and attach to this form.

1.	**Stamp Duty**

Place "X" in the appropriate box or boxes and complete the appropriate certificate.

☐ It is certified that this instrument falls within category ☐ in the Schedule to the Stamp Duty (Exempt Instruments) Regulations 1987

☐ It is certified that the transaction effected does not form part of a larger transaction or of a series of transactions in respect of which the amount or value or the aggregate amount or value of the consideration exceeds the sum of £ ☐

☐ It is certified that this is an instrument on which stamp duty is not chargeable by virtue of the provisions of section 92 of the Finance Act 2001

2. Title Number(s) of the Property *Leave blank if not yet registered.*

3. Property

4. Date

5. Transferor *Give full names and company's registered number if any.*

6. Transferee **for entry on the register** *Give full name(s) and company's registered number, if any. For Scottish companies use an SC prefix and for limited liability partnerships use an OC prefix before the registered number, if any. For foreign companies give territory in which incorporated.*

Unless otherwise arranged with Land Registry headquarters, a certified copy of the Transferee's constitution (in English or Welsh) will be required if it is a body corporate but is not a company registered in England and Wales or Scotland under the Companies Acts.

7. Transferee's intended **address(es) for service (including postcode) for entry on the register** *You may give up to three addresses for service **one** of which **must** be a postal address but does not have to be within the UK. The other addresses can be any combination of a postal address, a box number at a UK document exchange or an electronic address.*

8.   The Transferor transfers the Property to the Transferee

9. Consideration *Place "X" in the appropriate box. State clearly the currency unit if other than sterling. If none of the boxes applies, insert an appropriate memorandum in the additional provisions panel.*

☐ The Transferor has received from the Transferee for the Property the sum of *In words and figures.*

☐ *Insert other receipt as appropriate.*

☐ The transfer is not for money or anything which has a monetary value

10. The Transferor transfers with *Place "X" in the appropriate box and add any modifications.*

☐ full title guarantee   ☐ limited title guarantee

---

11. Declaration of trust *Where there is more than one Transferee, place "X" in the appropriate box.*

☐ The Transferees are to hold the Property on trust for themselves as joint tenants

☐ The Transferees are to hold the Property on trust for themselves as tenants in common in equal shares

☐ The Transferees are to hold the Property *Complete as necessary.*

---

12. Additional provisions *Insert here any required or permitted statements, certificates or applications and any agreed covenants, declarations, etc.*

---

13. Execution *The Transferor must execute this transfer as a deed using the space below. If there is more than one Transferor, all must execute. Forms of execution are given in Schedule 9 to the Land Registration Rules 2003. If the transfer contains Transferee's covenants or declarations or contains an application by the Transferee (e.g. for a restriction), it must also be executed by the Transferee (all of them, if there is more than one).*

Application by purchaser[a] for official search with priority of the whole of the land in a registered title or a pending first registration application

Land Registry

OS1

Land Registry _____ Office

Use one form per title.
If you need more room than is provided for in a panel, use continuation sheet CS and attach to this form.

1.   Administrative area and postcode if known

2.   Title number *Enter the title number of the registered estate or that allotted to the pending first registration.*

3.   Payment of fee [b]*Place "X" in the appropriate box.*

☐ The Land Registry fee of £ [   ] accompanies this application.

☐ Debit the Credit Account mentioned in panel 4 with the appropriate fee payable under the current Land Registration Fee Order.

☐ By Direct Debit under an authorised agreement with Land Registry.

For official use only
Impression of fees

4.   The application has been lodged by:[c]
Land Registry Key No. (if appropriate)
Name
Address/DX No.

Reference[d]
E-mail

Telephone No.	Fax No.

5.   If the result of search is to be sent to anyone other than the applicant in panel 4, please supply the name and address of the person to whom it should be sent.

Reference[d]

6.   Registered proprietor/Applicant for first registration *Enter FULL name(s) of the registered proprietor(s) of the registered estate in the above mentioned title or of the person(s) applying for first registration of the property specified in panel 10. If there are more than two, enter the first two only.*

SURNAME/COMPANY NAME:

FORENAME(S):

SURNAME/COMPANY NAME:

FORENAME(S):

7. Search from date *For a search of a **registered title** enter in the box a date falling within the definition of search from date in rule 131 of the Land Registration Rules 2003.*[(e)] *If the date entered is not such a date the application may be rejected. In the case of a **pending first registration** search, enter the letters 'FR'.*

8. Applicant *Enter FULL name of each purchaser **or** lessee **or** chargee.*

9. Reason for application I certify that the applicant intends to: *Place "X" in the appropriate box.*

☐ P purchase   ☐ C take a registered charge

☐ L take a lease

10. Property details *Address or short description of the property.*

11. Type of search *Place "X" in the appropriate box.*

☐ **Registered land search**
Application is made to ascertain whether any adverse entry has been made in the register or day list since the date shown in panel 7.

☐ **Pending first registration search**
Application is made to ascertain whether any adverse entry has been made in the day list since the date of the pending first registration application referred to above.

12. Signature of applicant
or their conveyancer   **Date**

Explanatory notes

(a) "Purchaser" is defined in Land Registration Rules 2003, r.131. In essence, it is a person who has entered, or intends to enter, into a disposition for valuable consideration as disponee where: (i) the disposition is a registrable disposition (see Land Registration Act 2002, s.27), or (ii) there is a person subject to a duty under the Land Registration Act 2002, s.6, to apply for registration, the application is pending and the disposition would have been a registrable disposition had the estate been registered.
An official search in respect of registered land made by a person other than a "purchaser" should be made in Form OS3.

(b) Cheques are payable to 'Land Registry'. If you hold a credit account but do not indicate that it should be debited, and do not enclose a cheque, the registrar may still debit your account.

(c) If you hold a credit account and want the official search certificate sent to an address different from that associated with your key number, enter your key number, reference and telephone number but otherwise leave panel 4 blank. Complete panel 5 instead.

(d) Enter a maximum of 25 characters including stops, strokes, punctuation etc.

(e) Enter the date shown as the subsisting entries date on an official copy of the register or given as the subsisting entries date at the time of an access by remote terminal.

Practice Guide 12 'Official Searches and Outline Applications' contains further information.

Application by purchaser[a] for official search with priority of part of the land in a registered title or a pending first registration application

Land Registry

OS2

Land Registry _____ Office

Use one form per title. If you need more room than is provided for in a panel, use continuation sheet CS and attach to this form.

1.	**Administrative area and postcode** if known
2.	**Title number** *Enter the title number of the registered estate or that allotted to the pending first registration.*

3.   Payment of fee[b] *Place "X" in the appropriate box.*

☐ The Land Registry fee of £ [ ] accompanies this application.

☐ Debit the Credit Account mentioned in panel 4 with the appropriate fee payable under the current Land Registration Fee Order.

☐ By Direct Debit under an authorised agreement with Land Registry.

For official use only
Impression of fees

4.   The application has been lodged by:[c]
Land Registry Key No. (if appropriate)
Name
Address/DX No.

Reference[d]
E-mail

Telephone No.	Fax No.

5.   If the result of search is to be sent to anyone other than the applicant in panel 4, please supply the name and address of the person to whom it should be sent.

Reference[d]

6.   Registered proprietor(s)/Applicant(s) for first registration *Enter FULL name(s) of the registered proprietor(s) of the registered estate in the above mentioned title or of the person(s) applying for first registration of the property specified in panel 10. If there are more than two, enter the first two only.*

SURNAME/COMPANY NAME:

FORENAME(S):

SURNAME/COMPANY NAME:

FORENAME(S):

7.   Search from date *For a search of a **registered title** enter in the box a date falling within the definition of search from date in rule 131 of the Land Registration Rules 2003.*[(e)] *If the date entered is not such a date the application may be rejected. In the case of a **pending first registration** search, enter the letters 'FR'.*

8.   Applicant *Enter FULL name of each purchaser, or lessee, or chargee.*

9.   Reason for application I certify that the applicant(s) intend(s) to: *Place "X" in the appropriate box.*

☐ | P | purchase   ☐ | C | take a registered charge

☐ | L | take a lease

10. Property details *Address or short description of the property:*

Part to be searched – complete either (a) **or** (b) below
(a) Where an estate plan has been approved:

(i)   the plot number(s) is/are

(ii)   the date of approval of the estate plan is

OR

(b) Address or short description of the property as shown   on the attached plan.

NOTE: A plan in duplicate must be supplied when (b) above is completed.[(1)]

11. Type of search *Place "X" in the appropriate box.*

☐ **Registered land search**
     Application is made to ascertain whether any adverse entry has been made in the register or day list since the date shown in panel 7.

☐ **Pending first registration search**
     Application is made to ascertain whether any adverse entry has been made in the day list since the date of the pending first registration application referred to above.

**12. Signature of applicant
        or their conveyancer** _____   **Date** _____

Explanatory notes

(a) "Purchaser" is defined in Land Registration Rules 2003, r.131. In essence, it is a person who has entered, or intends to enter, into a disposition for valuable consideration as disponee where: (i) the disposition is a registrable disposition (see Land Registration Act 2002, s.27), or (ii) there is a person subject to a duty under the Land Registration Act 2002, s.6, to apply for registration, the application is pending and the disposition would have been a registrable disposition had the estate been registered.
An official search in respect of registered land made by a person other than a "purchaser" should be made in Form OS3.

(b) Cheques are payable to 'Land Registry'. If you hold a credit account but do not indicate that it should be debited, and do not enclose a cheque, the registrar may still debit your account.

(c) If you hold a credit account and want the official search certificate sent to an address different from that associated with your key number, enter your key number, reference and telephone number but otherwise leave panel 4 blank. Complete panel 5 instead.

(d) Enter a maximum of 25 characters including stops, strokes, punctuation etc.

(e) Enter the date shown as the subsisting entries date on an official copy of the register or given as the subsisting entries date at the time of an access by remote terminal.

(f) The plan should show its orientation and be drawn to a stated scale preferably not less than 1/1250 for urban areas and 1/2500 for rural areas. It should clearly show by edging or colouring the extent to be searched and show sufficient details to identify the position relative to existing physical features depicted on the Ordnance Survey map and, where appropriate, show floor level(s) with sufficient dimensions to define the extent. The plan should be a copy of the plan that will be used in the protected instrument.

Practice Guide 12 'Official Searches and Outline Applications' contains further information.

**Application for an
official search
of the index map**

Land Registry

Land Registry _____ Office

If you need more room than is provided for in a panel, use continuation sheet CS and attach to this form.

1.	**Administrative area**

2.	**Property to be searched**
	Postal number or description
	Name of road
	Name of locality
	Town
	Postcode
	Ordnance Survey map reference (if known)
	Known title number(s)

3. **Payment of fee** *Place "X" in the appropriate box.*	**For official use only**
☐ The Land Registry fee of £ [ ] accompanies this application.	Impression of fees
☐ Debit the Credit Account mentioned in panel 4 with the appropriate fee payable under the current Land Registration Fee Order.	
☐ By Direct Debit under an authorised agreement with Land Registry.	

4.	**The application has been lodged by:**
	Land Registry Key No. (if appropriate)
	Name
	Address/DX No.
	Reference
	E-mail

Telephone No.	Fax No.

<table>
<tr><td>

5. If the result of search is to be sent to anyone other than the applicant in panel 4, please supply the name and address of the person to whom it should be sent.

Reference
</td></tr>
<tr><td>

6. I apply for an official search of the index map in respect of the land referred to in panel 2 above and shown _____ **on the attached plan.**

Any attached plan must contain sufficient details of the surrounding roads and other features to enable the land to be identified satisfactorily on the Ordnance Survey map. A plan may be unnecessary if the land can be identified by postal description.
</td></tr>
<tr><td>

7.   Signature of applicant _____   **Date** _____
</td></tr>
</table>

Explanatory notes

1.   The purpose and scope of Official Searches of the Index Map are described in Practice Guide 10 'Official searches of the Index Map' obtainable from any Land Registry office. It can also be viewed online at www.landregistry.gov.uk.

2.   Please send this application to the appropriate Land Registry office. This information is contained in Practice Guide 51 'Areas served by Land Registry offices'.

3.   Please ensure that the appropriate fee payable under the current Land Registration Fee Order accompanies your application. If paying fees by cheque or postal order, these should be crossed and payable to "Land Registry". Where you have requested that the fee be paid by Credit Account, receipt of the certificate of result is confirmation that the appropriate fee has been debited.

© Crown copyright (ref: LR/HO) 2/07

First registration application

Land Registry

If you need more room than is provided for in a panel, use continuation sheet CS and attach to this form.

1.	**Administrative area and postcode** if known

2. Address or other description of the estate to be registered

On registering a rentcharge, profit a prendre in gross, or franchise, show the address as follows:- "Rentcharge, franchise etc, over 2 The Grove, Anytown, Northshire NE2 9OO".

3. Extent to be registered *Place "X" in the appropriate box and complete as necessary.*

☐ The land is clearly identified on the plan to the _____
Enter nature and date of deed.

☐ The land is clearly identified on the attached plan and shown _____
Enter reference e.g. "edged red".

☐ The description in panel 2 is sufficient to enable the land to be clearly identified on the Ordnance Survey map

When registering a rentcharge, profit a prendre in gross or franchise, the land to be identified is the land affected by that estate, or to which it relates.

4. Application, priority and fees *A fee calculator for all types of applications can be found on Land Registry's website at www.landregistry.gov.uk/fees*

Nature of applications

in priority order	Value/premium £	Fees paid £
1. **First registration of the estate**		
2.		
3.		
4.		
	TOTAL £	

Fee payment method: *Place "X" in the appropriate box.*

I wish to pay the appropriate fee payable under the current Land Registration Fee Order:

☐ by cheque or postal order, amount £ _____ made payable to "Land Registry".

☐ by Direct Debit under an authorised agreement with Land Registry.

FOR OFFICIAL USE ONLY
Record of fees paid

Particulars of under/over payments

Fees debited £

Reference number

5. The title applied for is *Place "X" in the appropriate box.*

☐ absolute freehold   ☐ absolute leasehold   ☐ good leasehold   ☐ possessory freehold

☐ possessory leasehold

6. Documents lodged with this form *List the documents on Form DL. We shall assume that you request the return of these documents. But we shall only assume that you request the return of a statutory declaration, subsisting lease, subsisting charge or the latest document of title (for example, any conveyance to the applicant) if you supply a certified copy of the document. If certified copies of such documents are not supplied, we may retain the originals of such documents and they may be destroyed.*

7. The applicant is: *Please provide the full name of the person applying to be registered as the proprietor.*

Application lodged by:
Land Registry Key No.(if appropriate)
Name (if different from the applicant)
Address/DX No.

Reference
E-mail

Telephone No.	Fax No.

FOR OFFICIAL USE ONLY
Status codes

8.   Where you would like us to deal with someone else *We shall deal only with the applicant, or the person lodging the application if different, unless you place "X" against one or more of the statements below and give the necessary details.*

☐ Send title information document to the person shown below

☐ Raise any requisitions or queries with the person shown below

☐ Return original documents lodged with this form (see note in panel 6) to the person shown below
If this applies only to certain documents, please specify.

Name
Address/DX No.

Reference
E-mail

Telephone No.	Fax No.

9.   Address(es) for service of every owner of the estate. The address(es) will be entered in the register and used for correspondence and the service of notice. *In this and panel 10, you may give up to three addresses for service **one** of which **must** be a postal address but does not have to be within the UK. The other addresses can be any combination of a postal address, a box number at a UK document exchange or an electronic address. For a company include the company's registered number, if any. For Scottish companies, use an SC prefix, and for limited liability partnerships, use an OC prefix before the registered number if any. For foreign companies give territory in which incorporated.*

Unless otherwise arranged with Land Registry headquarters, we require a certified copy of the owner's constitution (in English or Welsh) if it is a body corporate but is not a company registered in England and Wales or Scotland under the Companies Acts.

10. Information in respect of a chargee or mortgagee *Do not give this information if a Land Registry MD reference is printed on the charge, unless the charge has been transferred.*
Full name and address (including postcode) for service of notices and correspondence of the person entitled to be registered as proprietor of each charge. *You may give up to three addresses for service; see panel 9 as to the details you should include.*

Unless otherwise arranged with Land Registry headquarters, we require a certified copy of the chargee's constitution (in English or Welsh) if it is a body corporate but is not a company registered in England and Wales or Scotland under the Companies Acts.

11. Where the applicants are joint proprietors *Place "X" in the appropriate box*

☐ The applicants are holding the property on trust for themselves as joint tenants

☐ The applicants are holding the property on trust for themselves as tenants in common in equal shares

☐ The applicants are holding the property *(complete as necessary)*

12. Disclosable overriding interests *Place "X" in the appropriate box.*

☐ No disclosable overriding interests affect the estate

☐ Form DI accompanies this application

Rule 28 of the Land Registration Rules 2003 sets out the disclosable overriding interests that you must tell us about. You must use Form DI to tell us about any disclosable overriding interests that affect the estate.

The registrar may enter a notice of a disclosed interest in the register of title.

13. The title is based on the title documents listed in Form DL which are all those that are in the possession or control of the applicant.

Place "X" in the appropriate box. If applicable complete the second statement; include any interests disclosed only by searches other than local land charges. Any interests disclosed by searches which do not affect the estate being registered should be certified.

☐ All rights, interests and claims affecting the estate known to the applicant are disclosed in the title documents and Form DI if accompanying this application. There is no-one in adverse possession of the property or any part of it.

☐ In addition to the rights, interests and claims affecting the estate disclosed in the title documents or Form DI if accompanying this application, the applicant only knows of the following:

14. *Place "X" in this box if you are NOT able to give this certificate.* ☐

We have fully examined the applicant's title to the estate, including any appurtenant rights, or are satisfied that it has been fully examined by a conveyancer in the usual way prior to this application.

15. We have authority to lodge this application and request the registrar to complete the registration.

**16. Signature of applicant
or their conveyancer** _____ **Date** _____

Note: Failure to complete the form with proper care may deprive the applicant of protection under the Land Registration Act if, as a result, a mistake is made in the register.

© Crown copyright (ref: LR/HQ/CD-ROM) 6/03

**Application for official
copies of register/plan or
certificate in Form CI**

Land Registry

OC1

Land Registry _____ Office

Use one form per title. *If you need more room than is provided for in a panel, use continuation sheet CS and attach to this form.*

1.	**Administrative area** if known
2.	**Title number** if known
3.	**Property** Postal number or description
	Name of road
	Name of locality
	Town
	Postcode
	Ordnance Survey map reference (if known)

4.   Payment of fee *Place "X" in the appropriate box.*

☐ The Land Registry fee of £ ☐ accompanies this application.

☐ Debit the Credit Account mentioned in panel 5 with the appropriate fee payable under the current Land Registration Fee Order.

☐ By Direct Debit under an authorised agreement with Land Registry.

For official use only

Impression of fees

5.   The application has been lodged by:
Land Registry Key No. (if appropriate)
Name
Address/DX No.

Reference
E-mail

Telephone No.	Fax No.

6. If the official copies are to be sent to anyone other than the applicant in panel 5, please supply the name and address of the person to whom they should be sent.

Reference

7. Where the title number is **not** quoted in panel 2, place "X" in the appropriate box(es). As regards this property, my application relates to:

☐ freehold estate   ☐ caution against first registration   ☐ franchise   ☐ manor

☐ leasehold estate   ☐ rentcharge   ☐ profit a prendre in gross

8. In case there is an application for registration pending against the title, place "X" in the appropriate box:

☐ I require an official copy back-dated to the day prior to the receipt of that application   **or**

☐ I require an official copy on completion of that application

9. **I apply for:** *Place "X" in the appropriate box(es) and indicate how many copies are required.*

☐ ____ official copy(ies) of the **register** of the above mentioned property

☐ ____ official copy(ies) of the **title plan or caution plan** of the above mentioned property

☐ ____ a certificate in Form CI, in which case **either**:

☐ an estate plan has been approved and the plot number is _____

or

☐ no estate plan has been approved and a certificate is to be issued in respect of the land shown _____ on the attached plan and copy

10. Signature of applicant _____ **Date** _____

**Cancellation of entries
relating to a
registered charge**

Land Registry

DS1

This form should be accompanied by either Form AP1 or Form DS2.
If you need more room than is provided for in a panel, use continuation sheet CS and attach to this form.

1. Title Number(s) of the Property	
2. Property	
3. Date	
4. Date of charge	
5. Lender	
6. The Lender acknowledges that the property is no longer charged as security for the payment of sums due under the charge	
7. Date of Land Registry facility letter, if any	
8. *To be executed as a deed by the lender or in accordance with the above facility letter.*	

© Crown copyright (ref: LR/HQ/CD-ROM) 6/03

**Release of part
of the land from a
registered charge**

Land Registry

DS3

This form should be accompanied by Form AP1.
If you need more room than is provided for in a panel, use continuation sheet CS and attach to this form.

1.	**Title Number(s)**

2.	Property **released from the charge** *Insert address, including postcode, or other description of the property released from the charge.*

The property is defined *Place "X" in the appropriate box and complete the statement.*

☐ on the attached plan and shown *State reference e.g. "edged red".*

☐ on the title plan(s) of the above title(s) and shown *State reference e.g. "edged and numbered 1 in blue".*

3.	Date

4.	Date of charge

5.	Lender

6.	**The Lender acknowledges that the property defined in panel 2 is no longer charged as security for the payment of sums due under the charge**
7.	Date of Land Registry facility letter, if any
8.	Additional provisions *Insert any agreed provisions as to rights granted or other matters.*

9.	*To be executed as a deed by the lender or in accordance with the above facility letter.*

© Crown copyright (ref: LR/HQ/CD-ROM) 6/03

**Application to
change the register**

Land Registry

If you need more room than is provided for in a panel, use continuation sheet CS and attach to this form.

1. Administrative area and postcode *if* known

2. Title number(s)

3. If you have already made this application by **outline application**, insert reference number:

4. This application affects *Place "X" in the appropriate box.*

☐ the **whole** of the title(s) *Go to panel 5.*

☐ **part** of the title(s) *Give a brief description of the property affected.*

---

5. Application, priority and fees *A fee calculator for all types of applications can be found on Land Registry's website at www.landregistry.gov.uk/fees*
Nature of applications numbered   Value £   Fees paid £
in priority order
1.

TOTAL £
Fee payment method: *Place "X" in the appropriate box.*
I wish to pay the appropriate fee payable under the current Land Registration Fee Order:

☐ by cheque or postal order, amount £ _____ made payable to "Land Registry".

☐ by Direct Debit under an authorised agreement with Land Registry.

FOR OFFICIAL USE ONLY
Record of fee paid

Particulars of under/over payment

Fees debited £

Reference number

---

6. Documents lodged with this form *Number the documents in sequence; copies should also be numbered and listed as separate documents. Alternatively you may prefer to use Form DL. If you supply the original document and a certified copy, we shall assume that you request the return of the original; if a certified copy is not supplied, we may retain the original document and it may be destroyed.*

---

7. The applicant is: *Please provide the full name(s) of the person(s) applying to change the register. Where a conveyancer lodges the application, the applicant is the client, not the conveyancer.*

---

8. The application has been lodged by:
Land Registry Key No. (if appropriate)
Name (if different from the applicant)
Address/DX No.

Reference
Email

Telephone No.	Fax No.

FOR
OFFICIAL
USE ONLY
Codes
Dealing

Status

9. Where you would like us to deal with someone else *We shall deal only with the applicant, or the person lodging the application if different, unless you place "X" against one or more of the statements below and give the necessary details.*

☐ Send title information document to the person shown below

☐ Raise any requisitions or queries with the person shown below

☐ Return original documents lodged with this form (see note in panel 6) to the person shown below
If this applies only to certain documents, please specify.

Name
Address/DX No.

Reference
Email

Telephone No.	Fax No.

10. Where you would like us to notify someone else that we have completed the registration of this application *Place "X" in the box and provide the name and address of the person to whom notification should be sent.*

☐ Send notification of completion to the person shown below

Name
Address/DX No.

Reference
Email

11. Address(es) for service of the proprietor(s) of the registered estate(s). The address(es) will be entered in the register and used for correspondence and the service of notice. *Place "X" in the appropriate box(es). You may give up to three addresses for service **one** of which **must** be a postal address but does not have to be within the UK. The other addresses can be any combination of a postal address, a box number at a UK document exchange or an electronic address.*

☐ Enter the address(es) from the transfer/assent/lease

☐ Enter the address(es), including postcode, as follows:

☐ Retain the address(es) currently in the register for the title(s)

12. Disclosable overriding interests *Place "X" in the appropriate box.*

☐ This is not an application to register a registrable disposition or it is but no disclosable overriding interests affect the registered estate(s) *Section 27 of the Land Registration Act 2002 lists the registrable dispositions. Rule 57 of the Land Registration Rules 2003 sets out the disclosable overriding interests. Use Form DI to tell us about any disclosable overriding interests that affect the registered estate(s) identified in panel 2.*

☐ Form DI accompanies this application

The registrar may enter a notice of a disclosed interest in the register of title.

13. Information in respect of any new charge *Do not give this information if a Land Registry MD reference is printed on the charge, unless the charge has been transferred.*

Full name and address (including postcode) for service of notices and correspondence of the person to be registered as proprietor of each charge. *You may give up to three addresses for service **one** of which **must** be a postal address but does not have to be within the UK. The other addresses can be any combination of a postal address, a box number at a UK document exchange or an electronic address. For a company include company's registered number, if any. For Scottish companies use an SC prefix and for limited liability partnerships use an OC prefix before the registered number, if any. For foreign companies give territory in which incorporated.*

Unless otherwise arranged with Land Registry headquarters, we require a certified copy of the chargee's constitution (in English or Welsh) if it is a body corporate but is not a company registered in England and Wales or Scotland under the Companies Acts.

14. Signature of applicant or their conveyancer _____ **Date** _____

© Crown copyright (ref: LR/HO) 7/05

Disclosable overriding interests   **Land Registry**

This form should be accompanied by either Form AP1 or Form FR1.

1.	**Property**

2.	**Title number(s)**

3. **The applicant is:** *Please provide the full name of the person applying to be registered as proprietor or to change the register.*

    The application has been lodged by:
    Land Registry Key No. (if appropriate)
    Name (if different from the applicant)
    Address/DX No.

    Reference
    E-mail

Telephone No.	Fax No.

FOR OFFICIAL USE ONLY
Codes
Dealing

Status

4. **In the panels below, please give details of any disclosable overriding interest that affects the estate to which the application relates.**

   Use panel 5 to tell us about any lease that is a disclosable overriding interest.

   Use panel 6 to tell us about any other disclosable overriding interest. You may use as many Forms DI as necessary.

   The registrar may enter notice of a disclosed interest in the register of title.

5. **Please list below all unregistered disclosable leases in date order, starting with the oldest. You may use as many Forms DI as are necessary.**

   Please lodge a certified copy of either the original or the counterpart of each lease disclosed.

   NB: If a previously noted lease has determined, the notice of it will only be cancelled on receipt of a Form CN1.

	Description of land leased	**Date of Lease**	**Term and commencement date**
e.g.	**Flat 1, garage 3 and bin store**	**24.06.2002**	**5 years from 24.06.2002**
a.			
b.			
c.			
d.			
e.			

6.	**Please list below any disclosable overriding interests which you have not included in panel 5**
a.	*Description of interest. For example, a legal easement.*
	_____
	_____
	arising by virtue of _____
	_____
	_____
	Deed or circumstances in which the interest arose.
	[affects the land shown _____ on the enclosed plan].
b.	*Description of interest. For example, a legal easement.*
	_____
	_____
	arising by virtue of _____
	_____
	_____
	Deed or circumstances in which the interest arose.
	[affects the land shown _____ on the enclosed plan].
c.	*Description of interest. For example, a legal easement.*
	_____
	_____
	arising by virtue of _____
	_____
	_____
	Deed or circumstances in which the interest arose.
	[affects the land shown _____ on the enclosed plan].

Index